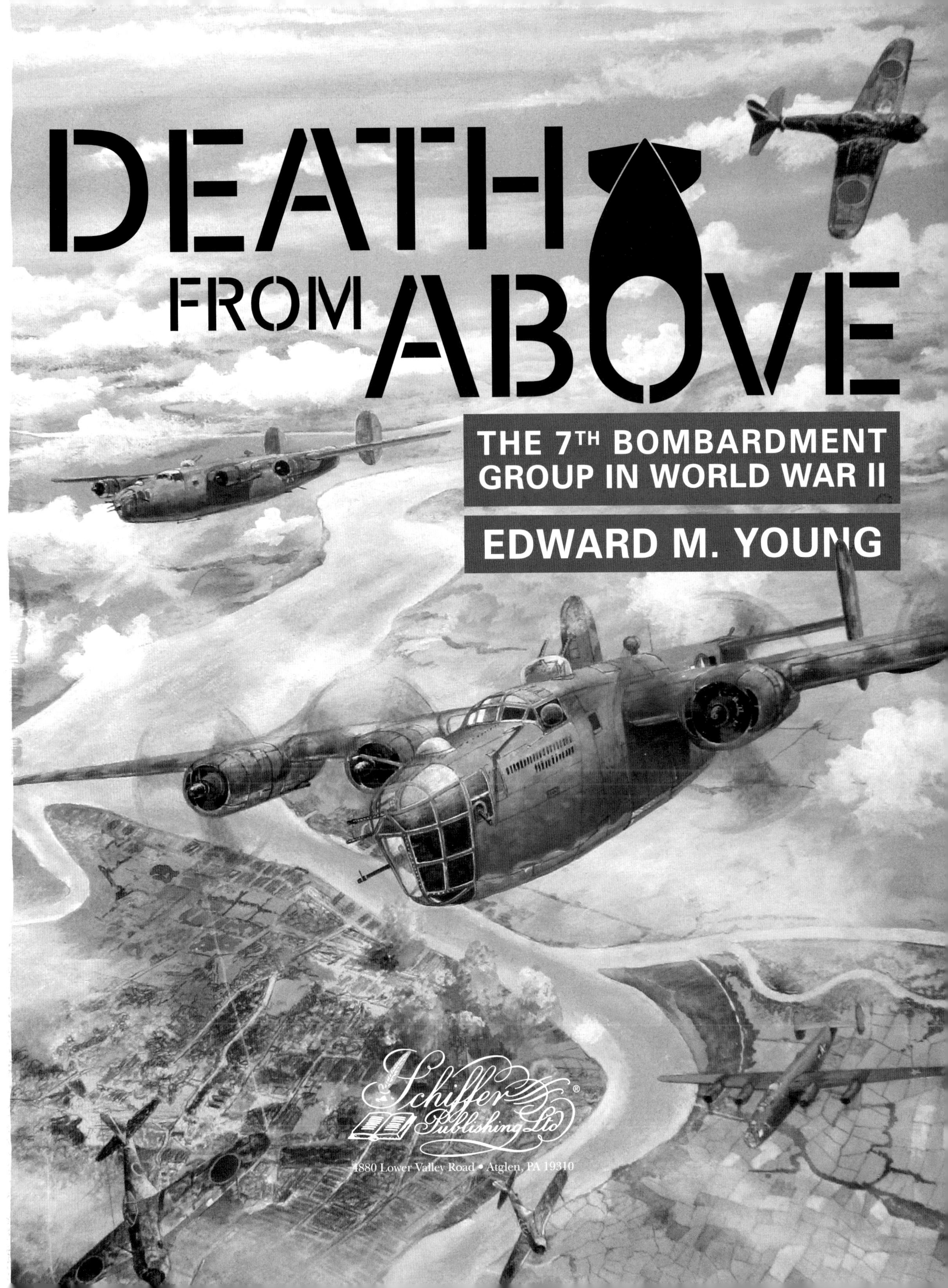

DEATH FROM ABOVE

THE 7TH BOMBARDMENT GROUP IN WORLD WAR II

EDWARD M. YOUNG

Schiffer Publishing Ltd
4880 Lower Valley Road • Atglen, PA 19310

Library of Congress Control Number: 2014935681

Type set in Ulissa, Humanst & Georgia

ISBN: 978-0-7643-4635-4
Printed in China

Published by Schiffer Publishing, Ltd.
4880 Lower Valley Road
Atglen, PA 19310
Phone: (610) 593-1777; Fax: (610) 593-2002
E-mail: Info@schifferbooks.com

Dedication

In memory of those who built the 7th Bombardment Group
in peace and those who served with the Group in WWII

Acknowledgments

This history of the 7th Bombardment Group grew out of more than 20 years of research and writing on the air war over Burma during WWII. To my great regret, by the time I began work on a more detailed history of the 7th Group, many of the Group's wartime members had passed away and the 7th Bombardment Group (H) Historical Foundation had been dissolved. This history is written in their memory. I wanted to record their experience of war and put this experience and their achievements in context, so that their story will not be forgotten. I hope that in reading this account, their families may learn a bit more about what their fathers or grandfathers did as young men to contribute to victory over Japan so many years ago. A number of people provided valuable assistance in the preparation of this history. I would particularly like to thank Colonel Thomas Sledge, USAF (Ret'd.), formerly a bombardier with the 9th Bombardment Squadron during 1942-43, for sharing his memories and photographs from his tour in India. Dr. Mary Elizabeth Ruwell, Academic Archivist and Chief, Special Collections, at the United States Air Force Academy, gave me access to the papers of the 7th Bombardment Group (H) Historical Foundation and kindly gave me permission to use photographs from the Group's extensive collection. Jim Augustus, who maintained the excellent 7th Bombardment Group (H) website and whose father was a member of the 7th Bomb Group in India, generously shared an extensive collection of material about the Group, including several privately printed memoirs and some excellent photos. Dan Hagedorn, Senior Curator at the Museum of Flight, dug into his extensive files on the Douglas B-18 for material he had collected on the 7th Bombardment Group. Also at the Museum of Flight, Ms. Amy Heidrick, Photo Archivist, provided a number of photos of 7th Bombardment Group aircraft from the prewar and WWII eras. At the San Diego Air and Space Museum, Nelson Chase responded cheerily to numerous requests for photos from the museum's extensive collection. The staff of the Hamilton Field Military Museum opened their own files on the 7th Bombardment Group and allowed me to copy several photos from the Group's years at Hamilton Field. In the Netherlands, my old friend Gerard Cassius sent me several photos taken in Java during 1941-42. Other important sources of photographs were the Still Pictures Branch at the National Archives and Records Administration, the Air Force Historical Research Agency at Maxwell AFB, and the Australian War Memorial in Canberra, Australia. I would like to express my sincere thanks to the staff of all three institutions for their assistance. Maria Brown, Chief Cartographer at Kroll Map Company in Seattle, did a superb job designing the maps that accompany the text. Sarah Serazawa worked on the translation of several memoirs by pilots from the Japanese Army Air Force's *64th Sentai*, who fought against the 7th Bombardment Group over Burma. Steve Ellis took time to read a draft of the book and made many useful suggestions to improve it. I would also like to acknowledge the website www.B24Bestweb, an invaluable tool for tracking down individual 7th Bombardment Group airplanes. To my wife Candis, I offer my deepest gratitude for her patient support and encouragement for this and many other projects.

CONTENTS

INTRODUCTION

The United States Army Air Forces went to war committed to the doctrine of daylight precision strategic bombing. This belief in the efficacy of precision attacks on selected industrial targets to undermine an enemy nation's ability to prosecute a war was enshrined in AWPD/1, the Army Air Force's air war plan developed in August 1941.[1] Four officers—Col.. Harold George, Lt. Col. Kenneth Walker, and Majs. Haywood Hansell and Lawrence Kuter, all former instructors at the Air Corps Tactical School serving in the Air War Plans Division—put the plan together in a little over a week. In the event that the United States went to war against Germany and Japan, AWPD/1 called for the Army Air Force to deploy a substantial force of heavy bombers in a strategic bombing campaign against the German and Japanese industrial fabric. The plan assumed that fleets of heavy bombers, flying at high altitude in tight defensive formations, but without fighter escort, could penetrate deep into enemy territory to destroy vital industrial targets, transportation systems, and power supplies to disrupt the enemy's economy, thereby bringing production of war materials to a halt.[2] The advocates of strategic bombing believed that an effective bombing campaign might even force an enemy nation to surrender without the need for invasion and the horrendous casualties that most observers believed would follow in a battle between two armies.[3] Acceptance of AWPD/1 at the highest levels of Government represented a hard-won victory for the air power advocates. These men, many of whom were to take up senior commands in the war against Germany and Japan, had long argued in favor of strategic bombardment in the face of opposition from the Army and the War Department. Development of the strategic bombardment concept took place during the interwar years at the Air Corps Tactical School, where theories about air power were proposed, fiercely debated, and refined into doctrine. Throughout the 1930s, the Army Air Corps tested and practiced these theories of air power in the Army Air Corps' operational units and annual maneuvers. The small number of bomber groups in the prewar Air Corps helped work out the tactics of aerial bombardment with the aircraft they had available, limited in both number and capability for most of the period. Only toward the end of the decade did the

Army Air Corps begin to acquire the four-engine heavy bombers that appeared to finally offer the technical ability to make strategic bombing a reality. Five months after AWPD/1 was approved, the Army Air Forces' leaders would have the opportunity to put their theories, their equipment, and their faith in strategic bombardment to the test in a real war.

The 7th Bombardment Group was an integral part of the process of developing the doctrine of daylight precision strategic bombing and its application in WWII. As one of the Army Air Corps' few active bombardment groups during the period between the wars, the 7th Bombardment Group helped create the techniques and tactics of aerial bombardment the Army Air Force used during WWII. From its formation June 1, 1928, until the beginning of the war with Japan December 7, 1941, the 7th Group flew nearly every type of heavy bomber in the Air Corps inventory. The Group successfully made the transition from the biplane bombers of the early 1930s—not far removed from the bombers of WWI—to the more capable all-metal, multi-engine bombers that came into service later in the decade. The 7th Group and the other heavy bomber groups served as a laboratory for air power. These units were a mechanism for the transmission and transformation of the air power doctrine developed at the Air Corps Tactical School into standard tactics to be applied in wartime. The 7th Group tested, practiced, and taught these tactics during exercises and maneuvers. In addition, the 7th Group and other prewar bomber groups served as training grounds for the wartime leaders of bombardment aviation. Many of the men who commanded Air Forces, Air Divisions, and Bombardment Wings, Groups, and Squadrons during WWII served their apprenticeships in the 7th Bombardment Group.

The 7th Bombardment Group's wartime service began during the attack on Pearl Harbor (December 7, 1941) and continued until the very end of the war August 15, 1945. Only a small number of Army Air Force units had as long a record of active service. The 7th Group spent the entire war fighting against the armed forces of Japan. Operating first from Java in early 1942, the Group transferred to bases in India and became part of the Tenth Air Force in the China-Burma-India Theater. Flying B-24 Liberators, the 7th Group flew bombing missions deep into Burma and Thailand. The 7th Group's experience of war was different from what the air power theorists had envisioned. The B-24s did not have the range to reach Japan, so they could not destroy the industries vital to the Japanese war economy. While there were few "strategic" targets in Burma or Thailand, India-based heavy bombers could still have an impact on Japan's ability to prosecute the war in Burma and protect its newly-won territories. Instead of bombing industrial plants, the 7th Group concentrated on the Japanese lines of communications bringing supplies into Burma for the Japanese Army and Army Air Force units fighting there. Far from having fleets of heavy bombers available, the Tenth Air Force deployed only a single heavy bomber group out of India through the entire war. During its first year of combat out of India, the 7th Group could rarely put up more than a dozen airplanes on a single bombing mission, and normally flew missions with less. Permanently destroying carefully selected targets proved far more difficult than prewar bombing theorists had expected. The job was even more difficult when so few bombers were available. Even though American bombing technology was the best in the world, it was still, until very late in the war, inadequate to the task.[4] Not only were many of the targets—especially bridges—difficult to hit with any precision, but the Japanese proved adept at making rapid repairs. The same targets had to be bombed again, and again, and again. This became a long, relentless war of attrition. While unescorted daylight bombing missions proved feasible against weak Japanese fighter opposition, the 7th Group learned the same painful lesson as other bomb groups in other theaters of war: high altitude, speed, heavy armament, and tight defensive formations did not make bombers invulnerable to enemy fighters. Only toward the end of the war did circumstances—more aircraft and combat crews available, a change in tactics and bombing technology and, critically, Allied air superiority over Burma—permit the 7th Group to inflict significant and sustained damage to the Japanese communication system with minimal losses. The 7th Bombardment Group fought a long, hard war in a mostly forgotten theater of war fraught with political controversy and conflicting Allied interests and objectives. Flying missions of unparalleled distance as a matter of course with small numbers of bombers; at times through appalling weather, with little chance of escape if forced down over enemy territory; with events and activities of other air forces in other theaters of war often overshadowing their own achievements; at the end of the longest supply route in the Army Air Forces and often with the lowest priority for aircraft, men, and equipment, the men of the 7th Group went about their work resolutely and with determination. They contributed in no small measure to the ultimate defeat of the Japanese Army in Burma.

CHAPTER ONE

A LABORATORY FOR AIR POWER: BUILDING A BOMBARDMENT GROUP

Building the 7th Bombardment Group

Designated a bombardment group on March 24, 1923, while on inactive status, the 7th Bombardment Group began a new incarnation as an active air unit through the Army Air Corps Act of 1926. The 7th Bomb Group could trace its lineage to the First Army Observation Group that served in France during 1918.[1] Demobilized in April 1919, this unit was reactivated October 1, 1919, as the 1st Army Observation Group—one of the seven groups the War Department authorized for the Army Air Service—and was established at Langley Field, Virginia, with the 50th and 88th Observation Squadrons.[2] On March 26, 1921, the Group was redesignated the 7th Group (Observation), but it remained active for only another five months. That same year, Congress initiated sharp cutbacks in the size of the United States Army. As a result, the Air Service placed a number of units on the inactive list, including the 7th Group, which was inactivated August 30, 1921.[3] While remaining on the inactive list, the Group went through two changes in designation, becoming the 7th Observation Group January 25, 1923, and then, two months later, being redesignated the 7th Bombardment Group.[4]

In the aftermath of WWI, the Army Air Service underwent a period of seemingly inexorable decline in strength and capability. At the Armistice in November 1918, the Air Service had a total strength of 190,000 officers and men, with 78,000 serving overseas; by June 1919, the Air Service had shrunk to 27,000 officers and men, and would shrink even further.[5] Under the National Defense Act of 1920, Congress authorized a strength for the Air Service of 1,516 officers and 16,000 enlisted men.[6] Over the next few years, the Air Service would have difficulty meeting even this level. Having fought the war to end all wars, with thousands of surplus aircraft and engines in storage, and with no threats to the nation on the horizon, a majority of Congressmen saw little reason to spend money on the armed forces beyond what was considered necessary to maintain the traditional small peacetime force. Appropriations for the Air Service declined from $33 million for Fiscal Year 1921 to $12.9 million for Fiscal Year 1923 and remained at that level for the next two years.[7] As the years went by, the supply of surplus WWI aircraft ran down, while the aircraft in service began to wear out. Although the Air

Service had begun to introduce newer pursuit and observation aircraft in 1925 in small numbers, by that time the majority of the Service's aircraft were obsolete and badly in need of replacement. Concern for the state of the Air Service and agitation for not only new equipment, but a formal Government policy toward military aviation reached a peak during 1925, with the congressional Lampert Committee investigation, the controversial court martial of Brig. Gen. William Mitchell, the most outspoken proponent of air power, and the President's Aircraft Board (the Morrow Board), President Calvin Coolidge's response to Mitchell's criticisms. In the House and Senate, several bills to address the weaknesses of the Air Service were combined into the Army Air Corps Act. President Coolidge signed the Act into law July 2, 1926.[8]

The Act changed the name of the Army Air Service to the Army Air Corps, created the position of Assistant Secretary

An aerial view of Rockwell Field on North Island in the late 1920s. The Army Air Corps maintained an air depot here, sharing the field with the U.S. Navy. By the end of the 1920s, congestion had become a major problem. (3B-21051, Record Group 342FH, National Archives and Records Administration (NARA)

of War (for Air) in the War Department, and most importantly, approved a five-year expansion program to build the Air Corps up to a level of 1,650 officers, 15,000 enlisted men, and 1,800 airplanes, allocated among 20 new tactical units. The expansion program brought the number of authorized Air Corps squadrons up to 52. This included activation of four new bombardment squadrons. Under the program, the Air Corps planned to establish two bombardment wings—one on each coast—comprised of one bombardment group and one pursuit group, each group consisting of three squadrons. But in approving the Air Corps Act, Congress did not allocate any appropriations for expansion. The Air Corps would still have to depend on its annual appropriation from Congress as part of the President's overall budget submission. The five-year program ran into delays from the outset. President Coolidge, anxious to reduce government spending, ordered that the Air Corps expansion program be delayed until Fiscal Year 1928 (July 1, 1927, to June 30, 1928).[9] Without appropriations for men or aircraft, the Air Corps could not complete the formation of a new bombardment wing on the west coast, so the Air Corps did what it could; it made a start. Testifying in April 1928 before the House Committee on Military Affairs on the Air Corps Bill for Fiscal Year 1929, Maj. Gen. James Fechet, Chief of the Army Air Corps, and F. Trubee Davison, Assistant Secretary of War (for Air), told the Committee that it was the Air Corps' intention to establish a bombardment group headquarters, a bombardment squadron, and a pursuit squadron at Rockwell Field in California, with the longer term plan of transferring the bombardment group to March Field once the flying school there had been transferred to a new facility being built at San Antonio, Texas.[10] In June 1928, the last month of Fiscal Year 1928, it activated three new units as the first elements of its planned bombardment wing.[11] To equip its existing and planned bomber squadrons, the Air Corps placed an order with the Keystone Aircraft Corporation for 35 twin-engine Keystone Light Bombardment airplanes, consisting of 18 LB-6 airplanes with 536 h.p. Wright R-1750 Cyclone engines and 17 LB-7 airplanes with the 525 h.p. Pratt & Whitney R-1690 Hornet engines, as well as an order with the Curtiss Aeroplane and Motor Company for 12 Curtiss B-2 Condor bombers with 633 h.p. Curtiss Conqueror engines.[12]

On June 1, 1928, the Air Corps activated the 7th Bombardment Group and the first of its intended component units, the 11th Bombardment Squadron.[13] At the same time, the Air Corps activated the 95th Pursuit Squadron, and in the absence of its planned parent pursuit group, assigned the squadron to the administrative control of the 7th Bombardment Group. The new units were assigned to Rockwell Field, where the Air Corps maintained an air depot, sharing the base on North Island—near Coronado, California—with the Navy. Staff at Rockwell immediately began preparing buildings and a tent camp to receive troops assigned to the new units. The first increment of 92 enlisted men arrived from March Field, California, on June 25th, where they were assigned to Headquarters, 7th Bombardment Group, and the 11th and 95th Squadrons. Within a few weeks, the 7th Bombardment Group Headquarters had 35 men, while the 11th Bombardment Squadron had 115 men and the 95th Pursuit Squadron 114.[14] Capt. H.M. Elmendorf, a well-known Air Corps pursuit pilot who had served at Selfridge Field with the 1st Pursuit Group, was appointed commander of the 7th Bombardment Group and concurrently commander of the 95th Pursuit Squadron.[15] Capt. R.H. Pritchard assumed command of Headquarters, 7th Bombardment Group, and Capt. E.C. Black was placed in command of the 11th Bombardment Squadron.[16]

The Douglas O-2 series was chosen as a replacement for the venerable Dehavilland DH-4 in the Army's observation squadrons. Douglas built 140 O-2H aircraft between 1927 and 1929 which served in a number of Air Corps and National Guard observation squadrons. (00026726, Courtesy San Diego Air & Space Museum)

The 11th Bombardment Squadron was one of the small number of bombardment squadrons that had seen active service in France during WWI. The squadron was organized at Kelly Field, Texas, on June 26, 1917, as the 11th Aero Squadron. Shipped overseas—first to England and then to France—in August 1918, the 11th was equipped with American-built DeHavilland DH-4 day bombers. Before going into combat, the squadron adopted as its insignia the character Mr. Jiggs carrying a bomb under his arm, from the comic strip "Bringing Up Father" created by George McManus, who was a member of the squadron. On September 10, 1918, the 11th Aero Squadron was assigned to the 1st Day Bombardment Group. From that date until the Armistice on November 11th, the squadron flew 32 bombing missions in support of American Army offensives in Lorraine, St. Mihiel, and the Meuse-Argonne, being credited with 13 victories over German fighters. At the end of the War, the 11th returned to the United States with the 1st Day Bombardment Group, redesignated the 2nd Bombardment Group in 1921. The 11th Squadron served at Langley Field, Virginia, until 1927, when the squadron was placed on the inactive list and its personnel transferred to March Field in Riverside, California, to support the flying school set up under the Army Air Corps' five-year expansion program.[17]

Officers assigned to the newly-activated 11th Bombardment Squadron began arriving at Rockwell Field in July, comprising a mix of experienced Lieutenants, newly-appointed Second Lieutenants recently graduated from flying school, and reserve officers from several cities on the West Coast who were called up for eight months of active duty.[18] Aircraft for the new squadron came in slowly, as well. In the absence of enough aircraft to supply the 11th with bombers, the Air Corps assigned a small number of Douglas O-2 observation airplanes. The squadron commander, Capt. E.C. Black, went by rail to the San Antonio Air Depot, where he picked up an O-2 for his squadron, arriving back at Rockwell July 22nd with a flying time of 11 hours and 45 minutes.[19] Enough O-2 aircraft were on hand for the squadron to make its public "debut" on August 16th, when the 11th participated in the dedication of Lindbergh Field—San Diego's municipal airport—as part of a parade of

82 Air Corps aircraft which flew over the field at noon, followed by 140 Navy aircraft also from North Island.[20] Much of the rest of the year was taken up with routine flying, including some short cross-country flights, though the *Air Corps News Letter* for November 24, 1928, noted that at a Halloween costume party at the Rockwell Field Officer's Club, Capt. E.C. "Red" Black, 11th Squadron commander, took the honors dressed as a French maid pushing around 2nd Lt. Baxter in a baby carriage, with Baxter dressed as an infant.[21]

At the end of the year, the 11th Squadron began assisting in the preparations for an experimental exercise in aerial refueling and long distance flight. At the suggestion of Capt. Ira Eaker, Maj. Carl Spaatz[22] had requested and received permission from Maj. Gen. James Fechet, Army Air Corps commander, to try for a new world air endurance record using air-to-air refueling. Needing a week of good weather for the flight, Spaatz and Eaker chose Rockwell Field as the base for the attempt. The Air Corps prepared a Fokker C-2A three-engine transport as the endurance plane and two Douglas C-1 transports as the refueling planes. The Fokker was dubbed "Question Mark," given the unpredictability of the experimental flight. In addition to Spaatz, who would oversee the refueling, the crew of the "Question Mark" consisted of Capt. Eaker, Lts. Elwood Quesada and Harry Halverson as pilots, and S/Sgt Roy Hooe, mechanic. From the 7th Bombardment Group, Capt. Hugh Elmendorf, Group commander, was placed in charge of all ground support operations, while Capt. E.C. Black was made responsible for night operations in support of the flight. Lt. Odas Moon, from the 11th Bombardment Squadron, was appointed pilot of the second Douglas C-1 refueling airplane; many other officers and enlisted men of the squadron took on other duties. The "Question Mark" took off at 7:28 a.m. on January 1, 1929, from the metropolitan airport at Van Nuys, California, and set off for Rockwell Field. The airplane did not land again until 2:07 p.m. on January 7th, having remained aloft for 150 hours, 40 minutes, and 14 seconds, flying a circuit between San Diego and Los Angeles. During its week aloft, the "Question Mark" received gasoline and oil in 42 refueling contacts, eight during the night. Lt. Moon did the first refueling flight and flew several test flights to determine the maximum load of gasoline the C-1 could carry, as well as additional refueling flights during the week. The flight broke every endurance record and received wide publicity.[23]

Lt. Howard Keefer (right) was one of the pilots of the "blackboard plane", a Boeing PW-9D used to pass messages on to the "Question Mark". Captain Hugh Elmendorf stands on the left. (Peter M. Bowers Collection, Museum of Flight)

The Atlantic Fokker C-2 "Question Mark" used in the January 1929 endurance flight. (Museum of Flight)

After supporting the flight of the "Question Mark," the 11th Bombardment Squadron took the first steps toward becoming an operational bombardment squadron. The Air Corps had decided to allocate ten of the new Keystone LB-7 bombers to the 11th Squadron. In late January, Lts. Odas Moon and William Kingsbury left Rockwell Field and traveled by rail to the Keystone factory at Bristol, Pennsylvania, to pick up two LB-7 aircraft and ferry them back to Rockwell.[24] During the 1920s and 1930s, the Air Corps made a practice of having squadron pilots pick up aircraft at the manufacturer's factory and fly them back to their bases, gaining valuable cross-country flying experience. In preparation for the arrival of their new bombers, the squadron set up a bombing range on a corner of Rockwell Field towards Point Loma for low altitude bombing practice.[25] Moon and Kingsbury spent several months at the Keystone factory, where they were joined in late March by Lt. Eugene Batten. Finally, at the beginning of April, the first three LB-7 bombers were ready and the three 11th Squadron pilots flew them across the country in stages, with Kingsbury arriving April 3rd, Moon April 5th, and Batten April 11th.[26] The *Air Corps News Letter* correspondent at Rockwell Field proudly wrote that "The 11th Bombardment Squadron flew in formation over Rockwell Field in real bombers—LB-7s—for the first time on April 12th. The three huge Keystone Panthers, powered by P&W 'Hornets,' caused considerable attention to be directed skyward as they roared over Coronado and vicinity on their premier flight."[27] A week later, to give squadron officers more experience in their new bombers, the three LB-7s made a cross-country flight to Phoenix and Tucson, Arizona, carrying nine officers and six enlisted men, returning to Rockwell Field on April 21st.[28]

The 11th Bombardment Squadron began to receive the Keystone LB-7 bomber in April 1929. The Squadron's insignia, Mr. Jiggs from the comic strip *Bringing Up Father*, is painted on the nose below the front gun position. (00025514, Courtesy San Diego Air & Space Museum)

The Keystone LB-7 was, for its time, a large aircraft, with a wingspan of 75' and a length of 43'. A twin-engine biplane built of steel tubing with fabric covering, the LB-7 could carry 2,000 pounds of bombs and was armed with five machine guns. The LB-7's deficiencies as a bomber were its limited speed, range, and service ceiling, though for its time it was comparable to the bombers of other nations and was hailed in the press as "...the most formidable air dreadnaught to be constructed in the United States..."[29] The LB-7's top speed of 110 mph at 5,000 feet altitude was actually slower than the DeHavilland DH-4 of WWI. Its range was 432 miles with a full bomb load and its service ceiling was 13,325 feet.[30] Nevertheless, the Keystone biplane bombers became the standard Army Air Corps bombers between 1927 and 1932, primarily because of "...their low cost, economical operation, and stable flying qualities."[31] They were by no means comfortable to fly in. Harold Bowman, who joined the 11th Bombardment Squadron as a young 2nd Lieutenant in 1929, recalled that the LB-7s "...not only had air-cooled engines but was air cooled in every other way. With open cockpits, open gun turrets, and open bomb bays, it was as air-filled as a hoop skirt in a whirlwind. Crew members were encumbered with seventy-five pounds of clothing and equipment: helmets, goggles, face masks, fleece-lined leather flying suits and boots, thick mittens, oxygen hoses running through the face masks to be gripped between the teeth, headsets, silk neck scarves and parachutes. Pilot and co-pilot sat side by side only partially protected by the windshield. The copilot crawled down to the lower deck at the proper time to serve as bombardier."[32] The LB-7s, with their air-cooled Pratt & Whitney Hornet engines, were also incredibly loud. As one former pilot remembered, "the first of the series had no collector rings and exhaust pipes. The exhaust came out of short stacks directly into the ears of the pilot and copilot, who sat between the engines. It was literally deafining."[33] The exhaust stacks of the air-cooled engines proved to be the "Achilles Heel" of the early Keystone bombers; their fabric covering proved to be highly flammable. Sparks or cinders from the exhaust could, and did, easily set the airplane on fire. Later versions offered an improvement. The 7th Bombardment Group would fly several models of the Keystone bomber until 1934, when an entirely new generation of more modern and more capable bombers made their appearance.

Shortly after receiving its first bombers, the 7th Bombardment Group received a new commanding officer. On May 6, 1929, Maj. Carl Spaatz assumed command of the 7th Group and its two assigned squadrons, while Capt. Hugh Elmendorf reverted to commander of the 95th Pursuit Squadron.[34] At the time, Spaatz was one of the Air Corps' leading experts on pursuit aviation, having flown pursuits in France during WWI, where he achieved three victories over German fighters, later serving as commander of the 1st Pursuit Group. Spaatz took up his new appointment as the Air Corps

The cockpit layout of a later Keystone B-6A, which is illustrative of the series. The control wheel could be swung over to the left side when it was the copilot's turn to fly. (3B-28079, RG 342FH NARA)

Major Carl Spaatz stands to the far right with a group of Air Corps officers at a demonstration at Langley Field in May 1928, a year before taking over command of the 7th Bombardment Group. (02-S-00652, Courtesy San Diego Air & Space Museum)

was beginning to revise its doctrine of air power and making the first halting steps toward the development of theories of strategic air bombardment. His experiences with the 7th Bombardment Group would enable Spaatz to contribute to the development of these theories in the following years.[35]

Four days after arriving at his new command, Spaatz departed Rockwell Field with a formation of airplanes from the 11th Bombardment Squadron and the 95th Pursuit Squadron for Wright Field, Ohio, to join the Air Corps' 1929 annual maneuvers.[36] The 11th Squadron sent off its six LB-7 bombers, while the 95th Squadron's flight consisted of 15 recently arrived Boeing P-12 and older PW-9D pursuits. Three transports from the Headquarters Squadron accompanied the fighters and bombers. The maneuvers in Ohio, running from May 15th to May 25th, were the largest combined exercise involving ground troops and the Air Corps held to that date, and the first to have air units assigned to both opposing forces. Air Corps units from all over the country flew in more than 200 aircraft to equip the Blue Force and the Red Force under the overall direction of Brig. Gen. Benjamin Foulois, Assistant Chief of the Air Corps. The 95th Pursuit Squadron joined the 2nd Bombardment Group, the 3rd Attack Group, and the 9th Observation Group as part of the Blue Force based at Wright Field, while the 11th Bombardment Squadron became part of the Red Force with the 1st Pursuit Group and the 15th and 16th Observation Squadrons, based at North Field, near Columbus.[37] The state of Ohio was divided in two, with the Red Army defending the eastern half of the state and the Blue Army the western half. Over the course of the maneuvers, both the Blue and Red air forces were heavily engaged in daily missions to practice both offensive and defensive tactics, culminating in an attack on a mock ground force using live bombs and ammunition. While F. Trubee Davison, Assistant Secretary of War (Air), praised the maneuvers, saying "from a tactical viewpoint, the experienced gained in these maneuvers has been of inestimable value...", at least one knowledgeable observer doubted whether officials had gleaned the larger lesson that air forces were weapons of attack and should be employed in that capacity.[38] Echoing themes that were part of the Air Corps' own developing theory of air power, the writer argued that the full effect of this lesson from the last war "...should do much for building up of larger and larger air forces, for it will provide a weapon which can strike with lightning rapidity and deliver its blow in what in former times was called non-combatant territory where not only the food and machines of war are gathered and stored, but where the spirit which keeps wars going is engendered."[39]

One of the most interesting features of the maneuvers was an attempt at long-range bombing using aerial refueling, in a practical test of the success of the flight of the "Question

Mark" earlier in the year. The Material Division at Wright Field modified a Keystone LB-7, adding two fuel tanks in the rear fuselage with a gasoline intake in the top of the fuselage, close to the rear gunner's position. A system of pumps fed the gasoline in the rear tanks into the airplane's main tanks in the wings. The plan was to have the LB-7 take off from Wright Field and meet up with a Douglas C-1 refueling plane over Washington, D.C., then fly on to New York City to drop flares over New York Harbor. The bomber would be refueled in the

A line up of the Keystone LB-7s of the 11th Bombardment Squadron, two Fokker C-2 and a Douglas C-1 transports, and the Boeing PW-9D pursuits of the 95th Pursuit Squadron at Rockwell Field circa 1929. (00025498, Courtesy San Diego Air & Space Museum)

air again on its return flight to Wright Field, having covered a distance of some 1,300 miles non-stop. Lt. Odas Moon, a member of the 11th Bombardment Squadron who had flown the second refueling airplane during the "Question Mark" flight, was chosen to fly the LB-7, while Capt. Ross Hoyt, who had flown the first refueling plane, would repeat his role flying the C-1. Practice flights around Wright Field proved the concept and the modifications to the LB-7. Unfortunately, on the chosen day (May 21st), the weather proved uncooperative. The refueling plane could not get off the ground. Moon got through the weather to New York, where he dropped three flares over Governor's Island, headquarters of the Army's 2nd Corps area, around 2125, then flew to Bolling Field, Washington, where he landed.[40] The next day, Moon and Hoyt flew up from Bolling Field to provide New York City with a demonstration of aerial refueling, actually refueling one time, then demonstrating the process of hooking up four more times while a radio broadcaster from the National Broadcasting Corporation flew nearby in another Air Corps airplane, describing the action.[41] The long-range flight Moon and Hoyt had attempted would become routine thirty years later.

Keystone LB-7 bombers from the 11th Bombardment Squadron flying in formation over California. In a day when airplanes were still relatively small and few in number, a formation of these large bombers was an impressive sight. (00025506, Courtesy San Diego Air & Space Museum)

The 11th Bombardment Squadron returned from the maneuvers in Ohio at the end of May and began a regular training program of formation flying and aerial gunnery, interspersed with occasional cross-country flights, continuing this program for the remainder of the year. This would be the squadron's and the 7th Bombardment Group's pattern for much of the next decade. Pilots would fly as often as possible to practice and refine their individual skills. Squadron, and later Group exercises would integrate individual aircraft into larger formations. The squadrons and the Group would practice and refine offensive and defensive tactics in preparation for the annual Air Corps maneuvers, where senior commanders could test command and control of large air units. Proficiency in bombing, gunnery, and navigation would also be practiced and tested throughout the year. At this time, the Air Corps did not have specialized bombardiers or navigators; pilots were expected to do their own navigating and bombing. In addition, they were expected to demonstrate proficiency in aerial gunnery. The standards were set out in the Training Regulations manual TR 440-40, *Air Corps Aerial Gunnery and Bombing*. Attaining proficiency to meet the standards depended on the annual ammunition and bombing allowances allocated to the squadron. Bombing practice

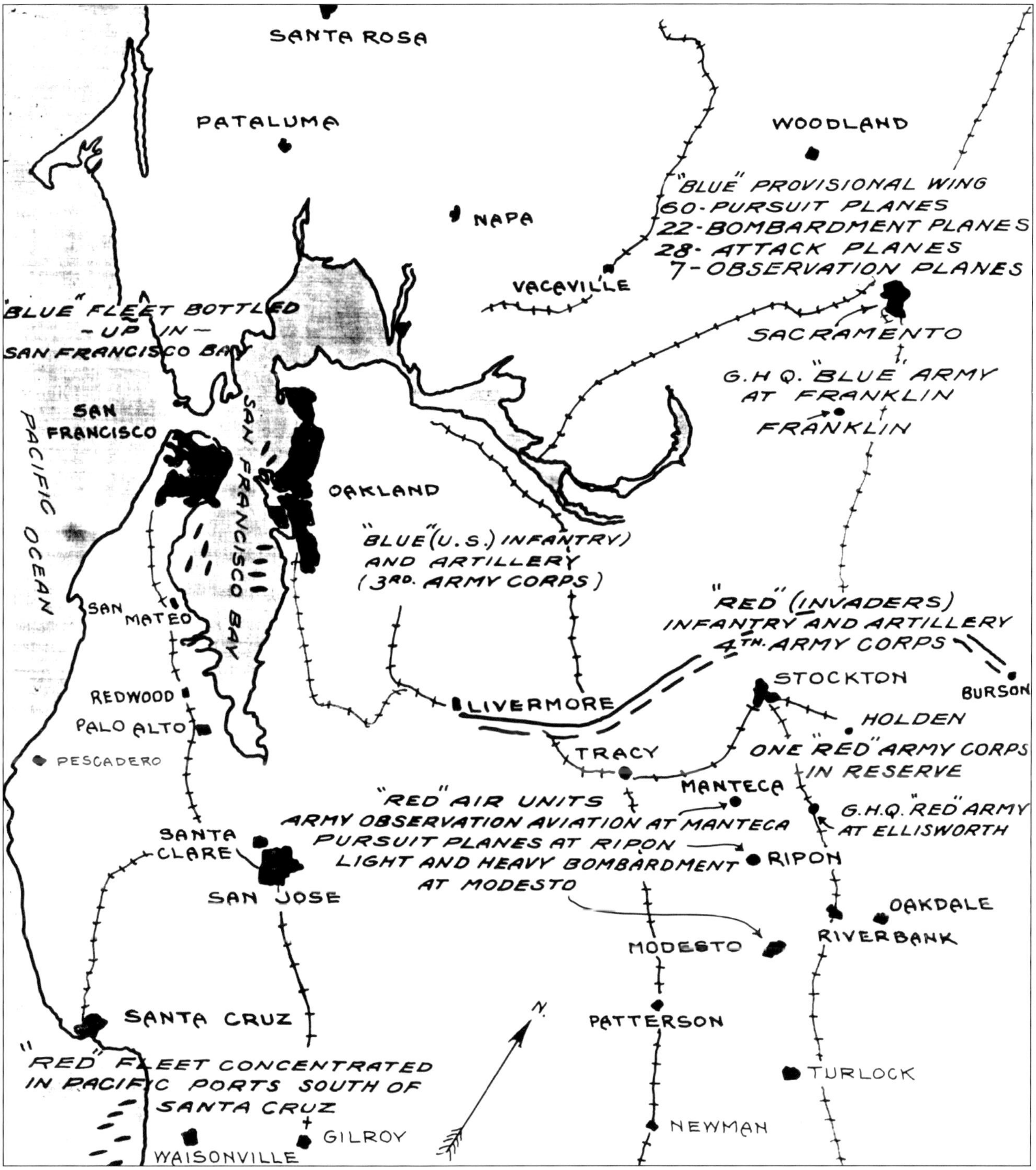

The plan for the April 1930 Army Air Corps Field Exercises showing the location of the Red and Blue forces around the San Francisco area. (3B-10961, RG 342FH,NARA)

consisted of low altitude bombing at 300 feet, aiming at a white disc 12' in diameter; intermediate altitude bombing at 5,000 feet at a white disc 30 feet in diameter in the center of a larger white ring 200 feet in diameter; and what was then termed high altitude bombing at 8,000 feet against the same target.[42] Pilots aspired to be awarded the rating of Expert Aerial Bomber and Expert Aerial Gunner. When possible, the Air Corps held annual matches in May, where pilots from Attack, Bombardment, Observation, and Pursuit squadrons competed against each other.

The Air Corps was keen to demonstrate to the American public the reality of air power and the prowess of its pilots, and give the public a glimpse of its equipment.[43] This took the form of publicizing the annual maneuvers and incorporating mass flights over nearby cities and towns and participating in public events, such as the opening of municipal airports. This had the benefit of maximizing the value of cross-country

The four Group commanders at the 1930 maneuvers (left to right): Major Hugh Knerr, 2nd Bombardment Group; Major Davenport Johnson, 3rd Attack Group; Major Carl Spaatz, 7th Bombardment Group; and Major Ralph Royce, 1st Pursuit Group. (3B-10985, RG 342FH, NARA)

training flights. During the summer of 1929, the Air Corps introduced a policy that required pilots to make at least one long-range trip a month, covering a distance of 500 miles each way in order to practice and gain experience in navigation.[44] There was some debate within the Group as to whether it was better to rely on one's navigation or to add extra minutes to a flight by following a railroad instead, the difference being that pilots stood "...to lose a week if forced down in some of those big wide 'open spaces' out here in the West."[45] The 7th Bombardment Group participated regularly in cross-country flights to public events. That summer, Maj. Spaatz led a formation of six P-12 pursuits and three LB-7s over Los Angeles, then to the Grand Central Airport at Glendale, California, to perform maneuvers overhead for a visiting convention of members of the Elks; formations of LB-7s attended the opening of several airports in the region, three bombers with an escort of P-12s from the 95th Pursuit Squadron flying to the opening of the Denver airport in October.[46] Other flights that Fall involved a series of tests to determine fuel and oil consumption and air speeds for the LB-7 at various altitudes from 5,000 to 10,000 feet. The 11th Squadron conducted tests of the bomber's load carrying capacity, setting a record for an LB-7. One bomber carried a load of 6,200 pounds made up of three enlisted men, 2,200 pounds of fuel, 2,700 pounds of bombs, six machine guns, and additional ballast.[47]

The most pressing problem the 7th Bombardment Group faced was the rapid attrition of the 11th Bombardment Squadron's LB-7 aircraft. On September 2, 1929, LB-7 serial number 29-6 burned to the ground when the left engine backfired, igniting the fabric on the left wing.[48] A second bomber was wrecked in an attempt to land spare parts and a repair crew on a dry lake bed where a 95th Pursuit Squadron pilot had crash-landed.[49] The risk of fire in the LB-7 was an ongoing problem. The 11th Bombardment Squadron suspended its training program for three weeks in November to allow longer exhaust stacks to be installed in the LB-7s that extended back out over the rear edge of the lower wing, instead of ejecting exhaust directly over the wing. The Material Division at Wright Field sent out an engineering officer to confer with Maj. Spaatz and his staff on the engine exhaust stack installations.[50] The visitor, a Capt. R.G. Breene, left December 2nd; ironically, nineteen days later, the 11th Squadron lost another LB-7 to fire. Then, in the first week of March 1930, the Squadron lost two LB-7s to crashes on consecutive days. Taking off on March 4th as a member of a three-plane formation, Lt. William Groen, Jr.'s LB-7 somehow damaged one of its landing gear. Those on the ground could see the problem, but Groen was unaware of the damage. Capt. Hugh Elmendorf, C.O. of the 95th Pursuit Squadron, took off with another pursuit pilot, and through a series of maneuvers got the attention of the LB-7's crew, one of whom saw the damaged landing gear and sent Groen a note. Groen circled the field, then came in for a landing, gently putting the LB-7 down on the remaining gear until the airplane slowed down and settled on the broken gear, wrecking the wing, but without injury to the crew.[51] As a result, when the annual Air Corps maneuvers began in April, the 11th Squadron had only five LB-7 bombers available.

The Army Air Corps' 1930 Field Exercises were ambitious in scope, if not in the number of airplanes involved. For the first time, all four Air Corps branches—Attack, Bombardment, Observation, and Pursuit—would be combined in the maneuvers, and also for the first time, the Air Corps would organize a Wing command to experiment with the coordination of operations by multiple units of bombers and pursuits. Brig. Gen. William Gillmore, Assistant Chief of the Air Corps, was placed in command of the First Provisional Wing. This temporary organization would also be in charge of the maneuvers. Mather Field, near Sacramento, was chosen as the base for the exercise. The units involved were the 1st Pursuit Group from Selfridge Field in Michigan, the 2nd Bombardment Group from Langley Field in Virginia, the 3rd Attack Group from Fort Crockett in Texas, the 7th Bombardment Group from Rockwell Field, and the 91st Observation Squadron from Crissy Field in San Francisco, creating a force of more than 150 aircraft of all types. The maneuvers, scheduled to be held from April 1st to April 24th, were divided into three phases. During the first week, training would focus on practice within the individual squadrons and groups, including air discipline for operating from a congested airfield. During the second week, the groups would be assigned various tactical problems and test out new tactics developed for each branch. The third week would involve a mock battle in and around San Francisco, based on a tactical problem involving attacks and defense against a supposed enemy force that had captured much of Southern California. The climax of the exercise would be a defense of San Francisco from a supposed naval attack. At the end of the exercises, the Air Corps planned public displays over San Francisco and Los Angeles.[52]

One of the more interesting aspects of the 1930 Air Corps maneuvers was the experimental use of radio for directing tactical units. The Air Corps had tried out ground to air radio communications on several occasions during the late 1920s, but the radio sets available were heavy and bulky, limiting their tactical use.[53] The standard SCR-133 set weighed 70 pounds, while the SCR-134 weighed 100 pounds—suitable for a bomber or transport, but difficult to fit in a pursuit plane.[54] The ability to exercise command and control of units in the air was fairly limited; flight commanders communicated through the use of visual hand signals, or rocking the wings of their airplanes to get the attention of the other members of their flight, and communication between flights of different kinds of aircraft was even more difficult. Radio thus held great promise, if it could be made practical. Maj. Carl Spaatz was one of the pioneers of this development.[55] At the end of 1929, with the assistance of a radio engineer from the Army Signal Corps, Spaatz had all the LB-7 bombers in the 11th Squadron, the 7th Bombardment Group Headquarters Fokker C-2 transport, and one P-12 pursuit outfitted with radios.[56] On December 27, 1929, the 11th Squadron sent a formation of bombers on a cross-country flight up to Crissy Field at San Francisco. During the flight, the bombers were in regular contact with ground stations, receiving hourly weather reports from the Western Air Express radio system along the way.[57]

At the end of the April 1930 maneuvers, the 1st Provisional Wing's units flew south to give several demonstration flights in and around Los Angeles. Here a formation of LB-7 bombers flies in review over March Field. (3B-11005, RG 342FH, NARA)

A formation of Keystone LB-6/7 and Curtiss B-2 bombers flying over Mills Field, San Francisco, in a public demonstration on April 19, 1930. Some 125,000 people visited the field to witness the flying. (3B-10982, RG 342FH, NARA)

Pilots of both the 11th and 95th Squadrons worked out a list of 100 words that could be heard distinctly over the radio against engine noise to use in addition to Morse Code and began regular practice with radio communication. The problem of fitting the bulky radio into the P-12s was partly solved by fitting Capt. Hugh Elmendorf's airplane with both sending and receiving radios and fitting only receivers into the airplanes of his five element leaders. Elmendorf could then receive and confirm commands and pass them on to his element leaders, who passed on the commands to their flights using hand signals. During some working-up exercises before the April maneuvers, Maj. Gen. Fechet, Chief of the Air Corps, went up in one of the 11th Bombardment Squadron's LB-7s, and with Maj. Spaatz sitting behind him, directed a formation of 18 pursuit planes of the 95th Squadron while flying between Los Angeles and Rockwell Field.[58]

The units detailed for the maneuvers began arriving at Mather Field at the end of March. The 2nd Bombardment Group flew out one LB-6, six LB-7s, and eleven B-2 bombers from Langley Field, the 3rd Attack Group brought its A-3 attack planes, and the 1st Pursuit Group had 22 P-1C pursuits and 18 brand new P-12s picked up at the Boeing plant in Seattle and flown down to Mather Field. The 7th Bombardment Group contributed 22 P-12s from the 95th Squadron and four LB-7s from the 11th Squadron. Several transports from the

A Curtiss B-2 "Condor" bomber of the 96th Bombardment Squadron, which passed on nine of its Condors to the 11th Bombardment Squadron at the end of the April 1930 maneuvers in California. (3B-24362, RG 342FH, NARA)

Headquarters Squadron, who had been flying a shuttle service carrying supplies between Rockwell Field and Mather Field, accompanied the Group. After a week of practice flying, the assembled units took up tactical problems. The bombardment squadrons practiced bombing runs against railroad bridges and junctions, airfields, and simulated attacks on shipping in San Francisco harbor. As part of the final week's exercise against the imaginary invasion force to the south, the bombers concentrated on disrupting communications links that an invading force could use to move north. On some missions, attack planes escorted the bombers to practice "taking out" anti-aircraft units before the bombers began their bombing runs. The bombers also practiced defensive formations against pursuit attack, working out a "V" formation with planes stepped down from the leader so as to expose a pursuit attacking from the rear to the concentrated fire of the formation's rear gun turrets. Throughout the maneuvers, the First Provisional Wing operated independently from any ground forces, in effect practicing as an independent, self-supporting military force. On April 19th, the entire force of 150 airplanes flew in a mass formation over the city of San Francisco to Mills Field, with the pursuits making mock attacks on the bomber formations.[59] For the senior officers and unit commanders, the annual maneuvers provided valuable experience in the mobilization of air units, the logistical challenges of maintaining a unit in the field away from its home base, and the problems involved in coordinating different units as part of a larger air plan.

At the end of the maneuvers, the 2nd Bombardment Group's 96th Bombardment Squadron traded aircraft with the 11th Bombardment Squadron. Accidents with the LB-7s had reduced the 11th Squadron to half its strength. Rather than assign more LB-7s from other bombardment squadrons to the 11th Squadron, the Air Corps decided to transfer nine of the eleven Condors the 96th had brought from Langley Field to the 11th. The 11th Squadron in turn gave its five remaining LB-7s to the 96th to fly back to Virginia. Prior to the maneuvers, the Air Corps had given a contract to the Keystone Aircraft Company for 73 new improved bombers based on the earlier LB-6/7 series and had decided to allocate 20 to the 2nd Bombardment Group. These new models, designated the B-3A when the Air Corps dropped the Light Bomber classification later in the year, were to be delivered to the 2nd Bombardment Group early in 1931, leaving the 96th Squadron to soldier on with the older LB-7s for the remainder of 1930.[60]

Members of the 11th Bombardment Squadron stand in front of one of the Squadron's new Curtiss B-2 Condors in the fall of 1930. The Squadron's "Mr. Jiggs" insignia has been painted on the nose of the bomber. (7th Bombardment Group (H) Historical Foundation, USAFA McDermott Library)

A formation of nine B-2 Condors flying along the California coast. The 11th Bombardment Squadron was often called on to provide aerial reviews for visiting dignitaries and public ceremonies across southern California. (3B-24383, RG 342FH, NARA)

Powered by two Curtiss Conqueror 675 h.p. liquid-cooled engines, the Curtiss B-2 Condor was bigger, faster, and carried a heavier bomb load than the LB-7. Although superior in performance, the B-2 was more expensive than the LB-7 and

A Curtiss B-2 Condor from the 11th Bombardment Squadron being loaded with bombs at Fort Sill, Oklahoma, during the bombing tests conducted in October 1930. (3B-24367, RG 342FH, NARA)

would not fit into existing Air Corps hangars; a selection panel chose the Keystone bomber over the Curtiss, but the Air Corps went ahead and gave Curtiss a contract for twelve B-2s.[61] The pilots of the 11th Bombardment Squadron preferred the Condor over the Keystone; the Condor was more pleasant to fly and had fewer mechanical problems than the LB-7s.[62]

The 11th Squadron took to their new mounts with alacrity. On May 23, 1930, after a month's practice, the Squadron sent off six Condors to join 18 P-12s from the 95th Squadron for an aerial review over Coronado for the visiting Building and Loan Convention involving half an hour of formation flying.[63] A more dramatic display followed around two weeks later. The 7th Bombardment Group organized a mock air battle over Los Angeles as part of the ceremonies for the dedication of Mines Field, Los Angeles' first municipal airport. The 11th Bombardment Squadron sent off six Condors to fly over the city at 15,000 feet. The P-12s of the 95th Squadron were flying high above at 30,000 feet. After a radio signal from the bombers, the P-12s dived down to attack imaginary anti-aircraft positions, then soared back up to escort the bomber formation in its attack on the city. The formation then flew over the assembled dignitaries at the airport. A radio link with a local radio station enabled one of the officers flying in one of the Condor bombers to explain over the air what was happening during the demonstration.[64]

More practical applications of the new Condors began October 1st, with the start of the formal training season. In preparation, the 11th Bombardment Squadron painted its Condors with striking yellow markings on the nose and engine cowlings and added the famous "Mr. Jiggs" insignia. That day, the 11th and 95th Squadrons conducted an aerial review for Maj. Barton Yount, commander of Rockwell Field, and Maj. Carl Spaatz. Three days later, Spaatz had both squadrons engage in a tactical problem, directing their movements from a newly-arrived Fokker C-7 transport plane that had been fitted out with radio receiving and transmitting equipment. In the middle of the month, the 7th Bombardment Group conducted a test of anti-aircraft equipment in cooperation with the 63rd Anti-Aircraft Regiment. The 95th Squadron stationed one flight of P-12s at United Airfield in Burbank to intercept flights of three Condors with a flight of P-12s as escorts. The Condors flew night missions to give the anti-aircraft regiment more practice. A week later, Lt. Charles Howard, the 11th Squadron's newly-appointed commander, took three Condors to Fort Sill, Oklahoma, where the Air Corps and the Army Ordnance Department were holding ten days of bombing tests to examine the effect of various sizes

An 11th Bombardment Squadron B-2 in flight carrying a 2,000-pound bomb during the bombing tests at Fort Sill. (3B-5865, RG 342FH, NARA)

of bombs on hard surfaces. The rocky hills surrounding the area of the fort provided an excellent testing ground. During their time at Fort Sill, the three 11th Squadron crews dropped a large number of bombs, ranging from 300 to 2,000 pounds. As pilots normally were allocated only 32 practice bombs and a few live bombs per year, this was a special opportunity.[65]

March Field

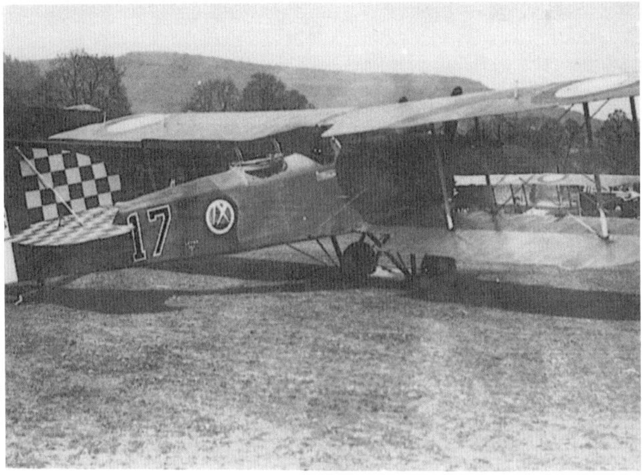

A Breguet 14A2 of the 9th Aero Squadron at Trier, Germany, in 1919, showing the Squadron's insignia of three searchlight beams forming the Roman numeral IX, relating to the Squadron's role in night bombardment. (7th Bombardment Group (H) Historical Foundation, USAFA McDermott Library)

Completing the formation of the 1st Bombardment Wing and its component units took time. In the years following the passage of the Army Air Corps Act, funding and the lack of adequate officer personnel acted as constraints on the organization of tactical units, and as a result, the plans envisioned at the beginning of the Air Corps' expansion fell behind schedule.[66] The Air Corps' original intention was to have established the 1st Bombardment Wing at March Field, with one bomber and one pursuit group, but it was not until 1931 that the next steps could be taken towards this objective. For Maj. Carl Spaatz and the officers and men of the 7th Bombardment Group, the year would be one of change, transformation, and movement involving a protracted transition from Rockwell Field to March Field, all against the need to maintain the Group's on-going training program and preparations for the annual Air Corps maneuvers.

As a first stage in the process, on April 1, 1931, the Air Corps activated the first of several new units, beginning with the 1st Bombardment Wing.[67] The same day, the Air Corps activated the 9th and 31st Bombardment Squadrons at March Field and assigned them to the 7th Group, to bring the Group up to its full complement of three squadrons.[68] Both squadrons traced their origins back to WWI. The 9th had begun life May 31, 1917, as the 9th Aero Squadron. Sent to England in 1918 for further training, the Squadron went to France during the summer of 1918 and converted to the French Breguet 14A2 bomber. The 9th Aero Squadron flew its first mission over the lines September 14, 1918, and from then until the Armistice flew night bombing and reconnaissance missions.[69] After serving with the Army of Occupation in Germany, the Squadron returned to the United States and was placed on the inactive list in June 1922. The 31st Squadron had been activated June 13, 1917, and had also gone to France in 1918, but did not see combat, serving as a training squadron at the Army Air Service center at Issoudun until the end of the war, when the Squadron returned to the United States and was demobilized.[70] Following activation, Capt. Leo F. Post was appointed commander of the 9th Bombardment Squadron and Capt. Earle G. Harper commander of the 31st Bombardment Squadron.[71] Over the next few months, regular and reserve officers and recent graduates of the advanced flying schools joined the squadron. The Air Corps did not have enough bomber aircraft to equip the two new squadrons. As an interim solution, each squadron received ten new Douglas O-38B observation aircraft.[72] The O-38B's Pratt & Whitney Hornet engine gave the airplane a top speed of 143 mph, about 15 miles an hour faster than the Breguet 14 of WWI.[73]

The 7th Bombardment Group would not complete its move to March Field for another eight months. The Group's movement to its new home was part of a complicated series of other moves. During 1931, the Air Corps undertook a consolidation of its flying training programs, moving its primary flying training schools at Brooks Field at San Antonio, Texas, and March Field in California to the newly-built Randolph Field, occupying a larger area outside of San Antonio.[74] Although construction had begun in 1929, Randolph

A Douglas O-38B observation plane that formed the initial equipment of the 9th and 31st Bombardment Squadrons at March Field. (Peter M. Bowers Collection, Museum of Flight)

Field did not begin flying training until November 2, 1931. The primary flying school at March Field did not move to Randolph until September 1931. In July 1931, the Air Corps

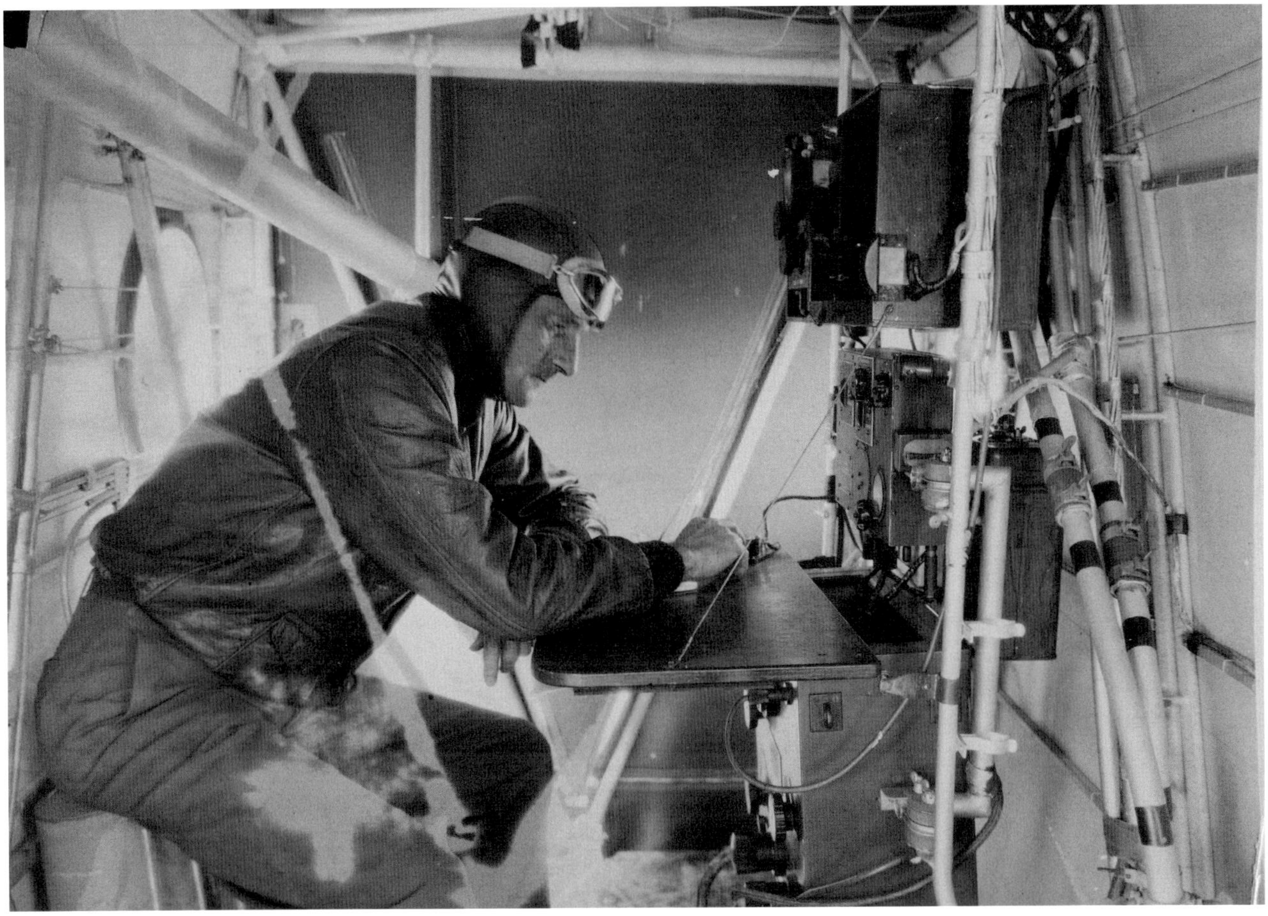

Major Carl Spaatz sending out messages on board the 7th Bombardment Group's Fokker C-7A command ship, which could carry the heavy and bulky radio equipment of the day. By early 1931, the Group had shifted entirely to voice communications. (02-00638, Courtesy San Diego Air & Space Museum)

had also activated the 17th Pursuit Group and two new pursuit squadrons (the 34th and the 73rd) as the component pursuit group for the 1st Bombardment Wing and transferred the 95th Pursuit Squadron from the 7th Bombardment Group to be under the 17th Pursuit Group.[75] With new squadrons forming and the primary flying school moving out, bringing all the units and personnel of the 7th Bombardment Group to one base took some time. With the integration of new units and a major move on the horizon, and the transfer of personnel to March Field accelerating, the 7th Group still had to maintain its own training program in anticipation of the 1931 Air Corps maneuvers planned for the month of May.

The Air Corps maneuvers planned for 1931 were the most ambitious yet undertaken. While previous maneuvers had focused on tactical problems, the goal for the 1931 maneuvers was to explore the challenges of operating the largest air unit then authorized, an Air Division. As the Air Corps did not yet have an operating wing in existence, this was an ambitious challenge, but one the Air Corps' leaders were keen to pursue, conscious as they were that when America went to war in 1917, few Army officers had any experience working with full divisions, much less a corps or field army. By its table of organization, an Air Division would have 2,238 airplanes, 4,000 officers, and 28,000 enlisted men, a force nearly double the size of the existing Air Corps at that date. By employing all but one of the Air Corps squadrons in the continental United States, one flight from each of 19 National Guard observation squadrons, and by creating an observation and pursuit group and an attack and bombardment squadron from the advanced flying school at Kelly Field, the Air Corps came up with a force of 667 airplanes, 692 officers, 69 flying cadets, and 643 enlisted men. Out of this mix, the Air Corps organized ten groups composed of 32 squadrons. These ten groups, with a transport group and the National Guard flights, were designated the 1st Provisional Air Division. These units were divided up and assigned to four temporary larger provisional units for the period of the maneuvers. These were the 1st Provisional Pursuit Wing, the 11th Provisional Bombardment Wing, and the 21st and 22nd Provisional Observation Wings. This force, though well below the

A Fokker C-7A transport plane, the type that Spaatz used as his radio command plane. (Peter M. Bowers Collection, Museum of Flight)

authorized strength of an Air Division, still presented real challenges with regard to basing, coordination, communication, and supply that would test staff at all levels of command. The initial plan called for a concentration in the area around Wright Field, followed by movement to the New York area, New England, and the Chesapeake Bay area. The maneuvers were scheduled to run for two weeks beginning in mid-May.[76]

In the first weeks of the new year, the staff of the 7th Bombardment Group devised an intensive training program for the 11th Bombardment and the 95th Pursuit Squadron involving formation flying, altitude flights, tactical missions, and cross-country navigation exercises and radio communication exercises.[77] For the altitude flights, the 11th Squadron pilots took their B-2 Condors up on a series of flights to measure the rate of climb and maximum height that could be obtained in two hours, and to familiarize the pilots with the use of oxygen at high altitudes.[78] On one flight, a Lt. J.A. Ronin coaxed his B-2 up to an altitude of 24,940 feet, well above the specified absolute ceiling for the B-2 of 19,400 feet and surely a record for the B-2.[79] The two squadrons cooperated with bombing and gunnery practice, the pursuits towing sleeve targets for the B-2 gunners to fire at. When the bombers went out to practice bombing against a target anchored at sea, the pursuits practiced by dive-bombing the shadows the bombers created on the surface of the ocean with 25-pound bombs.[80]

Maj. Spaatz continued developing radio communications with both squadrons. During the early months of 1931, the Group coordinated most of its training exercises using radios installed in the Condors and newer, smaller radios in the P-12 pursuits. Spaatz could coordinate the movements of both squadrons using either the Group's Fokker C-7A transport command ship or a P-12 fitted out with radio equipment. The Group and the two squadrons maintained their own ground stations to maintain communications once the squadron pilots

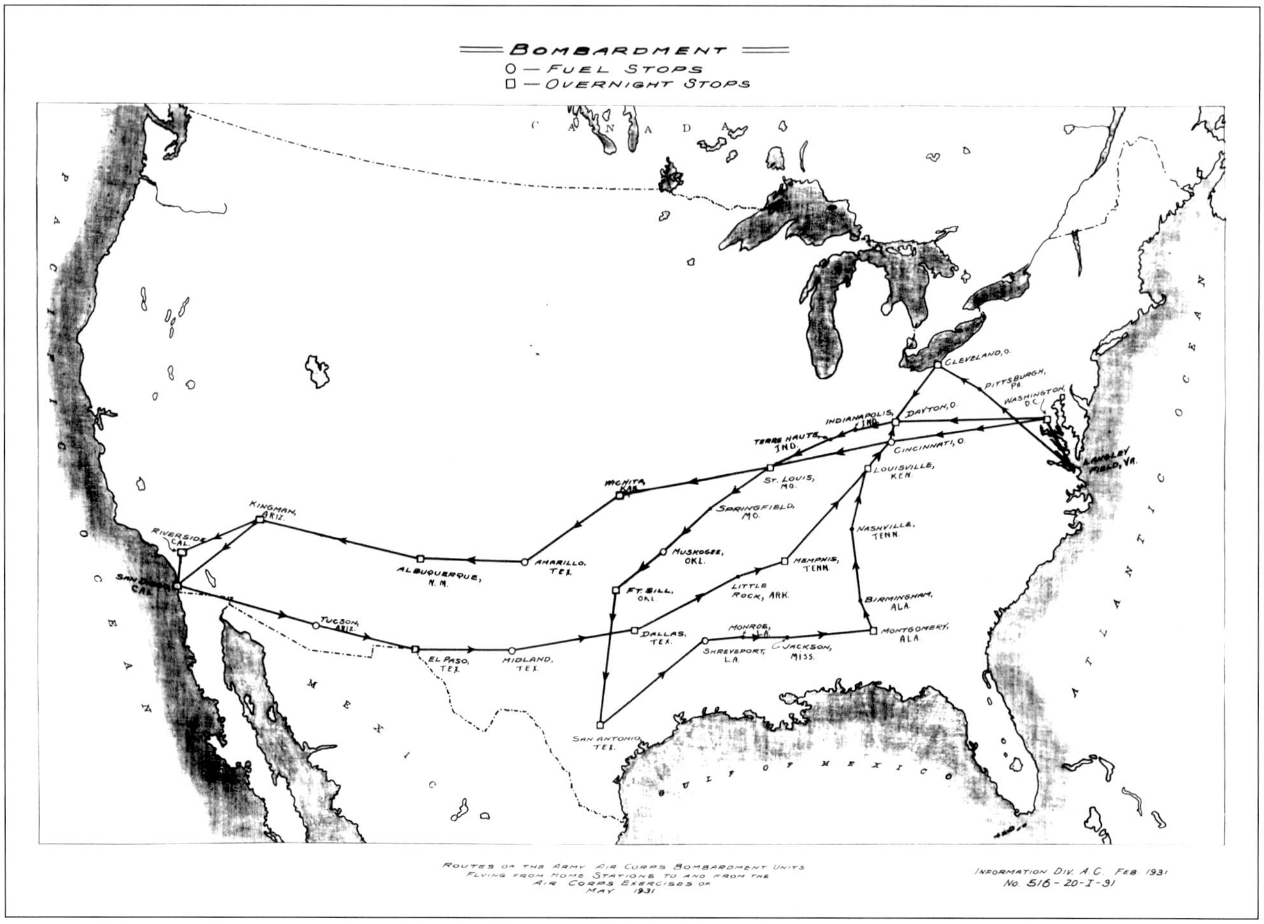

were airborne on training exercises or cross-country flights. Coming back from a long flight to Tucson, Arizona, the 11th Squadron was in radio contact with the Squadron's ground station for the entire flight. In another series of experiments

A formation of 11th Bombardment Squadron B-2 bombers taken during the 1931 Air Corps maneuvers. Poor weather dogged the maneuvers for much of the time. (3B-24382, RG 342FH, NARA)

undertaken during the last two weeks of March, the Group investigated the ability to direct pursuits against a bomber by radio. The 11th Squadron would send up a Condor bomber to fly out of visual range of Rockwell Field, but remain in radio contact, providing altitude, location, and course. The ground station would then pass this information on to the pursuits, directing them toward the bomber for a successful interception.[81]

Preparations for the 1931 annual maneuvers went into high gear toward the end of April. Brig. Gen. Benjamin Foulois was appointed commander of the 1st Provisional Air Division, with Lt. Col. Frank Andrews as his Chief of Staff. Maj. Spaatz was appointed Deputy Chief of Staff, so Maj. Joseph McNarney, commander of the Primary Flying School at March Field, filled in as temporary commander of the 7th Bombardment Group.[82] The 11th Bombardment Squadron was assigned to the 2nd Bombardment Group to give the 2nd a full complement of four bomber squadrons. For the maneuvers, the 7th Bombardment group was made up of the newly-formed 9th and 31st Squadrons with their O-38s and a special provisional squadron from Kelly Field—also with O-38s—all acting as "bombers."[83] The Group had a long cross-country flight to get to Dayton. Since the Secretary of War had ordered that a large part of the 1931 maneuvers entail demonstrations to give the public a view of the Air Corps and its activities, the 7th Group made an overnight stop at Dallas to give the public there a chance to inspect the Group's B-2 Condors and O-38 aircraft.[84] Lt. Charles Howard, commander of the 11th Bombardment Squadron, arranged a radio link-up with a local Dallas radio station to broadcast a description of the flight as the massed formation approached the city.[85]

The squadrons participating in the maneuvers began arriving at Wright Field in mid-May and immediately began practicing formation flying in group strength. At Wright Field, a Composite Demonstration Group was organized with one attack, one bombardment, and one pursuit squadron to put on an exhibition of aerial combat tactics. Competition to be

An 11th Bombardment Squadron B-2 Condor. The copilot salutes the photographer. The photograph illustrates how unprotected the crews were from the elements. (3B-24372, RG 342FH, NARA)

selected was intense. The 11th Bombardment Squadron was chosen to represent bombardment aviation and the 95th Pursuit Squadron narrowly beat out the 36th Pursuit for the honor, with the 13th Attack Squadron completing the Group.[86] May 18th, the Air Division put on its first review, with 300 airplanes

An 11th Bombardment Squadron B-2 flying over Atlantic City, New Jersey. (7th Bombardment Group (H) Historical Foundation, USAFA McDermott Library)

An aerial photograph of March Field taken a few months after the 7th Bombardment Group moved from Rockwell Field. (3B-18591, RG 342FH, NARA)

flying over the Fairfield Air Depot in front of huge crowds. Poor weather delayed a move to Chicago until May 20th, when the 1st Provisional Air Division moved up to several municipal airports around Chicago. Despite blustery weather the next day, the entire Air Division took off and formed up for a fly past down the shore of Lake Michigan past hundreds of thousands of residents of Chicago, taking a full hour to complete the review. After leaving Chicago, the Air Division flew back to Wright Field. The Composite Demonstration Group returned to the lake front to put on its own exhibition. As the Associated Press reported:

> ...the crowd was not denied its thrills. The Ninety-Fifth Pursuit Squadron of Rockwell Field, Cal., the Eleventh Bombardment Squadron of Rockwell Field and the Thirteenth Attack Squadron left the rest of the division south of the city and returned to the downtown section. Out over the lake in view of thousands of office workers these squadrons first flew in close formations, their wing tips seeming almost to touch. Nine heavy bombers, ominous looking craft that in war time carry 2,000-pounds of explosives each, flew low, setting up a great roar with their eighteen motors. Twelve attack planes, faster, more agile, waged mimic warfare on ground personnel. Up among the clouds the eighteen single seated pursuit ships cavorted under the leadership of Capt. F. O'D. Hunter, one of the few remaining war aces still in the service. Swerving quickly, banking so that only their yellow backs were visible at times, these tiny speedsters demonstrated everything in the army air repertory...[87]

From Wright Field, the Air Division flew on to the New York area, deploying to bases on Long Island. The Division repeated the aerial review it had given in Chicago May 23rd, flying past Manhattan down the Hudson River while the Composite Demonstration Group gave an exhibition over newly-opened Floyd Bennett Field. At New York, the Air Division became part of an elaborate war game Gen. Douglas MacArthur, Army Chief of Staff, had devised to test the Army Air Corps' ability to respond rapidly in defense of America's coasts.[88] Although the Air Corps had been assigned a role in coastal defense, throughout the 1930s, this continued to be a source of controversy between the Army and the Navy. In January 1931, MacArthur reached an agreement with the Chief of Naval Operations, freeing the Navy from responsibility for coastal defense and increasing the role of the Air Corps.[89] The scenario MacArthur had devised involved an enemy invasion fleet approaching New England, then proceeding south along the East Coast. Weather again dogged the maneuvers, but the Air Division moved to airfields around Boston for two days of operations and an aerial review over the city. The scene then shifted back to the New York area, with the Division conducting operations around Atlantic City, where the war game ended. The maneuvers finished in Washington, D.C., with a mass aerial review over the city after the Composite Demonstration Group had completed its half-hour exhibition. Over the course of two weeks, the Air Division's aircraft had flown almost 38,000 hours and cumulatively covered nearly four million miles, with only three aircraft damaged beyond repair. The 11th Bombardment Squadron had participated in five exhibitions of aerial tactics, all enthusiastically received. The Squadron ended the maneuvers at Langley Field, home of the 2nd Bombardment Group, whose pilots cast a longing eye at their former B-2 Condors, "...because they still have a soft spot in their hearts for them."[90]

The 11th Bombardment Squadron employed its B-2 bombers for numerous exercises and aerial reviews around Southern California from Rockwell Field and the Squadron's new home at March Field. (00040402, Courtesy San Diego Air & Space Museum)

In a widely published article titled "Radio-Controlled Sky Battles of the Next Great War" published after the maneuvers, Maj. Carl Spaatz described the vast change in tactics that radio had brought about since the end of WWI. Contrasting wartime flights with what the 1st Provisional Air Division had just demonstrated, Spaatz wrote: "...the picture of great swarms of airplanes wandering blindly towards the fighting front has changed to one of well-organized units, flying precise, highly maneuverable formations, which are strictly controlled. However many planes may be in flight, all are responsive to the orders of the commander at a moment's notice while within a radius of two hundred miles...In the next war, instead of each pilot fighting his own battle in his own way, large formations will move as units, resembling well-drilled infantry regiments. The commander, office and all, will actually be in the sky."[91] Though Spaatz was mistaken about a commander having a flying office, his vision of vast formations moving across the sky under the control of one commander was prophetic.

Pilots of the 9th Bombardment Squadron in front of one of the Squadron's Douglas O-38 observation aircraft at March Field in 1931 with the original insignia from World War I, showing an airplane bombing a German town by night. The airplane and the town were later removed on government orders and the insignia simplified to show only the three searchlight beams forming the Roman numeral IX. (7th Bombardment Group (H) Historical Foundation, USAFA McDermott Library)

After something of a hiatus over the summer following the maneuvers on the East Coast, the 7th Bombardment Group launched its new training season in early September. With the move to March Field now imminent, the following weeks were hectic. The Primary Flying School at March Field departed for Randolph Field October 25, 1931, and the 7th Bombardment Group began its relocation that same day.[92] Just prior to the move, Maj. Spaatz was appointed commander of the 1st Bombardment Wing, relinquishing command of the 7th Bombardment Group October 29, 1931, to Maj. Joseph McNarney, who had assumed temporary command of the Group during the May maneuvers. Like Spaatz, McNarney was a graduate of West Point and had learned to fly in 1916, serving in France during 1918, then spending much of the 1920s at what became the Air Corps Tactical School on the War Department General Staff before becoming commander of the Primary Flying School at March Field in 1930.[93] In other command moves, Lt. Younger A. Pitts took over command of the 9th Bombardment Squadron from Capt. Leo F. Post, who took command of the 70th Service Squadron. In late November, Spaatz's good friend, Henry "Hap" Arnold, was promoted to Lt. Colonel and assumed command of March Field.[94]

While undergoing the move to March Field, the 11th Bombardment Squadron still maintained a busy training schedule, participating in several exercises during mid-November that illustrated typical flying experiences of the day. The 11th Squadron took on the task of testing the new L-1 Type bomb sight. As their new home at March Field lacked a bombing range, the 11th Bombardment Squadron and its B-2s commuted each day from March Field back to Rockwell for the tests.[95] Pilots from the 31st Squadron joined the tests to gain experience. Over the course of eight days, three bombing teams dropped 116 100-pound and 300-pound bombs from 6,000, 9,000, and 12,000 feet. That same week, the 11th Squadron cooperated with the 63rd Coast Artillery (Anti-Aircraft) in a test of their sound detectors and search lights. The 11th sent up three Condors to fly over March Field at specified intervals and at altitudes ranging from 6,000 to 10,000 feet. When the sound detectors picked up the sound of airplane engines, the search lights would come on and seek out the approaching bombers. Although the crews were wearing some 50 pounds of heavy flight suits, they reported that "...this 'Sunny California' stuff does not apply at this time of year."[96]

The consolidation of the 7th Bombardment Group at March Field brought "real" bombers for the 9th and 31st Bombardment Squadrons. The aircraft allotment plan for Fiscal Year 1932 called for 12 Keystone B-3A, eight Keystone Y1B-4A, and ten B-4A bombers by June 30, 1932.[97] Flying their Douglas O-38s east and returning with a Keystone bomber, pilots of the two squadrons began ferrying the aircraft across the country during December 1931. The ferrying task went on for the next several months, with pilots picking up bombers from the 2nd Bombardment Group at Langley and new B-4A airplanes directly from the Keystone factory in Pennsylvania until both squadrons had received their full allocation. These ferry trips were coveted assignments. Normally, cross-country flights were limited to a radius of 500 miles from base; on a ferry flight, a young pilot was on his own with an entire country to cross and received a payment per mile to the factory and back.[98] Adapting to the larger Keystone bombers was not without its pains, as there were three accidents involving B-3As at March Field within a space of two weeks in December 1931.[99] By the following February, crews of the 9th Bombardment

A Keystone B-4A bomber of the 9th Bombardment Squadron. The B-4As began arriving in early 1932. The "sanitized" version of the 9th Squadron's emblem has been painted on the nose. (Peter M. Bowers Collection, Museum of Flight)

Squadron had gained sufficient experience with their new B-3A bombers to begin working on simulated tactical problems. Newly-promoted Capt. Younger Pitts took his squadron up to make simulated bombing runs on railroad yards, dock facilities, and factories around the Southern California area and made a cross-county flight to Yuma, Arizona, where the squadron made runs against the Southern Pacific railroad yard.[100]

While the 9th and 31st Squadrons had been converting to their new aircraft, the 11th Bombardment flew a mercy mission that won Lt. Charles Howard, Squadron commander, the McKay Trophy the following year. In mid-January 1932, a series of severe snow storms cut off the roads into the western and southern Navajo and Hopi Reservations in northern New Mexico and Arizona, leaving thousands of residents without food. The Commissioner of Indian Affairs in the Department of the Interior contacted the War Department for help. The War Department instructed March Field to mount a relief expedition. On January 16, 1932, Lt. Howard led six B-2 bombers, a Ford C-4A transport, and an O-38 observation plane to Winslow, Arizona. Emergency ration packs were made up containing 48 pounds of flour, 10 pounds of sugar, 4 pounds of salt pork, 10 pounds of coffee, 10 pounds of beans, 10 pounds of dried fruit, and 2 pounds of baking powder. The first attempt to drop these supplies wrapped in a burlap sack failed, so the supplies were wrapped in two sacks, much like a blanket roll, and ten sacks were attached to shackles in a B-2's bomb bay. With local residents and agents from the Bureau of Indian Affairs as airborne guides, the six B-2s flew 15,000 miles between January 16th and 21st, dropping 30,000 pounds of ration packs to isolated houses and communities.

The 31st Bombardment Squadron also began receiving Keystone B-4A bombers in early 1932. The skull and crossbones squadron emblem is on the nose. (Peter M. Bowers Collection, Museum of Flight)

The sorties involved flying at low altitude over rough terrain in very cold weather in open cockpit airplanes. Commendations for the Squadron's successful efforts came in from all involved in the rescue effort, which was an early demonstration of the possibilities of aerial resupply.[101]

The continuation of the Depression brought about strict economies in all areas of the Federal Government, and as a result, the Air Corps did not have enough funds to support a major exercise during 1932.[102] This provided the 1st Bombardment Wing with an opportunity to conduct its own training program, with tactical exercises aimed at coordinating the 7th Bombardment Group and the 17th Pursuit Group. After completing their squadron and group training programs, the two Groups turned to the training schedule for the 1st Bombardment Wing that Maj. Spaatz and Lt. Col. Arnold had devised. The exercises involved the coordination of units via radio from bases around the March Field area, other radio problems, and the defense of March Field against attack. Arnold was particularly keen to have the Wing's squadrons practice operating away from their home field living under field conditions.[103] During May, Maj. Spaatz conducted two weeks of maneuvers out of Rockwell Field with 57 pursuits and 27 bombers.[104] The officers and men lived in a tent city for the period while transport planes operated a daily shuttle service between Rockwell Field and March Field, bringing in needed supplies. After completing the maneuvers, Spaatz had one bombardment and one pursuit squadron remain at Rockwell for a month of intensive training in bombing and gunnery. The 11th Bombardment and 95th Pursuit Squadrons went first, followed by the 9th Bombardment and 34th Pursuit, then the 31st Bombardment and 73rd Pursuit. At the end of the training period, all 43 bomber pilots of the three bombardment squadrons achieved an Expert ranking, considered to be a remarkable achievement, since the majority had less than two years of active service in bombardment squadrons.[105]

As an added bonus, and no doubt to provide some diversity in the training, that same summer, Maj. McNarney sent his bombardment squadrons on a tour of the region's natural beauty. In May, the 11th Bombardment Squadron took its B-2s on a tour of Death Valley and the Sierra Nevada Mountains, past Mount Whitney to Yosemite Park. The Squadron toured the park by automobile, returning in their B-2s a month later. June 29th, the 9th Bombardment Squadron took off for a long cross-country flight to the Grand Canyon carrying Maj. McNarney and five newsreel cameramen as guests. The bombers descended into the canyon, flying 1,000 feet below the rim, and flew up and down several times to give the cameramen a photo opportunity.[106]

The new training year began again in September, in the new Fiscal Year. A Wing exercise in October demonstrated the variety of tactics that Arnold, Spaatz, McNarney, and Capt. Frank O'D. Hunter, commander of the 17th Pursuit Group, tried out with the Wing's squadrons. The occasion was the visit of Brig. Gen. Oscar Westover, Assistant Chief of Staff of the Air Corps and second in command to Maj. Gen. Foulois, who was on an inspection tour of Air Corps installations in the West. October 26, 1932, the Wing staged a night bombing raid against March Field, with search lights from Battery "A", 63rd Coast Artillery (AA) providing the defense and several hundred spectators in attendance. Operating from a dispersed field, the 7th Bombardment Group's three squadrons approached the field from separate routes, converging over the field at 7:00 p.m. at high altitude. As a diversion, the 17th Pursuit Group sent in several formations of pursuits at lower altitude, to distract the sound locators and search lights. With the pursuits buzzing around below them, the bombers flew over the field, dropping flares in lieu of bombs. The diversion worked, and only one bomber was caught in the search lights and deemed destroyed. During Westover's visit, the 31st Bombardment Squadron took him out over the Pacific Ocean to watch the 7th Bombardment Group bomb towed targets from an altitude of 12,000 feet.[107]

For a young Air Corps officer in the early 1930s in the depths of the Depression, life was not particularly onerous. One historian described the typical day for a flyer: "Flying began at about 8:00 a.m. and continued until 11:30 a.m. when the officers went to lunch. The pilots usually relaxed in the officer's club until about 1:30 p.m. and then returned to the office, hangar, or flight line for another two hours. At about 3:30 p.m. the duty day normally ended. Nearly all officers had their weekends free, as well as a half day off on Wednesdays, and almost no one worked at night."[108] Squadron officers usually had one or more extra duties to attend to on a daily or weekly basis as assistant Armament, Communications, or Engineering officers, in addition to other administrative functions they might be assigned. To enhance their training and knowledge, officers were occasionally sent to service schools for a period of weeks or months to study technical subjects or to acquire skills, such as navigation. But there was still plenty of time for relaxation. At the time, throughout the Air Corps there was heavy emphasis on sports and pilots keeping fit. Many squadrons had their own sports teams for

A B-2 from the 11th Bombardment Squadron flying over the Sierra Nevada Mountains in May 1932 on a scenic cross-country flight. (3B-24409, RG 342FH, NARA)

A month later, the 11th Bombardment Squadron returned to fly through Yosemite Valley, creating some stunning photographs. (3B-24410, RG 342FH, NARA)

The lounge at the officer's club at March Field in 1934. (3B-19624, RG 342FH, NARA)

March Field's proximity to Los Angeles and Hollywood had its compensations. These young starlets paid a visit to the 11th Bombardment Squadron in late 1931. (7th Bombardment Group (H) Historical Foundation, USAFA McDermott Library)

baseball, tennis, or golf, with regular matches against other Air Corps, Army, or Navy units. There were frustrations, mostly relating to pay, promotion, and flying hours. During the Depression years, all Army officers had to take cuts in pay or take unpaid leave; annual flying hours were cut as well for additional economies.[109] Promotion during the 1920s and early 1930s was glacial. With a fixed number of officers allocated to the entire Army and promotion based primarily on seniority, it could take years for a 1st Lieutenant to make Captain. With a "log jam" of more senior officers in field grade positions, promotion to higher ranks was also blocked. As a result, in the Air Corps 1st Lieutenants commanded squadrons in place of Majors and Captains commanded Groups in place of Lt. Colonels. This did not change until 1935, when the Congress passed legislation that mandated promotion from 2nd to 1st Lieutenant in three years and from 1st Lieutenant to Captain after seven years and created more field grade officer positions.[110] The difficulty Spaatz and other Air Corps commanders faced during these years was not only pay and promotion, but simply obtaining enough qualified officers and enlisted men to keep their units up to strength. While the Air Corps had created almost all the tactical units it had planned, manning these units continued to be a problem. At the end of the Air Corps' five-year expansion program, the units at March Field under Spaatz's command had 118 officers out of 218 required under the table of organization. Overall, the Air Corps was 22 per cent below its goal for regular officers and 33 per cent below its goal for rated pilots.[111] Reserve officers, who normally served a year on active duty after completing their flying training, helped fill the gap, but their numbers were also entirely dependent on Congressional appropriations.

As the Depression deepened, President Herbert Hoover ordered extensive cuts to the Federal Government's budget to maintain a balanced budget and reduce the Government's budget deficit as its revenues declined sharply. The military were not exempt from spending cuts. Budget problems made it increasingly difficult for the Army Air Corps to obtain the funds it felt it needed to complete the five-year expansion program.[112] For Fiscal 1931, the Air Corps requested an

The Douglas XB-7 was a bomber version of the Douglas XO-35 observation airplane to meet a possible Air Corps requirement for a high-speed light bomber. (00005534, Courtesy San Diego Air & Space Museum)

appropriation of $54 million; the Bureau of the Budget approved an allocation of $35.8 million for submission to Congress.[113] For the following year—the final year of the expansion program—the Air Corps asked for $64 million and was granted $31.5 million.[114] The need to strictly economize forced a curtailment of flying hours and delays in the purchasing of airplanes and in bringing existing tactical units up to strength. Although the amount of appropriations Congress approved during the Air Corps' five-year expansion program was close to the original estimates of the cost of the program, the Air Corps had not achieved all the expansion program's objectives by the end of the five-year period. While the Air Corps was in a better position than it had been at the start of the expansion program in 1927, with more tactical units, more and better aircraft, and a greater number of officers and enlisted personnel, many of the units the Air Corps had activated remained below their authorized strength.[115]

Through most of 1932, the Group was still flying eight of the Curtiss B-2 Condors in the 11th Bombardment Squadron, while the 9th and 31st Bombardment Squadrons flew a mix of one Keystone Y1B-4A, one Y1B-6A, and 22 Keystone B-4As.[116] The Condors had led a charmed life with the 11th Squadron; in four years the Squadron lost only one B-2, and that came at the end of 1932, when 2nd Lt. George Campbell was forced to ditch his bomber off the coast after losing an engine during a low-altitude speed test.[117] In 1930, the Air Corps had placed an order with the Douglas Aircraft Company for a twin-engine, long-range observation airplane. Douglas had developed this airplane in response to the XO-27, a rival design from the Fokker-Atlantic Company. The Douglas design, the XO-35, was a gull-wing monoplane with retractable landing gear powered by two Curtiss Conqueror engines of 600 h.p. The engines were fitted in underwing nacelles with metal bracing to attach the nacelle to the wing. The fuselage was a metal semi-monocoque. With a top speed of 178 mph at sea level, the XO-35 could easily outstrip the elderly Keystone bombers. Based on the estimated performance of the observation version, the Air Corps had Douglas build a second airplane as the XB-7, a potential high-speed light bombardment airplane. The XB-7 was a transitional aircraft, with an open cockpit for the pilot and copilot/bombardier and two open turrets for the front and rear gunners. While the XB-7 was still being built, the Air Corps ordered seven airplanes designated Y1B-7 for testing in service with an operational bombardment squadron. The first Y1B-7 arrived at March Field in December 1932 and was assigned to the 11th Bombardment Squadron. Three more arrived in January 1933, and apparently went to the 31st Bombardment Squadron; two more Y1B-7s came to March Field at the end of the year. The transition to the new bombers, the first with retractable landing gear, appears to have gone without a problem. A few weeks after their arrival, Maj. Spaatz flew a Y1B-7 to Randolph Field on a cross-country navigation exercise, and a few day later led a flight of two Y1B-7s and four P-12s to Bolling Field in Washington, D.C.[118]

During May 1933, the 7th Bombardment Group participated in two major exercises: the Joint Anti-aircraft-Air Corps Exercise on the East Coast and the annual Air Corps Exercises on the West Coast. In the anti-aircraft exercises, the Air Corps and the Coast Artillery tested air and ground measures for air defense involving a ground warning system, pursuit interceptors, anti-aircraft guns, sound locators, and search lights from the Coast Artillery.[119] The exercise drew 113 airplanes from bombardment, attack, and pursuit groups around the country and included two of the Air Corps' newest bombers undergoing service testing. The 2nd Bombardment Group sent part of the 49th Bombardment Squadron with five Boeing Y1B-9 bombers, while the 7th Bombardment Group

The Air Corps ordered seven Y1B-7 bombers from Douglas for testing in service. Six aircraft were delivered to March Field for service with the 11th and 31st Bombardment Squadrons. (00005555, Courtesy San Diego Air & Space Museum)

The 11th Bombardment Squadron's B-2 Condors in Ohio for the Joint Anti-aircraft-Air Corps Exercises April-May 1933. The new camouflage pattern can just be made out on the fuselages of the Condors. (3B-24380, RG 342FH, NARA)

sent the 11th Bombardment Squadron with its nine B-2 Condors and a formation from the 31st Bombardment Squadron with at least three of the new Y1B-7s to form the 2nd Provisional Bombardment Group, with an attached squadron of attack planes included.[120] On their way to Patterson Field, near Dayton, Ohio, where the Air Corps units were concentrating, the 11th and 31st Bombardment Squadron aircraft stopped at Fort Riley, Kansas, where they had temporary water-soluble camouflage applied in a pattern of dark green, olive drab, and purple with light blue undersurfaces.[121] The bomber squadrons formed part of the Blue air force. This force was to launch a series of attacks on Fort Knox—representing a major rail center—165 miles away. The Red air force was defending Fort Knox with the 1st Pursuit Group's P-6E and P-12E pursuits. Capt. Claire Chennault, then a pursuit instructor at the Air Corps Tactical School, had set up a warning network around the Fort Knox area with ground observers and a system for plotting enemy airplanes that would alert the pursuit squadrons to the location of the enemy bombers. Coordinating three different types of bombers with different speeds and getting them to execute a combined raid at a specific time proved to be challenging. After several weeks of practice flying, the exercise got underway May 16th, when several flights of Blue force bombers launched attacks against Fort Knox. While some of the bombers were intercepted through the warning net, three formations got past the pursuits to attack Fort Knox. In one instance, three P-12s from the 27th Pursuit Squadron dove on a Y1B-7 from the 31st Squadron engaged in jamming radio transmissions from a Red Force airfield. The Y1B-7 pilot opened his throttles and "literally walked away" from the attacking P-12s.[122] Over the course of the exercises, however, as the warning system and the intercepting pursuit pilots gained experience, they intercepted the bomber formations more frequently. By the end of the exercise on May 24th, the Red Force had located 27 enemy bomber formations and performed successful interceptions on 17.[123] Although the exercises had demonstrated the potential of a combined warning system and interceptors to disrupt bomber formations, the upcoming maneuvers on the West Coast would lead the Air Corps commanders there to the opposite conclusion.[124]

Y1B-7s of the 3rd Bombardment Squadron at the Joint Anti-aircraft-Air Corps Exercises. (Museum of Flight)

The annual Air Corps exercises on the West Coast had multiple objectives: tactical problems in coastal defense, the dispersion and coordination of air units, and a test of what had up to that point been only conceptual—the General Headquarters Air Force. The concept had emerged during WWI from ideas for an air force to conduct missions beyond the battle line. In 1920, the Army set up plans for a GHQ Reserve, with an aviation component "...to be used as a centrally controlled strike force and for reconnaissance..."[125] In theory, this headquarters would take command of tactical air units normally allocated to Army Corps commanders, an approach that ran counter to existing Army doctrine. The GHQ Air Force would report directly to the Army Theater Commander in Chief. In the early 1930s, the Air Corps lacked a command structure that could rapidly mobilize tactical units, concentrate them, and direct them against an attacker.[126] Maj. Gen. Benjamin Foulois, who became Chief of the Air Corps in 1931, proposed the idea of a General Headquarters Air Force. The GHQ Air Force would take command of all attack, bomber, and pursuit units from Corps commanders to form a concentrated strike force to operate against any potential invader at any point around the country. The idea meshed with Gen. MacArthur's 1932-33 initiative to divide the United States into four defense sectors, each with its own field army. A GHQ Air Force would be able to rapidly deploy to whichever defense sector needed support. With long-range reconnaissance and long-range bombers, an air force could locate an enemy force while it was still at sea and attack it before it reached the shore. While the purpose of a GHQ Air Force was to enhance the role of air power in coastal defense, in effect, it sanctioned independent air operations, a thorny subject and a source of on-going strife between the Army's General Staff and those Air Corps officers who had been supporters of an independent air force. There was an additional concern that a GHQ Air Force might distract the Air Corps away from what the General Staff considered to be the Air Corps' primary mission: the support of the ground forces. Despite these reservations, there was a growing awareness that a GHQ Air Force might well have significant advantages in time of war. While the General Staff continued to consider the idea, in early 1933, the War Department approved an Air Corps request to form a provisional GHQ Air Force during the 1933 annual maneuvers as an experiment.[127]

For the 1933 Air Corps maneuvers, Brig. Gen. Oliver Westover, Assistant Chief of the Air Corps, was appointed commander of the General Headquarters, with Lt. Col. Henry Arnold as his Chief of Staff. The Air Corps had hoped to hold the annual maneuvers in the Pacific Northwest, but a shortage

GHQ Air Force (Provisional) staff (left to right): Major Clarence Tinker, G-2; Major Jacob Rudolph, G-4; Brigadier Oscar Westover, Commander; Lt. Col. Henry Arnold, Chief of Staff; Major Arnold Krogstad, G-1; and Major Ralph Royce, G-3. Tinker and Royce would both command the 7th Bombardment Group in the years to come. (3B-22320, RG 342FH, NARA)

of funds restricted operations to the area around March Field. Participating units included the 1st Bombardment Wing from March; the 2nd Bombardment Wing from Langley—less the units participating in the anti-aircraft exercises; the 3rd Attack Wing from Barksdale Field; and the 12th Observation Group, with the newly-formed 19th Bombardment Group from Rockwell Field attached for long-range reconnaissance. Altogether, the GHQ Air Force had 322 aircraft at its disposal from three bombardment, one attack, three pursuit groups, and one observation squadron. Most units arrived at March Field by May 7th, settling in for a brief stay in a tent city at the north end of the airfield before dispersing to airfields all around the Los Angeles area May 9th. The tactical problems for this year's maneuvers involved the defense of a coastal area from attack by sea and air. An Army mine laying vessel, used to plant and maintain mine fields in harbors as part of coastal fortifications, served as an enemy "aircraft carrier" that had to be located and attacked, while different attack, bombardment, and pursuit units served as "enemy" air forces for some of the problems. The maneuvers emphasized the rapid concentration of dispersed forces and their deployment under GHQ Air Force control. As an example, on May 11th, Brig. Gen. Westover directed a concentration of the three wings for a simulated attack on enemy ships off Long Beach. The 2nd Bombardment Wing rendezvoused over Long Beach, with the bombers at 3,000 feet and the pursuits higher up, then proceeded to Mines Field, the bombers climbing to 7,000 feet and the pursuits to 10,000 feet. At Mines Field, the 1st Bombardment and 3rd Attack Wings joined the formation; all the pursuits climbed to 10,000 feet and the bombers formed up at 7,000 feet, with the attack airplanes below. The entire formation then moved to its objective.[128]

The 7th Bombardment Group was active most days, practicing attacks on airfields and ships at sea—missions that would be required for coastal defense against an invading force. The Group represented an invading enemy's air force May 12th and participated in a joint mission with the 2nd Bombardment Group on May 15th to attack March Field, with Maj. McNarney in command of both bombardment groups. Observation planes from the 12th Observation Group acted as an early warning network, radioing reports of the bomber formations to the pursuit squadrons, who took off to intercept. The pursuits deployed over Riverside, in the hills west of March Field. The pursuits saw the bombers just before they reached their objective. As the pursuits came in, McNarney split his formation into smaller flights. These eluded the pursuits long enough to come in over the airfield in simulated bombing runs.[129] The night of May 18th, the 7th Group cooperated with the 12th Observation Group to locate the Army mine layer, playing the role of an enemy fleet approaching the coast off Catalina Island. Once the observation planes had located the enemy, the 7th Group came in to make bombing runs against the ship. Five days later, the bombardment groups and the attack group again practiced launching attacks against a ship at sea, following directions from the observation airplanes once they had located the vessel. Several exercises involved the pursuit squadrons practicing interceptions of the bombardment groups. On the last day of the exercises,

Aircraft assembled at March Field for the 1933 Air Corps exercises. (3B-19620, RG 342FH, NARA)

During 1933, the Army Air Corps approved a design the 7th Bombardment Group submitted for the Group's insignia. The design, shown here, featured a crest with a bomb piercing a cloud to indicate bombardment, the mission of the Group. The shield contained a band in orange yellow on a field of ultramarine blue (the colors of the Air Corps). The band came from the flag of the French province Lorraine, where the Group's squadrons had been stationed during WWI. Three black crosses, representing the battle honors credit to the unit—Lorraine, St. Mihiel, and Meuse-Argonne—adorned the band. The 7th Bombardment Group chose as its motto the Latin phrase *Mors Ab Alto*, "Death from Above", as another indication of the Group's mission and its spirit. (Author's collection)

A card showing the 7th Bombardment Group's insignia in color, with gold replacing the orange yellow, from the Group's time at Hamilton Field in the later 1930s. (Author's collection)

the 7th Group borrowed a squadron from the 2nd Bombardment Group to practice operations at its full wartime strength of four squadrons. The main exercises ended May 27th. A smaller group of 57 airplanes, including the 7th Bombardment Group, flew up to the Puget Sound area for several days of staff exercises, using the smaller number of airplanes to represent larger formations. June 1st, a formation of bombers from the 2nd, 7th, and new 19th Bombardment Group flew in formation over Seattle, "...like a swarm of monstrous bees"... as *The Seattle Daily Times* commented.[130] This first test of GHQ Air Force and a balanced striking force of attack, bombardment, pursuit, and observation aircraft was deemed a success, demonstrating the Air Corps' ability to rapidly organize and deploy a striking force in defense of strategic areas along the West Coast.[131]

In the middle of the exercises, Lt. Col. Arnold was informed that 3,000 young men from the Civilian Conservation Corps (CCC) were about to descend on March Field, and that they would have to housed, fed, clothed, and organized into camps to carry out their conservation work.[132] President Roosevelt had organized the CCC shortly after his inauguration in March 1933 to provide temporary employment for young men whose families were on relief. The young men chosen for the CCC program went to work on conservation projects around the country, building trails in state and national parks, planting trees, working on soil conservation, and other projects. Arnold immediately pulled the 17th Pursuit Group out of the exercises and set the Group's officers to working with the CCC men. When officers of the 7th Bombardment Group returned from the exercises in Seattle, they, too, were pulled into working with the CCC. By the end of June, there were 7,000 young men in what had been designated the March Field District, with Lt. Col. Arnold in command of 25 CCC camps. With 29 of 88 regular officers at March Field serving as camp commanders and another 22 serving on Arnold's staff, the training program for the 1st Bombardment Wing ground to a halt.[133] The 7th Group's three squadrons were consolidated into the 11th Bombardment Squadron so that some squadron training could continue. For many officers, service in the CCC camps lasted until October, when the Army called up Reserve officers to replace the Air Corps officers. While disruptive of the training routine, the experience of working with the CCC and commanding 200 young men at each CCC camp did have its benefits. As General Arnold recalled in his memoir, "The Air Corps learned a lot from handling those boys. Officers who had never before thought of anything very seriously, except flying an airplane, suddenly found themselves faced with administrative and human relations problems."[134] This experience would be invaluable a few years later when, during the war-time expansion, hundreds of thousands of young men entered the Army Air Forces, as it had then become, and needed to be hurriedly organized and trained.

The Air Mail Emergency and the End of an Era

Following the Air Corps West Coast exercises, there were several changes in command affecting the 7th Bombardment Group. Maj. Spaatz gave up command of the 1st Bombardment Wing to Lt. Col. Henry Arnold and went to Washington to take up an appointment in the Office of the Chief of the Air Corps. The actual transfer of command appears to have taken

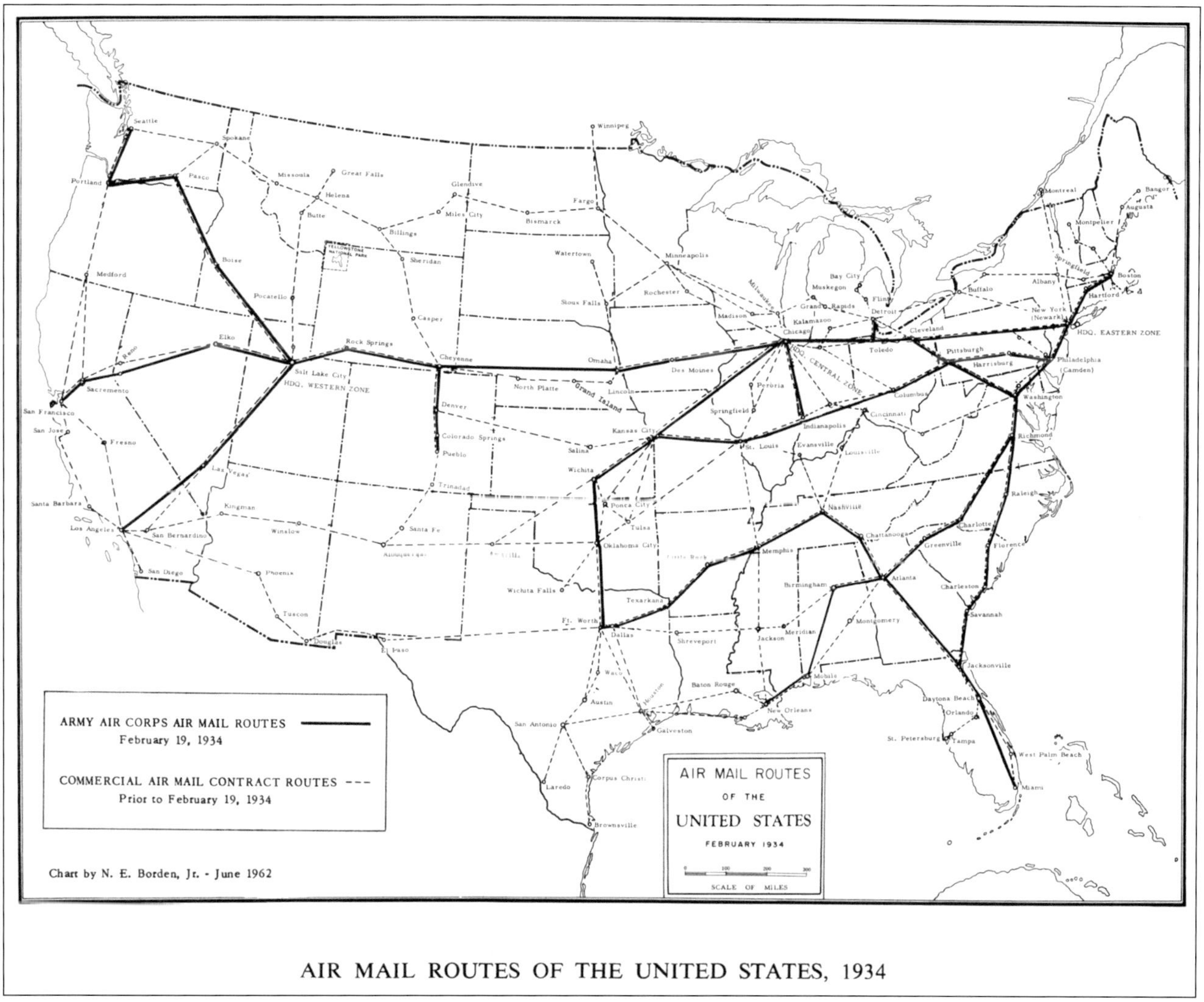

The Army Air Corps Mail Operation set up 17 routes around the country, as shown on this map. (Source: Borden, *Air Mail Emergency 1934*)

place in January, but Spaatz stayed on to command the Wing during the May exercises.[135] Then in July, Maj. Joseph McNarney was sent to the Army War College as an instructor, giving up command of the 7th Bombardment Group to Maj. Leo Walton. Walton had served in the Army Air Service in WWI, commanded a pursuit squadron during the 1920s, and had been the assistant commander of the Primary Flying School at March Field. During the same month, Lt. Charles Howard, who had commanded the 11th Bombardment Squadron since May 1930, gave up command to Capt. Robert E. Selff. In September, Maj. Charles T. Philips took over command of the 9th Bombardment Squadron and in January 1934, Maj. Harold D. Smith became commander of the 31st Bombardment Squadron. These men—Walton, Selff, Philips, and Smith—were in command when the 7th Bombardment faced its most challenging test since its activation.[136]

A B-2 Condor bomber from the 11th Bombardment Squadron flying the mail between Los Angeles and Salt Lake City over Air Mail Route 4. This was the Condor's "Swan Song"; within a few months they would be withdrawn from first line service. (3B-24379, RG 342FH, NARA)

Loading mail onto a Y1B-7 of the 31st Bombardment Squadron. The Y1B-7 was better equipped for carrying the mail, as it was considerably faster than the Condor and Keystone bombers. (00005559, Courtesy San Diego Air & Space Museum)

On Friday, February 9, 1934, the Second Assistant Postmaster General, Harllee Branch, asked Maj. Gen. Benjamin Foulois to a meeting that afternoon. Branch explained to Foulois that the President was considering cancelling the air mail contracts with the commercial airlines, based on concerns that the contracts had been awarded unfairly through collusion, concerns that had emerged from Congressional hearings under Senator Hugo Black. Branch put a question to Foulois: could the Air Corps carry the air mail in place of the airlines? Foulois said yes, if the Air Corps was given some time to prepare. Later that afternoon, President Roosevelt issued an Executive Order cancelling all domestic air mail contracts and ordering the Air Corps to take over the transportation of the mail during the period of the emergency. The airlines were given ten days' notice that their contracts would end February 19th, and the Air Corps was instructed to begin carrying the mail that same date.[137] Foulois may have felt that he had no choice but to respond to the emergency as a matter of duty, but in accepting the task, he was about to put the Air Corps to a severe test that was in many ways beyond its capabilities, "...sending it to do a twenty-four hour job for which it was not even remotely prepared."[138]

Foulois and his staff immediately set to work establishing a system to transport the mail designated the Army Air Corps Mail Operation. Brig. Gen. Oscar Westover took command. The country was divided into three zones (Eastern, Central, and Western) and a reduced network of 17 routes covering 11,000 airway miles was established. Lt. Col. Henry Arnold was appointed commander of the Western Zone, covering the area from Cheyenne, Wyoming, to the West Coast cities. This zone had 20 stops along its assigned routes, requiring 11,922 miles of flying every day. All Air Corps units were put on immediate alert. There were only ten days to put the system in place: determining stops; selecting airfields, airplanes, and pilots; allocating maintenance crews among stations; arranging for living quarters; giving pilots a chance to familiarize themselves with the routes they were to fly; and a host of other details. Arnold selected Salt Lake City as his headquarters for the Western Zone. Few of the aircraft available were suitable to carry the mail or had the speeds equal to the commercial aircraft the airlines used. Only the Y1B-7s, the Curtiss A-12 attack plane, and the hurriedly introduced Martin Y1B-10 bomber approached the performance needed. The remaining attack, bomber, observation, and pursuit aircraft selected had to be hurriedly modified to accommodate sacks of mail. Air Corps airplanes lacked many of the blind flying instruments that were standard for airlines; these instruments were rapidly installed. Worst of all, few Air Corps pilots had experience flying in bad weather. While the Air Corps did conduct training in instrument flying and night flying, most flying was done in good weather with good visibility. Compounding the problems to come was the Air Corps' heavy reliance on young Reserve Officers, many only a few months out of flying school and serving their required year of active service. These pilots had minimal experience flying in weather.[139]

The 7th Bombardment Group contributed men and planes to the Western Zone. Maj. Leo Walton, Group commander, was placed in charge of a transport group to ferry men and supplies to stations throughout the Zone, while Maj. Charles Philips took on the Salt Lake City to Seattle route.[140] Drawing from the bombardment and pursuit groups in the 1st Bombardment Wing and National Guard observation squadrons, Arnold had 120 pilots and 50 airplanes at his disposal for the mail run. In an interview with the press, Arnold admitted that he and his pilots faced a difficult task, particularly as so few pilots had extensive experience with either the routes they were to fly or with weather. "We are greatly handicapped," Arnold told the press, "Lack of experience and speed will provide handicaps hard to surmount, but we'll do the best we can."[141] The 7th Bombardment Group's airplanes were assigned to several routes within the Western Zone. In addition to ferrying supplies, the Group's Curtiss Condor and Keystone bombers flew the mail over Air Mail Route 4—the Los Angeles-Salt Lake City route—despite their slow speed. The faster Y1B-7s in the 31st Bombardment Squadron were set to work carrying the air mail over several sectors in the Western Zone, including the Salt Lake City-Seattle route; six of the similar Y1O-35 observation planes were also assigned to the Western Zone. February 13th, Maj. Philips led a formation of five Y1O-35 fast observation airplanes over the Salt Lake City-Seattle route to familiarize the pilots, noting that for carrying the mail, the observation planes were likely to be replaced with bombers.[142] One of the 31st Squadron's Y1B-7 aircraft was involved in one of three fatal accidents that occurred February 16, 1934, even before the Air Corps' Air Mail Operation got underway. That evening, 2nd Lt. James Eastham was undertaking a night training flight along the Salt Lake City-Seattle route via Boise-Pasco-Portland-Tacoma. Taking off from Salt Lake at 19:30, Eastham was flying near Jerome, Idaho, when the weather worsened, with rain and

A Keystone Y1B-4A from the 31st Bombardment Squadron. The Keystones were slowly withdrawn during the second half of 1933. (Peter M. Bowers Collection, Museum of Flight)

poor visibility. Eastham tried to locate the airfield near the town, but in his search for the field inadvertently flew too low and hit a tree. The airplane crashed, killing Eastham.[143]

Other deaths followed in quick succession. Before the first bag of mail had been delivered, six pilots had been killed. More accidents occurred once the Air Corps began flying the mail. The onset of severe winter weather—the worst in years—was one contributing factor. The resulting outcry from newspapers across the country and from Congress forced President Roosevelt to order a curtailment of the Army Air Corps Mail Operation March 9th. Maj. Gen. Foulois instituted more stringent safety precautions, but the damage to the Air Corps' image had already been done. The Air Corps continued flying the mail into May. Moderating weather and better-trained pilots brought better results, but the overall record was poor: 12 pilots killed, 66 airplanes lost or damaged in crashes (including two more Y1B-7s from the 31st Bombardment Squadron), and only 66 per cent of scheduled flights completed.[144] From a public relations standpoint, the Air Mail Emergency was a disaster for the Air Corps, yet it did create an awareness that the Air Corps was deficient in both equipment and pilot training. In the midst of the crisis, the Secretary of War, George H. Dern, set up a special board to report on the state of the Air Corps and identify areas of improvement. Dern appointed Newton Baker, formerly Secretary of War during WWI, as its chairman. The Baker Board, as it was called, began its investigations in April, and after hearing testimony from a wide variety of witnesses, issued its report in July 1934. The Baker Board's recommendations echoed those of the Drum Board of the previous year, calling for an increase in the authorized number of aircraft for the Air Corps from 1,800 to 2,320, more training in instrument and bad-weather flying, more flying hours per year for pilots, and more realistic training, as well as measures to deal with the officer shortage and the problems of promotion. More importantly for the future, the Baker Board strongly backed the immediate formation of a General Headquarters Air Force to control all combat units in the Continental United States. While clearly addressing the problems the Air Corps faced at the time, the Baker Board's recommendations lacked credibility without adequate funding. Several years would pass before the changes needed could be made.[145]

For the Army Air Corps and the 7th Bombardment Group, the year 1934 marked a transition—the ending of one era and the beginning of another. While the five-year expansion program authorized in 1926 and finally completed after delays in 1933 had brought many improvements to the Air Corps, the results remained less than what many airmen had hoped for. The Air Corps had expanded the number of its tactical units. The bombardment arm now had three bombardment groups (2nd, 7th, and 19th), with a fourth (9th Bombardment Group) to be organized in 1935. However, these groups were under-strength in men and equipment and their formation had taken longer than planned. The experience of the 7th Bombardment Group in this regard was not atypical. On the more positive side, the Air Corps had, during this period, "... obtained a mission, aerial coastal defense, that justified the creation of a centrally controlled strike force, the GHQ Air Force..." that pointed toward a larger mission: strategic bombardment.[146] The 7th Bombardment Group had played an active role in developing and refining the tactics for coastal defense through its unit training and participation in the annual Air Corps maneuvers. In the years ahead, the Group would continue to serve as a laboratory for experiments in air power doctrine and the development of tactics. The larger mission that many officers in the Air Corps were now seeking, however, would require airplanes with greater performance, as the Air Corps' experience during the air mail emergency had so dramatically proven. But this change, too, was on the horizon. The biplane era was ending. The technological revolution in aircraft that was transforming commercial aviation was about to begin in the Air Corps. The 7th Bombardment Group's Curtiss and Keystone bombers, only a small advance over their WWI forbearers, had seen their day. Already in September 1933, these relics from another era had started to leave the Group, transferred to the advanced flying school at Kelly Field.[147] Later in 1934, the 7th Bombardment Group would begin a new era with the arrival of 30 all-metal monoplane Martin bombers. These airplanes represented a significant leap in performance and capability. Over the next seven years, the 7th Group would be at the forefront of the technological and tactical developments that would form the basis of air power doctrine the Air Corps would adopt as its principal mission and that its successor, the Army Air Forces, would attempt to implement in war: unescorted, daylight precision bombing.

CHAPTER TWO

A LABORATORY FOR AIR POWER: BIGGER AND BETTER BOMBERS

The Revolution in Aircraft Technology and Air Power Doctrine

The early 1930s witnessed a revolution in aircraft design and a dramatic increase in performance and capability. The revolution was less the result of a single technological breakthrough than the synergistic application of a number of technological developments, the result being the establishment of the all-metal monoplane as the predominant airplane type for commercial and military applications. Among these developments were advances in aerodynamics and streamlining, the switch to all-metal, stressed-skin, semi-mononoque construction, the use of retractable landing gear, variable pitch propellers, and engines of increasing power and reliability.[1] With the constrained funding the Depression had imposed on government, these new technological improvements were applied to aircraft designed for the commercial airlines for fast air mail and improved passenger comfort and safety. The epitome of this dramatic change was the Douglas DC-1, first flown in July 1933, with an air speed nearly 100 mph faster than the 7th Bombardment Group's Keystone B-4As. In one stroke, the Air Corps' principal bomber had become obsolete. Within its funding constraints, however, the Air Corps had begun to move in this new technological direction with the acquisition of six Boeing Y1B-9 airplanes in 1932, the Air Corps' first all-metal monoplane bomber with retractable landing gear. The Martin XB-907, ordered a year later, proved to be the better airplane, once it incorporated modifications from Wright Field engineers who designed a stronger, larger wing and recommended an enclosed cockpit and gun positions. The Air Corps placed an order with Martin in January 1933 for 48 bombers. The Martin B-10 and B-10B, with the Martin B-12 equipped with Pratt & Whitney Hornet engines in place of the B-10's Wright Cyclones, became the Air Corps' standard bomber during the mid-1930s. When the Martin entered service in 1934, it could fly faster, farther, and higher than any bomber then in service with the Air Corps, or in service with most of the world's air forces. Not only could it out-fly other bombers, the Martin could fly faster than almost every pursuit in the Air Corps, the one exception being the recently introduced Boeing P-26.[2]

The entry of the Martin B-10 into service in 1934 coincided with a changing emphasis within Air Corps doctrine toward the primacy of bombardment aviation. For much of the 1920s, air power and the Air Corps were seen as subordinate to the Army ground forces. The role of the nation's military in war was to destroy an enemy's will and ability to resist through the destruction of the enemy's armed forces. The official view within the War Department and the Army General Staff was that air power would contribute to the destruction of an enemy's will to resist through coordinated action with the ground forces, who would ultimately decide the outcome; the infantry remained the "queen of battle."[3] The role of bombardment aviation was to conduct attacks on tactical targets in direct support of ground operations, or through attacks on "strategic" targets, defined broadly as targets beyond the battle line, such as the supplies the opposing army required, lines of communication to move those supplies, or enemy airfields and bases.[4] There was no question of an independent role for an air force. As the emphasis was on the tactical employment of air power, pursuit aviation was seen as the primary focus for an air force, given that the pursuit's mission of achieving air superiority over the battlefield allowed the other air arms—attack, bombardment, and observation—to achieve their respective missions.

The 7th Bombardment Group's new Martin B-12 bombers began to arrive toward the end of June 1934. A B-12 bomber from the 11th Bombardment Squadron on a flight from March Field with the Squadron's Mr. Jiggs insignia prominently displayed on the nose of the airplane. (3B-24554, RG 342FH, NARA)

In the years after WWI, air power theorists in England and the United States began to work out a more prominent role for air forces independent of the ground armies. Air operations, in their view, held the potential for making a far greater impact in war than merely providing support for ground operations. Because of its speed, freedom from the constraints of geography, and ability to carry heavy loads, the airplane, and specifically the bomber, could carry destruction deep within an enemy's territory, striking at the very heart of an enemy's morale and the resources it needed to resist.[5] The theory developed the conviction that "...using air power to strike heavily at the vital points of a nation's structure rather than conducting exhausting wars of attrition was a means of achieving the military objective at the least possible cost."[6] In the United States, Brig. Gen. William Mitchell became the most forceful advocate of this theory of air power and for an independent air force. Freed from the need to provide support for the ground forces, an independent air force could concentrate on strategic bombing operations, destroying the enemy's military capacity and will to resist. After his court martial in 1925, Mitchell's acolytes in the Army Air Corps continued to develop his theories at the Air Corps Tactical School, the center for the debate of air power theories and the development of air power doctrine for the Air Corps.[7] By 1930, the Air Corps Tactical School had come to accept the primacy of bombardment aviation over pursuit. In 1933, in the journal *U.S. Air Services*, Lt. Kenneth Walker, an instructor in bombardment aviation at the Air Corps Tactical School and one of the leading spokesmen for the theory of bombardment, wrote, "by reason of the great striking power of the bombardment airplane, bombardment aviation is the basic arm—the backbone of any air force. The operation of this basic component of an air force will, in any major war, be paramount."[8] An air force, Walker argued, is best employed against the resources an enemy needed for the prosecution of a war. "Destruction of the means by which any armed force is supplied, moved, and made ready to operate," he postulated, "eliminates that force as a threat."[9] Walker went on to articulate a view that was becoming prevalent among bomber advocates: "...a determined air attack, once launched, is most difficult, if not impossible to stop when directed against land objectives."[10] With a force of antiquated biplane bombers, Walker's statements required an extraordinary leap of faith, but with a new generation of modern bombing aircraft that could fly higher, faster, farther, and carry a greater load of bombs, and that appeared to be relatively safe from interception, his ideas seemed within the realm of possibility.[11] The prospect of even more capable bombers emerging from continued technological development encouraged this viewpoint. During the mid-1930s, Walker and other Air Corps Tactical School instructors, such as Maj. Donald Wilson and Capt. Harold George, continued to refine their arguments into a doctrine that emphasized "...sustained, precision attacks by heavy bombers against the industrial structure of an enemy nation...," a doctrine of long-range, unescorted, daylight precision bombing by a centralized air force operating independently of the ground forces.[12]

The doctrine of the primacy of strategic bombardment developed at the Air Corps Tactical School was by no means officially accepted outside the school. For the War Department and the General Staff, an independent role for the Air Corps, much less an independent air force, was an anathema. Though there was a growing recognition of the power of more modern airplanes and some sympathy for the Air Corps' desire to exercise greater control over its own forces, neither the Drum Board nor the Baker Board had supported independence for the Air Corps.[13] The 1931 MacArthur-Pratt agreement and the support for the formation of a General Headquarters Air Force had, however, become "...the thin edge of a wedge for the Air Corps in its quest for expanded responsibility and material."[14] The Air Corps' mission of coastal defense provided the rationale for the development and procurement of long-range bombers for reconnaissance and attacks on a potential enemy invasion force far from America's shores. In addition to the tension with the War Department about official definitions of air power doctrine, the Air Corps would engage in a vigorous effort to obtain ever more capable long-range bombers, to the detriment of other types of aircraft. The War Department resisted this effort until shortly before the outbreak of WWII.

The activities of the 7th Bombardment Group during the second half of the 1930s can best be understood against this background of doctrinal and technical development. As the doctrine of strategic bombardment developed at the Air Corps Tactical School, the bombardment groups were the laboratory where tactics were developed and tested. With higher speeds and higher altitudes came questions of the best bombing formations to employ for offensive and defensive purposes. While the bomber advocates came to believe that bombers had become less vulnerable to pursuits, they nevertheless worked on formations that would maximize a bomber formation's collective fire power. The ability of formations to hit small targets with precision—the foundation of the American doctrine of strategic bombing—had to be practiced assiduously with the newly-introduced Norden bombsight. Higher speeds and altitudes compounded the problem of bombing accuracy. To fulfill its role in coastal defense, bombers had to be able to locate their targets at sea. This required extensive training in reconnaissance and navigation. From the perspective of performing an independent air mission, the General Headquarters Air Force had to practice the rapid concentration and coordination of these units. Overlaying these problems of employment was the need to bring into regular use airplanes of increasing complexity with more training in some of the weaknesses the Air Mail Emergency had disclosed— instrument flying, for example.[15]

The Martin Bomber Arrives

The Air Corps had initially planned to assign ten Martin B-10 bombers and 20 B-12 versions to the 7th Bombardment Group at March Field during 1934, but decided to equip the Group entirely with the 32 B-12 bombers the Air Corps had ordered,

The cockpit of a B-10 provided a new luxury to bomber pilots: a closed canopy to keep out the rain and wind. (060511-F-1234S-011 National Museum of the United States Air Force)

possibly to avoid the maintenance complications of operating the same aircraft with different types of engines.[16] Several of the YB-10s—the service test model that were hurriedly delivered to the Air Corps during the Air Mail Emergency—appear to have returned to March Field after the Air Corps stopped carrying the mail in May 1934. Some of these aircraft, with several enlisted men from the 9th and 11th Bombardment Squadrons, participated in the Army Alaskan Flight. Led by Lt. Col. Henry Arnold, the flight departed from Bolling Field in Washington, D.C., July 19, 1934, and returned August 20th. Spending 21 days in Alaska, the Flight conducted a photographic survey and successfully demonstrated the Martin bomber's long-range capability. The B-12s, initially designated YB-12, began to arrive at March Field toward the end of June; after some months, the YB designation was dropped and the bombers became B-12s.[17] Bombers modified with an extra fuel tank in the bomb bay were designated B-12A. Within a few weeks of their arrival, the 7th Bombardment Group's pilots were putting their new Martins through their paces.

For a young pilot fresh from flying the older Keystone bombers at advanced flying school at Kelly Field, the new Martin bomber was a thrill and a challenge. Edward Virgin

The rear cockpit of the B-10 housed the navigator-copilot's station and space for a rear gunner. (060511-F-1234S-032 National Museum of the United States Air Force)

A close-up of a B-12 from the 9th Bombardment Squadron showing the entry to the bombardier's compartment. Once inside there was no other exit, which made a wheels-up landing something to be avoided. (Peter M. Bowers Collection, Museum of Flight)

graduated from Kelly Field in February 1934 and was assigned to the 7th Bombardment Group. He made his first solo flight in a B-12 July 5, 1934. Years later, he recalled his first impressions and his memories of what the Martin was like to fly:

> We began getting deliveries of our Martin B-10s and B-12s in the summer. They were beautiful to behold... It is hard to find words to describe the order of magnitude advance in the modern airplane over even the B-7, which was far, far ahead of the Keystones...I was just four months out of the flying school and was checking out in a B-12—man, I had arrived.
>
> The B-10s were real dreamboats. The ground handling characteristics were excellent—good brakes and small differences in throttle settings coupled with excellent forward visibility and no tendency for ground loops made for fast, straight-ahead taxiing and formation takeoffs, as well as fast clearing of the runway after landing. The in-flight visibility was even better. The controls were effective and the forces reasonable (you could say well harmonized), making it an excellent close-formation airplane day and night. The plane was an excellent bombing platform because of its stability around all three axes. Directional changes, as requested on the PDI [Pilot Direction Indicator] from the bombardier, could be made quickly. The airplane was very forgiving in every respect, not having any vicious characteristics even in a power-off stall. It would stall straight ahead with adequate warning (buffet). This resulted in a good, safe airplane during landings.[18]

The Martin carried a crew of four: pilot, co-pilot (who also served as bombardier and navigator, depending on the mission), radio operator, and gunner in three compartments, each isolated from the other. The bombardier's compartment in the nose held a base for the Norden bombsight and a manually operated turret with a single .30 caliber machine gun. The pilot's cockpit sat just forward of the bomb bay and was entered by climbing up the left side of the fuselage and onto the left wing. The rear compartment held the navigator/copilot's station with equipment for dead-reckoning or celestial navigation and a seat, control wheel, and basic flight instruments, so the copilot could take over flying on long-distance flights. Behind the copilot's station was an upper machine gun on a flexible mount and a tunnel gun underneath. The radio operator had his station in this rear compartment, as well. The main weakness of the Martin was the inability of the crew to change stations. The nature of the mission

The three compartments in the B-10/B-12 for the copilot/bombardier, pilot, and the copilot/navigator and gunner were not interconnected, a major weakness of the Martin bomber. (3B-24564, RG 342FH, NARA)

determined the compartment the copilot flew in, limiting his flexibility and his utility.[19]

The 7th Bombardment Group had its first real test of its new bombers a few weeks after Lt. Col. Arnold returned to March Field in late August from the Army Alaska Flight. In light of the evolving doctrine emerging from the Air Corps Tactical School and the introduction of the Martin bomber and the new Boeing P-26 pursuit, Arnold wanted to conduct a series of operational experiments looking at the tactics of bombers and pursuits in attack and defense to test then-current assumptions against the reality of modern aircraft.[20] Arnold had the tools he needed at hand at March Field: the 7th Bombardment Group and the 17th Pursuit Group. Over a period of two months, using the full complement of airplanes from both groups, Arnold arranged and carried out 26 interception problems around the March Field area. The problems involved interceptions of a bomber formation approaching from known and unknown directions and altitudes, with the pursuits directly in front of and to the flank of the objective. To simulate an observation network on the ground, the bomber formations radioed their positions as they approached March Field; this information was passed on to the pursuit squadrons after a slight delay. The tests demonstrated that to affect a successful interception at the speeds the bombers were now flying, the pursuits had to have as much advance warning as possible. The closer to the objective the bombers were before the pursuits received warning, the more difficult it was to intercept the bomber formation. Even though the P-26 had a speed advantage over

The 7th Bombardment Group's Martin bombers at March Field in November 1934, shortly after the tests of bombardment and pursuit tactics. (3B-19617, RG 342FH, NARA)

the Martin, it was not so great as to ensure success in all cases; the tests found that "...if Pursuit fails to intercept and permits Bombardment to get between it and the objective, it is practically impossible for Pursuit to overtake Bombardment before the attack is delivered."[21] The bombers experimented with several formations to determine the maximum number of guns that could be brought to bear, finding that some form of stepped-down formation seemed to offer the best protection

A formation of B-12 bombers from the 11th Bombardment Squadron. During Arnold's tests the bombers flew in flights of six, varying their formations to test defense against pursuit attack. (Museum of Flight)

against an attack, a formation that came to be called "Javelin Down". Three bomber squadrons in formation were deemed the minimum number required to mount an effective defense. The tests, though not without flaws, seemed to confirm the view that modern bombardment aircraft had minimal risk of interception. Arnold came to the conclusion that the then-current pursuit tactics were inadequate, and given the higher speeds of modern airplanes close range firing had become "... almost an impossibility."[22] In one section of his report on the tests he stated, "it is extremely doubtful if single-seater Pursuit planes, even though they have a 50-mile excess of speed over the bomber, can prevent a formation of modern Bombardment planes from reaching their objective or destroy the planes either en route to or returning from their objective."[23] Actual experience during the coming war would show that the bomber advocates were all too sanguine about the balance of advantages between the bomber and the pursuit, particularly in their estimation of the effect of defensive fire against attacking pursuits.

One of the most interesting aspects of Arnold's operational tests was the use of the 7th Group's B-12 bombers to simulate multi-seat fighters. The tests seemed to demonstrate the limitations of single-seat pursuits in attacking bomber formations; Arnold wanted to explore the possibility of using multi-seat fighters that could bring multiple guns to bear from different angles. Arnold had one of the Group's squadrons act as fighters, while the other two flew as the bomber formation. For purposes of the test, the bombers flew at a slower speed to give the "fighter" aircraft a 30-mph speed advantage. Using camera guns, the "fighters" experimented with attacks on the bomber formation from the flanks, from the rear, and in combination, as well as the possibility of overhead bombing attacks against a formation of bombers.

A view of Hamilton Field as it looked in 1935. (3B-18830, RG 342FH, NARA)

The conclusion was that multi-seat fighter attacks would be effective if all guns on the fighter could be brought to bear and if the attack concentrated on the rear of the bomber formation. Though Arnold recommended development of a multi-seat fighter and higher-caliber guns, the airplane that ultimately came out of this line of development, the Bell FM-1, proved unsuccessful.[24]

In early October, the 7th Group experienced its first fatality with its new bombers. On October 2, 1934, Maj. Charles Philips, Group commander, was leading a formation of 18 B-12s on a cross-country flight from March Field up to Yosemite and return. Flying over the Sierra Nevada Mountains, the formation encountered turbulence. Capt. Richard Selff, commander of the 11th Bombardment Squadron, was leading a flight of six aircraft when suddenly the wing on Selff's B-12 collapsed, sending the airplane crashing into the mountains below. Only one crewman, Cadet Fay Olmstead, bailed out. As a precaution, the Air Corps grounded the Group's B-12s until an inspection could be completed.[25] Capt. Arthur G. Hamilton replaced Selff as squadron commander.[26]

That same day, the Secretary of War announced the organization of the General Headquarters Air Force, following the recommendation of the Baker Board, and the transfer of all combat units to the new command. The new GHQ Air Force would have three wings to cover the United States: the 2nd Bombardment Wing at Langley Field, Virginia, with the 2nd and 9th Bombardment Groups and the 1st and 8th Pursuit Groups to cover the East Coast; the 3rd Attack Wing at Barksdale Field, Louisiana, with the 3rd Attack Group and the 20th Pursuit Group to cover the southern region; and the 1st Pursuit Wing (as the 1st Bombardment Wing had been redesignated August 18, 1933) with its component units, the 7th Bombardment Group and the 17th Pursuit Group at March Field, and the 19th Bombardment Group at Rockwell Field to cover the West Coast. Included in the announcement was the news that as part of the reorganization of Army Air Corps units, the 7th Bombardment Group would be moving to Hamilton Field, outside San Francsico.[27]

Hamilton Field

The idea of having an airfield in the San Francisco area made strategic sense, given the Air Corps' mission of coastal defense, but the initial impetus for building an airfield was jobs, not defense. In 1929, the Board of Supervisors of Marin County, on the peninsula just north of San Francisco, offered to buy 776 acres of land and give it to the Army Air Corps for an airfield.[28] Delays in acquiring all the land the Air Corps wanted and in obtaining funding during the early years of the Depression put off the 7th Bombardment Group's move to Hamilton Field until the fall of 1934. The base was located north of San Rafael, overlooking San Pablo Bay. The hangars, administrative and maintenance buildings, offices, mess and officers' club, and accommodations for officers and enlisted men were built in the Spanish Mission style popular at the time. Featuring white stucco with red tile roofs surrounded by rolling hills and oak trees, upon its completion Hamilton Field was considered one of the finest Army Air Corps bases in the country.[29]

November 4, 1934, a month before the Group's move, Maj. Clarence Tinker was appointed commander. Tinker had transferred to the Army Air Service in the early 1920s, after serving several years in the Infantry. He had commanded the Advanced Flying School at Kelly Field, and in June 1933 had taken over command of the 17th Pursuit Group at March Field, where his pursuit squadrons had worked closely with the 7th Group. In preparation for the move, on November 17th, Tinker led a flight of 16 Martins from all three of the Group's squadrons from March Field to Hamilton Field to inspect their new facilities.[30] Because of the fatal crash in October and the precautionary grounding of the Martins, when 24 of the

A line of Martin B-12 bombers from the 31st Bombardment Squadron, shortly after arriving at Hamilton Field in early December 1934. (Author's collection)

A ski-equipped B-12 from the 11th Bombardment Squadron takes off from a snow-packed runway. (3B-11086, RG 342FH, NARA)

Group's bombers left March Field permanently December 1st, they carried only a pilot and radio operator, not a full crew. On arrival at Hamilton Field, the Martins were immediately grounded for structural inspections.[31] The rest of the officers and men arrived by rail and truck December 4th. Officers and men were immensely pleased with their new home.[32]

The New Year brought new tests for the 7th Bombardment Group. In late January, the 11th Bombardment Squadron's commanding officer, Capt. Arthur Hamilton, took three Martin B-12s, including one from the 9th Squadron, to join the Cold Weather Test Flight in Michigan. This formation of 17 service aircraft of different types evaluated operations in extremely cold weather. The operation started February 1, 1935, at Selfridge Field, Michigan, under the command of Maj. Ralph Royce. The B-12s were fitted with skis attached to the landing gear to enable them to land on snow-packed runways. This arrangement did not work as well as planned, as the landing wheels protruded beneath the skis, acting as a brake and creating a huge amount of drag when taking off. For the next several weeks, the airplanes operated out of a number of civilian airfields around Michigan and into Wisconsin, North Dakota, and Minnesota. The weather cooperated for most of the test period, providing freezing temperatures well below zero and plentiful snow. The tests came up with useful recommendations for maintenance, clothing, and winter flying equipment. One of the main requests was for a redesign of the ski installation on larger aircraft. In the air, the skis proved to be as big a drag as the wheels were in the snow. On one

Wearing cold weather gear, three crewmen inspect the skies attached to their 9th Bombardment Squadron B-12. Note the polar bear emblem of the Cold Weather Test Flight to the right of the 9th Squadron's insignia. (3B-11088, RG 342FH, NARA)

Personnel of the Cold Weather Test Flight in February 1935 standing in front of a B-12 from the 9th Bombardment Squadron. Major Ralph Royce is standing just beneath the bombardier's window. (3B-11096, RG 342FH, NARA)

occasion, Capt. Hamilton radioed Maj. Royce, saying, "the P-26s have passed us, the P-12s and Observation have gone by, and the Attack is just going by. Now, then, under ordinary circumstances, without these skis we could outrun any of you, but, by golly, if the Transports go by I'm going to jump!"[33]

February 15th, ten Martin B-12As from the 31st Bombardment Squadron under the command of Capt. Harold Smith, who had been appointed squadron commander the month before, left Hamilton Field on the first stage of what was to be a

Lt. Col. Clarence Tinker's personal Martin B-12. Tinker named all his airplanes "Bird-O-Prey". This B-12 was his eleventh, and may have been the airplane he would later belly land at Rockwell Field. (3B-24483, RG 342FH, NARA)

planned long-distance flight from Washington, D.C., to the Panama Canal via Miami, Florida. The 1,100-mile flight from Miami to Panama was to be made over the Caribbean, out of sight of land. On the return, the Squadron hoped to fly non-stop from Panama to Washington. The purpose of the trip was to replicate the long-distance flight from Washington to Alaska the previous summer, demonstrating the Air Corps' ability to reinforce America's outlying possessions. In addition, it would test the range and fuel consumption of the B-12A, as well as give crews extensive practice in navigation. The Squadron's B-12As were equipped with a 500-gallon tank fitted into the bomb bay to extend the bomber's range. The crews spent ten days training at Rockwell Field, where their aircraft were fitted with controllable pitch propellers, the latest radio equipment, and radio compasses. The crews undertook training in flying on instruments under the instruction of Air Corps specialists. As a practice, on February 20th, the Squadron made a 1,200-mile flight over water, leaving Rockwell Field at 10:45 a.m. and flying out over the Pacific Ocean north to San Francisco. After heading inland to circle Hamilton Field, the Squadron flew back to Rockwell Field over the ocean, landing at 4:30 p.m.[34] The Squadron reached Langley Field February 28th and waited for good weather over the Caribbean. To the Squadron's frustration, the flight was cancelled at the last minute due to lack of funds.[35]

The General Headquarters Air Force—authorized the previous fall—was established March 1, 1935, with Brig. Gen. Frank M. Andrews, promoted from Lt. Colonel, as its first commander. With the activation of the GHQ Air Force, all component wings became regional sub-commands and were redesignated without specific categories, the 1st Pursuit Wing becoming simply the 1st Wing.[36] The 1st Wing's component units remained the 7th Bombardment Group at Hamilton Field, the 19th Bombardment Group at Rockwell Field (moved to March Field later in the year), and the redesignated 17th Attack Group, with one addition. To provide the Wing with the capability to perform long-range reconnaissance as part of its mission of coastal defense, the 88th Observation Squadron at Brooks Field, Texas, was attached to the 1st Wing, though the Squadron remained at Brooks Field until September. As the 88th Aero Squadron, the unit had served as a Corps observation squadron on the Western Front during WWI, flying French Salmson observation aircraft. Returning to the United States after the War, the Squadron had been redesignated the 88th Observation Squadron in 1921 and had served with various Army divisions and observation groups. At the time, the Squadron was equipped with O-19 and O-35 observation aircraft, but the apparent intention was to re-equip the Squadron with the Douglas OA-4 Dolphin amphibian, as the Squadron was shortly redesignated the 88th Observation Squadron (Long Range, Amphibian).[37]

Long-overdue promotions came with these organizational changes. Formation of the GHQ Air Force included authorization to promote the commanders of the 1st and 2nd Wings to temporary Brig. Gen.; Lt. Col. Henry Arnold gained the new higher rank. The War Department also authorized temporary promotions within the tactical units of GHQ Air Force to those officers who held ranks below the rank authorized for the position. Through this measure Maj. Tinker received a temporary promotion to Lt. Colonel and the 7th Bombardment Group's three squadron commanders—Capts. John M. Davies (9th Bombardment), Arthur G. Hamilton (11th Bombardment), and Harold D. Smith (31st Bombardment)—were all promoted to Major. 1st Lieutenants who were acting as Operations Officers or senior flight leaders received temporary promotions to Captain.[38]

The nature of the GHQ Air Force's mission determined much of the 7th Bombardment Group's training for the next several years. The rationale for creating a GHQ Air Force was to create "...a highly mobile force of great striking power."[39] For all tactical units assigned to GHQ Air Force, "...the object of all planning and training...is to create a powerful, highly mobile striking force ready at all times for immediate action on M-Day."[40] GHQ Air Force planners set three criteria for tactical units to be instantly available. A unit should:

a. Take off with all its airplanes from its home station within forty-eight hours of receipt of the order.

b. Fly to the designated concentration area at cruising speed, with minimum stop-overs for fuel and oil, at such intervals as are dictated by the range of the planes.

c. Take off to perform a normal operating mission against the enemy within twenty-four hours after arrival within the concentration area.[41]

Achieving greater mobility and instant availability would require more training and more flying hours, with more frequent field exercises and maneuvers to be held away from a unit's home field, practices that Arnold had already been practicing with the 1st Wing for several years. Following the lessons learned in the Air Mail Emergency, flying hours would become more demanding, with more hours devoted to navigation, instrument flying, and the use of radio beams. Individual pilots and crews would still have to attain the specified minimum standards for bombing and gunnery, but in a shift with past practice, competition would now be between units, rather than between individuals. To make tactical units more mobile, many maintenance staff were shifted to service squadrons and a station complement. At Hamilton Field, the 69th Service Squadron was activated to join the existing 70th Service Squadron, serving the 7th Bombardment Group and its squadrons.[42]

Brig. Gen. Arnold wasted little time, holding his first Wing Concentration at Hamilton Field March 22nd, with 51 P-26 Pursuits from the 17th Attack Group, 12 bombers from the 19th Bombardment Group, and 13 bombers from the 7th Group. Arnold had the three groups practice a coordination and communications problem based on the assumption that an enemy fleet had been located off the coast of San Francisco. The 17th Attack Group flew up to Hamilton Field to provide protection for the bombers of the 7th and 19th Bombardment Groups while they refueled between missions. The following month, on April 13th and 14th, the 1st Wing held its second concentration—this time at March Field—with some 150 of the Wing's aircraft taking part. The 88th Observation Squadron flew in from Brooks Field to participate in the 1st Wing maneuvers for the first time. After a hiatus of several months, the next Wing concentration took place from June 18th to June 20th in the Los Angeles area. Lt. Col. Tinker led 16 Martins from the 11th and 31st Bombardment Squadrons south, the 11th going to Mines Field and the 31st to Long Beach. The 88th Observation Squadron flew in again from Brooks Field and was attached to the 7th Group for the tactical problems Arnold had established for them. The fourth in the series of Wing maneuvers was the most ambitious. Arnold planned a Wing concentration at Salt Lake City, Utah, for all units in the Wing from July 22nd to the 25th. The maneuvers included flights to Wyoming, Idaho, and Nevada to familiarize the pilots with the area and to gain experience in cross-country flying. In preparation for the maneuvers, Lt. Col. Tinker put the Group's squadrons through their quarterly load test, taking their bombers up to a specified altitude with full military load of 2,000 pounds of bombs, followed by a series of bombing and gunnery competitions. The morning of July 22nd, 17 bombers took off from Hamilton Field for Salt Lake City, with Tinker leading in his *Bird-O-Prey*. The 7th Bombardment Group, in two V echelon formations, arrived over the city at 1:40 p.m., to be met by a crowd of more than 5,000 at the municipal airport. The next day, the group flew to Cheyenne, Wyoming, and returned to Salt Lake City via Denver, while the 17th and 19th Groups made other cross-country flights around the region. The 7th Bombardment Group's pilots flew singly back to Hamilton Field, had their planes worked on overnight, and flew to a Wing concentration at March Field the next day.[43]

In between the 1st Wing concentrations, the 7th Bombardment Group conducted its own group and squadron exercises, as well as regular training in bombing, gunnery, and navigation. GHQ Air Force had instructed the Wings to incorporate logistical problems in Group and Squadron maneuvers to investigate the challenges of and gain experience in supplying units in the field. In May, the Group went to Mather Field for an extended 10-day exercise over the Sacramento area. Lt. Col. Tinker dispersed his squadrons to different bases (the 9th to Mills Field at San Francisco, the 11th to Stockton, and the 31st to Suisun), then coordinated their concentration over a focal point by radio from his *Bird-O-Prey*.[44] The challenge of the exercise was to insure that all

Martin B-12s of the 9th, 31st, and 11th Bombardment Squadrons on line prior to a quarterly full load test in April 1935, shortly before the 1st Wing Concentration held that month. On the far right are three B-7 bombers. (Courtesy Hamilton Field Military Museum)

three squadrons, coming from three different bases, arrived over the focal point at the same time. During the exercise, Tinker varied the focal point each day. Tragedy struck May 28th, when a bomber from the 31st Squadron crashed near

Martin B-12 and B-10 bombers from the 7th and 19th Bombardment Groups at the 1st Wing Concentration at Hamilton Field in April 1935. (3B-18797, RG 342FH, NARA)

Sequoia National Park, killing the pilot, 2nd Lt. Edgar Root, the radio operator, Pvt. Guy Porter, and two newsmen who were aboard filming the Squadron's formation flight. The other members of the Squadron saw Root's airplane fall out of formation and start circling at a steep angle, then flip over and go into a flat spin from which there was no escape; some suspected that the passengers in the rear cockpit may have become entangled in the flight controls.[45] Over the summer, Tinker sent out each of the Group's squadrons on tactical field exercises to practice operating from remote locations, with the Group's service squadrons providing maintenance and logistical support. In June, the 11th Squadron spent a week at Coalinga, California, where the weather was so hot all maintenance had to be completed by 7:00 a.m. in the morning, followed by the 9th Squadron, who went to Visalia and had the same problems with high temperatures. The 31st Squadron was more fortunate, spending a week at Medford, Oregon. From Medford, the Squadron flew long-range bombing missions to different targets in the area.[46]

To become the powerful striking force it intended to be and to implement the evolving doctrine of daylight precision bombing, GHQ Air Force required its crews to be proficient in bombing, navigation, and gunnery, as well as flying their aircraft to the high standards General Frank Andrews wanted.[47] The new, revised Training Regulation TR 440-40 contained more demanding and rigid requirements for obtaining Expert ranking. Reaching this standard took long hours and constant practice. The Air Corps philosophy at the time was that all pilots had to become bombardiers, on the theory that to be effective, a pilot had to understand the problems of the bombardier and the bombardier had to understand the problems of the pilot to insure proper coordination.[48] The 7th Bombardment Group had been handicapped in reaching the required level of proficiency in bombing. The demands of the CCC Program, the Air Mail Emergency, and the lack of bomb sights for its Martin bombers until early 1935 meant that the majority of the younger officers and enlisted flight crews had participated in only a few bombing exercises.[49] Compounding the problem was the gradual introduction of the new Norden Model XV bomb sight. The Group not only had to provide basic instruction in bombardment for the more inexperienced crews, but train all pilots and enlisted bombardiers in the operation of the new Norden bomb sight. With the arrival of bomb sights and ground training devices, the Group set up an elementary ground instruction course, followed by eight hours on the training devices. Successful completion of this phase led to the ten-hour advanced course. Prior to the introduction of the Pilot Direction Indicator (PDI), the men who served as bombardiers had to learn and practice guiding a pilot on to the target (at the time, the Army Air Corps had no specialist bombardier position; other pilots or enlisted men who qualified acted as bombardiers). Pilots and bombardiers were required to practice bombing from the air at a target adjacent to Hamilton Field in San Pablo Bay; more

As part of the training directive from GHQ Air Force, the 7th Bombardment Group's squadrons practiced flying and bombing from high altitudes. The Martin bomber's lack of a heating system required this 31st Bombardment Squadron crew to wear heavy fur-lined clothing with their oxygen masks. (00005714, Courtesy San Diego Air & Space Museum)

often, they used a bombing range set up at Mather Field, where the squadrons could spend a week to ten days qualifying crews in the requirements of TR 440-40. In the belief that bombing in future wars would be conducted from higher altitudes above the usual 8,000 to 10,000 feet, the 1st Wing directed bombing practice to be conducted at those altitudes

The training program for Fiscal Year 1936 placed a heavy emphasis on navigation. The 7th Bombardment Group received three Douglas OA-4 Dolphin amphibians to practice navigating over the ocean. (3B-223529, RG 342FH, NARA)

and on longer range flights. The training instructions also directed the Group to practice salvo bombing by elements, squadrons, and the full group, dropping on a signal from the lead bombardier. Following this directive, the Group's squadrons flew a significant number of bombing missions at altitudes that required the use of oxygen—from 15,000 to 20,000 feet, and on one occasion from 23,000 feet. Pilots and bombardiers found that flying and bombing with precision from these altitudes while wearing bulky clothing, sucking oxygen through a tube, and using the microphone to transmit instructions proved to be demanding and fatiguing. Not surprisingly, bombing accuracy from higher altitudes was only deemed satisfactory.[50]

Despite shortages of the proper equipment and airplanes, the Group put nearly as much emphasis on navigation training as on bombardment. A Navigation School was set up to train small groups of officers in dead reckoning navigation, the final test requiring the student to intercept a commercial vessel at sea around 200 miles offshore. To provide an airplane for navigation practice, the Group was assigned three Douglas YOA-4 aircraft. In addition, one Martin bomber was fitted out with equipment for dead reckoning navigation. The Wing, Group, and Squadron exercises carried out during the year away from Hamilton Field, as well as regular cross-country flights, gave pilots additional experience in navigation. The amphibians were available for rescue should a bomber go down at sea and often accompanied the bombers on missions out over the ocean.[51]

In late September 1935, the 88th Observation Squadron, under the command of Maj. Calvin E. Griffin, completed its move from Brooks Field, Texas, to Hamilton Field with five regular and seven reserve officers. Although assigned to the 1st Wing, the Squadron was attached to the 7th Bombardment Group for administrative purposes. At Brooks Field, the Squadron had a small complement of six aircraft, consisting of the remaining Douglas Y1O-35 observation aircraft and Y1B-7 bombers that had been transferred from the 31st Bombardment Squadron. At Hamilton Field, the Squadron apparently took over the Group's OA-4B amphibians. Soon after its arrival, the Squadron began intensive training in navigation and long-range reconnaissance, with particular attention to the problems of navigating over water. The Squadron set up its own radio station to maintain direct contact with aircraft flying training missions out over the Pacific Ocean.[52]

That same month, Lt. Col. Tinker had a narrow escape during a public air show at March Field on September 5, 1935—one of many the Group participated in around the state of California to promote public awareness of the Air Corps. P-26s from the 17th Attack Group made mock attacks on a formation of B-12s Tinker was leading in *Bird-O-Prey XIII*. As Tinker was about to land, the radio operator called him to say that while the right landing gear was down, the left gear was still locked up. Tinker had noticed the problem from his

After transferring to Hamilton Field in October 1935 for attachment to the 7th Bombardment Group, the 88th Observation Squadron apparently took over the Group's Douglas OA-4 amphibians. This OA-4 has the 88th Observation Squadron's cowboy riding a bronco insignia on the nose. (Courtesy Hamilton Field Military Museum)

instruments. In trying to get the landing gear to cycle properly, the right landing gear jammed four-fifths of the way up. Repeated attempts to get both gear down failed. Tinker realized he would have to make a crash landing, though no one had ever made a belly landing in a B-12 before. He ordered his passengers, one of whom was the Medical Officer on his first flight in an airplane, to jump, the two men in the rear cockpit going out the bomb bay. With great presence of mind, Tinker flew his bomber to Rockwell Field, where he knew the Air

The 88th Observation Squadron flew a mix of the remaining Douglas Y1B-7 bombers and Y1O-35 observation airplanes. (7th Bombardment Group (H) Historical Foundation, USAFA McDermott Library)

Corps had better repair facilities than at March Field. He made an excellent wheels-up landing and within six weeks his plane had been repaired and was back in the air.[53]

In early November, Brig. Gen. Arnold organized two weeks of field exercises for the 1st Wing in the San Joaquin Valley as a test of the maintenance system's ability to maintain tactical units in the field for extended periods of operation. The exercise provided a test of different bombing methods and served as a warm-up to the planned GHQ Air Force maneuvers scheduled for December. At a luncheon given at Bakersfield in honor of the visiting airmen, Brig. Gen. Arnold gave a vivid description of what the next war would be like, describing how "...wave after wave of gigantic bombers will shower devastation upon railroads, factories, arsenals, and docks." The anti-aircraft guns might knock out the first, second, or even third wave of bombers, Arnold said, "...but on and on they will come, these flying fortresses with their tons of bombs and many will get through, to spread devastation throughout the land."[54]

Conducted from November 4th to the 17th, the exercises began with the 1st Wing's units moving to dispersed bases around the San Joaquin Valley, on the assumption that their main bases would be the immediate targets of any invading force. The 7th Bombardment Group's headquarters were at Merced, with the Group's squadrons and their 20 Martin B-12 bombers based there and at Visalia and Coalinga. The 88th Observation Squadron was stationed at 1st Wing headquarters at Fresno. During the first few days of the exercises, the tactical problems involved coordinating the rendezvous of units en route to bomb targets at Muroc dry lake in the Mojave Desert. In other exercises, the squadrons assembled over the main Group airfield before flying to the target. The 1st Wing practiced bombing by individual bombardiers, then pattern bombing by flights, squadrons, and Groups using a designated lead aircraft, all the other bombardiers dropping their bombs when the lead bombardier dropped his. The airplanes bombed from an altitude of around 12,000 feet against circular targets and against a life-size battleship outlined in white on the desert floor. After the maneuvers were over, the 7th Bombardment Group returned to Hamilton Field for maintenance, then went back to Muroc, where the Group set up camp to conduct more bombing tests based on the results of the maneuvers. The focus was mainly on formation bombing, using 100- and 300-pound practice bombs and bombs made out of concrete weighing 600, 1,000, and 2,000 pounds. By the end of the tests, the Group could fly a formation of two nine-plane squadrons and drop eighteen 300-pound bombs against the battleship target with a good concentration.[55]

GHQ Air Force held its first concentration in South Florida from December 2 to December 15, 1935.[56] The participating units brought less than their full complement of airplanes, with around 160 airplanes participating in the exercise; those units lacking more modern aircraft did not participate in the maneuvers. The first phase was the concentration itself. Brig. Gen. Frank Andrews wanted to test GHQ Air Force's ability to complete a concentration within 24 hours. On the West

Pattern bombing of a battleship target on Muroc Dry Lake by a combined formation of 7th and 19th Bombardment Group Martin bombers. (3B-5763, RG 342FH, NARA)

Coast, representing the 1st Wing, the 7th and 19th Bombardment Groups were consolidated into the 7th Provisional Bombardment Group with 29 Martin bombers. Lt. Col. Tinker flew the 7th

Group contingent to March Field to join the 19th Group's planes and crews. Covering a distance of 2,500 miles, the

Brigadier General Henry Arnold and Lt. Col. Clarence Tinker in January 1936, just before Arnold was transferred to Washington, D.C. Arnold's airplane carries the insignia of the 1st Wing. (Courtesy Hamilton Field Military Museum)

formation left March Field at 12:15 p.m. December 1st and flew to Vero Beach, Florida, north of Miami, in 21 hours and 50 minutes, with three refueling stops at Fort Bliss in Texas, Barksdale Field in Louisiana, and Maxwell Field in Alabama. This was believed to be a record for a mass flight of aircraft. The 2nd Wing, with only pursuit planes, was based at Miami, and the 3rd Wing with its attack aircraft at Fort Pierce just south of Vero Beach. For the next ten days, the units of GHQ Air Force worked on tactical problems involving attack and defense, with the pursuit formations attempting to defend Miami from attack. Working with the attack planes from the 3rd Wing, the 1st Wing bombers flew several different types of bombing missions against Miami, including a night raid over the port facilities and longer-range missions to "targets" in the northern part of the state and as far as Georgia. On one mission, the bombers left Vero Beach, crossed the state to bomb Tampa, then turned and flew southeast to bomb Miami in coordination with the attack planes. They covered 650 miles in 3 ½ hours of flying. Defending close to target, the pursuits regularly intercepted the bombers over Miami, but when interceptions were attempted at greater range from the city, it became easier for the bombers to split their formation and evade interception. At the end of the maneuvers, several GHQ Air Force units remained in Florida to participate in the All-American Air Races at Miami, flying formations for the assembled crowds.[57] The most valuable lesson of the maneuvers was the logistical challenges involved in maintaining a large force in the field. This would have lasting implications for Air Corps leaders in the years ahead. As the *Air Corps News Letter* noted in its review of the lessons of the Miami air maneuvers, "...while the Air Force is the most mobile and effective of the new engines of war, its service, care and supply increases greatly as its size is augmented...Tactical use of small air formations is a relatively simple matter, but combined strategical and tactical use of large fleets is going to demand much preparation."[58]

GHQ Air Force did not hold maneuvers during 1936. Instead, the individual wings and groups conducted their own concentrations and maneuvers, often as part of larger Army or Navy exercises. For the 7th Bombardment Group, it was a year of continuous training in the basic skills of bombing and navigation, combined with training in operations away from the Group's base at Hamilton Field. The Group's squadrons continued to use Mather Field for their bombing practice, working on the requirements for TR440-40 while operating from a different airfield for two weeks. In addition, Lt. Col. Tinker sent the squadrons out to other small airfields in California for a week of work on tactical problems. Later in the year, the squadrons undertook longer cross-country flights of a week to ten days around the West to practice navigation. The 11th Bombardment Squadron made a long ten-day trip from Hamilton Field to Denver, Colorado, and return with side trips to Missoula, Montana, and Albuquerque, New

Officers of the 11th Bombardment Squadron at Hamilton Field. (7th Bombardment Group (H) Historical Foundation, USAFA McDermott Library)

Mexico, during August, while the 31st Bombardment Squadron flew to Boise, Idaho, via Reno, Nevada, for a week of flights around the area to examine airfield facilities.[59] One of the 11th Squadron's pilots on this long trip was Lt. Harvey Alness, who would later command the 7th Group in WWII. More importantly, the Group participated in several exercises involving two key aspects of the Air Corps' mission: tests of precision bombing and coastal defense.

In 1934, the Bombardment Aviation text at the Air Corps Tactical School emphasized daylight strategic bombing; not the enemy's armies, but its national will and industrial system. Two years later, the Bombardment text addressed the need to attack a nation's "vital centers"—factories, communications systems, and power sources—to disrupt an enemy nation's ability to make war.[60] Precision bombing also applied to the Air Corps' assigned mission: coastal defense and the destruction of enemy naval vessels. In the mid-1930s, the Air Corps combined the Martin bomber and the Norden bomb sight, which seemingly made the evolving air power theory of daylight precision bombing a reality, but the technology had to be tested and combat techniques perfected. During his period in command of the 1st Wing, Brig. Gen. Arnold used the 7th Bombardment Group to experiment with different bombing techniques on targets laid out on Muroc Dry Lake; these experiments continued after Arnold was transferred to Washington, D.C., in January 1936.[61] Through these tests, Arnold came to realize that bombing accuracy declined as the bombers flew at higher speeds and higher altitudes to avoid both anti-aircraft fire and interception. An analysis of bombing accuracy conducted later in the decade would show that a doubling of the bombing altitude would result in a near doubling of the radial error, or the distance between a bomb's point of impact and the target. Arnold developed the technique of grouping his bombers in larger formations and bombing in salvos, using quantity of explosives to partly overcome the problems of bombing accuracy.[62] The advocates of daylight precision bombing failed to fully comprehend, or chose to ignore that almost all the bombing practice was done at relatively low altitudes, in good weather; bombing was accurate "...only in excellent weather against a clearly outlined, undefended target in the middle of wide-open terrain."[63] As experience would show, bombing accurately through weather, flak, and fighters would be an entirely different proposition.

Loading a 2,000-pound concrete practice bomb under the wing of a B-12 bomber from the 11th Bombardment Squadron. Concrete bombs were used extensively in tests over Muroc Dry Lake. (7th Bombardment Group (H) Historical Foundation, USAFA McDermott Library)

Brig. Gen. Henry Clagett, who took over from Arnold as commander of the 1st Wing at the end of February 1936, participated in the Wing's first concentration of the year in March: ten days of field exercises at Muroc Dry Lake with the 7th Bombardment Group and the 17th Attack Group. The objectives of the exercise were to test the handling and performance of the B-12 loaded with heavy bombs and to investigate precision bombing and bomb patterns from altitudes between 15,000 and 18,000 feet.[64] Capt. Philip Schwartz, the 1st Wing's ordnance officer, had developed concrete bombs for the tests weighing 600, 1,100, and 2,000 pounds.[65] The 7th Bombardment Group was scheduled to fly 18 bombing missions using the outline of a battleship on the ground as a target. The planned missions would examine the results of airplanes bombing independently with 300-pound bombs and the three types of heavy concrete bombs, and airplanes employing salvo bombing by flights, squadron, and the entire group. Part of the tests involved determining the maximum practical operating altitude of the B-12 with different combinations of bombs. To make some of the missions more realistic, two involved flights of 2 1/2 hours: one flown with two 1,100-pound concrete bombs and one with a single 2,000-pound concrete bomb.[66] The Group returned to Muroc in August for more bombing tests, Lt. Col. Tinker taking 18 bombers to join nine aircraft from the 19th Bombardment Group to form three nine-plane squadrons. The Group practiced bombing by squadron salvo from an altitude of 12,000 feet, flying in a stepped down javelin formation, dropping bombs in train sighting on the lead plane in the formation. Each bombing run was photographed obliquely from low altitude and vertically from the bombers. To simulate a ship moving at 30 knots, three trucks drove across the lake bed at 150-foot intervals, the bombardiers sighting on the dust clouds the trucks raised.[67] Later in the Fall, the 9th Bombardment Squadron conducted tests for the 1st Wing to determine the pattern of bombs dropped from various formations outlined in the Air Corps Tactical School's bombardment manual. With aircraft from its sister squadrons, the 9th Squadron used a nine-plane formation on the bombing range at Mather Field. Using practice bombs with black powder charges and carefully measuring the distance between the center of the target and the impact point of the bomb, the Squadron practiced varying the distance and interval of each aircraft within a formation, stepped up and stepped down formations, and variations in speed and altitude. To keep bomb release as simultaneous as possible, two lights were installed in the bomb bay doors of the lead airplane: one to signal the time for sighting on the target and the other to signal bomb release.[68] The information from all these tests, and those from other bomb groups, went into the preparation of tactics manuals for bombardment aviation and into the institutional memory of the Air Corps and its commanders.

The 7th Bombardment Group at Fort Lewis, Washington, for the Joint Coastal Frontier Defense Exercises in November 1936. The 88th Reconnaissance Squadron's four Douglas OA-4B aircraft can be seen on the right. (Courtesy Hamilton Field Military Museum)

A practical test of the Group's navigation training for coastal defense came in mid-July, when Lt. Col. Tinker planned a Group interception of a ship at sea. The USS *Meigs*, an Army transport ship approaching San Francisco, was to be the target. Position reports from the *Miegs* were plotted daily, along with weather reports, and showed that the ship would be in position to be intercepted the morning of July 17th. At 8:30 a.m. that morning, Tinker ordered the 88th Observation Squadron to send off an airplane to locate the *Meigs* based on its probable position around 190 miles west of the Golden Gate. An hour later the Group took off, following the navigation airplane, intercepting the *Meigs* an hour and seven minutes later. After intercepting the ship, Tinker dropped smoke bombs and a container of aluminum powder to make a target for individual bombing with 110-pound practice bombs. He took the precaution of having one 88th Squadron OA-4B amphibian take off and fly with the Group to the intercept point, with two more flying ahead of the Group on the flight back to Hamilton Field.[69]

In the Fall, the 13th Naval District, covering the Pacific Northwest, organized the Joint Coastal Defense Exercise to train Naval air and sea forces, the Coast Guard, and Army Air Corps units in the tactics and skills they would need to defend the Puget Sound area. The scenario of the exercise assumed a hostile force had sent submarines and smaller surface vessels to attack shipping off the coast. The 7th Bombardment Group was designated as the air striking force. The Group sent the 11th and 31st Bombardment Squadrons, each with six bombers, and attached a flight from the 9th Squadron to each to make up two nine-plane squadrons. The 88th Squadron brought its four OA-4B amphibians and two Martin bombers for long-range reconnaissance. All were based at Fort Lewis, Washington. Prior to the beginning of the exercise November 3rd, the Group arranged for an Army mine laying vessel to tow a target out at sea to give the squadrons practice bombing a moving target. Procedures for the exercise involved Navy patrol planes from Sand Point Naval Air Station in Seattle flying out to the operating area to search for "enemy" ships. The patrol planes sent back contact reports to Navy headquarters in Bremerton, who ordered the 7th Bombardment Group to attack. This opportunity provided useful training in inter-service coordination. The Pacific Northwest's typical winter weather interfered with the exercise, limiting flying to only a few days and frustrating the pilots. On the most successful day (November 7th), though the patrol planes were grounded due to fog, the Group was given the location of the target vessel some 50 miles off the coast. The Group took off

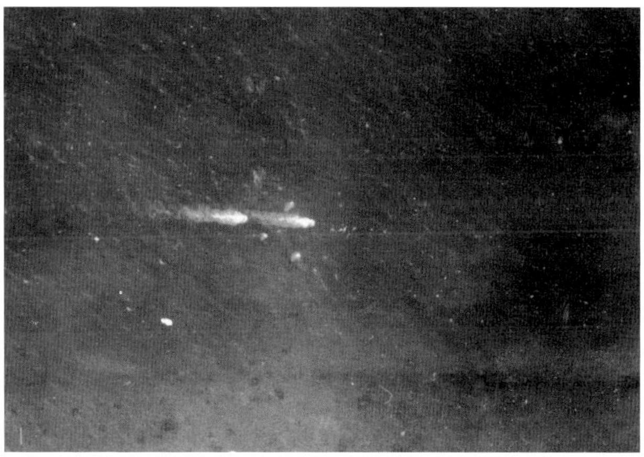

Bombing practice from an altitude of 7,000 feet against a target ship being towed at sea. (Gp-7-SU-(Bomb) November 1936, Albert F. Simpson Historical Research Center, Air Force Historical Research Agency, Maxwell AFB, AL)

from Fort Lewis with two of the amphibians along for safety and went into a search formation. With the target located, the bombers dropped 45 practice bombs. Returning to Fort

Lt. Col. Clarence Tinker's brand new Martin B-10B bomber *Bird-O-Prey XIII* at Boeing Field in Seattle, June 1936. Tinker was visiting the Boeing factory after displaying the newest Air Corps bomber at a National Defense Week demonstration held in Spokane, Washington, at the end of May. (Peter M. Bowers Collection, Museum of Flight)

Lewis, the bombers were hurriedly refueled and rearmed and took off again for another attack before returning to the airfield.[70]

The exercise gave the 7th Group good practice in attacking shipping. The most effective formation proved to be a column of three flights echeloned in altitude, flying 1,000 feet above and below the lead flight. If the flights converged on the target from slightly different directions, this greatly increased the chances of scoring a hit. If a ship turned left or right it would still be vulnerable to bombing, and having the flights at different altitudes made a difficult target for the ship's anti-aircraft guns. The Air Corps officers found it frustrating to engage in attacks on smaller vessels, believing that proper targets for bombardment were larger capital ships or aircraft carriers. They were confident that two squadrons of nine airplanes each could disable a capital ship if 60 per cent of the airplanes were able to release their bombs, although they admitted that heavier anti-aircraft fire would no doubt reduce the accuracy of bombing. Experience would later prove that Air Corps officers were far too optimistic in their faith in the effectiveness of level bombing against ships at sea. From the higher altitudes that wartime bombers would fly from to avoid flak and fighters, even stationary ships would prove to be difficult targets.[71]

During the second half of 1936, the 7th Bombardment Group underwent several changes in equipment, organization, and command. At the end of May, the Group began turning in its Martin B-12s and re-equipping with the Martin B-10B, the main production version of the Martin bomber that had more powerful Wright Cyclone engines of 775 h.p. The Air Corps had ordered 103 B-10Bs in 1934 for service with all four of the Air Corps' bombardment groups. Performance was basically the same as the B-12. The re-equipment allowed at least some of the older B-12s to be transferred to the 88th Observation Squadron, along with a few of the new B-10Bs. Experience in coastal defense exercises had called into question the idea of equipping the long-range reconnaissance squadrons with airplanes that were incapable of carrying bombs and that did not have the same speed and range as the bombers they were supporting. The November joint exercises with the Navy in the Pacific Northwest supported this conclusion.[72] In August, the War Department announced a reorganization of the Air Corps to be effective September 1, 1936. Part of the plan was a reorganization of the maintenance and support personnel at the group level, shifting from service squadrons to an air base squadron concept. To enhance their mobility, tactical units were relieved of most of their administrative responsibilities. These and other services and supply functions were transferred to an air base squadron. The new air base squadrons would have responsibility for servicing units at their home station and from airfields within a 200-mile radius. The 69th and 70th Service Squadrons that were part of the 7th Bombardment Group were deactivated, along with the Station Complement, Hamilton Field, to become the Headquarters and Headquarters Squadron, 7th Bombardment Group, and

Lt. Col. Clarence Tinker and Captain Kenneth Walker, who would take command of the 9th Bombardment Squadron in October 1936, stand in front of Tinker's new Martin B-10B, believed to be 34-72. (Courtesy Hamilton Field Military Museum)

the Base Headquarters and 5th Air Base Squadron.[73] Some of the maintenance personnel from the two Service Squadrons returned to the bomber squadrons. The 88th Observation Squadron (Long Range, Amphibian), along with the other long-range observation squadrons attached to the GHQ Air Force Wings, was redesignated the 88th Reconnaissance Squadron.[74]

Command changes affected the 7th Bombardment Group at all levels. In July, Brig. Gen. Delos Emmons replaced Brig. Gen. Henry Clagett as commander of the 1st Wing, a post he would hold until March 1939. That same month, Col. Davenport Johnson arrived at Hamilton Field to take up the post of Base Commander, relieving Lt. Col. Tinker of one of his two assignments. At the end of August, Tinker was promoted to Colonel and transferred to Washington, D.C., relinquishing command of the 7th Group. Col. Johnson took over temporary command of the Group until November, when Lt. Col. George Stratemeyer, who had been serving as Johnson's executive officer, was appointed to command the Group. Stratemeyer was a West Point graduate who had joined the Aviation Section of the Signal Corps in 1916. He completed the Air Corps Tactical School course in 1930, then went on to the Army's two-year course at Command and General Staff School, remaining there until his transfer to Hamilton Field in July 1936. In October, Capt. Kenneth Walker, one of the leading advocates of strategic bombing during his tour as an instructor at the Air Corps Tactical School who had been serving on the 7th Group's staff, took over command of the 9th Bombardment Squadron from Maj. John Davies. That same month, Maj. Newton Longfellow, a recent graduate of the Air Corps Tactical School, took command of the 88th Reconnaissance Squadron, giving the 7th Bombardment Group its third ACTS graduate. A month later, Maj. James Taylor replaced Maj. Harold Smith as commander of the 31st Bombardment Squadrons, completing the command moves that year.[75]

Soon after taking over the Group, Lt. Col. Stratemeyer had a narrow escape. Returning from a practice mission in Tinker's old airplane (B-10B *Bird-O-Prey XIII*), Stratemeyer was about to land at Hamilton Field when one of his engines failed, followed quickly by the other engine. With no altitude and no alternative, Stratemeyer put the airplane down into San Pablo Bay in shallow water about a mile offshore. He and his crew were uninjured and were rescued by the base's crash boat, available for just such an emergency.[76] The incident didn't faze him and he was soon putting his squadrons to work. On their return from the joint exercise in the Pacific Northwest, he ordered them to undertake field exercises from different fields around the area. The 9th Bombardment Squadron spent a week at Stockton, the 11th Squadron was at Modesto, and the 31st Squadron was at Fresno. All practiced bombing, formation flying, gunnery, and interception problems. The 88th Reconnaissance Squadron spent a week at Redding working on patrol and reconnaissance missions. At Fresno, the 31st Squadron held an open house for 25,000 people to acquaint them with the Air Corps' activities. After the New Year, following GHQ Air Force training directives to emphasize individual training, the squadrons began intensive work on dead reckoning navigation and instrument flying, with each squadron setting up a navigation school to teach the theory, followed by practice missions. Inclement weather disrupted the flying schedule and led to the loss of a B-10B and crew.

Colonel Davenport Johnson (left) and Lt. Colonel George Stratemeyer at Hamilton Field. Johnson commanded the 7th Group for two and a half months before relinquishing command to Stratemeyer in November 1936. (Courtesy Hamilton Field Military Museum)

Flying a night mission January 4, 1937, 2nd Lt. Herbert Knieriem from the 11th Bombardment Squadron was alerted to the approach of heavy winds and blinding rain squalls and ordered to return to Hamilton Field. The squall hit as Knieriem was making his approach, sending the aircraft crashing into San Pablo Bay some seven miles north of the field. Knieriem and his radio operator, Private Hartley Roberts, were both killed.[77]

With the next series of GHQ Air Force maneuvers a few months away, during February and March, Lt. Col. Stratemeyer devised a series of tactical navigation problems to exercise the entire Group and test its efficiency. In the first exercise,

The 9th Bombardment Squadron's air and ground crews at the 1937 GHQ Air Force 1937 maneuvers. (SQ-Bomb-9-SU-PH-1932-42, Albert F. Simpson Research Center, Air Force Historical Research Agency, Maxwell AFB, AL.

just before take-off, the squadrons were given an assembly point and assigned separate routes to take to the initial point. The assigned navigators had 20 minutes to work out their courses and times to arrive at the assembly point from the initial point exactly 80 minutes later. Stratemeyer was waiting at the assembly point. Upon arrival, the squadrons were organized into a group formation for the return flight to Hamilton Field. A week later, Stratemeyer had each aircraft fly individually to each squadron's initial point to give the navigators more training. At the squadron initial point, the squadrons formed up and flew to the Group assembly point designated by latitude, longitude, altitude, and time. There the squadrons formed into a group column and flew toward their target, an enemy "aircraft factory" in San Pablo Bay off Hamilton Field. The Group flew in an echelon right formation, stacked up from 9,000 to 12,000 feet, each aircraft flying 500 feet from the other in the flight. After bombing, each aircraft turned sharply to the left so that their route of departure was close to the route of attack of other airplanes in the formation, thereby presenting a more confusing target for enemy anti-aircraft. In a third exercise Stratemeyer devised, he experimented with making multiple passes over the target from an unspecified higher altitude. In the first two passes aircraft bombed individually, the third pass using the squadron salvo technique. Practice, and more practice, experimenting with different tactics, trying to determine what worked and what didn't; the 7th Bombardment Group's effort continued month after month.[78]

GHQ Air Force decided to hold its 1937 annual maneuvers on the West Coast during May. Frank Andrews, who had been promoted to Major General, wanted to test tactics and the efficiency of the recently-organized air base system's ability to supply and maintain units in the field. For a more realistic test, Andrews wanted to practice with units at their full strength, flying missions of three to six hours, similar to what they would encounter in actual combat. Since few units in the GHQ Air Force were actually at full strength, some having as few as one flight available, aircraft and units were combined to bring Groups to full strength. The 7th Bombardment Group assigned the 9th and 31st Squadrons to the maneuvers and borrowed the 32nd Bombardment Squadron from the 19th Bombardment Group to make up a full group. The squadrons operated from bases at Fresno, Stockton, and Merced, California. The 3rd Attack Group was based around Bakersfield and the 1st Pursuit Group at Muroc Dry Lake. In total, 450 officers, 3,400 enlisted men, and 260 airplanes took part. Tactical exercises took place between May 10th and May 21st. For purposes of the exercise, Muroc Dry Lake substituted for Los Angeles, with factories, docks, and other facilities outlined in lime on the lake bed as targets. Additional targets were set up at the Great Salt Lake in Utah. The 1st Wing was assigned the pursuit units and charged with defending Muroc Dry Lake, while the 2nd Wing was given the 7th Bombardment Group and the 3rd Attack Group as the attacking force. On the opening day of the tactical exercises, Lt. Col. Stratemeyer led 27 Martin B-10B bombers from the 7th Group to attack an "aircraft factory" at Muroc Dry Lake with 54 Northrop A-17 attack planes in support. The bombers came in at altitudes from 8,000 to 12,000 feet. Boeing P-26 and Consolidated PB-2 pursuits intercepted the bombers using camera guns. The pursuits found intercepting the bombers a challenge when the Martins flew at higher speeds, but still managed several successful interceptions. The *Los Angeles Times* reported that "only" five of the bombers were claimed as destroyed. This represented a loss rate of nearly 20 per cent.[79] Several days later, the 7th Group flew a low-level night mission to the same target, following up with a second attack in mid-morning. For added experience, the 7th Group flew several longer, six-hour missions to the targets at the Great Salt Lake in Utah, spending

Two Douglas B-18s belonging to the 11th Bombardment Squadron at Hamilton Field, 1937-38. (Courtesy Hamilton Field Military Museum)

much of the flight on oxygen flying at 21,000 feet, somewhat out of the ordinary range of practice missions. The air base squadrons at Hamilton Field and March Field worked admirably, ten Douglas C-33 transport planes flying supplies to various auxiliary airfields throughout the period of the maneuvers. The maneuvers provided valuable practice in bombardment and attack tactics and their coordination, and in interception tactics, but also gave evidence that the units involved were both undermanned and under-equipped for all the demands that were placed on them.[80] The GHQ Air Force maneuvers were something of a swan song for the 7th Group's Martin B-10s. After nearly three years flying the Martins, they were due for replacement with a more modern aircraft, the Douglas B-18.

The Douglas Aircraft Company began working on a design for a twin-engine bomber (the DB-1) during 1934, in parallel to the development of its commercial transports, the DC-1 and DC-2.[81] Douglas submitted its design to the Army Air Corps in response to the Air Corps Circular Proposal 35-26, issued in September 1934, calling for a new multi-engine bomber that could meet the needs of the coastal defense mission, and in the Air Corps' mind, the evolving doctrine of long-range bombing. The Air Corps wanted a bomber that had good speed, the ability to fly at higher altitudes than the Martin B-10B, the range to cross the continental United States without stopping, and the ability to carry several tons of bombs.[82] The Douglas DB-1 was in competition with the Martin Model 146 and the Boeing Model 299, forerunner of the B-17. After testing at Wright Field during the latter part of 1935, the Air Corps Evaluation Board selected the DB-1 for acquisition in quantity. December 21, 1935, the War Department announced that Douglas Aircraft had received a contract for ninety new bombers, designated the B-18, while the Boeing Company was awarded a contract to provide thirteen of its four-engine design for service test.[83] The contract with Douglas was later increased to cover 132 airplanes. Over the years, considerable controversy has developed around this decision. The Boeing Model 299 was what the Air Corps bombardment advocates were looking for, an airplane that had the potential for truly long-range, strategic bombing missions, able to fly at speed at high altitude, with seemingly adequate defenses against opposing pursuits. Although Maj. Gen. Benjamin Foulois recommended the purchase of 65 of the new Boeing bombers, the crash of the Model 299 before the completion of flight testing precluded the purchase of more than thirteen airplanes as the Y1B-17 service test model.[84] Over the next several years, the debate over the purchase of additional B-17s became a point of serious contention between the Air Corps and the War Department; senior Air Corps officers pushed for more B-17s and the War Department resisted the Air Corps' attempt to expand its mission into long-range strategic bombing.[85] From the War Department's perspective, the Douglas bomber, designated the B-18, was perfectly adequate for the mission of coastal defense and support of the ground forces, had received the Air Corps' approval, and more critically, could be purchased in greater

The cockpit of the B-18 was more complex than that of the Martin B-10 to allow for safer flying on instruments by either pilot or copilot. (3B-25124, RG 342FH, NARA)

quantities than the B-17 because of its lower cost. In his annual report issued December 8, 1935—shortly before the contracts for Fiscal Year 1936 were announced—Secretary of War George

A B-18 from the 11th Bombardment Squadron on a practice mission over California. The B-18 was one of the first airplanes delivered to the Air Corps in natural metal finish. (7th Bombardment Group (H) Historical Foundation, USAFA McDermott Library)

Dern called for a new five-year airplane procurement program for the Army Air Corps and recommended that 800 modern airplanes be purchased each year to bring the Air Corps up to the level of 2,320 serviceable airplanes recommended by the Drum and Baker Boards.[86] With four Air Corps bombardment groups to re-equip and bring up to full strength, purchasing a greater number of B-18s, rather than a smaller number of B-17s, would do more to reach this goal; Congress authorized the purchase in June 1936.[87]

While not much faster than the Martin B-10B, the Douglas B-18 was a considerable improvement over the older Martin bomber. The B-18 had a higher service ceiling, but more critically, double the range with the same bomb load. For defensive armament, the B-18 carried three .30 caliber machine guns in a nose turret, a retractable dorsal turret, and a ventral gun position—a fairly typical arrangement for the time. As a bomber, the B-18 was comparable to contemporary bombers serving in other air forces in Europe and Japan. Where the B-18 offered a quantum leap over the Martin B-10B was in crew arrangement, crew comfort, and the complexity more commonly associated with contemporary commercial air transports. In contrast to the cramped and isolated compartments of the Martin, the B-18 featured side-by-side seating for the pilot and co-pilot in an enclosed, heated cockpit featuring sound-proofing, a bombardier's and gunner's position in the nose, and positions for the radio operator and navigator just aft of the flight deck. The rear of the fuselage held a bunk for crew rest—a novelty. The wide fuselage allowed free movement between the different crew positions. As the *Air Corps News Letter* noted in an issue a few months after the B-18 entered service, the new multi-engine, multi-place airplanes entering service were placing new requirements on its pilots. The newsletter said, "...the piloting of these airplanes requires not only familiarity with and knowledge of all the instruments and accessories common to commercial transports, but also mastery of literally hundreds of purely military devices. The present-day pilot must not only be able to fly the airplanes, but he must direct the work of many other members of the crew and be competent in case of need to man any of their positions."[88] Perhaps the most important contribution the B-18 made to the development of the Air Corps in the years before WWII was the extensive experience it provided to so many pilots in managing and coordinating a crew. This experience was invaluable in preparing pilots for the challenges of the larger B-17s, B-24s, and B-29s introduced a few years later.

In January 1937, Col. Davenport Johnson, commander of Hamilton Field, announced to the local press that 35 of the big new Douglas bombers would be assigned to replace the Martins; the first contingent of nine airplanes would arrive in May.[89] For whatever reason, it took longer for the full complement of B-18s to make it to Hamilton Field than expected. The first B-18 for the 7th Bombardment Group arrived July 9, 1937, with three more arriving that month and another five during August. The next batch of eight bombers did not arrive until November, with a further six during January 1938. The last B-18 arrived in June, giving the Group 21 airplanes on hand and allowing it to bid farewell to its last two Martin B-10s.[90] Earlier, the arrival of the B-18s and the subsequent freeing-up of more Martin B-10Bs from other squadrons enabled the 88th Reconnaissance Squadron to relinquish its last three Douglas O-35s, then the oldest airplanes in the GHQ Air Force inventory.[91] As soon as the new bombers arrived at Hamilton Field, the pilots began practice flights to familiarize themselves with their new airplanes. The War Department specified new levels of proficiency for pilots of the B-18, requiring them to have at least five years of flying experience and 1,250 flying hours.[92] With tongue planted firmly in cheek, the Hamilton Field correspondent to the *Air Corps News Letter* reported on a new practice for flying the new B-18s these demanding requirements had brought about:

> Recent requirements regarding flying qualifications have necessitated a deviation from the usual flying procedure. Until such time as they are qualified to use both, co-pilots are flying B-18s on one engine, in order to build up their time for multi-motored equipment. Of course, qualified pilots take off and land the plane on two engines, but turn the ship over to the co-pilot in the air for single motor flying. The fact that the 7th Bombardment Group is conducting extensive single-engine performance tests, of course, is of considerable aid in affecting the above qualifications."[93]

For younger pilots coming to large multi-engine airplanes for the first time, the B-18 was a relatively straightforward

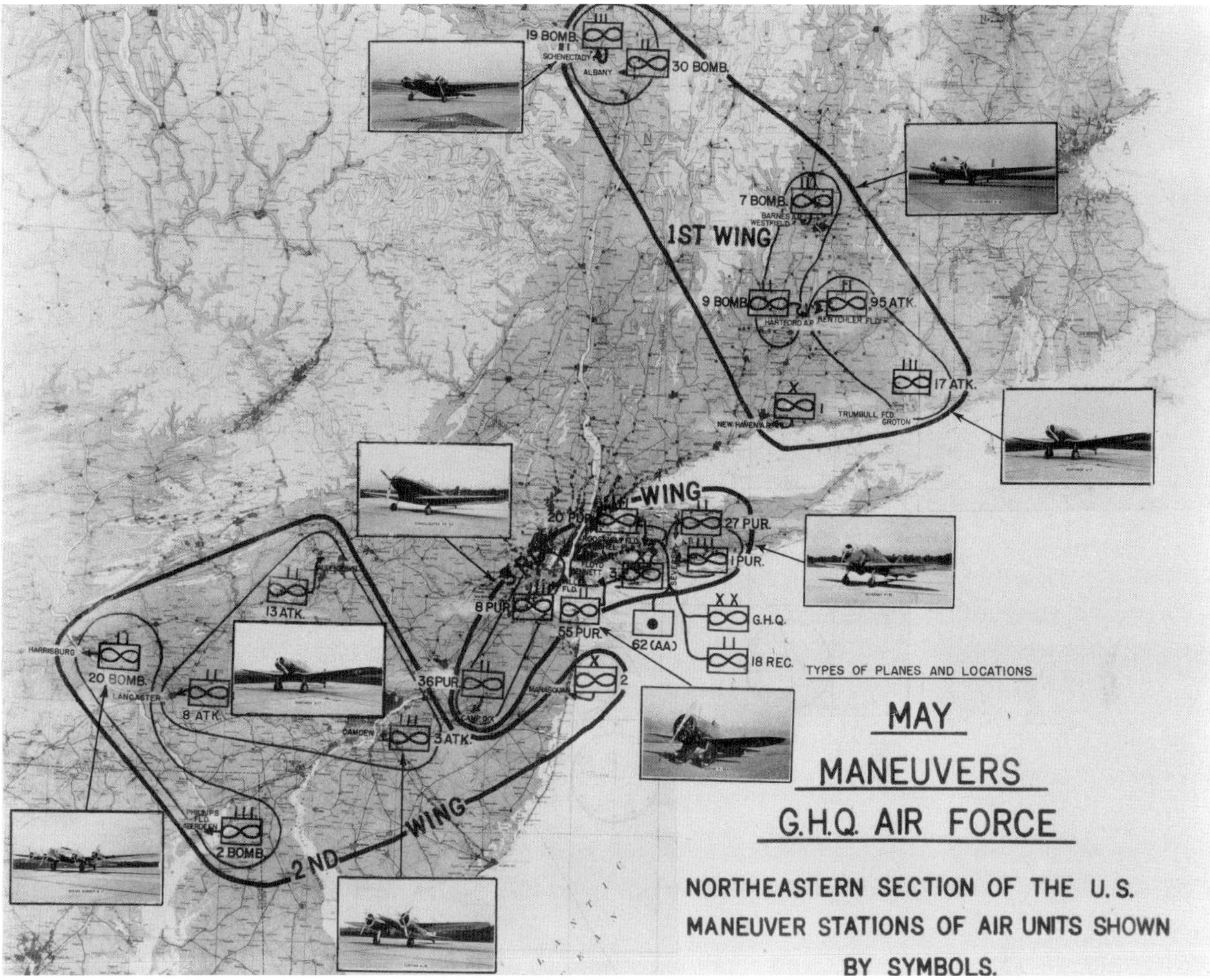

A map showing the locations of the different wings involved in the 1938 GHQ Air Force maneuvers in New England. The 7th Bombardment Group was based at the Barnes National Guard field in Westfield, Massachusetts. (3B-11140, RG 342FH, NARA)

aircraft with few vices, a good airplane in which to gain valuable experience. As one pilot recalled, "the B-18 was not an exciting airplane, but it was reliable. It looked sturdy and squatty and was. It had an honest stall with a polite amount of warning... the B-18 was our steadfast ally. It patiently tolerated our youthful exuberance, our mistakes, and our occasional recklessness... It forgave us all but our most egregious errors."[94]

For the rest of the year, the 7th Group's squadrons flew regularly to build experience on the B-18s. Local practice missions and longer cross-country flights helped the crews move on to the Fiscal Year 1938 training program. The 88th Reconnaissance Squadron obtained a few airplanes in early 1938. Continuing the emphasis on building individual navigation proficiency, the Group again set up a navigation school in the fall for all pilots not already qualified. The course covered 60 hours of dead reckoning and celestial navigation, with 20 hours of air navigation exercises. The goal was to train pilot/navigators to be able to plot their position to within one mile in a hundred and arrive at a point to within one minute of each hour from the start of the exercise. With the coastal defense mission in mind, after forty hours of instruction students were required to fly a number of missions out over the Pacific Ocean to practice what they had learned. The final interception problems involved finding commercial ships at sea based on position reports sent in every twelve hours. The Group's pilots apparently regularly practiced intercepting ships heading for San Francisco while still several hundred miles offshore. To provide an airplane that could double as a rescue plane and a navigational trainer, and that could keep up with the B-18s, the 7th Group received a single Sikorsky Y1OA-8, a larger twin-engine amphibian.[95]

There were other changes as well. Over a period of three months during the summer of 1937, the 11th Bombardment Squadron went through three commanders. Capt. Donald W. Benner took up the position more permanently in early September. In January 1938, the 9th Bombardment Squadron's commander, Capt. Kenneth Walker, was transferred to the Hawaiian Department. Maj. Thad V. Foster, who had been serving as Group Adjutant, took command of the 9th Squadron in March. The biggest change was the transfer of the 31st Bombardment Squadron to the 5th Composite Group in Hawaii. To strengthen the composite groups in Hawaii and Panama, in January 1938, the War Department ordered two squadrons based in the continental United States to relocate. The move took place quickly. The War Department's orders came out January 20, 1938, and the 31st Squadron left Hamilton Field February 1st. The gap created by the 31st Squadron's departure remained until late 1939. The 7th Group was left with only two bombardment squadrons (the 9th and the 11th) and the attached 88th Reconnaissance Squadron.[96]

The 7th Bombardment Group's B-18s in formation. The airplanes were given a special camouflage scheme for the 1938 GHQ Air Force maneuvers in New England. (Museum of Flight)

In early February 1938, the 7th Bombardment Group debuted four of its new B-18s at Barksdale Field, Louisiana, for the students of the Air Corps Tactical School in a demonstration of attack, bombardment, and pursuit aviation.[97] Three months later, the Group flew to the East Coast to participate in the 1938 GHQ Air Force maneuvers, the largest yet attempted. Maj. Gen. Frank Andrews planned the maneuvers as a test of GHQ Air Force's ability to defend an area against a hypothetical attack by a coalition of "Asiatic and European powers" who had assembled a fleet off the Northeast Coast. After an assembly at 18 airfields scattered around six northeastern states in early May, the maneuvers were scheduled to begin May 12th and last for five days. More than 3,000 officers and men and 217 airplanes participated.[98] The 7th Bombardment Group sent ten B-18s to the maneuvers—all that could be sent with the crews then available—drawn from the 9th, 11th, and 88th Squadrons. The 7th Group's bomber contingent went to Barnes Field in Westfield, Massachusetts. After arriving, all aircraft received extensive camouflage to act as "enemy" aircraft from the attacking Black Force: five in day camouflage and five in night camouflage.[99] In addition, to provide more transport aircraft for the maneuvers, the 7th Bombardment Group organized the 2nd Provisional Transport Squadron with five B-18s and personnel drawn from the Group headquarters squadron and the 9th Bombardment Squadron, with Maj. Newton Longfellow, commander of the 88th Reconnaissance Squadron, in command.[100] The B-18s could carry fifteen men and a good load of supplies. The 7th Group used the B-18s extensively to ferry personnel and equipment from Hamilton Field to the maneuvers. The bombers made four cross-country trips, and once in the northeast transported men and materials among the airfields.

Flying from their base in Massachusetts and from temporary bases in New York State, the 7th Group's B-18s acted as enemy Black Force bombers, attacking the Blue Force's bases in the New York City area. At 3:00 a.m. on March 12th, the opening day of the maneuvers, three B-18s made a night attack on Mitchell Field, the headquarters of GHQ Air Force, while other 7th Group B-18s made "raids" later in the morning on the airports in Boston and Providence, Rhode Island, and later on the Philadelphia Navy Yard. That same day, three B-17 Flying Fortresses from the 2nd Bombardment Group intercepted the Italian ocean liner *Rex* 750 miles off the coast of New York, to the ire of the U.S. Navy. The high point for the Group occurred May 16th, on a night bombing raid. Three B-18s made an attack on Farmingdale, Long Island. The city fathers arranged a blackout for the first time during any Air Corps maneuvers. Just before the Group's bombers came over the town, their undersides painted black,

A 9th Bombardment Squadron B-18 flying over Spokane, Washington during the August 1938 1st Wing maneuvers in the Pacific Northwest. (Courtesy Hamilton Field Military Museum)

reconnaissance planes dropped flares to illuminate the town. Search lights sought out the bombers coming in above, apparently without success. The next day, the Group staged

An enlisted man holds "Teddy", the 7th Bombardment Group's mascot during the late 1930s. Over the course of his service with the Group, Teddy accumulated several hundred hours in the B-18, and had his flight record carefully recorded. (GP-7-SU-(Bomb) 1937-1941, Albert F. Simpson Research Center, Air Force Historical Research Agency, Maxwell AFB, AL)

a bombing mission to the Army arsenal at Aberdeen Proving Ground, near Washington, D.C., flying on to drop practice bombs on the ranges near Langley Field, Virginia. The maneuvers ended with a fly-past by 144 airplanes over New York City.[101]

While the 1938 maneuvers provided valuable experience to both the tactical units and the staff of GHQ Air Force, and improvements in the ability to coordinate a large number of units operating out of widely dispersed airfields, the maneuvers could not help but reveal some major weaknesses. Hanson Baldwin, defense correspondent for the *New York Times*, commented that the Army "...really has as yet no air force, but merely the good beginning of one."[102] In reality, GHQ Air Force had only 300 combat planes available, and only 217 participated in the maneuvers. These 217 planes had to simulate 700 airplanes, the number that would have been available if all the units involved in the maneuvers had been at their full strength. The GHQ Air Force and its tactical units were still short of staff, both officers and enlisted men. During maneuvers, the higher headquarters had to borrow officers and men from the tactical units to make up their staffs. As an example, the 1st Wing's bombardment squadrons in the 7th and 19th Bombardment Groups were operating as five airplane squadrons, eight airplanes below their authorized strength.[103] Former WWI pilot Cy Caldwell, writing for *Aero Digest*, was critical of the lack of realism in the maneuvers, as well as the lack of adequate numbers of aircraft. In an article on the maneuvers for the June issue of the magazine, Caldwell said, "...Well, it was good fun and a good show, but the real implications of it were all missed by the public—who took it as a show, as an amiable game of make-believe among a group of sporting gentlemen... These are but the simple beginnings of Air Power, these antics we see today, and in five years we will look back and marvel that we took such tiny doings as war maneuvers seriously."[104]

In August, the 1st Wing held its own maneuvers from August 8th to the 15th in the Pacific Northwest to practice long-range reconnaissance missions and to give the Wing's crews an opportunity to become familiar with the terrain and airfields in the region. Brig. Gen. Delos Emmons planned for 71 airplanes, 75 officers, and 225 enlisted men to take part from the 7th and 19th Bombardment Groups, the 17th Attack Group, and the 38th and 88th Reconnaissance Squadrons. Wing headquarters, the 19th Group, and the 38th and 88th Reconnaissance Squadrons were to be based at recently-opened McChord Field, near Fort Lewis, Washington. The 7th Group sent 15 B-18s to Felts Field in Spokane and the 17th Group went to Pearson Field, at Vancouver, Washington. On August 9th, the three groups made a leisurely 750-mile circuit of Washington State and northern Oregon—one in the morning and two in the afternoon—making a mass formation flight over Portland, Seattle, Spokane, Walla Walla, and the Naval base at Bremerton, west of Seattle. The next day, the Wing organized a public bombing demonstration at McChord Field, destroying a dummy "factory" with practice bombs, but also starting a grass fire that caused the event to be halted. On August 12th, the 7th, 17th, and 19th Groups made a massed flight over four Northwest states, meeting up over Great Falls, Montana, then flying a circuit around Billings, Livingstone, and West Yellowstone to Missoula, then on to Idaho and back to Spokane, where the 17th and 19th Groups split off to return to McChord and Pearson Fields. After a day opening the field to the public to inspect the Wing's airplanes, the units returned to their home fields August 15th. Four days later, Lt. John G. Armstrong, from the 11th Bombardment Squadron, with Lt. David H. Walker as his co-pilot, took off in a B-18 on the Douglas bomber's first non-stop transcontinental flight, arriving at Mitchel Field on Long Island at 10:18 a.m. August 20th, after a flight of 15 hours and 38 minutes over a distance of 2,570 miles. As happened to the B-18 all too often, the flight was not a record, as a B-17 Flying Fortress had already covered the same distance in 11 hours.[105] That August, Lt. Col. George Stratemeyer gave up command of the 7th Bombardment Group to attend the Army War College. Lt. Col. Joseph McNarney, who had commanded the Group during 1931-33, returned to his old command, although his tenure would prove to be short.[106]

Preparing for War

The GHQ Air Force's maneuvers in the spring of 1938 took place against a background of rising tensions in Europe and all-out war in Spain and China. In March, Nazi Germany had annexed Austria in the Anschluss. Hitler followed this with increasing demands on the Czechoslovakian government on behalf of the Germans living in the Sudetenland, with the ultimate goal of annexing the Sudetenland into the Third Reich. German pressure on the Czechs continued over the summer months, leading to the crisis of September 1938. That summer saw the second anniversary of the brutal Civil War in Spain, where aircraft of both the Republican and Nationalist forces were playing an active role in the conflict. Airplanes of the German Legion Condor and the Italian *Aviazione Legionaria* had engaged in the deliberate bombing of civilians in Spanish cities, notably Guernica, Madrid, and Barcelona. In China, the same summer months saw the first anniversary of the Sino-Japanese Incident, a full-scale war in all but name. By July, the Japanese Army had advanced well down the Yangtze River, with the Imperial Japanese Army Air Force and Naval Air Service providing air support and undertaking long-range bombing campaigns as in Spain against Chinese cities. With relations between the Axis powers of Germany, Italy, and Japan and the European democracies steadily deteriorating, it seemed that Europe was heading inexorably toward war.

A glimpse of the future. A brand-new Boeing B-17B that stopped at Hamilton Field in August 1939 en route to the 2nd Bombardment Group in Langley, Virginia.(SQ-Bomb-11-SU-PH-5, Albert F. Simpson Research Center, Air Force Historical Research Agency, Maxwell AFB, AL)

Ironically, with the likelihood of global conflict becoming more of a reality, the summer of 1938 represented something of a nadir for the Air Corps' effort to win support from the War Department for the further development of the long-range bomber and the acquisition of more Boeing B-17s. The interception of the Italian ocean liner during the May GHQ Air Force maneuvers, intended as a demonstration of the capabilities of the B-17 for coastal defense, backfired. The event triggered a reaction from the Army's General Staff, who saw it as an attempt to win support for purchasing more long-range bombers the General Staff did not want, and from the Navy, which was jealous of its own role in coastal defense.[107] Gen. Marlin Craig, Army Chief of Staff, issued verbal orders that the Air Corps was not to fly missions beyond 100 miles off the coast, though he apparently did not put this order in writing and proved amenable to its modification on a case-by-case basis.[108] In June, General Craig asked the Joint Army-Navy Board to consider the question of developing long-range bombers. On June 29, 1938, the Joint Board told Gen. Craig that "...it saw no probable military requirement for aircraft larger than the B-17...the Air Corps would be called upon to perform many missions which could be executed successfully

A 7th Bombardment Group B-18 flying over San Francisco during 1938. This is likely to be the Group Commander's aircraft. It carries the Group Insignia on the side of the fuselage. (3B-25027, RG 342FH, NARA)

by planes of lesser range and lower cost than the B-17."[109] Money that the Air Corps wanted to develop even larger and longer-range aircraft than the B-17 could be better employed purchasing greater numbers of smaller aircraft. Consistent with current practice, the War Department used funds already allocated for the purchase of two Boeing XB-15s and an even larger prototype bomber to acquire more Douglas B-18s.[110] On June 30th, the War Department ordered an additional 77 Douglas B-18As, on top of an outstanding order for 177 B-18As issued in June 1937.[111] When Maj. Gen. Oscar Westover urged a reconsideration of the War Department's position, arguing that the Secretary of War's intention to increase Air Corps strength to 2,320 airplanes had included a provision for larger bombers, he was told that the Air Corps could use the Secretary of War's program as a guide for budget planning; however, no four-engine bombers were to be purchased during Fiscal Year 1940 and 1941.[112]

A few months later, President Franklin Roosevelt and events in Europe reversed the General Staff's opposition to the long-range bomber. The Munich Crisis of September 1938 saw the British and French Governments capitulate to Adolf Hitler's demands for the Sudetenland to be returned to Germany. To avoid war, the British and French forced the Czech government to accede to Hitler. Prime Minister Neville Chamberlin returned to London with the signed agreement, asserting his belief that it represented "...peace in our time."[113] Europe had come close to war, averting it at the last minute; but in the eyes of many observers, Munich was only a postponement. President Roosevelt did not believe the Munich Agreement would create a lasting peace and had little faith that Hitler would refrain from new demands for territorial aggrandizement. He saw the crisis as "...an interlude between threats in which the democracies must rearm."[114] Roosevelt was impressed with how the threat of the Luftwaffe and aerial bombing had contributed to the British and French willingness to give in to Hitler's demands. Roosevelt concluded that greatly strengthened American, British, and French air forces would be the only deterrent against German aggression.[115] At the end of September, the President called a meeting of his senior cabinet officers and military leaders, including Brig. Gen. Henry Arnold, representing the Air Corps after the death of Maj. Gen. Westover a week before. The President told those attending the meeting that he believed airplanes were the only implements of war that would influence Hitler and wanted the American aviation industry to move immediately toward mass production of 10,000 airplanes a year, increasing to 20,000.[116] More importantly, Roosevelt wanted more long-range bombers, arguing that if the United States was to be responsible for the air protection of the entire hemisphere, it needed that capability.[117] In November, the President called another meeting with General Marlin Craig (the new Deputy Chief of Staff), Brig. Gen. George Marshall, and Maj. Gen. Arnold (recently promoted to Chief of the Air Corps) to outline his planes for the Air Corps. Roosevelt wanted the Air Corps to have an authorized strength of 20,000 airplanes, but believed that Congress would approve no more than 10,000. Over the following months, Arnold and the General Staff persuaded the President that planes alone were insufficient; the Air Corps would need air crews to man the planes and men to maintain and support them.[118] In addition, the Army itself badly needed modernization. On January 12, 1939, in a special message to Congress, President Roosevelt called for appropriations of $525 million for defense in light of changing world conditions, with $300 million to be allocated for the purchase of 3,000 new airplanes for the Army Air Corps and $10 million for training additional pilots.[119] In response, the Congress raised the Air Corps' authorized strength to 5,500 airplanes, 3.203 officers, and 45,000 enlisted men and appropriated funds for procurement of 3,251 airplanes, to be accomplished by June 1, 1941.[120] The Army Air Corps began mobilizing for war.

The Group Commander's airplane leads a mass formation of the 7th Bombardment Group over the hills of California in September 1938. (3B-25003, RG 342FH, NARA)

It took time for new planes, new pilots, and new enlisted men to filter down to the GHQ Air Force's tactical units, but the Air Corps' mobilization soon began to have an impact on the 7th Bombardment Group. In March 1939, Maj. Gen. Arnold pulled Lt. Col. McNarney back to Washington to help work out the details for the Air Corps' expansion.[121] Maj. Earl H. DeFord replaced him for the next six months. The plans that Arnold and his staff worked out called for an increase in Air Corps combat groups from 14 to 24, comprising five heavy bombardment groups, six medium bombardment groups, two light bombardment groups, nine pursuit groups, and two composite groups, with 13 groups going to GHQ Air Force and 11 groups to overseas commands.[122] In April 1939, GHQ

Air Force announced plans to activate fifteen new combat squadrons and three transport squadrons during the coming year to equip new combat groups and bring older combat groups up to strength. Within the 1st Wing, the 7th Bombardment Group was redesignated 7th Bombardment Group (Heavy) and assigned a third bombardment squadron, while the 19th Bombardment Group at March Field also added the (Heavy) designation and added two additional bombardment squadrons.[123] The 17th Attack Group was redesignated the 17th Bombardment Group (Medium) and selected for transfer to the newly-opened McChord Field in Washington. The 20th Pursuit Group was transferred from Barksdale Field to March Field and designated to provide cadre for the formation of a new pursuit group (the 35th Pursuit) at Moffett Field.[124] Each heavy and medium bombardment group was assigned a reconnaissance squadron operating the same type of airplane.[125] Despite its re-designation as a heavy bombardment group and the intention to re-equip the Group with heavy bombers, there were no B-17s available. As of April 1939, the Air Corps had 13 B-17s in service with the 2nd Bombardment Group and 39 B-17Bs on order. In August, the Air Corps placed an additional order with Boeing for 38 B-17C models, two months after the first B-17B entered service. That year, the Air Corps initiated development of a new heavy bomber that would feature prominently in the 7th Bombardment Group's future. Asked to become a second source for building the B-17, the Consolidated Aircraft Company responded with its own heavy bomber design. The Air Corps ordered a prototype as the XB-24 in March 1939, seven YB-24s in April, and 38 B-24As in September. The new heavy bombers would not enter service in any number until later in 1940.[126]

A line of B-18As of the 11th Bombardment Squadron at March Field for a 1st Wing concentration exercise in May 1940. The Squadron's emblem, "Mr. Jiggs", can be seen on the side of the fuselage. (3B-25090, RG 342FH, NARA)

The 7th Bombardment Group had to wait until the end of 1939 to receive its first B-17. The Group had begun replacing its Douglas B-18s with the newer B-18A model in November 1938, and by the end of April 1939 had acquired 22 B-18As, with the final ten airplanes arriving in September. While news of the Air Corps' expansion surely created no little excitement within the Group at the prospects for new airplanes and promotions, the Group's squadrons continued the more mundane task of completing the training program for Fiscal Year 1939. The Group received new pilots and they needed to be trained to operational standard. In March 1938, for example, the 9th Bombardment Squadron had only two fully trained crews and only ten officers in the Squadron; by June 1939, the number of officers in the 9th Squadron had grown to 36, and in the 11th Bombardment Squadron to 39.[127] In compliance with the GHQ Air Force's Training Directive, 16 officers completed the bombing program to become experts, bringing the number of expert pilot bombardiers in the squadron to 27, while all 36 officers had completed the dead reckoning navigation course and 14 had completed a course on celestial navigation.[128] More officers and enlisted men would be joining the Group in the months ahead. To fill the cockpits and maintain the thousands of airplanes on order, the Air Corps needed a huge increase in pilots, air crews, and trained mechanics. On June 1, 1939, Secretary of War Woodring announced that the Air Corps planned to recruit 24,644 enlisted men over the coming year, while also recruiting new pilot trainees from colleges around the country and extending the service of Reserve officers.[129]

A B-18A belonging to the 88th Reconnaissance Squadron in late 1939. (SQ-Bomb-11-SU-PH-6, Albert F. Simpson Research Center, Air Force Historical Research Agency, Maxwell AFB, AL)

In August, the 7th Group received a new commanding officer and the welcome news that the Group would soon receive its first B-17s.[130] Lt. Col. Ralph Royce arrived at Hamilton Field from the Philippines, where he had been serving as Air Officer. A West Point graduate, Royce had joined the Aviation Section of the Signal Corps in 1915 and commanded the 1st Observation Group in France during WWI. Like Carl Spaatz, much of his service after the war had been in pursuits,

The staff of the 7th Bombardment Group at Hamilton Field in 1940. Left to right: 1st Lt. Arthur Pierce, 2nd Lt. Robert Northcutt, Capt. Austin Straubel, Capt. Stanley Robinson, 1st Lt. Gene Tibbetts, Maj Earl DeFord, and Lt. Col. Ralph Royce, Group Commander. Robinson and Straubel would command the Group in Java in early 1942 where both would be killed in action. (7th Bombardment Group (H) Historical Foundation, USAFA McDermott Library)

including command of the 1st Pursuit Group during the early 1930s. The Group's pilots had an opportunity to take a closer look at their prospective new airplane August 9th, when Lt. Col. Robert Olds flew in a new B-17B from the Boeing factory in Seattle en route to the 2nd Bombardment Group at Langley Field.[131] While at Hamilton Field, Olds tested the new runway, taking off the B-17 at a gross weight of 50,000 pounds in about 17 seconds using less than two-thirds of thc runway surface. The next day, Olds left at 6:30 a.m. on a non-stop flight to Langley, completing the trip in ten hours and 49 minutes.[132] A month after taking command, Lt. Col. Royce led 15 B-18As from the 9th and 11th Squadrons and the Headquarters Squadron on an exercise in the vicinity of Spokane, Washington, to practice bombing transportation targets. Sending the 9th Squadron on to Boise, Idaho, and the 11th to Salem, Oregon, with the few airplanes of the Headquarters Squadron at Pendleton, Oregon, Royce arranged a Group rendezvous over Spokane at 3 p.m. in the afternoon. Spending two nights in Spokane, the Group practiced attacks on the large railroad yard located five miles north of the city.[133]

The first B-17B for the 7th Bombardment Group arrived in mid-November, ten weeks after the outbreak of war in Europe on September 3, 1939. Maj. Earl DeFord picked up the airplane at the Boeing factory in Seattle and flew it back to Hamilton Field. The B-17B, equipped with turbo-superchargers, flew at much higher altitudes than the B-18, reaching a top speed of 292 mph at 25,000 feet. This capability appeared to confirm the bombardment advocates' belief that high speed and high altitude would offer protection from fighter interception. Over the next several months, the B-17Bs arrived in small numbers. The Group ultimately received twelve aircraft, distributing these among the different squadrons. As the B-17Bs started coming on board the 7th Bombardment Group, so too did the Group's third bombardment squadron. On October 20, 1939, the Air Corps activated the 22nd Bombardment Squadron at Hamilton Field with Maj. John B. Hart as commander.[134] With some pilots transferred from the 9th Squadron and a trickle of newly-trained pilots and enlisted men, the 22nd started working up to full strength. The Squadron flew its first training mission December 5th, when Hart and his crew took a B-18A out on a cross-country navigation exercise to San Antonio, Texas, and experienced their first formation bombing practice December 18th.[135] The 7th Group had its first opportunity to put its new B-17s to use during joint Army-Navy war games in central California in January 1940, the first of a series of large-scale war games planned for that year. Beginning January 15th, the exercise was the most extensive ever held to that date, involving more than 10,000 Army troops, 80 Navy ships, and the four units of the 1st Wing reinforced with a squadron of eight B-17s from the 2nd Bombardment Group.[136] The 1st Wing was part of the Blue Force, defending against the invading Black Force. The Army-Navy exercise ended January 22nd, but the 1st Wing continued with its own maneuvers over the Sacramento Valley for an additional four days, its units dividing up into defending and attacking forces. One of the more interesting aspects of the exercises was the

The 7th Bombardment Group began to re-equip with the B-17B in November 1939. This airplane has yet to receive the Group designation on the tail. (7th Bombardment Group (H) Historical Foundation, USAFA McDermott Library)

movement of an entire battalion of troops of the 65th Coast Artillery Regiment from Hamilton Field to March Field using

A row of 7th Bombardment Group B-17Bs at March Field for the May 1940 1st Wing concentration exercise. The first aircraft is from the 9th Bombardment Squadron, and the second B-17B in line belongs to the 88th Reconnaissance Squadron. (3B-24873, RG 342FH, NARA)

the B-18s of the 7th and 17th Bombardment Groups as transports.[137]

From May 2nd to 4th, the 1st Wing held a Wing concentration at March Field, working on tactical problems involving the defense of San Clemente Island from an invading force.[138] Six days later, a real and vastly different scale of invasion erupted in Europe when the German Army and Luftwaffe struck the Netherlands, Belgium, and France. On May 16, 1940, President Roosevelt addressed Congress, calling for a force of 50,000 airplanes for the Army and the Navy and a production capacity of at least that many airplanes annually. In response, as the Congress approved the appropriation of more funds for national defense, the Air Corps revised its expansion plans upward, first to 41 combat groups and then to 54 combat groups with 4,000 airplanes, 16,800 officers, 187,000 enlisted men, and 15,000 aviation cadets.[139] This was only the beginning, as the number of combat groups, planes, and pilots was subject to constant upward revision; the number of combat groups would quadruple once America was at war. The 54-group plan alone called for 12,000 pilots, 2,500 bombardiers, and 1,030 navigators for heavy and medium bombardment groups.[140] In the summer of 1940, the Air Corps was short of everything it needed to meet the ambitious goals the President had set: airplanes, experienced personnel to train the flood of new aviation cadets, officers and enlisted men in a vast range of specialties, commanders and staff for the new combat groups hurriedly forming, facilities to house training schools and tactical units, and above all, time. The experience of the Air Corps' expansion between 1939 and 1941 was "...a race against time in a desperate effort to overtake Axis air forces which had long been on a war basis."[141]

The 7th Bombardment Group, like other tactical units, would provide cadres to staff the newly-forming combat squadrons and groups in the 1 1/2 years left before the United States entered the war. While necessary, this did take some of the more experienced officers away from the Group just as it was going through its own expansion. As the training schools ramped up, the Group absorbed a steady stream of new pilots and enlisted men; fourteen new pilots joined the Group in July alone. During 1940, to relieve the burden of training pilots as navigators and pilots and enlisted men as bombardiers—the practice during the 1930s—and to allow the bombardment groups to concentrate on unit training, the Air Corps established specialized schools to train non-pilot specialists in these disciplines.[142] Specialization made sense in view of the complexity of the larger heavy bomber aircraft entering service. More combat groups, more aircraft, and more men required more facilities. In a few months of operating the B-17B, the 7th Bombardment Group discovered that the runways, taxiways, and aprons at Hamilton Field couldn't adequately support a fully-laden B-17.[143] Since rebuilding the runways would take too long, the War Department arranged for the 7th Group to transfer to the Municipal Airport at Salt Lake City, Utah, announcing the move August 26, 1940.[144] At the same time, the War Department stated that, as part of the Air Corp's ongoing expansion, the Group would be raised to its authorized strength of 172 officers and 1,083 enlisted men as trained personnel became available.

The 7th Bombardment Group brought six of its B-17s to Seattle, Washington from their new base at Fort Douglas, Utah, in February 1940 as a salute to national defense workers. The bombers went to Boeing Field to give the employees of Boeing Aircraft Company and their families a chance to see what they had built. (Museum of Flight)

This was an increase of 50 officers and 483 enlisted men. The 7th Group's departure from Hamilton Field allowed the 20th and 35th Pursuit Groups to move in. The move was completed quickly, with the 7th Group and 88th Reconnaissance Squadron completing the move by September 11th, initially to Fort Douglas, outside Salt Lake City, until facilities at the Municipal

The 7th Bombardment Group's B-17s fly in formation near Mount Rainier, south of Seattle, Washington. (Museum of Flight)

Airport could be completed. Improvements included building a bigger taxi ramp, new hangars, mess halls, and barracks.[145] The Group's airplanes arrived in a mass flight from Hamilton Field, with eleven B-17s and ten B-18s greeted by a crowd of 20,000 people.[146] Maj. Gen. Arnold arrived October 7th to inspect the unit in its new home and witness an aerial review of the entire Group.[147]

The Group wasted little time getting back to its training regime, although the lack of necessary buildings at the Municipal Airport hampered flying, as did the onset of winter weather. The squadrons carried out their maintenance and administrative duties from a tent city hurriedly set up at the airport until temporary facilities could be built. Prophetically, the move was described as "...a nature somewhat similar to that which may be encountered in time of war, and as such has proven of inestimable value."[148] While waiting for the new Wendover Bombing Range to be completed, the Group set up a gunnery range and three auxiliary bombing ranges on salt flats and islands in the Great Salt Lake and put them to use for day and night bombing practice. Pending the arrival of specialist navigators from the new schools, the newest pilots went through an intensive course in dead reckoning navigation, with long-distance flights to Mitchell Field, on New York's Long Island, as a navigation exercise. All flight crews had to learn to fire the .50 caliber machine gun, which equipped all the gun positions on the newer B-17Cs except the nose position, with the first C model arriving at the end of 1940. By the end of March 1941, the Group had three B-18s, seven B-18As, one B-18 and B-18A for towing targets for gunnery practice, and twelve B-17Bs, four B-17Cs, and three B-17Ds distributed among the three bombardment squadrons and the 88th Reconnaissance Squadron.[149] There were personnel changes, as well as new units coming into being. January 15th the Air Corps activated the 39th Bombardment Group (Heavy) and the 42nd Bombardment Group (Medium) at Salt Lake City, promoting Maj. Newton Longfellow from the 88th Reconnaissance Squadron to command the 39th Group and Maj. John B. Hart, who had been the first commander of the 22nd Bombardment Squadron, to command the 42nd Group. In April, Lt. Col. Ralph Royce was promoted to Brigadier General and placed in command of the 20th Bombardment Wing, activated the previous December as part of the Air Corps' expansion from four to seventeen wings in the continental United States.[150] The new wings were distributed among four air districts: Northeast, Northwest, Southeast, and Southwest. These became the First, Second, Third, and Fourth Air Forces March 26, 1941. The Group's executive officer, Maj. Earl DeFord, was promoted to Lt. Colonel and again took command of the Group for the following six months. The commanders of the 9th and 11th Squadrons (Majs. Elmer Adler and John Warren) also moved on to new assignments.[151]

Operation Plum

During July 1941, President Roosevelt asked the newly-created Army Air Forces for an estimate of the Air Force's needs relating to the statement of strategic principles for cooperation with the British Commonwealth in the event of America's entry into the war stemming from discussions that Spring in Washington.[152] In its response, the Air Force's Air War Plans Division prepared AWPD/1 (Air War Plans Division, Plan Number One), an estimate of the Air Force's requirements and a statement of the doctrine of air warfare that would dictate their use. The American and British staff meetings had resulted in the ABC-1 report. This report called for the defense of the Western Hemisphere and the United Kingdom, strong defensive positions in the Middle East, India, and the Far East, and the maintenance of sea communications around the globe.[153] Offensively, the American and British staffs agreed on what became known as the "Germany First" strategy. As the dominant power in the Axis, Germany would be defeated first, with operations in other areas subordinated to this primary strategic objective.[154] Developed over seven days by four graduates of the Air Corps Tactical School, all strong advocates of strategic bombardment, AWPD/1 called for a sustained strategic bombing campaign against Germany using daylight precision bombing against key industrial systems, stating that the "...basic conception on which this plan is based lies in the application of air power for the breakdown of the industrial and economic structure of Germany."[155] Though AWPD/1 also called for the development of tactical air power

During 1941 the 7th Bombardment Group received additional B-17C and B-17D aircraft for its three bombardment squadrons and the 88th Reconnaissance Squadron, though not enough to bring the Group up to full strength. (Museum of Flight)

to support a land invasion of Europe, should that be necessary, and despite the growing evidence from the European war that the reality might well prove far different from its rhetoric, the Army Air Forces would go to war with unescorted, daylight precision strategic bombing as its core doctrine.[156] The War Department's approval of the plan later in the year represented a victory for the air power advocates.

Although agreeing on the need to defeat Germany first, the Roosevelt administration could not ignore ominous developments in Asia and America's deteriorating relations with Japan, though there was little that could be done, given the strong isolationist sentiment at the time. In September 1940, the Japanese had taken control of the northern half of French Indochina and formally joined the Axis powers through the Tripartite Pact. In response, Roosevelt placed an embargo on shipments of steel, scrap iron, and aviation fuel to Japan. Following the German invasion of Russia on June 22, 1941, the Japanese occupied the southern half of French Indochina. In response, the United States banned oil exports to Japan, a move that contributed to the Japanese decision to attack the United States. With the Soviet Union locked in a struggle for survival and with the war in Europe sharply limiting the military forces the European colonial powers could deploy in Southeast Asia, Japan seemed bent on expansion. This placed America's Philippine colony at increasing risk. The War Department had begun a belated reinforcement of the Philippines in late 1940, sending more troops and fighter squadrons. In July 1941, President Roosevelt appointed retired General Douglas MacArthur as commander of the United States Army Forces in the Far East and converted the Philippine Department Air Force into the Air Force, United States Army Forces in the Far East. By building American air power in the Philippines, particularly the number of heavy bombers, Roosevelt hoped to restrain Japan.[157]

During the summer of 1941, the Army Air Forces developed a plan to send four heavy bomber groups with 272 airplanes, along with two full pursuit groups with 130 airplanes, to the Philippines by February 1942.[158] On July 24, 1941, Roosevelt's Secretary of War, Henry L. Stimson, urged the President to transfer B-17s to the Philippines to strengthen the Philippine defenses in the belief that more heavy bombers would act as a deterrent to Japan.[159] At the time, not one of the bombardment groups in the United States had its full complement of even the early B-17Cs and Ds, though a better version in quantity was on its way. In August 1940, the Air Corps had placed an order with the Boeing Aircraft Company for 277 improved B-17Es, featuring an enlarged tail for better control at high altitudes, a tail gun position, and powered turrets. An amended contract signed a month later added 235 more B-17s, with a delivery date of April 1941 for the first aircraft.[160] Supply problems delayed the delivery of the first B-17E until the end of September. The situation in the Far East was deemed so urgent that the Air Force could not wait for the B-17Es to arrive to reinforce the Philippines.[161] The 19th Bombardment Group (the 7th Bombardment Group's old partner in the 1st Wing), then stationed at Albuquerque, New Mexico, was ordered to the Philippines. With the 19th Group yet to complete its training, in early September, the 14th Bombardment

A 7th Bombardment Group B-17D on a practice bombing mission over the salt flats of the Great Salt Lakein the latter part of 1941. (Museum of Flight)

Squadron (H), part of the 11th Bombardment Group, left Hickam Field in Hawaii with nine B-17Ds under the command of Maj. Emmett O'Donnell, Jr. for a pioneering flight across the Pacific Ocean to Clark Field in the Philippines via Midway

Island, Wake Island, and Port Moresby in New Guinea. The squadron arrived at Clark Field September 12th.[162] In mid-October, the 19th Group, under the command of Lt. Col. Eugene Eubank, began the long flight across the Pacific route with six B-17Cs and 20 B-17Ds from its 30th and 93rd Bombardment Squadrons. Those squadrons completed their move by November 5th.[163] On arrival, the 19th Group absorbed the 14th Bombardment Squadron and the 28th Bombardment Squadron, which had been in the Philippines for several years. On November 16, 1941, the Air Force activated the Far East Air Force to replace the Air Department of the Philippines. Maj. Gen. Louis Brereton, who had arrived in the Philippines the month before, took command.[164] At the same time, V Bomber Command was activated to control the heavy bomber groups destined for the Philippines. Since the 19th Bombardment Group arrived first, the Group's commander, Lt. Col. Eubank, served concurrently as commander of V Bomber Command, until turning over command of the Group in December to Maj. O'Donnell. Then it was the 7th Bombardment Group's turn.

In late October, the 7th Bombardment Group was alerted to prepare for two years of overseas service—destination "Plum", as the Philippines were designated. After hurried preparations, the ground echelon of 1,098 officers and men from the 7th Group and the 88th Reconnaissance Squadron left Salt Lake City by troop train November 13, 1941, arriving in San Francisco two days later.[165] On the evening of November 20th, the men boarded the Army transport ship USS *Republic* with men from the 147th and 148th Field Artillery battalions of the Texas National Guard, setting off the next day for the Philippines. While the ground echelon was leaving, the Group's air echelon proceeded to Seattle to pick up brand new Boeing B-17Es, ferrying them back to Salt Lake City; the Group's B-17Cs and Ds were transferred to other bombardment groups for training. The Group was now under the command of Maj. Stanley Robinson, who had taken over from Lt. Col. DeFord October 6th. Just after the ground echelon left, the 88th Reconnaissance Squadron lost its commander when Maj. Robert Pirtle was killed bailing out of one of the squadron's B-18s caught in a storm. Capt. Richard Carmichael was transferred from the 9th Bombardment Squadron to take command of the 88th, shortly to leave for the Philippines. The 88th Reconnaissance Squadron, then stationed at Tucson, Arizona, had been chosen as the next unit to make the crossing

The officers of the 9th Bombardment Squadron line up in front of one of the Squadron's B-17Ds in October 1941. Two months later, they would exchange their older B-17s for the new B-17E, and head off to war in Java. (SQ-Bomb-9-SU-PH-1932-1942, Albert F. Simpson Research Center, Air Force Historical Research Agency, Maxwell AFB, AL)

along the Pacific route, in company with the 38th Reconnaissance Squadron, attached to the 19th Bombardment Group. At 1000 on December 5, 1941, the Fourth Air Force ordered the 88th Squadron to send six B-17Es and crews to Hamilton Field—the jumping off point for flights to Hawaii—for immediate departure for "Plum". Two additional crews were flown to Hamilton, where they picked up two new B-17Es.[166] The 38th Reconnaissance Squadron arrived at Hamilton Field the same day with eight B-17Cs and B-17Es.[167] Later on December 5th, the 7th Bombardment Group was instructed to send all remaining air crews at Salt Lake City to the Sacramento Air Depot, where they would receive their full allotment of airplanes to take to the Philippines. As several crews were away picking up new B-17s in Seattle and on detached service, only six crews left Salt Lake City immediately by train for Sacramento that night, arriving the next evening. Around noon on Saturday, December 6th, the 7th Group received urgent instructions to transfer all remaining personnel to Sacramento by any available means of transport. The ferry crews picking up new B-17s in Seattle were ordered to fly directly to Sacramento. By using commercial airlines, utility planes, and planes borrowed from the 42nd Bombardment Group, the 7th Group got everyone to Sacramento by 0300 on Sunday, December 7th.[168]

The need to install long-range fuel tanks and reported headwinds between California and Hawaii delayed the take-off until the next day, December 6th. Disturbed at the delay in getting the B-17s to the Philippines, General George Marshall, Army Chief of Staff, sent Maj. Gen. Hap Arnold to reinforce to the crews the urgency of their mission and to tell them frankly of the dangers they might face.[169] Arnold told the crews they might well run into trouble along their route to the Philippines and might have to use their guns.[170] When Maj. Truman Landon, 38th Squadron commander, asked why they weren't then carrying ammunition for the guns, Arnold replied that they needed all the fuel they could carry for the flight to Hawaii, and that the greatest danger would be the second leg of the flight, when they would be flying over the Japanese mandated islands between Wake and Port Moresby.[171] The airplanes began taking off at 1700 at ten minute intervals. Two airplanes from the 38th Squadron and one from the 88th Squadron, the airplane of Lt. Frank W. Potter, developed mechanical problems and remained behind. One aircraft from the 88th Squadron, piloted by Lt. Richard Ezzard, had to turn back after taking off, leaving six B-17Es from the 88th, with Capt. Richard Carmichael leading Lts. Harold N. Chaffin, Frank P. Bostrom, Robert E. Thacker, Harry N. Brandon, and David G. Rawls and four B-17Cs and two B-17Es to make the long 14-hour flight to Hawaii with a skeleton crew of pilot, co-pilot, navigator, flight engineer, and radio operator.[172] The crews settled back, the navigators knowing it would be some time before they could pick up Station KGMB from Honolulu, the station's music acting as a radio beam to aid their navigation.[173]

Within 24 hours, America would be at war with Japan, a war that the 7th Bombardment Group would continue to fight until the very last day of the conflict in August 1945. All the training of the previous years, all the practice missions, the classes in bombardment and navigation, all the maneuvers, the hours spent in B-10s, B-18s, and B-17s, and the doctrine of daylight precision bombardment would now be put to the test of war. The men who had trained and guided the 7th Bombardment Group and built up their own experience during the formative interwar years—Carl Spaatz, Joseph McNarney, Clarence Tinker, Davenport Johnson, George Stratemeyer, and Ralph Royce—would all take up high positions in the Army Air Forces during the war. Spaatz would rise to command all the U.S. Strategic Air Forces in Europe. But in the main, the work of taking the bomber squadrons and groups into combat, of trying to make daylight precision strategic bombing work and modifying it under the pressures of war when it didn't fell to the younger men, the Captains and Lieutenants who had joined the Army Air Corps during the 1930s. These were the men thrust into command in the heat of battle. They would guide the 7th Bombardment Group through combat in a distant theater of war on missions far different from what the Army Air Corps' prewar air doctrine had envisioned. For the 7th Group, there would be no massed formations of bombers destroying the industrial fabric of Germany or Japan. As the men of the 7th Group and the men of the entire Army Air Forces would discover, the reality of war would prove to be vastly different from the controlled maneuvers they had experienced in peace time.

CHAPTER THREE

TO WAR IN JAVA

Pearl Harbor

As the B-17s neared Hawaii the morning of December 7, 1941, they could pick up Hawaiian music being broadcast over station KGMB to help them locate the island of Oahu. The 38th Reconnaissance Squadron's flight was the first to arrive. Maj. Landon, leading the flight, saw what he thought was a flight of fighter aircraft coming out to meet them. To his surprise, the fighters began firing on the B-17s and a voice shouted over the intercom, "Damn it, those are Japs!"[1] The B-17s hurriedly took evasive action, trying to land wherever they could. Five airplanes landed at Hickam Field, where strafing Zeros set Capt. Raymond Swenson's B-17C on fire, and one B-17C came in to land at Bellows Field, running off the runway.[2] The 88th Reconnaissance Squadron arrived a short time later. Seeing Pearl Harbor under attack, Capt. Richard Carmichael and Lt. Harold Chaffin avoided Hickam Field and landed at Haleiwa Auxiliary Field, on the north shore of Oahu. Lts. Harry Brandon and David Rawls got into Hickam Field during a lull in the Japanese attack, while Lt.

A well-known photo of two Aichi D3A Type 99 Carrier Attack aircraft (VAL) passing a B-17E of the 38th Reconnaissance Squadron on their way to attack Pearl Harbor. (111-SC-127014, Records of the Office of the Chief Signals Officer, Record Group 111, National Archives and Records Administration)

Men unload their bags and equipment from a B-17E that managed to land on Hickim Field during the attack on December 7, 1941. (111-SC-127011, RG 111, NARA)

Robert Thacker apparently landed at Wheeler Field. Shortly thereafter, Thacker made a quick flight into Hickam.[3] Coming in to Hickam Field, Lt. Frank Bostrom was surprised to see fires burning and was told not to land. Circling the field, he asked the tower what was going on, and was told that the field was under attack. Quickly pulling away, Bostrom flew to the northwest, deciding to wait until the attack was over, but learned that Hickam was being attacked again. "We flew in and out of broken cumulus clouds," he recalled, "hoping not to be observed, for we had no means of defense. But two minutes later we were attacked by a Japanese pursuit coming in from the rear. We outmaneuvered him, but three other ships came on us, two of them succeeding in firing at us. We were using full power and our gas was nearly exhausted, so we broke away from the clouds and were warned by the radio operator that another Japanese plane was on our tail. We knew we'd better land or we never would."[4] Spotting a golf course below them, Bostrom skillfully put his big B-17 down on the fairway.

The attack on Pearl Harbor brought the 7th Bombardment Group's transfer to the Philippines to an abrupt halt. The immediate need was to protect Pearl Harbor and the Western United States from a possible follow-on Japanese attack that at the time seemed more than likely. At Pearl Harbor, the men of the 88th Reconnaissance Squadron began flying patrol missions December 9th. The next day, the crews were temporarily assigned to the 31st Bombardment Squadron, part of the 5th Bombardment Group; they would remain at Pearl Harbor, flying long distance patrols for several more weeks.[5] In the United States, the Fourth Air Force, covering the Southwest, and the Second Air Force, covering the Northwest, were immediately responsible for the defense of the West Coast and protection of the major cities with the limited forces they had available. A Western Defense Command was set up four days after the attack on Pearl Harbor.[6] When news of the attack on Pearl Harbor came in around noon on December 7th, the 7th Bombardment Group's airplanes at Hamilton Field and the Sacramento Air Depot were immediately ordered to disperse to the airfield at Muroc Dry Lake, arriving there at 0200 on December 8th.[7] At Muroc, the B-17s were hurriedly loaded with bombs and ammunition, with the combat crews working throughout the night. As soon as an airplane was loaded, it set off on anti-submarine patrol 350 miles west of San Francisco.[8] There were rumors flying about Japanese fleets off the coast of California. On the morning of December 9th, the Group was ordered to take off and attack a Japanese force reported off the coast of southern California, but this was countermanded to sending three bombers on a reconnaissance of the area. That afternoon, the Group was ordered to send nine airplanes to attack a force of one Japanese cruiser and three destroyers reported off Huntington Beach, only to have the airplanes recalled when this report, too, proved false. The planes struggled back to their base through awful weather. Patrols continued on December 10th. Meanwhile, more B-17s flew to the Sacramento Air Depot to have additional armament installed in preparation for departure to "Plum". As there were no maintenance personnel at Muroc when the 7th Group arrived, the combat crews refueled and rearmed their planes. Regular patrols, the constant countermanding of orders, poor weather, and maintenance work were exhausting.[9]

Members of the 7th Bombardment Group's ground echelon found out about the attack on Pearl Harbor while at sea. The *Republic* had arrived in Honolulu November 28th, where the troops on board were given a four-hour pass to see some of the city. The next day, the ship left as part of Convoy No. 4002, along with seven other transports loaded with troops, supplies, and aircraft all bound for the Philippines. The cruiser USS *Pensacola* escorted the convoy, headed for the Fiji Islands.[10] Around 11 a.m. December 7th, an announcement came over the ship's loudspeakers that Pearl Harbor had been attacked. On the *Republic*, the artillery men broke out their 75mm cannon and arranged several on deck, with others manning the ship's few guns. Men from the 88th Reconnaissance Squadron were assigned to a water-cooled .50 caliber machine gun. While the Army and Navy debated where the convoy should go, the ships continued on to Suva, in the Fiji Islands, arriving December 13th. The convoy was then ordered to Brisbane, Australia, where the Air Corps troops on board the *Republic* would disembark with their equipment to wait for instructions. On the afternoon of December 23rd, the 7th Group's ground echelon disembarked and marched to temporary accommodations at the Ascot Race Track. When it seemed doubtful the convoy could get through to the Philippines, on December 29th, the men from the 9th and 88th

Squadrons were sent to Amberly Field, some 30 miles from Brisbane, and the men from the 11th and 22nd Squadrons went to nearby Archer Field. With no B-17s to service, the ground echelon was put to work assembling Douglas A-24 dive bombers (the Army Air Forces' version of the Navy SBD Dauntless) and Curtiss P-40 fighters that had arrived in crates with the convoy.[11]

Disaster in the Philippines

A wrecked 19th Bombardment Group B-17C or D at Clark Field in the Philippines, taken from a contemporary Japanese propaganda volume. (via the author)

The Japanese air attacks on American airfields in the Philippines that began December 8, 1941, and continued for five successive days devastated the Far East Air Force; by December 13th, the Japanese had established effective air superiority over the Philippines.[12] On December 8th, as the Far East Air Force's B-17s at Clark Field were preparing for a raid against Japanese air bases on Formosa, the Japanese attacked, and in two hours of bombing and strafing destroyed 12 B-17s—a third of the 19th Bombardment Group's strength—and 34 out of 92 P-40 fighters.[13] The continued loss of fighters made the air bases in Luzon vulnerable to Japanese attack, forcing Maj. Gen. Louis Brereton to withdraw his few remaining B-17s to Del Monte airfield on Mindanao, south of Luzon. Del Monte had been the intended base for the 7th Bombardment Group. Between December 11th and 18th, the 19th Bombardment Group flew only two missions against the Japanese. With the Japanese having achieved air superiority over the Philippines, Brereton ordered the remaining B-17s to Australia to avoid their destruction. The 19th Bombardment Group began withdrawing December 17th. Four B-17s narrowly avoided destruction during a Japanese strafing attack on Del Monte field December 19th.[14] Despite these setbacks, the United States had no intention of giving up the Philippines. President Roosevelt requested that all possible reinforcements should be sent to the Philippines as soon as possible. On December 15, 1941, the War Department informed General MacArthur that 65 new B-17 heavy bombers and fifteen Consolidated LB-30 bombers (the export version of the B-24), requisitioned from British orders, would be sent to him by February 21, 1942.[15] The Japanese capture of Wake Island December 23rd cut the only proven route across the Pacific Ocean, delaying the departure of B-17s for the Philippines.[16] Until a new more southerly route could be improvised, heavy bomber reinforcements would have to travel the long route across the South Atlantic from Africa to India, then from India to the Netherlands East Indies. The ferry program, designated Project X, would be carried out in two stages: first, the transfer of the fifteen LB-30 bombers; and second, the transfer of the 65 B-17s as they became available from the Boeing factory and after modifications at the Sacramento Air Depot. The 7th Bombardment Group became part of this movement of aircraft.

The 7th Group resumed moving to the Philippines. Six B-17Es from the 22nd Squadron left Hamilton Field for Hickam Field December 18, 1941, where they were held up with the fall of Wake Island and retained in Hawaii for patrol duties.[17]

LB-30 AL 576, one of the aircraft requisitioned from the British order and assigned to the 11th Bombardment Squadron at Tucson, Arizona, in December 1941. (00025565, Courtesy San Diego Air & Space Museum)

Prior to this flight, on December 14th, a fifteen-airplane squadron was organized to fly the LB-30 bombers out to the Philippines. The 11th Bombardment Squadron served as the nucleus with additional crews from the 9th and 32nd

Bombardment Squadrons and the 38th and 88th Reconnaissance Squadrons, under the command of Maj. Austin Straubel.[18] Straubel hurried to Washington for briefings with the Air Ferry Command, which was setting up the route across Africa

The 11th Bombardment Squadron's pilots had only a few days to transition to the LB-30 before they headed off on their ferry flight to the Far East Air Force. (00025562, Courtesy San Diego Air & Space Museum)

and India. The crews selected for the 11th Squadron flew their B-17Es to the Sacramento Air Depot, where they were transferred to pilots from the 5th Bombardment Group to make the flight to Hawaii. The 11th Squadron crews flew to Tucson, Arizona, to begin transition training on the LB-30. The British Government had placed several orders for the Consolidated LB-30, the export version of the B-24 Liberator bomber, amounting to 139 airplanes. Roughly equivalent to the B-24A, the LB-30 had provision for two hand-operated .50 caliber machine guns in the tail, two in the waist position, a two-gun Martin turret, one tunnel gun, and one in the nose. The LB-30s, however, lacked turbo-superchargers for the airplane's four Pratt & Whitney R-1830 Twin Wasp engines, limiting the airplane's operational ceiling.[19] After the Pearl Harbor attack, the Army Air Forces requisitioned 75 LB-30s from British contracts. Consolidated Aircraft pilots flew the airplanes to Tucson, where the company had established a modification center at nearby Davis-Monthan Field. Here the LB-30s had guns—including a Martin upper turret—armor, radios, oxygen systems, and Norden bombsights installed, while the 11th Squadron pilots began flying the airplanes whenever they could. When the modifications were completed at Tucson, the crews flew their airplanes to Wright Field in Ohio to get additional American equipment installed.

Finally, on December 28th, Maj. Straubel, with Lts. Horace M. Wade and John E. Dougherty, arrived at the Ferrying Command base at McDill Field, near Tampa, Florida. At Tampa, they prepared for their flight to Karachi, India, the point where the airplanes would come under Far East Air Force's control. The route took them to Karachi via Trinidad-Belem-Natal-Accra-Khartoum to Aden, in the Middle East. After final checks, including the removal of 3,000 pounds of excess equipment, the three pilots took off for Trinidad at midnight, December 30th, arriving at Karachi seven days later on January 6, 1942. At Karachi, the crews received maps of India and the Netherlands East Indies and instructions to fly to Bangalore, in southern India, then on to Java. After a day spent on maintenance at Bangalore, the three LB-30s took off at 1730. On January 9, 1942, they arrived at Bandoeng, in central Java, around 1000 in the morning of January 10th, after flying through tropical storms and severe turbulence that nearly forced them back. The next morning, the three crews flew to Malang, in eastern Java, where they reported to Lt. Col. Eugene Eubank, commander of the 19th Bombardment Group and V Bomber Command.[20] Three days later, on January 14th, five 7th Group aircraft arrived in Java. Maj. Conrad F. Necrason—a former pursuit pilot and newly-appointed commander of the 9th Bombardment Squadron—and Lt. John L. DuFrane, also from the 9th, flew their B-17Es to Java via the South Atlantic-Africa-India route, having actually left Tampa the day before Straubel and his LB-30s. The LB-30s had the range to fly from Ceylon directly to Java; the B-17s had to fly from India to Palembang, on the island of Sumatra, refuel at the Dutch airfield there, then fly on to Java. Arriving from the opposite direction were two more B-17Es from the

LB-30 AL 576 at Tucson. The twin .50 caliber machine guns in the newly-mounted Martin turret can just be seen on the upper fuselage just behind the wing. 1st Lt. William E. Bayse flew this airplane to Java in January 1942. (00025563, Courtesy San Diego Air & Space Museum)

22nd Bombardment Squadron in Hawaii, which had been released to fly to Java via the new Pacific route, via Palmyra Island, Canton Island, Fiji, New Caledonia, Townsville, and Darwin in Australia, then on to Java. Maj. Kenneth B. Hobson, 22nd Squadron commander, and Lt. Jack W. Hughes, another

22nd pilot, landed within a few hours of Necrason and DuFrane. Lt. William E. Bayse, one of the pilots assigned to the 11th Bombardment Squadron from the 88th Reconnaissance Squadron, used the South Atlantic route to fly one of the 11th Squadron's LB-30s to Java. For young pilots and navigators who had relatively little experience over long expanses of ocean, desert, and jungle, this was an impressive achievement. Project X called for three B-17s to leave on the first and second days after the start of the project, then for three LB-30s and three B-17s to leave on each of the next five days, with the remaining 44 aircraft to leave at a rate of six B-17s a day as production deliveries and crew training for the ferry flights speeded up.[21]

Defending Java

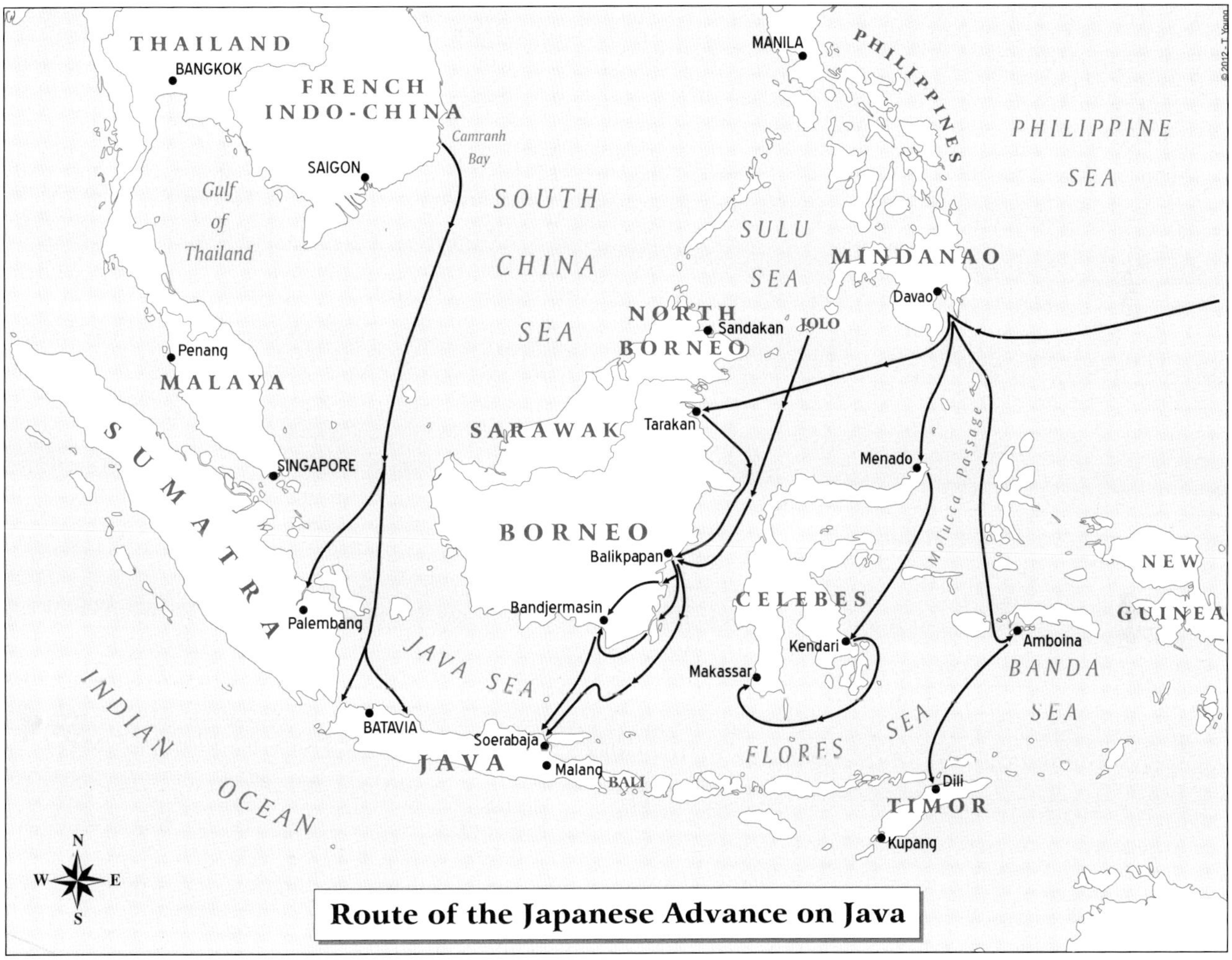

Route of the Japanese Advance on Java

By the time the 7th Bombardment Group airplanes arrived in Java, the Allied forces attempting the defense of Southeast Asia were in desperate straits. On December 8, 1941 (December 7th at Pearl Harbor), the Japanese had initiated a campaign that employed "...speed, surprise, and rapid exploitation..." integrating their air, sea, and ground forces in a series of "... brilliantly imagined thrusts that were to tear the Allies apart throughout the region."[22] Japan's principal objective in going to war was to seize the oil fields of the Netherlands East Indies as soon as possible and capture the vast and vital raw material resources of Southeast Asia. Without these resources, the Japanese could not hope to survive the conflict with the Western powers they thought was inevitable.[23] To establish the Greater East Asia Co-prosperity sphere and dominate Asia, Japan's Imperial General Headquarters knew the Japanese would have to undertake a campaign across a wide geographic area against the British, Dutch, and American forces defending their colonial possessions, evict the Western powers, and use the region's raw materials to build the weapons needed to protect their conquests.[24] After a rapid conquest, Imperial General Headquarters planned to establish a barrier stretching from Burma in the west across Southeast Asia to New Guinea and the Bismarck Islands, then up through the central Pacific to the Kuriles. The challenge was to accomplish this with limited military forces and transport the Japanese military had available. The Imperial Japanese Army and Navy worked out a plan that would achieve Japan's objectives in three phases:

1. **Phase One:** Initial operations to secure the western and eastern flanks of the planned assault on Southeast Asia through the neutralization of the American Pacific Fleet at Pearl Harbor and American air forces in the Philippines, seizure of Thailand as a base for an advance into southern Burma, and the invasions of northern Malaya and the Philippines;
2. **Phase Two:** Occupation of Malaya and capture of Singapore, capture of airfields in southern Burma, and preliminary operations to seize airfields for the advance on Java;
3. **Phase Three:** Capture of Sumatra, Java, and the rest of Burma, and the consolidation of the defensive barrier when all three had fallen.[25]

After two weeks of fighting, the Japanese had seized the strategic initiative and had established a dominant position against the Allies.[26] In their initial planning, the Japanese had estimated that it would take them 50 days to capture the Philippines, 100 days to capture Malaya and Singapore, and five months to complete the conquest of the Netherlands East Indies.[27] By the end of December, they were well ahead of their schedule. Having captured British North Borneo and

A contemporary postcard showing the Mitsubishi G3M Type 96 Attack Bomber on a mission over the southern front in early 1942. (Author's collection)

the Philippine islands of Davao and Jolo, the Imperial General Headquarters decided to begin the advance on the Netherlands East Indies with the main island of Java as the goal.[28] The Japanese planned a three-pronged advance to seize Java, using a strategy of pushing forward under the cover of air

The Mitsubishi G4M Type I Attack Bomber that equipped the *Takao Kokutai* and the detachment from the *Kanoya Kokutai*. (Author's collection)

power. The plan involved progressively seizing airfields closer and closer to Java, moving air units to the next newly-captured air base, and using these units to provide air cover over the naval forces and transports for the next stage in the advance. The Central Force would move down the coast of eastern Borneo along the Strait of Makassar, capturing the oil fields and airfields at Tarakan, Balikpapan, and Bandjarmasin. Bases at these locations would enable Japanese Navy bombers and fighters to strike Java. The Eastern Force would proceed down the Moluccas Passage to capture airfields in the Celebes, beginning with Menado, then Kendari, then Makassar. After the projected capture of Singapore, the Western Force would seize the airfields at Palembang in southern Sumatra, enabling the Japanese to then capture Java in a massive double envelopment. Air support was critical to the plan's success. Imperial General Headquarters assigned principle responsibility to the Imperial Navy's land-based *21st* and *23rd Kōkū Sentai* (Naval Air Flotilla) from the *11th Kōkū Kantai* (Air Fleet), with a combined total (at the beginning of the war) of three bomber (*Takao Kokutai*, *1st Kokutai*, and a detachment of the *Kanoya Kokutai*) and two fighter (*3rd Kokutai* and *Tainan Kokutai*) air groups (*Kokutai*) with 48 Mitsubishi G3M Type 96 Attack Bombers (Nell), 108 Mitsubishi G4M Type 1 Attack Bombers (Betty), and 107 Mitsubishi A6M2 Type 0 Carrier Fighters (Zero, later Zeke), with support from the aircraft carriers of the Second Carrier Division.[29]

The Allied response to the Japanese onslaught reflected, in the words of one historian, "...confusion, unreality, and weakness, shrouded by wishful thinking."[30] Allied forces in Southeast Asia were unevenly distributed, often under-strength and poorly trained, and lacked adequate modern equipment. The four countries directly involved in the region's defense—America, Australia, Great Britain, and the Netherlands—operated through five distinctly separate commands whose orders and objectives stemmed from separate national interests.[31] In an attempt to bring some degree of coordination to this disparate group, President Roosevelt and Prime Minister Winston Churchill and their Chiefs of Staff agreed at the Arcadia Conference in Washington, D.C., toward the end of December 1941 to form the America-British-Dutch-Australian Command (ABDA). The British General Sir Archibald Wavell, Commander in Chief, India, was given the thankless task of commanding ABDA and trying to stem the Japanese advance with what forces could be made available, a command that "...offered little chance of success and seemed likely to end in defeat and even disaster."[32] To balance nationalities within ABDACOM, Wavell selected Army Air Forces Gen. George Brett. Air Marshal Sir Richard Peirse was appointed ABDA-Air with Maj. Gen. Louis Brereton as his deputy, in addition to Brereton's other responsibilities. Within the American and British military leadership there was general agreement that the Allies had to hold the Malay barrier, stretching from Sumatra to New Guinea, to preserve the raw materials there for their own war industries and to prevent the Japanese from pushing beyond into Australia and Burma. There was growing concern that the Allies would be unable to send sufficient reinforcements to the region,

The ML-KNIL, the air arm of the Netherlands Indies Army, had one squadron of Curtiss Hawk 75s for defense, its main equipment being the Brewster 339D Buffalo. Both types were inferior to the A6M2 Type 0 Carrier Fighter. (Peter M. Bowers Collection, Museum of Flight)

particularly fighter aircraft needed to regain air superiority, before the Japanese could complete their plan of conquest, which seemed to move inexorably forward without hindrance.

When General Wavell activated the ABDACOM headquarters at Bandoeng, in central Java, on January 15, 1942—a few days after the first 7th Bombardment Group aircraft had arrived on the island—the situation was already dire. In the two weeks since the 7th Group's pilots had left the United States, the Japanese Army had pushed back the British Commonwealth forces in Malaya, bottled up the American

The ML-KNIL's Curtiss CW-21B had an excellent rate of climb, but were overwhelmed in combat by the superior A6M2 Type 0 Carrier Fighter. (Peter M. Bowers Collection, Museum of Flight)

Army on the Bataan Peninsula on Luzon, and had begun the first phase of the invasion of the Netherlands East Indies, capturing Tarakan, on the east coast of Borneo and Menado in the northern Celebes, on January 12th.[33] From airfields at these two locations, the Japanese could launch attacks on Balikpapan and Kendari and provide cover for amphibious landings. Wavell had precious little with which to delay, much less stop the Japanese naval forces and transport convoys advancing on Java. The *Militaire Luchtvaart van het Koninklijk Nederlands-Indisch Leger*, or ML-KNIL, the Dutch Army's aviation branch in the Netherlands, had around 70 older Martin 139W bombers—the equivalent of the Army Air Corps B-10B—now hopelessly obsolete for the task at hand, with some 150 fighters of American origin (Brewster Buffalos, Curtiss Hawk 75s, and CW-21Bs), none of which could stand up to the A6M2 Type 0 Carrier Fighter and the Imperial Japanese Navy's superbly trained pilots.[34] Apart from a small Allied naval force, Wavell's only other option was to use the heavy bombers of the V Bomber Command's 19th and soon to arrive 7th Bombardment Groups. In view of the looming Japanese threat, Brereton decided to move the V Bomber Command to Java.[35]

The 19th Bombardment Group, temporarily based at Batchelor Field near Darwin, in northern Australia, was ordered to transfer to Java to undertake attacks on the Japanese forces moving south on the Netherlands East Indies. The 19th Group's remaining eleven B-17s (a single B-17C and ten B-17Ds) started flying to Java December 30, 1941, using

The large grass runway at the Singarsari air field near Malang, in eastern Java. (Courtesy of Gerry Cassius)

the airfield at Singosari, just outside the city of Malang, in eastern Java, as their base.[36] The Group flew its first mission out of Java January 4, 1942, when eight planes took off to bomb Japanese shipping building up at Davao. The aircraft stopped at Samarinda, on the east coast of Borneo, to refuel on the way.[37] The bombers claimed one destroyer sunk and three hits on a heavy cruiser.[38] The 19th Group flew its next mission, again to Davao, on January 8th, refueling at Kendari. Weather made bombing difficult and the crews were not able to confirm any hits. The crews returned to Malang January 10th to learn that the shipping they had seen on January 4th at Davao was part of the invasion force now heading for Tarakan and Menado. Seven B-17s went out the next day, but four lost the formation in bad weather. The remaining three bombed a convoy through the clouds before encountering a flight of Zeros that attacked the bombers for 30 minutes.[39] One of the airplanes returned to Malang later that day and the other two returned January 12th after stopping at Samarinda and Soerabaja, respectively.

The crews from the 19th Group were delighted to see the newly-arrived pilots from the 7th and their new airplanes, the first heavy bomber reinforcements to arrive in Java. For the crews of the 7th, their talks with the men of the 19th were sobering. They were impressed with the "enormous tiredness" in the faces of the men who had been in combat and under continuous pressure for over a month now.[40] Raymond Carr, the bombardier on Maj. Austin Straubel's airplane, recalled meeting up with several classmates from Bombardier School at Lowry Field: "They really had some tales to tell us about the Philippines and also the missions they had been running out of Java. It didn't sound at all good, and we began to get a picture of the trouble ahead...One of my classmates had just come in from a mission and said he was lucky, because their plane had been 'shot to hell'."[41] At least Malang was a good airfield, with comfortable barracks, decent food, two large hangars for maintenance, and long (4,000 feet) grass

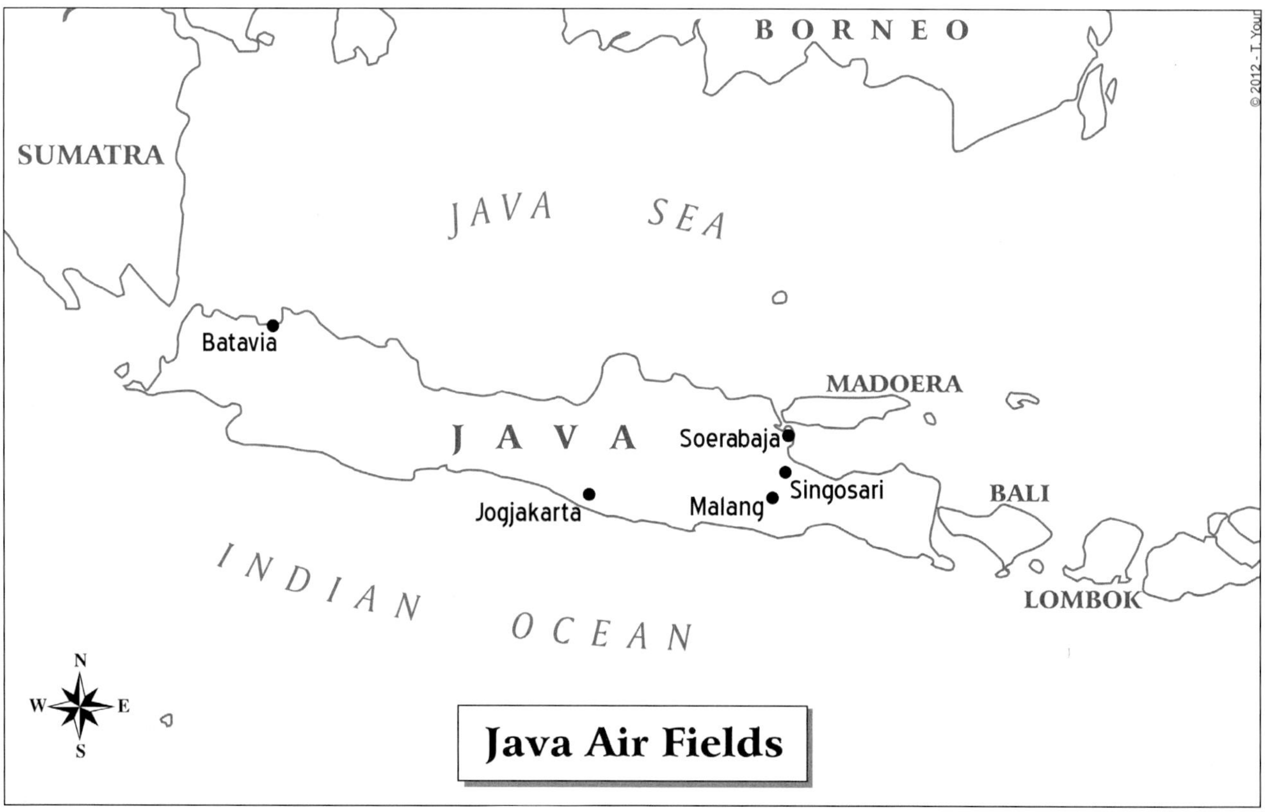

runways.[42] The problem for the men of the 19th Group and the new arrivals was the lack of maintenance men. The crews initially performed their own maintenance until men from

Mitsubishi A6M2 Type 0 Carrier Fighters preparing to take off on a mission. The 7th Bombardment Group had the misfortune to run into Zero fighters on the Group's first combat mission on January 17, 1942. (Via the author)

the 1st Battalion of the 131st Field Artillery, who arrived in Java without their field guns, were assigned to help the two bomb groups.[43] After arriving, the men of the 7th Group spent the next several days working on their airplanes, removing the long-range fuel tanks put in for the ferry flight, checking guns and bomb racks, and preparing for their first mission. The 7th Bombardment Group was to be based near the town of Jogjakarta, 150 miles to the west of Malang, but until there was an adequate number of maintenance staff available at Jogjakarta, the 7th Group stayed at Malang and operated alongside the 19th Group.[44]

There was little time to get acclimated. At V Bomber Command Eubank, recently promoted to Colonel, had wanted to give the new pilots some time to settle in, but the rapidity of the Japanese advance gave him no choice. With the Japanese steadily pushing the British Commonwealth forces down Malaya toward Singapore, Wavell ordered V Bomber Command to send its heavy bombers to attack the Japanese-occupied airfields in Malaya, using Palembang, on Sumatra, as a forward refueling base. Both Eubank and the bomber crews realized that the mission was essentially a futile exercise, but they had no choice.[45] At the same time, Japanese shipping at Menado, in the northern Celebes, posed an urgent threat. Eubank sent the 19th Bombardment Group on the Malaya mission and alerted the 7th Group pilots January 15th to fly a mission the next day with two B-17Es and the three LB-30s. The aircraft would land on Kendari, in the southeastern Celebes, to refuel and take on Dutch bombs. The Two B-17s, flown by Maj. Necrason and Lt. John DuFrane, were assigned to bomb shipping in Menado Bay, while Maj. Straubel took Lt. William Bayse and Lt. John Dougherty in their LB-30s to bomb the airfield at Langoan, twenty miles to the south of the town.[46] Their first mission proved to be a rude awakening.

The bombers took off from Malang a little after noon on January 16th and arrived at Kendari airfield around two hours later. The bombers were refueled, and with the help of Dutch personnel loaded with Dutch 100-kilogram (225-pound) bombs, the LB-30s taking twelve each and the B-17Es ten. The crews had a few hours rest, taking off at about 0315 on the morning of January 17th for Menado, using their landing lights to illuminate the runway. The B-17s lead the formation toward Menado, the two flights separating as they neared the town to attack their respective targets, the LB-30s, without super-chargers, flying at an altitude of 19,500 feet. As they came in over Menado Bay, the B-17 crews saw two large and two small Japanese transports with two more at the dock. Coming in on their bomb run at 0530, they approached into the sun from inexperience, blinding the bombardiers and forcing Necrason to make a second run. On the second attempt, they dropped their bombs on the transports below, though one airplane had six bombs fail to release from the bomb racks. The crews saw one transport capsize as they pulled off the target. On the way out they flew over Langoan airfield, where the airplane with the hung bombs dropped two on the airfield.[47] As the B-17s turned for Kendari, they ran into a flight of five A6M2 Zeros from the *3rd Kokutai* patrolling nearby; twelve more fighters were scrambled when the bombers appeared overhead. The Zeros kept up the attacks for 40 minutes, making continued passes from the rear quarter.

Major Austin Straubel sits in the cockpit of an early B-17 in 1940, when he was commander of "B" Flight in the 11th Bombardment Squadron. (From *The Bomber 1940*, via the author)

The B-17 crews later reported that 15 fighters had attacked them, including two "Messerschmitts". Petty Officer 3rd Class Shoichi Shoji and Airman 1st Class Seijii Tojiri attacked

Necrason's airplane, believing they had damaged it so severely it would not make it back to its base.[48] Petty Officer 2nd Class Katsujiro Nakano attacked Lt. DuFrane's airplane, which had

John Dougherty as a young 2nd Lieutenant in the 11th Bombardment Squadron. (From *The Bomber 1940*, via the author)

lost an engine on the bombing run, possibly from anti-aircraft fire. Nakano knocked out a second engine before DuFrane could escape into clouds.[49] Gunners on the two B-17s claimed five Zeros and one of the "Messerschmitts" shot down. Necrason's crew claimed five airplanes: four by the tail gunners and one by the bombardier. Necrason's tail gunner, Pfc. Arvid Hegdahl, claimed two Zeros. A 7.7mm bullet exploded one of his .50 caliber rounds, sending the pieces into his left leg. Hegdahl continued firing, then collapsed from the loss of blood. Master Sergeant Louis T. Silva, the 9th Bombardment's line chief and a long-serving member of the 9th Squadron, had insisted on flying on the mission because of the limited experience of the young gunners on Necrason's crew. Silva dragged Hegdahl out of his tail position, bandaged his wound, and gave him a shot of morphine. Taking his place in the tail position, Silva claimed two more Zeros shot down. For his actions Silva was awarded the Distinguished Service Cross at an age of nearly 60 years old.[50]

Necrason and DuFrane returned to Kendari to refuel, make repairs, and have their wounded treated. The *3rd Kokutai* staff assumed the B-17s would be using Kendari for refueling and sent out three A6M2s and a Mitsubishi C5M2 Type 98 Reconnaissance Plane (Babs) in the hope of catching the two bombers on the ground. Necrason was just about to take off and DuFrane and his crew were still working on the engines of their airplane when the Zeros swept in to strafe the airfield. Petty Officer 1st Class Masao Masuyama attacked Necrason's airplane repeatedly, but failed to bring it down. Necrason eluded his pursuer and returned to Malang later that day. The other Zeros strafed DuFrane's airplane, inflicting even more damage. When repairs proved impossible, the airplane was blown up two days later. Lt. Horace Wade flew in one of the 11th Squadron's LB-30s at night to take out DuFrane and his crew.[51]

Maj. Straubel and his flight arrived shortly after the B-17s had completed their bombing. Without clear directions as to the location of the airfield at Langoan, Straubel had to spend some time searching for the target. Fortunately, there were no Japanese fighter planes over the area, as they had apparently intercepted the B-17s. Encountering no anti-aircraft fire over the target, the three bombers had a clear run on the airfield. With his two wingmen flying 200 feet to his right and left, Straubel brought his formation over the airfield, all airplanes dropping on the leader at 0536 and seeing hits on the runway and the parking areas. Coming off the target, the LB-30s dropped down to 17,000 in order to pick up speed. The LB-30s ran into a flight of five A6M2s from the *3rd Kokutai*, most likely from the group of fighters sent off to intercept the B-17s. Coming in out of the sun, the fighters surprised the LB-30 gunners. In a five minute attack, the Zeros damaged Bayse's and Dougherty's airplanes before they could escape into cloud. Petty Officer 3rd Class Saburo Yahata attacked one of the LB-30s and saw smoke coming from three of the four engines

William Bayse when serving with the 88th Reconnaissance Squadron as a 2nd Lieutenant. (From *The Bomber 1940*, via the author)

before it went into a cloud; this seems likely to have been Dougherty's aircraft, who dropped out of the formation and turned to the right shortly before the fighters stopped their attacks.[52] As they headed back to Malang, Bayse fell farther and farther behind Straubel. Bayse reported "my ship was shot up badly. The damage to the ship slowed it up badly, about 10-15mph. There was a bad oil leak in the top of No. 1 engine. We found out after we were on the ground that the oil line had been shot away. We were unable to keep up with the lead ship and kept dropping back until lost from sight."[53] Bayse turned off to land at Makassar. Bayse lowered the wheels using the emergency system. On landing, the right wheel blew and the airplane swerved to the right. Full left rudder and left brake failed to bring the plane back, and it went on to plow through several bunkers, barricades, a ditch, and pile of dirt. The landing ripped off all three wheels, bent the propellers, and twisted the rear fuselage.[54] The airplane was far too damaged to be recovered. A Navy PBY from Patrol Wing Ten came up to take them back to Java with a load of salvaged parts. Dougherty had to crash land on an island, where he and his crew were rescued after several days and brought back on another PBY. With two out of three LB-30s lost on the mission, and in view of their weaker armament, lack of armor protection, and inability to fly at higher altitudes, the LB-30s were shifted to night bombing and reconnaissance missions.[55] On its first combat mission, the 7th Group had lost four out of six airplanes.

More B-17s arrived over the next several days. Lt. Robert Northcutt arrived January 18th. Maj. Stanley Robinson, 7th Group commander, arrived with two other B-17Es flown by Lt. D.R. Strother and Lt. Duane Skiles from the 9th Squadron on January 19th. Lts. Jack Bleasdale, Joseph Preston, and T.B. Swanson flew in three more B-17Es on January 21st. While the extra planes were welcome, the greater need was for maintenance personnel to service and repair them. The 19th Bombardment Group flew out some pilots and maintenance personnel from Del Monte Field on Mindanao (Maj. Hobson and Lt. Hughes went along on the mission, but had to turn back due to engine trouble), who were a welcome addition to the force at Malang. With the 7th Group's ground crews still in Australia, the Group's combat crews had to continue to work on their own aircraft before and after every mission. There was a lack of spare parts and tools, and the rainy season, then at its height, made both maintenance and takeoffs from the grass runways even more challenging. On January 18th, the 7th Group's ground echelon, having worked around the clock at Amberly and Archer Fields assembling A-24s and P-40s, sailed for Java. In preparation for their arrival, and as Malang was getting more crowded, the 11th Squadron began working to prepare the airfield at Jogjakarta, and the LB-30s shuttled personnel and supplies from Malang. Construction began on a 150 x 4,500-foot concrete runway. Until that was completed, the bombers had to use the frequently rain-sodden grass field. The field at Jogjakarta was well-supplied with bombs and fuel, but a memo to Col. Eubank noted that there was no .50 caliber ammunition and no oxygen available. The officers and men were quartered temporarily in a school in the town, with a local club providing food at a cost to the officers of two guilders a day. On January 23rd, Maj. Necrason brought in two B-17Es and crews from the 9th Squadron. On January 24th, Lt. Jerome Tarter arrived from the States in an LB-30 via the Africa route. Two days later Lt. Walter Sparks, Jr. brought in a B-17E from Africa, while Lts. Richard Ezzard and Clyde Kelsay—part of the enlarged 11th Bombardment Squadron—brought in two more LB-30s following the Pacific route. Ezzard came in fast on landing and had to use full brakes and the entire runway to bring his airplane to a stop, the nose gear breaking off in the mud at the end. The damage required two weeks to repair. Though the 7th Group had begun to base its aircraft at Jogjakarta, combat missions were still flown out of Malang. With the shortage of aircraft in both the 7th and 19th Groups, "larger" missions of more than three or four aircraft could only be accomplished using planes and pilots from both groups together.[56]

Major Stanley Robinson, the 7th Bombardment Group's commander at the outbreak of the war, seen here as a Captain with the Group in 1940. Robinson arrived in Java on January 19, 1942, and was killed in action ten days later. (From *The Bomber 1940*, via the author)

The end of Ole' 576. Lt. William Bayse flew LB-30 AL 576 out to Java from the United States, only to have it badly shot up during his first combat mission on January 17, 1942. The airplane's right tire blew on landing at Makassar, causing the plane to swerve off the runway. (00025573, Courtesy San Diego Air & Space Museum)

A photo from a 1942 Japanese magazine showing a wrecked B-17E at Palembang, possibly the aircraft that 1st Lt. Hughes wrecked on landing on January 22, 1942. (Via the author)

Maj. Robinson wasted no time getting into combat. He was "...a fine officer, with the offensive spirit in a very high degree..." who led from the front, being "...the type of leader incapable of asking more from his men than he expected of himself."[57] Robinson was fiercely proud of the 7th Group and intent on retaining its individual identity. Some degree of friction emerged, at least initially, and perhaps inevitably, when a new and untried group finds itself side by side with more experienced veterans (Lt. Jack Bleasdale wrote in his diary, "...they treat us as though we were a bunch of 'Dodos.'")[58] The friction carried over to relations between Maj. Robinson and Col. Eubank, particularly over tactics. The 19th Group had learned through experience to hit a target "high, fast, and *once*."[59] Col. Eubank's tactical doctrine was based on the bomber formation flying in tight formation, remaining level at the same altitude, and flying straight on to the target, sticking to the plan for the mission, something right out of the Air Corps Tactical School's view of how bomber formations should operate.[60] In contrast, Robinson "...held to the old philosophy that the leader of the mission should command all phases of the attack and make all tactical decisions during flight."[61]

Robinson went on his first combat mission January 22nd—three days after his arrival—a long mission to apparently bomb Japanese shipping off Balkipapan. Taking off at 0630 from Malang, Maj. Robinson led eight B-17Es and one B-17D, with six pilots from the 7th Group and three from the 19th Group, first to Palembang to refuel and take on bombs. The 7th Group's Lt. Hughes overshot the field and wrecked his bomber on landing. The airplane was stripped of parts and left at Palembang. Robinson led the remaining eight B-17s on to Malaya, returning to Palembang in the afternoon and then on to Malang the next day.[62] While they were away, Japanese naval vessels and transports arrived off Balikpapan, with its vital oil fields, and began landing troops January 23rd, following air strikes by the *21st Kōkū Kantai* and airplanes from the *2nd Carrier Division*. The next day, the Japanese seized Kendari, with the *21st Kōkū Kantai* moving to the airfield that evening. With bases at Balikpapan and Kendari, the Japanese could now dominate the southern half of the Makassar Strait and threaten the air route from Australia to Java.[63]

General Wavell ordered attacks on the Japanese invasion convoy off Balikpapan. V Bomber Command responded immediately to this new threat with what few aircraft it had available, but the results would be limited due to bad weather. On January 24th, Maj. Robinson led another mixed formation of six B-17Es from the 7th Group (with Maj. Hobson, Capt. Key, and Lts. Northcutt, Hillhouse, and Strother) and two B-17Ds from the 19th Group to attack shipping around Balikpapan. The flight claimed one transport sunk and one damaged. Running into Japanese fighters patrolling over Balikpapan that day, most likely from the *Tainan Kokutai*, the bombers claimed five enemy fighters shot down at no loss to themselves, though the Zero pilots would have better luck the next day. Returning to Malang at low altitude, Robinson fortuitously came across the 11th Squadron's missing Lt. Dougherty and his crew. On his return, Robinson arranged for a PatWing Ten PBY to pick them up the next day. The bombers went out again to Balikpapan January 25th, a mixed force of two B-17Es from the 7th Group (Maj. Hobson and Lt. Northcutt) and two from the 19th Group, along with three of the 19th's long-suffering B-17Ds, survivors of the Philippine battles still in service. The flight ran into Japanese fighters, again most likely from the *Tainan Kokutai*, who had moved to Balikpapan on January 24th.[64] Though no B-17s were lost, the formation was roughly handled. Hobson and Northcutt both landed their B-17s with wheels up near the town of Bangkalan, on the island of Madura, across from the city of Soerabaja, the main Dutch naval base. Lt. Hillhouse of the 19th Group had to land at Bandjermasin, south of Balikpapan, with his airplane badly shot up. That night, Lt. Horace Wade flew an LB-30 to Mindanao in company with a B-24A from Ferry Command loaded with badly needed supplies of ammunition and medicine taken on at Darwin. They returned to Darwin January 26th, carrying 40 airplane mechanics and two officers from the 19th Group stranded at Del Monte.[65] That same day the push continued, with Maj. Robinson and Lt. Strother taking off on another mission to Balikpapan in the early morning, only to turn back because of weather; two B-17Es and a single B-17 from the 19th Group went to Balikpapan a few hours later and also had to abandon the mission due to weather. Robinson led six B-17s—three B-17Es from the 7th and two B-17Es and a B-17D from the 19th—back to Balikpapan the next day (January 27th), his fourth mission in five days. The flight claimed one transport sunk, one damaged, and a cruiser damaged. Robinson did not fly the next day. Lts. Bleasdale and Preston joined three pilots from the 19th Group on a mission to bomb Japanese airfields in Malaya, stopping off at Palembang for fuel and bombs. By this point in the battle for Malaya, the mission had little chance of having any impact. The bombers were too few, and the British Commonwealth troops had already been ordered to retreat back to Singapore. To compound the sense of futility, the bomb sight in the lead bomber had not been correctly adjusted, so all bombs missed the targeted airfield. That night, Lts. Bayse and Tartar flew a night mission to bomb Kendari in their LB-30s. This appears to be the type's first attempt at night bombing, though the weather thwarted the mission.[66]

The next day, January 29th, another small formation of B-17s was due to return to Balikpapan to attack Japanese shipping, while two 7th Group crews (Lts. Bleasdale and Preston) joined three from the 19th for another mission to bomb airfields in Malaya via Palembang. The rainy season weather was not only difficult to fly through, but made bombing especially difficult, as the bombardiers were trying to locate and zero in on their targets through breaks in the clouds, rarely knowing if they had scored a hit. For the combat crews, "this uncertainty about achieved results, the unreliable intelligence they had to work with, the length of their missions, the lack of relief for combat crews, and the necessity of flying through the blind and violent heart of the vast equatorial front both on their way to the target and again before they could return to base, wore heavily on nerves already stretched fine."[67] It is not surprising that Robinson fought an order from Col. Eubank temporarily grounding him when he learned of the lack of experience of the crews assigned for this mission to Balkipapan. Of the four other pilots scheduled for the mission, only one—Lt. Cox of the 19th Group—had more than ten days experience in combat; one of the 7th Group's crews had arrived January 26th, and that of Lt. Habberstad had only arrived in Java the day before. Robinson pleaded with Eubank for permission to lead the mission, which Eubank reluctantly granted.[68] It would be Robinson's last. Lt. Duane Skiles, who was one of the relatively more experienced pilots on the mission, having been in Java all of ten days, wrote a report on how Maj. Robinson met his death:

"Maj. Robinson took Lt. Nyblades' place in Capt. Sparks' crew [who had arrived in Java January 26th] to act as a combination copilot, command pilot, and formation leader because of the inexperience of the other members of the crew in combat. On the first attack at 23,500 indicated, the bombs on Capt. Sparks' ship failed to drop. As all the bombardiers were instructed to drop on the leader, the attack was a failure. My ship was then designated as leader, and another attack was made with Capt. Sparks' ship as the rear ship of a Diamond Formation (four ships). The target was a Japanese cruiser already underway. It dodged just as the bombs were released and all missed. Enemy pursuit was active even before the first attack, and Capt. Sparks' ship was hit on #4 motor at some time during the second attack. He fell behind the formation, notified us by radio, and we slowed down to 130 m.p.h. (indicated). Pursuit were fighting furiously by this time, and it was four or five minutes before he rejoined the formation. His superchargers were gone, one engine out, the prop feathering system gone, and two men badly wounded. The No. 3 crew reported seeing large holes in the tail section and that the left elevator seemed to be entirely gone. We kept our power completely off and lost altitude down to 3,000 feet at 500ft/min. Pursuit abandoned the fight and the major notified us he was going to pull off to the right and 'zero his stabilizer'. He pulled off toward an island and appeared to be preparing to land on the beach. We followed about 3/4 mile away and saw the ship begin a slow left turn, which got steeper and steeper until it hit the sea in almost a vertical dive. There was an explosion and a huge gasoline fire on the water about 300ft in diameter and 500ft high, which burned for about two minutes. We circled the spot at low altitude, but nothing was observed except an oil slick."[69]

7th Bombardment Group ground echelon personnel working on the assembly of a Douglas A-24 Dauntless dive bomber at Archerley Field, Australia, in January 1942. (P000264_002-1, Australian War Memorial)

For his heroism and devotion to duty, Robinson was posthumously awarded the Distinguished Service Cross and the Distinguished Flying Cross. When Robinson's death was reported, Maj. Austin Straubel, leading the 11th Bombardment Squadron, was immediately appointed commander of the 7th Group. He would hold the position for five days.

A portion of the 7th Bombardment Group's ground echelon finally reached Java January 28th, the day before Maj. Robinson's final mission. The ground echelon—comprising the 7th Bombardment Group Headquarters and Headquarters

A Curtiss P-40E fresh out of its delivery crate and ready for assembly. (P000264_006-1, Australian War Memorial)

Squadron and the ground personnel of the 9th, 11th, and 22nd Bombardment Squadrons and the 88th Reconnaissance Squadron—had spent over a month in Brisbane. The engineering, armament, and radio technicians sent to Amberley and Archer Fields were put to work assembling A-24 dive bombers for the 27th Bombardment Group (Light) and P-40 fighters for the fighter squadrons on Java, off-loaded in wooden crates from the convoy the men had traveled with from Hawaii. None of the men from the 7th Group had ever worked on an A-24 or a P-40 before, much less assembled one, but they started working as best they could without proper tools or assembly instructions. Fortunately, an engineering officer from the Far East Air Force was available to provide some assistance, but he found the assembly process trying, as through inexperience the crews often made mistakes, attaching the wrong part in the wrong place, or failing to complete an assembly sequence correctly.[70] When the A-24s were assembled, they were found to be missing vital parts necessary for combat. The airplanes had been shipped with an insufficient number of trigger motors for their two nose-mounted machine guns, no solenoids, improper gun mounts, and incorrect bomb racks, among other defects.[71] Nor was there enough Prestone coolant for the P-40s; a fighter would be assembled, the radiator filled with Prestone, flight tested, then the radiator would be drained of Prestone to be used on another fighter. Despite all the problems, the 7th Group's men assembled 138 P-40s, 52 A-24s, and 5 C-53 transports with the assistance of a team of experienced P-40 crew chiefs who arrived at Amberley Field January 14th.[72] Finally, on January 20th, 250 officers and men from the ground echelons of the 11th and 22nd Squadrons boarded the SS *President Polk* for the trip to Java. Arriving at Soerabaja, the men were split up—110 from the 11th Squadron going to join their unit and the 7th Bombardment Group at Jogjakarta, while the men from the 22nd Squadron were sent to Malang, where the 22nd had apparently been assigned to the short-handed 19th Group.[73]

Missions to Balikpapan continued without let up. The night of January 30th, Lts. Horace Wade and Richard Ezzard flew another night mission to bomb shipping in the area, though trying to find, much less bomb, Japanese ships in the dark of night, through clouds and rain, was asking a great deal, one record stating "results of mission doubtful."[74] On the 31st, six B-17Es went out with four crews from the 7th Group (Lts. Strother, Habberstad, Preston, and Bleasdale), along with two from the 19th Group. They flew up to Balikpapan, only to find the weather obscuring the target, but the Zeros found the B-17s and in a running fight, T/Sgt. J.A. Potters was killed and Pvt. Edwin Shipley was wounded on board Bleasdale's aircraft. Maj. Straubel went on his first mission as group commander the next day (February 1st), leading Lt. Northcutt from the 7th Group and four 19th Group B-17Es back to Balikpapan, only to have to abandon the mission again due to weather. That night, Lts. Daugherty, Kelsey, and Tartar took their LB-30s on a night mission to Balikpapan, and on this occasion had a certain degree of success. Dougherty claimed a ship sunk, while Tartar's crew saw some oil tanks and bombed them, setting them on fire. The 7th Group stood down February 2nd, while the 19th Group sent out eight B-17s to keep up the pressure on Japanese shipping at Balikpapan.[75]

The Tide Turns, Irrevocably

The situation facing ABDACOM in early February was dire. The Japanese drive down the Malaya peninsula—one of the most brilliant campaigns of the entire Pacific War—had succeeded in driving the British Commonwealth forces back into Singapore. The Japanese *25th Army*, under the command of General Tomoyuki Yamashita, stood on the shores of Johor, looking across at Singapore Island a short distance away. To the north, the Japanese had launched attacks into southern Burma, capturing the city of Moulmein on January 31st —the same day British forces withdrew into Singapore—and were threatening Rangoon. While American and Philippine troops under General MacArthur were still holding out on Bataan, at this point, there was no hope of reinforcement; the Philippines had been lost. The Japanese occupation of Balikpapan and Kendari placed them in a position to directly threaten Java. After seizing the towns and moving their naval air units to the airfields, the Japanese paused in their advance. Their next move was to seize the island of Amboina, east of the Celebes, to give themselves another base for attacks on Java and Timor. Wavell's only hope of slowing the Japanese advance was to achieve air superiority over the area.[76] This depended critically on the ability to bring in more fighter planes from Australia over the air route to Java, a flight of more than 1,200 miles. The Far East Air Force had brought the 17th Pursuit Squadron (Provisional) with its P-40s to Java during January for the defense of Eastern Java.[77] More fighters were on the way, but it would take time to build up the island's air defenses to anything approaching adequacy, and the Japanese were not going to give the Allies time.

A photo from a contemporary Japanese magazine showing Japanese ground crew waving off an A6M2 pilot on his next mission. (Via the author)

On February 3rd and 5th, the Japanese launched an "air annihilation campaign" against the airfields in Eastern Java and the Dutch naval base at Soerabaja.[78] With drop tanks, the A6M2 Zero fighters of the *3rd* and *Tainan Kokutai*, based at Balikpapan, could accompany the Navy's G3M and G4M bombers based at Kendari to Eastern Java. On February 3rd, the A6M2s set off from Balikpapan to rendezvous with the bombers from three of the bomber *Kokutai* flying from Kendari to targets on Java. The *Takao Kokutai* sent 26 G3Ms to the naval base at Soerabaja, while 27 G3Ms from the *Kanoya Kokutai* headed to the airfield at Madioen and 19 G3Ms from the *1st Kokutai* to Singosari, near Malang.[79] The fighter *kokutai* split the escort: 27 A6M2s from the *3rd Kokutai* going to Soerabaja and Madioen, while 17 A6M2s from the *Tainan Kokutai* went to Singosari.[80] The Japanese bombers arrived over the naval base a little after 1000. A small force of seven Dutch Hawk 75As and twelve CW-21Bs, with six P-40Es from the 17th Pursuit Squadron, took off to intercept this force. The CW-21Bs claimed three of the *3rd Kokutai* A6M2s, but lost seven of their own airplanes in the process, while the Hawk 75As claimed a probable bomber and several damaged for the loss of five of their own airplanes; the P-40s claimed one bomber and one Zero for the loss of one P-40.[81] At Singosari, the air raid alarm sounded at 1015. The airfield was defenseless, with no anti-aircraft guns to protect it. At 1040, nine A6M2 Zeros appeared overhead, misidentified as "Type 97 Dive Bombers". The Zeros began strafing the field five minutes later. The bombers arrived at 1100 and began their attack. Three of the 19th Bombardment Group B-17s—two B-17Ds and a single B-17E—were destroyed in the attack; two loaded with bombs exploded within five minutes of each other and a third was set on fire. A fourth bomber, a B-17E damaged in the attack, burst into flames the next day and was completely destroyed. Worse, Lt. Cox, who had taken off in a B-17C on a local test flight, ran into the Zeros and was shot down ten miles south of the airfield with the loss of the crew.[82]

That morning, the 7th Group had sent out its first mission from Jogjakarta, the largest mission the Group had launched to date with nine airplanes (the crews were Hobson, Habberstad, Strother, Bleasdale, Sargent, Northcutt, Swanson, Preston, and DuFrane) under the command of Maj. Hobson, heading for Balikpapan. The target was a convoy off Balikpapan. Once again, weather interfered with the bombing. On this occasion, the bombers came in at high altitude, bombing from 30,000 feet, probably to reduce their chances of interception from the Zeros based at the nearby airfield. On the way back to Java they ran into the *Tainan Kokutai*'s formation of A6M2s returning from the mission to Singosari.[83] Two of the Zero fighters broke off to attack the B-17 formation, the bombers claiming two fighters shot down in the brief combat. An engine on Lt. Swanson's airplane was apparently hit during the fight, as it caught fire about an hour after leaving the target area. Five of the crew bailed out, but Swanson made a wheels-up landing on a beach on Arendis Island, southeast of Borneo. The eight aircraft that returned carried two wounded and a third man who died from oxygen complications. DuFrane and Strother landed at Soerabaja on their return, but the other airplanes flew on to Jogjakarta, where they learned that Japanese fighters had shot down Maj. Straubel in a B-18 he was flying to Soerabaja on his way to a conference. All on board died in the crash or from severe burns. Maj. Hobson replaced him as group commander, the 7th Group's third C.O. in six days. At the end of the day, the Far East Air Force had eight B-17s and one LB-30 available for combat.[84]

The 7th Group did not fly another bombing mission until February 8th. On February 4th, Lts. Wade and Crowder flew two LB-30s from Darwin to Mindanao, returning to Darwin and then on to Malang on February 7th with 21 officers and men from the 19th Bombardment Group stranded at Del Monte. The 19th Group took off on a mission to Balikpapan February 5th, but ran into a formation of Zeros and abandoned the mission after the upper turrets on two of the aircraft failed to operate and one airplane had its oxygen system shot out. To their intense frustration, the next day (February 6th), the crews of the 7th Group took nine B-17s off from Jogjakarta to avoid a possible air raid on the field and spent six hours droning back and forth over the sea south of Java. Having lost six bombers on February 4th, V Bomber Command received more reinforcements from the United States in the following few days: two more LB-30s flown across the Pacific route by Lts. Paul Cool and Elbert Helton for the 11th Bombardment Squadron and five B-17s that flew over the Atlantic route: three for the 7th Group (Capt. F.M. Harrison and Lts. William Prichard and R.H. Beck) and two for the 19th Group. The 19th Group flew a mixed bombing and reconnaissance mission February 7th, searching for an aircraft carrier reported to be southeast of Makassar without success. The next day, February 8th, became known as "Black Sunday" among some members of the 7th Group and V Bomber Command.[85]

For the pilots of the *3rd* and *Tainan Kokutai*, the stout B-17 Flying Fortresses they encountered during the early months of the war proved to be difficult enemies, strongly built with good fire power, especially to the rear quarter, providing good protection. Above all, the B-17s proved exceedingly difficult to shoot down. One of the Navy fighter pilots who worked hard to develop the tactics needed to combat the B-17s was Petty Officer 1st Class Kandiyohi Tanaka of the *Tainan Kokutai*. An experienced fighter pilot who claimed 12 victories in the air war in China, Tanaka joined the Air Group in October 1941 and participated in the fighting over the Philippines and in the Netherlands East Indies, where he encountered the B-17s for the first time over Balikpapan.[86] January 24, 1942, P.O. Tanaka was part of a flight that intercepted the mixed 7th and 19th Group B-17 formation Maj. Robinson was leading to bomb shipping in the Makassar Strait. Tanaka and his fellow pilots spent 20 minutes attacking the B-17s in repeated passes from above, without success. Tanaka himself fired numerous bursts into one airplane without inflicting any apparent damage. On his seventh pass he saw the bomber shake slightly and then fall on another airplane in the formation, sending both into the sea, though on that day neither the 7th nor the 19th Group lost any B-17s (in turn, the B-17 crews claimed five fighters shot down, when in fact none were lost). On landing, Tanaka was surprised to find that his own Zero fighter had been hit thirteen times. Ten days later, Tanaka was apparently one of the *Tainan Kokutai* pilots who strafed the 19th Group B-17s at Singosari. Making a pass at a B-17 from the front, he was astonished to see the big bomber burst into flames. It occurred to him that the way to destroy a B-17 was through a frontal attack, avoiding the firepower from the rear quarter.[87] This realization no doubt came to other pilots at the time who must have seen or experienced the single .30 caliber machine gun in the nose of the B-17E provided for attacks from the front quarter. The first test of this new tactic came February 5th against the 19th Group's mission that day to Balikpapan. Eight Zeros from the *Tainan Kokutai*'s *2nd Chutai* encountered the American formation east of Soerabaja on their way to attack the naval base while the B-17s were climbing for altitude.[88] Instead of making the usual stern attacks, the Zeros flew alongside the B-17s, out of range, then began making individual frontal attacks, avoiding all attacks from the rear.[89] On this occasion, the 19th Group was lucky and lost no airplanes. On the February 8th mission, the 7th Group's luck ran out.

A formation of B-17s heads out for on a mission during the Java campaign. The V Bomber Command rarely had more than nine aircraft operational. (Courtesy of Gerard Cassius)

The mission that day was to bomb the airfield at Kendari, the base for the Japanese Navy bombers attacking eastern Java. The 7th Group sent out nine B-17s from Singosari at 0735, with recently promoted Capt. John DuFrane leading the mission (a number of 7th Group senior Lieutenants were apparently promoted to Captain around this time, including Bleasdale, Strother, Bayse, and Crowther, among others). As they began their slow climb up to altitude, Bleasdale's airplane lost an engine and had to return to Singosari, leaving the other eight airplanes to continue on to Kendari. That same morning, Lt. Hideki Shingo led off nine A6M2s and one C5M (Petty Officer Tanaka was one of the pilots on the mission) from the *Tainan Kokutai*'s base at Balikpapan on a mission to strafe the Allied airfield at Denpassar on Bali, a transit point on the air route from Darwin to Java. The Japanese fighters ran into the bad weather typical of the season and abandoned the mission, Lt. Shingo apparently deciding to make a sweep over Soerabaja instead. On the way the fighters chanced upon the B-17 formation, then flying at 14,000 feet. According to one account, the Zeros paced the B-17s for a time while both formations climbed to 17,000 feet, separating into two flights to sandwich the B-17s between them. Using the lessons learned over the previous few days, the fighters began making coordinated attacks from the front quarter, at times with another fighter coming up from underneath simultaneously.

A photo of John DuFrane, Jr., who was killed leading the 7th Bombardment Group mission on February 8, 1942, when he was a 2nd Lieutenant with the 88th Reconnaissance Squadron. (From *The Bomber 1940*, via the author)

The Zero pilots pressed their attacks dangerously close to the B-17s, in one case clearing the wing of one B-17 by a mere 20 feet. DuFrane, possibly reacting to previous V Bomber Command criticism of formation leaders who deviated from their orders, kept the formation on course and took no evasive action, apart from closing up and climbing.[90]

On the fighter's second pass, the Zeros concentrated on DuFrane's lead B-17. The bomber burst into flame as the bomb bay tank ignited. The other pilots saw smoke coming from the bomb bay and then a mass of flame erupted. The plane continued to burn even after the tank was jettisoned. Six of the crew bailed out and the other combat crews saw the Zeros fire at the men in their parachutes. DuFrane's B-17 pulled away from the formation in a steep diving turn and exploded in mid-air. Capt. Donald Strother, also recently promoted, took over the lead, turning the formation to the right toward a cloudy area, maneuvering into the head-on attacks in the hopes of spoiling the Zeros' aim. Soon after, his airplane was hit in another frontal pass, a bullet exploding an oxygen tank and blowing out the hydraulic system and the bomb release mechanism. Capt. Preston's bomber was hit, setting the bomb bay tank on fire, but he jettisoned the tank and his bombs, avoiding an explosion. In another frontal attack, Lt. William Prichard's aircraft, flying a wing position in the second element of the formation, caught fire and spiraled down out of the formation, exploding soon after. One member of the crew bailed out. Prichard was on his first combat mission. The remaining six airplanes reached a cloud formation, where they lost the Zeros, remaining in formation until heavy rain and turbulence made it impossible. The airplanes staggered back to Java individually. Lt. Paul Lindsey's airplane was so badly damaged in the tail section that both Lindsey and his copilot had to hold the controls to hold the airplane steady. Flying into turbulence, the airplane went into a spin, with the navigator, copilot, and tail gunner all baling out. Lindsey stuck with his airplane and recovered control at 7,000 feet altitude. He returned to Singosari, having found his way without the benefit of a navigator, map, or his copilot. One airplane landed at another field due to weather over Singosari, but of the five that returned to the base, four had sustained damage in the combat. The crews claimed five Zeros shot down, though in fact only two were hit and damaged. The Zeros claimed two bombers shot down and three probables, credited jointly to all nine pilots, including P.O. Tanaka and another Petty Officer who would become one of the Imperial Navy's leading aces, Saburo Sakai.[91]

The mission of February 8th proved to be the costliest the V Bomber Command flew out of Java.[92] The command had been fortunate not to have lost any bombers on previous encounters with the Zero. The critique of the mission stated that it was "...the best executed attack so far encountered... Coordinated attacks from head-on and front quarters were the first attacks of this nature reported by friendly forces in this area," the attacks on the February 5th mission having been done individually.[93] The mission revealed weaknesses in the B-17's armament. The remote control Bendix belly turret that equipped the early versions of the B-17E proved completely ineffective. The high closing speeds between the B-17s and the Zeros was "...so great that the top turrets could not traverse fast enough to fire on the enemy during head-on attacks."[94] The single .30 caliber machine gun in the B-17E's nose was the only effective forward defense, and although the crews on the February 8th mission claimed two Zeros shot down with the nose guns, the crews had realized that one small caliber machine gun was effectively useless against a fighter armed with multiple machine guns and cannon at a closing speed of over 300mph. More critically, the report on the mission noted that at altitudes below 20,000 feet, the fighters held the advantage and could choose the method of attack; above 20,000 feet, this advantage was lessened and most attacks at that altitude had come from the rear and the sides, where the B-17's defensive armament was more effective.[95] Looking at the outcome of the mission—two bombers shot down and four more damaged, two severely, and the mission abandoned well short of the target—an astute observer might have questioned the Air Corps' core doctrine and underlying faith in unescorted, daylight precision bombing missions.

That night, Lts. John Dougherty, Richard Ezzard, Jerome Tartar, and Paul Cool took off from Jogjakarta between 2230 and 2300 on a mission in search of enemy shipping around Makassar, in the southern Celebes. Tartar had to return when he had trouble with his airplane's landing gear, but the others

Lt. William Prichard, formerly with the 88th Reconnaissance Squadron like John DuFrane, was killed on February 8, 1942, on his first combat mission. (From *The Bomber 1940*, via the author)

searched the area without success. On their return flight, two of the crews saw naval vessels off the south coast of Java, possibly including an aircraft carrier. A B-17 sent out on reconnaissance the next morning confirmed that these were friendly ships. While the rest of the Group stood down, most likely to make repairs on airplanes damaged in the mission of February 8th, the LB-30s went out on another night mission on February 9th, with Lts. Elbert Haltom, Murray Crowder, Jerome Tartar, and William Bayse going off after a Japanese aircraft carrier reported to be in the Makassar Strait, northeast of Tarakan, off the coast of Borneo. Tartar again had trouble with the gear on his airplane and had to return early, but the others flew on. Two dropped bombs and ran into heavy anti-aircraft fire, one of the airplanes receiving a hit on the propeller. For the next several nights, the LB-30s continued to bomb Japanese shipping, the targets getting closer and closer to Java.[96]

The reports coming in to the men of the 7th and 19th Groups was uniformly bad. On February 8th, the Japanese launched their invasion of Singapore, Great Britain's supposedly impregnable fortress. In the Netherlands East Indies they had resumed their advance, capturing Makassar, in the southern Celebes, on February 9th and occupying Bandjermasin, on the south coast of Borneo, after an overland march February 10th. Within a week, the 3rd and *Tainan Kokutai* would move their A6M2s up to these forward air bases. Although bad weather over Eastern Java prevented any major raids, there were now almost daily air raid alarms at Jogjakarta. The combat crews went on alert each day at 0530, and on some days had to take their bombers away from the field in case of an enemy raid, adding to the strain. The 7th Group used Jogjakarta, Malang, and Madioen as bases, shuttling men and supplies between them. Missions continued, new crews arriving with replacement aircraft hurriedly thrown into combat within a few days. Between February 9th and 12th, six crews arrived and were assigned to the 7th Group. These were Lt. H.C. Smelzer, Lt. R.W. Evans, 2nd Lt. Richard Taylor, Lt. Clarence McCauley, Capt. C.A. Beran, and Lt. Harry Markey, who all brought in B-17Es over the Atlantic route.[97]

On February 10th, Capt. Strother led six B-17s from Jogjakarta to attack an aircraft carrier still reported in the Makassar Strait. Bad weather and insufficient fuel ended the mission. Three of the planes developed mechanical problems and the rest, who had already taken off, wasted too much fuel waiting for them. The next day, February 11th, the combat and maintenance crews were told they would be given 24 hours off from 1400 until 1430 for some badly needed rest, but then the 7th Group was notified to send what airplanes it had in commission to Malang, where they would be attached to the 19th Group for a mission February 12th. That night, Lts. Horace Wade and Richard Ezzard took off at 2235 and 2245 to search for and attack shipping off Makassar. Early the next morning, on one of the largest raids the V Bomber Command mounted out of Java, eight B-17s from the 7th Group (Capt. Strother led Capt. Hardison and Lts. Beck, Habberstad, Northcutt, and Swanson) with three from the 19th went out to bomb shipping in and around Makassar, taking off between 0030 and 0220. One flight, with Lt. Northcutt, Capt. Hardison, and Capt. F.M. Key from the 19th Group, claimed hits on a transport, but weather and darkness in the target area obscured the result. A few hours after the flight returned, Capt. Strother was found dead behind his quarters, having committed suicide with his .45 pistol.[98]

Strother's death had "a profoundly depressing effect" on the men at all the bases.[99] Strother had been a flight leader, promoted for his abilities, with eight missions to his credit. Physical exhaustion from the constant effort, frustration with the lack of spare parts and adequate personnel, missions frustrated or cancelled by bad weather, and the growing realization that all their efforts were having no effect on the Japanese increasingly demoralized the 7th and 19th Groups.[100] No doubt the fact that the 7th Group had lost two commanders in the space of a week had an impact. For pilots who had spent several years practicing and absorbing a belief in strategic bombing, "their conception of the strategic role of heavy bombardment was violated by the almost impromptu fashion in which the B-17s were employed."[101] At this low point, news reached the men that Singapore had surrendered.

The Japanese had not waited for Singapore's fall to make their next leap to Sumatra, their objective the vital oil fields at Palembang and its nearby airfield, P.1. Once captured,

Sumatra would be a base for an attack on Java from the West, part of the Japanese plan for a gigantic double envelopment. The loss of the airfields on Sumatra would be a blow to V Bomber Command, for then no more B-17s could fly to Java from India. On February 9th, a convoy of eight Japanese transport ships carrying part of an invasion force left French Indochina with their naval escort, followed by the main force in 13 transports two days later. News of these movements came just as the 7th Group was relocating to Jogjakarta from other bases on Java. On February 12th, four B-17s left Malang that morning for Jogjakarta, with the 7th Group headquarters and maintenance crews following. That night, after receiving reports of the Japanese convoy's possible location, V Bomber Command sent off three LB-30s—Lts. John Dougherty, Paul Cool, and Arthur Fletcher, now piloting his own airplane after serving as a copilot—to find and attack the convoy. The Japanese advance down the South China Sea was hidden under a weather front. The LB-30s returned to Jogjakarta, having been unable to locate their target. The morning of February 14th, V Bomber Command sent out a maximum effort—14 B-17s from its two bombardment groups—in the hope of catching the convoy at dawn. Eight B-17s from the 7th Group left Jogjakarta at 0215, followed by six from the 19th Group an hour later. They failed to see any sign of the convoy

A Japanese convoy carrying troops and supplies to the Southern front. Japanese shipping was the 7th Bombardment Group's primary target during the Java campaign. (Author's collection)

in the designated area, reported to be near the island of Banka, off the southeastern coast of Sumatra, and returned to their airfields. The planes were refueled and the crews were ordered to stand by. That morning, the Japanese began dropping several companies of paratroopers at points nearby Palembang, in the hope of seizing the airfields and the oil installations intact. The lead elements of the main Japanese invasion force were scheduled to arrive the following day, moving up the Moesi River to Palembang.[102]

For the next four days, V Bomber Command sent out every available airplane to disrupt the invasion force, only to have weather interfere with nearly every mission. On February 15th, the day after the paratroop landings, Capts. Basye and Crowther, with Lt. Markey (on his first combat mission) took off in three LB-30s from Jogjakarta between 0200 and 0215 to bomb enemy shipping off Palembang. After an hour and a half of flying on instruments, they abandoned the mission. A few hours later, five 19th Group B-17s took off from Malang at 0620 and found a convoy off the coast of Sumatra through the clouds. Bombing from 28,000 feet, the flight claimed hits on an auxiliary vessel and a cruiser, despite bombs hanging up on two of the bombers. Later in the morning, Capt. Bleasdale led off two other B-17s flown by Lts. Beck and Smelser to the same target, but had to abandon the mission when weather again interfered, making it impossible to fly in formation. That evening, Lt. Gen. Arthur Percival surrendered Singapore to General Tomouki Yamashita and his forces, the largest capitulation in British military history. This shocking development permanently damaged British prestige in the region. Over 130,000 Australian, British, and Indian troops went into captivity. News of Singapore's surrender probably filtered to the men of V Bomber Command during the next day, February 16th. Both groups went back to Palembang, the 19th Group running into the same front that had now covered the area for several days. The aircraft got to within 75 miles of the target area when the weather forced them back. The 7th Group had better luck and one of its best missions. Four B-17s took off from Jogjakarta and three from Madioen. Capt. R.E, Northcut led the formation, with Capt. Hardison, Lts. Beck, Schmid, and Lindsey, 2nd Lts. Magee and Snitkin, and Capt. Keiser from the 19th Group. The two formations rendezvoused and flew on to Palembang below the weather at a ceiling between 2,000 and 4,000 feet. Lindsey had to turn back when he lost an engine, but the others pressed on. After five hours, the formation arrived off the mouth of the Moesi River, where the sun finally broke through. The B-17s came in over part of the invasion force unloading troops and supplies off transports onto barges to head up the river. Despite light anti-aircraft fire that holed a few bombers, the B-17s attacked two transports, claiming both as sunk, then returned to strafe the troops on the barges. The formation returned to Batavia, the capital of Java, to refuel before flying back to Jogjakarta and Madioen. The 19th Group tried again the next day, only to be turned back once more by the weather. Eight P-40s did manage to get through the weather to bomb and strafe barges on the Moesi River. The bombardment groups tried again February 18th, the 7th sending out four B-17s from Madioen and the 19th sending out six from Malang, but both formations had to turn back because of bad weather, running into thunderstorms and ground fog in the target area. A few hours after the 7th

Group bombers returned to Madioen the Japanese raided the field. Three bombers got off in time, leaving two in hangars, where Japanese fighters strafed them, fortunately doing only minor damage.[103]

Maj. Gen. Brereton flew to Malang the afternoon of February 17th with Air Marshal Sir Richard Peirse to present awards to the two bombardment groups. As Brereton noted in his diary, many of the awards he read out to the men assembled in one of Malang's hangars under a deafening rain were posthumous, for men killed in the Philippines.[104] The next morning, before returning to ABDA headquarters at Bandoeng, Brereton had a sobering discussion with Maj. Morocco, V Bomber Command's senior flight surgeon. As Brereton recorded in his diary, Morocco's report "...was very discouraging. Combat replacement crews did not exist. Reinforcing aircraft contained only skeleton navigating crews. Fatigue and combat weariness had worn the men to their last ounce of resistance. Pilots returned from attacks crying with rage and frustration when a crewmember was killed or when weather or mechanical failures prevented successful completion of the mission. A flight commander, a fine leader, committed suicide. Boys were on the verge of mental and physical collapse. I felt I had every reason to be thankful that I would not be called upon to ask much more of them."[105]

B-17E 41-2488 burning after the Japanese attack on Singosari air field near Malang, Java, on February 20, 1942, one of five B-17s the Far East Air Force lost on that date. (7th Bombardment Group (H) Historical Foundation, USAFA McDermott Library)

Brereton knew the end in Java was near. The men of V Bomber Command had but two weeks left on the island. After the fall of Singapore, General Wavell realized the Japanese were likely to invade Java before the end of the month and that "...the successful defense of Java with the resources available and in sight was extremely doubtful..."[106] He recommended to the Combined Chiefs of Staff in London and Washington that an Australian Corps from the Middle East be diverted to either Burma or Australia, both vital to the continued prosecution of the war against Japan, and that a force of heavy bombers should be built up in Burma as soon as possible.[107] Having completed the capture of Palembang in two days, the Japanese wasted no time moving on to their next objectives: the islands of Bali and Timor, to the east of Java. On February 18th, a force of two transports with four destroyers as escort sailed out of Makassar for Bali, landing a small force on the island that evening. Three B-17s from the 19th Group took off at 0500 the next morning to strike the convoy, running into two Zeros from the *Tainan Kokutai* patrolling overhead, which attacked without effect. Lt. Mathewson bombed what he took to be a cruiser, claiming two hits. Four more B-17s took off from Malang an hour later, followed by two more around mid-day. In a break with previous practice, the 7th Group's LB-30s were thrown into the attack in daylight, the 11th Squadron sending out three of its LB-30 bombers from Jogjakarta with Capt. Helton, Capt. Tartar, and Lt. Cool to bomb shipping off Bali. The flight ran into a group of nine Zeros from the *Tainan Kokutai*. In the ensuing combat two bombers were damaged, forcing the flight to abandon the mission. Back at Jogjakarta, these two aircraft were deemed out of commission. Two B-17s assigned to the 9th Squadron, based at Madioen, also took off that morning for Bali and claimed hits on a cruiser while fighting off two Zeros. Lt. Harold Smelser joined Lt. Skiles on the mission, encountering the vaunted Zero for the first time, as he recalled in an interview later in the war:

> My first engagement with the enemy was at Bali, during a landing which was being made there. Six aircraft took off from Madioen to bomb the ports south of the island of Bali, but before we were away from Java, four had to return. Skiles and myself proceeded across the north of Bali at 15,000 feet due to the high clouds. [We] went around the east side of Bali and attacked from the East. On approaching the targets, we noticed one large boat, which we identified as a cruiser, in the middle of the Strait between Bali and the small islands south of Bali, and a small group of transports several miles away. At this time we saw no enemy aircraft and decided to divide to attack both targets.
>
> As I started my run on the cruiser, Lt. Skiles said on the radio "Look out! Here they come!" I looked up and saw the first of the Zero fighters coming head on. I realized that my bombs would be away in about 10 seconds and so took no evasive action until the light indicated that my bombs were falling. I then headed directly into the ships that were attacking me and ran to the clouds as fast as I could do so, diving head-on into each ship as it made its attack. I reached cloud cover in about two minutes (it seemed like ten years)

and rejoined Lt. Skiles. We proceeded through the clouds to our base and reported...Shortly after landing, we took off again because of a local air raid and finally returned when our gas was low."[108]

Waist gun positions on an LB-30. The gunners were named Fraley (left) and Terry, from the 11th Bombardment Squadron. (7th Bombardment Group (H) Historical Foundation, USAFA McDermott Library)

Lt. Kenneth Casper had been scheduled to join the 9th Squadron's mission to Bali, but his B-17 lost an engine warming up. The airplane was still on the airfield when the air raid alarm sounded. Casper and his crew ran to their airplane, apparently taking off on the three working engines to avoid the enemy attack. Since his airplane seemed to be handling without difficulty and was fully loaded with bombs, Casper decided that instead of simply cruising off the south coast of Java, he would head over to Bali, where he bombed a destroyer from 28,000 feet, claiming hits alongside.[109]

By this point in the campaign, with the bombers risking an engagement with Zero fighters on nearly every daylight mission, the crews had begun to make their own jury-rigged modifications to increase the B-17E's armament, particularly in the nose compartment, to deal with the Zero pilots' new tactic of head-on attacks. The nose of the B-17E contained four ball socket gun ports in the glass sections of the nose and on the side of the fuselage to allow the operator of the single .30 caliber machine gun to move the weapon from gun port to gun port to get a better angle on an attacking fighter. The bomber crews on Java began adding more .30 caliber guns in the nose, adding as many as six by using every gun port available. For even more fire power, some crews added a heavier .50 caliber machine gun pointed through the open ventilator window on the lower right side of the nose, tied in place with rope. When the B-17Es arrived in Java, they brought with them 25 and 50 round cans of .50 caliber ammunition for the two waist gun positions. These cans were completely inadequate for combat, having too little ammunition and imposing a dangerous burden on the gunners, who might have to stop in the middle of a fighter attack to replace an empty can. As a temporary expedient, many gunners simply left a can attached to their gun with the bottom removed to allow a complete belt of ammunition to feed into the gun. The Bendix remote control belly turret in the bottom of the fuselage behind the bomb bay proved to be completely useless. A gunner simply could not track a fast fighter through the remote sight. In the face of head-on attacks, many crews loaded the Bendix turret with tracer ammunition, pointed the guns forward toward the nose, and used a string to fire them whenever a Zero attacked. The crews found, however, that often the best defense against a head-on attack was to dive straight at the attacking fighter to throw off his attack. With the small formations the squadrons were flying this was practical, particularly as the B-17 proved to be more maneuverable than the pilots had expected. The pilots had learned to vary the formations they had practiced so often in peace time. The standard V-formation of three bombers, with the two wingmen flying at a 45 degree angle back from the leader, had to be altered in combat, as it blocked out the lead ship's line of fire. The crews flattened out the V until the airplanes were flying almost abreast of each other. The squadrons also found that the most effective defensive formation consisted of six airplanes using a Javalin Down formation. This gave the flight the ability to maneuver against enemy fighter attacks and still maintain cohesiveness. It brought the maximum number of guns to bear against the attack.[110]

In the afternoon, Japanese Army Air Force units brought forward to the Palembang airfields launched a raid on Bandoeng, with 28 Nakajima Ki-43 Type 1 Fighters from the *59th* and *64th Fighter Sentais* escorting nine Kawasaki Ki-48 Type 99 Light Bombers to the target. The Japanese aircraft destroyed two B-17s that had arrived that day from India: one on the airfield and one shot down in the air. A third newly-arrived B-17 was so badly damaged it was stripped for spare parts. These were the last B-17s to arrive in Java for the Far East Air Force. To add to the depressing news that day, Japanese carrier planes from the *Hiryu* and *Soryu* carried out a devastating raid on Darwin, Australia, followed later in the day by aircraft from the *21st Kōkū Sentai*. The attack sank ten ships and damaged another 25, destroying 23 airplanes in the air and on the ground.[111] That same day, February 19th, Maj. Gen. Brereton attended a conference with General Wavell, General George Brett, Deputy Commander of ABDA, and Air Marshal Sir Richard Peirse, ABDA-Air. Brereton told Wavell that "...the combat efficiency of the Bomber Command had been taxed beyond endurance...," and that he had decided to withdraw the American Air Forces in Java, as he viewed any further operations as not in the best interests of the United

States.[112] Brett and Pierce concurred with Brereton's decision. Wavell had hoped that the air forces could hold out for another two weeks, just to delay the Japanese that much longer. With Brett and Peirse in agreement with Brereton, Wavell acquiesced, asking only that Brereton delay for 48 hours to allow Wavell to consult with the Combined Chiefs of Staff, not just about the evacuation of the Far East Air Force, but the entire ABDA command.[113]

The hammer blows kept falling. The day after the raid on Darwin, V Bomber Command launched more raids on the Japanese force off Bali with the 13 bombers it had available: at Malang, seven B-17s; and at Madioen, three B-17s and three L-30s.[114] At 0645, Capt. Horace Wade led two other 11th Squadron pilots (Lts. Arthur Fletcher and Richard Hernlund) on another daylight mission to Bali in their LB-30s. Hernlund had been Maj. Straubel's copilot on the flight from the United States that must have seemed like ages before. For the first time since their arrival in Java, the bombers had some accompanying fighters: 15 P-40s who were escorting seven A-24s from the recently-arrived 91st Bombardment Squadron. The LB-30s claimed three direct hits on a cruiser and eight waterline hits, though no Japanese warship was sunk that day. Two hours later, Capt. Hardison led two other B-17s from the 9th Squadron to Bali, bombing a large transport that they claimed to have sunk. The 19th Group was active as well, sending out seven B-17s to Bali in the morning. In response, the *Tainan Kokutai*, quickly brought up to the airfield on Bali, sent out nine A6M2 Zeros to strafe the airfield at Malang, catching the 19th Group's B-17s on the ground shortly after they had landed. Keeping five fighters above as protection, four of the Zeros dove down to strafe the field, setting five of the bombers on fire. Three burned out completely, but while the ground crews extinguished the fires on the other two airplanes, they were so badly damaged they could only be used for spare parts.[115] During the day, Japanese troops landed at Kupang and Dili, on the island of Timor, followed by a paratroop drop on the airfield. By capturing Bali and Timor, the Japanese had cut the air route between Australia and Java. This eliminated the Far East Air Force's ability to bring in more P-40s for its now beleaguered fighter squadrons, or the A-24 dive bombers that might have been effective against the Japanese transports anchored off shore had the A-24s been available in adequate numbers. With Japanese fighters now based on Bali—around 430 air miles from Jogjakarta, and well within the range of an A6M2 with a drop tank—no Allied airfield in Eastern Java was safe from attack.

A Mitsubishi A6M2 *Rei-sen* (Zero) fighter from the 22nd *Kokutai* at a field in Malaya in early 1942. (P000618_001--1, Australian War Memorial)

Missions continued even as the Far East Air Forces began to make preparations for the evacuation of Java. The objectives for the next few days were Japanese shipping off Bali and the airport at Denpasar, where the Japanese had based their fighters and bombers. First to depart on February 21st were two LB-30s. Lts. Ezzard and Hughey took off from Jogjakarta around 0235 for Bali, but apparently couldn't locate any ships, so they dropped their bombs on a tent camp and the Denpasar airport. Seven Zeros from the *Tainan Kokutai* were scrambled to intercept the bombers, but could not catch them before they got away. Six B-17s from the 19th Group were next. As an indication of the difficulties both groups were having in maintaining their airplanes without adequate spare parts or maintenance personnel, soon after take-off one airplane lost two engines, another had a fire in the bottom turret, and a third bomber had its generator and electrical system go out. In the fourth bomber, a gunner passed out from lack of oxygen, leaving two B-17s to complete the mission. The two bombers climbed to 27,000 feet before approaching Bali, but couldn't find the airport from that altitude. The 9th Squadron sent off three B-17s with Lt. Swanson leading to attack either shipping or the Denpasar airport. Failing to see any ships, the flight bombed the airport from 26,000 feet, but clouds over the target obscured any results. During the day, Zeros from the *Tainan Kokutai* strafed the airfield at Malang in the morning, claiming three small aircraft destroyed, while later in the morning, Zeros from the *3rd Kokutai*, after completing an escort mission, returned to Malang, claiming a B-17 destroyed, though none were lost on this date. One of these formations also strafed Madioen, but failed to inflict significant damage. The next day, the 11th Squadron was not so lucky. Early on the morning of February 22nd, six Zeros from the *Tainan Kokutai* and three from the *3rd Kokutai* went out from Bali to strafe the airfield at Jogjakarta. The 11th Squadron had one LB-30 on the airfield (AL 576). This airplane was destroyed along with four Dutch CW-22 training airplanes; the Dutch had several Martin bombers damaged in the attack. During the day, the 19th Group lost four of its remaining B-17Ds when the *Tainan Kokutai*'s Zeros attacked the small airfield at

Pasirian, south of Malang, where the bombers had been sent for protection.[116] The air attacks on Bali had failed to have any real impact on the Japanese, who could now attack the Far East Air Force's airfields at will. Without adequate air defense—problematical now that the only air route to Java for the P-40s had been cut off—American high command in the region and in Washington had come to realize there was little point in bringing in more heavy bombers for V Bomber Command. A desperate attempt to deliver more P-40s by sea failed five days later when the USS *Langley*, carrying 36 P-40s, was sunk off the coast of Java.[117]

That same day, Maj. Gen. Brereton heard from General George Marshall, Army Chief of Staff, approving the withdrawal of the Far East Air Force to a place and at a time of Brereton's choosing.[118] Later Marshall sent additional instructions to insure that all air personnel and technicians "who cannot contribute to the defense of Java" be withdrawn, basically giving Brereton *carte blanche* to remove everyone he could to Australia.[119] In expectation of receiving Marshall's concurrence, Brereton had already instructed Col. Eubank to continue operations as long as an effective force existed, but to begin evacuating those officers, men, and aircraft not needed to sustain missions.[120] At the same time, General Wavell had decided to dissolve ABDA Command. Told that Burma was being withdrawn from his command and with control reverting to India in view of the Japanese invasion, Wavell pointed out to the Combined Chiefs that "...there was practically nothing left to command in the ABDA area."[121] With the agreement of the Combined Chiefs, Wavell held his last conference of the ABDA Command on February 23rd, where he informed his staff of his decision to dissolve his command on February 25th and return responsibility for the defense of Java to the Dutch Commanders-in-Chief. General Brett flew back to Australia the morning of February 23rd to take command of U.S. forces there. Brereton left the next day. Having suffered two defeats in the Philippines and in Java in a matter of a few months, Brereton wanted to go where he could start building up a force for an eventual assault on Japan. He and Brett believed the best place to do this was in Burma and China.[122] As he wrote in his diary: "...I was glad to leave. Everyone realized that it was a completely hopeless task to defend Java. My desire for some time had been to give the Japs territory and get back where we could reorganize the striking force, and I didn't care whether it was India or Australia. Brett gave me my choice and I picked India, maybe because I was sick of islands, even one as big as Australia."[123] That night, February 24th, Brereton left Java in an LB-30 with Capt. Murray Crowder as pilot and flew to Ceylon. Brereton took with him a small group of officers he wanted to use as the nucleus of the new air force he planned to build in India. From the bombardment groups he selected Lt. Col. Emmett O'Donnell, Far East Air Force Operations officer; Maj. Cecil Combs, commander of the 19th Bombardment Group, and Capts. Elmer Parsel, Donald Keiser, Earl Tash, and George Schaetzel; and from the 7th Bombardment Group Maj. Conrad Necrason and Capts. William Bayse and Horace Wade.[124] Some of these men flew out with Brereton and others flew to India over the next few days on other LB-30s. The next evening, Wade flew out General Wavell and several senior members of his staff. Brereton left Col. Eubank on Java to arrange the evacuation of all the remaining members of the Far East Air Force.

As preparations got underway, the 9th Squadron sent out two B-17s the morning of February 23rd to bomb Denpasar airport. Capt. Preston and Lt. Lewis (a third B-17 aborted the mission with engine problems) bombed from 27,000 feet by dead reckoning, as cloud obscured the target. While the missions continued, the evacuation started February 24th, when Capt. Hoevet of the 19th Group flew from Malang to Broome, Australia—chosen as the initial terminus—with the first batch of personnel. In Western Java, the Royal Air Force had evacuated to Java from Singapore and Palembang. The RAF was fighting off Japanese Army Air Force raids launched from the airfields on Sumatra, which the Japanese had just captured. A bombing raid on Bandoeng, in Java, destroyed two more B-17Es at the depot at Andir; a third B-17 used for spare parts was also destroyed. In Eastern Java, a PBY of PatWing 10 had gotten off a radio report of a large Japanese convoy off Makassar before being shot down. Six B-17s from

B-17Es burning at Andir aerodrome near Bandoeng, Java, on February 24, 1942. (via Gerry Cassius)

the 9th Squadron (Habberstad, Beck, and Smelser in "A" Flight and Hardison, Swanson, and Beran in "B" Flight) took off from Madioen and arrived over the area around 1100, seeing seven large transports and two smaller ones. The formation dropped 48 300-kg bombs from 27,000 feet and claimed two transports sunk. Early the next day, February 25th, while the LB-30s of the 11th Squadron stood down, the 9th sent off five

B-17s to bomb Bali. Mechanical problems and the pre-dawn darkness prevented three of the airplanes from joining up, but Lt. Kenneth Casper continued on with Capt. Preston. On the way Preston had an engine burst into flames. He put out the fire, but had to return to base. Casper went on alone, his second solo bombing mission over Bali. Coming in at 26,000 feet, the bombardier pressed the bomb release, only to have the bombs hang up for an instant because of frozen bomb racks; this caused them to fall beyond the target, doing no damage.[125]

Three men from the 11th Bombardment Squadron who escaped from Java to Australia (left to right): T.J. Stewart, C.R. Olsen, and J.H. Lindgren. (7th Bombardment Group (H) Historical Foundation, USAFA McDermott Library)

Before dawn on the morning of February 25th, two 19th Group B-17s took off to ferry personnel to Broome. That night, while Capt. Horace Wade flew out General Wavell, Lt. Richard Ezzard flew more men and equipment to Broome. For the next four days, the B-17s and LB-30s shuttled back and forth to Broome, ferrying personnel. Col. Eubank had told the men based at Malang that they would all be evacuated to Australia, the ground crews primarily by boat and the combat crews with their airplanes. In the afternoon of February 25th, the entire ground echelon of the 19th Group and some combat crews arrived at Jogjakarta to prepare for evacuation, while others waited at Malang for the bombers. The men of the 22nd Squadron had arrived an hour earlier, and 30 men and 15 officers from the 17th Pursuit Squadron before them, presenting the staff on the field with a problem of housing and feeding so many men. Eubank had arranged for a Dutch transport ship, the *Abbekerk*, to take his units to Australia out of the port of Tjilatjap, on the south coast of Java. The men reached the port in a large truck convoy and by train, including the ground echelons of the 11th and 22nd Squadrons. This left only a bare minimum of ground crews at Jogjakarta, Malang, and Madioen to service the remaining bombers. The *Abbekerk* set sail February 27th or 28th, undertaking a nerve-wracking solo voyage to Australia. The knowledge that Japanese bombers had just sunk the *Langley* and other ships in these same waters did not inspire confidence about the ship's chances, nor did an encounter with a Japanese reconnaissance plane that made several passes. Sick with fear, the men on board had a desperate wait until nightfall. To their great relief, the men arrived safely at Freemantle, on Australia's west coast, where they disembarked and transferred to an Australian camp 60 miles from Perth.[126]

The men left temporarily behind continued to service the aircraft and fly missions, though they knew the end of their time in Java was near at hand. With only a few ground crews left, the combat crews again had to service their own aircraft, grabbing a meal and some rest whenever they could. Word soon arrived that the Japanese invasion force they had long expected was on its way. The Japanese ships reported off Makassar on February 25th were part of the invasion force heading toward Java. The Japanese had organized two forces: a *Western Force* that set sail from Camranh Bay, in French Indochina, with 58 transports and an escort of cruisers and destroyers toward the west coast of Java; and the *Eastern Force*, with 41 transports and naval escort destined for the eastern end of Java.[127] Following their strike on Darwin, Vice Admiral Nagumo's four aircraft carriers of the *1st Kōkū Kantai* were at Kendari to support the invasion. The ships the 9th Squadron had attacked on February 24th had been part of the *Eastern Force* assembling for the invasion. Reports that the invasion convoy was moving toward Java reached V Bomber Command headquarters late in the afternoon on February 26th. At 1700, the 9th Squadron sent off Capt. Hardison with Lt. Barr from Madioen to attack part of the convoy. The two crews reported 18 ships in the target area northeast of Bawean Island, more than a hundred miles north of Java, and bombed them from 21,000 feet, missing by 100 feet. Just after midnight, at 0035 on February 27th, Capt. Dougherty took one of the 11th Squadron's LB-30s not being used to evacuate personnel to Australia and searched north of the Java coast for Japanese convoys. Finding nothing, Dougherty returned to Jogjakarta shortly after dawn. Four 19th Group B-17s took off shortly after, three planes returning to Jogjakarta with engine problems. One pilot continued on and finding the convoy of five large ships and smaller vessels, bombed from 30,000 feet, clouds obscuring the result. The 9th Squadron sent off two more B-17s from Madioen at 0730. Lts. McPherson and Kenneth Casper found five ships and made two runs from 26,000 feet, striking close to a large vessel on the first run, a large transport or cruiser. Clouds obscured their second run. The crews saw a large convoy of 35 ships in the area before they left. That day, V Bomber Command moved its headquarters to Jogjakarta, where maintenance crews began destroying airplanes that were no longer serviceable: two older B-17Ds, two B-17Es, and a single LB-30 that had all been damaged beyond repair. That night Capt. Elbert Helton, who learned of his promotion to Captain earlier in the day, took an LB-30 to attack the airport at Denpasar, bombing by moonlight from 7,000 feet and reporting five hits. The evacuation of personnel at Jogjakarta continued, with an LB-30 and three B-17s leaving before dawn on the last day of February. V Bomber Command would stay in Java two more days.[128]

Early on the morning of February 28th—the penultimate day for the 7th Bombardment Group in Java—news arrived that the Japanese had inflicted a decisive defeat on an Allied naval force, sinking two cruisers and three destroyers. There was now nothing that could stop the Japanese invasion force landing on Java. Nevertheless, the 9th Squadron sent off three B-17s from Madioen at 0640 in a repeat attempt to bomb the convoys off the north coast of Java. Capt. Preston had to return when his guns wouldn't work, leaving Lt. Skiles and Lt. Evans to go on. They bombed two transports they found from an altitude of 26,000 feet, claiming one sunk and one damaged. Ominously, they saw a convoy containing 35 transports and 11 warships heading towards Java. To the astonishment of some of the American pilots, the Royal Air Force flew in eight Vickers Vildabeests (a large single-engine biplane torpedo bomber that had entered RAF service back in 1932) and a single Fairey Albacore (a Royal Navy biplane torpedo bomber)—all from No. 36 Squadron—to join V Bomber Command's last few heavy bombers attacking the approaching invasion convoy.[129] Late that night, one B-17E from the 19th Bombardment Group and one LB-30 from the 11th Squadron flown by Lt. Hughey took off from Jogjakarta and headed north for the Japanese convoy. From Madioen, the 9th Squadron sent off five B-17Es flown by Capts. Hardison and Smelser and Lts. Beck, Barr, and Bevan. All the planes flew to the area and attacked individually. Bevan claimed one transport destroyed and possibly another, while Hardison attacked one transport and also claimed it as sunk. After searching fruitlessly, Smelser came across the convoy by accident when tracers from the escorting naval vessels came shooting up at him. He climbed to 15,000 feet and there below him was the convoy, silhouetted in the moonlight. He recalled later that the convoy "...was the most perfect target I had ever seen, as they were lined up two abreast and barely a ship's length apart and were steaming directly into the moon, so that they were in the reflection in the water—and I was away from the moon and they were unable to pick me up...Heavy anti-aircraft fire from the four naval vessels was so wild that we proceeded undisturbed to drop a stick of eight 600-pound bombs directly down the middle of the convoy."[130] Smelser claimed to have sunk at least four transports, though once again, the Japanese recorded no losses that night. On his return, he was impressed with the "...three ancient biplanes flown by the British—who swore they got them from the Singapore Museum...Those three flew across the convoy at 500 feet, returned, landed, looked at the hundreds of machine gun holes in their wings, laughed like hell, got another drink of whiskey and went back. These boys were Australians who were flying for the RAF..."[131]

March 1, 1942, was the 7th Bombardment Group's last day on Java and the last day for the 19th Group, the Far East Air Force, and the remaining pilots and ground crews from the 17th Pursuit Group. That morning, the Japanese invasion force began landing on the north coast of Java and moving inland, adding to the tension of those American air and ground crews waiting for evacuation. After the airplanes returned to the field from the night mission, the pilots grabbed a few hours rest, then had to take off again and stay away from their airfields to make sure they weren't destroyed in an air attack. The 9th Squadron sent off one last mission out of Madioen. Lt. Kenneth Casper and Lt. McPherson took off at 0900 for one more attack on the Japanese invasion convoy north of Java. Once again Casper had engine trouble, but this time he decided to return to the field. McPherson continued on, bombing from 27,000 feet, claiming one transport destroyed and another transport hit along the waterline. He returned to Madioen at 1440 as preparations were underway to evacuate the field. Shortly before McPherson landed, the Dutch officers at Madioen and Jogjakarta received orders to blow up the airfields to deny their use to the Japanese. All serviceable airplanes were ordered to move to Malang; Col. Eubank refused and kept his few airplanes where they were.[132] That afternoon, ground crews at Jogjakarta started blowing up aircraft that had been damaged and could not be repaired: three LB-30s and two B-17Es went in flames and smoke. The

The 11th Bombardment Squadron's LB-30 aircraft, AL515, that escaped to Australia, the last LB-30 to leave Java. Note the .50 caliber machine gun fitted in the nose. (00025564, Courtesy San Diego Air & Space Museum)

A photograph taken from the Japanese aviation periodical *Koku Asahi* showing wrecked Army Air Force bombers at Jogjakarta after Java's fall to the Japanese. (via the author)

The burned out remains of LB-30 AL576 at Jogjakarta from *Koku Asahi*. (via the author)

funeral pyre happily served as a beacon for the men of the 17th Pursuit Group, who arrived at Jogjakarta in two trucks and several cars, not knowing where the airfield was located, though the sight of what they assumed was the means of their deliverance going up in flames was discouraging.[133] That evening, Lt. Harold Smelser and Lt. Richard Beck flew in two B-17Es from Madioen; three more B-17s and two LB-30s followed, flown by Lt. Murray Crowder and Capt. Elbert Helton.[134] Two B-17s apparently flew directly from Madioen to Broome. Lt. McPherson's B-17E had broken its tail wheel; without one the big bomber could not take off. Apparently there was no replacement available, so Master Sergeants Louis Silva and Walter Ashby supervised the hurried construction of a wooden tail skid made from 2 x 4 and 4 x 4 chunks of wood wrapped with cable.[135] The makeshift skid worked, getting the plane off from Madioen and down to a safe landing in Australia.

The airplanes leaving Jogjakarta were all overloaded. The bomb bays had planks inserted for people to stand on in order to get more passengers on board each airplane; in one B-17 nine men crowded into the nose compartment.[136] Passenger lists had been carefully worked out for each airplane, but when all passengers were aboard 15 men from the 17th Pursuit Squadron remained on the field. By going from plane to plane and appealing to the crews, somehow places were found for all of them.[137] The heavily-laden B-17s took off first, then the two LB-30s took off around 0030 on March 2nd. As the planes flew off in the dark of night, they could see behind them explosions going off as the Dutch blew up the field.[138] Lt. Edward Habberstad, who left Java in the belly of a Liberator, later recalled his feelings that night. "Once out over the Indian Ocean", he said, "it was a feeling of relief and exhilaration. We had been granted a new lease on life."[139]

Aftermath

Dutch forces on Java surrendered to the Japanese March 8, 1942, three months to the day after the Japanese launched their offensive and two months ahead of their own schedule. As one historian wrote, "...thus ended a campaign that for the Allies was nothing short of a total, humiliating disaster."[140] While the American garrisons in the Philippines would hold out until April on Bataan and May on Corregidor, in a mere 90 days, the Japanese military had captured almost all of Southeast Asia. They would complete the conquest of Burma in early May, adding to their territory. The Japanese defeat of the British Commonwealth forces in Malaya and Singapore was "...by any standard one of the most brilliant feats of modern arms in the war, perhaps in modern military history. At every level—strategic direction, tactics, command, equipment, in the air, at sea, and on land—the Japanese decisively out-scored a British force..."[141] The Japanese plan had been based on concentrating their forces to attack key strategic points in the region under the cover of air power.[142] The Japanese Army had advanced in stages that were within reach of newly-captured airfields, leapfrogging from one airfield to the next captured airfield, rapidly bringing up their supporting Army and Navy air units. By the time the last

American soldier surrendered in the Philippines and the last British Commonwealth soldier withdrew into India in May 1942, the Japanese had inflicted an estimated 380,000 casualties (killed, wounded, and made prisoner of war) on the Allies for the loss of roughly 37,000 of their own forces, a ratio of nearly ten to one in their favor.[143] The Japanese Army and Navy now dominated an arc running from the Burma-Indian border in the west to the Bismarck Archipelago in the East and up through the Central Pacific to the home islands. The Japanese had established a defensive barrier around the resources they believed they needed to sustain that barrier "...until the enemy's will to continue the struggle was broken."[144] The Allies, principally America and Great Britain with her Commonwealth, now faced the daunting task of holding the line against any further Japanese expansion until such time as resources became available to enable Allied forces to shift over to the offensive. With the defeat of Germany paramount, that would take time.

Allied air power was far less effective and far less prepared for war than the Japanese. None of the Allied powers in the region had anywhere near enough bombers and fighters of adequate quality with proper maintenance support and supplies of spare parts, much less a defensive warning network to contest the Japanese advance. The Far East Air Force's two heavy bomber groups (the 7th and the 19th) had to cover an area ranging from the Philippines through the Netherlands East Indies to Malaya with fewer than 15 serviceable B-17 and LB-30 bombers, far too few to deal with the multiple prongs of the Japanese advance.[145] Though reinforcements did arrive during the Java campaign, they arrived piecemeal and barely kept pace with attrition; there were never enough skilled maintenance personnel, nor an adequate flow of spare parts to keep more bombers in service. A typical bombing mission saw five or six B-17s set off to a target and on occasion nine airplanes, but rarely more. In addition to their regular bombing missions, the Far East Air Force had to use its heavy bombers for reconnaissance and at times as transports, ferrying supplies and personnel from Australia, not to mention the times when the bombers had to fly for hours away from their home fields to avoid air attacks. All this added to the strain on men and airplanes. The frequent exercises away from their home fields so typical of the maneuvers during the 1930s failed to match the challenge of sustaining them more than 8,000 miles from the United States with a practically non-existent source of supplies. America was late in preparing for war and ramping up production of aircraft and the training of personnel. American forces in the Philippines and Java paid the price of America's unpreparedness.

There were problems with the deployment of heavy bombers as well. The reality of war that dictated the operations of the bombers in the Java campaign was far different from the air power doctrine the Army Air Corps had developed and practiced in the prewar years. The prewar theory: "...seems to have been limited primarily to operations carried out from fixed and well-equipped bases and against such targets as factories, refineries, and marshaling yards. This would have been strategic bombing. If heavy bombers were to be employed against shipping, the theory required the use of many aircraft, nine or more, in every formation. Thus, it was hoped, a ship would be caught in a pattern of bombs. Almost none of the pre-requisites for this type of bombing existed in the Pacific in January 1942."[146] Bombing ships from altitudes that were well above what the airmen had flown during training, in often poor weather, with anti-aircraft fire and the presence of enemy fighters proved to be exceptionally demanding and far more difficult than had been thought. It is also ironic that a force that ostensibly had as its primary mission during the 1930s the defense of American coasts from enemy fleets should have had such a difficult time attacking Japanese shipping. During the Java campaign, the heavy bombers claimed one destroyer, ten transports, and two other ships sunk, but the postwar Joint Army-Navy Assessment Committee's report on Japanese merchant and naval shipping losses shows that during that time, only two transports were lost to aircraft (credited to the Netherlands East Indies Air Force) and no naval vessels; the majority of Japanese shipping losses were due to submarines. Even had the Far East Air Force sunk all the ships it claimed, the numbers were far too small to have had any impact on what the Japanese had available. With all the problems of inadequate numbers, compounded by mechanical and weather problems that prevented 40 percent of the bombers dispatched from reaching their target, it is not surprising that bomber operations in the Philippines and Java were deemed to have failed.[147] Despite all the shortages of men and equipment, the problems, the frustrations, the fatigue, the loss of friends and commanding officers, the 7th Bombardment Group's pilots, crews, and maintenance personnel and their compatriots in the 19th Bombardment Group continued to the bitter end. They fought with gallantry and determination against a better prepared and substantially better armed foe.

On December 29, 1942, the War Department awarded the Distinguished Unit Citation to the 7th Bombardment Group for its performance during the Java campaign. The citation read:

> Opposing the full force of the numerically superior Japanese with all available aircraft, the 7th Bombardment Group participated daily in attacking the enemy whenever they found him during his prolonged drive through the Philippines and Netherlands Indies to Java. Long-range bombing attacks were executed in

the face of heavy antiaircraft fire and large concentrations of enemy fighter airplanes over the target areas. Despite extremely adverse weather and dangerous field conditions, hampered by lack of

A captured B-17 the Japanese restored to flying condition at Bandoeng, Java. (courtesy Gerry Cassius)

adequate personnel to maintain aircraft in continuous combat condition, many successful missions were performed by crews fatigued from daily flights against the numerically dominant enemy. During this period, great damage was inflicted on enemy aircraft, ground installations, warships, and transports. Combat crews exhibited the greatest bravery and resourcefulness; the ground units, in the face of heavy enemy fire, performed all duties with utter disregard of personal safety. The superior courage and devotion to duty shown by this bombardment group will always be worthy of emulation.[148]

The 7th Bombardment Group that went to war on December 7, 1941, was not reassembled after the Group's evacuation to Australia. The V Bomber Command had transferred its headquarters to Melbourne on March 2nd. Over the next week, the bombers and their crews and the ground echelons evacuated from Java gradually congregated there at the Royal Australian Air Force Base at Laverton before moving on to Townsville. On March 14, 1942, the personnel and units of the 7th Bombardment Group in Australia—basically all the air crews and the ground echelons of the 11th and 22nd Bombardment Squadrons—were merged into the 19th Bombardment Group; the remaining ground echelon of the 7th Group, 9th Bombardment Squadron, and the 88th Reconnaissance Squadron went to India.[149] Their story will be related in the next chapter. Lt. Colonel Kenneth Hobson, formerly commander of the 22nd Squadron, was appointed commander of the 19th Group. The aircrews that had remained with the 88th Squadron were also incorporated into the 19th Group at this time, though they had followed a different path to Australia. Following the attack on Pearl Harbor, the 88th and the 38th Reconnaissance Squadrons had been retained in Hawaii for patrol duties, with the later addition of several airplanes and crews from the 22nd Bombardment Squadron. In early February, twelve crews were attached to a U.S. Naval force (Naval Task Force ANZAC) to help protect the South Pacific convoy route to Australia and were sent to the Fiji Islands, where they flew patrols until February 18th.[149] The crews moved to Australia, where they undertook the first American bombing of Rabaul on February 23rd. On March 14th, they were reformed into the 40th Reconnaissance Squadron under the command of Maj. Richard Carmichael and assigned to the 19th Group.[151] Carmichael was appointed commander of the 19th Group later in 1942. Other pilots who had served with the 7th Group on Java continued to fly with the 19th Group, with Felix Hardison and Elbert Helton commanding the Group for short periods. John Dougherty, who had flown one of the first three LB-30s out to Java, was promoted to Major and Group Executive Officer.[152] A new 7th Bombardment Group would be built in India, assigned to a new air force in a new theater of war to continue the fight against the Japanese.

CHAPTER FOUR

INDIA AND THE TENTH AIR FORCE

China-Burma-India

After the fall of Singapore on February 15, 1942, Maj. Gens. Brett and Brereton became convinced that the best hope for the Allies was to launch an air offensive against the Japanese from Burma and China. Brett had sent one of his staff (Col. F.M. Brady) out to Burma to report on facilities and the possibility of stationing heavy bombers there.[1] Brady reported that heavy bombers could operate from the airfield at Akyab, on Burma's west coast, and by using the airfields at Magwe and Toungoo as advanced bases could reach Bangkok and Saigon, where the Japanese were unloading supplies for their armies.[2] From bases in China, it seemed feasible that heavy bombers could reach the Japanese home islands to strike directly at Japan's war industries. Brett sent Brereton to India on his own initiative to set up a new force to strike at the Japanese, but once again, the Japanese disrupted Brereton's plans and his timetable. British forces in Burma had been unable to stop the Japanese overland advance from Thailand. After a disastrous defeat at the Sittang River, General Sir Harold Alexander, who had just taken over command of British forces in Burma on March 5, 1942, decided to save his Army, abandoning Rangoon, the capital of Burma, and

A 7th Bombardment Group B-17 at the air field outside Karachi, where the Group was first stationed after withdrawing from Java in March 1942. (3A-35387, RG 342FH, NARA)

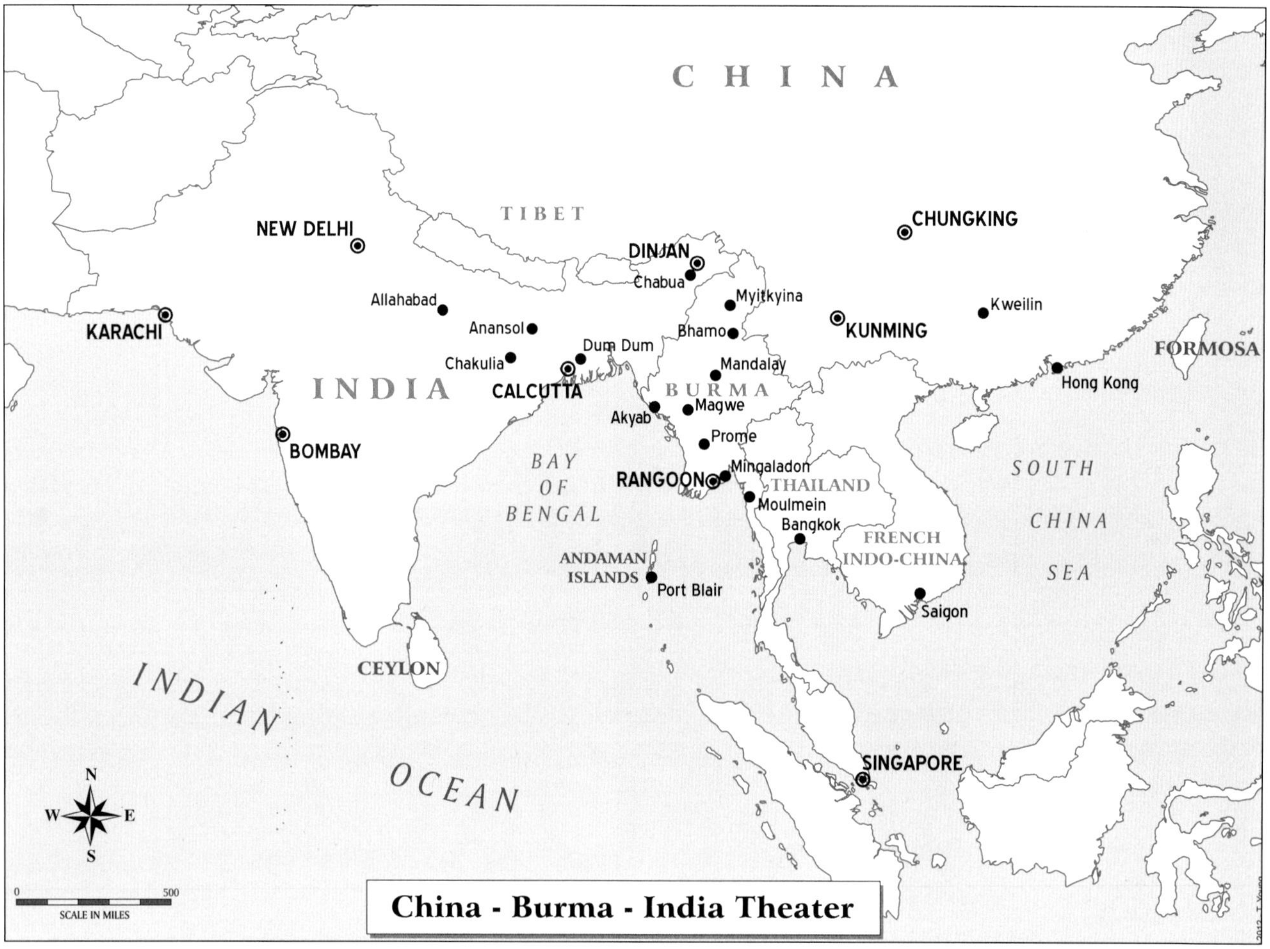

China - Burma - India Theater

retreating north.[3] The Japanese advance into Central Burma continued without letup. By the end of March, when Toungoo fell to the Japanese, air attacks had made the Royal Air Force airfields at Magwe and Akyab untenable.[4] While basing American heavy bombers in Burma to strike back at the Japanese—as Brett and Brereton had hoped—proved impossible, the United States had already decided that ensuring China remained in the war against Japan would be one of its principal war aims. To this end, the United States would need to provide even more assistance to the Chinese to strengthen their ability to resist the Japanese, including the provision of American air units to assist Chinese forces.

China's stand against Japanese rapaciousness and the sufferings of the Chinese people at the hands of the Japanese military had aroused the anger and sympathy of the American people and the American government, though there was little President Roosevelt could do to provide support to the embattled Chinese, apart from granting credits for the purchase of arms. In late 1940, with the growing prospect of war with Germany and Japan, President Roosevelt approved military aid to China, the amount of aid increasing with the passage of the Lend-Lease Act in March 1941. The Roosevelt administration agreed to the formation of the American Volunteer Group, composed of volunteers drawn from the Army Air Corps, Marines, and the Navy to fight as a unit of the Chinese Air Force.[5] Further assistance came in the form of an American military mission to China that began to arrive during September 1941 to assess the needs of the Chinese armed forces and aid in the effective use of Lend-Lease materials.[6] Between May and December 1941, the United States shipped around 67,000 tons of war material to China.[7] With America's entry into the war, China became an important component of American strategy for the war against Japan. Japan's on-going war in China tied down 23 of the Japanese Army's 51 divisions, who were maintaining a hold on the sizeable sections of China the Japanese had seized in their earlier conquests. Japan's commitment in China was a considerable drain on the country's limited resources.[8] The United States needed those Japanese troops to remain in China, given the decision to fight Germany first and remain on the defensive in the Pacific. In the first few months of the war, China appeared to be the only territory in Allied hands where it seemed possible to base aircraft to attack Japan. China might also serve as a jumping off point for the eventual invasion of Japan. With China assuming greater importance in American strategic planning, so too did the importance of ensuring the increasing flow of material to China. With the Japanese having captured all of its coastal ports, China's lifeline to the West was the Burma Road, an inadequate line of communication stretching from the port of Rangoon all the way to Lashio, on the Burma-China border. All Lend-Lease supplies from the United States had to travel by ship to Rangoon, where they were unloaded and trucked up to China. If this line was cut, as now seemed increasingly likely, there was no other overland route to get supplies into China; all supplies would have to be flown to China from bases in India. Ensuring China's continued participation in the war through the supply of military material, improving the effectiveness of China's military forces in their fight with the Japanese, and potentially basing American bombers and an invasion force in China became the capstones of American strategy. Thus, the defense of Burma and India became vital to sustaining the flow of supplies to China.

At the ARCADIA Conference in Washington in December 1941, President Roosevelt pressed for greater recognition of China's potential role in the war and for steps that would bring Generalissimo Chiang Kai-shek into Allied councils. The Combined Chiefs of Staff proposed creating a China theater of war under the Generalissimo, with a senior American officer to act as an advisor and liaison with other Allied forces.[9] Toward the end of January 1942, the War Department created the China-Burma-India Theater and appointed Lt. Gen. Joseph Stilwell to the position as Chief of Staff to Generalissimo Chiang Kai-shek, commander of all U.S. Army Forces in the Theater, with additional responsibility for all Lend-Lease aid to China. To provide support for Stilwell's multiple missions, the Army Air Forces assigned the Tenth Air Force, activated on February 12, 1942, to the China-Burma-India Theater. The Tenth Air Force's primary missions were to defend and maintain the air supply route from India to China, and conduct offensive air operations in China and from India as required in support of its primary mission.[10] At the same time, the Army Air Forces initiated a number of projects to expand air support for China and launch air attacks on Japan. As bombardment was the core of the Army Air Forces' air power doctrine, a heavy bomber component for the China-Burma-India Theater was part of the Army Air Forces' early planning. General Arnold initially appointed Col. Caleb V. Haynes to command the Tenth Air Force's heavy bomber group, to be made up from the units of the 7th Bombardment Group then in Australia.[11] Arnold directed Haynes to take a force of heavy bombers and transports to India for operations in China. Haynes's bombers, some erudite staff officer designating them Task Force Aquila (the Latin word for eagle), were intended to bomb Japan from bases in Eastern China, one of two plans to strike back at the Japanese, the other being Lt. Col. James Doolittle's carrier-borne B-25s.[12] The initiatives underway in the United States with the formation of the Tenth Air Force and those of Maj. Gens. Brett and Brereton to base heavy bombers in the China-Burma-India region merged with Brereton's arrival in India and his assumption of command of the Tenth Air Force on March 5, 1942.[13]

Something Old, Something New

When Brereton took command, he had available the LB-30 aircraft he had flown from Java, five B-17s that had been unable to fly on to Java after the capture of the airfields on Sumatra, a small nucleus of combat-experienced officers to help him build the Tenth Air Force, and a daunting logistical problem.[14] No other American air force had a longer line of communication back to the United States than the Tenth Air Force. Since the Mediterranean and much of the Pacific Ocean were now closed to Allied shipping, transports with supplies for the Tenth Air Force had to go around South Africa or Australia, a journey either way of some 13,000 miles that could take as much as two months.[15] Karachi, on the western side of India, had been chosen as the main port for American transport ships. The front line was another thousand miles to the east, requiring supplies to be moved by air, or by the barely adequate Indian railroad system. Nor were there an adequate number of airfields to support the units the Tenth Air Force planned to bring into India, nor an industrial infrastructure to support the needs of a modern air force.[16] Even before Brereton could begin to address these problems, his few aircraft were immediately put to use assisting the Royal Air Force's one transport squadron ferrying badly needed reinforcements into Burma. From March 8th to March 12th, the Tenth Air Force's bombers flew in 465 men from a battalion of the 1st Royal Inniskilling Fusiliers from India to Magwe, flying out with 424 civilian evacuees.[17] On the last day of the evacuation, the ground echelons of the 7th Bombardment Group Headquarters and Headquarters Squadron, the 9th Bombardment Squadron, and the 88th Reconnaissance Squadron arrived in Karachi, India, after a month-long peripatetic voyage from Australia. Here they began the work of building up a new 7th Bombardment Group.

After the ground echelons of the 11th and 22nd Squadrons left for Java in January, the remaining 7th Group ground echelon staff finished assembling the remaining P-40s from their crates and prepared for their own move to Java. On

The U.S.A.T. *Willard A. Holbrook* brought the 7th Bombardment Group's ground echelon from Australia to Karachi, India. (7th Bombardment Group (H) Historical Foundation, USAFA McDermott Library)

The *Willard A. Holbrook* had minimal armament. The men of the 7th Group mounted machine guns on deck in case of attack. (7th Bombardment Group (H) Historical Foundation, USAFA McDermott Library)

The airship hangar at Karachi airport where the men of the 7th Group were housed temporarily after arriving from Australia. (7th Bombardment Group (H) Historical Foundation, USAFA McDermott Library)

The tent camp at New Malier, seven miles west of Karachi airport, where the 7th Group moved after a few weeks in the airship hangar. (File 828.08 1942 Volume 1, Albert F. Simpson Historical Research Center, Air Force Historical Research Agency, Maxwell AFB, AL

February 4, 1942, the personnel were loaded on the U.S.A.T. *Willard A. Holbrook* at Brisbane and set sail on a voyage around Australia to avoid the Japanese aircraft moving into the Netherlands East Indies. The *Holbrook* had no armament of its own, so the men mounted .30 and .50 caliber machine guns on the deck and set up shifts to man the guns. The ship spent four days in Melbourne, where stevedores loaded bombs and torpedoes into the hold of the *Holbrook*, which was somewhat disconcerting to the men aboard, who imagined what would happen to them if a Japanese torpedo hit the ship. The ship left Melbourne on February 13th, joining a convoy of three other transports all bound for Java. The convoy stopped at Fremantle, in Western Australia, for four days, where the USS *Langley*, along with its cargo of P-40s, joined them. The convoy set sail for Java on February 22nd, but was immediately sent back to Freemantle. It was clear that Java could not be held, so a decision was reached to send the men and equipment to India. The convoy left Freemantle the next day, the *Langley* heading off on its fateful run to Java. Ten days later, on March 5th, the convoy arrived at Columbo, capital of Ceylon, where they again anchored for two days before heading to Karachi, the destination chosen to avoid the risk of running into Japanese air or naval forces in the Bay of Bengal. The *Holbrook* arrived in Karachi on March 12th, 36 days after leaving Brisbane.[18]

After disembarking at the port of Karachi, the men went into temporary quarters. The 7th Group Headquarters and Headquarters Squadron and the 9th Bombardment Squadron ground echelons went by truck to the old Royal Air Force airship hangar seven miles east of the city, where they were to establish their camp. The men of the 88th Reconnaissance

Squadron went to a tent camp at New Malir, seven miles further east. For the next few weeks, the men set about building a camp at the Karachi airport, setting up Indian-made tents and building mess halls, workshops, and administrative and medical offices from old airplane crates. The men moved into the new tent camp on April 2nd, as temperatures began to rise with the onset of the hot dry season. From May through July, temperatures are regularly over 90°F and often over 100°F. The heat added to the discomfort of mild skin diseases and stomach ailments (the "Karachi Kramp") that afflicted nearly everyone. Heat, sand and dust, and the constant shortage of spare parts made maintenance difficult. Keeping the B-17s in commission was a constant challenge. Shortly after arrival of the ground echelons, the 7th Group gained a new command structure, as the Group's two active squadrons (the 9th Bombardment and the 88th Reconnaissance) reorganized. On March 15th, Capt. Donald Keiser, one of the men from the 19th Bombardment Group Brereton brought from Java, was appointed commander of the 9th Bombardment Squadron. The next day, Capt. William Bayse, formerly with the 11th Bombardment Squadron and also from Java, took over the 88th Reconnaissance Squadron. A week later, Maj. Cecil Combs, another 19th Bombardment Group veteran, became commander of the 7th Bombardment Group.[19]

Airplanes for the Group began to dribble in from several sources. The B-17s that had already arrived in India and more that came through over the next two months on the Project X program—the program to get B-17s to Java—were sent to Karachi and assigned to the 7th Group. On April 7th, six B-17s and one B-24 assigned to Col. Caleb Haynes's Task Force Aquila arrived at Karachi (among the pilots were Haynes, Lt. Cols. Robert Tate, Robert Scott, Jerry Mason, and Torgas Wold, and Majs. Max Fennell and Donald Struther).[20] While waiting for confirmation of their mission, Maj. Fennell apparently made several flights into China to familiarize himself with the bases the Task Force might operate from, knowledge that would prove useful several months later. The loss of air bases in Eastern China that the Task Force had intended to use meant the B-17s could no longer reach Japan, so the project was cancelled and the B-17s turned over to the 7th Group and assigned to the 9th Bombardment Squadron. The addition of these six aircraft gave Brereton about 20 bombers, though a number were out of commission. The airplanes arriving at Karachi at this time were later models of the B-17E, some with the Sperry ball turret in the belly position in place of the Bendix remote control turret. This was a new feature for many of the maintenance staff from Australia, who had never seen a B-17E before. For some of

2nd Lt. Harry Burkhart, copilot on a B-17E that made the flight from the United States to Karachi in April 1942. (Author's collection)

Camp beds for the 7th Bombardment Group inside the Karachi airship hangar. Note the Vultee P-66 fighters intended for the Chinese Air Force being assembled on the other side. (File 828.08 1942 Volume I, Albert F. Simpson Historical Research Center, Air Force Historical Research Agency, Maxwell AFB, AL)

Boeing B-17Es intended for the 7th Bombardment Group at Kano in Nigeria, on their way across Africa to Karachi in April 1942. (7th Bombardment Group (H) Historical Foundation, USAFA McDermott Library)

An aerial reconnaissance photograph of the Japanese air field and naval base at Port Blair in the Andaman Islands, the target of the 7th Bombardment Group's first mission out of India on April 2, 1942. (Courtesy Col. Thomas Sledge, USAF Retd)

the ground personnel who volunteered for combat duty, training was on the job and makeshift at best. Wilbur Mayhew, who volunteered to serve as a ball turret gunner, read the technical manual on how to get into the ball turret, then had the airplane's tail gunner read the rest of the manual to him over the intercom while he practiced operating the turret.[21] The newly-arrived crews undertook further training on their arrival at Karachi to build their experience with the B-17. Brereton was frustrated that partially-trained combat crews had been thrown into combat during the Philippines and Java campaigns before they were ready. He recommended additional training in pilotage, gunnery, bombardment, and formation flying before combat crews would be allowed to go on combat missions.[22]

The question of the appropriate aircraft for the 7th Bombardment Group led to a change in its composition. Looking at the areas where the Tenth Air Force would likely operate over the coming months, Brereton concluded that medium bombers would be more effective than heavy bombers.[23] He based his requests for more medium bombers on the limited number of significant targets in the region and the lack of photographic reconnaissance aircraft required for successful long-range strategic bombing to measure results. And, since the P-40 fighters assigned to the Tenth lacked the range to escort bombers deep into enemy territory, Brereton also concluded that all bombing would be done at night. With their higher speed, mediums would have a better chance of evading interception. In the first few chaotic months of the war, with every Army Air Forces theater crying for reinforcements, Brereton's requests for medium bombers to be sent to India were initially turned down, but in April, the Army Air Forces agreed to turn the 7th Bombardment Group into a composite group with two heavy and two medium bomber squadrons.[24] Toward this end, the 11th and 22nd Bombardment Squadrons (H)—still nominally part of the 7th Group, though not active—were relieved from assignment to the Group. During early April, two new squadrons designated the 11th and 22nd Bombardment Squadrons (M) came into being with crews drawn from the 17th Bombardment Group and the 89th Reconnaissance Squadron training in the North American B-25 Mitchell medium bombers at Columbia Army Air Base in South Carolina.[25] In mid-April, the crews of the new 11th and 22nd Squadrons flew to Florida to prepare for flying the Atlantic-Africa route to Karachi as Project 157. The crews from the 11th Squadron were put under the command of Maj. Gordon Leland and those from the 22nd under Lt. Blair Sorenson. On May 1, 1942, the first airplanes set off on the long flight, most overloaded with extra equipment and supplies to maintain the airplanes once they were in India. Most of the crews arrived in Karachi by the end of May. Ground echelons for the two squadrons went by sea to Karachi, arriving in July.[26]

With the devastating raids on the Royal Air Force bases at Magwe and Akyab, by the end of March, the Japanese Army Air Force's *5th Hikōshidan* (Air Division) had effectively established air superiority over the front in Burma.[27] Following the fall of Rangoon on March 8th, the two divisions of the Japanese *15th Army* steadily pushed British forces back toward India and at Toungoo decisively defeated the Chinese divisions Chiang Kai-shek had sent to assist the British, thereby threatening the Allied flank. The situation was desperate and there appeared to be little hope of holding on, much less winning the country back. With the loss of Burma and the Burma Road—the only land route for Lend-Lease supplies to China—the defense of India became critical to American support of China. On March 24th, Maj. Gen. Brereton flew into Burma to meet with General Stilwell. When Brereton briefed Stilwell on the War Department's plan to bomb Japan from China with Task Force AQUILA (then on its way to India), Stilwell replied, "What the hell are we doing trying to go to Japan to bomb when we have a war on our hands right here?"[28] A few days later, back in India, Brereton learned that the Japanese were bringing transports up from Singapore to Rangoon and sending naval vessels and supplies to the Andaman Islands, in the Bay of Bengal, where the Japanese could threaten Allied shipping on the way to Calcutta. The Royal Air Force in India had just received a squadron of Wellington bombers, the only RAF long-range aircraft available as reinforcements, but the Wellington lacked the range to reach either the Andaman Islands or Rangoon. The only airplanes able to reach these targets were the 9th Bombardment Squadron's B-17s. Brereton decided to attack both Rangoon and Port Blair (the main port in the Andaman Islands) at night, to take advantage of the full moon.[29] He set April 2nd as the date for the mission to the Andaman Islands, the first opportunity for the 7th Bombardment Group since its arrival in India.

On April 1st, the 9th Bombardment Squadron sent eight B-17s and the 7th Group's single LB-30—all the heavy bombers then available—to Asansol, in Eastern India, 138 miles northwest of Calcutta to prepare for the missions to Port Blair and Rangoon.[30] The plan was to have six B-17s bomb Port Blair, a round trip of more than 1,600 miles, and two B-17s and the LB-30 go to Rangoon to bomb the dock areas, covering 1,500 miles to the target and back. Brereton led the mission to Port Blair with Maj. Combs as pilot of the lead aircraft, the other pilots on this flight were Lts. Willard Fountain, Delmar Rogers, James Keenan, and Charles Blankenhorn.[31] The night of April 2, 1942, the Port Blair mission took off first, beginning at 2150 under clear skies and a full moon. The two flights reached the Andaman Islands around 0330 on the morning of April 3rd, descending to their bombing altitude of 3,000 feet. As the bombers neared Port Blair approaching from the east, they could see five large ships in the harbor in the moonlight and a larger ship, which they identified as a Japanese cruiser, going out to sea. Brereton and Combs chose this vessel as their target, but the bombardier reported the sighting run to be too short, so they came in for a second run, claiming direct hits on the cruiser, while the other bombers attacked vessels in the harbor. The formation ran into anti-aircraft fire over the harbor and several fighters tried but failed to intercept the B-17s.[32]

Maintenance work on a 7th Group B-17E at Asansol, India, during 1942. (7th Bombardment Group (H) Historical Foundation, USAFA McDermott Library)

Major General Louis Brereton awards decorations to the men who participated in the raid on Port Blair, April 1942. (3A-34310, RG 342FH, NARA)

The mission to Rangoon got off to a bad start. Capt. Elmer Parsel, leading the mission, crashed on take-off from Asanasol. A large stump stood at the end of the runway on the right side. Parsel apparently saw this as he was trying to get his heavily-laden B-17 into the air. He got the wheels clear, but the tail of his B-17 caught the stump, ripping off one of the elevators. The plane rose a hundred feet in the air, then crashed down into a gully just off the runway, killing the entire crew, including Brereton's senior aide, Maj. Norman Lewellyn, who had insisted on going on the mission.[33] A second airplane experienced mechanical difficulties, so the mission was cancelled. The next night (April 3rd), six B-17s flew to Rangoon, carrying a mix of high explosive bombs and incindiaries.[34] This attack was successful, the bombers returning undamaged after having started fires in the dock area. Two weeks later, on the night of April 16th, the 9th Squadron undertook another night mission to bomb the Rangoon docks. Six B-17s flew to Asansol, but one had a mechanical problem, one airplane lost two engines, and a third got stuck in the mud on the airfield.[35] The other flight of three B-17s, with Maj. Donald Keiser (9th Squadron commander) leading the formation, took off and headed for Rangoon. After arriving in the Rangoon area, Maj. Keiser's aircraft would drop the first flares to illuminate the target for the two other airplanes. All three B-17s, bombing from different altitudes between 3,500 and 4,000 feet, dropped more flares as they went over. Keiser dropped his first flare south of the city, but this alerted the Japanese anti-aircraft and searchlights in Rangoon, who began throwing up a barrage of fire over the city. Writing later in the war, Capt. Thomas Rowan recalled the mission: "The whole show burst into our gaping faces. Scores of blue searchlights, turning in unison by automatic control, pierced and probed into the night, converging finally into a fountainhead, with our ship riding on top of it. I felt as conspicuous as an uninvited guest at a banquet who has somehow lost his trousers. The fireworks started instantaneously. We had not only found the target: we were the target!"[36] The bombers returned to base, reporting fires started in the target area.

These first missions, despite the loss of Capt. Persel and his crew, helped lift the morale of the men of the 7th Group. At Karachi, they had to put up with the heat, dust, poor food, and limited mail from home. When the bombers returned to Karachi from their Rangoon mission, Combs put his two squadrons through an intensive period of training and maintenance. The combat crews had classroom sessions five hours a day on a range of topics and practice and more practice in the air, concentrating on flying formation at high altitudes, bombing practice, and night landings.[37] To make the practice flights more productive, the 9th and 88th Squadrons flew reconnaissance missions out over the Arabian Sea, searching for American and British convoys bringing supplies to Karachi. The Imperial Japanese Navy's attack on the British Navy's base at Columbo and Trincomalee, on Ceylon, on April 6th and April 9th, made these reconnaissance flights more than simple exercises. On April 22nd, the ground echelons of the 9th Bombardment Squadron left Karachi by troop train for the air base at Allahabad, five hundred miles west of Calcutta. The 9th Squadron's air echelon transferred to Allahabad a week later. While this brought the Tenth Air Force's bombers a thousand miles closer to the front lines in Burma, they still had to stop at Calcutta to refuel on the way to their targets.

Local Indian dignitaries visiting the 7th Bombardment Group at Karachi. (File 828.08 1942 Volume 2, Albert F. Simpson Historical Research Center, Air Force Historical Research Agency, Maxwell AFB, AL)

To conform with the 7th Bombardment Group's new structure as a composite group, the 88th Reconnaissance Squadron was redesignated the 436th Bombardment Squadron (H) on April 22nd, remaining for the time being in Karachi.[38]

During April, five new B-17Es arrived from the United States to join the Group. Around the same time, the Group also gained the Task Force Aquila B-17s. Three B-17s were lost in accidents and more went out of commission. Maintenance problems persisted. The Group could rarely send out more than six B-17s on a mission. The sand at the Karachi airport was a particular problem, wearing down the engines on the B-17s and causing excessive oil consumption. As Wilbur Mayhew recalled: "the air intake for the engines was on the bottom, so sand was sucked in when the engines were run up on the ground. Soon the rings in the cylinders were so ground down, the planes left a huge amount of black smoke trailing behind them. Each engine had an oil tank that held 45 gallons of oil. Planes were grounded when they were using more than eight gallons of oil per engine per hour. Some missions were flown over Burma using all four engines on takeoff, feathering two engines on the way to the target, all four engines over the target, then the other two engines on the return trip in order to have enough oil to make the flight."[39]

A 7th Bombardment Group B-17E at Allahabad, India, being made ready for a mission in June 1942. (7th Bombardment Group (H) Historical Foundation, USAFA McDermott Library)

Even with the small number of airplanes available, the 9th Squadron resumed missions into Burma at the end of April, flying from Calcutta. In light of the precarious situation in Burma, the War Department had amended the Tenth Air Force's instructions and ordered Brereton to cooperate with the Royal Air Force in the defense of India, resulting in the 9th Squadron's move to Allahabad. On April 29th, a single B-17 made a daylight raid on Rangoon, remarkably without being intercepted. The next night, a single B-17 returned to Rangoon, dropping two tons of bombs on the dock area. May was a busy month, with the 9th Squadron flying 45 sorties during 14 missions and dropping 82 tons of bombs. The Rangoon docks remained a primary target: a single B-17 again making a daylight attack on May 1st, one bomber making a night raid on May 2nd, and two B-17s flying a night mission on May 3rd. These were little more than nuisance raids, as the few tons of bombs dropped on each mission could do little substantive damage. The night of May 4th, the bombers switched to attacking the former Royal Air Force base at Mingaladon, outside of Rangoon, with two B-17s claiming 40 airplanes destroyed and 25 damaged on the airfield, though Japanese records do not confirm these losses. Three B-17s returned to Mingaladon the next night. On May 8th, five B-17s made a dawn raid on the Rangoon dock area, flying through thunderstorms to drop ten tons of bombs without observing the results because of weather. A single bomber attacked the airfield at Mingaladon at the same time. The 9th Squadron switched its attacks to the airfield at Myitkyina, in northeast Burma, a planned fueling stop on the route from India to Kunming that the Japanese captured on May 12th. For three days (May 12th, 14th, and 16th), the 9th sent out four B-17s in daylight raids on the airfield. On May 14th, the four B-17s bombed from an altitude of between 24,000 and 27,000 feet, getting hits on the runway and buildings around the airfield, with three bombs exploding among parked aircraft.[40] Fortunately for the bombers, the Ki-43 Type 1 Hayabusa fighters of the Japanese Army Air Force's *64th Sentai* were occupied fighting elsewhere, so the B-17s missed enemy fighters. After a nine-day pause, probably for needed maintenance, the 9th Squadron returned to Rangoon the night of May 25th, with four bombers attacking the dock areas along the Rangoon River, while two more bombers attacked Mingaladon. During the last three days of the month, the 9th flew a night mission to the Myitkyina airfield on May 29th with four B-17s and sent three bombers to Myitkyina in daylight the next day, closing out the month with a night raid by five B-17s on the Rangoon docks.[41]

By the end of May, Burma had fallen. The Japanese *15th Army* had forced the Chinese divisions in Burma to withdraw back across the Burma-China border into Yunnan and north beyond Myitkyina into Assam, in India. On May 20th, British and Indian troops withdrew across the Chindwin River and back into India through the mountain ranges along the Burma-India border over the few available tracks to Imphal, where a road led back into Assam. The Japanese had captured Burma in a 5½ month campaign, inflicting another painful defeat on the Allies and cutting China's last lifeline. Burma's border with India ran for more than 1,000 miles through successive mountain ranges leading from the foothills of the Himalayas to the Arakan on the Bay of Bengal, presenting a formidable and seemingly impenetrable barrier devoid of roads. To the beaten and demoralized Allied troops, the re-conquest of Burma was the farthest thing from their minds. There was little that could be done at the time and much rebuilding to be done, but as General Stilwell famously said of the defeat in Burma: "We got a hell of a beating. It was as humiliating as hell. We ought to find out why it happened and go back!"[42]

For the Allies, the loss of Burma was a significant setback. At the time, there were serious doubts about China's ability to remain in the war without the supplies she so desperately needed. These now would have to travel over a precarious air route from India to China with the inadequate number of transport planes then available. The plan to use China as a base for air operations against Japan became an even greater challenge. Allied plans began to focus on two objectives: "... to recapturing at least enough of Burma to secure the air route and, if possible, to open a land route to China so as to keep her in the war—a most difficult military operation across the grain of a country of jungle-covered mountain ranges and broad rivers."[43]

For the 7th Bombardment Group, the war continued as before, even if the raids into Burma were now no more than a nuisance to the Japanese. On May 26th, Maj. Necrason was assigned to the 7th Group as Executive Officer. The next day, the 436th Squadron's ground echelon packed its bags and made the move to Allahabad to join the 9th Squadron, the air crews following shortly thereafter. At the same time, the 7th Bombardment Group headquarters was ordered to Calcutta,

Lt. Col. Conrad Necrason at his desk in Karachi. Necrason took over command of the 7th Bombardment Group on July 1, 1942. (File 827-306-1, Vol. 2, Albert F. Simpson Historical Research Center, Air Force Historical Research Agency, Maxwell AFB, AL)

leaving a small detachment at Karachi.[44] The Group flew only three heavy bomber missions during the month of June. On June 1st, five B-17s, most likely from the 9th Squadron, went out on a day mission to Rangoon to bomb the docks, but were unable to observe any results. Three days later, the 436th Squadron prepared three B-17s for another mission to the Rangoon docks, again during the day. One airplane failed to get off, but Capts. Frank Sharp and John Toomey continued on, running into bad weather over the Bay of Bengal and having to fly on instruments for 2 1/2 hours.[45] The weather over Rangoon was overcast, making it difficult to pick up the docks, so Sharp decided to attack Mingaladon airfield—the alternate target—and searched for a break in the clouds. He and Toomey found the Rangoon River and saw two transports ahead. As they prepared their bombing run, they saw Japanese fighters coming at them. This time, the *64th Sentai* had gotten off several Ki-43 Type 1 fighters. Sgt. Maj. Yoshito Yasuda attacked one of the B-17s several times before losing it in clouds.[46] Sharp was climbing back up to the overcast when one of the fighters, possibly Yasuda, knocked out his number 3 engine. The next attack knocked out the number 4 engine, the bomb bay doors stuck open, and the hydraulic system, radios, and rudder controls were damaged. To make matters worse, a fire had started in the nose. One of the waist gunners (Pvt. Francis Teehan) was hit in the chest and killed instantly, the first member of the 7th Bombardment Group to be killed over Burma, while the top turret gunner and the copilot were wounded. The navigator asked for permission to bail out. Sharp agreed to his request, the bombardier going out with the navigator. Sharp struggled on, heading up the Irrawaddy River—as he was unwilling to go far out over the sea with only two engines—gradually managing to gain altitude. As he flew north he came out into a patch of clearer weather 95 miles northwest of Magwe, where he ran into three Ki-27 Type 97 fighters from the *77th Sentai*, which were now based at the former RAF airfield.[47] Sharp was wounded in the attack. Escaping into a cloud, he ordered the remaining crew to jump. Sharp and his copilot, Lt. Herbert Wunderlich, who had decided to stay with him, flew on, hoping to find a flat area where they could make a crash landing. With darkness approaching and his gasoline almost gone, Sharp saw a small valley off to his left, where he and Wunderlich set their riddled and badly damaged B-17 down on rice paddies alongside a river. Climbing out, Wunderlich walked around to the nose and fired six shots from his .45 caliber pistol into the Norden bombsight to destroy it. The next day, they returned to bury Pvt. Teehan with the help of some local people who helped them make their way to meet up with a British Army major in command of a band of Chin guerillas. A 12-day horse ride brought the two men to a town in Assam, where a boat took them to the railroad for a train back to Calcutta. They arrived 28 days after they had taken off on their ill-fated mission. The six men who had bailed out were all taken prisoner, though only three would survive the war.[48]

A single B-17 attacked the town of Homalin on June 15th, and that same day four bombers went out to bomb the airfield at Myitkyina, though only two attacked.[49] Due to the missions flown in May and early June, the training program for new pilots, and the on-going struggles with sand, dust, and a lack of spare parts and spare engines, before the month was out, all the 7th Group's bombers were out of commission.[50] The onset of the monsoon over southern Burma compounded the difficulties of flying combat missions to Rangoon. The only aircraft available to the Group for offensive missions were the newly-arrived B-25s of the 11th and 22nd Bombardment Squadrons. On arrival in India the 11th Squadron was reorganized, adding more combat crews from the 22nd Squadron to bring the 11th up to full strength. On May 27th, the 11th Squadron sent six B-25s under the command of Maj. Leland to Allahabad to prepare for two weeks of operations in China. At Allahabad, the long-range bomb bay tanks were removed and the airplanes loaded with six 500-lb bombs. On June 2nd, Maj. Leland led the formation to Dinjan, in Assam, in northeastern India, the terminus for flights from India to Kunming. The operational plan called for the B-25s to fly to Kunming via Lashio, where they would bomb the Japanese airfield in the 11th Squadron's first combat mission. The mission ended in disaster.[51]

The flight took off from Dinjan at 0600 on the morning of June 3, 1942. Some 45 minutes later, the weather worsened and the aircraft became separated, but five aircraft reformed just before they reached Lashio. Descending through broken clouds, the aircraft made their bombing run over the airfield at 1,500 feet. The sixth aircraft came in over the airfield just after the others had finished bombing, bombing another runway, but encountering two Japanese fighters who had taken off to intercept. The top turret gunner damaged one of the fighters as it made a pass, but the other continued attacking the bomber, making ten passes and killing the radio operator before the B-25 could get away and head to Kunming. The five other bombers climbed up through the overcast and headed for Kunming. Flying at 10,000 feet through solid clouds, Maj. Leland ran into the side of a mountain, killing everyone on board. A split second later, the No. 2 airplane in the first element and the No. 1 airplane in the second element hit the mountain nearby. The other two airplanes saw the explosions of the crash and missed the mountainside by a few feet, catching a glimpse of grass and trees as they flew by. The two surviving airplanes flew on to Kunming, one landing safely and the other running out of gas in the clouds, the crew bailing out. They arrived at Kunming two weeks later. A week after William Bayse, now a Major, was sent to Kunming to take over command of the 11th Squadron. More B-25s made the flight to Kunming and the Squadron spent the rest of June preparing for operations in China, where the Squadron would be based.[52]

The remaining crews in the 22nd Squadron were attached to the Headquarters and Headquarters Squadron of the 7th Bombardment Group for special missions, such as flying coastal patrols and bombing and reconnaissance missions into Burma. On one of these missions, 2nd Lt. Clark Johnston took a B-25 with a mixed crew to strafe the Japanese airfield at Akyab, on the Burmese coast. Coming in at 50 feet, the bomber ran into heavy anti-aircraft fire. This killed a Sergeant from another squadron serving as bombardier in the nose of the airplane and knocked out the left engine. Johnston flew the aircraft back toward Calcutta, but had to crash land the bomber in the Bay of Bengal 21 miles off the coast. The men got into their life raft and paddled to shore, where they spent

The men of the 7th Bombardment Group used P-40 packing grates to make offices, tool rooms, and mess halls at their camp at New Malier in Karachi. The officer's mess was named after the famous Stork Club of New York City. (File 828.08 1942 Vol. 1, Albert F. Simpson Historical Research Center, Air Force Historical Research Agency, Maxwell AFB, AL)

six days living off their chocolate emergency ration bars and coconut milk. Somehow they were either spotted or got word back to the 7th Group. Necrason, recently promoted to Lt. Colonel, arranged to borrow a transport plane from the China National Aviation Corporation. With the CNAC crew aboard, Necrason landed on a nearby beach to pick up the survivors.[53]

As Brereton and his small staff tried to overcome the many problems they faced in building up the Tenth Air Force's meager supply of heavy bombers, he received an urgent order from the War Department on June 24th to proceed immediately to the Middle East with every available heavy bomber and assist the British forces defending Egypt.[54] On May 26, 1942, German General Erwin Rommel and his *Afrika Korps* had launched a devastating attack against British positions in Libya. Breaking the Gazala Line and capturing Tobruk, which had held out for months against German attack, Rommel forced the British Eighth Army into a humiliating retreat back to the Egyptian border.[55] It seemed, at the time, that the Allies might lose control of the Middle East; had the Middle East fallen, then the China-Burma-India Theater would have been isolated and cut off from its air ferry route. As the Combined Chiefs of Staff viewed the two theaters as interdependent, units assigned to one theater were considered as immediate reinforcements for the other, wherever the need was greatest.[56] The Tenth Air Force was stripped of all its operational heavy bombers. Brereton's Chief of Staff, Brig. Gen. Earl Naiden, took over command of what was left of the Tenth Air Force.

The 9th Squadron Goes Walkabout

Brereton left for the Middle East on June 25th, apparently taking several B-17s with him. Arriving in Cairo on June 28th, Brereton took command of the U.S. Army Middle East Air

The 9th Bombardment Squadron's B-17 *Jungle Jim* at Karachi in June 1942. (7th Bombardment Group (H) Historical Foundation, USAFA McDermott Library)

Force (USAMEAF). As fast as possible, eight more B-17Es at Karachi had newly-overhauled engines fitted and set off to the Middle East. The 7th Group's last remaining LB-30 and four newly-arrived B-24Ds followed shortly after, leaving eight B-17Es in India, all grounded for lack of engines and other spare parts, as the Tenth Air Force's remaining heavy bombers.[57] The urgent call from the Middle East drew off nearly all the combat crews in the 9th Bombardment Squadron with some additions from the 436th Squadron.[58] The bombers left on July 4, 1942, and flew to Lydda, an airfield outside of Tel Aviv in Palestine, where they were to be based while the threat to Egypt remained. The 9th Squadron was initially designated the Brereton Detachment, though within the Squadron the men called themselves "Brereton's Bastards" or the "Bengal Bombers".[59] Brereton also had under his command a small force of B-24Ds of the HALPRO Detachment led by Col. Harry Halverson. HALPRO was one of the special projects organized during the early months of the war to bomb Japan from bases in China. With the loss of Burma, the HALPRO Detachment was diverted to the Middle East, where it undertook the first American air raid on the oil fields at Ploesti in Rumania, the Army Air Forces' first true strategic bombing mission of the war.[60] As Rommel's army advanced toward Egypt, the HALPRO B-24s began night attacks in concert with Royal Air Force Wellington bombers on the ports of Benghazi and Tobruk in Libya, where supplies for the *Afrika Korps* and the Italian Army were unloaded from transports.

The 9th Bombardment Squadron's B-17s flew their first mission shortly after arriving at Lydda. Initially, as with the HALPRO Detachment, all bombing missions were flown at night. The B-17s would take off from Lydda in the afternoon and fly to Fayid—a Royal Air Force base in Egypt—for final briefing. On the night of July 2nd, four B-17Es that had arrived with Brereton a few days earlier attacked Tobruk along with six HALPRO B-24s, where they met light anti-aircraft fire. The 9th Squadron sent two B-17Es the next night back to Tobruk to bomb supply dumps, getting hits in the target area. Five nights later, on July 8th, the 9th Squadron sent three B-17s back to bomb Tobruk while the HALPRO B-24s went to bomb

A 7th Group B-17E 41-9049 at Allahabad, India. Lt. Elmer Morse flew this airplane from the United States to India at the end of April 1942. (7th Bombardment Group (H) Historical Foundation, USAFA McDermott Library)

Benghazi harbor. The 9th Squadron took its turn against Benghazi three nights later, but failed to find the target. As more bombers arrived, the 9th Squadron could sometimes

Major Max Fennell (left) and Major General Louis Brereton stand beneath Fennell's aircraft that he named *Fennell vs Rommel*, somewhere in the Middle East in the summer of 1942. (7th Bombardment Group (H) Historical Foundation, USAFA McDermott Library)

Men of the 9th Bombardment Squadron at Lydda, Palestine, where the Squadron was based during its time in the Middle East. (7th Bombardment Group (H) Historical Foundation, USAFA McDermott Library)

Engine change on a 9th Bombardment Squadron B-17E at Lydda, Palestine. (7th Bombardment Group (H) Historical Foundation, USAFA McDermott Library)

9th Squadron maintenance crews taking a watermelon break under the wing of one of the Squadron's B-17Es. (7th Bombardment Group (H) Historical Foundation, USAFA McDermott Library)

send out more than two or three B-17s on a mission. On the night of July 13th, the Squadron sent five B-17s for a raid on Tobruk harbor, where the bombing started two large fires in the target area. For the next two missions to Tobruk harbor on the nights of July 17th and 19th, the Squadron sent three B-17s on each mission. The B-17s missed any night fighters on these missions and the anti-aircraft fire varied from light to heavy, but failed to damage any of the 9th's aircraft.[61]

On July 20th, the HALPRO Detachment (now called the Hal Squadron) and the 9th Bombardment Squadron were combined into the First Provisional Bombardment Group under Col. Halverson. By this date the battle for Egypt had stabilized, with British forces holding the line at El Alamein, a hundred and fifty miles from Cairo. By advancing, Rommel's army had traveled farther and farther from its two principal supply ports: Benghazi, 600 miles to the west; and Tobruk, 350 miles west. The Allied air forces steadily pounded these critical ports and extended their coverage to several other ports in the Mediterranean where Axis convoys formed up for the voyage to North Africa. By this time, the First Provisional Bomb Group had 19 B-24s and nine B-17s, but only seven B-24s and three B-17s were in commission.[62] Reinforcements had reached Palestine with the arrival of the first squadron of the 98th Bombardment Group; the entire group would be in place by the end of the first week in August.[63] While the longer range B-24s of the Hal Squadron began reaching farther

9th Bombardment Squadron gunners taking some time off while at Lydda, Palestine, summer of 1942. (7th Bombardment Group (H) Historical Foundation, USAFA McDermott Library)

afield, the 9th Squadron's B-17s continued hitting Tobruk harbor. The 9th flew night missions to Tobruk on July 23/24 and 25/26, sending out four aircraft each night and getting strikes in the target area, and again on the nights of July 27/28 and 30/31, with three and then four aircraft—all that could be made operational. The Squadron attacked a convoy in Tobruk harbor on August 6th, and then had a respite from flying combat missions for three weeks, during a period when the British and German armies in Egypt took time to rest and rebuild their forces for the next battles. The crews of the Hal Squadron and the 9th Squadron were given two weeks' leave, allowing the maintenance crews time to get more aircraft back into commission.[64] The 9th Squadron returned to action on August 27th and 28th, with raids on an Axis convoy, then went after shipping in Candia Bay, on the north coast of Crete, on September 1st. As the Germans raced to build up their supplies, the heavy bombers of the First Provisional Bomb Group continued attacking Benghazi and Tobruk. The 9th Squadron flew six missions during the month of September. The night of September 13th, the 9th Squadron sent out five B-17s as part of a large Allied bombing effort against Benghazi and Tobruk involving the B-24s of the Hal Squadron, the newly-arrived 344th Squadron of the 98th Bombardment Group, and Royal Air Force Wellingtons. The mission was partly to cover a British commando raid on both harbors. The bombers made repeated runs over their targets as a distraction for the commandos. According to one source, Bf 109s attacked Lt. Joe Kramp's B-17, causing him to jettison his bombs over Tobruk harbor, by chance getting hits on a tanker.[65] Three days later, seven B-17s bombed Benghazi harbor in daylight, claiming hits on a transport that had just begun unloading its cargo, as well as on a medium-sized vessel nearby. One Bf 109 intercepted the formation, but the bombers escaped undamged.[66]

The 9th Squadron flew nine missions during the first three weeks of October before the Second Battle of El Alamein, striking at the harbors in Benghazi and Tobruk and attacking convoys en route to the two ports. Vessels in port were easier targets than ships at sea and brought more success. On a mission to Tobruk on October 14th, three B-17s got two direct hits on a large transport and demolished a lighter alongside the transport unloading supplies.[67] Weather began to interfere with the missions, the B-17s turning back on several occasions. On October 23rd, General Bernard Montgomery, who had taken command of the British Eighth Army in August, attacked German positions. The battle raged for twelve days, until the British broke through the German lines on November 4th, forcing the *Afrika Korps* into headlong retreat west. With his rear ports in disarray and his convoys under attack, Rommel had the *Luftwaffe* fly in desperately needed gasoline from Crete using Ju52 transports. On October 30th, the First Provisional Bomb Group sent out B-24s and B-17s to bomb the German airfields on Crete. Six B-17s attacked the airfield at Tymbaki through thunderstorms.[68] This was the 9th Bombardment Squadron's last mission in the Middle East. Brig. Gen. Clayton Bissell, who had taken over command of the Tenth Air Force on August 18, 1942, from Brig. Gen. Naiden, had been pressing for the return of the 9th Bombardment Squadron and the transfer of the Halverson

A later model B-17E of the 9th Bombardment Squadron at Gambut, Lybia. Note how the airplane's serial number has been painted out—a common practice in the Tenth Air Force at that time—and a British Royal Air Force insignia added on the tail. (7th Bombardment Group (H) Historical Foundation, USAFA McDermott Library)

Detachment to the CBI, but even with the arrival of the 98th Bombardment Group, Brereton had been reluctant to part with his most experienced squadrons.[69] Under an agreement worked out in September, the Tenth Air Force regained its transport aircraft diverted to the Middle East and the bulk of the 9th Bombardment Squadron's ground crews and a portion of the combat crews, while the crews of the Halverson Detachment remained in the Middle East. Members of the 9th Squadron began transferring back to Karachi on October 3rd, the last personnel arriving on November 3rd.[70] On November 2nd, the First Provisional Bomb Group was re-designated the 376th Bombardment Group (H). The 9th Squadron's crews remaining at Lydda became the core of the newly-activated 513th and 515th Bombardment Squadrons in the 376th Group.[71]

Treading Water

A 9th Bombardment Squadron B-17E in a sandbag revetment at Fayid, Egypt, in November 1942, after the Squadron's mission in the Middle East had ended. (7th Bombardment Group (H) Historical Foundation, USAFA McDermott Library)

The departure of the 9th Bombardment Squadron to the Middle East had left the 7th Bombardment Group with no heavy bombers capable of flying combat missions. The effort to build a heavy bomber group for the Tenth Air Force had to start all over again. During the remaining weeks of July and into August, a few of the eight remaining B-17s were slowly put back into commission, but they were limited to short training flights due to excessive oil consumption.[72] The Tenth Air Force resorted to borrowing two Fortress I airplanes (equivalent to the B-17C) from the Royal Air Force. These had made their way from England to the Middle East and then on to India.[73] They were used only for training. During July and August, the heavy bombers undertook only one mission, when a single B-17E flew to the Andaman Islands in an unsuccessful search for a Japanese seaplane tender reported in the area.[74] Only the 11th Bombardment Squadron was active, flying 11 missions during July and 17 during August against targets in China. A small detachment flying out of Dinjan, in India, completed 12 missions in July and another 11 in August.[75] From India, the 11th Squadron's B-25s, singly or in pairs, attacked the airfield at Myitkyina and the railroad at nearby Mogaung, where supplies for Japanese troops were unloaded.

Several organizational developments occurred during the summer of 1942 that pointed to a more active future for the 7th Bombardment Group. In June, General Henry Arnold and Rear Admiral John Towers, representing the Army Air Forces and the Navy, reached an agreement with Air Chief Marshal Sir Charles Portal, Chief of Staff of the Royal Air Force, on a proposed allocation of American Army Air units among the various theaters of war.[76] For the China-Burma-India Theater, the Army Air Forces planned to have one full group of heavy bombers with four squadrons and 35 aircraft and a full medium bomber group with 57 aircraft in four squadrons by September 1942, along with two groups of fighters with 160 aircraft by October 1942.[77] The Combined Chiefs of Staff approved the Arnold-Portal Agreement in early July. Although the crisis in the Middle East delayed implementation of these plans for the CBI, the Arnold-Portal Agreement set the stage for the restructuring of the 7th Bombardment Group from a composite heavy-medium group back to a heavy bomber group. For the CBI, the one drawback of the new plan was that the new squadrons needed to bring the 7th Group and the proposed medium bomber group up to full four-squadron strength would have to be raised within the CBI Theater. This meant

Short of aircraft, the 7th Bombardment Group borrowed two older Fortress I airplanes (equivalent to the B-17C) from the Royal Air Force for training flights. (Author's collection)

A B-25C of the 11th Bombardment Squadron prepares for a mission in China during the summer of 1942. The Squadron painted the famous "Mr. Jiggs" emblem on the noses of its B-25s. (RG 208-AA-Folder 12X-81, NARA)

that existing squadrons would have to provide cadre for their new sister units and the new units would have to be filled out with replacement crews and aircraft as they arrived from America. This process took several months. As a first step, the 341st Bombardment Group (M) was activated in India on September 15, 1942. That same day, two new squadrons were activated (the 490th and 491st Bombardment Squadrons (M)) and the 11th and 22nd Bombardment Squadrons were re-designated as medium bomber squadrons and transferred from the 7th Group to the new 341st Group.[78] Activation of new heavy bomber squadrons for the 7th Bombardment Group, however, was delayed until October.

The 7th Group would also receive a new bomber aircraft. The B-17 had proved to be less than satisfactory in the China-Burma-India Theater. The Flying Fortress lacked the range to reach targets in southern Burma and beyond with an adequate bomb load, while the dust and sand at airfields in India caused excessive oil consumption and wear on the engines, a problem that lack of spare parts and spare engines only made worse when engines had to be changed after only 20 flying hours.[79] By the end of September, the few remaining B-17s in the 7th Group had, for the most part, been out of commission for nearly three months. Brig. Gen. Bissell echoed Maj. Gen. Brereton's complaints about the B-17.[80] The Army Air Corps agreed to replace the 7th Group's B-17s with the B-24. The B-24 had the range to reach Rangoon and beyond. The Group would fly the B-24 for the remainder of the war. The prewar pilots who had trained on the B-17 preferred the Flying Fortress to the Liberator, but for the mechanics, the Liberator was easier to work on. The maintenance men found the B-24's Pratt & Whitney R-1830 engines easier to maintain than the B-17's Wright Cyclones.[81] Because of the demands of other theaters, it took several months for the conversion to be completed and the Group to be brought up to full strength. In September, two B-24Ds equipped with ASV search radar arrived in India for the 7th Group, though the ASV gear was shortly removed.[82] More B-24Ds followed: 16 arriving in October and five in December.[83] By the end of the year, the Group had 22 B-24s assigned and ten non-operational B-17s.

Lt. Col. Necrason took command of the 7th Bombardment Group on July 1, 1942, when Lt. Col. Combs transferred to Tenth Air Force headquarters. Necrason would lead the 7th Group for the next year and a half. A 1936 graduate of West Point, Necrason served as a pursuit pilot in the Philippines and the 35th Pursuit Group before joining the 7th Bombardment Group as a Captain in mid-1941. Promoted to major, he commanded the 9th Bombardment Squadron in Java. The stress and strain of the Java campaign left its mark on him; meeting up with Necrason in Karachi a month after leaving Java, Capt. James Tull, adjutant of the 7th Group's headquarters squadron, recalled that: "...the gay, young, and efficient officer whom we had left in Salt Lake City four months before now was grave, quiet, and looked five years older."[84] Necrason was a capable commander who won the respect of his men. As Charles Beauvais, a squadron mechanic, remembered him, Necrason "...was a fine officer and an inspiration to all of us,

B-17Es flying over India during the summer of 1942. (7th Bombardment Group (H) Historical Foundation, USAFA McDermott Library)

ground and air crews alike. If there was a particularly dangerous mission he was always in the lead ship. If there was a dangerous volunteer mission it was always the Colonel and whoever wished to volunteer."[85]

Necrason's task in the months after he assumed command was to oversee the operations of a group undermanned, under-equipped, and spread from Karachi to Calcutta. The 11th Bombardment Squadron was operating in China with the China Air Task Force. This unit was formed on July 4, 1942, with the remnants of the American Volunteer Group and pilots of the 23rd Fighter Group under the command of Brig.

Gen. Claire Chennault. The 22nd Bombardment Squadron was flying missions out of bases near Calcutta and from Dinjan, in Assam. With no heavy bombers available for combat

Major General Louis Brereton preferred the B-24 Liberator to the B-17 Flying Fortress for the China-Burma-India Theater because of the Liberator's longer range. (3A-33645, RG 342FH, NARA)

operations, the 7th Group headquarters moved back to Karachi from Calcutta on August 9th, leaving the 436th Bombardment Squadron at Allahabad. After the activation of the 341st Bombardment Group in September, the 7th Bombardment Group's Headquarters and Headquarters Squadron was disbanded, the personnel going to form the Headquarters 7th Bombardment Group and Headquarters 341st Bombardment Group. Personnel that were excess to requirements were organized into the Provisional Heavy Bombardment Squadron pending activation of the two heavy bomber squadrons for the 7th Group.[86] The Group did not begin to fly combat missions again until the end of October 1942.

The Tenth Air Force's headquarters was based in New Delhi, over a thousand miles away from the front lines in eastern India. Brig. Gen. Bissell realized the need for an organization located closer to the operating units to control and coordinate operations. With the end of the monsoon in September, he combined all the combat units in India into the India Air Task Force, to operate in a similar fashion to Chennault's China Air Task Force. He placed Col. Caleb Haynes in command.[87] Activated on October 3, 1942, the India Air Task Force had nine squadrons assigned from the 7th and 341st Bombardment Groups and the 51st Fighter Group. However, not one was fully manned, equipped, and ready for combat operations.[88] In the 7th Group, the personnel from the 9th Bombardment Squadron began arriving in Karachi from their Middle East sojourn on October 7th and continued to dribble in over the next several weeks. After arrival, they again officially became the 9th Bombardment Squadron. The Provisional Heavy Bombardment Squadron was disbanded and its personnel reassigned to the 9th Squadron to bring it up to strength. The 436th Bombardment Squadron began to receive its new B-24Ds and new combat crews during the month, the air echelon moving from Allahabad to a new base at Gaya, India. Permission to activate the two new heavy bomber squadrons finally came through, and on October 20, 1942, the 492nd and 493rd Bombardment Squadrons (H) came into being, with one officer and ten enlisted men assigned to each squadron at the New Malir camp outside Karachi on October 25th.[88]

The 7th Bombardment Group had been in India for eight months, with little to show for all the hard work the air and ground crews had undertaken. From April to early June, the 9th Bombardment Squadron had flown 23 missions to targets in Burma and the Andaman Islands, despite being constantly short of airplanes and spare parts. Over the next three months, the 7th Group carried out only two more missions. Just as offensive missions were finally getting underway, the crisis in the Middle East took all available aircraft and most of the combat crews, forcing the Group to build up a combat capability all over again. The maintenance crews had to cope with the scorching heat and sand and dust in Karachi and other bases in India, and the torrential monsoons that made flying and working difficult and dangerous from June into September. The constant shortage of parts and spare engines continued for months on end, often never even arriving in India. Other units pilfered shipments along the route from the United States to Karachi. In October 1942, the 7th Group

An early B-17E flying over India with the remote control belly turret extended. (Author's collection)

would start flying combat again and would continue flying missions out of India until the end of the war, nearly three years away.

CHAPTER FIVE

INDIA AIR TASK FORCE

A Plan of Action

Older B-17Es alongside the new B-24Ds at Gaya, the 7th Bombardment Group's base in India, in late 1942. The 7th Group retained several B-17Es well into 1943 and flew them on several combat missions until more B-24Ds arrived to equip the Group. (3A-33635, RG 342FH, NARA)

With the end of the monsoon in October, the question confronting the Allied and Japanese high commands was how to proceed in Burma. The Japanese had the more straightforward decision. In prewar planning, the Japanese high command had assumed that the Burma-India border would be the extent of their conquests in Southeast Asia. Following the successful capture of Burma, Malaya, and the Netherlands East Indies, Japan's overall objective was to establish a secure defensive position to defend its newly-conquered territories while developing these resources for Japan's war industries.[1] Japan now had a huge territory to defend with limited forces, especially air forces, and a limited amount of shipping to supply their now far-flung garrisons. In Burma, the Japanese *15th Army* was instructed to go on the defensive to prevent the Allies from launching counter-attacks into Burma from India or China.[2] The Japanese forces in Burma required a more secure supply route than the sea route up from Singapore. The sea route to Rangoon made

Japanese transports vulnerable to air or submarine attack. *Imperial General Headquarters* in Tokyo ordered the construction of a railway line from Thailand into Burma so that supplies could be transported from the port of Bangkok.[3]

For the Allies, the enormous logistical difficulties they confronted in the China-Burma-India Theater and conflicting national interests and objectives complicated the strategic options before them. No other Allied theater of war faced the logistical problems confronting British and American forces in India. In the first instance, the sheer distance from sources of supply in the United States and the United Kingdom remained an on-going problem even after the port of Calcutta was opened to shipping. A shortage of transport ships from 1942 well into 1943 meant fewer supplies could be shipped to India. Even had there been enough ships, the European and Mediterranean Theaters' first call on supplies of men, aircraft, and equipment of all types meant little remained for the Far East. Once supplies reached India at the ports of Karachi or Calcutta, they had to be transported over a road and rail system that was barely adequate to carry the normal flow of traffic in peacetime, much less the amount of supplies needed in war. To reach the forward airfields for the flight over the Hump to China, supplies moved by rail to a point on the Brahmaputra River, were unloaded and carried across the river by ferry, and loaded onto another train line for shipment to their destination. Supplying the front lines of the British IV Corps in Assam and the XV Corps in the Arakan was an even worse proposition. The mountain ranges that stretched from the foothills of the Himalayas to the Bay of Bengal created a barrier more than one-hundred miles wide between India and Burma, with only one road leading from the train lines to Imphal. From there only fair weather tracks led into Burma. Communications down the Arakan coast were marginally better. The border area was covered in jungle, rampant with disease, and barely passable during the May to October monsoon with its torrential rains. Within India there was a chronic shortage for much of 1942 and 1943 of engineering troops and equipment for the vital tasks of building more airfields for not only the Tenth Air Force, but for the air route to China over the Hump and for the expanding Royal Air Force in Northeast India, as well as better roads and railroads.[4]

The American objective in the China-Burma-India Theater had always been simple: to ensure that China remained in the war. With the fall of Burma, the United States had to re-open a connection from India to China. The flow of supplies was essential to prevent China's collapse, as seemed immanent in the fall of 1942 and early 1943.[5] A trickle of supplies had begun to flow over the air route from northern Assam to Kunming, the infamous Hump route. This amounted to only a few hundred tons a month, and it did not seem at the time that the air route, lacking both transport aircraft and an adequate number of airfields, could ever sustain China on its own. The solution seemed at the time to require driving the Japanese out of northern Burma to re-open a land route to China via the Burma Road. Lt. Gen. Stilwell developed a plan during July-August 1942 to retake Burma through a combined Chinese-British offensive involving 12 American-trained and -equipped Chinese divisions advancing from Yunnan into Northern Burma and then south; two more American-trained and -equipped Chinese divisions, and three British divisions, advancing from Assam toward Mandalay, in Central Burma; and a seaborne operation to capture Akyab, on the Burmese coast, followed by a landing at Rangoon to open the port and link up with forces advancing from the north.[6] The Chinese were keen to see Burma retaken and the Burma Road reopened, but Generalissimo Chiang Kai-shek was reluctant to contribute any large portion of the Chinese armies for the task; in certain cases he had only the most tenuous control over these armies. He was reluctant to arm and train the armies of his political rivals, preferring instead to husband his resources for the inevitable postwar battle with the Communists.[7]

The British perspective disagreed with American strategic objectives. For the British high command, the recapture of Burma was seen not as a means of reopening a land supply route to China as the Americans wanted, but as a stepping stone toward the liberation of Britain's other colonies in Southeast Asia—Malaya and Singapore.[8] British plans did not require a revitalized Chinese military and considered China's continued participation in the war unnecessary.[9] General Wavell had begun planning how to retake Burma soon after it fell. Looking at the severe and seemingly insurmountable logistical constraints of mounting an overland campaign through the jungle-covered, mountainous India-Burma border, Wavell and his planning staff came to see amphibious landings in lower Burma as the preferred avenue of approach.[10] As Prime Minister Winston Churchill would say of the idea of advancing through northern Burma to attack the Japanese, "Going into a swampy jungle to fight the Japanese is like going into the water to attack a shark."[11] The failure of the limited British advance in the Arakan coastal area in early 1943 seemed to confirm Churchill's views. Wavell's plan, called ANAKIM, involved a limited advance in Assam to hold Japanese troops there, the seizure of the airfields at Akyab to gain air superiority, and a seaborne landing at Rangoon to seize Lower Burma. ANAKIM, however, was dependent on three crucial factors: the establishment of air superiority over all of Burma, British naval control of the Bay of Bengal, and adequate numbers of landing craft and troops. None of these requirements could possibly be provided until the fall of 1943 at the earliest. Wavell, and later Churchill and other British planners began to think about bypassing Burma altogether in favor of Sumatra

Brigadier General Caleb V. Haynes, commander of the India Air Task Force. (File 827.306-1 November 1942-May 1943, Albert F. Simpson Historical Research Center, Air Force Historical Research Agency, Maxwell AFB, AL)

as a base for operations against Malaya and Singapore.[12]

To the frustration of the Americans, ANAKIM was to be postponed until the fall of 1943 and was finally dropped altogether as simply too ambitious for the limited resources available to the Far East. It appeared that nothing would be achieved during 1943 to aid China. President Roosevelt and the American Joint Chiefs of Staff began to work on other means of aiding China more quickly through the provision of more airplanes to Gen. Chennault, an increase in the number of transports assigned to the Hump route, and consideration of General Stilwell's plan to build a road from Ledo, in Assam, to connect with the old Burma Road at Lashio, capturing Myitkyina along the way. Beginning at the Trident Conference in May 1943 and finally the Quadrant Conference in August 1943, the British and the Americans agreed on a strategy for Burma that incorporated elements of several plans, but was much less ambitious than either Stilwell or Wavell had originally conceived.[13] For most of the year, apart from limited offensives in the Arakan, the first Wingate expedition, and Stilwell's initial advance with his American-trained Chinese divisions from Ledo in the fall of 1943, the main Allied response against the Japanese in Burma was the Royal Air Force and the Tenth Air Force's small but growing air campaign using their limited numbers of fighters, medium bombers, and heavy bombers.[14]

Lack of agreement on a comprehensive Allied strategy for operations in Burma complicated the task of the Tenth Air Force. Problems included the allocation of units and aircraft, the construction of new and better airfields, and the selection of targets. Brig. Gen. Clayton Bissell, commanding the Tenth Air Force, deferred to higher authority for their resolution, inevitably slowing down the process.[15] As one history of the China-Burma-India Theater commented: "each day of delay in agreeing on strategy meant that the Tenth would continue to fight on the principle of co-operation with the British and Chinese, rather than in an Allied command with them."[16] Fortunately for the Allies, the efforts of the Royal Air Force and the Tenth Air Force in Burma, though only loosely coordinated, proved to be complementary, in part due to the types of aircraft assigned to each force and their relative capabilities. In late 1942, the Royal Air Force had four squadrons of Blenheim and the similar Bisley light bombers, one squadron of Wellington medium bombers, and one squadron with a small number of Liberator heavy bombers available. With only a limited number of bombers, the RAF decided that its bombing policy should concentrate on reducing the capabilities of the Japanese Army Air Force in Burma.[17] Japanese airfields in Burma became the priority targets, the shorter-range Blenheims and Bisleys attacked forward area airfields by day, and the medium-range Wellingtons attacked airfields in Central Burma by night. As the RAF had so few operational Liberators, the Tenth Air Force's heavy bombers in the 7th Bombardment Group took on the task of attacking targets in lower Burma, principally Rangoon.[18]

Brig. Gen. Bissell had assigned the India Air Task Force two missions: primarily defending the air bases in northeastern Assam supporting the air ferry route from India to China, but the secondary mission was "...the destruction of hostile aircraft, shipping, and installations in other areas."[19] Caleb V. Haynes, promoted to Brigadier General on assuming command of the India Air Task Force, was a 1932 graduate of the Air Corps Tactical School and an experienced bomber pilot. Bissell gave Haynes wide leeway in the conduct of tactical operations. Haynes chose to use his small force of heavy bombers in the 7th Bombardment Group according to Army Air Forces strategic bombing doctrine. The Army Air Corps 1940 Field Manual FM 1-10, *Tactics and Techniques of Air Attack*, specified that: "...strategic objectives for air attack include elements of the enemy's armed forces, and facilities and establishments which support the operations of those forces and the enemy national structure."[20] There were few strategic targets in Burma that could be defined as part of the Japanese "national structure" or contributed to the production of war materials as the Army Air Corps prewar strategic bombing advocates had envisioned. The bombing campaign in Burma would have a different set of targets, principally the Japanese Army's line of communications system and the supplies brought over that system from Japan. Back in 1933, Lt. Kenneth Walker, Haynes's instructor at the Air Corps Tactical School and one of the Army Air Corps' leading bombing advocates, had outlined the basic form of the strategic air campaign that the Tenth Air Force carried out in Burma from 1942 until 1945. In his article for *U.S. Air Services*, Walker wrote the following:

The fact that logistics (the art of supply and

transportation) is the Achilles Heel of modern warfare is fast becoming recognized. Destruction of the means by which any armed force is supplied, moved, and made ready to operate, eliminates that force as a threat. There will be certain vital enemy objectives, which if destroyed will contribute most to the success of the combined arms of the nation. These objectives may be the hostile naval force which insures the maintenance of the enemy sea lines of communication; convoyed merchantmen transporting air and land forces to bases from which a blow can be struck against us; dock facilities, supply establishments and lines of communications on land necessary for the unloading, supplying and moving of hostile forces, operating airdromes of hostile air units. Successful air operations against such vital objectives will hamstring an enemy.[21]

The targets that Walker outlined—shipping, port facilities, supply dumps, and lines of communication—would all be objectives for the 7th Bombardment Group, indirectly supporting the fighters defending the Assam air bases and the British and Chinese armies in Burma through the destruction of the Japanese Army's and Army Air Forces' supplies and the system of moving those supplies where they were needed.[22]

The Japanese Army in Burma had its own logistical challenges. Mountain ranges on Burma's northern, western, and eastern borders had effectively cut the country off from its neighbors. In the prewar years, trade flows in and out of the country went by sea out of Rangoon, Burma's principal port. While the Japanese Army obtained a sizeable portion of its requirements from within Burma—principally food, clothing, and some fuel—all its weapons, ammunition, heavy equipment, and spare parts had to come by sea from Japan or Japanese factories in Manchuria. The distance from Japan to Burma was less than from the United Kingdom or the United States, but Japanese shipping still traveled more than 4,000 miles of ocean to reach Rangoon, passing around Singapore and through the Strait of Malacca to the Gulf of Martaban, then going up the Rangoon River to Rangoon. Although the Japanese could bring up supplies by rail from Singapore, until the railroad from Bangkok to Burma was completed late in 1943, the Japanese could not avail themselves of the ports in Bangkok or Saigon. Once in Rangoon or the few other smaller ports in southern Burma, supplies had to be moved to the front lines over the Burmese railroad system, a network of 2,000 miles of single-line track running from the Malay Peninsula to Myitkyina in the north, with a branch line off to Lashio in the northeast of the country. The two stages of the transportation system—shipping supplies to Burma, unloading supplies and storing them at port facilities, then arranging for the transfer of supplies from the coast to the front lines via the railroad system—gave the Tenth Air Force a plentitude of potential targets that would disrupt the flow of supplies along the Japanese line of communications. The longer-range B-24s of the 7th Bombardment Group took on the more distant targets in southern Burma, principally Rangoon, while the 341st Bombardment Group's medium-range B-25s took responsibility for targets in Central Burma. With Japan's limited number of transports shipping became a priority, followed by the ports within range of the B-24s. As Army Air Corps planners had envisioned as they worked up the doctrines of strategic bombing during the 1930s, the Burmese railroad system had vulnerable points all along the route. Beginning at Rangoon and at key towns along the route to the north were marshaling yards, depots, warehouses, and concentrations of rolling stock—suitable targets for heavy and medium bombers. Burma's north-south railroad line included numerous bridges along the route from Rangoon and the other southern ports to towns in central and northern Burma. Destroying a key bridge along the route would completely disrupt the flow of supplies. What the air planners had not envisioned nor realized in the course of the many exercises and bombing practices conducted during the 1930s was just how difficult it would be to destroy these types of targets, especially bridges, and how quickly they could be repaired.

Rangoon: the target for many a 7th Bombardment Group mission during 1942-43. Taken just after a bombing mission on December 20, 1942, the photograph is looking south past the city, down the Rangoon River to the Gulf of Martaban. (Courtesy Col. Thomas Sledge, USAF Retd)

The Tenth Air Force's campaign against the Japanese line of communications in Burma would be a relentless 2 ½-year battle of attrition, at first amounting to not much more than nuisance raids in the early months of 1943 before gradually building into an effective force capable of inflicting regular and sustained damage against key targets.[23]

The Bombing Campaign Begins: The Lin-hsi Mines Mission

Major Max Fennell's crew with their B-24 in China on the mission to bomb the Lin-hsi Coal Mines on October 20, 1942. (7th Bombardment Group (H) Historical Foundation, USAFA McDermott Library)

The 7th Bombardment Group's first mission for the India Air Task Force was not into Burma, but to China. The mission was an attempt to knock out one of the few vital industrial targets in China, the Lin-hsi coal mines in northern China. These mines produced 14,000 tons of coking coal a day for iron and steel plants in Manchuria and Japan. The mines were a perfect and worthy target for the doctrine of daylight precision strategic bombing, a critical economic node for the Japanese war industries. The specific target was the power plant and pumping station alongside the mines; their complete destruction would result in flooding the mines and disrupting production for months on end.[24] In early October, five newly-arrived B-24 crews assigned to the 9th and 436th Bombardment Squadrons and the Provisional Bombardment Squadron were chosen for the mission under the command of Maj. Max Fennell, who had previously flown several missions in China during the spring of 1942 before going with the 9th Bombardment Squadron to the Middle East. Fennell was brought back from the Middle East for the mission because of his experience flying over China. On his arrival at Karachi, he and his five crews began two days of intensive training, flying practice bombing missions to a small island off the coast to drop 100-pound practice bombs from 14,000 feet (the altitude selected for the mission). Brig. Gen. Bissell came to inspect the crews and their airplanes.[25]

On October 11, 1942, six B-24D bombers and their crews (Maj. Fennell, Capts. Joseph Pirruccello, James Ridgell, and Wesley Werner, and Lts. Elmer Morse and Merle O'Brian) flew to the 7th Bombardment Group's base at Allahabad, in Central India, where they picked up a spare airplane with Lt. Col. Cecil Combs as pilot, then flew to Dinjan, in northeastern Assam, the western terminus of the Hump route. Two days later, on October 13th, the six crews, with Combs flying the spare, headed off for Kunming. A small number of maintenance men went along with them to service their B-24s in China. Flying at 20,000 feet through broken clouds, Lt. Col. Combs's B-24 stalled in a climb, the big bomber starting a roll to the right. The copilot, 2nd Lt. Thomas Murphy—a big strong man who had already experienced being shot down in a B-25 over

Smoke rises from the Lin-hsi Mines after the bombing. (7th Bombardment Group (H) Historical Foundation, USAFA McDermott Library)

Akyab the previous June—got the airplane under control by continuing the roll. The B-24 did a complete roll to the right, narrowly missing the side of a mountain to the left. By sheer chance, the B-24 had come out of the clouds over a valley where there was space to complete the roll. The shaken crew continued on to Kunming.[26]

The crews had to wait several days at Kunming for good weather before proceeding to their jumping off base at Hsinching, near the city of Chengtu, 150 miles northwest of the city of Chungking. The weather finally cleared sufficiently on October 20th for the mission to Lin-hsi to begin. The B-24s took off at 0930, carrying 750-pound Russian-made bombs and three containers of small German-made incendiaries. Two hours out, the formation ran into a cold front, where they encountered heavy ice forming on the wings. After trying to break through, Maj. Fennell ordered the formation to return to base, rather than risk losing an airplane. They tried again the next day, and had good weather all the way to the target. The formation passed several Japanese airfields along the way, but no fighters rose to intercept them. Capt. Ridgell's plane aborted the mission due to engine trouble, but the others continued on. Arriving over the target, the bombers approached at 14,000 feet, each airplane making an individual run over the mines. As the bombers flew over the mines, the waist gunners threw the small German incendiary bombs out the waist windows, each container holding fifteen bombs. As they departed, the crews could see smoke rising from several fires. Though they struck the target, the bombs failed to destroy the power plant and the pumping station. Still, in one of the longest missions of the war to date—a journey of around 2,400 miles—the bombers had shown the Japanese that they could expect attacks over a far greater area than they had previously experienced. On their way back to India, the bombers took off from Kunming around 0230 on the morning of October 27th and bombed the Japanese-held airfield at Myitkyina shortly after dawn on their way to Calcutta and then their air base at Allahabad.[27]

Into Burma

At the end of October, the 7th Bombardment Group flew its first mission into Burma and its second combat mission with its new B-24s. Though it proved unsuccessful, it gave 2nd Lt. Thomas Murphy his third brush with disaster in only a few short months. The mission sent six B-24s from the 436th Squadron to bomb the docks at Rangoon (though the 436th

A new B-24D belonging to the 436th Bombardment Squadron in India (left to right): 2nd Lt. Tom Murphy (CP), 2nd Lt. William Berkeley (P), and 2nd Lt. Richard Weis (N), soon to be promoted to 1st Lt. (7th Bombardment Group (H) Historical Foundation, USAFA McDermott Library)

Squadron History records ten aircraft going out on the mission). The airplanes arrived over the target around 1755, but were unable to locate the docks due to bad weather, despite flying over the Rangoon area for 35 minutes. Returning to base, three aircraft apparently bombed Akyab. That evening, 2nd Lt. Murphy was flying as a copilot in Lt. William Berkeley's crew. Fifteen minutes before reaching Rangoon, a fire broke out in the nose of the aircraft when a parachute placed too close to the electric heater burst into flames. Lt. Francis Thompson, the navigator, put out the flames. Flying over the target area, all four engines on the B-24 suddenly cut out and the plane started descending toward Rangoon. Berkeley hurriedly worked the controls to get the engines going again, only to have them cut out a few seconds later, and the airplane resumed its slow downward glide. Fortunately, the engines started up again. The bombardier, M/Sgt. Howard Darby, jettisoned the bomb load and Berkeley headed the airplane out over the Bay of Bengal and back to base. When the bomber was still 100 miles away from Calcutta over the sea, the electrical system conked out, followed by the auxiliary electrical system and then the batteries. The radios went dead, there were no landing lights, and no governors for the propellers. On the instrument panel, only the flight indicator and the gyro compass (neither electric) were working. Murphy shined a flashlight on the panel so Berkeley could maintain course while the flight engineer tried unsuccessfully to get the electric power back on. They finally reached a city and started circling, looking for an airport. With no ability to identify themselves, the air defense network assumed they were an enemy bomber and sent up a Hurricane fighter to intercept. Continuing their good fortune, the fighter pilot apparently recognized the big airplane as a B-24 and turned away without firing. Soon

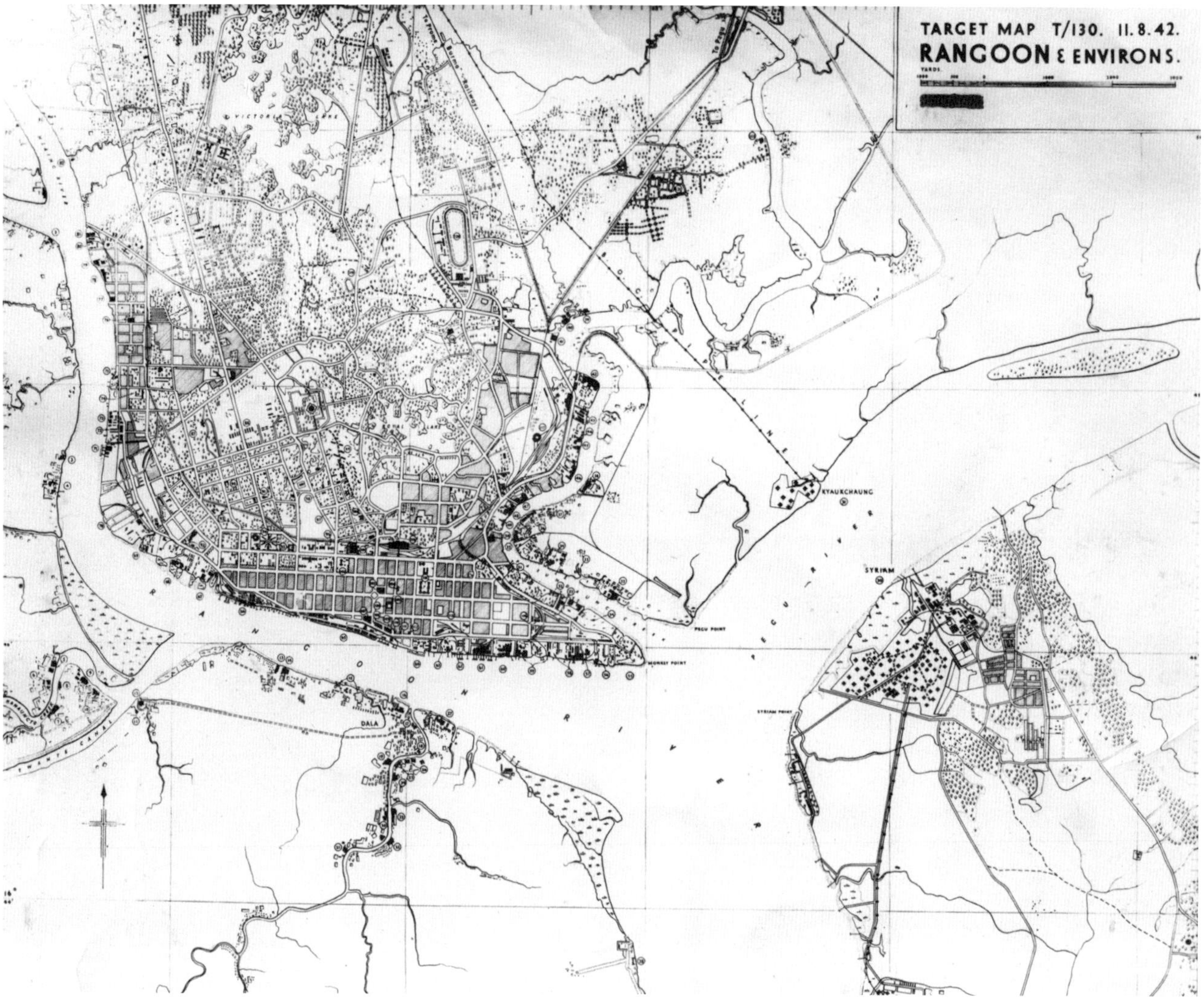

A target map of Rangoon from November 1942. The docks along the Rangoon River, in the center of the map, and the warehouses alongside were frequent targets for the 7th Group. (Courtesy Col. Thomas Sledge, USAF Retd)

afterwards, the number 3 engine on the B-24 started running away as the RPMs went past the danger limit. When the engine started to disintegrate Berkeley ordered the crew to bail out. By another stroke of luck a ground crewman had placed an extra parachute on board, so all nine crew members had good chutes. On bailing out, seven of the crew were knocked unconscious when the buckles on their parachutes, which they had not had time to properly adjust, hit them in the face. Wind scattered the men over the countryside, some landing in rice paddies, swamps, trees, or a lake. The next day, the men proceeded toward Calcutta, meeting up along the way at different stations on the train line. At Calcutta, they waited eight days for transportation back to their base. To their frustration, they paid their hotel bills out of their own pockets. This seemed a bit much after what they had been through.[28]

Rangoon would be a regular target for the 7th Bombardment Group for the next six months, until the onset of the monsoon weather in May. The Group flew more than 40 missions to targets in the Rangoon area before the rains came. Key targets in and near the city included ships in the Rangoon River, the docks and warehouses alongside, the Mahlwagon marshaling yards and railroad workshops, and the Pazundaung railroad bridge, which carried the rail line north to Mandalay.[29] The missions to Rangoon were long—nine to ten hours—covering a distance greater than that from England to Berlin. The bombers went out most often by day, without fighter escort, as there were no fighters in the CBI Theater with the range to reach Rangoon. The Group usually flew in loose formation most of the way to Rangoon over the Bay of Bengal, far enough off the Burmese coast to avoid Japanese fighters. Around 100 miles before reaching Rangoon, the bombers would climb to their bombing altitude of 23,000 to 25,000 feet. On reaching the Irrawaddy River Delta, the bombers would tighten the formation for bombing and come in over land toward the

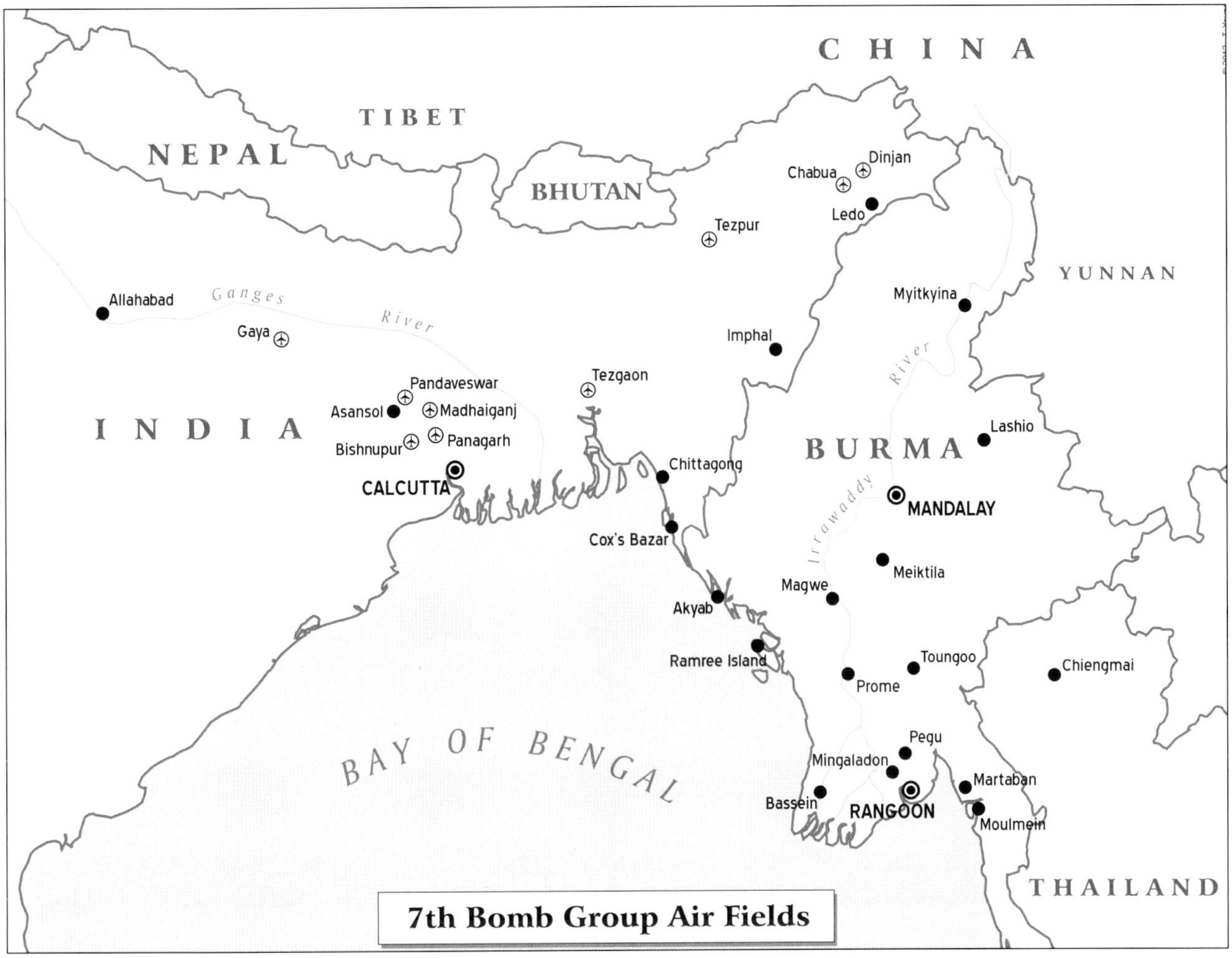

7th Bomb Group Air Fields

target, making a sharp turn and descent right after bombing to get back over the ocean as quickly as possible. At first Rangoon lacked air defenses, but as Allied raids increased the Japanese added anti-aircraft guns until the city became one of the hotter spots in the theater.[30] For some months, there were relatively few Japanese fighters assigned to the defense of Rangoon, enabling the 7th Bombardment Group to continue with unescorted daylight missions with acceptable losses.

The 436th Squadron flew two more missions to Rangoon in the first half of November 1942. The Squadron sent out six B-24s on November 6th to bomb the docks and nearby warehouses in a daylight mission. Two bombers took off from Alipore to join four taking off from Dum-Dum, near Calcutta. The bombers flew down the Bay of Bengal, slowly climbing to 25,000 feet before coming in over the Irrawaddy Delta. The bombers dropped twenty 1,000-pound bombs from 26,700 feet on the target area against light flak. Nine bombs fell into the Rangoon River and one hit a transport, claimed as sunk. Six bombers returned to Rangoon three days later, again bombing from high altitude at 26,800 feet. Each airplane dropped five 1,000-pound bombs, and again twenty bombs hit in the target area—the main docks and warehouses. Five bombs fell into the river and five hit the oil refinery at Syriam, just southeast of the city. For the first time, the bombers encountered Japanese fighters. Three fighters, most likely Japanese Army Air Force Ki-43 Type 1 Hayabusa (Ki-43-I)—given the name "Oscar" in the Army Air Forces' intelligence system for identifying Japanese airplanes then going into general use in the CBI and the Southwest Pacific—from the *64th Sentai*, then charged with the defense of Rangoon, came up to observe the bomber formation. One fighter attacked from the rear without effect; the bombers replied with some 1,500 rounds of.50 caliber fire.[31]

The early missions by the 436th Bombardment Squadron were something of a warm-up exercise, as the 7th Group was still not fully manned nor concentrated. At the end of October, the 436th Squadron had moved from Allahabad to a new base at Gaya, an airfield some 260 miles northeast of Calcutta. Having gathered crews and aircraft at Karachi for several weeks, the 9th Bombardment Squadron sent its air echelon to Gaya on November 14th, followed a few days later by Lt. Col. Necrason and the Group staff, leaving the 9th Squadron's ground echelon to pack up all equipment and await word on when to move east. The 436th Squadron's ground echelon arrived at Gaya on November 20th, servicing both squadrons

Returning from the first night mission to Bangkok, Thailand, November 26, 1942. (File 827.306-1, Albert F. Simpson Historical Research Center, Air Force Historical Research Agency, Maxwell AFB, AL)

for a period of a few weeks. The 7th Group's newest squadrons (the 492nd and 493rd) remained at Karachi in the cadre stage, helping newly-arrived crews through a short, two-week training period prior to their assignment to either the 9th or 436th Squadrons. Around the same time, the 341st Bombardment Group, with its one operational B-25 squadron in India (the 22nd Bombardment Squadron), was assigned to an airfield at Chakulia, southwest of Calcutta. On November 15th, Brig. Gen. Haynes moved the headquarters of the India Air Task Force from New Delhi to Barrackpore, near Calcutta, to be closer to his operational groups. Although the 7th Group had only 17 B-24Ds available in November, in addition to the ten non-operational B-17Es, and the 341st Group less than 20 B-25s, with two heavy bomber squadrons and one medium bomber squadron now operational, the India Air Task Force decided to launch a sustained air offensive against Japanese lines of communication in Burma, beginning with the heavy bombers.[32]

The first missions of the offensive took place on November 20, 1942. At 0700 that morning, Lt. Col. Necrason led eight B-24s from the 436th Bombardment Squadron to attack the railroad marshaling yards and engine repair shop at Mandalay. Each B-24 again carried five 1,000-pound bombs. The formation came in over the target at 27,000 feet, with scattered clouds below them. The yards were full of rolling stock. Dropping their bombs in train, the formation scored hits near the engine repair shop—six in the railroad yard in the midst of all the railroad cars—and ten hits in the warehouses near the repair shops. Despite only getting 50 per cent of their bombs in the target area, the mission was deemed a success. Two days later, on November 22nd, the 9th Squadron made its combat debut with the B-24 when Maj. Willard Fountain (squadron commander) took six bombers back to the marshaling yards at Mandalay. Clouds over the target forced the bombers to circle for 45 minutes, waiting for a break. Bombing from a lower altitude at 20,000 feet, the formation dropped thirty 1,000-pound bombs into the target area, getting more hits on the engine repair shops, the marshaling yards, and buildings in the area. As an example of the frustrations that could occur, three of the bombers salvoed all their bombs at once due to a malfunction in their bomb racks.[33]

The night of November 25th, the 7th Bombardment Group flew the Army Air Forces' longest mission of the war to date: a 2,700 mile round trip to Bangkok, billed as a "Thanksgiving Day celebration".[34] Lt. Col. Necrason led off three aircraft from the 9th Squadron and six from the 436th Squadron to bomb an oil refinery near the city that the Japanese were using to produce kerosene, aviation gasoline, and diesel fuel. The planes began taking off from the airfield at Gaya at 1800 at three-minute intervals. One aircraft had to return to the field with landing gear problems, but the rest continued on to the target, where they bombed individually from assigned altitudes, beginning at 12,000 feet and stepping up at a 200-foot spacing. All airplanes reported getting most of their bombs in the target area. The raid caught the Japanese completely by surprise, the returning crews reporting only

Briefing 7th Bombardment Group crews for a night mission to Rangoon in late 1942. (File 827.306-1, Albert F. Simpson Historical Research Center, Air Force Historical Research Agency, Maxwell AFB, AL)

"spasmodic" anti-aircraft fire. The last airplane landed at 1055 on the morning of November 26th, after nearly seventeen hours in the air.[35]

Three days later, the Group suffered its first combat loss of the new campaign. The 436th Squadron sent out six aircraft on a night bombing mission to Rangoon. The same night that the 7th Group went to Bangkok, three RAF Liberators from No.159 Squadron had gone out to bomb Mingaladon airfield as part of a series of RAF raids on Japanese airfields across

Burma. Four Ki-43s from the *64th Sentai* went up to intercept the bombers, claiming one shot down, though none were lost.[36] When the 436th Squadron airplanes arrived over

The Japanese naval base at Port Blair, in the Andaman Islands. The 7th Group flew its first combat mission out of India to Port Blair in April 1942 and returned on November 30, 1942. (File 827.306-1, Albert F. Simpson Historical Research Center, Air Force Historical Research Agency, Maxwell AFB, AL)

Rangoon around 0400 on the morning of November 30th, they ran into improved defenses, with heavy anti-aircraft fire and around 20 searchlights probing for the bombers. The crews saw eight enemy fighters flying parallel and above them, though only one apparently attacked, peeling off and coming in from the rear quarter. Five bombs definitely hit in the target area (the dock and warehouses), with another fifteen seen to fall in the area, though the bursts were unobserved. When the airplanes returned to Gaya later in the morning, 2nd Lt. Thomas Akarman's bomber was not among them. No trace of the airplane nor Akarman and his crew was ever found. The *64th Sentai* made no claims for any bombers shot down that night; more likely anti-aircraft fire damaged Akarman's aircraft over Rangoon, or it suffered some malfunction on its way back to base.[37]

Japanese shipping remained a high priority target for the India Air Task Force well into 1943. One of the goals of the IATF's bombing campaign was to interdict the enemy sea lanes to prevent Japanese ships operating in the Bay of Bengal or reaching Burmese ports. Part of this strategy included regular visits to the Japanese naval base at Port Blair, in the Andaman Islands, the goal of the 7th Bombardment Group's first mission out of India back in April. Allied intelligence had reported a Japanese naval auxiliary vessel in the harbor. Maj. Fountain took six of the 9th Squadron's B-24s to Port Blair on November 30th to go after the ship on a 12-hour flight to the target and back. Bombing from 18,000 to 19,000 feet, the formation claimed one direct hit and three near misses on the auxiliary vessel, believing they had sunk it. Six bombers from the 436th Squadron took the next trip to Port Blair eleven days later, when another report came in of naval vessels in the harbor. Six crews were hurriedly briefed, but on this occasion they came up empty. Clouds covered the area, making it difficult to locate any of the navy vessels reported to be there. Three of the airplanes dropped their bombs in the harbor area, while the other three brought theirs back to base.[38]

During December, the 7th Group went back to the Rangoon area on five separate missions to continue the attacks on the docks, railroad facilities, and the airfield at Mingaladon. Lt. Col. Necrason began the month taking six 436th Squadron airplanes to bomb a truck park near the village of Pyawbwe, around twenty miles southeast of the town of Meiktila, in central Burma, starting fires that were reported visible from

Bombs exploding among the warehouses along the Rangoon River on the mission of December 20, 1942. Note the Japanese transport ships moored alongside the docks. (File 827.306-1, Albert F. Simpson Historical Research Center, Air Force Historical Research Agency, Maxwell AFB, AL)

50 miles away. On the first anniversary of the attack on Pearl Harbor, the 9th Squadron sent six aircraft to bomb the docks and shipping at Rangoon, borrowing one aircraft and crew

The runway at Pandaveswar, where the 7th Group would remain, with one three-month interval, until the end of the war. (7th Bombardment Group (H) Historical Foundation, USAFA McDermott Library)

from the 436th Squadron, while Brig. Gen. Haynes and Lt. Col. Necrason led six aircraft from the 436th Squadron to bomb and drop leaflets at Mandalay with, unusually, an escort of five P-40 fighters, while other IATF and RAF squadrons hit other targets as part of the Pearl Harbor anniversary. Weather prevented both groups of bombers from completing their missions. The 9th Squadron failed to reach Rangoon, while the 436th ended up showering Mandalay with leaflets when clouds covered the marshaling yards. While the 436th went to Port Blair on December 11th, the 9th raided the Rangoon dock area. Maj. Fountain led six aircraft, bombing from 24,000 feet and getting 20 hits among the warehouses alongside the docks that started several fires.[39]

In mid-December, another change of station took place. On December 13th, the 9th Bombardment Squadron's air echelon moved from Gaya to a former Royal Air Force airfield at Pandaveswar—quickly renamed "Panda"—the squadron's ground echelon having arrived the previous day. Three days later, the Headquarters of the 7th Bombardment Group made the move. Panda was located near the town of Asanasol, 130 miles northwest of Calcutta. The field would be home to the 9th Squadron for most of its time in India. The 7th Group headquarters personnel who had remained in Karachi traveled to Panda by troop train. A month later, the 9th Photo Reconnaissance Squadron, equipped with F-4 Lightnings, arrived to share the field. Pandaveswar was hardly a garden spot. The airfield: "...lay in a furnace-like plain where temperatures up to 115° made heat exhaustion or worse a constant threat for those working on aircraft, where every movement of wind carried sand with it...where the sudden onset of the monsoon set the floors of the tents awash, brought out the snakes, and caused the open latrine pits to overflow."[40] A small village that was home to local farmers and workers in the nearby coal mines lay around 200 yards from the Group headquarters building. The Group frequently hired local labor for many of the manual tasks necessary to keep a bomb group functioning. To reduce the risk of damage from air attack, offices, maintenance shops, mess, and quarters were spread around the airfield. As the months went by living accommodations gradually improved. Working conditions remained difficult until the end of the war. Little could be done about the heat, the sand and dust, the humidity, and the rain during the monsoon season. The maintenance crews learned to wear light clothing and to stay out of the sun as much as they possibly could to avoid heatstroke. The high humidity most of the year caused parts to rapidly rust and corrode if not cleaned regularly. Mildew would cover electrical connections and cover .50 caliber ammunition. The Group was fortunate to have a good number of experienced mechanics, armorers, and technicians who knew their jobs and their aircraft inside and out, but many of the replacements coming into the group toward the end of 1942 were younger men fresh out of training schools with little practical experience.[41]

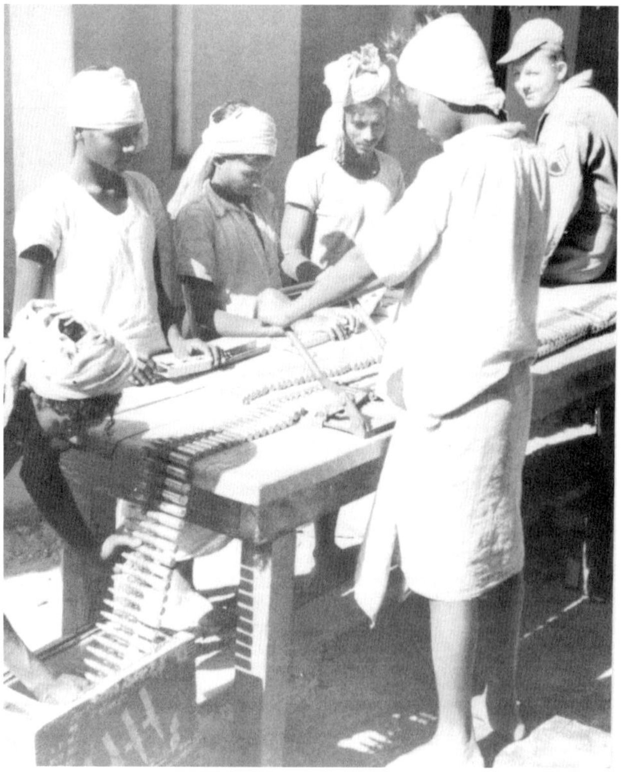

For some months, the 7th Bombardment Group was short-handed and had to rely on local labor for a multitude of tasks. Here, local Indian workers make up belts of .50 caliber ammunition. (7th Bombardment Group (H) Historical Foundation, USAFA McDermott Library)

Lt. Thomas Sledge, a bombardier in then Lt. William Delahay's crew, first in the 9th Bombardment Squadron and then in the 492nd Bombardment Squadron. Sledge would complete 45 missions with the 7th Group between 1942 and 1944. (Courtesy Col. Thomas Sledge, USAF Retd)

The docks in Rangoon were again the target of the mission on December 22, 1942, when the 9th Bombardment Squadron sent out five aircraft. (File 827.306-1, Albert F. Simpson Historical Research Center, Air Force Historical Research Agency, Maxwell AFB, AL)

Four new combat crews arrived at Pandaveswar that month after spending a week training in Karachi; all four were assigned to the 9th Bombardment Squadron. The experiences of one of these men, then 2nd Lt. Thomas Sledge, is representative of the new replacement crews arriving in India fresh from their hurried training in the United States. A student at the University of Texas at the time of the Pearl Harbor attack, Sledge was anxious to serve his country. Rather than join the long list of young men waiting to be pilots, Sledge chose to volunteer for training as a bombardier. Completing his 12-week training course at George Army Air Forces Base at Victorville, California, in the early summer, Sledge was assigned to the 303rd Bombardment Group and began training on B-17Es. He flew five to six hour missions practicing formation flying, gunnery, and practice bombing. During this period, Sledge received his only formal gunnery training: 30 minutes firing a .30 caliber machine gun out of the nose of a B-17E. Moving the machine gun from one gun port to another, Sledge accidently kept his finger on the trigger, blasting several holes in the Plexiglas frames of the nose. Shortly before the 303rd Group began to transfer overseas in August 1942, his crew flew back to Boise, Idaho, to pick up belongings they had stored there. Running into a thunderstorm, their B-17 broke up and all but one of the crew were killed. Now crewless, Sledge was sent to El Paso, Texas, to join a B-24 crew that lacked a bombardier. At El Paso, he joined 2nd Lt. Robert Kavanaugh's crew. Over the next several months, the Army Air Forces moved the crew from El Paso to Tucson, Arizona, to Topeka, Kansas. In between moves they did very little training. In early November, Sledge was transferred to Capt. William Delahay's crew. That crew was transferred to the 4th Ferrying Group at Nashville, Tennessee, where they picked up a new B-24D for the flight to India, leaving on November 14, 1942, as one of a formation of five aircraft. The pilots agreed to use the two-week flight to India, covering 72 hours of flying time, as a training exercise. The pilots flew in tight formation the entire way to practice their formation flying. Sledge worked with the navigator to gain experience in navigation and used cities, towns, and geographic features as aiming points to practice using his Norden bomb sight. Sledge and his crew arrived in Karachi on December 4, 1942, and 13 days later flew to Pandaveswar. Five days after arriving at Panda, Sledge went on his first combat mission, never having fired a .50 caliber machine gun and never once having dropped a bomb from a B-24.[42]

The 9th Squadron's first element got its bombs in the dock area, but the three airplanes in the second element missed the docks, the bombs falling into the Rangoon River. (File 827.306-1, Albert F. Simpson Historical Research Center, Air Force Historical Research Agency, Maxwell AFB, AL)

The 436th Squadron went back to Rangoon first, three airplanes attacking Mingaladon airfield, while six went over the city to bomb the railroad yards alongside the Irrawaddy River on December 20th. Bombing was poor on this occasion, with only 15 of 54 500-pound bombs falling in the target area, but starting fires nonetheless. The 9th Squadron sent five aircraft to Rangoon two days later to hit the docks and warehouses with only slightly better results. The bombers approached the city from the west, heading east on their bomb run. Sledge, who kept a small notebook where he wrote up a few details of each mission on his way back to base, recorded that the first two aircraft in the formation got 17 of 18 bombs in the target area, but the three planes in the following section dropped short, all 27 bombs landing in the Irrawaddy River. That afternoon he had his first introduction to flak, noting that it was "fairly intense" and, unusually for this period, Japanese fighters. Two Army Type 1 (Ki-43) Oscar fighters intercepted the formation 60 miles to the west of Rangoon as the bombers were withdrawing after their bomb run. The fighters did no damage to the bombers, but one Oscar was claimed as probably destroyed.[43]

The 7th Group ended the year with another long-range mission to Bangkok and an attack on shipping approaching Rangoon. In the Group's largest raid to date, 12 aircraft from the 9th and 436th Squadrons made the long flight to Bangkok on the night of December 26th. Capt. Delahay led three B-24s from the 9th Squadron to bomb the main railroad station in Bangkok, while Capt. Wesley Werner took three bombers to the naval dockyard on the Chao Phya River. Lt. Col. Necrason took six aircraft from the 436th Squadron to bomb the Bangkok Arsenal, which made various weapons and ammunition. Coming in over the city at staggered altitudes, the targets proved difficult to locate. Flying as bombardier in Capt. Delahay's crew, 2nd Lt. Tom Sledge noted that he was unable to see where his bombs hit because of clouds. Delahay made five runs over the railroad yards and three runs over the airfield at Don Muang, outside of Bangkok, the designated secondary target. Search lights came on but couldn't find the bombers, and anti-aircraft fire was light. The main risk was running into another airplane as the formations searched for their targets over the city. Sledge recorded in his diary: "Busch [Lt. Dewey Busch] came damn close to running into us over the

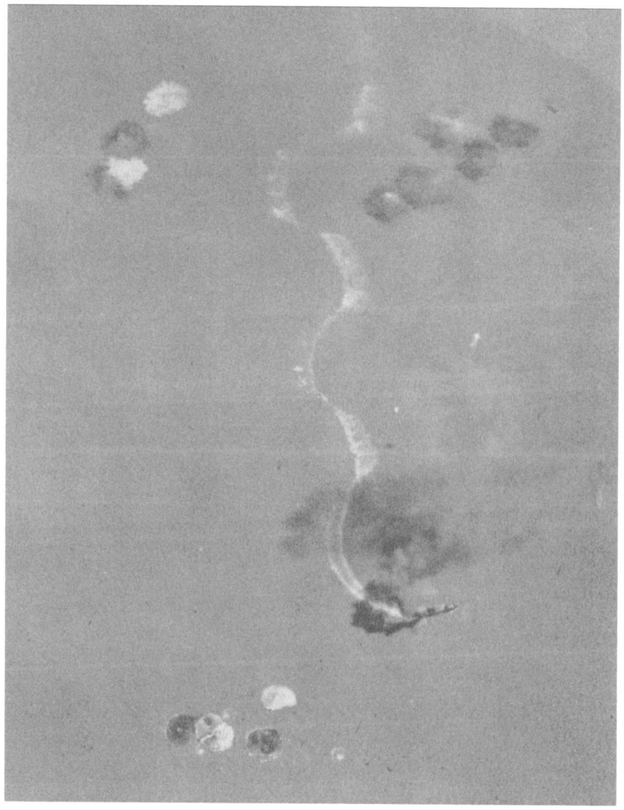

The 9th and 436th Squadrons attacked a Japanese tanker off the coast of Burma on December 29, 1942. The photograph shows the tanker maneuvering to avoid the bombs falling nearby. (File 827.306-1, Albert F. Simpson Historical Research Center, Air Force Historical Research Agency, Maxwell AFB, AL)

target because of flying at the wrong altitude."[44] The bombers returned to their base, having flown 14 to 15 hours. Two war correspondents went along on the mission: Darrell Berrigan from United Press and Toby Wiant of the Associated Press. The official Tenth Air Force communique issued after the mission stated: "...a large force of American four-motored bombers dealt a second destructive blow at Bangkok, Japanese-occupied capital of Thailand, smashing the naval dock area, a large arsenal and powder factory and the airfield..."[45] Wiant flew in Capt. Warner's airplane, writing of his experiences for the Associated Press, not without a bit of hyperbole. "From a grandstand seat in one bomber", he wrote, "I saw thousands of pounds of high explosive blast targets with devastating effect. Several fires were started and one of five bombs which scored direct hits on the arsenal illuminated the whole countryside far as the attacking bombers high above...A few searchlights swung their beams frantically over the Bangkok skies but were unable to locate the American bombers. I was in one of the bombers assigned to pound the naval dockyard located in the heart of the city along the Menam Chao Phya River. It was my first visit to Bangkok and I thoroughly enjoyed what we did to improve the scenery."[46]

At the end of the month, the 9th and 436th Squadrons were alerted to prepare to strike Japanese shipping. The India Air Task Force had received intelligence of a 6,000-ton tanker and a 5,000-ton freighter approaching Rangoon across the Gulf of Martaban. The 436th Squadron prepared three bombers with two bomb bay tanks and three with one bomb bay tank to extend the range. The six aircraft flew to Pandaveswar to join the 9th Squadron, taking off before dawn on the morning of December 29th in two flights: six aircraft to go after the tanker and six heading for the freighter. Engine problems forced one aircraft in each flight to turn back, but the others continued on. The first flight found the tanker approaching the Rangoon River. Bombing from 24,000 feet as the tanker maneuvered sharply below them, the formation got a direct hit and two near misses that straddled the ship but did not sink it. The five aircraft in the second flight had a similar experience. Bombing from a lower altitude, the formation got two near misses that damaged the ship and appear to have set it on fire.[47]

Since the inauguration of the India Air Task Force's campaign against the Japanese lines of communication in Burma on November 20, 1942, the 7th Bombardment Group had flown 16 missions to various targets. These early missions were designed to "...feel out the enemy, survey his lines of communications and test his defenses."[48] All of this had been done with the loss of one airplane and crew. Together, the heavy bombers of the 7th Group and the B-25 medium bombers of the 341st Group had dropped 198 tons of bombs on targets in Burma—not nearly enough to have a significant impact on the Japanese.[49] Neither group, however, was at full strength. The demands of other theaters with higher priorities than the CBI had made it impossible for the Army Air Forces to meet the goals spelled out in the Arnold-Portal agreement of having a fully manned and equipped heavy bomber group in India by October 1942. While the 9th and 436th Squadrons had

On December 29, 1942, six aircraft from the 9th and 436th Squadrons went after a large Japanese freighter, getting several near misses. (File 827.306-1, Albert F. Simpson Historical Research Center, Air Force Historical Research Agency, Maxwell AFB, AL)

received their full complement of officers and men, most of whom were entering combat for the first time, the 492nd and 493rd Bombardment Squadrons were still in cadre status. At the end of 1942, total aircraft strength amounted to 22 B-24Ds and ten still non-operational B-17Es. Only rarely could the squadrons send out more than six aircraft on a single mission. There were still shortages of spare parts, aircraft, and personnel. It would take more time and a lot of hard work for the 7th Bombardment Group to become effective, yet much had been accomplished since the India Air Task Force's activation. Having had to rebuild the Group to full strength all over again, the Group's accomplishments were significant. A formal bombardment group structure with four combat squadrons had been organized, two bases closer to the Group's operating area had been established and expanded, replacement aircraft and crews were acquired, and combat missions were renewed after a nearly five-month hiatus. What the Army Air Forces Historical Study said of the first year of the Tenth Air Force applied equally to the 7th Bombardment Group: "Despite the comparatively modest scale on which the accomplishments of 1942 must be measured, the promise of future exploits already suggested the importance of the foundations laid during this difficult period."[50]

Building Up the Group

The Allied commands in India could welcome in the new year with a certain degree of relief and begin their work with a greater sense of security. While the tactical positions along the Burma-India border remained more or less unchanged, India's overall strategic position had significantly improved.[51]

On January 3, 1943, the 436th Squadron bombed the railroad yards at Mandalay with excellent results. (File 827.306-1-Volume 2, Albert F. Simpson Historical Research Center, Air Force Historical Research Agency, Maxwell AFB, AL)

The British Eighth Army's drive from Egypt across Libya and the Allied landings in North Africa under Operation Torch had removed the threat of a collapse in the Middle East that could have threatened India. While the Japanese grip on Burma remained, the Japanese *15th Army* had been unable to expand deeper into India and the Imperial Japanese Navy had avoided further attacks in the Indian Ocean or the Bay of Bengal. In northeastern Assam, the threat to the air ferry route to China over the Hump seemed less immanent. While there was an on-going debate between the Americans and the British over strategy for the liberation of Burma, they agreed on the need to build up a base in India. Supplies and personnel to build better airfields and improve the ports and railroad system in India were beginning to arrive, with the promise of making the India base more effective in the months to come.[52]

The new year brought the combat debut of the 492nd and 493rd Bombardment Squadrons as the Group continued its campaign against the Japanese communications system. The missions conducted during January fit the pattern of November and December: strikes on railroad yards and Japanese shipping bringing supplies into Rangoon. On January 3, 1943, the 436th Squadron began operations, sending out six aircraft to the railroad yards at Mandalay with excellent results. Each aircraft carried the standard load of nine 500-pound bombs. Bombing from 14,000 feet against heavy but inaccurate anti-aircraft fire, the formation put all bombs onto the railroad yard, concentrated among a batch of freight cars in the southern section of the yards. The resulting flames and smoke were visible from 70 miles. Later in the afternoon, three bombers went out to hit shipping at Rangoon, attacking a 15,000-ton transport moving up the Rangoon River. The bombers claimed two direct hits and three near misses. The 9th Squadron went to Mandalay the day after with only four aircraft. Approaching the target, the crews could see the railroad yards still smoking from the 436th Squadron's attack the day before. Bombing from the lower altitude brought excellent results again. The Squadron placed 36 bombs in the target area and started a number of fires. Three days later, the 9th Squadron went out on a long mission searching for Japanese shipping. Four bombers flew to the Andaman Islands to scope out Port Blair. Finding nothing, they flew across the Gulf of Martaban to Moulmein, where they also drew a blank, unloading their bombs on the Moulmein docks.[53]

The 9th Squadron's mission of January 15, 1943, was Sledge's most memorable mission of the war, though he did not learn the full significance of the mission until years later. Allied intelligence had reported a convoy heading towards Rangoon. That morning, the 9th sent out seven B-24s on a search mission, one turning back with mechanical problems.

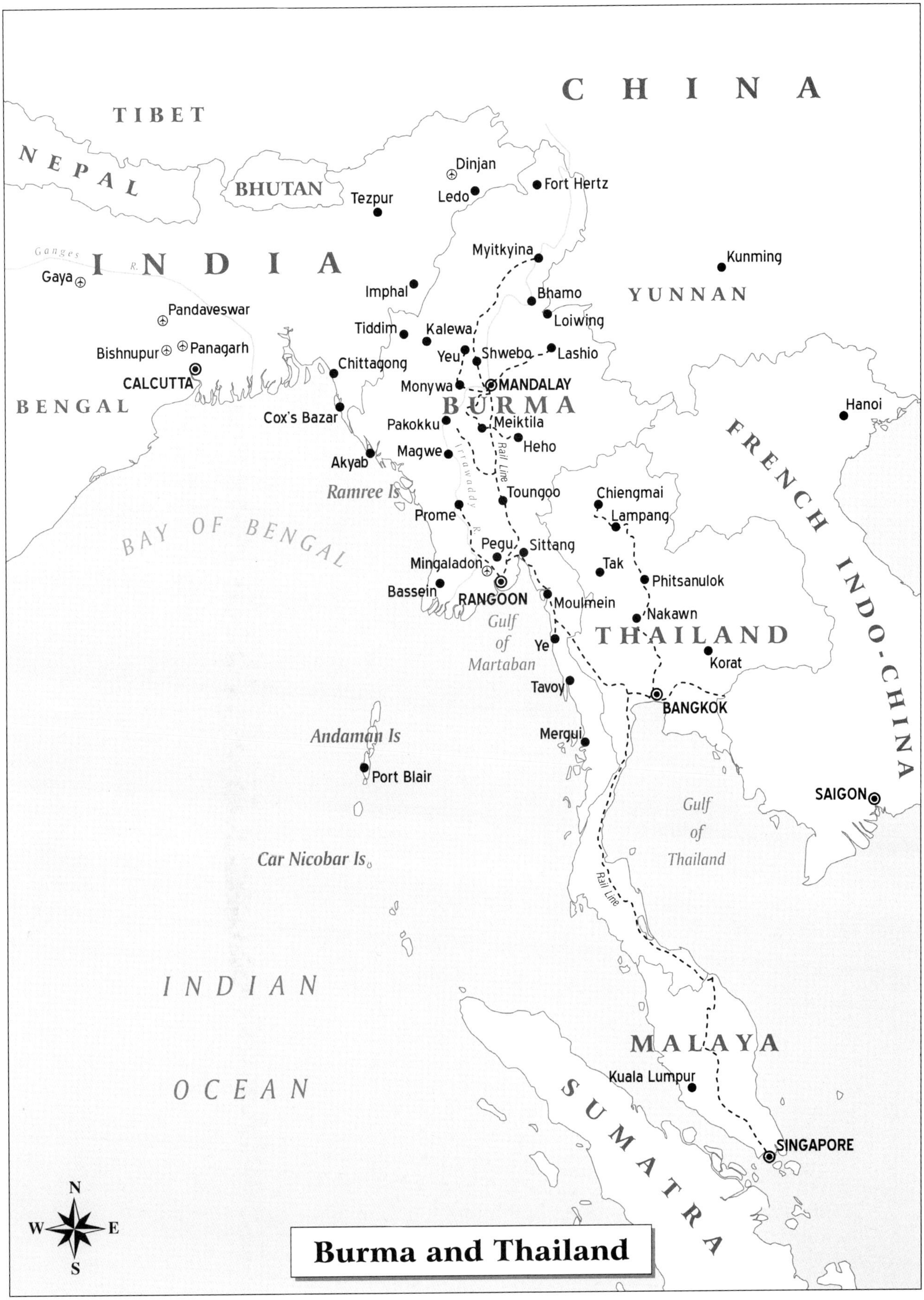

Burma and Thailand

Lt. Urbanks, Col. Necrason, and Captain Wesley Werner, CO of the recently formed 493rd Bombardment Squadron at Alipore in India, early 1943. (3A-48884, RG 342FH, NARA)

After flying for several hours down the Gulf of Martaban, the bombers came across two transports with several small naval escort vessels around 350 miles south of Rangoon. As Sledge, flying in Capt. Delahay's airplane, recalled:

> All of a sudden we ran across two Japanese freighters, big ships, with an escort that was shooting at us, small boats. But you could see them shooting at you...I started making my bomb run and the ship was turning. The ship could see the bombs coming out of the bomb bay and they could make a turn before the bombs could impact. So it was very difficult to hit a moving ship. He's watching you, and he's turning constantly one way or the other so that you can't get a good reading on him. And this was the first time I had ever bombed a moving ship. Now I had practiced bombing a moving target in bombing school. They had a little trainer thing that they could move. They couldn't turn it like a ship. So I told Bill Delahay, the pilot, "Bill, we got nine bombs. I don't want to drop them all on this first run. I'm going to take four bombs and see how we do." So we came back and we made a run.
>
> I could see that the ship was turning. I was trying to synchronize the bombsight. It was capable of synchronizing. You keep your cross hairs on the target, and if it is turning, why, the cross hairs will stay on there. But if he turns the other way, then you have to manipulate the bomb sight. So I was moving the bomb sight, put the selector on four bombs, put my trailer up, and the ship we saw was shooting at us. I could see the flashes off the top of the ship. So we came up and dropped the bombs and I'm looking through the bomb sight, and my bombs hit a long way behind the ship, not even close. I had a few choice words about that over the intercom. I said, "Well, let's go around and make another run, make it a little bit longer this time. So we did a 180 and turned around and I came back. As we were going in on the ship, he's turning, and I see a fire on the top of the ship. And I said, "how did that ship get on fire," because my bombs didn't even come close and nobody else is bombing him. I got everything set to drop the five bombs remaining, set the invalometer, the distance between each bomb, and came back around and made the bomb run, dropped the bombs, and looked down there and the bombs straddled the ship."[54]

The other airplanes in the flight hit the second transport, believing it to be disabled and possibly sinking. In this case, they were correct. They had fatally damaged the Japanese cargo ship *Nichimei Maru*, sinking it. What Sledge learned much later after the war was that both ships were carrying Dutch and American prisoners of war from the Netherlands East Indies to Burma to work on the railroad the Japanese were building from Thailand. He had narrowly missed killing fellow American soldiers, though sadly a number of Dutch POWs were killed in the sinking of the *Nichimei Maru*. The 436th Squadron went out the next day in search of another convoy, but found only a small coastal vessel; they bombed this, but missed.[55]

During January, the 492nd and 493rd Bombardment Squadrons finally became operational, after a fashion. Early in the month, the officers and men that made up the cadre of the two squadrons moved from Karachi to their new homes at the bases in India: the 492nd Squadron going to Gaya and the 493rd Squadron to Pandaveswar. At each base, the new squadron received a commanding officer and a number of veteran combat crews to form the core of the squadron. At Gaya, the 436th Squadron transferred ten officers and 79 enlisted men, 70 of whom were maintenance men, to the 492nd; the 9th Squadron transferred some crews as well, Capt. Bill Delahay among them. Capt. Joe Pirruccello, from the 436th Squadron, was appointed commanding officer of the 492nd on January 13, 1943, with Delahay as his operations officer. A few days later, nine combat crews and 291 enlisted men arrived from the United States as "fillers" for the squadron. By the end of the month, eight B-24Ds were on hand—four below authorized strength. At Panda, Capt. Wesley Werner became commanding officer of the 493rd Squadron, with Lt. William Berkeley of the jinxed October 28th mission as his Operations Officer. Again the 9th and 436th Squadrons contributed combat crews, the 436th transferring 12 officers and 16 enlisted men, with more combat crews and enlisted men arriving over the rest of the month. There were no B-24s available for the 493rd Squadron until well into February.

Instead, the 493rd was assigned three B-17Es for flying training and borrowed B-24s from the 9th Squadron to fly combat missions. The two new squadrons found shortages of just about everything they needed at their new bases: quarters, maintenance facilities, officers' and enlisted men's messes, recreation facilities, transportation, and aircraft. Officers and men lived in tents until more permanent quarters could be completed. The 492nd Squadron adopted as its squadron nickname "The Eager Beaver Bombing Company" and over the next several weeks "begged, borrowed, and built" what it required, the 493rd doing the same at Panda.[56]

The 7th Group's newest squadrons did not have to wait long before flying their first combat missions. The 492nd Squadron was first out of the box, borrowing four airplanes and a combat crew from the 436th Squadron to make up a nine-plane formation on a mission to bomb the docks and shipping at Rangoon, with Capt. Delahay leading. The bombers

Lt. William Berkeley and crew. Berkeley became Operations officer of the 493rd Squadron in January 1943 (left to right): William Berkeley, Clyde Cannon (CP), Richard Weiss (N), and Corrie (B); kneeling: Marvin Riehl (E), James Fisher (RO), John McNeil (G), Robert Fletcher (G), and Alfred Stank (G). (7th Bombardment Group (H) Historical Foundation, USAFA McDermott Library)

came over Rangoon in three flights of three aircraft, each with a separate target. Delahay's flight bombed a 5,000-ton freighter moored in the Rangoon River but missed, all their bombs hitting short on the south side of the river. The other flight dropped its bombs in the river near the freighter, managing to get two direct hits, while the third flight got 27 direct hits on the Sule Pagoda wharves along the riverside. Anti-aircraft fire was officially recorded as "heavy, intense, and fairly accurate", although Sledge, now a veteran of six previous missions, noted in his diary that there was very little AA over the target. Overall the day was deemed successful for a first combat mission, a good start for the Squadron. The next day, Capt. Pirruccello addressed the first squadron formation and gave a short talk to his men, saying "This is your squadron. It will be what you make it. Our job is to drop bombs on the enemy. If you do anything that interferes with dropping bombs on the enemy, then you are not doing your job. The success of the squadron is up to all of us."[57]

The 493rd Squadron had a ruder introduction to combat two days later. Borrowing seven aircraft and two combat crews from the 9th Squadron, Capt. Werner led the formation off at 0715 to bomb the Sule Pagoda wharves at Rangoon. For the first time, the bombers encountered sustained fighter attack. That morning, the pilots of the *3rd Chutai* (Squadron), of the Japanese Army Air Force's *50th Sentai*, were on alert at Mingaladon Airfield with seven Oscar fighters (at the time, the *50th Sentai* was still flying the Ki-43-I model of the Hayabusa). Among the pilots on alert that day was Sgt. Satoru Anabuki, who would become the *50th Sentai*'s leading ace over Burma. Anabuki and his fellow pilots were expecting to encounter the big American bombers that had been attacking Rangoon and were in high spirits about having a B-24, the newest American heavy bomber, in their grasp. After a false alarm in the morning, the seven pilots received a new report around 1400 local time of enemy four-engine bombers approaching Rangoon. Anabuki was one of seven pilots who were ordered to take off immediately and patrol over Rangoon. Climbing to altitude, he saw two formations of bombers: one of three aircraft in the lead and one of four aircraft trailing behind, to the west of Rangoon, heading north. His first impression was of a giant green body, gleaming in the sunlight. Climbing up above the lead formation, Anabuki's formation leader gave the signal to attack. The three Oscars dived down in an attack on the rear of the B-24s, as they had done before with other Allied bombers. They opened fire on the B-24s at 600 meters, firing continuously until they were close. Anabuki recalled getting hits in the cockpit area of the bomber he was attacking and seeing white smoke come out of both wings as he dived away from the formation. As he returned for another attack, one of the three fighters in his formation dived away, smoking, to return to Mingaladon. The B-24s dropped their bombs, hitting the wharves, with some bombs falling into the Rangoon River. For his next attack, Anabuki came in from the front and below, pulling up to fire into the bomber above him. He claimed to have seen black smoke coming out of the airplane. By now there were only three Oscars attacking the bombers as they withdrew from Rangoon, the others having been damaged by strong return fire from the B-24s. Anabuki apparently came around for a third attack, but his machine guns stopped working, so he withdrew. When he last saw the B-24s, they were heading back toward the Arakan. For Anabuki and his colleagues, the mission had been a sobering and frustrating experience. The B-24s had proved to be formidable opponents, stronger than expected. The Ki-43-I model had been hard pressed to catch these faster bombers at high altitude. The heavy return fire from the B-24's multiple .50 caliber machine guns had damaged all six of the Oscar fighters, forcing three of them to leave the fight. The Japanese fighter pilots had fired off all their ammunition and claimed four B-24s shot down, though none were in fact lost on the mission. The battle had not turned out as the Japanese pilots expected it would.[58]

The 493rd Squadron's report of the mission was almost dismissive of the fighter attack, recording that during the bomb run "...the formation was harassed by Japanese interceptors and anti-aircraft [fire], neither of which had the least effect on the formation."[59] The crews reported that four enemy aircraft had attacked the formation during the bombing run and had continued the attacks for some time on the way out of Burma. They identified the enemy fighters as two Oscars, one unidentified single-seat fighter, and one Type 97 Fighter (Nate) that stayed out of range. The crews reported that one Oscar had been definitely hit and was seen to dive away from the formation smoking, conforming to Anabuki's account. Two B-24s received minor damage. The bombing was less effective: the Squadron getting nine hits on the wharves, nine nearby, and the rest of the 61 bombs dropped on the mission falling into the Rangoon River or landing where they were unobserved.[60]

Bombing Bridges

Although still lacking its complete complement of aircraft, the 7th Group, with two more squadrons operational, could at least undertake more frequent missions. By early February, the 9th Bombardment Squadron had eleven B-24s, the 436th Squadron had nine, and the 492nd had seven.[61] With only three B-17Es available, the 493rd Squadron still had to borrow aircraft

Myitnge Bridge, the 7th Group's target for January 10, 1943. (File 827.306-1, Albert F. Simpson Historical Research Center, Air Force Historical Research Agency, Maxwell AFB, AL)

from the 9th Squadron. The on-going shortages of aircraft, spare parts, and maintenance crews meant that the squadrons could only occasionally send out more than six or seven aircraft on a mission; during these early months, a nine-airplane mission was considered a "big deal". The number of missions did gradually increase, with the Group flying 10 missions during January, 19 during February, and 23 during March. The Group began sending two or three squadrons to the same target area on the same day, bombing separate targets around Rangoon, for example, and sending squadrons to bomb the same target on successive days. This was important for the targets that occupied much of the Group's effort during February and March: railroad bridges.

Burma's railway transportation system had several vulnerable points along its route to the north. At this period of the war in Burma, Rangoon was the central point for supplies going to the Japanese armies at the front. At Rangoon, supplies were unloaded from transports and stored in the warehouses alongside the wharves, then taken to the marshaling yards for loading onto freight cars for the rail journey north. In effect, Rangoon was the "...key which could lock the Burma door to Japanese supplies."[62] The effort to disrupt the Japanese supply process in and around Rangoon, to lock the Burma door as it were, would continue for months, but the India Air Task Force's bombing effort in southern Burma was now expanded to disrupting the flow of traffic along the route through attacks on three key targets: the Pazundaung railroad bridge at Rangoon, the Myitnge railroad bridge south of Mandalay, and the Gokteik Viaduct on the railroad line to Lashio. Narrow bridges, carrying a single track, proved to be exceptionally difficult targets for high-altitude bombers.

The battle against the railroad bridges had actually begun in January with an attack on the Myitnge bridge on January 10, 1943, one of the few bombing missions carried out in coordination with the B-25s from the 341st Bombardment Group. The 436th Squadron attacked first, six aircraft dropping

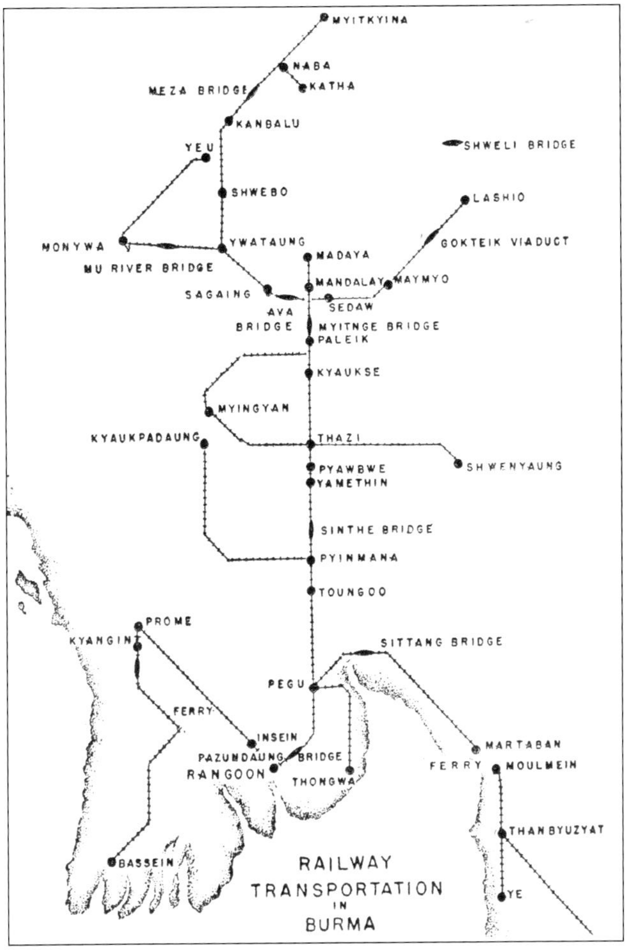

27 500-pound bombs and 12 1,000-pound bombs on the bridge from 15,000 feet. The bigger 1,000-pounders got three direct hits on the third span of the bridge, knocking it into the river below. The B-25s followed a half an hour later, but lacking the more accurate Norden bomb sights the B-24s carried, their loads failed to get more than a few near misses.[63] As a follow up to this attack, nine days later, the 9th Bombardment Squadron sent out four B-24s to bomb the important rail junction at Thazi, south of the Myitnge bridge. Bombing from the low altitude of 14,000 feet in the absence of any anti-aircraft fire, the bombers got four hits on the junction and more hits on the nearby warehouses.[64]

During February, the 7th Group went after the Myitnge Bridge on five missions, but failed to do more than add superficial damage to what had been accomplished on January 10th. Japanese Army engineers had raised the span that had been knocked into the river back up to the level of the bridge, but had not yet restored rail traffic over the bridge.[65] The 492nd Squadron went first, sending out seven bombers on February 4, 1943, but failed to hit the bridge. The B-25s joined them again, but were also unsuccessful. The 9th Squadron tried again the next day with six bombers, without result. The 493rd took its turn on February 12th, dropping 2,000-pound bombs for the first time in the CBI Theater. On this mission, the bombers had better luck. The Squadron dropped nine 2,000-pound bombs and 20 1,000-pound bombs from 17,500 feet, getting two hits on the bridge and demolishing one span. Two hits out of 29 bombs dropped indicates the difficulty of hitting so small a target. As an indication of the importance of the bridge to the Japanese supply system, in the interval between the February 5th mission and the 436th Squadron's mission on February 12th, the Japanese Army brought up a number of heavy anti-aircraft guns. Their barrage fortunately proved to be inaccurate. The 9th Squadron went back to the bridge on February 15th, and like the 436th, the seven B-24s carried a mixed load of 11 2,000-pound bombs and 18 1,000-pounders. This time the formation ran into heavy anti-aircraft fire over the target, but the gunners had a hard time tracking the formation, so no bombers were damaged. The bombing was admittedly poor, with the bombers failing to damage the bridge at all from an altitude of 16,500 feet. Ten days later, the 9th Squadron tried again, sending eight bombers in at a lower altitude of 12,500 feet to drop 57 1,000-pound bombs. Making two runs over the bridge in three separate formations in the face of intensifying and increasingly accurate anti-aircraft fire that damaged one airplane, the bombers got some hits on the northern and southern approaches to the bridge, but once again failed to damage the bridge itself.[66]

The 436th Squadron's Armament Section preparing a 2,000-pound demolition bomb for a mission while at Gaya, India, in early 1943. (7th Bombardment Group (H) Historical Foundation, USAFA McDermott Library)

After the 436th Squadron bombed the Myitnge bridge on March 6th, again without damaging the bridge structure, the 341st Bombardment Group took up the challenge, flying six missions against the bridge between March 8th and March 18th, but also without success, the medium bombers finally getting hits on the bridge on March 19th.[67] The 7th Group decided to launch a full effort on March 24th against the

The 493rd Squadron attacks the Myitnge Bridge on February 12, 1943, dropping 2,000-pound bombs for the first time in the China-Burma-India Theater. (File 827.306-1, Vol. 2, Albert F. Simpson Historical Research Center, Air Force Historical Research Agency, Maxwell AFB, AL)

Myitnge bridge with all four squadrons participating using 2,000-pound bombs. The 9th and 493rd Squadrons came in as separate six-airplane formations, bombing from 16,500 feet and 15,800 feet, followed by two formations of 12 B-24s from the 436th and 492nd Squadrons who bombed from 20,000 feet and 16,800 feet. The bombing missed the bridge, but damaged the northern and southern approaches. Using the main raid as a distraction, Colonel Necrason (recently promoted) and Capt. Werner took two of the 493rd Squadron's elderly B-17Es in what may have been one of the last E model Flying Fortress missions of the war: a low level attack against the nearby Ava bridge west of Mandalay. The Ava Bridge was a massive nine-span structure, the only bridge over the Irrawaddy River. The British Army had blown up the bridge during the retreat from Burma. The Japanese had built a temporary structure between the spans to allow for some vehicle traffic. The B-17s came in at 50 feet, with one of the bombers dropping 40 yards short of the bridge and the bombs on the other hanging up in the bomb bay. Machine-gun fire near the bridge hit one of the bombers but did only minor damage. Continuing on at low level, the two B-17s strafed a number of boats on the Irrawaddy River before turning for home.[68]

As both the heavy and medium bombers found to their frustration, "...try as they might, the percentage of hits on these narrow targets remained pitifully low; and if they were difficult to hit, they were infinitely more difficult to destroy."[69] Over the course of 39 missions, the B-24s and B-25s dropped 1,219 bombs on the Myitnge bridge, getting only 18 direct hits.[70] The medium bombers ultimately built up the better record, getting 17 hits in 254 sorties, while the B-24s, typically bombing from higher altitudes, got only one hit in 81 sorties, even with generally clear weather and minimal anti-aircraft fire.[71] For the rest of the year, the heavy bombers left attacks on the Myitnge bridge to their medium bomber cousins. Newer tactics and newer weapons developed and introduced in the last year of the war would go a long way to solving the problem of destroying bridges in Burma.

The Gokteik Viaduct was another difficult target. A steel bridge completed in 1900, the viaduct carried the important rail line to Lashio, bringing supplies to the Japanese armies on the Salween front in northeastern Burma and cargos of zinc and lead back to Rangoon. The Viaduct's ten spans were 2,260 feet in length and stood 335 feet high with a narrow single track. The 7th Bombardment Group flew its first mission against the Viaduct on February 20, 1943, with six aircraft from the 492nd Squadron and seven from the 493rd. The 493rd went in first, bombing from 15,500 feet with 1,000-pound bombs, but failed to get any hits. The 492nd came in four hours later, bombing from 10,500 feet with 2,000 and 1,000-pound

The Myitnge Bridge under attack again during March 1943. Narrow bridges proved to be exceptionally difficult targets to hit from medium or high altitude. (File 827.306-1, Vol. 2, Albert F. Simpson Historical Research Center, Air Force Historical Research Agency, Maxwell AFB, AL)

On March 24, 1943, Col. Necrason and Captain Wesley Werner took two of the 493rd Squadron's elderly B-17Es in an attempt to hit the Myitnge Bridge from low level. (7th Bombardment Group (H) Historical Foundation, USAFA McDermott Library)

bombs, but the lower altitude made no difference. The crews observed no hits. After turning over the target to the medium bombers of the 341st Group, who flew four missions against the Viaduct without success, the 7th Group returned on March 21st, with all four squadrons participating. Haze and clouds made bombing difficult, and six of the 21 aircraft sent out bombed the Myitnge Bridge as an alternate. The 15 aircraft that bombed the viaduct made three passes, dropping 40 2,000-pound bombs and getting two direct hits on the northern approach to the viaduct and a possible hit on one of the spans, but the viaduct remained operational.[72]

Of the three most vital bridge targets, the Pazundaung railroad bridge at Rangoon received the most attention, with the 7th Group flying thirteen missions against the bridge from February to May 1943. As a target, the Pazundaung Bridge had all the problems of the Myitnge Bridge and the Gokteik Viaduct: a long, narrow strip of steel and concrete across Pazundaung Creek that flowed into the Rangoon River. The first attempt to destroy the bridge came on February 27, 1943, when six bombers from the 436th Squadron and five from the 9th Squadron dropped 55 1,000-pound bombs on the bridge. The first flight's bombs hit short of the target. The second flight got two near misses that failed to damage the bridge. On the route out from the target, a single Oscar from an unknown fighter *Sentai* made a determined attack on the 436th Squadron's formation at 23,000 feet. Coming up from the lower right quarter, the Japanese fighter raked Lt. Rieno Aalto's bomber, killing his waist gunner, S/Sgt. Frank Faith, instantly and wounding his tail gunner, S/Sgt. Ray Lent. Aalto landed at Alipore airfield on his way back to base to get Lent to a hospital.[73]

The 493rd Squadron was the next to try, with nine B-24s dropping 45 1,000-pound bombs on the bridge, getting hits on the southern and northern approaches to the bridge but only near misses on the bridge itself. This, frustratingly, was the pattern for most of the missions against the bridge. After sending out single squadrons against the bridge without much success, on March 18th, the Group tried with three squadrons (the 9th, 436th, and 492nd), sending out 16 B-24s armed with nine 500-pound and 72 1,000-pound bombs to saturate the target. Bombing on the lead bombardier, the attempt brought somewhat better results, getting one to three direct hits on the bridge, as well as hits on both approaches. However, the 492nd Squadron's Sledge recorded in his mission diary that the mission was not successful; the 108 bombs dropped fell all over the target area and straddled the bridge. The Group went back to sending out single squadrons against the Pazundaung Bridge, the 9th Squadron flying two more missions and the 493rd one. The squadrons switched to carrying 2,000-pound bombs, but the results were little better. On its mission of April 17th, the 493rd Squadron made two bomb runs against the bridge: one to the south and one to the north, dropping 18 2,000-pound bombs, but again only getting hits on the approaches.[74] The men of the 7th Group were discovering, as were their colleagues in other theaters of war, that daylight precision bombing with the Norden bomb sight was, in the

General Henry "Hap" Arnold awarding decorations to the 7th Bombardment Group flyers at Pandaveswar on his visit to the Group in February 1943. (7th Bombardment Group (H) Historical Foundation, USAFA McDermott Library)

reality of combat as opposed to prewar practice missions, more akin to using a shotgun than a rifle.[75] As the Eighth Air Force was finding in Europe: "...the prewar myth of a bomb in a pickle barrel from 20,000 feet was quickly exploded, and, to the intense disappointment of the regulars, it became apparent quickly that to destroy, or even hit, a given target was going to call for a vastly greater weight of attack than had been dreamed of in prewar doctrine."[76] Seemingly minute errors in ground track, ground speed, or the timing of the fall of a bomb could cause it to miss its target by hundreds of feet; at high altitude, "...errors made precision bombing a matter of luck and providence."[77] High altitude attacks on bridges proved to be a misuse of the heavy bombers, which, with the equipment they had, were better suited to large area targets.[78]

Project Low

The lack of accurate intelligence on the movement of Japanese shipping, as well as weather and the distances involved hindered the India Air Task Force's ability to stop the flow of supplies into Rangoon. Tenth Air Force intelligence estimated that between 30,000 and 50,000 tons of enemy shipping moved through the Rangoon River every week.[79] It occurred to Col. Harold Wright, Tenth Air Force A-2 (Intelligence), that mining the Rangoon River and its estuary would be a valuable adjunct to the destruction of the Rangoon dock areas and the attacks on shipping. Mines could potentially damage shipping coming up the river on days and nights when the 7th Bombardment Group was active elsewhere. There were problems with the idea: first, the India Air Task Force lacked aerial mines; and second, the 7th Bombardment Group, the only American unit with aircraft capable of carrying mines as far as Rangoon, had never been trained in mine laying. Laying a pattern of mines successfully also required information on tides, river channels, and river depths. The India Air Task Force had none of this information available. Using his contacts in the Royal Air Force, Col. Wright found out there were aerial mines available in India; the RAF believed it would be possible to attach these mines in the bomb bay of a B-24, and, perhaps most importantly, among the RAF personnel in India were men who had been trained in aerial mining and had actual experience mine laying in Europe. The RAF offered to make these men available as instructors. At the naval base in Ceylon, the Royal Navy had supplies of the Type A Mark V 1,000-pound magnetic mines that could be dropped by parachute, as well as the appropriate charts of the Rangoon River to determine the optimum placement of mines. In early January 1943, Wright recommended that the 7th Bombardment Group's B-24s conduct a night low-level mining operation under cover of a high altitude bombing raid on Rangoon.[80] Maj. Gen. Bissell gave his approval and Col. Wright got the project underway, first getting the approval for the project from the Royal Navy, who were equally enthusiastic about the idea.

A number of technical problems had to be sorted out before a mining mission could be undertaken, mostly to determine if the mines could be successfully fitted into a B-24. By good fortune, the RAF had a Liberator II—the equivalent model to the USAAF B-24D—in Ceylon, where the Royal Navy stored its mines. A trial fitting determined that the B-24 could carry four mines in the rear section of the B-24's bomb bay, where the parachutes would not get caught up on any bulkheads. The RAF did a test drop from a Liberator II to confirm that the fittings would work and the mines would drop clear of the bomb bay. The Royal Navy worked out the best placement of the mines in the Rangoon River and made up charts for the

A crew waiting to take off on a mission in February 1943. (3A-34837, RG 342FH, NARA)

combat crews to use on their mission. The Royal Navy arranged to ship 50 mines to Calcutta for delivery to the nearby airfield at Alipore. The ideal conditions for the mission required a full moon over Rangoon and low tide in the Rangoon River, with the next full moon/low tide period due around February 20th. The India Air Task Force started making modifications to the standard bomb shackles to accommodate the Royal Navy mines. RAF armament officers went to Alipore to assist with the technical details and the final loading of the mines into the B-24s, while other RAF officers prepared technical manuals on the mines and instructions on aerial mining for the crews selected for the mission.[81]

Dubbed "Project Low", the first mining mission was scheduled for the night of February 22/23, 1943. As the diversion, six aircraft from the 436th Squadron arrived over Rangoon at 0215 and remained over the city until 0243, dropping bombs on the Rangoon dock area through the night haze and starting several fires. Two RAF Liberators from No. 159 Squadron contributed to the diversion. At the same time, Col. Necrason led six aircraft from the 493rd Squadron and five from the 492nd to the lower section of the Rangoon River, where it entered the Gulf of Martaban. The airplanes came in over the river individually at 300 to 500 feet to drop their mines. One aircraft had all four of its mines hang up in the bomb bay, but the other ten dropped 39 mines successfully (one mine dropped safe with its arming wires still attached) into the designated areas. The mines were set with delays of one to seven days. While it does not appear that this first mission resulted in sinking any Japanese ships, Allied intelligence noticed that no Japanese ships entered or left Rangoon between February 27th and March 3rd. The second mining operation took place a month later, on the night of March 26/27. The 436th Squadron again provided a diversion, with six airplanes staying over Rangoon for an hour, bombing by moonlight. The 492nd Squadron sent off six aircraft, successfully dropping their mines in the Rangoon River. The 493rd Squadron had assembled seven aircraft for the mission, but on its take off run the airplane flown by 2nd Lt. Jack Porter failed to clear some palm trees at the end of the runway at Alipore, the jumping off point for the mission. Porter's B-24 crashed, killing all but one member of his crew and blocking the field for the rest of the squadron. The 493rd completed its mining mission the next night. These first two missions—starting with Rangoon—were the beginning of very successful mining operations that over the next two years extended to ports along the Burmese coast and into the Gulf of Thailand, severely disrupting Japanese shipping. The damage was not simply the number of Japanese ships sunk, but the delays that rippled through the transportation system. Once mines were discovered in a harbor, no ships could enter or leave until the harbor had been swept and cleared, throwing shipping schedules into disarray and delaying the delivery of supplies and the shipment of critically needed raw materials back to Japan. After a slow start, mining operations would become a regular part of the 7th Bombardment Group's operations over Burma and Thailand during the following months.[82]

During the first few months of 1943, there were several changes of station among the 7th Group's squadrons. At the end of February, the 436th and 492nd Squadrons left Gaya for a new base at Bishnupur, located 65 miles southeast of Asansol. This brought the two squadrons closer to the 7th Group headquarters at Pandaveswar and knocked 220 miles off the distance the 436th and 492nd had to fly to their targets in southern Burma. The squadrons staggered their moves, with the 436th going first on February 24th and the bulk of the ground and air echelons arriving the next day; two days later, the Squadron flew its first mission from its new home. The 492nd moved in during February 26-28th, flying its first mission from Bishnupur on March 3rd. The 492nd did not stay at Bishnupur long, moving to another nearby base at Panagarh on April 25th. There were command changes as well. On February 4th, Maj. Earl Tash left the 436th Squadron to return to the United States and Maj. Harvey Watkins replaced him as commanding officer. In April, Maj. Pirruccello was transferred from command of the 492nd Squadron to take over the 9th Squadron at Pandaveswar, with Capt. William Delahay taking his place. The 9th Squadron had gone through three commanders in the space of five months with transfers to other commands. Pirruccello would remain as commander of the 9th Squadron until October 1943, while Delahay commanded the 492nd until December.[83]

Air Battles Over Rangoon

The increasing tempo of American heavy bomber raids on Rangoon and other targets in southern Burma presented the Japanese Army Air Force's *5th Hikōshidan* (Air Division) with something of a dilemma. The *5th Hikōshidan*, charged with the defense of Burma, had two single-engine and one twin-engine fighter *Sentai* available: the *50th Sentai* in the *4th Hikōdan* (Air Brigade); the *64th Sentai*; and the *21st Sentai* with a small number of Type 2 Two-seat Ki-45 twin-engine fighters (Nick) in the *7th Hikōdan*. With 50 to 60 Oscar fighters between them, the *50th* and *64th Sentais* had responsibility for air superiority over the battle front and the defense of Rangoon and southern Burma. In February 1943, the *64th Sentai* returned to the airfield at Toungoo from Japan, where the unit had converted to the Ki-43-II model of the Hayabusa, allowing the *50th Sentai* to withdraw temporarily to Java for its own conversion to the newest model of the Oscar, the Regiment's squadrons returning to Burma as quickly as they could. In early March, the *21st Sentai* brought its Type 2 Two Seat fighters to Mingaladon to strengthen the defense of Rangoon. More heavily armed than the lighter Type 1

Hayabusa, the Type 2 Two Seat Fighter (Ki-45, code named "Nick") carried two 12.7mm machine guns in the nose and a 20mm cannon in a ventral tunnel. From February to May, the fighters were heavily involved supporting the Japanese

7th Bombardment Group B-24Ds en route to Rangoon during 1943. (3A-33602, RG 342FH, NARA)

Army in the Arakan, where the British had made a limited but unsuccessful advance toward Akyab. The Japanese fighters flew fighter sweeps and escorted bombers to attack British airfields in the Arakan area. Fortunately for the 7th Bombardment Group, their commitments to supporting the Japanese Army meant that the two fighter *Sentais* could rarely supply more than a single *Chutai* (squadron) to join the few K-45 Nick fighters in the defense of Rangoon.[84]

The *50th* and *64th Sentais* were experienced fighter units, having been in combat from the first days of the war in Southeast Asia. The two fighter regiments had capable, aggressive pilots, but they would find the B-24 to be a formidable opponent for their lightly-armed Hayabusa fighters. Designed as a tactical fighter with the mission of establishing air superiority over the battlefield, the Hayabusa demonstrated exceptional maneuverability, a feature that had limited utility when intercepting heavy bombers. More critically, for its new role of defending Rangoon against the B-24s, the Oscar's armament was inadequate. The Ki-43-II, the latest version of the Oscar, had a more powerful 1,150hp engine that gave a 20mph increase in speed over the earlier model Ki-43-I. The fighter's two 12.7mm machine guns were inadequate for a single fighter to bring down a B-24, unless it could get a sufficient number of hits in critical areas like the engines or incapacitate the crew. Developing effective tactics to counter the B-24s took the Japanese fighter pilots time and an immense amount of frustration. The *64th Sentai* pilots had some experience against American heavy bombers during a brief stay in Singapore in the fall of 1942, when a number of pilots had the opportunity to practice attacks against a captured B-17 Flying Fortress that the Japanese had repaired to flying condition (ironically, this might have been one of the 7th Bombardment Group's damaged B-17s left in Java). Capt. Yasuhiko Kuroe, commander of the *3rd Chutai* and later Executive Officer of the *64th Sentai*, flew on board the B-17 and watched as his men made dangerously close passes from the front quarter which even he found frightening. The brief session with the B-17 sharpened the fighting skills of his pilots and improved their morale and their confidence.[85]

The battles between the Japanese Oscar fighters and the B-24s would test the Army Air Forces' doctrine of unescorted daylight precision bombing; the first rounds would go to the 7th Bombardment Group. In between its attacks on key bridges in southern Burma, the 7th Group continued to attack the important transportation system targets in Rangoon, frequently running into Japanese fighters. The first clash between the newly-returned *64th Sentai* and the 7th Bombardment Group's B-24s took place on February 8, 1943.[86] The 436th Squadron sent out six aircraft to bomb the Aklone docks at Rangoon, while six aircraft each from the 492nd and 493rd Squadrons bombed the Mahlwagon marshaling yards; three other aircraft from the 492nd bombed Mingaladon airfield as a diversion. After completing their bomb run, the 436th Squadron's formation ran into a group of Japanese fighters

The opposition: 64th *Sentai* fighter pilots admire a colleague's new haircut with a Type 1 Fighter Hayabusa (Ki-43) in the background. (Author's collection)

that they identified as six "Zeros" (another report lists three Zekes, two Mikes—the code name assigned in error to the German Bf 109 the Japanese were thought to be using—and one Nate). The fighters kept up the attack for thirty minutes as the bombers headed home, making individual attacks and closing to short range. The bombers claimed one Oscar shot down and probably two more. Most of the attacks were directed against the formation's second element. Lt. German's B-24 was riddled, the fuselage and rudder taking numerous hits. His radio operator, S/Sgt. Eugene Gladd, was killed. German's two waist gunners (S/Sgts. Melville Baker and Robert Dolph) were both wounded in the first fighter attack, Dolph getting a bullet in his thigh. Despite this painful and heavily bleeding wound, Dolph continued to man his own gun as well as Baker's until the fighter attacks were over. He then attended to Baker's wounds without considering his own until other members of the crew came back to help him. For the courage he showed on this mission, Dolph was awarded the Silver Star.[87]

On the February 8th mission, the 492nd Squadron observed three Oscars during its attack on the airfield at Mingaladon, but these fighters remained at a distance. Four days later, on February 12th, the 492nd Squadron followed the 436th to Rangoon, the 436th Squadron attacking the Mahlwagon marshaling yards while the 492nd attacked the Rangoon railroad station. After dropping their bombs, the 492nd Squadron's formation came under attack by what the crews

A Ki-43 Oscar fighter circles around the 7th Bomb Group formation to line up for another frontal attack. (7th Bombardment Group (H) Historical Foundation, USAFA McDermott Library)

identified as four "Zekes" and one "Mike". The Japanese fighters kept up their attacks for an hour. The B-24 crews claimed one fighter destroyed, seeing it disintegrate in the air, and saw a second fighter leave combat trailing a heavy cloud of black smoke. The gunners fired off 4,000 rounds of .50 caliber ammunition. There is no record of the *64th Sentai* losing any airplanes on either February 8th or February 12th, however.[88]

For the next several weeks, fighter opposition over Rangoon declined. The *64th Sentai* and the newly-returned *50th Sentai* were heavily involved in the fighting in the Arakan and attacks on the American airfields in northeastern Assam. As previously related, a single Oscar damaged one B-24 and killed one of

In a still picture taken from a remarkable film of a 7th Bomb Group combat mission, a silver Oscar fighter dives past a B-24 formation. (Courtesy Col. Tom Sledge)

the crew from the 436th Squadron on the February 27th mission to the Pazundaung Bridge. On March 3rd, the 436th Squadron went out to bomb the Mahlwagon marshaling yards with six aircraft, while seven aircraft from the 492nd bombed the Rangoon docks and nine aircraft from the 493rd went after the Pazundaung Bridge. Two Oscars attacked the 436th Squadron's formation shortly after its bomb run; they made one individual pass each without result. The Squadron claimed one fighter as probably destroyed. The 492nd Squadron ran into two Oscars 45 minutes after leaving the target, each aircraft making a single attack on the formation from the 3 o'clock position. The gunners fired 700 rounds, seeing tracers enter both enemy fighters, and claimed both as damaged. The 493rd experienced a determined attack by a single Oscar who seemed almost to be experimenting with a tactic for intercepting the big bombers. The 493rd Squadron's mission report for March 3rd recorded the following:

> Almost immediately after the lead plane of the first element had completed a 180° turn, leaving target, one (1) Oscar was observed to right and above formation. It attacked by making a diving turn to the left, then slipping in left direction, skidding by entire formation, but remaining above it, and falling below only after passing the last element. He then continued to turn to his left and resumed his approximate original position, though, perhaps, at a greater altitude and distance. The maneuver was thereafter twice repeated, and each time he appeared to direct his attack principally upon

the third element. On each attack he was met with heavy fire from the formation, and the second and third attacks were met by turning the formation into him. He never came in closer than 500 yards and fired only a small quantity of ammunition. His third attack ended in a steep dive and he was not seen again. Puffs of gray smoke from his engine were seen to precede each attack.[89]

The *64th Sentai* returned to Mingaladon on March 7th to take up the defense of Rangoon.[90] Over the next week, several more intense air battles took place over the city. On March 10, 1943, six aircraft from the 9th Squadron bombed the Pazundaung Bridge at Rangoon while four from the 492nd attacked Mingaladon airfield, where their bombs killed four men from the *64th Sentai*. During the bomb run, the 492nd Squadron's small formation came under attack. Some 12 to 14 Oscars intercepted the bombers and made repeated attacks over a period of 40 minutes, following the bombers from Mingaladon across the Irrawaddy Delta to the Bay of Bengal. Some attacks came from the rear, but for the first time the Oscars tried head-on attacks, starting from a position above

Another still picture from the same film shows the right waist gun firing at Japanese fighter planes. (Courtesy Col. Tom Sledge)

the formation and then breaking away in a sharp turn. The crews noted that the attacks appeared to be well planned, with the fighters flying in line with the formation but out of range, with a single airplane turning into the attack, followed by another. When the airplanes started in for the attack, puffs of smoke seemed to come out of the exhaust. This may simply have been the Oscar's nose-mounted machine guns opening fire. One of the bombers was hit 15 times, but none were seriously damaged. The gunners in the formation claimed three Oscars destroyed and three to four others as damaged, though the *64th Sentai* does not appear to have lost any aircraft on this occasion. The Squadron credited excellent evasive tactics, the weight of the defensive fire, and the tight formation with saving the bombers from even greater damage.[91]

The mission of March 12th brought the first contact with the newly-arrived Ki-45 twin-engine fighters (Nick) of the *21st Sentai*, based at Mingaladon. The 436th Squadron went out on a mission to bomb the Pazundaung Bridge at dusk. In poor visibility the bridge was difficult to make out, so three aircraft dropped their bombs on the Mahlwagon marshaling yards. During the bombing run, an Oscar and a single Nick intercepted the formation, launching attacks on the first element. The Nick made two passes: the first from the 9 o'clock position, pulling up to pass over the formation. The Nick then came in from the 2 o'clock position. When the formation turned into the Nick's attack, the Nick pulled up into a stall, where it was hit and went into a dive with smoke coming out of the airplane. The crews claimed this airplane as destroyed. The Oscar made a single pass from directly ahead of the formation, climbing over the formation and racing past, with several gunners claiming hits on the airplane as it went by. The Oscar was seen to dive away in a slow, twisting dive and was claimed as a probable.[92]

The *64th Sentai* was called back to support an air offensive operation over the Arakan from the base at Magwe, probably on March 13th, leaving the *21st Sentai* and its Ki-45 fighters for the defense of Rangoon. That day, the twin-engine fighters made a highly effective and coordinated attack against the 9th Squadron, resulting in the loss of two B-24s and their crews, the first 7th Bombardment Group B-24s lost to Japanese fighters. The mission was to attack the Pazundaung Bridge. For some reason, only four aircraft went on the mission and bombed from the lower-than-normal altitude of 16,200 feet, arriving over the target right at noon. Just before the formation started its bomb run, five to seven Nicks intercepted the bombers and began to make well-coordinated attacks against the B-24s. Most of the attacks came from the front—from the 10 o'clock and 2 o'clock positions—the fighters passing underneath or through the formation after their attack run. The attacks were carefully coordinated, with airplanes making feint attacks from the rear quarter or from the sides to draw off the top turret from the real frontal attack. The Nicks made 15 to 20 attacks on the formation as it withdrew from Rangoon back to the Gulf of Martaban to the south. The gunners claimed one Nick destroyed, one probably destroyed, and several more damaged, but the 9th Squadron lost two B-24s. Capt. James Baldwin's airplane and that of Lt. Willard Short were fatally damaged in the attack. The two bombers made it out to the Gulf of Martaban but crashed into the sea, killing both crews. The two surviving bombers—one damaged with one gunner killed and two wounded—stayed with the two damaged bombers until they were about to crash into the sea. Interviewed shortly after his return from the mission, Lt. Paul Paskey, navigator in Lt. Gordon Wilson's airplane, said: "We didn't see them until we started our bombing run. They were 2,000

An illustration of the frontal attack on Col. Conrad Necrason's B-24 on March 31, 1943. (From Consoldiated Aircraft Corporation's *Plane Talk* March 1944)

feet above and dived steeply on us. They made pass after pass from all directions. I have never been so busy in my life. I shot up nearly all my ammunition." His colleague, bombardier Lt. Raymond Maloney, said: "I dropped all my bombs—as did all the others—then went to work with my machine gun. The air was full of lead, ack-ack, and smoke. We didn't have time to get scared then, but we were mighty shaky after we landed."[93]

The Nicks of the *21st Sentai* had no luck on their next encounter with the 7th Group five days later on March 18th, when the combined force of 16 B-24s from the 9th, 436th, and 492nd Squadrons went to Rangoon to bomb the Pazundaung Bridge. Four Nick fighters and a single Oscar made repeated attacks on the formation for nearly an hour, getting one cannon hit on a 9th Squadron B-24. Upon return, the 9th Squadron claimed the Oscar as destroyed and other gunners claimed damage to one of the Nicks. Once again, the Japanese fighters concentrated on frontal attacks from the one o'clock and two o'clock positions. Frontal attacks proved effective on the next encounter between Japanese fighters and the B-24s on March 31, 1943. That day, the 7th Group sent out all four squadrons to bomb the railroad bridge at Pyinmana, in central Burma, with the 492nd Squadron leading 24 aircraft. Weather interfered with the mission, the combined formation breaking up into single elements, each proceeding to the target area on their own, where haze made bombing difficult. By coincidence, Capt. Kuroe was leading 13 Oscar fighters from the *64th Sentai* on a mission to Chittagong from their base at Toungoo when they ran into several formations of B-24s. Seeing the bombers below him, Kuroe immediately ordered his fighters to attack. Col. Necrason was leading an element of four aircraft from the 493rd Squadron. As Necrason's element began its bomb run on the bridge, three Oscars launched a frontal attack on the bombers from ten o'clock above, while a second element of three came in from the two o'clock position, passing over the bomber formation at the end of their attack. Shortly after this attack, a single Oscar made a determined run on the lead ship, coming in head-on from above and firing all the way. An explosive shell hit the front canopy, penetrating the window and splintering on the armor plate behind Col. Necrason, the fragments wounding him in the neck and right shoulder and hitting his co-pilot, Maj. Bailey, in the scalp. Although bleeding from his wounds, Necrason flew back to base. The Oscars continued attacking the formation, coming in from the front and the beam, passing over the formation to attack another element of B-24s behind Necrason's formation. The crews observed that the attacks appeared to be well-coordinated. The Oscars worked in pairs: one pair coming into the attack from one side of the formation, crossing over after their run to the other side, while another pair came in from the opposite direction in succession. It seemed as if, in making frontal attacks from the 10 o'clock and 2 o'clock positions, the Oscars were using the lead aircraft in the element as a screen for the main attack on the airplanes flying alongside. It appears that the Oscar fighters in this attack were from the *2nd Chutai*, under the leadership of Capt. Hideo Miyabe, *Chutai* commander. Miyabe's aircraft and those of his two wingmen were all hit during their attack on the 493rd Squadron's

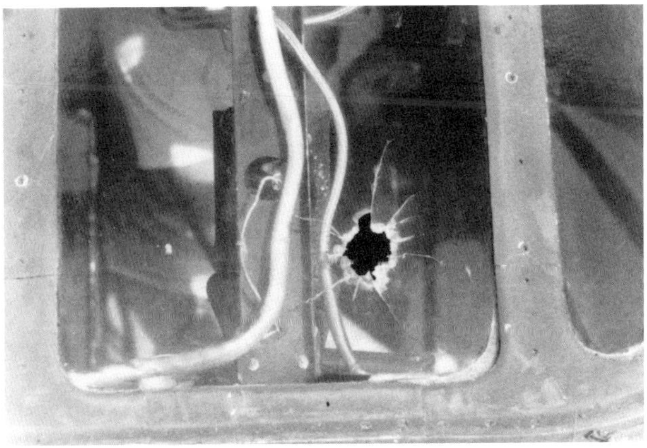

The cockpit window of the B-24D Col. Necrason was flying, showing where the Japanese 12.7mm shell entered the cockpit. (7th Bombardment Group (H) Historical Foundation, USAFA McDermott Library)

formation. Miyabe had to force land when his engine stopped. His wingmen force landed as well, one slightly wounded.[94]

Capt. Kuroe and his wingman attacked a B-24 in another formation, probably from the 9th Squadron. Kuroe made a rear attack—a dangerous approach—but hit one airplane's rear turret before his own aircraft was hit from return fire from other B-24s in the formation. He and his wingman continued to attack the bomber they had singled out. Kuroe made a frontal attack, finally bringing it down. This was the airplane of Lt. Lloyd Jensen, who bailed out with three other members of his crew. Years later, Jensen's co-pilot, 2nd Lt. Owen Baggett, stated that while floating down in his parachute he had fired at an Oscar that was circling his parachute after strafing some of the crew once they bailed out. Baggett claimed

On the way to targets in Burma out over the Bay of Bengal, the B-24s would fly in loose formation until it was time to make their run in to the target. (Courtesy Col. Tom Sledge)

to have shot it down. As the Oscar closed on him, Baggett pulled out his .45 caliber pistol and fired at the Oscar pilot in the cockpit, claiming that the Oscar immediately pulled up in a stall and spun down to the ground. However, no Japanese fighter pilot was killed that day and no Oscar was lost in a crash, though several were damaged.[95]

The *64th Sentai* pilots were beginning to work out tactics to use against the B-24s. The pilots had found attacking the B-24s immensely frustrating and even discouraging for pilots who were inculcated in the spirit of attack. On one occasion, five Oscar pilots fired close to 1,000 rounds against a B-24, only to see the American bomber fly on serenely as if nothing had happened.[96] Given the disparity in fire power—a single Oscar attacking a formation of six B-24s pitted its two 12.7mm machine guns against roughly 60 in the bombers putting out a formidable amount of return fire—going up against a bomber formation took considerable fortitude. One Japanese fighter pilot later recalled that the long, high wings of the B-24 appeared to him like an opponent with outstretched arms, calling out to him, "Come and get me!" It seemed as if the B-24s simply absorbed the bullets coming from the Oscars. The interceptions of the B-24s over Rangoon were exhausting and of limited success. Capts. Kuroe and Miyabe, and their pilots, debated the best way to attack a B-24, searching for a method that would be more successful. Through trial and error, they came to realize that attacks against the rear of a B-24 formation were extremely dangerous and likely to be fatal to the attacking pilot. The best approach was from the front, where the B-24 was less well armed. Frontal attacks, however, were difficult to execute, even for an experienced pilot. With the Oscar fighter's limited armament and the rapid closing speeds, a pilot could fire only a few bursts before he flew past the aircraft that was his target. The only advantage the Oscar had in a frontal attack was that its machine guns were fixed, and thus easier to aim than the flexible or turret guns in the B-24. Kuroe and Miyabe emphasized that frontal attacks had to be determined and calculated, demanding the utmost concentration in order to hit the vulnerable engines or cockpit crew. Kuroe urged his pilots to disregard the wall of fire coming up at them, the "infinite number of lights" that appeared in front of them from right to left as they attacked a formation, and throw themselves into the attack to "eat the bombers". Miyabe recommended concentrating all the attacks on one airplane on the right of the bomber formation; if that bomber could be knocked out, it would reduce the amount of return fire coming from the formation and enable renewed attacks at less risk. The tactics the *64th Sentai* developed for frontal attacks against the B-24s using concentrated fire would prove to be effective. However, to inflict real damage on the B-24s, the fighter *Sentai* required more fighters than were available in early 1943.[97]

The Americans were learning as well. The operational conditions the 7th Bombardment Group faced in its attacks over southern Burma and the tactics that the Group developed as a result were different from what the prewar doctrine of daylight precision bombing had envisioned and from the strategic bombing operations the Eighth Air Force in England was undertaking. The prewar tactics manual, *Tactics and Technique of Air Attack*, designated the bomb group as the normal unit of tactical employment.[98] While recognizing the principle of economy of force, which dictated the use of the smallest number of aircraft, the manual noted that "...the chance of successfully accomplishing the assigned mission increases with the size of the force dispatched, and this consideration indicates the dispatch of ample force."[99] American air power doctrine looked to the employment of massed formations of bombers to destroy key enemy targets. The Eighth Air Force based its combat formations on the bomb group and employed multiple groups; the day that the 7th Bombardment Group sent four squadrons of 24 aircraft to bomb the bridge at Pyinmana on March 31, 1943, the Eighth Air Force sent out five bomb groups with 103 B-17s and B-24s to bomb Rotterdam. As the Eighth Air Force gained strength over the course of 1943, the number of bomb groups and the number of aircraft deployed on bombing missions would steadily increase; by the end of the year, the Eighth was sending out over 20 bomb groups with more than 500 bombers on a single mission, numbers the Tenth Air Force could never equal.[100]

For most of 1943, the 7th Bombardment Group lacked airplanes. As indicated earlier, for reasons of maintenance and shortages of parts, the Group's squadrons could normally send out only six or seven airplanes on a mission. The Group also found that most of its targets in Burma were relatively small. As a result, bombing with larger formations of bombers would only have resulted in too wide a pattern of bombs and much wastage. For much of 1943, the Group employed the squadron, not the full group, as its standard tactical unit. In the course of 89 missions between October 1942 and the end of April 1943, the Group sent out more than three squadrons on only four missions. This was practical in part due to the relatively small number of Japanese fighters assigned to the defense of Rangoon, but it did mean that targets had to be hit repeatedly to limit repairs. The 7th Group relied on the 9th Photo Reconnaissance Squadron's photographic coverage of key targets for bomb damage assessment.

The 7th Group also found through experience that the best defense for the bombers was not the combined fire power of a bomber formation, as the prewar theorists and exercises had supposed, but evasive maneuvers. This was one principal benefit of flying in small squadron formations. The 7th Group developed effective evasive tactics that required disciplined

Over the target, the B-24s would close up into a tight defensive formation to obtain a closer bomb pattern and to maneuver against attacking Japanese fighters. (Courtesy Col. Tom Sledge)

flying and absolute formation integrity using the Javelin Down formation, with three airplanes in the first element and three to four in the second element following below. The aim of the evasive tactics the group developed was to throw off the Japanese fighter attacks. As Col. Necrason wrote in a report on his return to the United States in early 1944: "The only

Loading belts of .50 caliber machine gun rounds in the B-24's Consolidated tail turret. Japanese fighters rarely attacked from the rear quarter in order to avoid fire from the tail guns. (7th Bombardment Group (H) Historical Foundation, USAFA McDermott Library)

thing lethal about a fighter is its nose. If you plan your maneuvers so that you reduce to a minimum the length of time that the nose of the fighter is pointed toward your formation, evasive tactics are a success." Necrason did not have a high opinion of aerial gunnery. Accurate gunnery proved to be far more difficult than expected at the actual combat speeds the bombers and fighters flew at. "It is a great mistake", he argued, "to fly straight and level in order to maintain a steady shooting platform for bombardment gunners. The gunners just aren't that good!"[101]

As previously indicated, the squadrons would fly a loose formation flying down the Bay of Bengal toward targets in southern Burma, slowly climbing to bombing altitude as they neared the target and pulling into a tight formation for bombing. When equipped with the B-24D, the squadrons would bomb from an altitude of 22,000 to 25,000 feet, where the relative speed advantage the Oscar fighters had over the B-24D was not as great as at lower altitudes. After bomb release, the formation would exit the target area at the fastest speed possible while still maintaining a tight formation. The B-24s could never prevent the Japanese fighters from attacking, but a high-speed exit could limit the fighters to only three or four passes during a 40 to 60-minute battle.[102] The evasive tactics the Group developed, as outlined in Col. Necrason's report, bear quoting in full:

"1. A cardinal rule for defense is: *'to maintain the integrity of the formation.'* Evasive tactics are also a highly desirable means of defense, and, since the size of the formation determines the amount of maneuvering that can safely be done, it follows that large and small formations require different flying techniques.

2. Many of the early missions were, of necessity, made by small formations of six to nine planes. It was found that a six-plane formation with well-trained crews was highly maneuverable and that violent evasive tactics can be used without jeopardizing the formation. Several instances have occurred where the bombers have engaged in a 50- to 60-minute running battle and the attackers rarely got their nose pointed toward the formation, much less got any hits, due to the evasive tactics taken.
3. The great majority of Jap attacks are begun from the one to two o'clock and ten to eleven o'clock positions. To minimize the effectiveness of this pass, a steep diving turn into the attacker not only bares all the top turrets to reckon with the attacker, but also closes the distance gap between bomber and fighter to such an extent that the fighter, in most case, will not be able to complete his turn in toward the formation and, consequently, never gets his nose pointed anywhere near the formation. The ideal situation is to be able to anticipate the enemy attack and make the diving turn just before the beginning of the pass. The fighter himself is then in a predicament and has no choice but to dive out or away from the bomber formation.
4. Another method of evasion sometimes used is to delay the pass by turning at the proper moment away from the fighter. The Jap fighter usually spends a good deal of time catching up with the formation and reaching the favored frontal position for beginning the attack. This he will do by flying wide of the formation, on either side and just out of range of the bombers guns. By making a turn 20° to 30° away from him as he pulls up to approximately the four o'clock or eight o'clock position, the fighter is left facing the tail of the formation. *The Jap apparently regards a tail attack on a B-24 formation with high disfavor, so his only alternative is to move out wide of the formation and catch up again.* The time consumed in accomplishing this is all in favor of the bombers."[103]

This Army Air Force aircraft recognition training photo, using a model of the Ki-43 Oscar, gives an idea of what B-24 crews would have seen in a frontal attack. (3B-35039, RG 342FH, NARA)

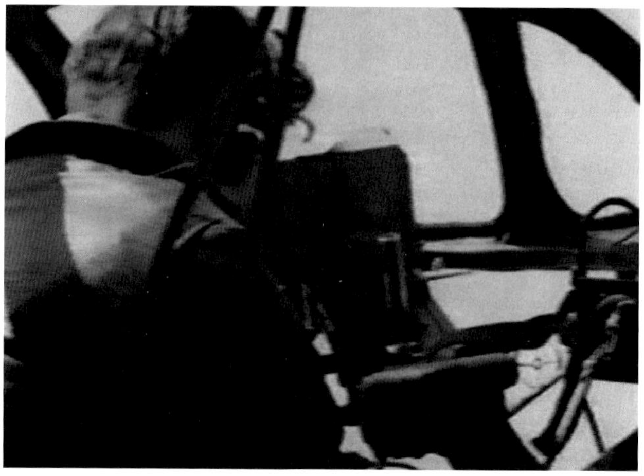

The bombardier in the nose of a B-24D prepares for the bomb run. The nose area was cramped, but provided excellent visibility for the bombardier and the navigator that was lost in later B-24 models. (Courtesy Col. Tom Sledge)

Within the 7th Group, the squadrons made it standard practice to have one individual in each bomber control the return fire during a fighter attack. On most airplanes the navigator took this responsibility, standing in the nose of the airplane with his head in the astrodome so that he could see and call out the number and direction of enemy fighter attacks. The tail gunner monitored fighters out of the line of vision of the navigator in the nose, calling out these fighters as they maneuvered out of range to position themselves for the next frontal attack. In the nose, the bombardier had responsibility for manning the nose-mounted machine guns, though there was little time, given the high closing speeds, for the bombardier to get many shots off, much less to get in a well-aimed burst. Tom Sledge recalled that all he really tried to do was send out bursts of tracer to "scare" the Japanese fighters, hopefully more than they scared him, as their approaches seemed certain to result in a head-on collision. Charles V. Duncan, Jr., a copilot on Lt. Stewart's crew in the 9th Bombardment Squadron, had his own memories of experiencing the frontal attacks the Japanese fighters came to prefer on one of his missions in early 1943:

> Japanese pursuit planes were already at our altitude and waiting, as we pulled out of range of the ack-ack... It was difficult to be sure just how many there were, because the attacks came in strings of two or three planes each, and they were repeated. The agile little planes would fly parallel to our formation, usually out of range to our right. After pulling well ahead of us, and gaining a slight altitude advantage, they would wheel, and come boring in from near head-on. When they came within range from this 11 o'clock to 1 o'clock position, little winking red lights shown on their wings, and at the top of the engine cowling. Often they would rock their wings back and forth, perhaps on the assumption this made more chance of hits, perhaps feinting an early break-away. Just when it appeared inevitable that there must be a mid-air collision, they would snap over on their backs, and dive down and away from our formation. They would disappear for a while, but soon re-appear, climbing to our right to repeat the process. It seemed to take nearly ten minutes for them to complete the cycle.
>
> It seemed impossible that they got so few hits; or for that matter, that the twin 50's in our top turrets got so meager results in opposing them. Possibly the reason these toe-to-toe shoot-outs were not more destructive, probably may have been the rate of closure. We usually flew at 160 to 180 mph indicated air speed. But in the thin air four miles up, our actual ground speed was nearer 250 mph. The opposing fighters would have been 100 mph faster. The rate of closure, therefore, was perhaps close to 600 mph. As a result, even with multiple rapid-firing guns, only a relatively few effective slugs could be fired by either side. The near straight down break-away gave the tail turret (and later, the ball turret) only a fraction of a second to line up a target. Any success they had would be largely accidental. But in spite of that, the frontal attacks were to prove more lethal to the B-24 than any other kind of attack.[104]

Lt. Robert Kavanagh and his crew, who were shot down on the mission of May 1, 1943. (7th Bombardment Group (H) Historical Foundation, USAFA McDermott Library)

The 7th Group's battles with the Japanese fighters lasted into May and the onset of the monsoon weather. The Group

A photograph taken from the Japanese aviation magazine *Koku Asahi* showing Lt. Kavanagh's B-24D after its successful crash landing in Burma. (Via the author)

held its own during the month of April, losing no bombers to fighter attack. With the *50th* and *64th Sentais* heavily involved supporting the Japanese Army in the Arakan and escorting Japanese Army Air Force bombers on raids against RAF airfields, there were fewer fighters available for the defense of Rangoon. On the few missions where the Japanese rose to intercept the B-24s, the bombers ran into only half a dozen fighters, rarely more. On April 17th, the 493rd Squadron encountered three Oscars while on a mission to bomb the Pazundaung Bridge. The Oscars made three individual attacks on the first element and one individual attack on the second element over 25 minutes without damaging any of the bombers. Following this raid the Group carried out three night missions, the 492nd Squadron bombing the Rangoon central railroad station on the night of April 18th and starting large fires, while on the night of April 21st, the 436th and 493rd Squadrons flew to Bangkok to bomb the arsenal at Bangsue. Weather interfered with the mission and prevented several of the bombers from reaching the target. The next night, April 22nd, the 9th and 492nd Squadrons bombed the Mahlwagon marshaling yards in Rangoon, the bombers attacking individually. While searchlights and anti-aircraft fire sought out the bombers, no fighters attempted to intercept. On the next daylight raid on Rangoon on April 26th, the *21st Sentai* sent up four Nick fighters to intercept a formation of six B-24s from the 492nd Squadron. The usually inaccurate anti-aircraft gunners got in a couple of good bursts, damaging the number 4 engine on the second airplane in the first element. As the formation left the target (warehouses near the central railroad station), the damaged airplane's engine was smoking heavily

A B-24D flying over Toungoo during April 1943. (File 827.306-1, Albert F. Simpson Historical Research Center, Air Force Historical Research Agency, Maxwell AFB, AL)

and the propeller had been feathered. About ten minutes later, the four Nick fighters appeared to the right of the formation, flying around 1,000 feet above the bombers. The Nicks began making individual attacks in a shallow dive: four coming in from the one o'clock position and two from the eleven o'clock position, raking the formation before passing over it to the rear. The fighters tried unsuccessfully to concentrate on the damaged bomber trailing smoke from its engine. Despite making six attacks and pressing each attack home, the Nicks inflicted only minor damage to the B-24s, with two airplanes taking hits in the wing. One fighter was seen to dive away from the formation with its engine smoking.[105]

The next battle with Japanese fighters brought the loss of another B-24. In late April, the *64th Sentai* apparently sent some of its fighters back to Mingaladon for the defense of Rangoon, the fighter regiment's *2nd Chutai* taking up the duty. On May 1st, the 492nd Squadron sent out eight aircraft to bomb shipping near the Sule Pagoda wharves at Rangoon. Five airplanes dropped their bombs on a ship near the wharves, getting good hits in the target area, while three airplanes bombed a ship moored in the Rangoon River just off the wharves, achieving several direct hits and near misses. Coming in for their bombing run at 23,500 feet, the formation ran into intense and accurate anti-aircraft fire; ahead they could see pursuits waiting to attack; these were a small number of Oscars from the *2nd Chutai*. As soon as the bombing run was over, five Oscar fighters began making individual runs, four attacks coming from the front quarter from the eleven o'clock to the one o'clock positions and one fighter coming from the six o'clock position. On one of these early passes, the Oscars shot out two engines on Lt. Robert Kavanagh's airplane. Sgt. Miyoshi Watanabe, who apparently made the initial attack on the rear of the formation, continued to fire at the rear of Kavanagh's airplane, despite the danger from the rear turret. Watanabe finally closed with the big bomber and deliberately rammed the rear turret with his airplane, surviving the encounter to force land his badly damaged fighter. Calling for help, Kavanagh dived toward the ground to escape his attackers. Capt. William Delahay, leading the mission, dived the formation after Kavanagh to provide some protection, but to no avail. Lt. Hirao Yukimoto and Warrant Officer Y. Takahama made repeated attacks on the damaged bomber, last seen entering clouds with three Oscars following. The formation flew off the coast for an hour, hoping that Kavanagh would make it out, but after losing a third engine he had no choice but to crash land, setting his airplane down in rice paddies near Bassein. Only three members of Kavanagh's crew survived the war. One crewman was killed in the action and four died as prisoners of war. This was another unpleasant contrast between the air war over Burma and the air war over Europe. For the men flying out of England particularly, there was a chance that if they were shot down over occupied territory they could link up with the Resistance and make their way to Spain and a return to England; American and

Early morning briefing for a mission over Burma in May 1943. Note the seven target folders on the table in front. The 7th Bomb Group's squadrons would normally send out six to seven B-24s on a mission. (3A-36248, RG 342FH, NARA)

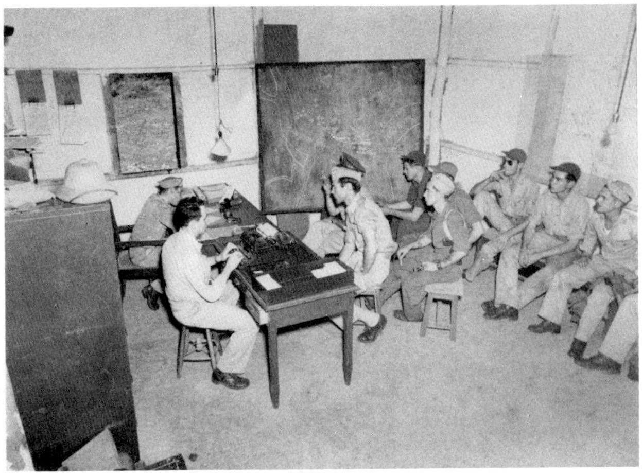

Interrogation for a 436th Squadron crew following the May 1, 1943, mission to bomb shipping at Rangoon. A rough chalk map of Rangoon has been drawn on the blackboard. (3A-36249, RG 342FH, NARA)

British flyers going into Burma had no hope of escape. The Burmese people, until very late in the war, routinely turned over Allied air crew to the Japanese, whose treatment of captured soldiers and airmen was abominable.[106]

The 9th and 493rd Squadrons extracted some revenge on a May 7th mission to bomb the railroad yards at Toungoo, near the *64th Sentai*'s main base. The two squadrons sent out 17 airplanes, but five had to turn back with various problems. The remaining 12 airplanes joined up and attacked the target as a single formation, the 493rd Squadron taking the lead. Bombing from an altitude of 21,800 feet, the formation got 66 direct hits in the target area, starting large fires. Coming off the target, the formation saw three to five Oscars and a single Nick below them waiting to attack. In most previous missions, the B-24s had resorted to diving away from the target after the attack to gain speed as part of their evasive maneuvers. As the Japanese fighters appeared to be waiting for this maneuver, the formation leader remained at altitude, forcing the fighters to climb up to the same level as the bombers, thereby gaining a little more time and shortening the distance to the Burmese coast. The Nick stayed away from the formation, but the Oscars made six determined frontal attacks from the 11 o'clock, one o'clock, and two o'clock positions; one fighter attacked the rear of the formation. In a change from previous tactics, on a number of the frontal attacks the Oscars came in at the same level as the bombers, or slightly lower. This made it more difficult for the top turrets to return fire. In addition, probably to confuse the gunners, several Oscars made feint attacks, seeming to come in directly but then breaking off. Lt. Alfonso Perez was a bombardier in Lt. William Larkin's 9th Squadron crew on the mission that day. After the mission he described the attack in his diary:

We were out of the target area when someone called, "Pursuit at 9 o'clock." I peered out, but couldn't see a thing, still someone kept reporting it, "It's up at 10 o'clock now and is climbing. "It looks like he is coming in!" Then all of a sudden I saw him. A speck in the distance, moving parallel to us and apparently trying to make up his mind whether to come in or not. He was at about 11 o'clock when he made his turn to come in. I could see our tracers reaching out for him. He kept coming; he was high—it seemed like he was going to crash right into the formation, as bullets were flying at him from all directions. He came straight, straight. Suddenly, just as he seemed about to crash into the second element, he flipped on his back and miraculously went through the second and third elements. He came out directly underneath our right wing, trailing black smoke. All possible guns were on him, including ours. He headed back and later, our rear gunner reported the pilot had bailed out and the plane had spun in. That was all for him, but there were more around to reckon with.

> There was another one at 2 o'clock and he was getting ready to make a pass. He finally came in pointing straight for the No. 2 element [aircraft] going under him and cutting to the right so that again I could see him plain as day as he flipped over under our right wing. I was on the floor gun, so I failed to shoot at him, as he was out of reach of my line of fire. I noticed that Goris [Lt. William B. Goris, Navigator] couldn't get him lined up either with the right gun from where he stood, so I decided to take his gun over, as I could get better shots from my position. "They never come in underneath us anyway," I thought, so I may as well get in on the fun."
>
> The third Zero [*sic*] was by this time up ahead at 2 o'clock, preparing to make his pass. I saw him get in front at about 1 o'clock and tracers began leaping for him. He seemed to be enticing the gunners to shoot at him. From where I was he seemed to be in range, but in all probability he wasn't, because the tracers were forming a pattern all around him and if he had been in range he would surely have gone down.
>
> He returned back to the 2 o'clock position, where he stayed for a while. I was almost hoping that he'd come in under my wing so that I could get a burst at him, since I was now manning the right nose gun. Finally, he started to come in. His pass was the same as the lead ship. In to No. 2 element from 2 o'clock and underneath us, flipping over under our right wing. Just as he flipped over I put my gun on him, pulling the trigger, and nothing happened. "Damn it." Goris had set the gun and I didn't remember to put it on "Fire". I thought, "I hope I get another chance like that, next time I'll get him."

A B-24D taxies in after a mission. A fixed, forward-firing machine gun has been added on the lower left side of the nose. (3A-33641, RG 342FH, NARA)

By this time we were coming up over the coast. I thought maybe they'd go back. But no, here was another one streaming up ahead to come in again. After he got into position he flew along with us for several minutes and came in. His attack was the same as the last one, only this time I was ready. I saw him come, picked him up, and let him have a can full. I could see the tracers sinking right into him. Satisfaction flowed right through me. Granger, our rear gunner, was also on him with a hail of lead. We never saw him again. Later, some of the gunners said they saw a Zero get caught in some cross fire and disintegrate that must have been ours. Anyway, I'm claiming part credit. That was the last pass made at us. Our ship came in with everyone safe, not even a scratch to show what we had been in. Some of the other ships got slightly shot up and a couple boys got hurt but not seriously. It was a very successful and eventful day. The fighter attack lasted 50 minutes.[107]

That day, the *64th Sentai* had one fighter shot down and another badly damaged in a crash landing.

The 7th Group had another success four days later. The 436th Squadron went out to bomb the Mahlwagon marshaling yards at Rangoon on May 7th, running into intense anti-aircraft fire that damaged five airplanes. Two Oscars intercepted the formation and unusually made five attacks from the seven o'clock position, with no bombers being damaged. The gunners claimed one of the Oscar fighters damaged. Then, on May 11th, the 9th and 493rd Squadrons went back to Rangoon to bomb the Syriam oil refinery south of the city. As the bombers began their bomb run—the 9th Squadron at 23,800 feet and the 493rd at 21,000 feet—the crews could see three Oscar fighters climbing up to meet them. The bombing on this mission was excellent, nearly all bombs falling into the target area and starting several fires, with columns of black smoke rising several thousand feet. After the bombing run the Oscars came in, making three frontal attacks, but on this occasion the attacks were half-hearted and not pressed home. In response, as the Oscars came in the lead airplane would drop its nose so the top turret could have a clear shot at the on-coming fighter. The bomber formation also tried a new evasive maneuver, moving 10 degrees away from the fighters paralleling the formation to force them to have to set up their attack all over again. The maneuver successfully delayed the fighter attacks. As he passed through the formation, return fire hit Lt. Hirao Yukimoto's Oscar, forcing it down. Yukimoto attempted to bail out at lower altitude but waited too long, jumping from 500 feet to his death. His airplane was seen to crash into the ocean off Rangoon. This was the last aerial combat the 7th Group experienced before the monsoon.[108]

The mission of May 11th was the 7th Group's last successful mission to Rangoon for the month. Although the weather had begun to worsen, signaling the beginning of the monsoon season, the Group kept up a steady pace of bombing missions across central and southern Burma. The bombers hit Myitkyina and Lashio and went back to the Toungoo railroad yards. The India Air Task Force was anxious to inflict as much damage as possible on the Japanese before the monsoon weather curtailed operations. In mid-May, the IATF provided support during the last phase of the Arakan campaign. In concert with the RAF, operating by day and night, the 7th and 341st Groups took on the task of bombing Japanese lines of communication in the Irrawaddy Valley in Operation Wimpole from May 18th

Lt. Edward McCoy's B-24D (41-11925) crashed on take-off for a mission, spewing 500-pound bombs around the airplane, though none were armed. (Courtesy Col. Tom Sledge)

to May 20th, a three-day blitz of nearly constant attacks.[109] The 7th Group sent out single squadron formations of six to nine aircraft to bomb railroad yards, oil facilities, towns, and factories in the Irrawaddy Valley that might be providing supplies to the Japanese Army, flying twelve missions in total. The missions were fairly straightforward, with no fighter opposition and little anti-aircraft fire. In an attack on the town of Magwe on May 19th, ten bombers from the 492nd Squadron came in behind a formation from the 436th Squadron, who were bombing Magwe instead of their primary target due to weather. The 9th Squadron started several large fires, a huge column of black smoke rising to 10,000 feet after the bombers withdrew. At the end of Operation Wimpole, the British Army commander sent the following message to the RAF and the India Air Task Force: "Most grateful for your joint efforts in Operation Wimpole from 18 to 20 May. Ground intelligence reports confirm result in Japanese casualties most effective and whole effort appears definitely to have restricted further forward movement of enemy in any numbers and to have seriously upset their supply arrangements."[110]

An attempted night mission to Rangoon by the 9th and 436th Squadrons as a cover for a joint 492nd and 493rd Squadron mining mission to the Rangoon River resulted in most of the aircraft turning back because of weather. The 492nd and 493rd brought their mines back to base. The last missions of the month—attempts at sea sweeps off the Rangoon estuary—had to be cancelled due to weather. This would be the pattern for the next several months.[111] The India Air Task Force's heavy and medium bombers could look to steadily improving results from the bombing campaign that began in November 1942. Collectively, the 7th Bombardment Group and the 341st Bombardment Group had flown 35 sorties in November at the start of the campaign, dropping 73.5 tons of bombs. During May 1943, the two groups completed 813 sorties, dropping 1,097.5 tons of bombs. From November to May, 445 tons of bombs had been dropped on targets in Rangoon. While not a huge amount of bombs relative to efforts in other theaters, the damage was considerable and contributed to reducing the flow of Japanese supplies into the port. Allied intelligence estimated that shipping tonnage going into Rangoon had shrunk from around 60,000 tons a month in August 1942, before any bombing had been undertaken, to around 5,000 tons a month in May 1943. For a period of nearly five weeks during March and April 1943, no ships came into Rangoon at all. The heavy bombers had been unable to completely close the port of Rangoon, but they had severely restricted shipping traffic. That was a significant accomplishment, given their limited numbers.[112]

Monsoon Madness

Burma is subject to the Southwest Monsoon. Beginning in late May to early June and lasting until late September to early October, the monsoon season brings torrential rains and storms almost daily over northeast India and much of Burma. Between June and August, it can rain nearly every day over southern Burma, with only four or five hours of sunshine. The extreme weather played havoc with aerial operations. Flying from India down the Bay of Bengal, an airplane had to work its way through successive rain squalls and cloud formations full of turbulent air. Often the 7th Group's bombers would fly several hours through turbulent weather, only to find their designated target covered in clouds, forcing them to turn around and make the same grueling flight back to base. As Charles Duncan recalled: "Formation flying had been hard physical work, with no power assists on the B-24. Instrument flying began to replace formation flying as the sweat job. Stewart [Duncan's pilot] and I would take ten or fifteen minute turns at it in the most turbulent air. This sometimes went on for over four hours without a break. The automatic pilot was of no use for either formation or instrument flying in rough air. At times, we would be forced to fly only a few hundred feet off the water of the Bay of Bengal for several hours."[113] In early July, Duncan went on a mission to bomb Akyab, on the Burmese coast. "We were lucky enough to be able to bomb from 6,000 feet", he wrote, "but the rest of the trip was made below 1,000 feet...We then set a direct course

Lt. David Kellogg at the controls of his B-24. Kellogg went on to command the 9th Bomb Squadron and was shot down on a mining mission to the Gulf of Thailand on May 8, 1944, spending the rest of the war as a POW. (7th Bombardment Group (H) Historical Foundation, USAFA McDermott Library)

B-24Ds of the 9th and 493rd Squadrons taxi out for a mission from their base at Pandaveswar. (3A-33640, RG 342FH, NARA)

back, over the Bay. For three hours we flew in rain of varying density, just off the water. But we could not see the water over the nose, only by looking down from the side windows. It was instrument flying all the way."[114]

Given the unpredictability of the weather over southern Burma, many of the missions the 7th Group flew during the peak months of the monsoon were a combination of sea sweeps around the estuary of the Rangoon River and over the Gulf of Martaban, combined with bombing whichever target might be clear of weather if no ships were found. Crews were routinely given a primary, a secondary, and sometimes even a third possible target to bomb. The squadrons went back to sending out small formations of aircraft—six to seven on a mission—as the weather often required formation instrument flying. Even a small formation often had trouble getting through the weather and often some or all of the airplanes would be forced to turn back. A formation would sometimes have to split up because the weather was bad. The airplanes would often be unable to reform after breaking out into clearer skies. On one mission in June, the Group sent out 30 aircraft drawn from all four squadrons; only five got through to the target. One of the few benefits of the monsoon weather was that it affected the Japanese as well, limiting the number of interceptions.

During June, the 7th Group flew missions on only 11 days. The weather during the first half of the month was especially bad. The Group flew no missions between June 2nd and 11th, and for the entire month, eleven missions had to be abandoned due to weather. Because the monsoon rains made the transport of supplies over Burma's limited road network difficult, the Japanese were forced to rely even more on the railroad system. As a result, railroad facilities throughout Burma became a major objective for the India Air Task Force's heavy and medium bombers over the next several months. A key target during the month for the 7th Bombardment Group was the railroad yard at Thanbyuzayat, a small town on the Burmese coast south of Moulmein. Thanbyuzayat was being built up as the terminus for the Burma-Thailand railroad between Bangkok and Moulmein. The Group made three attempts to get through to Thanbyuzayat, weather disrupting the first two. The 9th and 493rd Squadrons tried on June 12th. The 9th Squadron had to abandon the mission, but the 493rd got through. Maj. Werner led six aircraft from Panda to Thanbyuzayat, flying at 1,000 feet on instruments for much of the way through heavy rains and cloud before breaking into clearer weather near the Rangoon River estuary. An overcast over the target forced the bombers down to 4,000 feet for their bomb run, but with no anti-aircraft fire the bombers had a clear run on the target, getting most of their bombs on the south end of the railroad yards. The 492nd Squadron tried the next day, only to run into impenetrable fronts. They battled these fronts for several hours before turning back. All four squadrons went back to Thanbyuzayat on June 15th, but only five of 30 aircraft managed to reach the target, hitting in the railroad yards and a few warehouses nearby. Success came on the third attempt. The 9th Squadron sent out six airplanes and the 436th Squadron sent out seven on June 26th. As the 9th Squadron came in over the railroad yards at the low altitude of 3,600 feet, the crews saw a train going past the railroad station just as the bombs were released. The bombs fell directly onto the moving train, blowing it into the air and heavily damaging the tracks in the yard alongside. Bombing from 8,500 feet, the 436th added to the destruction. The next day, the 492nd Squadron made it to Thanbyuzayat, getting 38 to 43 hits on the west side of the railroad yards and damaging the tracks and the storage areas west of the station. The Group also bombed several other railroad marshaling yards in support of the efforts of the 341st Group's medium bombers to disrupt the rail system in central Burma. Small formations of B-24s penetrated the weather to hit the yards at Mandalay (twice), Yamethin, and at Monywa before the end of the month.[115]

July brought a modest improvement in the weather. The 7th Group was able to fly missions on 17 days during the month as opposed to 11 days in June and doubled the number of airplanes sent out, completing 145 sorties compared to 70 in June.[116] Railroad installations were again the main focus of the heavy bomber attacks, beginning on the first day of the month when the 9th and 492nd Squadrons returned to Thanbyuzayat to bomb the railroad yards. The primary target had been the Syriam oil refinery south of Rangoon. When the formations arrived in the target area, however, they found Rangoon clouded over, so headed to Thanbyuzayat—the secondary target—where they bombed successfully, but ran into surprisingly accurate anti-aircraft fire for the first time. One Nick fighter from the *21st Sentai* tried to intercept the

492nd Squadron, but the Squadron kept a tight formation and fought off the lone fighter. The squadrons returned after flying 11 ½ hours. The next day, July 2nd, the 436th and 493rd Squadrons headed out to bomb the Syriam oil refinery. The 436th Squadron got through to the target, bombing from 15,000 feet with fair results. The formation saw one Nick fighter in the area, though it did not attack. After bombing the refinery, the formation headed back out to sea, running into heavy clouds. Capt. Vick Winter's B-24 was last seen going into a cloud bank. A short while later, the rest of the formation heard a radio call "Any B-24 for help!"[117] Winter's plane was never seen again; he may have had the misfortune to run into one or more of the Nick fighters. The 493rd Squadron could not find a break in the clouds over Rangoon, so went on to Thanbyuzayat, the secondary target, where they found moderately good weather and a very determined Nick fighter. Coming in at 10,700 feet, the Squadron put almost all its bombs in the railroad yards, doing heavy damage. Coming off the target, the crews saw a single Nick approaching from the north, and as the Squadron history recorded, "...another exciting adventure was about to take place." The Nick made six passes against the formation in an attack that lasted 30 minutes. Four passes came from the front quarter, the Nick pressing home the attack, then passing over or through and underneath the formation. The enemy fighter came as close as 25 feet above the B-24s, despite intense fire from the

Sitting on a 2,000-pound bomb used for attacks on bridges at Panagarh in 1943. Left to right: Joe Murray, bombardier; Robert McIntosh, bombardier; Earl Rainbow, navigator; and Edward McCoy, pilot, all from the 492nd Squadron. (7th Bombardment Group (H) Historical Foundation, USAFA McDermott Library)

gunners. Several gunners noticed that the Nick's rear gunner would open fire on the B-24s as the Nick sped past the formation. All agreed the pilot showed "unusual daring and skill" in his attacks. Remarkably, only one B-24 was damaged; Lt. Ingham's airplane picked up one bullet in the leading edge of the wing.[118] For the rest of the month, the Group continued the attacks on the railroad yards in central Burma, hitting Mandalay and Ywataung several times, as well as making several attacks on warehouses and supply dumps, where it was assumed the Japanese were storing supplies they could

Col. Conrad Necrason, 7th Bomb Group commander, and Major William Delahay, 492nd Squadron commander, present a medal to Lt. John Miller at Panagarh in 1943. (7th Bombardment Group (H) Historical Foundation, USAFA McDermott Library)

not deliver over the railroad network. Despite the lack of results on previous missions, several bridges were added to the target list. The Myitnge Bridge received several visits, once again without demonstrable results, although the 341st Group's B-25s finally destroyed the bridge on July 23rd in a medium-altitude attack.[119]

The slow-down in missions during June and July enabled the squadrons to undertake special training programs and arrange for leave for some of the crews who had been flying without a break since the beginning of the year. More awards came through for the combat crews. While there had been several awards for conspicuous acts of bravery, in the main, the 7th Group used a standardized approach, awarding medals based on total flying hours. After completing 100 operational flying hours, an individual was awarded the Air Medal; after 200 operational flying hours came the award of the Distinguished Flying Cross; and after 300 hours, an Oak Leaf Cluster to the Air Medal. By June, a number of men were approaching the required number of hours, so during the monsoon months awards of the Air Medal and the Distinguished Flying Cross came regularly. Promotions came through as well, many men advancing a rank in grade.[120]

Training covered a broad range of topics and skills. The squadrons initiated refresher training for radio operators and flight engineers, a special course in ship identification with a

492nd Squadron bombardiers who were awarded the Distinguished Flying Cross. Several of the bombardiers are enlisted men, a legacy of the prewar Army Air Corps. (Courtesy Col. Tom Sledge)

The 7th Bomb Group began sending combat crews to rest camps in the foothills of the Himalaya mountains, where the men could get two weeks of complete relaxation. (Author's collection)

competition thrown in. The winner received an extra allotment of cigarettes. A special course in pistol marksmanship was set up for all officer and enlisted combat crewmembers, followed by a course in skeet shooting. In between their training assignments and combat missions, every other day the combat crewmembers spent several hours cleaning their .50 caliber machine guns to make sure none developed rust from the higher humidity and rain from the monsoon. During June, the 7th Group made arrangements with the 51st Fighter Group to send several fighter pilots and P-40 fighters on detached service for a program of aerial gunnery training. The 25th Fighter Squadron sent three pilots with three P-40s for several weeks of training. The fighters made gunnery passes on the B-24 formations, giving the gunners practice in tracking fighter attacks. The aerial gunnery training continued into July.[121]

With new combat crews arriving regularly, the "old hands" in the Group were given two weeks leave at U.S. Army rest camps in the foothills of the Himalaya mountains. The higher altitudes brought a welcome relief from the heat and humidity of Bengal. The rest camps gave the men a chance to fully relax, if only for a short period, with excellent food, physical activity if it was wanted, or time to simply sit around and watch the clouds drift by.[122] Calcutta was a shorter trip for those so inclined, with all its exotic sights, sounds, and smells. In an age when very few Americans traveled overseas, India was a wonder to many of the young men who found themselves stationed there. However, most considered the grinding poverty and lack of sanitation appalling. The squadrons held regular sporting events, particularly baseball games, for entertainment and for physical exercise, so the crews kept fit. There were inter-squadron games and games with other Army units in India. The "Eager Beavers" baseball team from the 492nd Squadron became regional U.S. Army champions in

In an age when few Americans traveled overseas, the sights, sounds, and smells of India were exotic and unlike anything most of the men of the 7th Bomb Group had ever seen before. These men are watching a snake charmer on a street in Calcutta. (7th Bombardment Group (H) Historical Foundation, USAFA McDermott Library)

Lt. Tom Sledge, 492nd Bomb Squadron, opens a can of American beer, a rare and welcome treat even if warm. (Courtesy Col. Tom Sledge)

June, when they defeated a team from the 393rd Port of Embarkation Corps 18 to 1. In August came the "great day", when a shipment of American candies, gum, and toiletries arrived at the PX at the different bases. Carefully rationed so all might partake of a little reminder of home, a shipment of American beer arrived around the same time, to be enjoyed warm, as there was no means of chilling it.[123]

Sea Sweeps and a Swan Song

Allied intelligence was concerned the Japanese would use the monsoon weather to conceal ships moving into Rangoon. During good weather, the 7th Bombardment Group's attacks on Rangoon had forced Japanese shipping to move cautiously up the Malay coast from Singapore and hug the Burmese coast up to Rangoon, mostly by night.[124] Storms and overcast skies over the Gulf of Martaban allowed single ships and convoys to slip into Rangoon undetected. With the limited number of bombers available and without detailed intelligence, it was difficult to adequately cover the area from the Andaman Islands to the Gulf of Martaban. During August and September, the 7th Group conducted regular sea sweeps, searching for Japanese shipping, with some success. The regular assignment of targets on land made these sea sweep missions economical in terms of fuel, bombs, and wear and tear on aircraft and crews. As an experiment, the 492nd Squadron received one B-24D equipped with radar for conducting sea searches in company with the standard B-24s the Squadron flew. During August, the squadrons began receiving later models of the B-24D with a Sperry ball turret with twin .50 caliber machine guns under the fuselage in place of the single .50 caliber tunnel gun in the earlier models. The increased defensive firepower was a welcome addition.

The sea sweeps began in earnest in late July. On July 23rd, the 436th Squadron sent five aircraft to sweep the Gulf of Martaban as far south as Pagoda Point, off Tavoy, about 120 miles south of Moulmein, on the southern Burmese coast. The flight came across two Japanese transport ships, each

The 7th Bomb Group received a small number of B-24D "Snooper" airplanes to assist in sea searches. (7th Bombardment Group (H) Historical Foundation, USAFA McDermott Library)

around 200 feet long, and claimed several near misses and one direct hit. The 492nd Squadron took the next sea sweep four days later, sending out nine airplanes over the Gulf of Martaban. The weather was so bad that the formation had to split up, each bomber proceeding individually. Capt. Disher, who was leading the mission, and Lt. Bonsteel ran into Oscars during their mission. Disher got away without damage, but Bonsteel had his ship shot up and his bombardier, Lt. McIntosh, slightly wounded. Bonsteel's top turret gunner, T/Sgt. Steinkellner, claimed one Oscar destroyed and one probably destroyed during the fight.[125] The next day, July 28th, the 493rd Squadron had the first of few successes achieved against Japanese ships during the monsoon months.

That morning, Maj. Werner, 493rd Squadron commander, led Lts. Olsen and Berlette on a sea sweep down to the area around Tavoy, where Allied intelligence had reported Japanese shipping. Nine aircraft from the 9th Squadron patrolled the same general area, but Werner's small flight had better luck, thanks to accurate intelligence. Working their way through heavy weather, the flight found a Japanese freighter near an island some 15 miles off the coast with a small Navy vessel as escort. They estimated the freighter to be around 3,000 tons and 250 feet long. Werner ordered Olsen and Berlette to climb up just below the 4,000-foot ceiling and make individual runs over the transport. Berlette went in first, dropping six 500-pound bombs. These landed along the starboard side of the ship. The transport was veering sharply in an attempt to evade the bombers when Olsen came in on his bomb run at 3,000 feet. Olsen's bombardier got at least one direct hit on the transport and possibly another, causing it to lose steering control. The ship turned east to head for the coast, listing to starboard with smoke pouring out of the engine compartment. Werner came in to administer the *coup de grace* in a low-altitude attack. Coming in at masthead height at 200 mph, Werner's bombs, with eight- to eleven-second delayed action fuses, hit the ship directly amidships. Three minutes later the *Tamiskima Maru* (1,931 tons) sank stern first. Werner and his two wingmen flew back to Pandaveswar at 700 feet most of the way through heavy rain and turbulence, landing after 12 hours and 40 minutes in the air.[126]

After several inconclusive sea sweeps and the cancellation of several missions due to weather, the 492nd and 493rd Squadrons headed out again to the Gulf of Martaban on August 13th to search for Japanese shipping along the coast. The 9th Squadron had found nothing a day earlier, dropping its bombs on the railroad station at the town of Ye, south of Moulmein, on the way back to base. Capt. Rote, leading four aircraft from the 493rd, reached the area south of Pagoda Point first, where the formation found a 150 to 175-foot long freighter estimated to be around 1,000 tons. Rote had the other three pilots make their attacks on the ship from 4,000 feet, but none got any hits, only near misses. Rote then came in at low level, and he, too, missed the ship. Turning for home, the bombers ran into a single Oscar fighter south of Pagoda Point. Lt. Koichi Mori from the *1st Chutai* of the *64th Sentai*, which had remained at Mingaladon for the defense of Rangoon while the rest of the unit withdrew to Palembang in Sumatra and Sungei Patani in Malaya to rest and train, was flying near the area. Whether he was there by chance or to intercept the bombers is unclear.

B-24D #20 from the 9th Bomb Squadron. This early model B-24D has a .50 caliber tunnel gun, later replaced with the Sperry ball turret. The 7th Bomb Group routinely painted out the serial numbers on its early B-24s. (Peter M. Bowers Collection, Museum of Flight)

The bombers were flying at an altitude of 1,000 feet when they spotted the Oscar coming at them from the north and above their formation. The Oscar began a diving attack from the 1 o'clock position into a hail of gun fire from the combined top turrets and nose guns. Mori may have been killed instantly,

Captain Disher and his crew from the 492nd Squadron with their B-24D *Hanger Queen*. (3A-34849, RG 342FH, NARA)

as his Oscar never pulled out of its dive, continuing on to crash into the sea. Following the combat, Rote contacted the 492nd Squadron's formation, heading to the same area, and alerted them to the Japanese freighter. The six aircraft came in and claimed two direct hits and a near miss, leaving the ship on fire and, they believed, sinking. On August 16th, the 9th, 492nd, and 493rd went out on sea sweeps. The 9th Squadron sent out four aircraft, one turning back. The other three continued on to the Gulf of Martaban, where they came across two small freighters but failed to sink them, getting 12 near misses. These left one ship listing and one appearing to have stopped. They came in low to strafe the two ships before heading back. The 492nd also went to the Gulf of Martaban, also finding two small ships that were bombed and strafed. Capt. Rote again led the 493rd Squadron to the coast off Rangoon, where the formation found a six ship convoy. Flying toward the convoy under an overcast sky, the bombers ran into six Oscars, most likely assigned to escort the convoy up the Rangoon River. The Oscars attacked immediately, hitting Rote's airplane in the nose area, seriously wounding Lt. William McDonald, his bombardier, and Lt. Guy Spotts, his navigator. As the formation had been briefed to bomb on McDonald—the lead bombardier—the mission had to be abandoned, most airplanes jettisoning their bombs as they headed back to base. Lt. McDonald died from his wounds the next day.[127]

After several fruitless sea sweeps and several bombing missions to targets in central Burma, the 493rd sent out two airplanes on August 25th, with Capt. Rote leading Lt. Bailey, on a long mission to Car Nicobar Island, south of the Andaman Islands—an approximately 1,800-mile round trip from Pandaveswar. Arriving over the island, they saw a 300-foot freighter anchored off the southeast corner of the island with barges unloading cargo and a small gunboat nearby. Rote and Bailey made individual bombing runs at 3,000 feet, each dropping six 500-pound bombs. At least three bombs hit the ship, setting it on fire. This was the *Heito Maru*, a 4,468-ton freighter that sank soon after the attack. As the bombers departed, the gunboat belated sent up anti-aircraft fire. Rote took Bailey down on a strafing pass over the island, shooting up a barracks, the Japanese camp on the island, and several trucks. Rote and Bailey returned to Pandaveswar, having flown 12 hours and 55 minutes. Rote led another flight of three airplanes back to Car Nicobar on September 3rd, and was lucky to return home from the mission. The targets were any ships that could be found and shore installations. Rote's two wingmen (Lts. Berlette and Stokes) bombed from 4,500 feet, getting hits on a pier and three near misses alongside a 100-foot boat. After bombing, the two planes came down to strafe installations on the island. Rote was coming in at 1,500 feet on his bomb run when he ran into a hail of anti-aircraft and small arms fire that knocked out one of his engines.

Two B-24s from the 493rd Bomb Squadron found and bombed a Japanese transport ship near the Car Nicobar Islands, August 23, 1943. (3A-37550, RG 342FH, NARA)

Jettisoning his bombs, Rote found that he could not feather the engine. Limping back to base, he had the crew throw out all ammunition to lighten the airplane. Rote finally made it back to land at Calcutta.[128]

7th Bomb Group B-24s attacking Akyab on August 28, 1943. (3A-37499, RG 342FH, NARA)

A break in the monsoon weather in early September resulted in one of the most effective missions against Japanese shipping. A reconnaissance mission over Rangoon on September 5th revealed four transports, including two large freighters, moored in the Rangoon River. On September 6th, the 7th Group dispatched all four squadrons and on this occasion grouped all four into a single formation. The 9th Squadron's Lt. Alfonso Perez recorded the mission in his diary:

> The target was to be the railroad yards, but at the last moment they changed it to shipping as they received a report that two boats were sighted on the river. We took off at 0600 in order to get in before the weather started closing in. it looked like this time we were destined to get in. The weather looked very good and as we hit the coast it was very probable that the cloud coverage would permit good sighting. There were again twenty-eight airplanes in the formation, each squadron having its own target. It was really a thrill to look out the window and see those babies looking so defiant, so powerful flying alongside of us in a perfect V formation. Such a feeling of confidence and pride came over me...
>
> In the distance I could see the Rangoon River and Rangoon itself. I picked it up with my glasses. I could see a larger boat anchored right in the middle of the stream and we were heading right for it. The bomb bays slid open and we were on the run. I could see flashes of fire coming out of the ship; she was shooting at us...The flak was bursting all around. The sky was black with it and damn accurate too—right on our wings! Somebody called up "Pursuit at 3 o'clock and below." At the moment I just thought "I'll worry about him later." Right now the problem at hand was to bomb these ships. We kept getting closer. I felt a jump in the ship as the bombs went out. Bombs were raining down from all the ships. I looked down. I saw a train go off to the left, missed. But here came another. One mushroom of water after another crawled up to the ship and ended up with two direct hits in the bow. Then the ship was surrounded by bomb bursts all around. I looked over to the right and the same thing was happening to the other boat. Two boats hit and sinking. We closed our doors and swerved away. The ack-ack still persistently trying to catch us.[129]

The bombing had been successful, with the 436th, 492nd, and 493rd Squadrons getting five direct hits and three near misses on the larger of the two ships, leaving it in flames. This was the *Milan Maru* of 5,467 tons, which sank in the Rangoon River a few hours later. The 9th Squadron bombed the smaller ship (the *Annan Maru*, 2, 941 tons), getting a direct hit and several near misses that set the ship on fire. The *Annan Maru* also sank that afternoon.[130]

Bombing ships moored in the Rangoon River. The photograph shows what a difficult target ships proved to be. (Courtesy Jim Augustus)

The fighters came in right after the bomb run, a mix of Oscars and Nicks from the *64th* and *21st Sentai*. The fight lasted for an hour. As the 492nd Squadron's history recorded, the fighter attacks "...were pressed relentlessly from all quarters above and below and all around the clock. All told around 30 passes were made, some being pressed to within 50 yards."[131] Lt. Perez was in the thick of the action:

> I looked out and saw the first 'zero'; his silver wings shining with the red ball on each tip. He was gaining altitude to make his first attack. He came in but it was just a sort of feeler. As he went under I looked out the fight window and saw my first I-45 [Nick fighter]. A twin engine nose heavy fighter. It looked pretty larger as it attacked the element on our right. I noticed that Lt. Bailey was flying all alone on the left. I thought to myself "You better get in the cloud or you'll get shot down." One I-45 made a pass at him tracers out—the Jap rolled under his belly—Bailey was still up there. Then I saw one I-45 coming straight at us from 12 o'clock. I let him have one short burst to get my range on him. As he got closer I froze my finger on the trigger and followed him in. Whether I got him or not, I don't know. He passed underneath us.
>
> They kept coming and coming. I was holding my floor gun when I felt a splattering of glass. I looked back at Goris [Lt. William B. Goris, navigator]. He was holding his arm. He made a sign to show he wasn't badly hurt. I went to charge the gun; the charging handle had been shot off. I looked around. There was a hole in the windshield as big as a small fist. How that bullet missed me, I'll never know. Here came another twin engine Jap. He was coming straight at the pilot's quarter. Closer and closer he came. I could see his nose blazing from the cannon fire. Goris and Russell [T/Sgt. Louis Russell, engineer and top turret gunner] were pumping tracers all around him. He came so close I could actually see the pilot. One hundred yards, 50, 10, and over. Not one bullet did he get into us, but I'll bet he got plenty as he passed by us. The battle lasted from 1050 to 1135. One zero remained. He followed us to the Bay, made one last futile pass and turned home.[132]

The attacks ended 50 miles south of Rangoon. Remarkably, only a few of the B-24s had been damaged in the fighter attack and only two were damaged by the anti-aircraft fire. The crews said it was the most intense and accurate opposition they had ever encountered over Rangoon. The bombers claimed one Oscar and one Nick as destroyed and two Oscars and one Nick as probably destroyed. It is not known whether the *21st Sentai* lost any Ki-45 fighters that day, but the *64th Sentai* had one definite loss. Lt. Shunji Takahashi continued to attack the B-24s as they withdrew from Rangoon. Over Bassein, squadron members saw him shoot out two engines on one of the bombers (none of the 7th Bombardment Group's squadron histories mention a plane losing two engines) and then return in a head-on attack, during which he was killed. It is possible he attacked the 493rd Squadron's formation, whose gunners claimed an Oscar as probably destroyed after seeing an explosion in the cockpit.[133]

The sea sweeps carried out during the rest of September failed to turn up any shipping.

With the monsoon season nearing its end and with recent losses, the Japanese may have decided to pull their shipping back from Rangoon. Poor weather over the Gulf of Martaban, however, was more likely the reason why there were no results from the sea sweeps, as a number of missions failed to reach the shipping lanes. The Group carried out 13 more sea sweeps during the rest of the month; another six sea sweeps were abandoned due to weather. Although in many cases the primary target could not be bombed due to weather, the 7th Group still flew more missions with more aircraft and dropped more bombs on targets in Burma than it had since the start of the monsoon. The Group flew 41 missions during the month:

The maintenance crew for the 9th Bomb Squadron's B-24D *Destiny's Tot* add another mission to the total. The 7th Bomb Group had a practice of painting bomb symbols on its aircraft in rows of fifteen. (3A-34970, RG 342FH, NARA)

double the number flown in June with three times the number of sorties. At 954 tons, the combined total bomb tonnage for the heavy and medium bomber groups was near to the May record of 1,097 tons.[134] The 7th and 341st Groups continued their attacks on Japanese lines of communication in central and southern Burma. On several missions, the B-24s backed up the B-25s on the same target. India Air Task Force intelligence estimated that the combined B-24 and B-25 attacks on the Burmese rail system cut transportation over the railroads by 65 per cent.[135] The attacks on the railroad system forced the Japanese to turn to Burma's rivers to transport supplies up the Irrawaddy and other rivers. The river boats quickly became pray to marauding Royal Air Force Beaufighters, causing further disruption to the supply system.

While the weather was improving, it still caused a number of missions to be abandoned or for the squadrons to bomb alternate targets. In some cases this resulted in excellent results. On September 4th, the Group scheduled all four squadrons to bomb the Syriam oil refinery at Rangoon, but

The 9th Bomb Squadron's B-24D *Destiny's Tot* flying over India. (3A-33754, RG 342FH, NARA)

poor weather over the target forced the aircraft to look for other targets. The 9th and 436th Squadrons turned back from Rangoon to bomb the railroad yards at Letpadan, northwest of Rangoon on the rail line from Rangoon to Prome. The 9th Squadron's bombing was excellent, all bombs falling in the target area, destroying a section of the railroad track and several warehouses. A week later, on September 11th, the 492nd Squadron attacked the railroad yards at Pyinmana, on the Rangoon-Mandalay railroad line north of Toungoo, getting excellent results on the second run over the target. Most bombs fell on the north end of the yards, starting several fires and one huge explosion. The 436th Squadron had been assigned the same target, but when the weather prevented them from bombing Pyinmana, the B-24s hit the oil installations at Chauk, on the Irrawaddy River near Magwe, starting two large fires and columns of smoke that could still be seen when 40 miles away. On September 14th, the 9th and 492nd Squadrons combined to attack the Japanese barracks at Myitkyina, again with excellent results. The 436th and 492nd Squadrons joined the B-25s on September 19th to bomb the barracks and railroad yards at Monywa, on the Chindwin River, the 492nd dropping 100-pound demolition bombs. The combined force dropped nearly 50 tons of bombs on the target, starting a number of fires and hitting a 70-foot long river boat. The 9th Squadron went back to the Thanbyuzayat railroad yards on September 25th, getting good hits. On the return flight, the formation of seven B-24s ran into seven Oscars, but held off the fighters, who did little damage to the bombers. At the end of the month, the 7th Group made two attempts to return to the Rangoon docks. On September 26th, the 9th, 492nd, and 493rd Squadrons tried for Rangoon, only to turn back because of weather, dropping their bombs instead on the railroad yards at Letpadan. The 492nd and 493rd tried again three days later, this time with the 436th Squadron, only to abandon the mission when the weather proved impossible to penetrate.[136]

These last missions were the swan song for the India Air Task Force. A new organization, Army Air Forces, India-Burma Sector, replaced it, with a new commander, Maj. Gen. George Stratemeyer. The reorganization of the Army Air Forces command structure represented an attempt to cope with the complex military, operational, administrative, and political realities of the China-Burma-India Theater. While these command changes had little immediate impact on the 7th Bombardment Group, Maj. Gen. Stratemeyer's arrival in India coincided with a shift in Allied strategy for the war in Burma and the belated creation of a more unified Allied command structure. Though it would take several more months to implement, by the end of the year, the 7th Bombardment Group would become part of a combined American and British bomber force, designated the Strategic Air Force. While waiting for this new organization to be established, the 7th Group would fly some of its most costly combat missions of the entire war.

CHAPTER SIX

STRATEGIC AIR FORCE

Allied Plans and Japanese Preparations

The organization of U.S. Army forces in the China-Burma-India Theater was "...not the result of logic and the best military thinking but one demanded by the political exigencies involved."[1] With far-flung combat operations reaching from China across India, the air transport operation over the Hump, and supporting units spread from Assam to Karachi, the command and administrative structure was complex, to say the least. The men serving in the theater came to say that CBI actually stood for "Confusion Beyond Imagination". In March 1943, in response to demands from Generalissimo Chiang Kai-shek and promises from Brig. Gen. Claire Chennault on what he could achieve with a force of 500 aircraft, the China Air Task Force was split off from the Tenth Air Force to give Chennault his own separate command (the Fourteenth Air Force) and promotion to Major General. The Air Transport Command had taken over the operation of the Hump route from the Tenth Air Force. This left the Tenth Air Force with responsibility for combat operations out of India over Burma in defense of the Air Transport Command's bases in Assam, the service units supporting both the Tenth and Fourteenth Air Forces and the training of Chinese pilots in India. The Tenth Air Force, with headquarters in New Delhi, and the Fourteenth Air Force, headquartered in Kunming, both reported to Lt. Gen. Joseph Stilwell as Theater Commander, who had his headquarters in Chungking; the Air Transport Command's Hump operation reported directly back to Air Transport Command in the United States. The long-standing friction between Clayton Bissell, commander of the Tenth Air Force, and Claire Chennault compounded the problem and became a matter of public comment. Overlaying these complexities was the need to coordinate operations, services, and strategies with the British government and British armed forces in India, who provided the vital base for American Army Air Forces units and the flow of supplies to China.[2]

With plans for an offensive in Burma moving ahead, senior Army Air Forces leaders wanted to place a senior Army Air

New commanders (left to right): Major General George Stratemeyer, Army Air Forces, India-Burma Sector and later Air Commander, Eastern Air Command; Major General Howard Davidson, Tenth Air Force; and Admiral Lord Louis Mountbatten, Supreme Allied Commander, South-East Asia Command. (3A-48793, RG 342FH, NARA)

Forces officer on Stilwell's staff as an advisor on air matters and to provide for better administrative control.[3] Stillwell was in agreement, but Generalissimo Chiang Kai-shek objected to the senior air officer having control over the Fourteenth Air Force. This led to the division of the Army Air Forces in the China-Burma-India Theater into the China Sector and the India-Burma Sector. Maj. Gen. George Stratemeyer, the former commander of the 7th Bombardment Group who had been serving as General Arnold's Chief of Staff, was appointed to the newly-created position of Commanding General, Army Air Forces Units, India-Burma Theater and Air Advisor to the Asiatic Theater Commander, a new Headquarters for this unit being activated on July 28, 1943. At the same time, the Army Air Forces used the reorganization to remove Maj. Gen. Clayton Bissell as commander of the Tenth Air Force, replacing him with Brig. Gen. Howard Davidson, brought out from the United States. On August 20, 1943, General Stilwell announced the formation of Headquarters, Army Air Forces, India-Burma Sector, with Maj. Gen. Stratemeyer commanding. Under this command were the following units: Tenth Air Force, China-Burma-India Air Service Command (Provisional), and the China-Burma-India Air Forces Training Unit. In his announcement, Stilwell added that the Tenth Air Force would transfer its headquarters from New Delhi to Calcutta to replace the India Air Task Force. In his new role, Stratemeyer took on multiple responsibilities: operations of the Tenth Air Force, administration of the CBI Air Service Command, provision of supplies and maintenance to the Fourteenth Air Force, training pilots for the Chinese Air Force, coordination with the Air Transport Command Hump operation, and providing advice to Stilwell on air operations.[4]

These organizational changes took place as the Allies were considering the larger strategy for offensive operations in Burma and putting in place a unified command structure for Southeast Asia at the Quadrant Conference in Quebec, held from August 17 to 24, 1943. At the Trident Conference in May, the Combined Chiefs of Staff had agreed to reduce the ambitious ANAKIM plan to a more limited operation to retake northern Burma with the goal of re-establishing an overland route to China from Ledo in Assam to link up with the old Burma Road. In addition, the Allies intended to capture Myitkyina to improve the air route to China. The Quadrant Conference confirmed this decision, though without agreement on what would follow. The plan was based on a three-pronged advance: Stilwell's Chinese divisions coming down from Ledo to capture Mogaung and Myitkyina; the Chinese forces in Yunnan crossing the Salween River into Burma; and the British IV Corps advancing across the Chindwin River. An amphibious operation to capture Akyab and Ramree Island on the Burmese coast would complement the capture of northern Burma. The Quadrant Conference also agreed to a long-range penetration operation under the command of Orde Wingate in support of Stilwell's advance toward Myitkyina. All these operations were to begin in February 1944.[5]

There had also been acceptance in principle at the Trident Conference of the need for a new command arrangement to more effectively prosecute the war against the Japanese in Burma, especially in light of the offensive operations planned for 1943-44. This would be an Allied command similar to that in the Mediterranean to allow for better coordination of forces. After several months of discussions, the American and British participants agreed at the Quadrant Conference to set up a Supreme Allied Command for Southeast Asia designated Southeast Asia Command (SEAC), with Vice Admiral Lord Louis Mountbattan as Supreme Commander, Lt. Gen. Stilwell as Deputy Commander, and a joint Anglo-American staff. Air Chief Marshal Sir Richard Peirse, Commander in Chief of the Royal Air Force in India, was appointed Air Commander Southeast Asia. Maj. Gen. Stratemeyer's position and the Army Air Forces, India-Burma Sector's role in the new Southeast Asia Command were initially ambiguous. Since the rationale for the existence of the Tenth Air Force was to provide support for the forces in China, American leaders were reluctant to have Tenth Air Force units placed under British command, whose sole mission was ostensibly the re-conquest of Burma. They preferred to leave Army Air Forces units under Stratemeyer, who reported directly to Stilwell as commander of all American forces in the CBI. Mountbattan was thus placed in the odd situation of giving orders to the American Army Air Forces units assigned to SEAC through General Stilwell and not through his SEAC air commander. Until the integration of the Tenth Air Force units and Royal Air Force units could be worked out, Stratemeyer exercised command of the Tenth Air Force independently of the Royal Air Force, and through the Tenth, the 7th Bombardment Group.[6]

The Japanese, too, were making plans. After conquering Burma, the Japanese *15th Army* had gone on the defensive. With the possibility of a multi-pronged Allied advance into Burma from Assam, Yunnan in China, and the Arakan, in March 1943, the Japanese Army set up a new organization (*Burma Area Army Headquarters*) to coordinate units defending these separate geographic areas along Burma's frontier with India and China. After the first Wingate operation showed that the mountainous region along the Assam-Burma border and the Chindwin River failed to serve as a barrier to an advance into Burma, Lt. Gen. R. Mutaguchi, newly-appointed commander of the *15th Army*, proposed that the Japanese Army push its defensive line deeper into the

The Japanese Army Nakajima Type 2 Fighter Ki-44 (Tojo). The *64th Sentai* received a small number of Type 2 fighters in the fall of 1943 for the defense of Rangoon. (Author's collection)

mountains and launch an offensive against British bases in Assam. After much debate, *Imperial General Headquarters* gave its approval to a plan (Operation *U-Go*) to capture the British base at Imphal. This was intended to prevent the British offensive into Burma the Japanese expected to be launched during the forthcoming dry season in early 1944.

The Kawasaki Type 2 Twin Engine Fighter Ki-45 (Nick) that equipped the *21st Sentai*. (Author's collection)

An attack on British forces in the Arakan (Operation *Ha-Go*) would precede the advance on Imphal to tie down British troops there. A successful offensive, however, would require additional Army divisions and a substantial increase in supplies and support units along the tenuous line of communications north from Rangoon to the front lines.[7]

As a result of increasing Allied air power, the Japanese could no longer be assured of maintaining air superiority over all of Burma. Since most of the Japanese aircraft and bases in Burma were out of range of Allied fighters, the Japanese still held the initiative in terms of when and where they could launch attacks.[8] The combined forces of the Army Air Forces and the Royal Air Force were now numerically superior to the JAAF's *5th Hikōshidan*, which had approximately 370 aircraft in Burma and Thailand against 719 aircraft for the USAAF and the RAF.[9] In planning for air operations leading up to the Army's offensives against the Arakan and Imphal in early 1944, the *5th Hikōshidan* had three main objectives: to neutralize Allied air forces through attacks on Allied air bases, to disrupt the flow of supplies over the Hump route, and protect supplies flowing into Burma through the port of Rangoon and over the soon-to-be-opened Burma-Thailand railroad.[10] In a conference of air commanders called to study the problem of how best to deploy its air strength, the *3rd Kōkūgun* (3rd Air Army), responsible for all air operations in Southeast Asia, it became evident that the *5th Hikōshidan* lacked a sufficient number of fighter aircraft to serve as escorts to Japanese Army bombers attacking Allied airfields in the Arakan and Assam and to provide an adequate defense of southern Burma.[11] Accordingly, the *3rd Kōkūgun* arranged for two additional fighter *Sentais* to be sent to Burma: the *33rd Sentai* arriving in Burma during October from the China Theater and the *204th Sentai* transferring during November. With aircraft production increasing back in Japan, the fighter units in Burma had added more aircraft and replacement pilots, giving the *5th Hikōshidan* a nominal strength of around 160 Hayabusa fighters, a small number of the Type 2 Fighter (Ki-44 Tojo), and the dozen or so Type 2 Two Seat Fighters (Ki-45 Nick) of the *21st Sentai*.[12]

By now, the *64th Sentai* was firmly committed to frontal attacks as the best method of combatting the B-24s. Although it required a cool, calculated, and determined attack—and not every pilot was capable of executing a frontal attack—the method had proved to be the most effective means of bringing down the big bombers. In the months prior to the monsoon, too few fighters had been available to make much impact on even a small B-24 formation. In four months of combat, the *64th Sentai* had shot down only four B-24s.[13] However, the fighter *Sentais* in China, flying against the B-24s of the 308th Bombardment Group, had shown what could be accomplished with an adequate number of Oscar fighters. Borrowing the tactics the *50th* and *64th Sentais* had developed over Burma, the Oscar-equipped *25th* and *33rd Sentais* had scored several notable victories by using weight of numbers against small bomber formations. On August 24th, the two *Sentais* shot down four of seven B-24s attacking Hankow and on September 15th, over Hanoi, the Oscars shot down three of five bombers, a fourth crashing on landing back at Kunming.[14] With more fighters available, the *5th Hikōshidan* would have its own notable successes in the remaining months of 1943.

The End of the Monsoon

With the end of the monsoon in early October, the 7th Group returned to the campaign against the Burmese railroad system. During the monsoon season, the squadrons had slowly received replacement aircraft and combat crews, so that by early October, they had a full complement of 12 aircraft each. The number of aircraft in commission increased as well, with more aircraft and improved maintenance. Despite the arrival of more combat crews, the Group was still short of the required number. The full complement for a bomber squadron was 18 combat crews, thus 72 for the entire group. By the beginning of October, the 7th Group had between 50 to 55 crews available for operations.[15] As a result, the squadrons were still unable to send out more than six to seven aircraft on a mission. If one or two aircraft had to turn back because of mechanical difficulties, the few remaining aircraft continuing on to the target were often too few to inflict significant damage. In October, possibly in recognition of this fact, the Group began to fly more missions involving two or more squadrons. Ten two-squadron missions and five full Group missions were flown during the month, a notable increase. At the end of September 1943, the 436th Squadron moved from Bishnupur to Panagarh to join the 492nd Squadron when the Royal Air Force reclaimed Bishnupur for its own uses.[16] This enabled a fairly easy pairing of the squadrons, with the 9th and 493rd Squadrons often flying together from Pandaveswar and the 436th and 492nd pairing up from Panagarh. With the arrival of new combat crews and the departure of a few men back to the United States, some in the squadrons began to entertain hopes that the units might all be going home soon, but Col. Necrason put an end to such speculation. In remarks to the 493rd Squadron, he "...plainly illuminated the enormity of the task before us..." as the Squadron's history recorded.[17]

Bomb bay doors open, B-24D *Sittin' Bull* from the 9th Bomb Squadron starts its run in on the Rangoon docks in the fall of 1943. (3A-33755, RG 342FH, NARA)

During October, the Group concentrated on attacks on railroad yards, flying ten missions to targets in central and southern Burma. Shipping remained a priority, with attacks on shipping at Rangoon. When the improved weather allowed better photographic coverage of the Burmese ports, enabling more accurate intelligence on Japanese shipping movements, the Group cut back on the sea sweeps it had flown during the monsoon. And for the first time in several months, the Group attacked Japanese airfields. Throughout the month, Japanese fighters frequently intercepted the Group, the fighter *Sentais* having returned to Burma from rest and re-equipping elsewhere. The Japanese fighter units defending Rangoon had the advantage of knowing that the American B-24s were likely to bomb Rangoon at a predictable time. Since the bombers did not wish to return to their bases after dark, most missions to Rangoon began at dawn, the bombers arriving over Rangoon sometime before or after noon. The squadrons began to refer to the "'Goon at Noon Club", eligible to any crewman who had flown over Rangoon at that hour. The 436th Squadron history noted that during the month "...the Japs seemed to be very eager. They pressed their attacks home in a whole-hearted manner, and seemed to be very interested in grabbing some glory."[18] Both sides would claim victories and suffer losses during the month.

The weather slapped at the 7th Group one last time at the beginning of October. On the first day of the month, all four squadrons went out on sea sweeps. While the 436th and 492nd Squadrons conducted unsuccessful searches, weather forced the 9th and 493rd Squadrons, sent out to bomb Port Blair, to abandon the mission. They dropped their bombs on Bassein instead on the return to base. Shipping in the Rangoon River was the target for an all-squadron mission on October 3rd and again on October 4th, Japanese fighters intercepting the bomber formations on both days. On the first mission on October 3rd, four Oscar fighters attacked the 9th Squadron's formation just after its bombing run. The Squadron had no trouble fending off the attacks. The Oscars on this day "... seemed not to be up to par with previous fighters engaged by the Ninth...", the Squadron recorded. The Group claimed two fighters destroyed and one probably destroyed for one bomber slightly damaged in the attack, though no Japanese fighters were actually lost that day.[19] The Group returned to Rangoon again the next day. Five airplanes had to turn back with various mechanical problems, but the remaining 22 aircraft bombed ships in the Rangoon River near the Ahlone docks, missing the ships, but hitting the docks and warehouses nearby. Ten minutes after leaving the target five Oscars and two Nick fighters intercepted the formation and kept up a running fight for 40 minutes, making six or seven passes from the front. Once again, the 9th Squadron described the attacks as "... displaying no special eagerness to battle".[20] The 9th Squadron claimed two Oscars destroyed and one damaged, the 492nd claimed one Oscar probably destroyed and one damaged, and the 493rd claimed an additional two fighters damaged, clearly firing on the same aircraft attacking the formation. On this date, the intercepting Oscars were from the *50th Sentai*, just returned to Mingaladon from Malaya. In one of the frontal attacks, Capt. Yoshihiro Takanarita, commander of the *1st Chutai*, was killed.[21]

For the next week, the 7th Group went after railroad yards. On October 7th, the 436th and 492nd Squadrons sent 13 aircraft to bomb the yards at Pyinmana with excellent results, hitting the tracks, rolling stock, and buildings alongside the yards. Two days later, the 436th Squadron sent seven airplanes to bomb the Sagaing railroad yards on the branch line from Mandalay to Myitkyina, returning on October 11th with the 493rd Squadron to drop 108 500-pound bombs from 19,750 feet. Almost every bomb hit within 700 feet of the aiming point and left a huge column of smoke behind as the squadrons

The crew of *Sittin' Bull* after completing the bomber's 50th combat mission. (3A-34795, RG 342FH, NARA)

turned for home. The bombers encountered moderately accurate flak over the target, one aircraft sustaining minor damage. The 9th and 493rd Squadrons went out to bomb the Toungoo railroad yards on October 13th. The 9th made it to Toungoo, getting all bombs in the target area, but clouds prevented the 493rd from bombing; instead, the 493rd bombed the railroad yards at Prome. In between these missions, the 9th Squadron had one of the Group's rare successes bombing a bridge. The target was the Meza River Bridge, southwest of Myitkyina. With no enemy opposition, the squadron had time to make a careful and uninterrupted approach to the target at an altitude of 8,000 feet. In a change of tactics, the formation split up into elements of two aircraft, so that each element could make a separate pass over the target. Even from 8,000 feet, the bridge looked like "...a toothpick across the river."[22] The three elements dropped 42 500-pound bombs, knocking out three spans at one go. Bombardier Lt. Max Herrman received credit for hitting the bridge directly with his bombs, a rare feat.[23]

If the fighter attacks in the first part of the month had seemed to be half-hearted to some, the 9th and 493rd Squadrons ran into a hornet's nest on a mission to Rangoon on October 14th. The mission called for all four Group squadrons to attack shipping in the Rangoon River, with the Pazundaung foundry and motor works as the secondary target. The 9th and 493rd Squadrons went in first, followed by the 436th and 492nd around 45 minutes later. Finding no shipping in the Rangoon River, the 9th and 493rd Squadrons proceeded to the Pazundaung

A veteran B-24D with some 40 bomb symbols beneath the cockpit lands after a mission. Local Indian labor was used to improve the 7th Bomb Group's airfields. (7th Bombardment Group (H) Historical Foundation, USAFA McDermott Library)

foundry and motor works; "riding the gauntlet of ack-ack" on the bomb run, the two squadrons dropped most of their bombs in the target area, starting a number of fires. Pulling away from the target, the formation ran into nine Oscar fighters (the B-24 crews invariably identified or simply called these fighters "Zeros") from the *64th Sentai* and seven Nick fighters from the *21st Sentai*. The ensuing fight lasted more than an hour, and in a display of unusual determination, the Japanese fighters pursued the bombers until well out to sea.[24]

9th Squadron bombardier Lt. Alfonso Perez was once again in the middle of the battle, recording his impressions in his diary:

> We took off at 0700, assembled with the other squadron, and got on course. The Burmese coast was first sighted at about 1115. By this time I was all set: my bombsight was ready, chest pack was on, and all guns checked. We came in the long way, circling around Pagoda Point in order to come in on the mouth of the Rangoon River so as to spot any shipping that might be present. I was hoping with all my might that we did not find some out here because, frankly, I was in no mood to go into Rangoon. It just isn't a healthy spot now or before. I guess I didn't hope hard enough, or else the Japs didn't want to cooperate. Anyway, the river was clear and we had to go in.
>
> We came directly on course for the target. I had plenty of time to set up my range so that I had it all killed long before the bomb release line. I thought those bombs would never go out. The Ack-Ack bursts were right on us and getting closer, still we were straight and level. I felt the ship hit once. It just launched up and to the right. I saw a "Zero" climbing up to meet us under our right wing. Suddenly, a streak of silver flashed by the nose. A "Zero" had surprised us coming out of the sun. Nobody even shot at him. The bombs started falling. Three of mine hung. I shoved down the salvo handle. The bombs were away. We had now stopped working for the government, we were now working for ourselves. The bombs hit square on the target! I closed the bomb bays and started looking for interceptions. I didn't have to look long. Five of them were lining up on our side. Then they started coming in without let down. I saw one I-45 [Ki-45 Nick] come in from 11 o'clock. Tracers were just soaking into him, yet he kept coming; turning on his back, he dived underneath us. He was trailing smoke. I hoped he was finished.
>
> There was a "Zero" that was coming in just left of 12 o'clock. I called up Larkin [Perez's pilot, flying a B-24D that had a fixed .50 caliber machine gun in the nose the pilot could fire]: "There is one almost in front of you." "Yea, I see him, I'll swing over and see what I can do." He did. The nose just shuddered as he pressed the trigger. At least 50 rounds were assimilated by that son of...heaven. He dove down and to the left and headed for home very much discouraged... These are just a few of the attacks that I remember most vividly. In all, there were between fifteen to twenty passes at our particular element."[25]

A 492nd Bomb Squadron B-24 on the way back to Madhaiganj. (7th Bombardment Group (H) Historical Foundation, USAFA McDermott Library)

On this mission, most of the attacks on Perez's formation came from the left side of the formation, where the navigator, Lt. William Goris, was manning the left nose gun. As Perez noted in his diary: "...this left me with little to do but to watch and sweat them out. If they ever got a good burst inside that nose I'd be a cooked goose. I just stand there in the most forward part with no more protection than what the Plexiglas can afford, which is none. As they came in all I could do was watch and say to myself I hope he misses. All the way in I'd watch his nose flashing like a blinker light as he poured out the lead. As they'd go by I'd think to myself, 'Well I survived that one,' and wait looking around for the next one. It became pretty much of a strain when you do this for an hour which was the length of the battle."[26]

The 493rd Squadron took the brunt of the fighter attack. Lt. Harold Goad was flying in the first element of the 493rd formation when his airplane came under attack and was badly damaged, with two engines set on fire and hits in the fuselage setting fire to the bomb bay tank. The fire burned a hole in the fuselage. Through the gap, another crew could see one of Goad's crew heroically hacking at the supports holding the tank in the bomb bay. This effort freed the tank and it dropped away, but too late to save Goad's airplane. Goad held formation as long as he could, but then turned away and fell off to the right when the bomber was past saving to avoid the other B-24s. A short time after the left wing came off, the airplane and the fuselage and right wing went spinning away, disintegrating a few seconds later. Miraculously, the men in the forward section of the B-24 bailed out. Goad, his copilot (2nd Lt. William Schrader), navigator 2nd Lt. Clarence King, bombardier 2nd Lt. Russell Gebert, and flight engineer S/Sgt. Francis Sawyer survived to become prisoners of war in Rangoon and were liberated at the end of the war. This was the first loss for the 493rd Squadron. Every airplane in the 493rd's formation was damaged in the fighting, though again, remarkably, no one else was injured. Two airplanes landed at Calcutta as a precaution. Between them, the 9th and 493rd claimed one Oscar and one Nick fighter destroyed, three fighters probably destroyed, and ten damaged; an indication of the intensity of the combat, though the Japanese do not have appeared to have lost any fighters during the battle. Weather interfered with the 436th and 492nd Squadrons' approach to Rangoon. The 436th bombed the railroad yards at Prome instead, while the four aircraft from the 492nd that made it off on the mission bombed Ramree Island.[27]

The 9th Squadron took its turn to go through the mill four days later, on October 18, 1943. The target that day was the airfield at Heho, northeast of Toungoo, and the base for the Oscar fighters of the *50th Sentai*. Seven aircraft from the 9th Squadron took off from Pandaveswar with seven from the 493rd; three of these aircraft turned back before reaching the target. Because of cloud cover the formation made two runs over the target, dropping 210 100-pound bombs over the airfield on the second run. After the B-24s turned for home, eight Oscars, most likely from the *50th Sentai*, intercepted the formation. The fighters concentrated their attacks on the 9th Squadron in a fight lasting 40 minutes. During the attacks, 2nd Lt. William McHenry's airplane was hit hard and began falling behind the formation. Several Oscars concentrated on the crippled bomber. As one Oscar finished an attack on McHenry's airplane, the left wing was seen to collapse, sending the bomber through the clouds below. McHenry, his copilot

Lt. Harold Goad (standing right) and his crew from the 493rd Squadron. Goad and several of these men were shot down on October 14, 1943. Left to right, back row: Lt. Walter McCoy, navigator; Lt. John Kelly, bombardier; Lt. Albert English, copilot; and Lt. Harold Goad (POW); kneeling: T/Sgt. Omar Austin, gunner (KIA); S/Sgt. Francis Sawyer, flight engineer (POW); T/Sgt. Robert White, radio operator (KIA); S/Sgt. George Marshall, gunner (KIA); and Frank Chiarello, gunner (KIA). (7th Bombardment Group (H) Historical Foundation, USAFA McDermott Library)

2nd Lt. Arthur Zipperian, and his navigator 2nd Lt. Irving Raubitschek failed to make it out of the airplane and were killed. The rest of the crew bailed out and were taken prisoner. All but one man, who died in captivity, survived the war. Two other aircraft were moderately damaged, one landing at Calcutta on the way back to base; three more suffered minor damage. The 9th Squadron claimed one fighter destroyed and three damaged. The 493rd came through the fight unscathed, with no damage to aircraft or personnel. The Squadron claimed one fighter confirmed destroyed, one probable, and one damaged, though it appears the *50th Sentai* lost no airplanes on this date.[28]

For the next five days, the 7th Group attacked railroad yards. The targets were some of the smaller railroad yards on the branch lines from Mandalay to Myitkyina and Mandalay to Ye-u—specifically the yards at Monywa, Ye-u, Kanbalu, and Naba—and the yards at Prome and Myingyan, in southern Burma. In attacking these targets, the 7th Group was reinforcing the work of the medium bombers of the 341st Group, the B-25s bombing these railroad yards on a regular basis. These railroad yards were small but fruitful targets, where locomotives and rolling stock were kept when idle and where goods were off-loaded and stored until they could be trucked up to the front.[29] The 436th and 492nd Squadrons attacked the railroad yards at Monywa on October 19th, but the bombing was poor. The 492nd hit the barracks area, but the 436th apparently failed to get a good pattern on the railroad yards, in what the Squadron

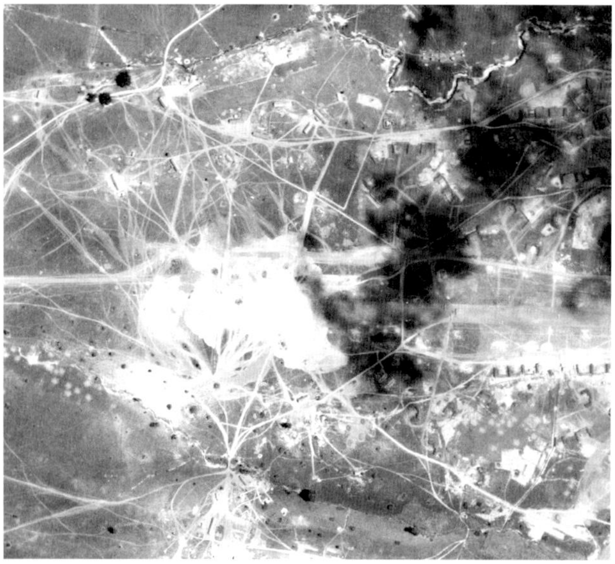

The Japanese Army air field at Heho, where the 9th Bomb Squadron lost a B-24 on October 18, 1943. (Courtesy Jim Augustus)

history deemed "...the first poor mission pulled by the squadron in quite some time."[30] Coincidently, the 9th and 493rd Squadrons had the same experience the next day, bombing Kanbalu. Ten aircraft from the two squadrons dropped 72 500-pound bombs, missing the railroad yards by a wide margin. The squadrons redeemed themselves over the next few days. The 436th and 492nd Squadrons bombed the yards at Myingyan on October 21st, putting their bombs into the center of the target. Maj. Werner led the 493rd Squadron to Prome on October 22nd. Bombing from 13,000 feet in the absence of any anti-aircraft fire, the Squadron achieved excellent results, hitting the main station, surrounding buildings, and the tracks. The 9th Squadron went back to Kanbalu on October 23rd, also getting excellent results on its second trip to the target by reducing the bombing altitude to 10,000 feet.[31]

Toward the last week of October, the 7th Bombardment Group began to receive small numbers of new B-24J models to replace the older B-24Ds. The B-24J was equipped with a nose turret with two .50 caliber machine guns to better cope with frontal attacks—the main defensive weakness of the earlier D models—as well as a ball turret in the belly position. The B-24J was something of a mixed blessing to the crews. While the additional firepower in the nose was definitely welcomed—the 493rd Squadron at first believed it would cause the Japanese fighters to abandon their frontal attacks—the added weight of the two turrets and other equipment made the J model heavier than the D (around 4,000 pounds heavier in terms of empty weight).[32] As a result of the added weight, the B-24J was slower than the B-24D. Combining the two types in the same formation caused problems, as some pilots had difficulty adjusting to the B-24J's slower speed and its increased fuel consumption.[33] The 7th Group found that the B-24J's practical bombing altitude was lower than that of the B-24D. Using the B-24D, the Group routinely bombed from an altitude of 23,000 to 25,000 feet. With the B-24J, the Group found that it was impractical to bomb from altitudes greater than 20,000 feet. The performance difference forced a change in tactics. With the B-24Ds, the squadrons would leave the target area as fast as possible while still maintaining formation; with the B-24Js, flying at a lower altitude and slower speed, the formation left the target at lower power settings and concentrated only on maintaining formation integrity. At 20,000 feet, the Oscar fighters were only just beginning to lose efficiency, and for this reason the Oscars could "...fly rings around the B-24J even at increased power settings..."[33] As one squadron recorded, "...the old Ds gave wonderful service and were reluctantly parted with..."[34]

For the bombardier and the navigator, the B-24J was not an improvement. Tom Sledge recalled that the nose compartment on the B-24J was "...a pain in the butt. There simply wasn't enough room."[35] The nose area in the B-24D,

Star Duster (B-24J-10-CO 42-73072) was one of the first J models assigned to the 493rd Bomb Squadron, arriving in November 1943. (Courtesy Jim Augustus)

though cramped with all the equipment and machine guns, at least had the benefit of providing excellent visibility. The navigator had a good view forward and by looking out over the bombsight, the bombardier could easily assist the navigator in identifying landmarks on the way to and from the target.

In the B-24J, the navigator had only two small side windows, while the front windows for the bombardier under the front

Maintenance crew working on another newly-arrived B-24J. (7th Bombardment Group (H) Historical Foundation, USAFA McDermott Library)

turret offered about a third as much visibility as in the B-24D. The bombardier could either kneel over his bomb sight or lie down to operate it, effectively blocking the view of the navigator out the front windows. The problem of forward visibility was an issue that Consolidated attempted to address but never fully solved. As soon as a number of the new B-24Js arrived, the squadrons set up training programs to familiarize the crews with their new aircraft and to give the gunners experience with the new nose turret.

Flying more multi-squadron and full group missions led to a revision in formation tactics. The 7th Group adopted what it called the Group Diamond Formation when flying to and from the target when there was little risk of interception. With six to seven airplanes per squadron, the Number Two squadron would fly to the right of the lead squadron about 500 feet higher; the Number Three squadron would be stepped down 500 feet on the left. The Number Four squadron flew in the slot position behind the other three squadrons, initially flying 1,000 feet below the formation, but when this proved to require excessive power to stay up with the lead squadron, the Number Four squadron shifted to a position to the right of the Lead squadron and in trail with the Number Two squadron. As the group formation approached the target, the Number Four squadron would drop back down into the slot position to form a more compact formation. Immediately after bombs away, the group would shift into the Group Defensive Formation as it flew away from the target. The Number Two and Three squadrons would move in almost in line with the Lead squadron, but fly slightly below, while the Number Four squadron flew in the slot below the Lead squadron and could move laterally from side to side to avoid attacks and cover any crippled ships that dropped out of the squadrons above.[36]

For months, the 7th Bombardment Group had been flying unescorted, daylight precision bombing missions partly according to stated Army Air Forces strategic bombing doctrine and partly due to the lack of any long-range fighters in the CBI that could escort the bombers to targets in southern Burma. Up to the end of the monsoon, this practice had been successful against limited Japanese fighter opposition, the 7th Group having lost only four B-24s to Japanese fighters from January to September 1943. The aggressive interceptions on October 14th and 18th, with larger numbers of fighters and concentrated frontal attacks, causing the first bomber losses since May, indicated that the good fortune the 7th Group had experienced up to that point might not last much longer, particularly with more Japanese fighter units arriving in Burma. Fortunately for the crews of the 7th Group, American long-range fighters finally arrived in the theater. After many requests for P-38 fighters, the Tenth Air Force was finally given permission to activate two twin-engine fighter squadrons (the 449th and 459th Squadrons) on August 20, 1943.[37] The 459th Squadron became the fourth squadron of the recently-arrived 80th Fighter Group, drawing its pilots and ground crews from the 80th Group and the 385th Fighter Squadron from the 311th Fighter-Bomber Group, also just arrived in

The 7th Bomb Group devised an attachment beneath the B-24's tail turret to catch ejected .50 caliber bullet cases to prevent them from falling on the airplanes flying in lower formations. (3A-33834, RG 342FH, NARA)

India.[38] The P-38 Lightnings were shipped in from the Mediterranean. The 311th Fighter-Bomber Group's three squadrons were equipped with the A-36 Invader, the dive bomber version of the P-51 Mustang, and the P-51A. While the mission of the 311th Group was to defend the airfields in Assam and provide support to Stilwell's Chinese forces

Long-range fighters finally arrived in India in October 1943, when P-38 Lightnings began to equip the 459th Fighter Squadron, activated the previous month. (111-SC-267021, RG 111, Records of the Chief Signals Officer, NARA)

advancing from Ledo, the long range of the P-51A made it a suitable escort for the B-24s on their missions to Rangoon. The 459th Squadron became operational and available to escort the bombers toward the latter part of November; the P-51As of the 530th Squadron from the 311th Group would be called on as well when needed.[39]

The 7th Group would have benefited from long-range fighter escort when the Group sent all four squadrons to Rangoon on October 26th. On October 24th, the crews had been briefed to attack shipping at Rangoon the next day. They remained on alert until 1000 on the morning of October 25th, waiting for the latest intelligence. By then it was too late to take off for Rangoon and return before dark, so the mission was postponed. At 0700 on the morning of October 26th, the squadrons began departing, each squadron sending out seven aircraft. In the 9th Squadron, two aircraft turned back due to mechanical problems. One of the new B-24Js, unable to keep up with the formation, turned back and bombed a secondary target instead. That morning, the Japanese transport *Dover Maru* (3,212 tons) was moored in the Rangoon River near the Ahlone docks. It appears that an F-5 Lightning reconnaissance airplane from the 9th Photographic Reconnaissance Squadron may have flown ahead of the bombers to confirm the presence of the transport.[40] Coming in over Rangoon at 21,500 feet, the formation could clearly see the ship in the river. The 9th, 436th, and 493rd Squadrons bombed the ship, getting several direct hits and near misses, with other bombs landing in the nearby dock area; the 492nd Squadron dropped its bombs on the docks and the central railway station. True to form, as the formation pulled away from the target the fighters came in.[41]

Photo reconnaissance for post-strike evaluation was vital to successful strategic bombing. The 9th Photo Reconnaissance Squadron was based at Pandaveswar alongside the 7th Bomb Group for a period of time during 1943. (File 827.306-1, Albert F. Simpson Historical Research Center, Air Force Historical Research Agency, Maxwell AFB, AL)

The 311th Fighter-Bomber Group arrived in India in September 1943 with one squadron, the 530th Fighter-Bomber Squadron, equipped with P-51A Mustangs, which also had the range to escort the 7th Bomb Group to Rangoon. (3A-34906, RG 342FH, NARA)

This was the largest interception to date. Though the accounts vary, it appears that the *64th Sentai* sent up at least nine Ki-43 Oscar fighters and possibly as many as 15, while the *21st Sentai*'s contribution was five to seven Ki-45 Nick fighters. The battle lasted 45 minutes, as the bombers withdrew back to the coast. The 9th Squadron escaped unscathed, but the other squadrons suffered several losses. In the 436th, 2nd Lt. Carl A. Smith, a bombardier in Lt. Cordell's airplane flying in the second element, was killed when a fighter raked the bomber, apparently also injuring the navigator, 2nd Lt. Wardle. The 493rd had four bombers damaged and one bombardier wounded and the navigator knocked out by an explosive bullet.

The 492nd lost an airplane and crew. The number two engine on Lt. Roy Vaughn's B-24 was hit in one of the passes and knocked out. Seeing the damaged B-24 continue to fly on, Cpl. Tomio Kamiguchi, one of the youngest and greenest pilots in the *64th Sentai* and flying an older model of the Oscar, decided to ram the bomber to knock it down. Making a pass from the 3 o'clock position, Kamiguchi hit the B-24 with his wing near the waist gun position, cutting the airplane in half. Incredibly, Kamiguchi survived. He bailed out of his fighter and landed safely, later receiving praise from the general commanding the *5th Hikōshidan*, though his fellow pilots thought his actions were rash in the extreme.[42] Vaughn's crew was not so fortunate. Only the bombardier, 2nd Lt. Gustaf Johnson, bailed out and survived as a prisoner of war.[43] Two days later, the 436th Squadron lost an airplane and crew in a tragic accident. The target that day for a full Group mission was the Japanese Army headquarters and railroad yards at Toungoo. On the second bomb run over the target, a three-plane element from another squadron drifted over the second element of the 436th Squadron's formation, apparently unaware of their sister bombers below them. A 500-pound bomb dropped from above hit Lt. James Reese's airplane between the Number 2 engine and the fuselage. Reese's bomber burst into flame and dropped out of the formation to explode a thousand feet below, killing the entire crew.[44]

Three young lieutenants who all started with the 436th Bomb Squadron in the fall of 1942 (left to right): Lt. Harry Burkhart, copilot; Lt. Raymond Rote, pilot; and Lt. Jerome German, bombardier. (Via the author)

Toward the end of October, a small number of crews and men in each of the 7th Group's four squadrons received the welcome news of their transfer back to the U.S.A. Apparently, at this time the Group did not have a definite policy setting out a specific number of missions to be completed during a tour of duty. This position probably related to the shortage of combat crews and the slow arrival of replacements.[45] By this time, using the 9th Squadron as an example, most of the crews had accumulated more than 300 operational hours and flown around 35 missions, while some had over 400 hours and more than 45 missions. One or two of the oldest serving crews had even flown more than 50 missions and were still flying.[46] By the end of November, fatigue caused a number of crews to be grounded. Lack of a policy had an adverse impact on morale, the crews coming to think they would have to fly until "...reported missing and the circumstances that entails, or of flying until 'washed out' by the Flight Surgeon."[47] As an operational analysis of the Group completed a few months later stated: "It may be true that losses in other theaters are higher but it does not follow that total flying hours or missions should be proportionately higher in this theater... Environment, living conditions, and tension built up after long missions, fate of lost crews, and the frustration of unsuccessful missions during the monsoons, are all factors affecting morale...If adequate crews are made available and a rotation policy instituted, the effectiveness of the Group as measured by operational sorties over primary targets will doubtless be materially increased."[48] The squadrons chose several of their longer-serving crews to return to the U.S., giving hope to those

Captains Harry Burkhart and Jerome German (middle and right) say farewell to their friend Captain Ziegmont (left) nearly a year and some forty or more missions later. (Via the author)

remaining that one day their turn would arrive. In response to a request from the United States for an airplane with a distinguished combat record to undertake a bond-buying tour across the country, the Group selected a representative B-24D, "Sittin' Bull" from the 493rd Squadron. Known as "Old 26" for having completed 56 missions, this aircraft had flown two missions to Bangkok and Car Nicobar Island. The airplane received a new name, "Rangoon Rambler", and with it a mixed crew from the 9th and 493rd Squadrons left for the United States in early November.[49]

The end of the monsoon brought somewhat cooler and less humid weather and a renewed interest in sports among the squadrons, softball being the most popular, with regular games between officers and enlisted men, pilots and bombardiers against copilots and navigators, and between squadrons. Volleyball and tennis were also favorites, and the squadrons set up regular tournaments. An ample supply of beer, liquor, and other PX supplies did wonders to boost morale, as did the arrival of two Red Cross girls permanently assigned to the 9th Squadron. In between missions, officers and enlisted men worked to improve their living quarters and

Major General George Statemeyer (middle) bids farewell to Captain Raymond Rote (left) and a scratch crew of combat veterans who flew B-24D *Sittin' Bull*—renamed *Rangoon Rambler*—back to the United States for a bond tour. (3A-34796, RG 342FH, NARA)

entertainment facilities. In the 9th Squadron, the officers continued work on a new officers club, while the enlisted men completed work on their own club, dubbed the "Jungle Junction", in place of the earlier "Flying Cobra's Club", which had given the 9th Squadron its nickname, "The Flying Cobras", adopted in September. Col. Necrason opened the club at the end of the month with suitable ceremony and a dance. In the 493rd Squadron, a great deal of effort went into building and fitting out new offices and new quarters that were larger and more comfortable and were located closer to the airfield at Pandaveswar. There were two changes in command during October. In the 9th Squadron, the squadron commander, Maj. Pirruccello, was promoted to Group Executive Officer, with Capt. Allan Lathan, Squadron Operations Officer, replacing him, while in the 436th Squadron, Lt. Col. Clyde Box, who had only replaced Maj. Harvey Watkins in August, was ordered back to the United States. Capt. Richard Henning, a former member of the Squadron who had been transferred to the 492nd, was brought back to replace Box.[50]

The air battles in October had been a foretaste of what lay ahead for the 7th Group. As the 9th Squadron's history noted: "...where we once thought of enemy fighters as a possibility, it became last month a certainty..."[51] During November, the Group would find that Japanese fighter attacks were "...more severe and savage."[52] For the first half of the month, the Group added attacks on airfields and a resumption of mining missions to its operations. The month began with a Group mission to bomb the railroad yards at Myitnge on November 2nd. Weather caused the Group to separate: the 9th Squadron hit the alternate target a Ye-u, while the 492nd and 493rd followed the 436th Squadron to bomb the town of Kalewa, on the Chindwin River. The next day, the 9th and 493rd Squadrons attacked the airfield at Loiwing, south of Lashio, both squadrons getting excellent results. The Group conducted two mining missions to the Rangoon River and its estuary on the nights of November 6/7 and 8/9, sending out five aircraft on each mission. A few airplanes ran into intense small arms fire flying at low altitude over the river, but most of the mines were laid successfully. The second airfield strike took the Group to Mingaladon airfield near Rangoon, home of the *21st* and *64th Sentais*. Unusually, this was a night mission, the first for some months. The Japanese sent up several Oscar and Nick fighters to intercept the bombers as they came over the field individually, bombing from 10,000 to 14,000 feet. The bombers carried a mix of 500- and 100-pound demolition bombs and 120-pound clusters of 20-pound fragmentation bombs, dropping 105 of the latter over the airfield. The crews found the anti-aircraft fire concentrated and accurate. The 493rd Squadron's Lt. Busch and his crew had a narrow escape when an anti-aircraft shell went through one of the wings on their B-24 to burst above their airplane, doing only minor damage. The 492nd Squadron's aircraft eluded the fighters, but the other squadrons had several aircraft damaged and crewmen wounded in fighter attacks.[53]

Heho airfield was the next target on November 11, 1943. The attack triggered an angry response from the Oscars of the *50th Sentai*. Although the Group lost no airplanes on the mission, Tom Sledge, the bombardier on Maj. Delahay's crew in the 492nd Squadron, recalled it as the worst he ever flew. For one crew in the 9th Squadron and one in the 492nd, it proved to be exceptionally harrowing. The squadrons began their take-off around 0745, flying to the target at 14,000 feet and climbing to 15,000 feet for the bomb run. The 26 aircraft in the Group were organized in four flights. The plan for the mission called for the 492nd Squadron, flying as D flight in the rear of the formation, to swing out and away as the main formation reached the initial point for the bombing run on Heho, some 16 miles south of the airfield. The 492nd would bomb nearby Aungban landing ground, joining back up with the main formation as the latter turned left after bombing Heho. There were some clouds over the airfield, causing the main formation to come in north of its designated IP. This threw off the 492nd Squadron's planned attack on the Aungban landing ground, as it would have required the Squadron to make a sharp 180° turn away from the main formation in order to hit the target. Maj. Delahay apparently tried to make the turn before realizing it wouldn't work and turned back to the main formation again as the other flights started dropping their fragmentation clusters over Heho field. When Maj. Delahay made his turn toward Aungban and then reversed to turn back to the main formation, the 492nd Squadron flight was temporarily scattered and fell behind the other squadrons just as at least ten Oscars from the *50th Sentai* hit the formation head on. The Oscars made repeated passes from the front quarter against the 492nd airplanes, now strung out and desperately trying to catch up with the Group formation ahead of them. All the squadron formations were in fact strung out and losing altitude to gain speed as they headed back toward India. The Oscars made several passes on Delahay's B-24, his gunners claiming one Oscar shot down. Lt. Larkin was flying as part of Maj. Delahay's element. His B-24 received several head on attacks, the Oscars coming in from the 10 o'clock to 2 o'clock positions. During one of the attacks explosive bullets entered the cockpit, severely wounding Larkin and his flight engineer, T/Sgt. Mickelson, and instantly killing his copilot, Lt. John A. Podawiltz. Lt. Miller, the bombardier, took over the controls and flew the damaged bomber back to the Royal Air Force airfield at Chittagong, where Larkin revived sufficiently to make a successful landing. The crew counted 70 holes in their damaged bomber.[54]

By an unfortunate coincidence, Lt. Robert Graves's crew in the 9th Squadron went through the same experience. Graves was assigned to the number three position in the Squadron's first element, flying on the left of the lead bomber in one of the new B-24Js. To make it easier to fly formation on the lead airplane, Graves swapped places, with his copilot, Lt. Cy Kurth, taking over the right seat. Coming in on the bomb run at 16,500 feet, seven Oscars and two Nick fighters attacked the formation. T/Sgt. Doug Labat (flight engineer) was in his top turret tracking a fighter off to his left as it came in to attack when he heard Kurtz call out another fighter coming in at 1 o'clock. This fighter hit the auxiliary tank in the wing, setting

A B-24J, possibly Lt. Grave's airplane, damaged in the November 11, 1943, mission to bomb Heho airfield. (3A-33583, RG 342FH, NARA)

it on fire. As the second Oscar came around for a frontal pass, Labat tracked the fighter's approach with his twin .50 caliber machine guns. His account of what followed was featured in an article in *Air Force*, the Army Air Forces' monthly magazine:

> I opened up and poured a long burst that seemed like 600, but was probably 60 rounds into the Jap. Our nose turret wasn't firing at the Zero [*sic*]; I wondered why. [Staff Sgt. William Burtch was killed by the first Zero as he, like Labat, was tracking the second Jap plane.] My guns were so hot the turret cut out; I hit the reset button and threw more lead at him as he kept coming in at our nose until I was sure he was going to pull one of those 'For the Emperor' tricks and ram us.
>
> The terrific crash of an explosive shell, flying glass, and debris around my legs, the rush of cold air, and a burst of flame from the Jap as some of my shells exploded his gas tanks all happened simultaneously. When it seemed too late, the Zero pulled up just enough to miss us, hurtling over my guns like a Roman candle on the Fourth of July.
>
> I knew we were hit bad now; our wing was still burning. Before I could get out of my turret to see what had happened, the right wing dropped and we slid off in a skidding dive underneath the other planes in our formation. Then I couldn't get out of my turret because the negative "G" had me plastered against the top. By reaching down to the ammunitions boxes, I finally managed to pull myself down out of the dome as our radio command set was screeching "Bail out, bail out before it's too late, bail out, you don't have a chance, bail out.[55]

Lt. Charles Duncan was flying as copilot in the airplane in the No.2 position in the lead element and saw what was happening to Grave's bomber. Duncan was watching the same Oscar as it came in to attack, expecting it to come in on his airplane, but for some unknown reason the fighter chose Grave's bomber on the left hand side of the element. As Duncan remembered: "Before I could glance away to see where he [the fighter] went, the plane on the left wing of the lead plane was banking to the right, or directly toward me. Quickly, not slowly, the left wing of that opposite B-24 lifted, and I could see that its #1 engine was on fire, flame trailing the wing at least ten feet. Then the plane was darting toward me, and I was hauling back on the control column with all my strength. Had I not, the other plane would have collided with us, fuselage to fuselage. But I got my ship up just enough to clear the flaming wing coming toward me and let the other plane slide across to the right, under me. I risked a quick glance out the side window to my right at the stricken B-24. It continued in a graceful arc, still in a steep right bank. Before it had disappeared from view, it seemed to nose down and was losing altitude. I could risk looking no longer. Lt. Graves was the pilot of that plane and Lt. Cyrus "Cy" B. Kurth the copilot—another of my Cadet days classmates. But I had to devote full time to keeping on the lead plane's wing. Zeros [*sic*] now seemed to be all around us."[56]

B-24Js taxi out for a mission in the fall of 1943.
(Courtesy of Jim Augustus)

Pulling himself down into the cockpit, Labat found a chaotic scene. "It was bad", he recalled. "Blood was spattered over everything, and maps and papers were flying around in the blast of air coming through a shell hole in the windshield. Kurth was slumped forward over the stick, Graves was wavering in his seat, and we were dropping fast." An explosive bullet had come through the windshield, hitting Kurth in the face and killing him instantly. Fragments from the bullet had wounded Graves in the neck. He told Labat, who had leaned over to pull Kurth away from the control wheel, "For God's sake, get him out of there." Labat pulled Kurth out of the seat, climbed back into it, took over the controls, and slowly pulled the bomber out of its dive. Graves, who was barely conscious, helped Labat level the airplane at 8,000 feet. Fortunately, the dive extinguished the fire in the wing, but unknown to Labat, two Oscars had followed the wounded bomber down and hit the airplane in more places, remarkably without wounding anyone else in the crew. However, the hydraulic system was damaged and the propeller governor on the Number 3 engine had frozen. Graves brought the B-24 near another squadron formation for protection. He told Labat to return to his turret to defend the bomber.[57]

At this point the navigator, Lt. Grant Erwin, hearing no responses on the interphone, climbed up to the cockpit to find Graves flying the airplane on his own. Erwin, who had gained some flying experience with the Royal Canadian Air Force, slipped into the left seat and helped Graves fly. This was timely, as at that point a Nick fighter came in from 12 o'clock. Labat fired at the Nick as it came on, getting some hits as Graves maneuvered the bomber away from the attack. The Nick dived past the B-24 and did not return. Two B-24s dropped back to provide protection as two more Oscars made attacks, the combined gunfire of the three bombers fending them off. With the attacks over, Labat relieved Erwin in the left seat so that Erwin could navigate the plane back to a base. Lt. Cecil Day, the bombardier, came up to man the top turret in Labat's place. Labat continued flying the airplane, correcting Graves' occasional movements of the controls to keep the airplane on course. Nearing Chittagong, two Oscars followed the bomber, but pulled away as the bomber started descending. On the approach to landing, the crew couldn't lower the landing gear. Labat turned the controls over to Lt. Erwin and went back to the emergency crank and after some effort got both of the main landing gear down, though only one would lock. Graves was just conscious enough to make the landing with Erwin's assistance, barely missing a dike just before the runway. Without full hydraulic pressure—the instruments indicated only 800 pounds of hydraulic pressure, less than the minimum of 850 pounds recommended in the pilot's manual—Labat told Graves and Erwin to keep their feet on the brakes, as they would have only one application of pressure. As the airplane came to a stop Graves passed out. Interviewed later, Labat commented: "Those crewmates of mine really deserve a lot of credit; they kept calm when most guys would have fallen apart. They did a wonderful job bringing us back home." For their efforts to save their airplane and fellow crewmates, Labat, Erwin, and Day were awarded the Silver Star.[58]

With the intensity of the Japanese fighter attacks and the larger number of fighters intercepting the bomber formations, the 9th and 492nd Squadrons were fortunate to have avoided losing any aircraft during the mission of November 11th. Having lost three bombers during October and now facing greater numbers of Japanese fighters, as the *5th Hikōshidan* brought in more fighter units, someone in the higher command level within the 7th Bombardment Group or the Army Air Forces India-Burma Sector appears to have begun to question the wisdom of making continued unescorted, daylight missions into Burma now that long-range escort fighters were available, even though the Group's squadrons were now fully equipped with the better-armed B-24J. On November 13, 1943, the 7th Group flew a mission with a fighter escort for the first time. Six P-51As from the 530th Fighter-Bomber Squadron, 311th Fighter-Bomber Group escorted 14 B-24s from the 436th and 492nd Squadrons to bomb the railroad workshops at Myitnge railroad yards. A few Japanese fighters attempted to intercept the bomber formation, but the Mustangs drove them off with no claims by either side.[59] The next day, the Group received dramatic proof that unescorted missions to targets in southern Burma where Japanese fighters were present in force were no longer viable.

The November 14th mission's target was the Japanese Army barracks in the town of Maymyo, east of Mandalay, on the road and railroad line to Lashio. The mission was intended to be a joint one with B-25s from the 490th Bombardment Squadron with an escort of six P-51As from the 530th Fighter-Bomber Squadron. The B-24s apparently went to the target first, followed by the B-25s. Maj. William Werner, CO of the 493rd Squadron, led the mission. One aircraft from each 7th Group squadron had to turn back with mechanical difficulties, leaving 12 B-24s to continue the mission. The formation arrived over Maymyo around noon, only to find the target area covered in clouds. Werner led the two squadrons on two runs over the area, hoping for a glimpse of the target through the clouds, but without success. Werner decided to go to the secondary target: Pakkoku, southwest of Mandalay. A misunderstanding arose between the two bomber squadrons. Combined with other undisclosed mistakes and the clouds in the area, this caused them to become separated. The Mustang escort followed the 9th Squadron, leaving the 493rd on its own. Some five minutes after the squadrons separated, at around 1215, the six B-24Js in the 493rd Squadron's formation ran into a force of what the surviving crews estimated to be 15 to 20 fighters, although surviving records identify these as only seven Oscars from the *50th Sentai*. The fighters had scrambled on receiving word of the approaching bombers. While few in number, their attacks were devastatingly effective, though the *50th Sentai* did not escape unscathed. The Oscars made concentrated frontal attacks on the B-24s, as well as attacks from the side and the rear quarter. Lt. George Kimball's aircraft appears to have been the first to fall. Kimball's aircraft was hit hard at 1220, possibly in the second head-on attack the Oscars delivered. His airplane dived straight into the ground from 10,000 feet, killing all on board. The bombers downed two of the attacking Oscars, Sgt. Ushitaro Sato and Sgt. Maj. Ofusa bailing out of their stricken fighters. Sgt. Sato's parachute failed to open. The third fighter in the section, flown by Lt. Furue, was also hit and severely damaged, forcing him to crash land nearby. The leader of the second section of Oscars, Lt. Hagashima, was also hit and forced to bail out. But the Oscars had inflicted mortal damage to two more B-24s. Maj. Werner's airplane had two engines knocked out. He attempted to stay with the formation as long as he could, but his airplane slowed and headed down, as did Lt. Willis McLoughlin's B-24. The rest of the formation (Capt. Busch and Lts. Berlette and Shaw) tried to stay with their wounded comrades as they descended, but the end was inevitable. Nearing the Chindwin River, Werner appeared to be attempting a crash landing when his airplane's wing struck a tree, exploding. By some miracle, Werner and seven other members of his crew survived the crash; tragically, as happened with others unfortunate enough to be shot down over Burma, five of these survivors died as prisoners of the Japanese. McLoughlin also attempted to put his B-24 down nearby, but in the ensuing crash he and his crew were killed. The fighter attacks continued on the remaining three aircraft, who survived by staying at low level and resorting to violent maneuvering. This was the costliest mission the 493rd had ever undertaken. Three complete crews were missing. Maj. Werner had commanded the 493rd since January 10, 1943. He had completed 52 combat missions and

The 436th Bomb Squadron gets a good pattern on the railroad workshops at Myitnge on November 13, 1943. (File 830.551, Albert F. Simpson Historical Research Center, Air Force Historical Research Agency, Maxwell AFB, AL)

Strings of bombs walk across the air field at Lampang, Thailand, on November 20, 1943. (USAF)

flown 475 combat hours when he was shot down; apparently he had refused an earlier opportunity to return to the United States, preferring to remain in command of the Squadron. In less than an hour, the 493rd Squadron had lost three B-24s to Japanese fighters; in a little more than a month, the 7th Group had lost six.[60]

After a critique of the November 14th mission, the Group sent all four squadrons out on November 16th to bomb the Japanese Army barracks at Meiktila, a major administrative center for the *15th Army*. The formation of 19 bombers that reached the target again had an escort of P-51 fighters. When three Oscar fighters attempted to intercept the bombers, the Mustangs drove them off, claiming two destroyed and a third as probable. As the 9th Squadron's history stated, "this show alone did much to up the morale of the squadron."[61] Two days later, the bombers returned to Pyinmana to bomb the railroad yards, without an escort this time, but without running into any Japanese fighters. The 9th Squadron had a frustrating time when the lead bomber's bomb sight went out before completing the bomb run. Only two other bombers got their bombs on the target. The other squadrons bombed with excellent results, destroying tracks and rolling stock. Continuing their "Cook's Tour" of Southeast Asia, the Group sent the 9th and 493rd Squadrons to bomb the airfield at Chiengmai, in northern Thailand, for the first time, while the 436th and 492nd bombed the airfield at Lampang to the south. The 492nd Squadron turned back due to a fuel shortage, but the other squadrons continued on. Clouds on the way to the target provided cover for the formation, which arrived over the airfields to find no opposition from fighters and only meager anti-aircraft fire. The bombing destroyed a number of aircraft at each airfield, most likely belonging to the Royal Thai Air Force, as the Japanese at the time did not base their aircraft at Chiengmai or Lampang. After returning to their home airfields, all four squadrons stood down to prepare for a major effort against Rangoon.[62]

The Assault on Rangoon

While still working on how best to integrate the Army Air Forces units in the India-Burma sector with the Royal Air Force in the new South East Asia Command, in early November, Maj. Gen. Stratemeyer proposed to Air Chief Marshal Sir Richard Peirse, Commander in Chief, Air Command Southeast Asia, that the Army Air Forces and the Royal Air Force join together in a combined attack on Rangoon. Stratemeyer envisioned a series of coordinated missions spread over several days, the AAF heavy bombers attacking during the day and the RAF by night, with the following objectives:

A) Destruction of vital communications facilities.

B) Elimination of as much enemy air power as possible.

C) Destruction of all important port facilities.[63]

Achieving Stratemeyer's objectives of inflicting maximum destruction required more heavy bombers than he had available in India. To add weight to the attacks, Stratemeyer proposed to Gen. Chennault, commander of the Fourteenth Air Force, that he temporarily transfer B-24s from the 308th Bombardment Group from China to India to cooperate with the 7th Bombardment Group.[64] A gasoline shortage in China had limited the number of missions the 308th Group could undertake, so Chennault agreed. Planes from the 308th began arriving in India on November 20th, and by November 24th, all four squadrons were in place. The 373rd and 425th Bombardment Squadrons took up residence at Pandaveswar, the crews helping to inaugurate the 493rd Squadron's new enlisted men's club, "The Slipstream", while the 374th and 375th Bombardment Squadrons went to Panagarh. Over the next several days, the 7th Group intelligence officers briefed the crews from the 308th Group on conditions over Burma

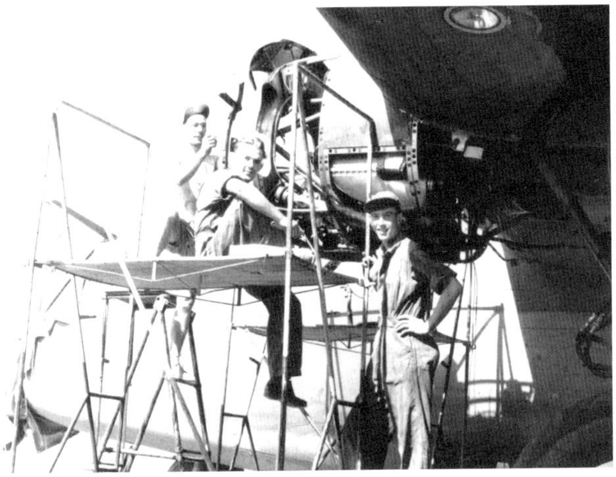

Engine change on a B-24. The maintenance crews worked out in the open throughout the year, during the intense heat of the dry season and the pouring rain of the monsoon. (7th Bombardment Group (H) Historical Foundation, USAFA McDermott Library)

and provided information and photographs of the intended targets. The 308th Group also received new B-24Js, giving each of the Group's squadrons nine B-24Js and three to four B-24Ds.[65] Stratemeyer also decided, for the first time, to add the B-25s of the 490th Bombardment Squadron to the attacks on Rangoon, arranging for the medium bombers to refuel at Chittagong, on the Bay of Bengal, so that the city would be within their range.

Staff officers from the Tenth Air Force and the RAF's Bengal Command, who had operational control of the Royal Air Force's heavy and medium bombers, worked up the plans for the raids on Rangoon. Since the 308th Bombardment Group would be available for a short period, the combined AAF/RAF bomber force could only hit a limited number of targets in the time available.[66] The specific targets selected for attack in the Rangoon area were carefully chosen based on an analysis of previous raids on Rangoon and an assessment of what would be most damaging to the Japanese. The Insein Locomotive Works—the only facility in Burma that could repair damaged locomotives—received the highest priority. Destruction of the Works would have a direct and significant impact on the Burmese railroad system, compounding the problems the Japanese were already facing from the loss of locomotives and rolling stock through the growing Allied air campaign against the railroads. With double the number of B-24s available, the Tenth Air Force now had the capability to inflict even greater damage to the docks and warehouses along the Rangoon River, the targets of many previous 7th Bombardment Group missions. The planners chose the Botataung Docks, on the western side of the dock area, as the main target. The bombers would begin in this area and continue bombing to the east, potentially destroying a huge section of the dock area. The RAF's Liberators and Wellington bombers were assigned the important Mahlwagon marshaling yards for their missions, as the yards were relatively easy to locate by night. Aware of the increasing number of fighters the Japanese were bringing into the Rangoon area, the P-38H Lightnings of the 459th Fighter Squadron and the P-51A Mustangs from the 530th Fighter-Bomber Squadron were assigned to escort the bombers to Rangoon.[67] The operational plan called for attacks over six days and five nights against the three main targets: the Insein Locomotive Works, the Mahlwagon marshaling yards, and the Botataung and other docks. The 7th and 308th Groups were to furnish 28 B-24s from each group for the missions. Each group would fly its own formation, with one group following closely behind the other. The main Japanese airfield at Mingaladon and the newer airfield the Japanese had built nearby at Zayatkwin were the targets of the first planned mission in the hope of destroying Japanese fighters and airfield installations prior to the main attacks. D-Day was set for November 25, 1943. The 7th and 308th Bombardment Groups would attack the airfields in two waves: the 7th Group going in first to Mingaladon and the 308th Group following to bomb Zayatkwin, all B-24s loaded with 30 100-pound bombs. That night, the RAF bombers would make their first attack on the Mahlwagon marshaling yards. The attacks would continue for five to six days, ending around D+8 with a night mining mission to Rangoon and Moulmein.[68]

Despite being at the end of one of the Army Air Force's longest supply lines, the maintenance crews in the 7th Bomb Group did an exceptional job keeping the maximum number of airplanes serviceable. (7th Bombardment Group (H) Historical Foundation, USAFA McDermott Library)

Bad luck and bad weather disrupted the first day's operations. At Pandaveswar, the 9th and 493rd Squadrons, part of the first wave attack, were scheduled to take off first, while the 308th Group's 373rd and 425th Squadrons were getting their briefings; once the field was clear, the 373rd and 425th would take off as part of the second wave. Appallingly, the 9th Squadron lost two B-24s on take-off, killing the crews in Lt. John S. Crall's and 2nd Lt. William Balfe's aircraft. Lt. Crall may have been the first to take off, his airplane exploding immediately after at the west end of the runway. The airplane's bomb load continued to explode for several minutes. The tower switched the take-off to the other direction (west to east), but tragically, once again the first airplane to take-off—possibly 2nd Lt. Balfe—overran the end of the runway, ran over a railroad track, and burst into flames, his airplane's bombs also continuing to explode for some time after the crash.[69] The 373rd and 425th Bombardment Squadrons conducted their briefings in a nearby building with the sound of frequent explosions in the background.[70] Two more of the 9th Squadron's airplanes had to turn back with mechanical difficulties, as did five more airplanes from the 7th Group's other squadrons. Seven aircraft of the 24 aircraft the 308th Group sent off also had to turn back. There was some confusion with the escort; the bombers managed to link up with the P-38s, but the P-51s were late getting off. The bombers went on without them. The P-51s caught up with the bombers later on. Nearing Rangoon, the two Groups found both targets covered in overcast. The 7th Group abandoned the mission, while the 9th Squadron bombed Akyab on its return flight to Pandaveswar and the 436th Squadron bombed the airfield at Minhla as an alternate target, claiming one Oscar fighter shot down that attacked the formation. In the target area, the four ships that made the flight from the 492nd Squadron ran into three Oscars, but the P-51s drove them off, claiming one as probably destroyed. The 492nd brought back their bombs, as did the 493rd Squadron, which lost one aircraft during the mission. Shortly before reaching the target area, Lt. Tom Ingham's airplane was seen to lose an engine. Ingham continued to fly with the formation, then gradually lost altitude. He was last seen entering clouds near the Chin Hills, on the Burma-India border. He and his crew were never found. Ten airplanes from the 308th Group got a glimpse of Zayatkwin airfield through a break in the clouds and dropped 224 100-pound bombs in the general area. The remaining 308th Group aircraft also bombed Akyab on their return. An hour after the B-24s had left, nine B-25s from the 490th Bombardment Squadron, with an escort of 12 P-51As from the 530th Fighter-Bomber Squadron, bombed Mingaladon, destroying two Japanese fighters on the field. The Mustangs ran into the Ki-43s from the *64th Sentai* and the Ki-45s from the *21st Sentai* while they were attempting to intercept the B-25 formation. The P-51 pilots claimed one Nick fighter destroyed and a second Nick and an Oscar as probably destroyed for the loss of two Mustangs, including the 311th Fighter-Bomber Group's commander, Col. Harry Melton. Gunners on the B-25s claimed one fighter destroyed, three probably destroyed, and two more damaged.[71]

The burned-out remains of one of the two 9th Bomb Squadron B-24s that crashed on take-off on November 25, 1943. (Courtesy of Jim Augustus)

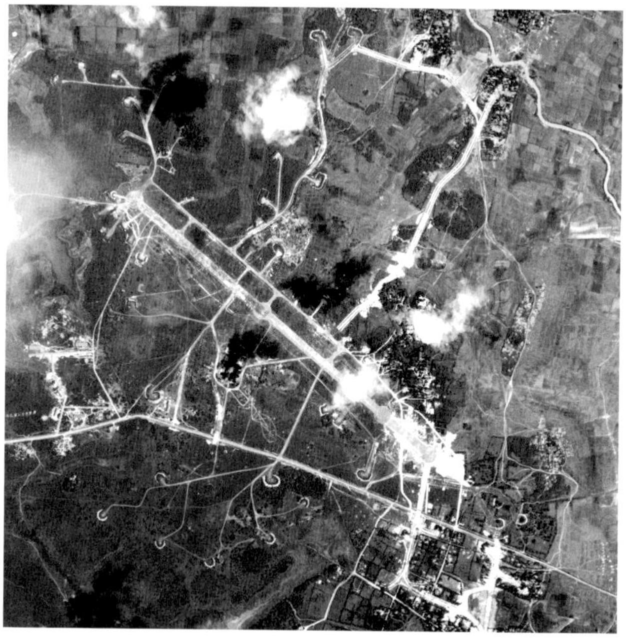

The Japanese Army Air Force air field at Zayatkwin, near Rangoon, the 308th Bomb Group's target on November 25, 1943, the first day of strikes against targets around Rangoon. (Courtesy Jim Augustus)

The first day's effort had been filled with frustration and disappointment, with the loss of three B-24s and two P-51s for only minimal damage to the Japanese, who were now fully alerted to the presence of a large force of heavy bombers and the prospect of more raids on Rangoon.[72] Continued bad weather over the Rangoon area forced the cancellation of

Believed to be a photograph of Lt. Stephen's B-24 about to crash land in the Bay of Bengal after having two engines shot out over Rangoon on November 27, 1943. (Courtesy Jim Augustus)

missions on November 26th, throwing the entire schedule into disarray, though during the night RAF Wellingtons bombed the Mahlwagon marshaling yards. On November 27th, the two groups renewed the attack, hitting the Insein Locomotive Works. In the largest single bombing mission to date, 25 B-24s from the 7th Group and 23 from the 308th Group flew to Rangoon with an escort of eleven P-38s from the 459th Squadron and five P-51As from the 530th Squadron. The 492nd Squadron led the 7th Bombardment Group formation, with the 436th Squadron in the B position, the 493rd in the C position, and the 9th Squadron in the D position in the rear of the formation. During the bombing run the formation encountered enemy fighters: eight Ki-43 Oscars and one Ki-44 Tojo from the *64th Sentai* and five or more Ki-45 Nick fighters from the *21st Sentai*. The fighters attacked the bombers for around 40 minutes, making repeated and determined frontal attacks. The 9th Squadron claimed four fighters destroyed and two more probably destroyed, while the 493rd claimed one Oscar as a probable and three more damaged. During the fighter attacks on the 493rd Squadron's formation, Lt. N.P. Wagner, a bombardier, was killed instantly when a machine gun bullet hit him in the head in an attack that damaged the airplane in which he was flying. In one of the attacks on the 493rd, Japanese fighters knocked out two engines in Lt. Stephen's airplane. Leaving the target, the formation tried to give Stephen cover, but as he descended the escorts took over, covering him out over the coast, where Stephen made a crash landing in the Bay of Bengal near Foul Island, south of Akyab. A British motor torpedo boat rescued Stephen and his crew three days later. The 308th Group claimed one Nick and five Oscars destroyed and another three fighters probably destroyed for the loss of two B-24s: one from the 373rd Squadron and one crew from the 374th Squadron. The P-38s had a difficult time, losing two of their number to the Japanese fighters for no gain, while the five P-51s claimed three single-engine fighters destroyed, a Nick and another Oscar probably destroyed, and an Oscar damaged for the loss of two P-51s. The Japanese lost one Oscar, one Tojo, and at least one Nick fighter. The B-25s came in after the heavy bombers had finished their bombing, their escort of ten P-51As claiming one Nick destroyed, two Oscars probably destroyed, and one damaged for the loss of two P-51s. Despite the fighter opposition, the bombing had been excellent. Allied intelligence estimated that 70% of the workshops had been destroyed.[73]

The next day, November 28th, the target was the Botataung docks. The 7th Group came in over the target first, bombing from 19,000 feet with excellent results. A smaller number of Japanese fighters, estimated at four Nicks and eight Oscars, intercepted the formation about 15 minutes before bombs away, but the escort of ten P-51As prevented many of the Japanese fighters from pressing their attacks. Only one bomber, in the 436th Squadron, sustained much damage, though the 530th Squadron lost one Mustang during the mission. With the control cables in his B-24 shot away, Lt. Agee made an emergency landing at Chittagong on the way back to base. After a one-hour battle with the fighters, the 9th Squadron claimed one probable and two damaged, while the 493rd Squadron claimed one Oscar destroyed. Intense anti-

Lt. Stephens and his crew were rescued after three days in their life rafts. (Courtesy Jim Augustus)

aircraft fire over Rangoon damaged one aircraft in the 493rd Squadron. Coming in behind the 7th Group, the 308th found the target area obscured by smoke, but the 22 bombers that reached the target area dropped most of their bombs in the area, adding to the destruction. Although the escorting Mustangs claimed four fighters shot down, Japanese records indicate none were in fact lost. Returning to Pandaveswar and Panagarh, the two Groups stood down for two days of maintenance. The hard-pressed 7th Group maintenance crews had to work on double the number of B-24s. During the night of November 28th, RAF Liberators and Wellingtons bombed the Insein Locomotive Works.[74]

Unknown to Allied intelligence, the *5th Hikōshidan* was planning a major attack against Calcutta and had called in as reinforcements the *204th Sentai*, equipped with Ki-43 Oscar fighters, as well as bomber and fighter units from the Imperial Japanese Navy.[75] The *204th Sentai* was assigned to the airfield at Toungoo, arriving at the end of November. This gave the *5th Hikōshidan* more than 50 single and twin-engine fighters for the defense of Rangoon. After two days of rest, the 7th and 308th Groups headed back to Rangoon on December 1, 1943, with the Insein Locomotive Works and nearby warehouses and storage areas as the targets. Once again, the 7th Bombardment Group led the mission, 21 aircraft going on to the target after six had turned back before what proved to be the Group's costliest mission of the war, despite the presence of an escort of six P-38s and eight P-51As who arrived after a delayed refueling. The Japanese fighters, adequately warned of the approaching bomber formation, rose up in full force to intercept: three full *Chutai* from the *64th Sentai*, the full *204th Sentai*, and more than a dozen Ki-45s from the *21st Sentai*. That day, the 9th Squadron was leading the 7th Group formation, coming in on the target on a north-south run at 19,000 feet, as the B-24Js were unable to bomb from the higher altitudes of the B-24Ds. This approach enabled the Japanese fighters to attack out of the sun, at their best altitude, coming within firing range almost as soon as the formation spotted them.[76] By now masters of the frontal attack, the *64th Sentai* finally had enough fighters to inflict real damage on the B-24 formation, even with the Oscar's relatively weak armament. The Oscars concentrated on the lead element of the 9th Squadron's formation. One after another, with the *204th Sentai* following, the Oscars quickly shot down the lead airplane of Capt. Bill Wright, the 9th Squadron's Operations Officer, and his two wingmen, 2nd Lts. Carl Carpenter and George Elliot. Experience made little difference in an attack like this: Wright had many missions under his belt, Elliot was in his third month of combat, and Carpenter was on his second combat mission. Elliot and his crew were killed when their B-24 burst into flames and went down out of control. Of the remaining twenty men in Wright's and Carpenter's crew, six survived the war as prisoners of the Japanese. Wright and five of his crew bailed out of their airplane, Wright dying later while a POW. Carpenter's airplane exploded in mid-air; only the bombardier, 2nd Lt. Clarence Clyborne, and the navigator, Lt. Grant Erwin, bailed out. Both were captured, but Clyborne

A B-24 tail turret damaged by anti-aircraft fire. (7th Bombardment Group (H) Historical Foundation, USAFA McDermott Library)

Bombing the Botataung dock area in Rangoon on November 28, 1943. (3A-37743, RG 342FH, NARA)

died at the end of December. Four crewmen were wounded on the three bombers that survived the attack. It was the 9th Squadron's worst mission of the war. In one week the Squadron had lost five airplanes, nearly half its strength.[77]

Capt. Richard Henning, CO of the 436th, led his squadron's formation that day. Seven aircraft took off from Panagarh in the morning, but only three reached the target. Over Rangoon, anti-aircraft fire hit Lt. John McLauchlen's B-24 in the left wing. With the wing smoking from a possible engine fire, McLauchlen's airplane dived out of the formation, running into Japanese fighters who immediately attacked. Capt. Yasuhiko Kuroe, the *64th Sentai*'s executive officer, led the attack. Kuroe fired at the B-24 and saw one engine stop, but return fire hit his Ki-43, causing one of his landing gear to drop down. The two other pilots in his section, W.O. Kinoshita and W.O. Yamazaki, took up the attack, but ran out of ammunition before they could not bring down the big bomber. Kuroe came in again and sent McLauchlen's airplane crashing into the jungle with no survivors. The 492nd Squadron got through the fighter attacks unscathed, but the 493rd Squadron was not as fortunate. Lt. Granville Stringfellow was leading the 492nd's formation of five aircraft that day, two having turned back with mechanical difficulties. The 493rd came under a ferocious attack that lasted more than an hour. The crews estimated the Japanese attacking force as ten Nicks and 20 Oscar fighters (the crews identified these as 15 Oscars and five Zekes). The Japanese fighters hit the formation at the same altitude of 19,000 feet about ten minutes before the bombers reached the Insein Locomotive Works. The fighters made between 30 and 40 passes on the formation, almost all from the front. The 493rd Squadron's gunners claimed two Oscars and a Zeke destroyed, two Oscars probably destroyed, and two damaged, but the 493rd lost one B-24J. Like Lt. McLauchlen, anti-aircraft fire hit Lt. Stringfellow's B-24 just before reaching the target. With his right wing smoking badly, Stringfellow dove out of the formation, running into Japanese fighters as his damaged airplane descended. The Japanese pilots pressed their attacks and Stringfellow's airplane exploded. Two men were seen to bail out of the airplane, but enemy fighters strafed them in their parachutes. Only one man—a Lt. Col. Everett Plummer, Stringfellow's copilot, who appears to have been attached to the Squadron just for this mission—survived the explosion and bailed out. The Squadron's intelligence officer, Capt. John Lasell, had also joined Stringfellow's crew for the mission and was killed.[78]

The 308th Bombardment Group had the misfortune to lose its formation leader, Maj. Paul O'Brien, just before the start of the bomb run. Lt. Kurosawa, from the *64th Sentai*, led his ten or more Oscar fighters in the attack on the 308th Group's formation of 28 B-24s, concentrating on the lead bomber and quickly shooting down O'Brien's aircraft, which exploded, killing the entire crew. In the confusion that followed, the five other aircraft in his formation passed over the target without dropping their bombs, as did another formation of six aircraft. All eleven later dropped their bombs on Akyab on the return flight. The following formations did bomb the primary target despite continued fighter attacks; the crews described these attacks as "very aggressive".[79] The fighters damaged nine of the 308th Group's bombers before the P-51 escort arrived to drive them off. One heavily damaged B-24 had to land at Chittagong on the return flight. The 308th Group's gunners claimed six Oscars shot down, while the escorting fighters claimed two Oscars and a Nick fighter destroyed and a second Nick as a probable for the loss of one P-51A. The *64th Sentai* lost Lt. Sanae Ishii, who was killed by return fire from the bombers, and had another Ki-43 shot down, the pilot bailing out successfully. Five more of the *64th Sentai*'s Oscars were damaged in the fighting. Losses in the *21st* and *204th Sentais* are not known. In turn, the Japanese pilots claimed ten B-24s, two P-51As, and two P-38s shot down.[80]

The Insein Locomotive Works at Rangoon, the target of the mission of December 1, 1943. (Courtesy Jim Augustus)

Following the December 1st mission to Rangoon, RAF bombers went out to bomb the towns of Bassein and Moulmein and the airfield at Heho on the nights of December 2nd, 5th, and 6th, while the 9th and 493rd Squadrons sent out eight aircraft to mine the Rangoon River estuary and the harbor at Moulmein on the night of December 4th. These were the concluding missions of the "Rangoon blitz". On December 7th, the 308th Bombardment Group's squadrons began leaving India to return to China. The results of the attacks were not

Lt. Granville Stringfellow (standing right) and his crew, lost on December 1, 1943. (7th Bombardment Group (H) Historical Foundation, USAFA McDermott Library)

as great as Maj. Gen. Stratemeyer had hoped to achieve. Weather had thrown off the schedule of missions, and as the 308th Group could stay in India for only a limited time, it proved impossible to carry out the initial operational plan. While damage to the Insein Locomotive Works was extensive, the attacks had not knocked out the Rangoon dock areas, nor had they inflicted significant losses on the Japanese fighter force defending Rangoon. Allied intelligence estimated that the Japanese had lost close to 50 fighters, but the actual losses were probably around a dozen Oscar and Nick fighters. At this point in the war, these losses could be replaced without great difficulty. The escorting fighters were too few in number, and in the face of larger numbers of Japanese fighters were often hard-pressed. Statistically, the bomber losses were not deemed to be excessive, with 12 B-24s lost in 205 sorties, a loss rate of 5.8 per cent overall; the loss rate went over 10 per cent on only one mission on December 1st (though through the cruelty of fate, or chance, the 9th Squadron was hit especially hard), though for an Air Force still operating at the far end of a long supply line, these losses were hard to quickly replace.[81] Among the operational lessons learned during these missions was the need to improve the scheduling of the escorts to accommodate the delays in refueling at advanced bases. The most important lesson, however, was the same conclusion other Army Air Forces bomber units around the world were learning at great cost: the prewar doctrine of unescorted daylight bombing was untenable against determined fighter opposition.[82] It was now clear that as long as the Japanese maintained a formidable number of fighters in the area for the defense of Rangoon, the B-24s could no longer undertake missions to the city without fighter escort.

The Strategic Air Force

Following the last mission of the Rangoon raids, most of the 7th Group effectively stood down until a mission on December 12th. On December 6th, 12 aircraft from the 436th and 492nd Squadrons flew a mission to Port Blair in search of Japanese shipping. Finding no ships in the harbor, they dropped their bombs on military installations on nearby Chatham Island. Ten minutes after leaving the target, five fighters intercepted the B-24 formation. These were most likely A6M5 Zero fighters from a detachment of the *331st Kokutai*, the Imperial Japanese Navy having taken over responsibility for the defense of Port Blair from the Japanese Army Air Force in July. The B-24s fought off the Zeros in a 40-minute battle without apparent damage to either side. Six days later, a Group mission went out to bomb the Myittha Railroad Bridge on the Rangoon-Mandalay railroad line south of Mandalay, despite previous experience indicating the difficulty, if not futility, of attacking bridges from high altitude. Only 18 aircraft went on the mission, indicative of the decreasing number of combat crews available. The 9th Squadron sent out four aircraft, as did the 492nd, while the 436th and 493rd sent out five each. As in previous missions, the bombing failed to damage the bridge. On this mission, the Group had an escort of eight P-38s, which

The December 15, 1943, attack on the Chaulk oil refinery. The 436th Bomb Squadron missed and dropped their bombs in the Irrawaddy River. (3A-37551, RG 342FH, NARA)

was fortunate, as eight to ten Oscar fighters intercepted the formation and made repeated attacks during a 30-minute fight. The bombers claimed one Oscar destroyed and three probably destroyed. The 9th Squadron bore the brunt of the

Crews arrive at the Operations building for debriefing following one of the December 1943 missions. (3A-36199, RG 342FH, NARA)

attacks. Three of its four bombers landed at Chittagong on the return flight; one aircraft had one crewman wounded and one killed. On the evening of December 13th, the four squadrons sent out 17 aircraft individually to bomb the Japanese airfield at Heho, getting good patterns on the runway and buildings. A mission to bomb the oil installations at Chauk, on the Irrawaddy River, southwest of Mandalay, with 20 bombers followed on December 15th, this time with an escort of 14 P-38s from the 459th Fighter Squadron. As the 492nd Squadron recorded in its monthly history, "morale suffered no loss by the sight of 14 P-38s..."[83] The target was a difficult one to pick up. While the other squadrons hit the pumping stations and workshops with good results, the 436th Squadron had the misfortune of seeing its bombs fall into the river alongside. The next day, 19 bombers went out to bomb the cement works at Thayitmyo, on the Irrawaddy River between Magwe and Prome, once again with an escort of P-38s. Bombing from 15,000 feet in clear weather with no opposition, the squadrons achieved an excellent pattern, completely destroying the target. The missions of December 15th and 16th coincided with the announcement of a new air organization for South East Asia Command that at long last integrated the American and British air units flying out of India: the Eastern Air Command.[84]

The most important benefit to the Allied air campaign that came out of the raids on Rangoon was the cooperation between the Army Air Forces and the Royal Air Force. For the first time, the two air forces had coordinated their attacks on a series of related targets. While the RAF made a comparatively smaller contribution—66 Liberator and Wellington sorties compared to 205 sorties for the AAF—the joint missions were "...a good omen for the theater."[85] During 1943, the strategic bombing effort had been conducted "...without the advantage of a unified air command and with no overall strategic direction."[86] While the 7th and 341st Bombardment Groups, who accounted for nearly 60 per cent of the total tonnage of bombs dropped on Japanese targets in Burma during 1943, had inflicted considerable damage on the Japanese lines of communications, the system was still functioning, albeit at a much reduced level. By the fall of 1943, Allied bombing had destroyed 65 per cent of the Burmese railroad system, making it difficult for the Japanese to supply their armies at the front.[87] The war of attrition, such as it was, could be measured not simply in the dock areas, marshaling yards, bridges, or rolling stock destroyed, but in the more intangible effects on the entire system of supply: "upset train schedules, delays caused by damage to bridges and trackage, loss of supplies, and necessity of employing so much equipment and so many laborers in repair work affected the enemy war effort."[88] But the bombing campaign had not yet reduced the flow of supplies into Burma to a level that would seriously impede the operations of the Japanese armies. This would require more heavy bombers and better coordination of effort, and finally, this came to pass.

The delay in integrating Army Air Forces in the India-Burma Sector and Royal Air Force units into a single command was due primarily to the reluctance of Stilwell and Stratemeyer to subordinate units to South East Asia Command that were

A tired crew sits at debriefing, December 1943. (3A-36200, RG 342FH, NARA)

intended, from the American viewpoint, for the defense and support of China. It took many weeks and numerous conferences to work out an agreement that was more or less acceptable to all. On December 12, 1943, Admiral Lord Louis Mountbatten issued a directive ordering the integration of

Col. Conrad Necrason awards medals to members of the 436th Bomb Squadron shortly before he gave up command of the 7th Bomb Group. (3A-34262, RG 342FH, NARA)

the Tenth Air Force and the Royal Air Force's Bengal Air Command into a new organization (Eastern Air Command), with Maj. Gen. Stratemeyer as commander, reporting to Air Chief Marshal Sir Richard Peirse as Commanding Officer, Air Command South East Asia. The role of Eastern Air Command was to control and coordinate all air operations into Burma. Under Eastern Air Command were four subordinate units that Stratemeyer listed in his General Orders Number One on December 15, 1943:

A) The Strategic Air Force, under the command of Brig. Gen. Howard Davidson from the Tenth Air Force, comprising the 7th and 341st Bombardment Groups and the RAF's Liberator and Wellington squadrons of No. 221 Group (in January 1944, these squadrons were placed under No. 231 Group).

B) The Third Tactical Air Force, under the command of Air Marshal John Baldwin, formally commander of the Bengal Air Command, containing all RAF and AAF fighter and fighter-bomber squadrons.

C) The Troop Carrier Command, under Brig. Gen. William Old, with all AAF and RAF transport squadrons.

D) The Photographic Reconnaissance Force, under the command of Group Captain S.G. Wise, RAF (appointed in February 1944).[89]

In his first order to his new command, Maj. Gen. Stratemeyer said:

> A resourceful, able, and wily enemy must be blasted from the jungles of Burma and driven from the skies in days to come. His lines of communication must be obliterated, his shipping destroyed, his will to resist crushed... Every ounce of energy of every man in this command will be required to accomplish this purpose... We must establish in Asia a record of Allied air victory of which we can be proud in the years to come. Let us write it now in the skies over Burma.[90]

The task assigned to the new Strategic Air Force continued to be: "...the conduct of an air offensive over Burma and adjacent territory in conformity with a plan to destroy enemy air forces and air installations, selected rail, river and road communications, depots and other maintenance facilities."[91] While this mission statement listed a number of objectives, the principal objective of the Strategic Air Force was the disruption of the Japanese transportation system in and into Burma, a task only the heavy bombers of the Allied air forces were capable of undertaking.[92] This mission was essentially what the 7th Bombardment Group had been engaged in for the past year, but with the formation of Eastern Air Command, the Allied air effort could at last be directed toward an integrated program of interdiction.[93] The Strategic Air Force operated on the principle that its efforts should be concentrated on the most important transport lines and that attacks should be aimed at achieving a continuous, rather than a temporary disruption of traffic.[94] The operational staff came to develop five rules to use as a guide in planning missions: first, there were only a certain number of targets that could be used to confuse the Japanese; second, missions should be aimed at striking the most important communications targets first; third, as the railroad system was the most important means of communication for the Japanese Army in Burma, railroads would be attacked with greater frequency; fourth, missions against the railroads would attempt to isolate larger segments of the railroad lines to prevent the transfer of supplies across a single break in the line; and fifth, the best targets were those that were most vulnerable and difficult to repair, particularly railroad bridges.[95] The Strategic Air Force tried to carry out its principle mission and adhere to these five rules to the extent it could, though over the following six months, developments in the ground war would often cause a change in priorities. During its first six months of operations, the Strategic Air Force carefully selected targets that would achieve the following objectives:

A) Denial of water transportation;

B) Destruction of rail transportation;

C) Denial of road communication;

D) Destruction of airfields and other military installations;

E) Destruction of industrial and stores areas;

F) Direct support of ground forces.[96]

To accomplish this mission, the Strategic Air Force had, a month after its inception, 48 B-24s in the 7th Bombardment Group, 37 B-25s in the 341st Bombardment Group, 31 Liberator bombers in No. 184 Wing and No. 185 Wing, RAF, and 33 Wellington bombers in No. 175 Wing, RAF.[97]

Integration of the 7th Bombardment Group into the Strategic Air Force unfortunately coincided with a sharp drop in the number of combat crews available. In the Army Air Forces, a full complement of crews amounted to 18 for a heavy bomber squadron and 72 for a heavy bomber group of four squadrons. During most of 1943, the 7th Group had been operating with less than 70 per cent of the combat crews required, the number rising to over 80 per cent for only two months (October and November).[98] Following the Rangoon missions, many crews rotated back to the United States or to other assignments, having flown more than 300 combat hours. In a reversal from the lack of aircraft experienced earlier in the year, rotations and combat losses saw the number of combat crews in the Group drop from around 60 in early December to a little over 30 by early January 1944, less than

Col. Necrason in the cockpit of a B-24. Necrason took command of the 7th Bomb Group when it was little more than a handful of tired B-17Es and led the Group through its first year of combat. (7th Bombardment Group (H) Historical Foundation, USAFA McDermott Library)

50 per cent of the number required. The 9th Bombardment Squadron was hit particularly hard; losses and rotations during the month left the Squadron with only six combat crews. Apparently during December 1943, only two new crews joined the Group as replacements. This situation continued well into 1944; adequate numbers of replacement crews did not arrive until May. As a result, the squadrons sent out fewer aircraft on each mission, typically only four to six B-24s per squadron. During January, the Group sent out more than 20 aircraft on only one mission. After flying over 300 sorties per month from September through November, the total number of sorties dropped to 205 in December, 228 in January, 126 in February (in part due to a special training program), climbed to 218 sorties in March, then dropped again to 131 sorties in April 1944.[99]

There were several changes in command at the turn of the year, as the 7th Group began working as part of the Strategic Air Force. Col. Necrason, who had led the Group since July 1942, relinquished command to return to the United States for assignment. In a little over two years, Necrason had risen from captain to colonel. He had participated in the frantic preparations for war, the dark days in Java, and the slow and at times frustrating reconstruction of the 7th Bombardment Group in India as the Tenth Air Force's sole heavy bomber group. In his administrative and combat roles he had performed admirably. In tribute, the 9th Squadron recorded in its history that Necrason's departure: "...left the entire outfit with a sense of regret. Colonel Necrason, who has served with the Group since before the battle of Java, and served well, earned not only the respect and admiration due an officer of his rank, but the sincere respect and sincere admiration due a man of his caliber. We feel that nothing more need be nor could be said."[100] Maj. William Delahay, who had relinquished command of the 492nd Squadron at the end of December 1943 and transferred to 7th Group Headquarters as Deputy Group Commander, replacing Lt. Col. Joseph Pirruccello, formally took over temporary command of the 7th Group on February 8, 1944.[101]

Toward the end of January, Col. Necrason sent a farewell letter to every member of the Group, saying the following:

1. It is with great reluctance in mind, but with pride in my heart, that I now take leave of the Seventh Bomb Group.
2. Only through everyone's combined efforts have we made the enviable record that will forever stand foremost in my opinion and in the opinions of several people higher than me.
3. We have done much and performed well. No praise is too high for you men of the Seventh. It has been cheerful and pleasant to serve with you men. We have had our sad moments in our losses, but they have not, and never will be, in vain.
4. Keep the Group where it is now—a fine outfit, full of spirit and camaraderie, forever striking with deadly effect upon the enemy.
5. My memories of the Seventh will always be the finest, and no position in the Army will grant me more pride and honor than I have had serving with you men of the Seventh.[102]

Col. Necrason, his commanders, and the officers and men of the 7th Bombardment Group had established a solid reputation for the Group. Reporting to now-Maj. Gen. Davidson on an inspection of the 7th Group, an Army Air Forces Colonel from Washington stated the following:

> The 7th Bomb Group (H) is to be commended for their accomplishments, since the war began. I was deeply impressed with the high caliber of personnel in all staff positions, the combat and ground crews. They

are aggressive, most cheerful and cooperative. Without exception, members of this group know their job and nothing deters them until it is done. If conditions and equipment are not up to their standards they themselves correct the deficiency... The bases are comfortable, clean, neat and orderly. They are maintained and improved without the aid of additional base personnel normally required at an Air Corps station.[103]

In the 9th Squadron, Capt. Allan Lathan, who had commanded the Squadron for only two months, gave up command to Capt. David Kellogg, from the 436th Squadron, at the end of December. Kellogg, a veteran with more than

The "wheels" of the 7th Bomb Group stand next to the Group's insignia in early 1944. Left to right: Maj. William Delahay, CO 7th Bomb Group; Capt. David Kellogg, CO 9th Bomb Squadron; Capt. Robert Bailey, CO 493rd Bomb Squadron; Capt. James Griffith, CO 436th Bomb Squadron; and Capt. John Stephen, CO 492nd Bomb Squadron. (7th Bombardment Group (H) Historical Foundation, USAFA McDermott Library)

400 combat hours, at first was not warmly received, but quickly won the respect of the men in the Squadron. In early January 1944, the commander of the 436th Squadron, Capt. Richard Henning, transferred to Group Headquarters as Assistant Operations Officer. In February Henning, the first member of the Group to exceed 500 combat hours, was promoted to Major and became Group Operations Officer. His replacement in the 436th was Capt. James Griffith, Jr. from the 492nd Squadron. In the 492nd, Capt. John Stephens, formerly with the Royal Canadian Air Force, who had joined the 7th Group in March 1943, replaced Delahay as squadron commander. These men, with Capt. Robert Bailey commanding the 493rd Squadron, would guide the 7th Group through the first few months of operations as part of the Strategic Air Force.[104]

To bring the 7th Group's squadrons closer together, the 436th and 492nd Squadrons left their base at Panagarh for a new airfield at Madhaiganj, 15 miles to the northwest but only around seven miles from Pandaveswar. The move took place in two stages: the 436th Squadron moved first on December 13, 1943, while the 492nd Squadron followed on January 22, 1944. The men of both squadrons found the barracks and buildings to be better than at Panagarh. Madhaiganj would be home to the 436th and the 492nd until June 1944.[105]

From mid-December 1943 to the onset of the monsoon in mid-June 1944, the 7th Group supported the objectives of the Strategic Air Force. The missions to different types of targets were flown concurrently. They can be viewed as a separate but coordinated effort to isolate the Burma battlefield. The starting point continued to be the destruction of Japanese shipping and port facilities within range of the B-24s. This forced the Japanese to rely on the railroad system, particularly the line running from Bangkok to Moulmein for moving supplies into Burma. With the Japanese Army increasingly dependent on the railroads, attacking railroad yards, key bridges, track lines, and locomotives and rolling stock had a cascading effect on the entire supply system. Damage to the railroad system drew off labor and engineers from other projects and resulted in delays in the delivery of critical supplies. As supplies accumulated in dumps these became lucrative targets. To create conditions wherein the bombers could undertake operations over Burma and Thailand with relative impunity required a comprehensive campaign to establish air superiority. This became more critical as the weight of supplies shipped over the Burma-Thailand rail line steadily grew after the line opened in October 1943. The Japanese Army in Burma required, daily, 490 tons of supplies for its ground forces and 113 tons of supplies for the Japanese Army Air Force units in Burma.[106] This total of 603 tons per day was within the Burmese railroad system's carrying capacity of 900 tons per day.[107] Cutting the daily tonnage by 50 per cent or more would have a decided impact on the Japanese Army's fighting capacity, weakening the Army's ability to resist Allied advances. The rail line from Thailand into Burma had three main weaknesses: first, there were no side lines that went around the major marshaling yards if they were blocked; second, the main line itself was a single track, so that destruction at any point along the route would cut the flow of supplies into Burma; and third, the route passed over a large number of bridges, so that the destruction of one or more would sever the line and trap locomotives and rolling stock in between, subjecting them to destruction as well.[108] As the months wore on, the Burma-Thailand railroad line would become an increasingly important target.

Direct attacks on shipping were few and far between, though in the first few months of 1944, the 7th Group flew a number of sea sweeps to the Andaman Islands, southern Burma, and the Gulf of Thailand when photo reconnaissance airplanes or RAF general reconnaissance flights reported ships or convoys. The first such mission of the New Year took place January 4th, when the 9th Squadron sent two airplanes on a sea sweep to the Andaman Islands without result. That same day, the 436th Squadron sent out its "sniffer" ship—a B-24 equipped with search radar—to search the area south of the Gulf of Martaban; seven aircraft were placed on alert in case the search airplane found any ships. The "sniffer" found only a 100-foot long patrol boat, but having no bombs on board, the aircraft descended for a single strafing pass. The next day, the 493rd Squadron sent out a sniffer and a standard B-24J with a full bomb load to search for shipping near the Cocos Islands, north of the Andamans. Both ships were hurriedly recalled when the Group received news of a convoy at Port Blair. All four squadrons went out on the mission, but turned back when they ran into bad weather.[109]

On January 23rd, the Group responded to a report of a large freighter in the harbor at Mergui, along the coast of southern Burma, a round trip of over 2,000 miles from the Group's bases in India. Capt. Benjamin Joy, Operations Officer in the 436th Squadron, requested and received permission to have the 436th attempt a low level attack. The 436th Squadron was first off at 0920, followed by the 492nd Squadron at 1030 and the 9th and 493rd Squadrons from Pandaveswar around the same time. The bombers arrived over Mergui around 1700. Coming in at low level with their bombs fused for eight- and eleven-second delay, the 436th aimed for the large freighter, but all bombs missed. Leaving the freighter behind, the six B-24s found two smaller coastal vessels, strafing them until one was sunk and the other left on fire. Coming off the target, the formation ran into four Ki-43 Oscar fighters from one of the JAAF *Sentai* defending southern Burma. The Oscars made a frontal attack on the first element of the 436th's formation, hitting Capt. Joy's B-24 and setting it on fire. Joy's airplane headed down with smoke pouring out. Joy appeared to be attempting a crash landing on a section of beach nearby, but when the plane hit the water offshore it disintegrated. Only the flight engineer, T/Sgt. Grant Butcher, survived the crash to be taken prisoner. Shortly after the three other squadrons, with the 492nd leading, came in at between 8,300 and 9,000 feet on their bomb runs. The 492nd got two or three near misses, but the 9th Squadron got four direct hits and the 493rd got one or two, sinking the *Seikai Maru*, a cargo ship of 3,180 tons. The mission lasted nearly 13 hours.[110]

After concentrating on other missions during February, the 7th Group went back to sea searches in early March to the area around Ko Sichang, an island in the Gulf of Thailand about 75 miles southeast of Bangkok, off the town of Siracha. The Japanese were using the island as an anchorage to unload supplies from cargo ships. On the night of March 7th, the 493rd Squadron sent out four B-24Js to make the 2400-mile round trip to the island to attack shipping reported there. Capt. Robert Bailey, squadron commander, led off at 1635. Arriving near the island later that night around 2340, the four airplanes found several ships and made individual runs against them for the next hour. Bailey found a 300-foot freighter and hit the stern. Continuing on, he narrowly missed a nearby tanker with two bombs. The second aircraft bombed a smaller coastal vessel in Siracha harbor and claimed this as sunk, while the third made two runs on a freighter underway south of Ko Sichang, claiming two near misses. The fourth aircraft bombed a small island, mistaking it for a large freighter. The next day, the *Juyo Maru*, a large freighter of 5,457 tons, was reported sunk by a mine in the area, but may have been damaged on the mission the night before. The next night, March 8th, the 436th and 493rd Squadrons went back to Ko Sichang, but the birds had fled. Lt. Barrett's aircraft ran out of fuel on the return flight, but Barrett made a successful crash landing 20 miles south of Calcutta, avoiding any injuries to the crew.

The last shipping attack took place April 15th against ships reported at Port Blair, in the Andaman Islands. The Group sent 12 aircraft: three from each squadron. Arriving over the harbor at 12,000 feet, the formation saw one large freighter

The 436th Squadron strafing Japanese coastal vessels off Mergui on January 23, 1944. (File 830.551, Albert F. Simpson Historical Research Center, Air Force Historical Research Agency, Maxwell AFB, AL)

and several smaller ships nearby, but could get no more than near misses from their bombing. Coming off the target, three to four Zero fighters intercepted the formation, making five passes in all: four from the front for 15 to 20 minutes. The 9th Squadron's element took the brunt of the attack. On their first pass, the Zeros shot out the No. 2 engine on Lt. Stanley

Allison's B-24, leading the element. Coming back in their second pass, the Zeros set the No.1 engine on fire. The rest of the formation tried to cover Allison's damaged airplane, but

The Mark 13 Aerial Mine. Mining proved to be the most effective means of disrupting Japanese shipping. (Via the author)

his B-24 had been hit too hard. The bomber dropped out of the formation and went down rapidly to crash in the sea below. Four men bailed out, but only the navigator, 2nd Lt. Charles Kaufman, survived. Lt. Michael Gavrity's B-24 had its hydraulic system shot out, but he made a skillful landing back at Pandaveswar.[111]

By early 1944, repeated attacks and damage to the dock facilities forced the Japanese to abandon Rangoon as an operating port; the risk to shipping had become too great.[112] With Rangoon no longer tenable, the Japanese turned to the smaller ports of Moulmein, Tavoy, and Mergui, in southern Burma. However, the B-24's long range put even these smaller ports at risk, as the January 23rd raid on Mergui had demonstrated. Much of the sea-borne supplies could now only move along this sea route using smaller and less efficient coastal vessels. In Thailand, Bangkok, Ko Sichang, and the small port of Sattahip further to the southeast were pressed into service. As these facilities came under attack, the Japanese came to depend on Saigon, in French Indochina, imposing further delays on the flow of supplies to Burma. Supplies from Saigon traveled by truck to the rail head at Phnom Penh in Cambodia, then to Bangkok and over the rail line into Burma.

The 7th Bombardment Group's first joint mission as part of the Strategic Air Force involved a combined night raid with the Royal Air Force on the new government dock area in Bangkok on the night of December 19, 1943. This mission marked the first long-distance debut of the Group's B-24Js. The Group sent 20 airplanes; 19 bombers reached the target, but found bombing difficult in the ground haze and light from a low moon. In late February, the 9th Squadron went out on a night mission to bomb the ferry terminals at Moulmein, while the 492nd Squadron attacked the ferry terminals on the opposite side at Martaban. The night was one of the darkest nights the crews had ever experienced. Three of the 9th Squadron's four airplanes found the target area and got good hits, starting a number of fires, but the 492nd had problems finding their target and only a few bombs landed in the area. The Moulmein jetties were the target in late April, when the 436th Squadron sent out three aircraft on a night mission with fair results. In an example of a different type of attack against shipping, on the night of March 6, 1944, Capt. David Kellogg, 9th Squadron commander, led four aircraft to Prong Island, 50 miles southeast of Bangkok, to bomb oil storage tanks used to refuel freighters coming into Bangkok. Kellogg and two other planes made it to the target, two dropping their bombs from 5,000 feet, while Kellogg went in at low level. All three observed hits in the target area but failed to start any fires. The bombers returned to Pandaveswar after an average flying time of 16 hours and 15 minutes.[113]

Aerial mining offered the most effective means of denying port facilities to the enemy. Using the 7th Group and RAF Liberator squadrons flying at night, the Strategic Air Force undertook a systematic program to mine the harbors the Japanese were using in Burma and Thailand. The missions to the Gulf of Thailand to mine the seas around Ko Sichang and Sattahip were exceptionally demanding, requiring flights of 14 hours or more.[114] On reaching the target area, the bombers would have to descend to low altitude to drop their mines in a precise pattern as close to the designated dropping point as possible, no mean feat at night. Using different types of mines, including some with delayed activation, the mining campaign

Major David Kellogg, CO of the 9th Bomb Squadron, seen kneeling on the right along with his crew in front of their aircraft *Leaping Lena*. Kellogg was shot down in this aircraft on May 8, 1944. (7th Bombardment Group (H) Historical Foundation, USAFA McDermott Library)

compounded the problems for the limited number of Japanese minesweepers available.[115] The 7th Group's first mining missions in this expanded program began in early January 1944, when the 436th and 492nd Squadrons laid mines in the Chao Phya River that led from the Gulf of Thailand to the port of Bangkok. On the night of January 8th, four 436th aircraft sowed their mines successfully. The 492nd sent five aircraft

The central station and marshaling yards in Bangkok, Thailand, a frequent target for the 7th Bomb Group during the war years. (USAF)

the next night, three successfully reaching the river and dropping their mines. After a two-month hiatus, the Group went back the Chao Phya River in April. Three aircraft from the 492nd Squadron dropped mines on the night of April 8, 1944, while one aircraft mined the harbor at Mergui with three others from the 436th Squadron and three from the 493rd Squadron. The 9th Squadron took its turn at mining Mergui on April 9th, then sent two aircraft to mine the harbor at Tavoy the next night, with the 493rd backing this up with two aircraft that mined Tavoy on the night of April 10th.[116]

In early May, the Group sent the squadrons to mine the anchorage at Ko Sichang and the small harbor at Sattahip. The 492nd Squadron went first on the night of May 5, 1944, three aircraft taking off at 30-minute intervals and dropping their mines successfully. Three aircraft from the 436th Squadron went out the next night, taking off at five-minute intervals. Over the target area, Lt Mueth's airplane had a malfunctioning bomb rack. His bombardier, Lt. Eldridge, went back into the bomb bay and released the mines one at a time with a screwdriver. Mueth made five passes to release them all. The 493rd sent three aircraft to mine the harbor at Sattahib on the night of May 7, 1944, but only one aircraft made it to the target, the other two returning with gasoline leaks. That same night, Maj. David Kellogg, who had accumulated more than 570 hours of combat time and who had just received an Oak Leaf Cluster to his Distinguished Flying Cross, led two other 9th Squadron aircraft to mine Sattahip as well. Flying as his copilot that night was Lt. Michael Gavrity, one of the Squadron's flight leaders. On the previous few missions, the other squadron crews had reported little opposition; only one airplane encountered some light machine gun fire. By chance, or by design, a Japanese gun boat was lying off the harbor that night. Kellogg made his run over the harbor at low altitude. After dropping his mines he headed south out to sea, passing between two small islands and unknowingly heading straight for the Japanese gunboat. The sound of engines probably alerted the crew, who opened fire with 20mm cannon as the big bomber flew over, setting fire to one wing and knocking out two engines. Kellogg had no choice but to ditch his airplane in the sea. He and one of his gunners, S/Sgt. Laurel Kinsey, survived the crash. The rest of his crew, all combat veterans with some having over thirty months of service overseas, were killed. As the Squadron recorded, "... the loss of these men cut deeply into the heart of the squadron."[117] Maj. William Kyes, a veteran of combat in the Southwest Pacific before coming to the CBI Theater, transferred in from the 493rd Squadron to replace Kellogg. Kyes' quiet efficiency did much to make up for Kellogg's loss.[118] The last mining missions before the monsoon were flown on the night of June 8, 1944, when the 9th Squadron sent three aircraft to mine the Mergui harbor and the 436th sent three to mine the Chao Phya River. Only one aircraft from each squadron made it to the target area: one turned back after four and a half hours when an engine failed and three turned back due to weather from the onset of the monsoon.[117] On April 25, 1944, Maj. Gen. Davidson, who had been promoted a few months earlier, received a letter from General Henry Arnold, Army Air Forces commander, who said the following:

> 1. The mining operations that are being conducted by the Tenth Air Force, and the results that are accruing from this work, are highly gratifying to me. They exemplify in the finest manner the versatility of the Army Air Forces, and their ability to utilize every available weapon to strike the enemy by day and by night.
>
> I desire that each individual who contributed to this effort, and particularly the crew members who are flying the missions, be extended my congratulations on a job well done. I am confident that your future aerial mine operations will be pressed home with the same vigor and determination, and will result in even greater success.[119]

The combined efforts of the 7th Bombardment Group and the RAF's Liberator squadrons against Japanese shipping and the Burmese and Thai port facilities proved successful. By the beginning of the monsoon in June 1944, the Japanese had effectively abandoned Rangoon, Moulmein, Tavoy, Mergui, and Bangkok as ports and would no longer send large cargo vessels into the Andaman Sea or the Gulf of Martaban, relegating what little supplies came through to smaller coastal vessels. And, just as supplies could no longer come into Burma by sea for the Japanese Army, far smaller amounts of the raw materials Japan needed for her war industries and the food to feed her people could return to Japan. The larger ships: "...would have been sunk had they appeared. The Japanese did not dare risk their dwindling tonnage to the bombs and mines of Allied air power. The effect was to sever one of the life lines of the Japanese empire."[120]

Attacks on the railroad system in Burma and Thailand continued unabated until the liberation of Burma in an effort that complemented the destruction of Japanese shipping. While the large marshaling yards at Mandalay, Rangoon, and Bangkok remained important targets, the squadrons in the Strategic Air Force developed new tactics to ensure the continuous disruption of the railroad system. The 7th Bombardment Group maintained its attacks on key marshaling yards in Burma and Thailand, but halted the ineffective high-altitude attacks on bridges. During most of 1944, bridge targets were left to the B-25 medium-bomber crews, who had developed much more effective low-level bombing techniques. Instead, the 7th Group took on a new mission: bombing the more distant Burma-Thailand railroad line at low level to destroy sections of track.

With the opening of the Burma-Thailand railroad line, the central station at Bangkok and the nearby marshaling yards at Bangsue became prime targets for the long-range heavy bombers. On the night of December 23rd, the Group joined RAF Liberators in an attack on the Bangkok railroad station. The still-depleted 9th Squadron had not yet received enough replacement crews to make up its losses so could only send three airplanes. The 436th sent six (with one returning early), the 492nd four airplanes, and the 493rd got six to the target. The airplanes took off at four- to five-minute intervals and flew to the target individually. The RAF Liberators had gone in first, so the target was already on fire and visible as the B-24s made their approach from 7,000 to 9,000 feet. Bombing was excellent, and the crews reported that the fires were still visible 100 miles from the target. After making their bomb run, a crew in the 493rd Squadron saw a single-engine fighter that followed the bomber for around five minutes before making a single, quick attack without result. The 9th and 493rd Squadrons returned to Bangkok on the night of January 10, 1944, to bomb the marshaling yards at Bangsue. Five aircraft reached the target and dropped their bombs in the area. A little over a week later, the 436th and 492nd Squadrons took their turn, heading out the night of January 19th to bomb the central railroad station again. Seven aircraft made it to the target, putting most of their bombs in the target area.[121] After these missions to Bangkok, Maj. Gen. Howard Davidson sent a letter of commendation to the 436th Squadron, no doubt expressing the gratitude he felt toward the entire group. In his letter Davidson said: "I wish to express my personal admiration and gratitude to the crews who have attacked Bangkok during the past two months. These long-range and exacting missions were no easy achievement, and it reflects great credit on the aircrews, and on the ground staffs who assisted them, that so gratifying and so consistent results were obtained."[122]

A 100-pound spike bomb, developed to destroy sections of railroad track when dropped from low level. (3A-33926, RG 342FH, NARA)

Within Burma, the Group concentrated on marshaling yards other than Rangoon, less important now that Japanese shipping had abandoned the port. The railroad yards at Mandalay, Monywa, and Moulmein were the main targets for the 7th Group, and the first two towns were also frequent targets for the RAF Wellingtons at night. Moulmein was the last stop on the Burma-Thailand railroad line. Supplies were off loaded at Moulmein and put on to ferries to carry them across to Martaban, where they were put back on railroad cars to travel over the Burmese railroad system. Mandalay was the central point where supplies would be loaded onto trains going east to Lashio and the Yunnan front and north to Myitkyina in the northeast part of Burma, where Gen. Stilwell's Chinese forces were advancing; and to Ye-u, on the Chindwin River, where the Japanese faced the British IV Corps. Monywa, on the Chindwin, was a smaller but important junction on the line to Ye-u. Damage to these three targets imposed immediate delays on the flow of supplies.

Monywa was targeted first. On the next to last day of 1943, the Group sent 20 aircraft from all four squadrons to bomb the railroad yards. One squadron carried 500-pound bombs and the three others dropped 100-pound fragmentation bombs. Bombing from an altitude of around 18,000 feet, the squadrons put most of their bombs in or near the target area, many hitting just to the east of the railroad yards. The crews had some question as to whether the 100-pound frags would do any real damage. The Group did not go back to Monywa until April 25, 1944, when six airplanes from the 436th and 492nd Squadrons bombed the railroad yards, while six airplanes from the 9th and 493rd Squadrons attacked the railroad sidings and supply dumps at Alon, a few miles to the north of Monywa. The yards at Mandalay were hit during a night mission on February 28, 1944. All four squadrons sent out aircraft, but haze and poor visibility over Mandalay made it difficult to find the target area or to assess any damage. The Group returned to Mandalay two months later on May 4th, in a mission coordinated with RAF long-range Beaufighter units. Once again, as a year earlier, by bombing the southern end of the marshaling yards the bombers hoped to trap locomotives and rolling stock so the Beaufighters could come in and strafe them. The Group sent only twelve aircraft, three from each squadron. Bombing from 17,700 feet, the 493rd Squadron's bombs missed the target completely, falling 2,800 feet northeast of the center of the railroad yards (the aiming point). The other three squadrons made up for the error, getting all their bombs on the southern section of the yards and getting direct hits on the switches. It is unclear, however, whether the RAF long-range fighters followed up the attack. Moulmein, the third but smallest target, was hit on two occasions: in night attack at the end of February and again in late April, when the 436th and 492nd Squadrons went out together in another night attack.[123]

All the missions to bomb marshaling yards were conventional, high-altitude precision bombing attacks. In February, the Group began training for a different mission that would see the B-24 used in a completely new role: low level attacks on the Burma-Thailand railroad line. In addition to knocking out key marshaling yards and bridges, Maj. Gen. Davidson and the Strategic Air Force staff wanted to destroy sections of railroad track along the main lines from Thailand into Burma and along the lines north to Mandalay and beyond. In low level attacks on the railroad lines, an airplane could place a conventional bomb in between the rails, but most bombs would simply hit the tracks and bounce off to explode nearby. Davidson needed some way to keep the bomb on the tracks in between the rails, rather than bouncing off the point of impact. After several tests with improvised metal fins for air brakes and flat noses weighted with concrete dropped from a B-25, Davidson came up with the idea of the spike bomb. Using a length of steel from old truck axles, local machinists crafted a 17-inch spike that screwed into the nose of a conventional bomb equipped with a delayed fuse in the tail. Dropped at minimum altitude directly onto the tracks, more often than not the spike bomb would stick between the rails, blowing a large gap in the rail line when it went off. The tactics developed for the use of spike bombs against a rail line involved dropping pairs of bombs at one- to two-mile intervals along a ten- to 15-mile section of track. As large segments of the lines were accessible only by rail and not by road, this greatly complicated the repair of damaged lines; repair crews could only repair one break at a time and had to repair one break before they could move on to the next. Davidson believed that: "...rail transportation in Burma can be seriously impaired, if not completely denied, by a methodical program of low-level spike-bomb attacks."[124]

The B-25s could cover most of the railroad lines in Burma, but only the B-24s could reach the Burma-Thailand railroad from bases in India. During February, the 7th Group's squadrons set aside several days to practice low-level attacks on railroad lines: both individual attacks and attacks in squadron formation using the local Indian railroad as a target. While the Squadron histories make no mention of the spike bomb at this time, it appears that using spike bombs was the intent of the practice missions. As the 9th Squadron recorded at the end of the month: "As yet we have not utilized the proficiency we obtained in this training. We are, never the less, looking forward to it with some anxiety."[125] The first opportunity came in late March. Still without replacements, the 9th Squadron's operations officer resorted to qualifying several copilots as first pilots and using extra crewmen to make up two new combat crews. The 436th Squadron took similar measures. The mission of March 23rd was a low-level attack on a segment of the Burma-Thailand railroad between Bangkok and Thanbyuzayat. This first low-level mission involved dropping 1,000-pound bombs on railroad bridges; these bombs may have had some form of spike attached.[126] Each B-24 was loaded with five 1,000-pound bombs and a bomb-bay fuel tank. Leaving their bases late in the morning to arrive over the target area just before dusk, three airplanes from each of the Group's four squadrons headed out. The

493rd diverted to bomb Moulmein due to poor weather, but the three other squadrons reached their stretches of the railroad and bombed individually. In its segment, the 9th claimed three bridges destroyed and apparently sections of the track as well, along with six railroad cars strafed. The two other squadrons bombed unspecified targets. Damage was difficult to determine in the gathering darkness.[127]

All four squadrons went back to the Burma-Thailand railroad on April 5th. The 9th, 436th, and 492nd sent three aircraft and the 493rd four, each squadron taking a different section of the line, where the airplanes descended to bomb individually. Once again, the squadrons left late in the morning to arrive in the target area just before dusk. This mission was more successful, but also more costly: the 9th and 493rd Squadrons both lost an airplane. Portions of the railroad line ran through valleys and gorges among the hills straddling the Burma-Thailand border, with the hills rising to 2,500 feet. The B-24s had to descend to lower altitude to hit the bridges and railroad tracks, not leaving much room to maneuver. The Japanese had placed machine guns and 20mm and 37mm anti-aircraft guns along the route and attached flak cars to some of the trains. The three airplanes from the 492nd escaped unscathed. They destroyed five miles of track using 100-pound spike bombs, strafing rolling stock and bashas (small buildings made from wood, bamboo, and thatch) as they flew along their sector of the railroad. One bomber in the 436th Squadron's formation carried a 2,000-pound bomb to cause a landslide down on the tracks, but when dropped the bomb failed to

One of the few color photos of a 7th Bomb Group B-24. This is B-24J *Babe*, which flew with the 492nd Bomb Squadron. (Mel Rappaport via Jim Augustus)

explode. Dropping down to low level, the airplanes destroyed several trains and bridges. With all bombs gone they continued on, strafing flak cars, machine gun emplacements, and camps along the route. On one of these runs, Capt. Schleier and his copilot, Lt. Col. Margrave, were both wounded in the arm when a burst of machine gun fire hit the cockpit of their B-24. A second bomber received hits in the wing tank and the bomb bay tank, but made it back to base safely.[128]

B-24J *Star Duster* flying over India some time in the first half of 1944. (Courtesy of Jim Augustus)

Lt. Stanley Allison, who would be killed ten days later, led the 9th Squadron's formation that day with Lt. Warren Kaufman, one of the Squadron's flight leaders, as one of his wingmen. Accompanying Kaufman was the Squadron's new intelligence officer, Capt. James Dorst, flying his first combat mission. The three airplanes ran into heavy ground fire on their bomb runs. After dropping two bombs on his first run, Lt. Kaufman's plane was hit and Kaufman was apparently wounded. His B-24 crashed into the ground and blew up. By some miracle three of the crew survived: the bombardier, 2nd Lt. Gene Gambale; and two of the gunners: S/Sgt. James McKernan and S/Sgt. Tyman Wells. McKernan and Wells survived their time as prisoners of war, but Gambale's Japanese captors beat him to death.[129] The 9th Squadron claimed two bridges destroyed and two probably destroyed, as well as a section of the track bed. Like the other formations, after bombing the remaining two airplanes went down to strafe locomotives, rolling stock, and any buildings they could find along the way. The loss of Lt. Kaufman on April 5th and Lt. Allison on April 10th—both flight leaders—dealt another hard blow to the 9th Squadron. Losses were terrible at any time, but to lose two flight leaders and two complete combat crews in quick succession with no replacements put a real burden on the Squadron.[130]

The 493rd Squadron commander, Capt. Robert Bailey, led four aircraft to the target, though one had to turn back due to a gas leak. Flying with Bailey as copilot was Col. Aubrey Dodson, the new commander of the 7th Bombardment Group, who had taken over command from Maj. Delahay on March

27th and was flying his fourth combat mission with the Group. The B-24s were loaded with 100-pound spike bombs. Covering a five-mile stretch of the railroad line from MS (Mile Stone) 25 to MS 20, one airplane made ten direct hits on the line of track. A second airplane then took over, covering the line from MS 20 to MS 12 and also getting ten direct hits. Bailey followed, covering the line from MS 12 to MS 6, his bombardier scoring eleven direct hits on the railroad track. As he neared the end of his run, 20mm and 37mm automatic weapons and machine guns opened fire on Bailey's airplane, punching holes in the B-24 just as the bombardier dropped the last bomb. Two 20mm shells hit the nose compartment, destroying the Automatic Flight Control Equipment (the autopilot), while another 20mm exploded an oxygen bottle in the rear of the airplane. Seconds earlier, a 37mm shell exploded in the waist gun position, fatally wounding S/Sgt. Warren Winkler. Machine gun fire knocked out the number 4 engine and punctured an oil line in the number 3 engine, causing a loss in power. Eight to ten 12.7mm bullets hit the right wing, holing the number 3 and 4 main fuel tanks. The heavily damaged bomber staggered back toward base and was last seen at 1910, flying at 3,000 feet. Bailey hoped to make an emergency landing at the closest base, but couldn't make it. In a remarkable feat of airmanship, Bailey successfully ditched his airplane—never easy in a B-24, especially at night. The nine remaining crew members got in their life rafts. Three B-24s searched for Bailey and his crew the next day without success, but late that night, the Squadron learned that a PBY Catalina had rescued them. After an interrogation they returned to the Squadron on April 10th, spending some time over the next few days briefing the other 7th Group squadrons about their experience.[131]

In a letter to Maj. Gen. Davidson, Maj. Gen. Stratemeyer complemented the 7th Group on its two attacks on the Burma-Thailand railroad. "I cannot let the opportunity pass", he wrote, "without complementing you on the excellent attack on the Moulmein-Bangkok railway. The fact that it was so successful in knocking out vital bridges, shows that it was carefully planned and well executed. The interdiction of this railroad cannot help but have an important effect on the fighting throughout Burma. Sir Richard Peirse, Air Commander-in-Chief, has asked me to send you his congratulations on the mission and, through you, to the 7th Group." Colonel Dobson added his own endorsement to Stratemeyer's letter, telling the men of his new Group: "...the successful attack upon the Moulmein-Bangkok railway could not have been possible without the fullest cooperation on the part of squadron staffs and ground personnel, as well as the combat crews which participated."[132]

On December 5, 1943, the Japanese carried out a major raid against Calcutta, a joint Army and Navy force inflicting considerable damage on the port area. The raid demonstrated that Japanese air power remained a potent force and a real threat to the air route to China and the planned advance of Allied forces into Burma.[133] To accomplish all the objectives set for it, Eastern Air Command had to achieve air superiority over the Japanese Army Air Force. While fighters played the main role in the campaign for air superiority, counter-air operations over Burma were a joint undertaking involving the heavy and medium bombers of the AAF and the RAF as well. Strategic Air Force bombers made regular raids on

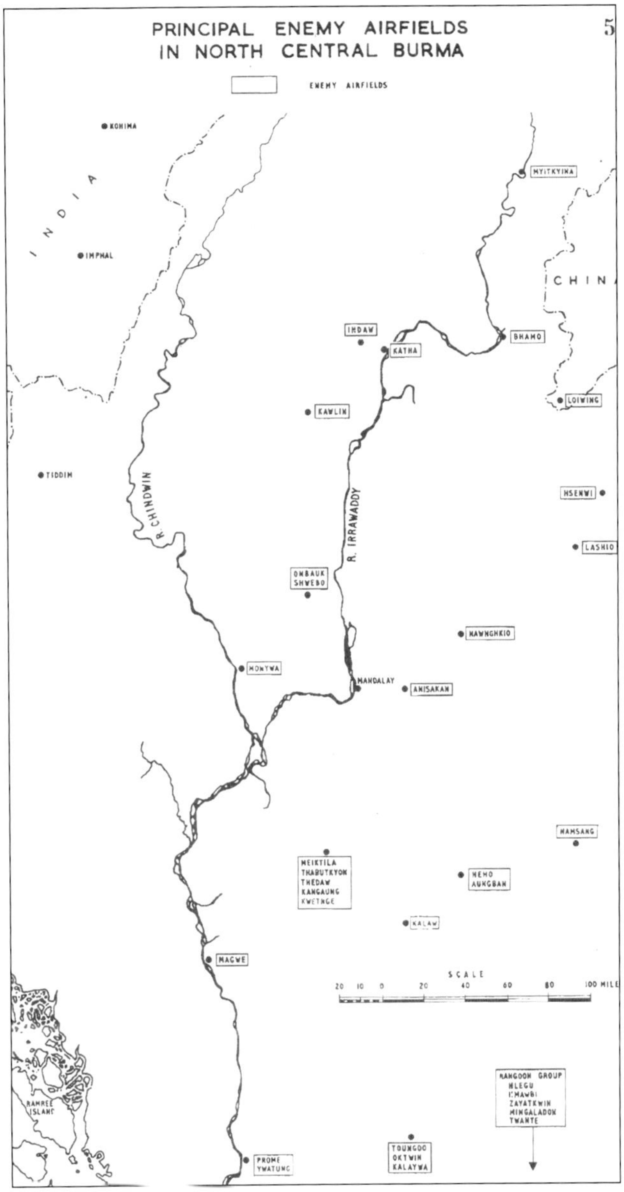

A map showing the principal Japanese Army Air Force air fields in Burma. (Air Historical Branch (1), Air Ministry: *R.A.F. Narrative: The Campaigns in the Far East, Volume IV, South East Asia (November 1943 to August 1945)* (London: Royal Air Force Air Force Centre for Air Power Studies, MLRS Books edition)

An aerial reconnaissance photograph of Don Muang air field taken in early 1944. (Via the author)

Japanese air bases in Burma and farther afield in Thailand. During the first three months of 1944, the 7th Group played a part in these attacks. While the Japanese became adept at making quick repairs, as they had done with bridges and railroads, the destruction from Allied bombing raids acted as a further drain on enemy resources and compounded the logistical problems facing the Japanese Army Air Force. The Japanese Army Air Force's main air installations in Burma were the air bases built in and around Rangoon. The JAAF had taken over Mingaladon after its capture, then built several more bases—Zayatkwin, Hlegu, and Hmawbi—in the area nearby. These bases, beyond the range of Allied fighters, served as maintenance and repair facilities, as well for defending Rangoon. The JAAF built a large number of forward airstrips closer to the front lines opposing the different Allied armies they faced in the Arakan, Assam, northeastern Burma, and against Yunnan. These forward airstrips gave the Japanese bomber and fighter *Sentai* great mobility, enabling them to move quickly from one field to another as required. In Thailand, the airfield at Don Muang, outside of Bangkok, provided a base well to the rear where Japanese units could rest and re-equip and new units could stage through on their way to Burma. After the capture of Burma the Japanese had greatly expanded Don Muang airfield, adding a new runway, extensive revetments, and many buildings.

From January to the first week of March 1944, the 7th Group flew ten missions to attack Japanese airfields in Burma and Thailand. The squadrons went out to Don Muang on three missions, bombing at night, since neither the P-38s nor the P-51s then available had the range to escort the bombers as far as Bangkok. Only small numbers of aircraft went on these missions. On the night of January 10, 1944, one airplane from the 9th Squadron bombed Don Muang, while two others attacked the Bangsue marshaling yards. Nine days later, the 9th and 493rd Squadrons returned to Don Muang, each squadron sending four aircraft, bombing individually. All four of the 9th Squadron's aircraft apparently found and bombed the airfield, but only two of the 493rd Squadron's aircraft could find the field. They did, however, do an excellent job. Coming in over the airfield between 10,000 and 10,500 feet, one airplane placed its bombs in the hangars and buildings on the northeast side of the airfield, while the other dropped a string of bombs through the revetments on the east side of the field. A month later, on February 10th, three airplanes from the 492nd went out to Don Muang, while the three other squadrons bombed the Ban Mah arsenal at Bangkok. Struggling with bad weather to and from the target and a dense haze, the bombers made two runs over the field. Mingaladon was the target on a night mission the last day of the month. The Group sent out 18 aircraft, but weather interfered with the mission, with only six aircraft managing to reach the target, dropping fragmentation bombs and incendiaries from medium altitudes.[134]

The Japanese forward airfields at Heho, Aungban, and Akyab, frequent targets of the Strategic Air Force's Wellington medium bombers, were the 7th Group's targets during February following the launch of the Japanese *Ha-Go* offensive in the Arakan. These night missions involved small numbers of aircraft, the squadrons sending three to four bombers on a mission. On the night of February 4th, the 9th and 493rd Squadrons bombed Heho airfield, while the 436th and 492nd attacked the nearby field at Aungban. The bombers carried loads of fragmentation and incendiary bombs and bombed from medium altitudes. Over Heho, three single-engine airplanes attempted to intercept the 9th Squadron's airplanes. One fighter chased Lt. Cawood's B-24 back toward India. Cawood claimed this fighter destroyed when, with the aid of his navigator, he ran the fighter into a mountain in the Chin Hills. Haze and darkness over Aungban made it difficult for the 436th and 492nd to locate the airfield, despite the use of

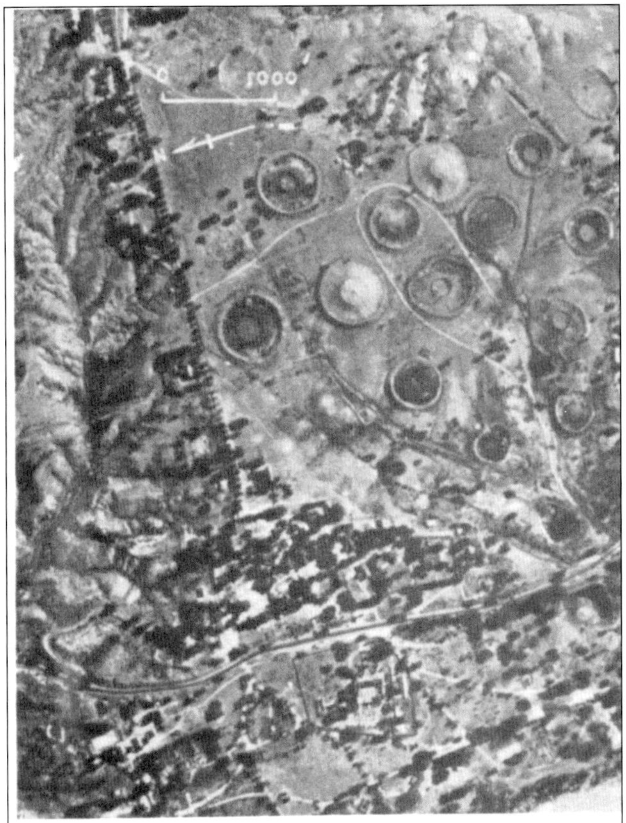

BEFORE: Oil fields and storage tanks at Thittabwe were target for a squadron mission on 2 January, first strike on this installation. Note camouflage nets over two tanks.

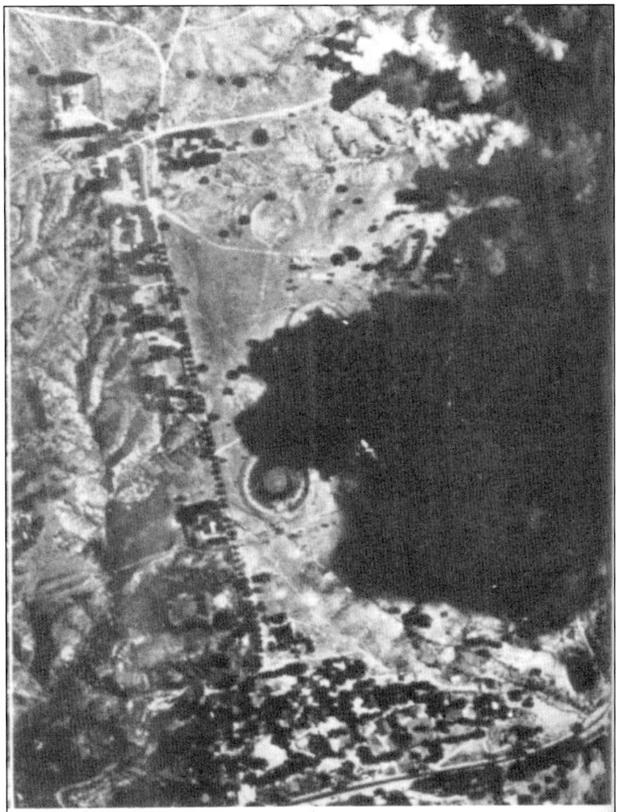

AFTER: Seven B-24s dropped 84 five-hundred-pound GP bombs from 18,500 feet with the results pictured above. AA fire over the target was slight and there was no interception.

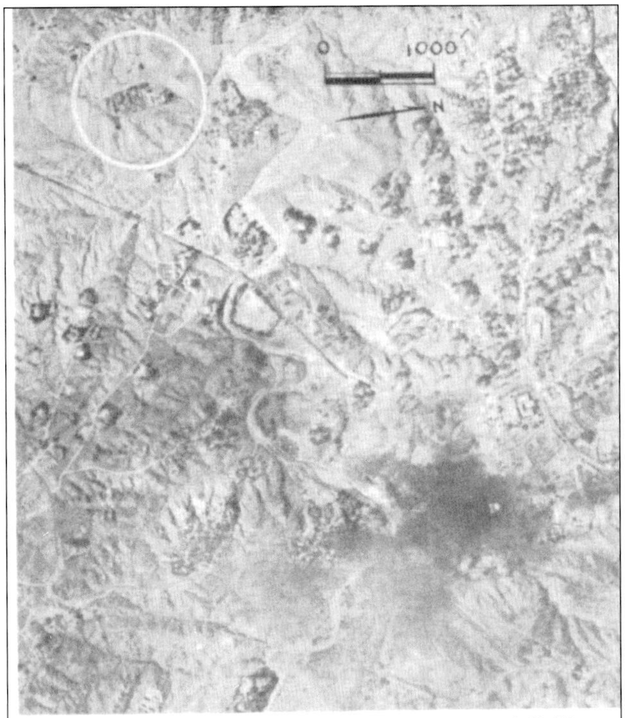

BEFORE: Strategic aiming point for squadron of B-24s on 2 January was Yenangyaung oil cracking plant, 600 feet long, 400 feet wide. River and railroad aided target location.

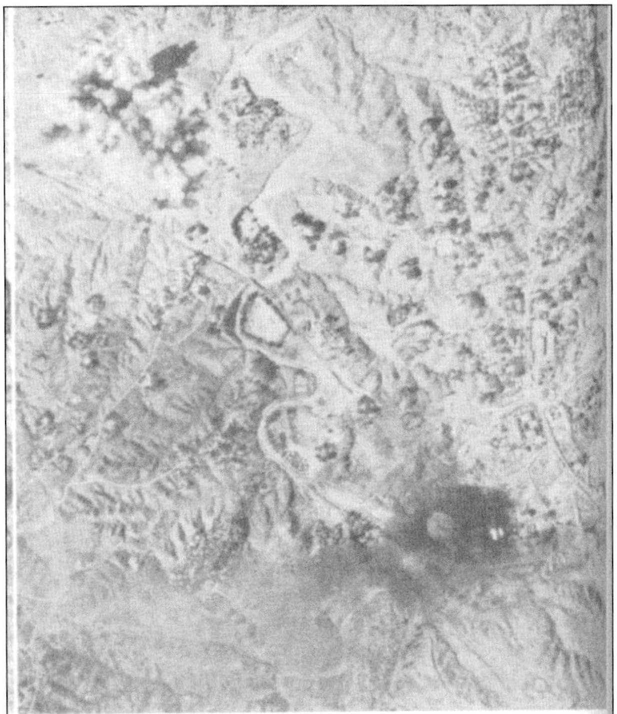

AFTER: Close concentration of bomb bursts completely obscures cracking plant. B-24s attacked with 500-lb. bombs from 19,100 feet. Result: total destruction of target.

Photos taken from the June 1944 issue of the Army Air Corps magazine *Impact* showing bombing during the 7th Bomb Group's attacks on the Burmese oil fields. (Via the author) parachute flares. Seeing searchlights over Heho, two of the 436th Squadron's airplanes bombed that field instead. The next night, the squadrons went back to the same targets with similar results. Haze over Aungban made bombing difficult, while the searchlights tracking the bombers over Heho made it easy to locate the airfield. All four squadrons went back to

A B-24J taxis out for a mission with the flight engineer keeping a sharp eye out along the narrow perimeter track. (Peter M. Bowers Collection, Museum of Flight)

Heho the night of February 13th. With practice, the Japanese searchlights coned several airplanes for a minute or more despite their evasive action. The crews saw one Ki-45 Nick fighter and several Oscars over the field, but only one Oscar attempted an attack on a bomber. The B-24 easily evaded the fighter with a sharp turn. All four squadrons bombed the airfield at Akyab on February 23rd, and in early March attacked Lashio and Loiwing—the airfields closest to the Yunnan front—on day missions. The 9th and 493rd Squadrons bombed Lashio with a welcome escort of P-40s from the Fourteenth Air Force, as interception was considered likely. The bombers got good hits on the runway. The 436th and 492nd Squadrons bombed Loiwing, also with a P-40 escort. The last mission against the airfields took place on the night of March 4th, when the four squadrons went out to bomb the airfields around Rangoon. The 9th and 493rd Squadrons covered Zayatkwin and Hlegu, while the 436th and 492nd attacked Mingaladon and Hmawbi. Taking off at five-minute intervals and bombing individually, most of the bombers reached their assigned targets, but a few dropped their bombs on other airfields when they were unable to find their primary. Over Mingaladon and Zayatkwin, the bombers ran into heavy anti-aircraft fire and active searchlights. One of the 493rd Squadron's pilots had a narrow escape over Mingaladon. Unable to locate Zayatkwin (the primary target), he found Mingaladon, only to be coned by up to 15 searchlights in the area that held his airplane for nearly eight minutes. Over the field four and possibly six Oscars intercepted the B-24. The fighters made repeated passes from the front and rear quarters, pressing their attacks but inflicting only minor damage. The pilot resorted to climbs and dives and finally a violent corkscrew maneuver to get away from the fighters, who stuck with the bomber until it went beyond the range of the searchlights. Due to poor visibility and a reluctance to give away their position to the fighters, the gunners on the B-24 held their fire while under attack. This was the 7th Group's last raid on a Japanese airfield until after the monsoon season. While the heavy and medium bomber attacks were helpful, what really broke the back of the Japanese Army Air Force during the first half of 1944 were the long-range fighter sweeps the Tenth Air Force's P-38s and P-51s undertook during March to May. The P-38Hs and later P-38Js of the 459th Fighter Squadron and the P-51As of the 530th Fighter Squadron and the First Air Commando Group attacked Japanese airfields in northern and central Burma, claiming 271 airplanes destroyed, 35 probably destroyed, and 118 damaged over three months. Newly-introduced Spitfires in the RAF fighter squadrons added to these totals in battles over the Arakan and Imphal. By the end of May, the Allied air forces had established air superiority over Burma. For the rest of the war, Allied heavy and medium bombers would carry out their missions with far less risk of interception.[135]

One of the few strategic targets in Burma, as defined by Army Air Forces doctrine, was the complex of oil fields and refineries around Yenangyaung and Chauk, on the banks of the Irrawaddy River north of Magwe, in central Burma. After capturing the oil fields in 1942, the Japanese had repaired the refineries to meet their need for gasoline and other fuels. The 7th Group had bombed Chauk on several occasions during 1943, most recently in December. Since the Japanese had repaired the damage, the Strategic Air Force called for more air attacks. In early January, the Group struck Yenangyaung twice, bombing the National Oil Company (N.O.C.) oil refinery, storage tanks, and pumping station on January 2nd and returning the next day to hit the British Oil Company (B.O.C.) refinery complex. Bombing from 18,500 to 19,100 feet in clear skies against inaccurate anti-aircraft fire, the bombing was rated excellent; almost all bombs fell in the small target area on both days. This was a difficult target, because the refinery was only around 250 square yards in total area, making it challenging to pick up from high altitude and difficult to hit with precision. In this instance, daylight precision bombing worked as intended. As the bombers left the oil fields after the first mission, they could see a column of smoke rising to 13,000 feet. The Group went back to bomb Yenangyaung again at the end of the month. This time the bombing was mixed: the 9th , 436th, and 492nd Squadrons dropped their bombs squarely or just near the target, again causing a huge column of smoke to rise up, while the 493rd Squadron dropped farther away. The Group returned to Yenangyaung and Chauk on April 3rd—weather having forced an attempt on the first of the month—while the 9th Squadron bombed a power station nearby. Bombing at an even lower altitude (around 14,500 feet) brought excellent results; the strings of bombs walked across the target area. Intelligence analysis believed that this mission destroyed the B.O.C. gasoline plant. On May 1st, the Group paid another visit to the oil fields; then, in a double attack, they hit Yenangyaung and Chauk on June 10th and 11th. At the beginning of the year, the refinery at Yenangyaung produced an estimated 5,000 barrels of gasoline a day; Strategic Air Force intelligence estimated that by early June, production had dropped to around 1,680 barrels a day.[136]

Although not originally intended as a major component of the Strategic Air Force's objectives, between January and May 1944, ground support missions on all three fronts in Burma made up the largest segment of the Strategic Air Force's effort. This accounted for 55 per cent of the bomb tonnage dropped from January to May.[137] Military installations, supply dumps and warehouses, and enemy positions all became targets. The number of missions flown against these targets and the tonnage of bombs dropped steadily increased as the battles in the Arakan, then Imphal, then in the northeast around Myitkyina intensified. As previously related, the Allied plans for 1944 had envisioned the capture of upper Burma to establish a land link with China. The plan called for Stilwell's Chinese forces to advance from Ledo to capture Myitkyina, while Chinese divisions in Yunnan, in southern China, advanced across the Salween River to clear the land route to China. The British 14th Army's IV Corps would undertake an advance across the Chindwin River. The plans included one or more of the amphibious operations Generalissimo Chiang Kai-shek insisted on to capture Akyab and Ramree Island, on the Burmese coast, for advanced airfields. A long-range penetration operation under the command of Maj. Gen. Orde Wingate would undertake a landing behind Japanese lines in support of these operations. The intent had been to confirm these plans at the Sextant Conference in Cairo at the end of November 1943. For a variety of reasons, including the need to cancel the planned amphibious operations due to a lack of resources, the Generalissimo refused to commit his Yunnan forces for what he saw as only a limited advance into Burma, not its full re-conquest. Admiral Mountbatten, SEAC commander, had no alternative but to cancel the original plans and replace them with three less ambitious operations, basically designed to contain the Japanese. Stilwell's force was to move toward the Myitkyina area allowing the construction of the Ledo Road behind them. IV Corps was to undertake a more limited advance up to the Chindwin River, while in the Arakan, the XV Corps would begin an overland advance toward Akyab. Wingate's long-range penetration force would assist one of these operations (it was soon decided to use Wingate's force to support Stilwell's advance). The advance in the Arakan would begin first, with the others to follow. The Japanese Army, in turn, planned for the *15th Army* to undertake a major offensive against the British base at Imphal (Operation *U-Go*) to prevent a British advance into Burma, while the *28th Army* pinned down British forces in the Arakan (Operation *Ha-Go*). The Japanese plan was to cut the British supply lines to Imphal, isolate the base, and destroy it. *Ha-Go* was scheduled to begin on February 4, 1944, with *U-Go* a month later in early March.[138]

For close support missions in support of the 14th Army, Army Air Force bombers started using depth charges to blast away the Japanese jungle positions. (3A-33905, RG 342FH, NARA)

The XV Corps was ordered to begin an offensive in the Arakan toward Akyab before the end of January 1944. In preparation, the 14th Army asked the Strategic Air Force to bomb a Japanese position near Kyauktaw, some 20 miles inland from the Bay of Bengal in the Arakan, north of Akyab. Earlier that month, the 341st Bombardment Group and two of its B-25 squadrons had been transferred to China to join the Fourteenth Air Force, leaving only one squadron of B-25 medium bombers in India, the 490th Bombardment Squadron. This reduced the number of medium bombers in the Strategic Air Force from 70 to 49, though not all were operational. It is likely for this reason that when asked for support Maj. Gen. Davidson called on the 7th Bombardment Group to help out. After two false starts due to weather, on January 17, 1944, the 7th Group sent the 9th, 492nd, and 493rd Squadrons with 13 airplanes. Bombing from 10,500 feet, the result was "perfect", as the 492nd Squadron recorded. In lieu of regular demolition bombs, the 493rd Squadron dropped 60 325-pound AN-Mk-17 depth charges. These had proved surprisingly effective against jungle targets. The next day, five airplanes from the 436th hit

Kyauktaw to complete the job, putting all their bombs on target. British forces successfully took the position after the bombing. The 14th Army called the Strategic Air Force back eight days later on January 26th to attack Japanese positions on a ridge near Razabil and at nearby Maungdaw, on the coast, in support of a British attack. Eight aircraft from the 9th and 493rd Squadrons went to Razabil, while eight from the 436th and the 492nd went to Maungdaw. At Razabil, 12 RAF Vengeance dive bombers marked the target area for the bombers, who came in at 8,300 feet. Seven B-25s followed the B-24s; 12 more Vengeances completed the bombing. The squadrons thought they had done a good job of bombing, but the 14th Army disagreed, as the attack did not succeed, despite the bombing and additional artillery and tank fire.[139]

The 7th Group was not called on to provide support to the ground armies again until early March. In February, as Wingate completed his plans for the insertion of two of the three brigades of his long-range penetration force behind enemy lines, the Strategic Air Force was alerted to be ready to provide support through operations against concentrations of Japanese forces that might move against Wingate's Special Force (officially the 3rd Indian Division, but better known as the Chindits).[140] To best support the advance of Stilwell's Chinese forces down the Hukwang Valley toward Moguang and Myitkyina, the Chindit brigades were to be air landed in gliders and C-47 transports near the railroad line from Mandalay to Myitkyina. There they could block the flow of supplies and reinforcements to the Japanese division fighting against the Chinese. The chosen area was around 80 miles southwest of Myitkyina. The fly-in was scheduled to begin on the night of March 5th, continuing for several days. On March 9th, while the landings were still in progress, the 7th Group bombed Japanese supply dumps at the towns of Kamaing and Mogaung, to the north of the landing area. Attacking these targets had the dual benefit of helping prevent the movement of supplies south against the Chindits or north toward the Chinese advancing toward Kamaing down the Hukwang Valley. The 9th and 493rd Squadrons bombed Kamaing with 11 airplanes. The 9th Squadron reported an excellent bombing pattern, but the 493rd had to make two runs over the target area when the second element couldn't get its bombs away on the first run. The Squadron classed the result as only "good". The 436th and 493rd Squadrons bombed Mogaung with eight aircraft, getting excellent results. The Group went back to Mogaung the next day, on what was for the time a relatively large group mission, with 22 airplanes making up the formation. On this occasion, Maj. Gen. Davidson joined the mission, flying as command pilot with the 436th Squadron's formation of seven aircraft in the Squadron C.O., Capt. James Griffith's bomber. From an altitude of 16,500 feet with no anti-aircraft fire, the Group's bombs covered the target area, hitting a railroad bridge, the tracks, and a large administration building and starting several fires, no doubt pleasing the General.[141]

Bombing a Japanese headquarters in early 1944 in support of the 14th Army. (3A-37534, RG 342FH, NARA)

The night of March 14th, the 7th Group joined RAF heavy and medium bombers in a raid on the major Japanese Army supply dumps nine miles north of Rangoon at Victoria Lake. This was another large mission, the Group sending out 22 airplanes to join ten RAF Liberators and 22 Wellington medium bombers. Most B-24s carried a mix of incendiaries and 100-pound demolition bombs. Attacking an important target close to Rangoon, the bombers ran into heavy anti-aircraft fire, searchlights, and enemy fighters. The RAF bombers apparently went in first as pathfinders, starting fires in the target area. Two bombers from the 436th also served as pathfinders to identify the target for the rest of the Group's airplanes. The B-24s bombed individually, having taken off a few minutes apart. The crews approaching the target could see flames and explosions from 25 miles away. The bombers went in at 12,750 and 14,500 feet around 0400, running the gauntlet of AA and searchlights operating from Rangoon and Mingaladon airfield. Several bombers were caught in the searchlight beams, finding that a violent turn to the left would momentarily free them from the lights from Rangoon and a violent turn to the right would get them out of the cone of lights from Mingaladon. In breaking free from one group of searchlights, the other group would invariably pick up the bomber again. One bomber was coned for three or more minutes and came under immediate fighter attack. Three single-engine fighters made several passes from the side and rear quarters. Crews reported seeing machine gun fire coming from the leading edges of the wings of some of the fighters. If not an optical illusion at night, these fighters may have been Type 2 Fighters (Ki-44 Tojo) from the *64th Sentai*, which had received a small number of Tojos the previous fall. The 493rd's aircraft escaped injury, but the fighters badly damaged two 492nd Squadron aircraft, fortunately without injury to the crews.[142]

The Japanese launched Operation *U-Go* on March 6, 1944, launching attacks against the IV Corps divisions advancing toward the Chindwin River. Lt. Gen. G.A.P. Scoones, commanding the IV Corps, ordered his forces to make a fighting withdrawal back to Imphal, where they would set up their defense against the Japanese attack. The Japanese plan for the capture of Imphal had one serious flaw: the advance of the three divisions allocated the *15th Army* was reliant on a logistical system that was judged to be "precarious" at best.[143] *Burma Area Army*, responsible for providing supplies, lacked the necessary administrative units to ensure that these supplies could reach the troops on a timely basis. The divisions could carry with them only a 20-day supply of ammunition, food, and other essentials. Lt. Gen. Mutaguchi, commanding the offensive, had arranged for an additional five days of supplies to be stored in dumps behind the Chindwin River, but the success of his operation and the survival of his divisions depended on the rapid capture of Imphal. Delays could prove disastrous; his divisions would find themselves "...in inhospitable country, without a supply line and opposed by a well-supplied enemy fighting on his own ground."[144] A delay in the advance also made supplies in rear area dumps all the more critical. For the next several months, Japanese dumps supplying the forces fighting against Imphal, Wingate's Special Force, and Stilwell's Chinese divisions became prime targets for the Strategic Air Force.

From March 17th to the 24th, the 7th Group flew four missions to bomb Japanese Army supply dumps in and around Kalewa, an important supply point on the one route from Mandalay to Imphal. As the Japanese Army Air Force was making regular attacks on Imphal with bombers and fighter escort, the B-24s welcomed an escort of P-38s on most of their missions. With no risk of interception and no anti-aircraft fire, the bombers could make their bombing runs at much lower altitudes—sometimes at 10,000 feet or less—usually resulting in excellent bombing, with a number of direct hits on buildings in the targeted area. On March 26th, Brig. Gen. Moore, Chief of Staff of the Tenth Air Force, accompanied the 492nd Squadron on a challenging Group mission to assist the 17th Indian Division retreating down the road from Tiddim to Imphal. The objective was to bomb the hillsides along the road in order to cause a landslide, blocking the Japanese advance. The Group sent 12 airplanes—three from each squadron—against this small and difficult target. Only the 436th Squadron picked out the target and dropped its bombs; the three other formations couldn't identify the correct spot and were reluctant to bomb in fear of hitting the British and Indian troops in the area. During the last week of the month, the Group returned to supporting Stilwell and Special Force: the 9th and 493rd Squadrons

A B-24J gets two new engines in its revetment. During the hot season temperatures out on the runway could reach 120°. (GP-7-SU-PH, Albert F. Simpson Historical Research Center, Air Force Historical Research Agency, Maxwell AFB, AL)

bombing the dumps at Mogaung on March 25th; the 436th and 492nd attacking Kamaing on March 27th; and the 9th and 493rd bombing Kamaing again the next day, dropping down to an altitude of 8,200 feet for their bomb run.[145]

During April, the 7th Group flew only four missions in support of the ground armies, attacking supply dumps near Kalewa twice and at Lashio once, but during May, the Group flew 15 ground support missions, mostly in support of Stilwell's advance on Myitkyina. By late April, Stilwell's Chinese divisions, with help from the American 5307th Composite Regiment—better known as "Merrill's Marauders"—had advanced down the Hukwang Valley and crossed over into the Mogaung Valley, working their way toward the town of Kamaing, some 20 miles from Moguang.[146] Stilwell's goal was Myitkyina, a key town on the Irrawaddy River that connected with the road to Lashio and the old Burma Road. Myitkyina had an airfield Japanese fighters had used to attack American transport planes flying over the air route to China, forcing them to fly the far more difficult higher altitude Hump route farther away. Capture of Myitkyina was critical to building a new overland route to China from Ledo. Stilwell decided in late April to send a force composed of Chinese troops and Merrill's Marauders over the Kumon mountain range (west of the town) to seize the airfield at Myitkyina in a surprise *coup de main* attack. Between May 10th and 15th, the 7th Group flew several night missions to Myitkyina. Each squadron sent a small number of aircraft at intervals to bomb the town for several hours at a time to disrupt the Japanese troops and distract them from the approaching Allied force. Stilwell's force captured the Myitkyina airfield on May 17th, but was too small to capture the town, the subsequent siege lasting into August. In support of the fight for Myitkyina and the Chinese and Special Force units now advancing on Mogaung, toward the end of May, the 7th Group flew three missions to bomb the railroad junction at Indaw, on the Mandalay-Myitkyina railroad line, to disrupt the flow of supplies to Japanese forces. The approaching monsoon weather sometimes made bombing difficult. At the beginning of May, the Group had flown two missions in support of IV Corps' defense of Imphal, hitting Japanese positions and supply dumps on May 8th and 9th. Toward the end of the month, the Group went out to bomb a Japanese road block on the Tiddim-Imphal road, but weather over the target prevented bombing. The bombers attacked the dumps at Kalemyo as an alternate. The weather was steadily worsening as the monsoon approached. Returning crews would report that the target was "12/10th's covered".[147] Several attempts to get through to bomb supply dumps had to be abandoned due to weather.[148]

Pecker Red, one of the 493rd Bomb Squadron's first and longest-serving B-24Js, with the ground crew midway through the airplane's long career. (Via the author)

Despite the shortage of combat crews during its first six months of operations as part of the Strategic Air Force, the 7th Group significantly contributed to achieving the Strategic Air Force's objectives. From the formation of the Strategic Air Force on December 15, 1943, until May 31, 1944, the American heavy and medium bomber units flew 2,024 sorties and dropped 3,300 tons of bombs on 129 different targets, while RAF bomber units dropped about the same amount.[149] With fewer RAF Liberator squadrons fully operational during the period, the 7th Group did most of the heavy-bomber work, striking important objectives that required the B-24's longer range. And for part of the period, from early January until mid-April, when the 12th Bombardment Group (Medium) arrived in India to replace the departed 341st Group, the 7th Group filled in for the missing B-25 medium bombers. While it is difficult to calculate the impact of the strategic bombing operations against the Japanese with precision, one estimate of the effect of the cumulative damage the AAF and RAF units in the Strategic Air Force inflicted on the Japanese communications system through their attacks on the railroad system is that these attacks stopped "...almost entirely the movement of supplies on the railways between Bangkok and Myitkyina from February to the end of May 1944".[150] This occurred at a time when the Japanese Army in Burma was in a desperate struggle against the 14th Army in the Arakan and Imphal, and against Stilwell's combined forces. During these battles, the Japanese Army had to rely on an already weak and inadequate system of supply. The most important development during these first few months of operations was the improved coordination and harmony between AAF and RAF units operating out of India. In his first report on Strategic Air Force operations, Maj. Gen. Davidson said, "the combination and coordination of the various units into a single, powerful striking force enabled us to hit the enemy more often and more disastrously than ever before."[151]

With the approach of the monsoon, the heat returned with a vengeance in April and May. The 436th Squadron recorded temperatures as high as 125 degrees; as the squadron historian commented: "the afternoon breeze off the fields resembles

Lost Angel, one of the first non-camouflaged B-24s in the 7th Bomb Group. Assigned to the 436th Bomb Squadron, the airplane brought its crew back on two engines from their first combat mission. (3A-34769, RG 342FH, NARA)

very closely that which comes from a blast furnace, 110 degrees in the shade is common everyday stuff."[151] The maintenance crews suffered the worst, as all work on the B-24s was done out in the open in concrete and earthen revetments that radiated the heat and glare. That they maintained a high rate of airplanes in commission is a tribute to their dedication. While many looked forward to the relatively cooler temperatures the monsoon would bring, for pilots, the

A mixed formation of older camouflaged and newer uncamouflaged B-24s setting out for a mission over Burma. (7th Bombardment Group (H) Historical Foundation, USAFA McDermott Library)

monsoon was a decidedly mixed blessing. The older crews, who had been through a monsoon season, were reminded of "...the weather hazards thru which they must fly again and the new crews, while eager, listen with profound respect to the old timers."[152] Some violent storms came in, the first and worst taking place on April 13th, as the 9th Squadron was hosting a large party. A lightning bolt hit the control tower, blowing out all the instruments, but the wind, rain, and hail failed to dampen spirits, perhaps due to the punch that was served "reportedly pulling 9gs". A few days later, a mission had to be cancelled while the airplanes were lining up on the runway when a storm blew in with 74mph winds and hail stones. As the weeks went on, once again, more missions had to be cancelled due to the weather. The crews repeatedly plowed through the weather, only to find their primary target covered over. Flying in the worsening weather was fatiguing. As the 9th Squadron history recorded: "the pilots are sometimes forced to fly on instruments for two to three hours. Much rain and turbulence being encountered in the heavy cloud formations. It is not uncommon for the wing tips to be obscured to the occupants of the plane and it is impossible to see the other planes in the formation, although only fifty feet away. This calls for consummate skill and care on the part of the pilot and causes increased tenseness on all personnel. When the men return from these weather aborted missions, they seem more fatigued than after battling Zeros and running through flak. There's something about 'Sweating out' a landing with 6,000 pounds of TNT that takes something out of a man."[153]

The heat and the approach of the monsoon weather were a few of the factors that contributed to a period of "strenuous griping" in April.[154] The shift in the practice of granting medals on the basis of accumulated hours instead of individual actions did have a positive effect on morale. A large number of men were awarded the Air Medal or the Distinguished Flying Cross during April. The change in policy made the combat crews look forward to accumulating the hours they needed to qualify for an Air Medal or a DFC. But the most pressing issue for many was the continued lack of a firm rotation policy. By April, all four squadrons had been operating for more than four months with a minimum of combat crews; only a few replacement crews had come in, and as previously related, the 9th and 436th Squadrons had resorted to qualifying copilots as first pilots and putting new crews together from extra individual crewmen. The operations officers were at times hard pressed to come up with enough crews to send out six planes on a mission. For some of the longer-serving men, April was their thirtieth month overseas, and many more were in the 25 to 30 month bracket. While a small number of men, usually with more than 400 combat hours, had been sent back to the United States, the Group still lacked a set policy on rotation. As Maj. Gen. Davidson explained in an all-Group meeting early in the month, the CBI Theater had no fixed rotation policy; men would be sent home when their replacements arrived.[155] When an announcement appeared in the 436th Squadron that those wishing to could sign up for a six-month extension could do so at any time, only one man signed the papers.[156]

In April 1944, the well-known Hollywood movie star Paulette Goddard visited the 7th Bomb Group while on a tour of the China-Burma-India Theater. (SQ-Bomb-11-SU-PH, Albert F. Simpson Historical Research Center, Air Force Historical Research Agency, Maxwell AFB, AL)

The newly-christened *Paulette*. This airplane was later lost in a crash after losing two engines. (Mel Rappaport via Jim Augustus)

The 492nd Bomb Squadron asked Miss Goddard to christen a new B-24J named in her honor with an appropriate and tasteful nose art image. (SQ-Bomb-11-SU-PH, Albert F. Simpson Historical Research Center, Air Force Historical Research Agency, Maxwell AFB, AL)

A 436th Bomb Squadron B-24J lands at the Squadron's new base at Tezagon. Around this time, the 7th Bomb Group adopted white and black or yellow and black check markings for each squadron: the 9th Squadron having white and black checks on the rudder with a horizontal yellow stripe and the 436th having yellow and black checks on the upper half of the vertical stabilizer, as shown here. The 492nd had white and black checks in the same position and the 493rd had yellow and black checks on the rudder. (3A-33739, RG 342FH, NARA)

The squadrons threw themselves into training and adjusting to new commanders. The 9th Squadron reintroduced a vigorous program concentrating on gunnery, aircraft recognition, and practice bombing in between missions. The 436th Squadron also put in a lot of practice flying, while the 492nd Squadron undertook a series of lectures in aircraft recognition, focusing on Japanese and British airplanes, as well as lectures on B-24 systems. In addition to a new Group commander in Col. Aubrey Dodson, there were several changes of command in the squadrons. In the 436th Squadron, Capt. James Griffith was transferred to Tenth Air Force Headquarters. Lt. Col. John Fitzwater, who had been flying with the 493rd Squadron, moved over to replace him. Tragically, Griffith was killed a month later in Calcutta checking out in a P-40. In the 492nd Squadron, Capt. John Stephens was promoted to Major and also transferred to Tenth Air Force Headquarters, with Capt. Hillard Gandy taking over as squadron commander.[157]

Relief for the older crews came toward the end of May, when all the squadrons received an influx of new combat crews and other personnel. After months of new crews dribbling in, the squadrons each gained six to seven new ones. Back in the United States, the training system finally reached high gear; the number of crews training in B-24s increased by 70 per cent from December 1943 to March 1944.[158] While a doubling of air crew casualties in the European and Mediterranean Theaters during the first few months of 1944 no doubt delayed the flow of replacements to the CBI, by May, the training pipeline was putting through a sufficient number of crews to supply all Army Air Forces theaters. The new crews that arrived in May, with more following in June, finally allowed the longest-serving men to return to the United States, to their great relief. One of those departing was Warrant Officer J.R. Yaney, who had served with the 7th Bombardment Group before the war, gone to Java with the 11th Bombardment Squadron, then to India in March 1942 with Maj. Gen. Brereton. So many new men arrived in the squadron at the end of May that the 9th Squadron joked that after 72 hours a new crew were considered "old men". The officer's quarters were overflowing with three men to a room, but no one complained.[159]

All four squadrons immediately began an intensive training program for the new crews to bring them up to operational standards. The new men received orientation lectures on the theater, as well as tactics and procedures from the more experienced crews. Practice missions stressed gunnery, bombing, and formation flying, especially the defensive formations the Group used in combat. The practice benefited the regular crews as well; pilots and copilots spent more time in the Link trainer. Bombardiers in the 9th Squadron practiced with a new bombing trainer the Squadron had built. The 436th Squadron used these practice flights to give some of the more experienced pilots the opportunity to fly as flight leaders and the bombardiers the experience of flying as a mission leader. The 492nd Squadron arranged for a P-40 to provide more realistic training for the new gunners, the fighter pilot making passes on the bomber formation using Japanese fighter tactics.[160]

Then, in early June 1944, in the middle of the training program for the new crews came a surprise announcement: the 7th Bombardment Group was being temporarily withdrawn from the Strategic Air Force and assigned to a new mission: hauling desperately needed gasoline to China for the embattled Fourteenth Air Force. On June 13th, Maj. Gens. Stratemeyer and Davidson visited the 9th and 493rd Squadrons at Pandaveswar and then the 436th and 492nd at Madhaiganj to personally inform the men of each of the squadrons and to impress on them the importance of this new mission. The June 10th bombing of Yenangyaung would be the Group's last bombing mission until the middle of October.[161]

Hauling Gas

Claire Chennault, as much an advocate for air power as his bomber brethren, firmly believed that air power held the key to the defeat of Japan. With a force of airplanes in China and adequate logistical support, he was convinced he could defeat the Japanese.[162] From bases in eastern China, Chennault believed he could cut off the flow of raw materials to Japan from Southeast Asia. Having defeated the Japanese Army Air Force in China, his forces could begin bombing the Japanese home islands. In the spring of 1943, Chennault and Stilwell presented their alternative plans for American support for China. Chennault's air power plan won out; Stilwell's plan to build up the Chinese armies would have been a lengthy process and President Roosevelt wanted more immediate aid to China. Stilwell and General George Marshall, head of the Joint Chiefs of Staff, pointed out that if Chennault's plan was as successful as Chennault argued it would be, then the Japanese were sure to retaliate and move against his airfields and the weakened Chinese armies were unlikely to be able to defend them.[163] In response, Chennault had Generalissimo Chiang Kai-shek promise President Roosevelt that Chiang's armies would halt any Japanese advance against the air offensive that the Generalissimo preferred over Stilwell's program of reforming the Chinese armies. Chennault accepted the Generalissimo's promise, though he later qualified it to include the availability of air support and a lack of Japanese reinforcements.[164] His confidence in the Chinese armies grew when in the fall of 1943, with the help of air support from the Fourteenth Air Force, the Chinese stopped a limited Japanese advance on the city of Chang-te.[165] But as he expanded his air operations and began an aggressive campaign against Japanese shipping off the China coast in early 1944, Chennault may have come to believe what he wanted to believe about the capability of the Chinese army to defend his airfields successfully.[166]

The Japanese were indeed planning for a major ground offensive in China to begin in the spring of 1944. There were multiple reasons for undertaking the offensive, named *Ichi-Go*; first, to take out Chennault's airfields to prevent further attacks on the Japanese lines of communication on land and sea; to prevent the new B-29 long-range bombers the Japanese knew were on their way from using these airfields to bomb Japan; and to open a land and rail route from China to the Japanese *Southern Army* in Southeast Asia.[167] The initial phase of the *Ichi-Go* offensive began in April, with Japanese troops pushing north from the city of Wuhan to establish the northern section of the land corridor; toward the end of May, the Japanese launched the second phase of the operation, heading south directly towards Chennault's airfields. Chennault warned Stilwell that the Fourteenth Air Force would need at least 10,000 tons of supplies over the Hump route, nearly double the monthly allocation, if the China airfields were to be held.[168] Chennault's fighters were now flying double the number of sorties they had flown only a few months earlier and their reserve stocks of fuel were getting dangerously low. The Fourteenth Air Force needed gas not only to fuel its fighters and bombers, but also the transports that were necessary to fly the gas to where it was most needed.[169] With the coming monsoon weather likely to curtail bombing operations over Burma and Thailand, there was good reason to divert the 7th Bombardment Group to transporting gasoline to China over the Hump.

The 7th Group's squadrons relocated soon after being notified of their new mission. To their great regret, they had to leave Pandaveswar and Madhaiganj and move to new bases closer to Chittagong, the receiving port for supplies of aviation gasoline for the Hump route. The 436th, 492nd, and 493rd Squadrons were assigned to Tezgaon, swapping places with the 12th Bombardment Group, whose squadrons moved to Pandaveswar and Madhaiganj, while the 9th Squadron moved to Kurmitola and the 434th Bombardment Squadron, from the 12th Group, relocated to Panda. Tezgaon and Kurmitola were approximately 200 miles east of Calcutta. The gasoline went by rail from Chittagong to the bases. On June 10, 1944, members of the Group staff flew to inspect their new homes and to begin working out the problems of moving from one base to another. A meeting with the 54th Service Group, charged with providing supplies, was discouraging. There was a shortage of spare parts and spare engines for the B-24s at Tezgaon and Kurmitola. Since the 12th Group typically bombed from medium altitudes, there was precious little oxygen for the longer high-altitude flights the B-24s would be making over the Hump route. The Group resorted to using an older B-24D to make daily runs to Tenth Air Force supply depots. Staff and squadron commanders met with their opposite numbers in the 12th Group on June 14th to plan the move. Everyone in the squadrons pitched in to pack up the supplies, records, equipment, and personal effects that would be needed. Soon B-24s were shuttling back and forth between the new and old bases, making three or four trips a day working with the B-25s of their sister squadrons in the 12th Group. The 436th Squadron worked out an arrangement with the 12th Group's 81st Squadron for each to load up an airplane with the equipment for the same department, fly to the new base, offload, then fly back with personnel and equipment belonging to the other squadron. In the midst of all the frenzied activity, the 493rd Squadron had a change in command: Capt. Frank Maholchic replaced Capt. Robert Bailey (Capt. Jack Bradley moved over from the 9th Squadron to replace Maholchic on August 23, 1944). The squadrons began the move on June 16, 1944; they were ready to begin gasoline hauling flights over the Hump by June 20, 1944.[170]

Pecker Red loading up equipment for the 493rd Squadron's move to Tezagon to begin hauling gas to China. (GP-12-HI (Bomb), Albert F. Simpson Historical Research Center, Air Force Historical Research Agency, Maxwell AFB, AL)

Not surprisingly, there were mixed reactions to the change in mission. While there was a general realization of the importance of flying gasoline to the Fourteenth Air Force, it was for many a disappointment. As the 9th Squadron history described it, a "...generally depressed state of mind prevailed."[171] This was particularly true for the bombardiers, old and new. As they were unnecessary for these missions, all were taken off flying. The older bombardiers: "...resent the inactivity and being relegated to the sidelines and the new ones miss the combat experience which is so necessary to put the finishing touch on their personal technique."[172] The newly-arrived crews faced a more difficult transition, having to cope with the confusion of moving to a new base and adapting to a completely new mission. Although dangerous, hauling gas over the Hump seemed "...tame to those who came here to do battle."[173] Still, the men overcame their disappointment and buckled down to their new task. Soon there was a healthy competition between them to see who could haul the most gasoline to China.

Pumping gas into the bomb bay tanks of a B-24J believed to be from the 9th Bomb Squadron for transport to China. (7th Bombardment Group (H) Historical Foundation, USAFA McDermott Library)

Moving aviation gasoline to China forced the 7th Group to improvise. Three 420-gallon bomb bay fuel tanks were put into the bomb bay; initially these could not be jettisoned, but later droppable tanks were installed for emergencies.[174] As there was a shortage of these larger fuel tanks when the Group first started flying over the Hump, the squadrons used P-40 drop tanks attached to the shackles in the bomb bay. This had a double benefit, as the Fourteenth Air Force's P-40s badly needed more drop tanks for their close support missions. For

The 7th Bomb Group fitted three bomb bay tanks into the B-24s to carry the gasoline over the Hump. (7th Bombardment Group (H) Historical Foundation, USAFA McDermott Library)

much of the period the gasoline for China arrived from Chittagong in drums. It took all night to fill a B-24, and the maintenance crews now had to take care of 13 to 16 aircraft as well. To reduce weight for take-offs and landings with a full load of fuel, the Group removed the belly turrets on the B-24Js and 60 per cent of the ammunition normally carried. The Group also cut the crew size for the Hump missions from ten men to seven and later to only five. Loaded with gasoline, the planes would fly to Kunming, China, to unload and make the return flight to Tezgaon or Kurmitola usually the same day. Later, to speed the delivery of fuel, planes flew to Liuchow, 200 miles closer to the front lines. The bombers unloaded their gasoline at Liuchow and flew to Kunming to stay the night, returning to India the next day. Two radio beacons, one at Imphal and one at Myitkyina, served as check points towards the Hump route, but after Myitkyina pilots and navigators were on their own until they reached Kunming. The runways at Tezagon and Kurmitola were just long enough for a B-24 to get off with a full load in the hot weather, but not by much. With a maximum load of fuel, the gross weights would often reach 72,000 pounds, well above the emergency maximum gross weight of 64,000 pounds specified in the B-24 pilot's manual.[175] Lt. Charles Niblett, a pilot with the 9th Squadron, recalled: "The length of the runways at both Kurmitola and Tezgaon presented a challenge to get the heavily over loaded B-24s off the ground. At Kurmitola the telephone line to Group headquarters hung from two poles, one on each end of the runway. It was a rather regular occurrence to wipe out communications with our landing gear."[176]

Once in the air, the pilot had to get his airplane over the Hump through some of the worst weather in the world. As the 9th Squadron's history for July 1944 recorded: "To the uninitiated and that includes the squadron at the inception of the operation, flying the 'Hump' seemed like a 'dry run' after the hazardous missions to which we have become accustomed. It is here noted that such an impression is entirely erroneous."[177] The weather was demanding, and sometimes dangerous. Going over the Hump required pilots to fly on instruments for six hours or more. Ralph Marshall, a newly-arrived pilot with the 493rd Squadron, recalled: "Flying the Hump was like no other flying experience, before or after. The course from Imphal to China was almost due east. The three main mountain ranges, just beyond Myitkyina, were parallel and aligned north-south. Two well-known rivers flowed through canyons between these ranges: first the Salween, then the Mekong. The winds at our flight altitude were usually west to east, with unpredictable speeds ranging up to 150mph. Created by these winds over the mountain ranges were unbelievable 'up' and 'down' drafts. We were given an assigned altitude and, at first, were expected to maintain it."[178]

An experienced pilot went along on a new pilot's first flight over the Hump; after that he was on his own. To help get started, the 7th Group arranged for the Air Transport Command to send ten experienced C-87(the cargo version of the B-24) pilots with many hours of flying the Hump to fly as copilots, first with the more experienced pilots in the Group, then with

Running a hose into the bomb bay to fill the tanks with gasoline. (7th Bombardment Group (H) Historical Foundation, USAFA McDermott Library)

the newer ones, so that every pilot had a veteran along for his first trip over the Hump.[179] A similar system was worked out for the Group's navigators, particularly important for many of the new navigators who had never flown in the Theater before. For the newly-arrived pilots, this first solo flight was a daunting experience. Carl Fritsche, who joined the 492nd Squadron in August 1944 with 293 hours on B-24s, was one of them. Writing of his first flight years later, Fritsche said: "As newly trained bomber pilots, most of us had never made an actual instrument let down, nor had we ever been in a storm cloud. On 14 August 1944 I made my first trip to China as a co-pilot so I could learn the route. The Hump was 'asleep', and we just had a few fair weather clouds to pass. On the next flight I took my own crew, and when I approached the Burma foothills I saw a solid line of black thunderheads reaching thousands of feet into the air. My last time in a Link trainer had been in April, so I had to make a couple of circles to build up my courage. I knew I couldn't stay there forever, so I headed straight into the boiling mass. Somehow I got through and when I came out on the other side, I saw a buddy of mine, on his way back in another B-24, circling to get up his courage. He radioed, 'If you can make it then I can too!' The Hump made you an instrument pilot or a casualty."[180]

From June 20th to the end of September, the 7th Group hauled gasoline to China almost every day. During this 102-day period, the Group made flights on 92 days, only stopping when weather over the Hump or in China proved insurmountable.[181] The squadrons started by sending two to four airplanes nearly every day on the run to Kunming. As the tempo of operations grew, the daily number went to an average of 18 planes a day. This was only possible because of

The windshield ices up at high altitude on a flight over the Hump. (Mel Rappaport via Jim Augustus)

the new crews that continued to arrive during July and August. For the first time in the war, the squadrons had their full complement of combat crews and sometimes more. During September, the Group had an average of 96 crews assigned and 80 available for operations.[182] In addition, the Group received more B-24s, giving the squadrons an average of 16 aircraft. The squadrons typically flew more than 100 round trips to China in a month, carrying 150,000 gallons or more of aviation gasoline. A healthy competition developed to see

Flying over the mountains between Kunming and Liuchow. The dangers didn't end after crossing the Hump. (Mel Rappaport via Jim Augustus)

who could carry the most fuel or make the most trips in the month. The 436th Squadron led the Group in the number of round trips and the amount of gasoline delivered. During September—the last month of the gas hauling operation—the 436th flew 156 round trips, carrying 234,000 gallons of aviation gas.[183]

Not surprisingly, there were accidents and losses. Taking off and landing a heavily-laden B-24 was not easy. The crushed-rock airfields in China cut up new tires after only a few landings. Several airplanes were written off on take-off or landing when the nose gear or main landing gear collapsed. The Group sent a small maintenance team to Kunming and had B-24s carry extra tires on their gasoline runs. The fields at Tezgaon and Kurmitola also had their share of accidents. On July 29, 1944, Lt. Tesh and his crew with the 436th Squadron had a narrow escape. Taking off from Tezgaon, the left tire blew and then the No.2 engine had a runaway prop and had to be feathered. Coming back to land, the left landing gear collapsed as the B-24 was rolling down the runway, causing it to swerve off to the left and catch fire. Fortunately, the crew made it out safely with only minor burns before the bomber was engulfed in flames. In August, Lt.Charles Mueth saved his B-24 and crew through a superb display of flying ability. On a regular flight to China on August 23rd, when Mueth's airplane was flying west of Imphal, the No. 4 engine had to be feathered due to a loss of oil. Mueth jettisoned his bomb bay fuel tanks and turned toward base, only to have the No. 2 engine start emitting smoke and oil. Mueth feathered this engine as well, brought his airplane back to Kurmitola on two engines, and made a perfect landing. For his exceptional airmanship, Mueth was later awarded an Oak Leaf Cluster to his DFC. A few weeks later, on September 18th, 2nd Lt. Edwin Eanes was taking off from Kunming when the nose gear on his B-24 collapsed. In the ensuing crash, the top turret collapsed and fell down on the navigator, 2nd Lt. Henry Shepard, and the radio operator, T/Sgt. Salvatore Maino, killing them.[184]

In the roughly 3 ½ months the 7th Group spent hauling gas to China, the Group lost 14 aircraft along the route, in addition to several more aircraft written off in landing or take-off accidents.[185] This was double the number of airplanes the Group had lost since it became part of the Strategic Air Force the previous December. In most cases, the crews bailed out safely to be rescued, sometimes after a trip of several days or weeks to get back to an air base, but others were less fortunate, 31 men losing their lives in these crashes. The 492nd Squadron suffered the most, losing six aircraft over the Hump route. The 9th and 436th lost four each; by chance, or luck, the 493rd didn't lose an airplane. The causes were various— fuel exhaustion, severe icing, mechanical problems, and engine failure, among them—but the accidents came with regularity, the Group losing two aircraft in June, five in July, five in August, and two in September.

The loss of any crew was always painful, but the death of a long-serving member of the Group was often worse. T/Sgt. Maino's loss hit the 436th Squadron's older crews particularly hard. Maino was a veteran with more than 400 combat hours,

A 436th Squadron B-24J unloading gasoline at Kunming in September 1944. (USAF)

yet was still flying, despite the arrival of newer crews. The older crews felt they, too, would run out of luck if they kept on flying. The Group still lacked a clear policy on rotation and the lack of one created, at least in the 436th Squadron, a "severe and dangerous morale problem". The Squadron history for September recorded the strong feelings on the issue, stating:

Taking off from Tezgaon on September 28, 1944, Lt. James L. Nemecek, 436th Bomb Squadron Operations Officer, had his left tire blow out on take-off. His B-24 slewed off the runway to the left, where the left landing gear collapsed. Fortunately no one was injured." (SU-Bomb-436-HI-Sept 1944, Albert F. Simpson Historical Research Center, Air Force Historical Research Agency, Maxwell AFB, AL)

"What we need and need immediately if we are to obtain the high level of morale necessary for combat work, is a definite policy as to the number of combat missions, or combat hours a man has to fly before he is returned to the zone of the interior. Within reason it makes little difference whether it be 350 hours or 550 hours, or, in terms of the number of missions, 40 or 60. What is needed is a goal, something to strive for, simply something definite, and last but not least, a policy that is uniform and common to all units operating in the theater."[186]

For the ground crews the situation was more complicated, as they had no standard to strive for, like the number of flying hours or missions completed in order to earn rotation home, nor did they have the same prospects of promotion. The Table of Organization dictated the allowed ranks for each department. To compound the problem, anyone designated for rotation to the zone of the interior was for some reason frozen in grade.[187] Despite these frustrations, all the maintenance and ground crews took great pride in their squadrons and in ensuring that their aircraft remained operational.

Hauling gasoline to China provided few opportunities for training for the Group's principal mission: bombing. The 7th Group apparently lacked a formal training policy. The training provided was deemed "spotty" in the view of an officer sent to evaluate the Group's training practices.[188] Training was done at the squadron level, and during this period almost all training was done through lectures. All the squadrons kept up a regular series of lectures on operational topics, principally aircraft recognition and gunnery, but also on targets in Burma and navigation, preparing for the day when they would return to combat operations. With every plane devoted to hauling

The 492nd Bomb Squadron's hardstand area at Tezgaon. The veteran B-24J, "Jungle Jig" sits on the right." (Courtesy Jim Augustus)

gas and maintenance crews working flat out, it was difficult to find time or an airplane for practice missions. This was a bigger burden on the newer combat crews, who arrived after the 7th Group had stopped flying bombing missions to haul gasoline. Having trained for combat in the United States, they arrived in the CBI to become, effectively, transport pilots. The new pilots and navigators did gain valuable experience flying over the Hump, but not in the skills they would need in combat. The pilots had a problem, in that the gas runs gave them little opportunity to practice formation flying, though a few of the squadrons tried to put in place a modicum of formation practice. The 9th Squadron tried to deal with this by having planes leaving for China take-off in sequence to practice joining up after take-off, one airplane acting as the leader while it circled the field and the others getting into formation for a brief time before heading individually to China.[189] But flying in formation used up more gas than flying individually, and gas was precious, so planes flew the Hump on their own. And it was a lot to ask a new pilot fresh from the United States to fly formation in a heavily overloaded B-24. Gunners were somewhat more fortunate. The 7th Group instituted a Group-wide gunnery training program involving an intensive ground school course and then a final exam during an operational flight when instructors would come along to test a gunner's ability to clear malfunctions correctly and quickly. However, there was little practice in aerial firing.[190] But for the bombardiers, with their highly specialized skills that had to be continuously honed to be maintained, there was no substitute for actual practice. Morale for the bombardiers in the Group, who had little to do apart from attending lectures, reached an all-time low toward the end of the monsoon. Despite much pleading from the bombardiers, no airplanes were made available for bombing practice and there were few bombing training devices to practice on.

The gas hauling operation finally came to an official end on October 1, 1944. With the end of the monsoon, the 7th Group returned to bombing and the Strategic Air Force. In the course of its gas hauling missions, the Group carried more than two million gallons of aviation gasoline to China, in addition to 800 P-40 drop tanks and 45,000 pounds of freight.[191] Commendations came in from Maj. Gens. Chennault, Stratemeyer, and Davidson, and from General Hap Arnold in Washington. When the 7th Group passed the million-gallon mark in August, General Arnold sent his thanks, saying: "My extreme appreciation goes to the heavy bombers of the Tenth Air Force for the outstanding job performed by them in August...Although they must consider this assignment a dull and thankless one, circumstances required it, and they have performed it as successfully as any combat job. It is my hope that these same heavies can return soon to the mission for which they were designed."[192] In expressing his own gratitude, Maj. Gen. Stratemeyer noted his long connection with the 7th Bombardment Group, saying: "As you know I at one time had the pleasure and gratification of commanding the 7th Group. Ever since that time I have paid personal attention to its exploits, invariably with a deep sense of satisfaction at the results. It may be hard for you and your personnel to realize the importance of the role you have been playing most recently. However, I assure you that without exception your work in the past few weeks has been the most important assignment in the history of your Group, an assignment which you have performed with outstanding success."[193]

While the aviation gasoline the 7th Group delivered to the Fourteenth Air Force was vital to its ability to continue flying combat missions, air power alone could not make up for the weak state of the Chinese Army, as General Stilwell had predicted. Poorly trained, poorly equipped, and often poorly led, the Chinese forces defending Chennault's airfields failed to stand up to the Japanese onslaught, despite a number of hard-fought defensive battles. In some cases, the Generalissimo refused to give supplies to some of the Chinese commanders in eastern China, not wishing to arm potential political rivals.[194] On August 8th, the city and airfield at Hengyang, one of the Fourteenth Air Force's most important bases, fell to the Japanese. The *Ichi-Go* offensive continued into the fall, with more airfields falling one after another. But for the 7th Bombardment Group, it was back to Burma.

CHAPTER SEVEN

BACK TO BOMBING

A New Plan for Burma

When the 7th Bombardment Group ceased bombing after the mission on June 10, 1944, the Allied armies in Burma were engaged in two critical battles at Imphal and Myitkyina. By October, when the 7th Group returned to the Strategic Air Force and bombing, these battles had been won, completely changing the strategic position for the Allies and the Japanese. In the Arakan, British and Indian troops had soundly beaten back the Japanese forces mobilized for Operation *Ha-Go*. Concentrating in a strongly-held defensive position and relying on air supply to replace the roads the Japanese had cut, the British forces held firm and did not retreat as the Japanese had expected them to. "For the first time", Field Marshal Sir William Slim, then 14th Army Commander, wrote in his memoir of the campaign, "a British force met, held and decisively defeated a major Japanese attack...British and Indian soldiers had proved themselves, man for man, the masters of the best the Japanese could bring against them..."[1] The same pattern, but on a much larger scale, repeated itself in the battle for Imphal. The Japanese *15th Army* threw three divisions into the attack on Imphal to destroy the base and the British and Indian troops protecting it. Lt. Gen. Mutaguchi, *15th Army* commander, expected the campaign to last three weeks; it went on for four months. The Japanese divisions succeeded in cutting off the road linking Imphal with its sources of supply in Assam, but once again, air supply made up the difference. The Japanese soldiers hammered at the gates of Imphal from early March to early July, only to withdraw in total exhaustion in the greatest defeat the Japanese Army had ever experienced up to that time. The *15th Army*, having sustained over 55,000 casualties, was a shattered force. Relentlessly pursuing the retreating Japanese through the monsoon rains, the 14th Army broke out of the mountain barrier along the Burma-India border and reached the Chindwin River, the last natural barrier before Burma's central plain, at the end of August. Imphal was the decisive battle of the war in Burma. Lt. Gen. Slim's overwhelming victory against the *15th Army* "...meant that Central Burma was open to him, and a campaign to retake Burma overland, which the British high command had flinched from for two years, became a real possibility."[2]

In the final months of the war in Burma, the Strategic Air Force made a concerted effort against Japanese lines of communication. The 7th Bomb Group would devote many missions to attacks on railroad bridges. (3A-37665, RG 342FH, NARA)

In the northeastern front, Stilwell's combined Chinese, American, and British force in the Northern Combat Area Command had also broken through the mountain barriers to stand at the northern end of Burma's central plain. Stilwell's Chinese and American troops had finally captured the key town of Myitkyina after a 2 ½ month siege. Myitkyina, on the banks of the Irrawaddy River, lay at the head of the rail line to Mandalay and Rangoon. From the town, a road went south to Lashio, on the Burma-China border. In capturing the airfield at Myitkyina, Stilwell's forces eliminated the threat to transports flying over the Hump. The Allies now had not only a new base for moving supplies through to China along the road from Ledo, but a new shorter and safer route over the Hump. Air Transport Command airplanes could fly at lower altitudes, carrying greater loads without risk of interception.[3]

The Allies now had opportunities hardly considered possible six months previously. Admiral Lord Louis Mountbatten's directives from the Combined Chiefs of Staff had only called for limited advances against the Japanese in northern Burma. As the extent of the Japanese defeat at Imphal became evident and with the capture of Myitkyina, the question confronting the Combined Chiefs of Staff was how best to take advantage of this new development and how far to push ahead into Burma. After some months of discussion and debate, a new directive for Mountbatten came out of the Octagon Conference at Quebec, where the Combined Chiefs of Staff met with Prime Minister Churchill and President Roosevelt. For the first time, the stated objective of South East Asia Command was the recapture of all of Burma, to be achieved through two main operations: Operation "Capital" and Operation "Dracula". A third, smaller operation called for clearing the Japanese Army from the Arakan. "Capital" called for an advance into central Burma in three phases to push the Japanese armies back to a position where they could no longer threaten the air staging post building at Myitkyina, nor the overland route to China. The ultimate goal of "Capital" was to establish a line running from Lashio to Mandalay, using the 14th Army's advance beyond the Chindwin and the Northern Combat Area Command forces driving southward, with this line to be achieved by the early 1945. "Dracula" called for an amphibious invasion, tentatively scheduled for March 1945, to capture Rangoon and push north to meet up with the Allied forces in central Burma, cutting the *Burma Area Army*'s supply lines and making the Japanese position in Burma untenable. Due to a shortage of resources "Dracula" was postponed until the fall of 1945, but plans for "Capital" went ahead.[4]

The Japanese, too, revised their strategy for Burma. With the loss of the Mariana Islands in June, Japan came within range of the B-29 long-range bombers that were sure to be based there. It was likely that the next major American offensive would be against the Philippines. Loss of the Philippines would threaten Japan's lifeline to Southeast Asia and its vital raw materials. The Japanese *Imperial General Headquarters* decided to prepare for the defense of the Philippine-Formosa-Okinawa-Japan area, concentrating maximum resources in the Philippines for a decisive battle against American forces. Unable to replace the losses inflicted on the *Burma Area Army* during its recent offensives, *Imperial General Headquarters* scaled back *Burma Area Army*'s plans to match its limited resources. The revised plan called for the army in Burma to maintain its hold on the strategic areas of southern Burma that were critical to the army's maintenance, namely the oil fields at Yenangyaung and the areas of rice production in the Irrawaddy River delta. *Burma Area Army* was to defend a line close to that specified for the Allied armies in Operation "Capital", stretching from Lashio through Mandalay to the oil fields. Toward the end of 1944, the Japanese Army and Army Air Forces units in Burma were told that they were effectively on their own; they could expect no more support from Japan.[5]

By this point in the war, the Allied air forces in India held an overwhelming advantage over the Japanese Army Air Force. In October 1944, Eastern Air Command had over 1,000 airplanes available in its Army Air Forces and Royal Air Force squadrons, including 491 fighters, 102 heavy bombers, and

83 medium bombers.[6] In contrast, the Japanese *5th Hikōshidan* had an estimated 42 aircraft in upper Burma and 69 aircraft in lower Burma, the majority Ki-43 Oscar fighters; an additional 108 aircraft, again mostly fighters, were based in Thailand, French Indochina, and Malaya.[7] Although there were occasional interceptions, Allied air superiority over Burma would never be seriously challenged. After the American invasion of the Philippines in October 1944 and U.S. Navy carrier strikes on French Indochina in early 1945, the Japanese Army Air Force withdrew more of its fighter *Sentai* from the Burma front, enabling the Allies to establish what amounted to aerial supremacy over Burma and Thailand. This greatly lowered the risk for Allied bombers who could, from the beginning of 1945, roam over their assigned area more or less at will.

During the monsoon period, there had been several changes within Eastern Air Command and the Strategic Air Force. Maj. Gen. Stratemeyer decided to split the 3rd Tactical Air Force into two separate commands: one for the northern front to support the Northern Combat Area Command and one to support the 14th Army for the advances into central

Air Commodore F.J.W. Mellersh, Air Commander, Strategic Air Force, June 1944-June 1945. (Via the Author)

Burma and the Arakan.[8] Accordingly, on June 20, 1944, the Tenth Air Force was reactivated as a tactical command and assigned all Army Air Forces fighter and medium bomber units, the 12th Bombardment Group leaving the Strategic Air Force for the Tenth. Maj. Gen. Davidson gave up command of the Strategic Air Force to devote all his time to the Tenth. Air Commodore (Air Cdre) F.J.W. Mellersh, Royal Air Force, who had been Davidson's Deputy Air Commander, took over as Air Commander, Strategic Air Force. The Royal Air Force's No. 231 Group became an all-Liberator bomber force when the last two RAF Wellington squadrons were withdrawn to convert to the Liberator. This gave the Strategic Air Force five squadrons of Liberators (Nos. 99, 159, 215, 355, and 356) in the bomber role, each equipped with the Liberator B. Mk. VI (equivalent to the Army Air Forces' B-24J), adding approximately 80 bombers to the heavy bomber force. With the rapid decline in Japanese air power reducing the chances of interception, the Strategic Air Force shifted strategic bombing, with the exception of mine laying, to daylight instead of night operations (this affected the RAF Liberator squadrons more than the 7th Bombardment Group).[9] This had the advantage of making it easier to pick out smaller targets the bombers would be going after in the months to come.

On October 18, 1944, Eastern Air Command issued Operational Directive No. 16 to the Strategic Air Force, covering its mission, objectives, and new area of operations. In line with the overall mission for South East Asia Command, the Strategic Air Force was to contribute to the "...destruction and expulsion of all Japanese forces at earliest date from Burma..."[10] The Directive laid out the following objectives in order of priority:

1. Naval and merchant vessels as targets of opportunity.
2. Communications into and within Burma, with continued sustained attacks against the BANGKOK/PEGU RAILWAY and PARALLEL RAILWAY in order to render them inoperable to the maximum extent, paying particular attention to the destruction of locomotives and rolling stock. Continued air attacks against *Chiengrai/Kentung* lines of communication, giving particular attention to the BAN DARA BRIDGE on the BANGKOK/LAMPANG RAIL ROAD and other critical points along the line.
3. Enemy air forces and installations.
4. Ports and shipping facilities.
5. Depots, dumps, and other military administrative facilities.
6. Mine laying operations as laid down by Eastern Air Command from time to time.[11]

As the tactical air forces covering the advance of the Allied armies into central Burma would now cover targets in this area, the Strategic Air Force's area of responsibility was moved eastward to cover Burma's eastern border with Thailand, Thailand itself, and Malaya; later, Rangoon and the delta area were added back. This shift allowed the Strategic Air Force to concentrate on the disruption of the railroad lines leading into Burma from Thailand and Malaya. With the flow of supplies from Japan sharply reduced, *Burma Area Army* had to rely on stocks in other parts of Southeast Asia. By building up the capacity of the railroad line running from Bangkok north to Chiengmai and using trucks to carry supplies into Burma, as well as herculean repair efforts along the Burma-Thailand railroad and the rail lines within Burma, the Japanese had increased the flow of supplies into Burma from 70,000 tons during the first half of 1944 to 113,000 tons during the second half.[12] The goal of the Strategic Air Force was to cut off this flow to the greatest extent possible. The effort to achieve this would occupy the 7th Bombardment Group for much of its remaining time in combat.

Back to Bombing

A mobile bombing trainer 7th Bomb Group bombardiers used to brush up their skills after returning to bombing operations in October 1944. (7th Bombardment Group (H) Historical Foundation, USAFA McDermott Library)

The 7th Bombardment Group's return to bombing operations was not as smooth as the Group would have liked, nor as effective as higher command expected. The announcement that the Group would return to its old bases and normal operations brought "...rejoicing among the old men and a tinge of excitement among the new..."[13] The squadrons spent the first week to ten days of October moving back to Madhaganj and Pandaveswar, the B-24s performing a reverse shuttle, flying twice a day loaded with equipment. The older crews were glad to be back "home", while the newer crews found the dryer weather on the plain a refreshing change from the humidity of Tezgaon and Kurmitola. It took several days for the squadron departments to set up again and for the B-24s to be made combat-ready with their belly turrets reinstalled. The squadrons then began training intensively to regain their "lost skills".[14]

When the Group began hauling gasoline to China, the Group staff had warned Maj. Gen. Davidson that the combat crews would have little opportunity to practice their basic combat skills—particularly formation flying—and would need a period of training before going back into combat. This was apparently promised, so the Group did not divert airplanes from hauling gas to practicing formation flying.[15] The influx of new crews between May and September compounded the training problem; during that time, the Group received 99 new crews. With so many older crews rotating back to the U.S., the overall level of experience, not surprisingly, declined. When the training program began in early October, the Group had only 18 experienced combat crews.[16] The newer pilots had spent little time flying in formation; the navigators had little experience in navigating to a precise schedule, lining up for a bombing run, or identifying targets; the gunners had next to no aerial gunnery; and the newer bombardiers had not dropped a bomb since leaving the U.S.[17]

The air crew training program concentrated on formation practice. The pilots started flying in elements of three airplanes, moving up to formations of six, practicing assembly, position, and changing lead airplane, as well as assembly into defensive formations. As the formation flying improved, the squadrons added training for the bombardiers and gunners. The Group had one bombing range where the bombardiers could practice, but the bombing altitude was limited to 10,000 feet due to the proximity of a nearby village. For experience at bombing from higher altitudes, the squadrons resorted to flying practice missions to nearby towns and cities in India where the bombardiers made dry runs on a selected target. This was, however, no substitute for real practice. The practice bombing missions were flown first with one, then with two and three elements, giving more practice in formation flying. Some, but not all of the gunners went on flights out over the Bay of Bengal using two B-24s. One airplane would fly at low altitude, casting a shadow on the sea below, while the other airplane made passes, allowing the gunners to fire at the shadow to practice deflection shooting. Ground training focused on operational procedures and intelligence on targets in Burma and Thailand. Bombardiers, navigators, and gunners had more training in their own specialties. The Group finally acquired working bombing trainers for the bombardiers, while the navigators concentrated on building target identification skills using photographs of targets the Group had bombed previously.[18]

The 7th Bomb Group's Gunnery School, where gunners could practice in the turrets they would operate in the B-24s they flew. (GP-7-HI(Bomb) May 1945, Albert F. Simpson Historical Research Center, Air Force Historical Research Agency, Maxwell AFB, AL)

The war intervened before the squadrons could complete their training. On October 18, 1944, the Strategic Air Force ordered the 7th Group to accompany 12 Liberators from No.231 Group in a joint attack on the newly-built jetties at the port of Moulmein the next day, October 19th. That day, the Group sent 24 aircraft, one returning because of engine failure. Col. Dodson flew with the 436th Squadron as copilot in Lt. Mueth's airplane. The Group's formation joined the RAF Liberators over the Bay of Bengal and proceeded to the target. The bombing was decidedly mixed. The 492nd Squadron did best, putting all its bombs on the target and destroying the buildings alongside the jetty and the nearby railroad tracks. The 493rd Squadron's bombs hit slightly south and to the east, but destroyed the railroad station and damaged the railroad yards. As the lead element in the 9th Squadron approached Moulmein, a cloud obscured the target. The lead bombardier picked up what he thought was the correct aiming point, but this turned out to be a large rice and saw mill 2,000 yards from the jetties. The 9th Squadron demolished the mill, but it was the wrong target. The 436th had problems as well, swinging to the left of the target due to the clouds and missing the target area completely.[19]

The Strategic Air Force had the bombers go back to the Moulmein jetties on October 22nd. On this mission, 24 B-24s from the 9th, 492nd, and 493rd Squadrons joined 12 Liberators from No. 355 Squadron, RAF. The 9th Squadron led the Group. The lead bombardier, who had missed the target three days before, dropped his bombs directly on the target from 8,000 feet. The other two squadrons followed suit, and although smoke from the 9th Squadron's bombs and those from the RAF Liberators partly obscured the target, they dropped their bombs very close to the target area, hitting one of the jetties squarely. Five minutes after leaving the target, eight to ten Japanese fighters attacked the Group's formation. These were Ki-43 Oscars from the *64th Sentai* and a number of new Type 4 fighters (Ki-84 Frank) from the newly re-equipped *50th Sentai* (the B-24 crews reported receiving fire from the wing

The Moulmein railroad jetties under attack on October 22, 1944. (7th Bombardment Group (H) Historical Foundation, USAFA McDermott Library)

guns of several fighters, corroborating the presence of the Ki-84s, equipped with two 20mm cannon in the wings). The attacks were well coordinated and pressed home, almost all attacks coming from the front quarter from 10 o'clock to 2 o'clock. Over the next half hour, the fighters made 30 to 40 passes against the formation, sometimes flying within 30 or 40 yards of the bombers. The 9th Squadron had two planes damaged and two men wounded, but claimed one fighter shot down. Flying a new defensive formation, the 492nd suffered

A 7th Bomb Group B-24 flying over clouds in the target area. (7th Bombardment Group (H) Historical Foundation, USAFA McDermott Library)

no damage, but the 493rd Squadron was hit hard. One of the enemy fighter passes set the No. 2 engine on Lt. Donald Blair's aircraft on fire. He pulled out of the formation and fell away to the left. His airplane was last seen heading toward clouds below with a fighter in pursuit. This fighter was one of the *64th Sentai*'s Oscars; at least two other fighters joined him in shooting down Blair's B-24, though Blair's gunners hit Cpl. Yamaguchi's fighter, sending it off smoking before they went down. Blair and his crew did not survive the crash.[20]

Sgt. Kato of the *64th Sentai* attacked one of the 493rd's B-24s, later describing this bomber as one of the lead aircraft. Other pilots watching Kato's attack saw the bomber swing away and collide with another B-24, both crashing. Maj. Jack Bradford, the squadron commander, was flying in the slot position that day when the 493rd formation came under attack. No one in the other airplanes noticed Bradford's B-24 getting hit, but Bradford's airplane slid over underneath the number three airplane in the element, remaining about 30 feet below. He then lost a bit of altitude and appeared to be attempting to swing back to the right to take up the slot position again. In doing so, the vertical stabilizer on his airplane hit the bomb bay area of Lt. Arthur Bodmer's B-24. Bodmer's No. 3 and No. 4 engines then cut off Bradford's tail section just behind the waist gun positions. Both airplanes spiraled down to crash in the sea below; both crews were killed. One of the remaining two airplanes in the 493rd Squadron's formation was damaged in the attack. The Group lost one airplane shot down, two in a mid-air collision, and had three damaged against one fighter claimed shot down, though none appear to have been lost. Observers on the mission judged the gunnery to be very poor.[21] Three days later, Capt. William Hillman, Jr. moved over from the 436th Squadron to take command of the 493rd.[22]

Lt. David Young was leading the 493rd that day and recorded the events of the mission in his diary when he returned to Panda:

> The 'Ninth" was supposed to bomb from 8,000' but went down to 7,000'. I was down to 7200' but climbed back up & Hart [Young's bombardier] really laid those bombs on them. The ack-ack was nothing to worry about so came out all together. Dropped at 1200.
>
> Just as I caught up with the Ninth I saw the pea shooters. Counted ten right off and then saw the first one break and come in. that was at about 1210 and the fun really started. Blair in #54 was hit first on about the second pass made. His #2 engines was really burning. He broke under me to the left and headed for a cloud bank.
>
> While that was going on Maj. Bradford either got hit or was crippled. He was flying the slot, went down and over to the left under Bodmer in #49 & pulled up under his plane. The Maj.'s vertical stabilizers (#45) rammed up into #49's bomb bay. The planes came apart after the props on #49 chewed the rear section from #45 at the waist windows. Both planes crashed straight into the bay. Four chutes blossomed from one plane. Hill saw all this happen. I never saw anything—too busy flying. I got a bullet hole in #4 engine cowling % one hole in the right wing root, damn close to Bob.
>
> Then we took an explosive shell just to the right rear of the top turret, fired from high & behind. The slug went out about a foot behind me. Boy was that a concussion, damn near blew me out of the seat. It shot out some electric lines and an oxygen line. Blew shrapnel all over the flight deck along with kapok [*sic*] lining. One other bullet went through the left wing. Well, that was 3 out of 5 which is no good! Went around the end of Pagoda Point and then home.

That stupid Major Kyes with the Ninth [the 9th Squadron's commander] started climbing during the attack and made us sitting ducks. Should've dropped altitude & gone like hell.

So Hill [Lt. Hill] and I slimmed out our gas and made it back O.K. No Bombay tanks made for calling it close. Hill landed at Calcutta to refuel and I don't know what happened to Blair, maybe he ditched. Take off at 0610 and killed the engines at 1715.[23]

On October 25th, the 436th and 492nd Squadrons bombed the rail yards at Paliek, near Ye-u, with the yards at Ye-u the secondary target. The planned initial approach went along the axis of the railroad, but an intervening cloud caused the 436th to make its attack at a 45° angle to the target, putting most of its bombs in the designated area. The 492nd found a cloud as it came in on the target. Deciding its approach was better aimed at the secondary target, the Squadron went for that, but its bombs hit slightly northeast of the aiming point, with only fair results. It was clear from these three missions that the Group needed more practice.[24]

The Group asked the Strategic Air Force for a list of lightly defended targets the squadrons could use for practice. The Group Operations staff selected three targets in Burma from a list the Strategic Air Force provided that would be relatively safe from fighter interception, would likely expose the new crews to some anti-aircraft fire, and would be small and difficult targets for the bombardiers and navigators to identify in time to make an accurate bombing run.[25] These missions would also give the newer pilots more practice in formation flying with loaded aircraft and in reassembling the Group after the bomb run. The first practice target was the Prome Dump No.6 at Sinde, just across the Irrawaddy River from the town of Prome. As intended, the target was difficult to pick out from the surrounding countryside. Broken clouds over the target area made it all but impossible to identify. The 9th and 493rd Squadrons went on this mission on October 25th. The formation leader missed the initial point, requiring a change in the bomb run. Most bombs missed the target area by 2,000 yards. On October 27th, the second practice mission went to Pakkoku, farther up the Irrawaddy toward Mandalay. This time, the 436rd and 492nd Squadrons took their turn. The results were unfortunately little better, the bombing again being judged unsatisfactory. The 9th and 493rd Squadrons had the third practice mission, to the supply dumps at Taungup. By design, the initial point and the target were difficult to identify. The 9th Squadron did well, getting an excellent pattern in the target area, but the 493rd Squadron's bombing was off, striking only the southwest edge of the target.[26]

Maj. Gen. Stratemeyer, who took a great deal of pride and interest in the 7th Group that he had once commanded, was apparently not pleased with the Group's recent performance. At a meeting on October 30, 1944, with Brig. Gen. Charles Stone, Chief of Staff of Eastern Air Command, and Brig. Gen. Alvin Luedecke, Assistant Chief for Operations, Plans, and Training for the Army Air Forces, India-Burma Sector, both of whom had served under Stratemeyer in the prewar 7th Bombardment Group, Stratemeyer brought up the 7th Group's poor bombing performance. Though it does not seem that Col. Dobson was entirely to blame for the situation (the 7th Group did not receive the training time it thought it needed), Stratemeyer, Stone, and Luedecke decided the 7th Group needed a new commander.[27] Stratemeyer proposed that Col. Harvey Alness take over from Dobson. Col Alness was another prewar 7th Group alumnus who had served as a junior lieutenant under Stratemeyer. He was then serving as Chief of Operations, Army Air Forces, India-Burma Sector. Stratemeyer called Maj. Gen. Davidson to a meeting the next day with Generals Stone and Luedecke and Col. Alness. At the meeting, Davidson was told that Alness was taking over command of the 7th Bombardment Group. Stratemeyer told Alness that "...I wanted the Group to be able to fly formation, to bomb, to fly on instruments, and to take-off and land at night", skills he apparently believed the Group was lacking.[28] Lt. Col. William Delahay was apparently appointed Acting Group Commander until Col. Alness arrived.

The Ban Dara Bridge under attack on November 1, 1944. One airplane from each of the 7th Bomb Group's squadrons went out on the mission. (File 825.08, Albert F. Simpson Historical Research Center, Air Force Historical Research Agency, Maxwell AFB, AL)

After the initial meeting with Stratemeyer and Luedecke and the decision to remove Col. Dobson as Group commander, Brig. Gen. Stone ordered Brig. Gen. Ray Clark, Air Inspector, Army Air Forces, India-Burma Sector to immediately conduct

One of the B-24s in the attack on the Ban Dara Bridge banks away after dropping a 1,000-pound bomb. (3A-37559, RG 342FH, NARA)

"...a thorough tactical, administrative and technical investigation..." of the 7th Bombardment Group to determine why the Group's combat and training missions had not come up to par.[29] Clark held three days of meetings with the Group Operations staff, all the squadron commanders, and squadron operations staff. Clark reviewed with them the recent combat and practice missions and the Group's training practices. Clark's inspection revealed that much of the problem was simply the Group's lack of proper training. The influx of new crews only exacerbated the training problem, as had the Group's preoccupation with the gas hauling mission. Clark found a lack of proper training facilities, equipment, and ranges. And in fairness, after the squadrons returned to their original bases the demands of war cut short the training period. Clark concluded that the Group's performance during October was, on balance, probably the best that could have been expected given the inexperience of most of the combat crews. He did believe, however, that the Group had been too informal in its training regime. While the Group covered a broad number of topics through its ground classes and lectures, a separate but concurrent report on the Group's training concluded that the ground instruction "...was unsystematic and did not follow any overall plan."[30] Neither the Group nor the squadrons had formally written guidelines for training pilots, bombardiers, navigators, or gunners. This same report criticized the attitude that "...there was no time for training...", as it interfered with all training efforts. Clark recommended that the Group produce written directives and standard training requirements for all aspects of combat crew training.[31] To be effective, training had to be structured, with clear standards and objectives, and pursued continuously, even in difficult circumstances.

Ironically, given the intense review and questioning of the 7th Group's performance, Col. Alness arrived a few days after the Group had performed one of its most difficult and rewarding missions. This was the destruction of the Ban Dara Bridge on the Bangkok-Chiengmai railroad line. Lying 284 miles north of Bangkok, the Ban Dara Bridge was the most important bridge on this railroad line that carried supplies north to Chiengmai and by truck into Burma. Built well before the war, the bridge was 780 feet long, with two spans of 240 feet each and a central span of 300 feet, all resting on two large concrete pillars. One pillar, placed in the middle of the Nan River, was the key to the bridge's destruction. If it could be destroyed, the central span and one of the side spans would collapse into the river. The pillar—an estimated 25 feet high and 30 feet wide—presented a difficult target, but the bridge's destruction would completely disrupt the flow of supplies going north. In late October, Air Cdre Mellersh, Air Commander, Strategic Air Force, called Lt. Col. William Delahay and Maj. Richard Henning, Group Operations Officer, to a meeting at his headquarters near Calcutta. Mellersh assigned the target to the 7th Group and told Delahay and Henning how important it was to knock it out.[32] Mellersh left the tactics up to them. Delahay and Henning planned two missions: the first mission had four airplanes attacking the bridge at low level just at dusk, flying a carefully planned route to achieve surprise; the second mission, in case the first failed to knock the bridge down, called for 36 airplanes to bomb the bridge from high altitude. The Group, and most likely the

The Ban Dara Bridge spans in the river following Lt. James Nemecek's final attack with the last of his bombs. (File 825.08, Albert F. Simpson Historical Research Center, Air Force Historical Research Agency, Maxwell AFB, AL)

Captain James Nemecek in January 1945, after his promotion to Captain. (SQ-Bomb-436-HI January 1945, Albert F. Simpson Historical Research Center, Air Force Historical Research Agency, Maxwell AFB, AL)

squadron operations staff, made a careful study of the bridge. They had a model built to determine the best approaches at low altitude. The operations staff took photographs to show what the bridge would look like at an altitude of 300 feet from different approaches. These photos were handed to the bombardiers at the briefing and taken with them on the mission.[33]

Each of the Group's four squadrons was requested to send one airplane. As the mission was considered dangerous, a call went out for volunteers. The four airplanes began taking off at 1030 the morning of November 1, 1944, each armed with five 1,000-pound bombs. Arriving over the bridge about an hour before sunset, the four bombers started their individual runs, heading almost due north on a course 20 to 30 degrees off the axis of the bridge. The attack continued for half an hour. The plan called for each airplane to drop one bomb on each run, going into a left hand pattern to come in again, in succession. Lt. Edward Thielson from the 9th Squadron and Lt. Delbert Anthony from the 492nd dropped their bombs, but missed the bridge. Capt. Hillman from the 493rd dropped two bombs from 100 feet above the bridge on his first run. One went into the river alongside and one detonated in the girder structure near the central pillar. On his second run, ground fire hit Hillman's airplane in the right side just behind the instrument panel, knocking out the electric circuits and all the instruments. The bombardier was planning to drop the 3rd and 4th bombs on this run, but hit the switch just as the electric circuits went out. Only the 3rd bomb dropped, hitting the river near the south end of the bridge. The ground fire was light but accurate. The B-24 gunners immediately started firing back, knocking out one machine gun position near the south end of the bridge. Hillman considered aborting his last run, but since the engines appeared to be working he went in again. The bombardier salvoed the 4th and 5th bombs, one hitting the bridge structure above the central pillar. Hillman flew back to Chittagong with his No. 4 engine stuck in high RPM for four hours and his No.3 engine throwing oil the entire time, but landed safely.[34]

It was now up to Lt. James Nemecek, Jr. of the 436th Squadron, flying with Capt. William Rector, an instrument flying instructor from Eastern Air Command who had volunteered to go on the mission as Nemecek's copilot. All the other airplanes had dropped their bombs and the Ban Dara Bridge was still standing. Nemecek's airplane had three bombs left. Nemecek, or his bombardier, decided to drop all three on their last run. Coming in on the bridge, machine gun fire from a position nearby shot out the bomber's hydraulic system and damaged the right side of the bomb bay, so that the bomb bay doors could not close. Lining up the key central pillar as his target, the bombardier let go his three bombs and scored a direct hit, demolishing the pillar and dropping the steel girder central span into the river. Nemecek circled the destroyed bridge so the crew could take photographs to confirm the damage. Capt. Rector flew the airplane back to Madhaganj and made a perfect landing at night, without brakes.[35] Commendations on the successful mission came in from Maj. Gens. Stratemeyer and Davidson and from Air Cdre Mellersh. A particularly heartfelt note of congratulations came from the Fourteenth Air Force's 69th Composite Wing and the 341st Bombardment Group, flying in support of the Chinese divisions fighting in southern China and on the Salween front. The message said: "We are shouting our cheers. Your Dara feat excellent. We have put 72 sorties on this target. The destruction at Dara is greatest accomplishment that could assist our efforts in these parts."[36] For their leadership and successful accomplishment of a hazardous mission, the four pilots were awarded the Silver Star.[37]

Col. Harvey Alness arrived to take command of the 7th Group on November 6, 1944. Alness's most important task was to bring the Group back up to the peak of combat efficiency. His arrival as the new Group commander coincided with a directive from Eastern Air Command ordering the entire Strategic Air Force to reduce operations and undertake a full scale training for all squadrons in the Force, Army Air

Forces, and Royal Air Force, who had switched to daylight missions. The directive called for attention to the following:

(i) Lead crews were to drop the maximum amount of bombs in order to bring their accuracy up to a high standard.

(ii) The remaining crews were to have the maximum amount of formation flying practice in order that the formations could bomb with the most effective pattern and accuracy.

(iii) All crews were to be capable of taking off and landing by night, particularly with loaded aircraft, and fly accurately on instruments.

(iv) The maximum amount of navigation and gunnery (cine camera gun) both in the air and on the ground was to be carried out.

(v) Squadron, Wing, and Force rendezvous with cross-countries were to be carried out and critiques were to be held after each practice in order to gain the maximum from those exercieses.[38]

The Strategic Air Force staggered the training schedule so that some squadrons would train while others continued flying combat missions, switching roles as a squadron completed the training program. In the 7th Bombardment Group, the 9th and 493rd Squadrons at Pandaveswar went back to training first from November 7th to November 22nd. The 436th and 492nd Squadrons at Madhaganj trained from November 22nd to December 5th. This second training program was more intensive than the training the squadrons had gone through the month before. The goal was to ensure that all crew members, but particularly the newer crews, from pilots to gunners, were "...thoroughly indoctrinated in the flying techniques peculiar to operations in this theater."[39] As the 436th Squadron's history commented: "...we must learn by constant practice, the art of working with other units on a much larger scale than has heretofore been possible. In addition to working with other units we ourselves need considerable experience in putting up 12 aircraft for a mission instead of the 3 or 6 plane missions we used in the past."[40] In addition to formation practice and a lot of low level work—a foretaste of the missions to come—the pilots spent time on night transition work and instrument flying. The bombardiers finally were given practice in high altitude bombing, synchronized by elements. Tragedy struck the 493rd Squadron during the training period. On the night of November 11, 1944, Lt. Edmund Powers was giving Lt. Walter South a night landing check flight, shooting night landings at Panda. On his second take-off, Powers braked and started raising his landing gear before he had cleared the runway. The plane settled back down on its nose, skidded off to the right, turned 180°, and broke up, killing Powers, South, and three other crew members.[41]

The ground school training was equally intensive. The Group finally obtained some working bombing trainers (several on hand had been missing their motors). These were made available to the bombardiers from 0800 to 1700 daily. Navigators brushed up their sextant skills, something the Group's previous training efforts had ignored. Flight engineers and radio operators had specialized courses twice a week, with written exams to test their knowledge, while gunners practiced working out turret mechanical problems and flexible gunnery at the Group gunnery school. There were additional lectures for crews on bail out procedure, navigation and bombing, map reading, and more gunnery.[42] In the middle of this second phase of training, Maj. Gen. Stratemeyer paid a visit to the 7th Group on November 21st, on the occasion of the Group's third anniversary overseas. Stratemeyer awarded medals to a large number of combat crews at a Group formation at Pandaveswar. Gathering the men together, he spoke of his days as commander of the 7th Bombardment Group in 1936-38 and reminded his listeners that "...the heavy bombardment tactics now in use in every theater were developed by the 7th Bomb Group back in '36 and '38."[43] The second period of training the 7th Group's squadrons undertook during November, combined with the experience of flying more

Major General George Stratemeyer awarding medals to men of the 436th Bomb Squadron on the occasion of the 7th Bomb Group's third anniversary overseas. (SU-Bomb-11-SU-PH, Albert F. Simpson Historical Research Center, Air Force Historical Research Agency, Maxwell AFB, AL)

combat missions during the month, apparently addressed the inadequacies that had emerged the month before. There were no further concerns about the Group's performance.

In addition to a new 7th Group commander in Col. Alness, there were other changes in squadron commands during October and November and more tragic accidents. In the 436th Squadron, Lt. Col. John Fitzwater, who had done an excellent job managing the influx of new crews and a new mission for the Squadron during the monsoon season, was transferred to Tenth Air Force Headquarters. Capt. David Brown, Operations Officer in the 492d Squadron, replaced him, but was tragically killed in the crash of the Group's PT-22 on November 29th, after less than four weeks in command. Brown was one of the most experienced pilots in the Group, having flown over 55 combat missions and over 500 combat hours. His loss was a blow, particularly as other experienced veterans continued to rotate back to the United States. Maj. Raymond Holsey, a veteran of two years on B-17s in the southwest Pacific with the Fifth Air Force, replaced him. Another crash took the life of Maj. Richard Henning, Group Operations Officer and former 436th Squadron commander, and another long-serving veteran of the 7th Group. Maj. William Kyes, commander of the 9th Squadron, was promoted to Lt. Colonel and moved to the Group to replace Henning. Capt. William Dabney, another combat veteran, replaced Kyes as 9th Squadron commander. Dabney had joined the Royal Air Force before America's entry into the war, later transferring to the 44th Bombardment Group in the Eighth Air Force. As a member of the 44th Group, Dabney flew on the famous August 1943 mission to Ploesti. At 22, he was one of the youngest squadron commanders in the Army Air Forces.[44]

These changes at the Group and Squadron level took place against a background of momentous changes in the China-Burma-India Theater command. The Japanese *Ichi-Go* offensive revealed a serious division in the command structure in China. Anxious to hold on to the Fourteenth Air Force's central and eastern China air bases to assist the war in the Pacific, the U.S. Joint Chiefs of Staff recommended that General Stilwell take command of all Chinese Army forces in China to stop the Japanese offensive. After initially accepting the proposal, Generalissimo Chiang Kai-shek changed his mind and demanded that Stilwell be recalled. This President Roosevelt agreed and Stilwell left China, and command of the China-Burma-India Theater, in mid-October. The War Department in Washington had apparently been considering splitting the CBI into two separate theaters, and with Stilwell's departure it became opportune to do so. Army Lt. Gen. Albert Wedemeyer took over as commander of the new China Theater and Chief of Staff to the Generalissimo on October 31, 1944. Four days previously, Lt. Gen. Daniel Sultan, Stilwell's Deputy Theater Commander, became commander of the new India-Burma Theater. Wedemeyer's mission was to provide support and advice to the Generalissimo and the Chinese armies fighting the Japanese and to continue air operations from bases in China. The India-Burma Theater, under Sultan, would remain the base for logistical support for the China Theater and would continue pursuing the objectives for the Northern Combat Area Command in the liberation of Burma. The successful invasion of the Philippines and the beginning of the long-range bombing campaign against Japan from bases in the Marianas would, however, reduce the importance of China in America's war against Japan.[45]

Bombing and More Bombing

The 7th Group's missions during November and December 1944 followed the Strategic Air Force's overall objective of attacking the Japanese line of communications into Burma. The Group flew more and more missions into Thailand to strike at the Burma-Thailand railroad from Bangkok to Moulmein and the line from Bangkok north to Chiengmai. These missions began what became known within the Group as the "Battle of the Bridges". From November 1944 through May 1945, the 7th Group repeatedly attacked bridges along the Burma-Thailand railroad line and other lines within Burma and Thailand. There were 271 bridges along the 457-mile route from Bangkok to the Burmese town of Pegu; 98 of these bridges were over 200 feet in length. The 458-mile line from Bangkok to Chiengmai crossed over 112 bridges, while the line from Singapore that went through the town of Jumbhorn, in southern Thailand—near the limit of a loaded B-24's range—to the town of Banpong, where the rail line from Singapore connected with the Bangkok-Moulmein line, had 114. The most promising section along the Burma-Thailand railroad was the 245-mile stretch of single track line between Banpong in Thailand and Thanbyuzayat in Burma. This line ran through the stretch of jungle-covered hills along the border between the two countries. There were no roads paralleling the rail line into Burma. If there were breaks in the railroad line, the Japanese could not easily shift supplies to trucks. The 7th Group would spend a lot of time bombing bridges along this route.

The Japanese became remarkably adept at repairing damaged bridges and building new ones using Allied prisoners of war and impressed Asians as forced labor. After completing the main line from Bangkok to Moulmein, the Japanese kept teams of prisoners and laborers at intervals along the railroad line to make repairs as needed. A full work crew under Japanese supervision could build a new wooden trestle bridge in six to eight days. As most of the bridges along the route were of the wooden trestle type, they could be quickly repaired.

The Japanese also took to building bypass bridges to minimize delays from disruptions along the line, sometimes even before the main bridge was destroyed. This meant the bombers had to return again and again to bomb the same railroad bridges.

A low-level attack on the Bilin Railroad Bridge, November 13, 1944. (3A-37527, RG 342FH, NARA)

As the months went on, the 7th Group developed new tactics and employed new technology to inflict the maximum amount of damage and impose the longest possible delays on the railroads bringing supplies into Burma.[46]

After the successful attack on the Ban Dara Bridge on November 1, 1944, the 9th and 493rd Squadrons sent out two aircraft from each squadron to the Bangkok-Chiengmai railroad on November 5th to attack two tunnels at MS 315 and MS 317, while the 436th and 492nd Squadron pairs went after the Geng Luang (Kaeng Luang) Bridge, southeast of Chiengmai. Both targets proved difficult to bomb accurately. Bombing from low level, the 492nd dropped five bombs within 100 feet of the north entrance to the tunnel and several more on the approach tracks, but the 9th Squadron found the terrain difficult for low level bombing and could only get close to the tunnels. Similarly, the 436th and 492nd Squadrons found it challenging to bomb the Kaeng Luang Bridge from low level. Trees, jungle, and hills obscured the bridge on the bomb run. The two 436th Squadron airplanes missed the bridge, while the 492nd did no better. Turning back to base, three single-engine fighters intercepted the two 492nd Squadron aircraft but did no damage. These were probably fighters from the Royal Thai Air Force defending Chiengmai.[47]

While the 9th and 493rd Squadrons went back to training for two weeks, the 436th and 492nd continued flying combat missions. During November, the RAF also pulled several of its Liberator squadrons out of combat for intensive training in daylight bombing and formation flying, leaving the Strategic Air Force with a smaller number of aircraft available for bombing. On November 13th, 18 aircraft from the 436th and 492nd Squadrons joined 20 RAF Liberators in an attack on four bridges along the railroad line from Pegu to Martaban. The 436th Squadron sent twelve airplanes to bomb two targets: the main steel girder and concrete railroad bridge near Bilin (the Squadron history records this as Hninpale), about halfway between Pegu and Martaban; and a wooden trestle bypass bridge being built 2,000 yards to the north. Lt. Mueth led the formation, with Col. Alness flying as his copilot. The 492nd went after two bridges near Mokpalin, northeast of Pegu, while the RAF Liberators went after locomotives and rolling stock along the route. The two 7th Group squadrons flew together down the Bay of Bengal, crossing into Burma and flying north of Rangoon to avoid any Japanese fighters. The P-38s of the 459th Fighter Squadron flew a diversionary sweep over Mingaladon to keep the Japanese fighters busy. The 492nd split off toward Mokpalin, while the 436th crossed the Gulf of Martaban to reach Bilin. Lt. Mueth and the first two elements bombed the main railroad bridge, while the second two elements went after the bypass bridge. Coming in at low altitude, Lt. Mueth's flight knocked out the central concrete pillar after several individual runs, sending the railroad bridge into the river below. Owing to a misidentification, the second flight bombed an unused road bridge farther to the north.

With the bridge in the water, the 436th Bomb Squadron heads off to another target. (3A-37525, RG 342FH, NARA)

The 492nd Squadron sent six airplanes to hit Bridge #41 near Mokpalin. When Lt. Veach (in the lead ship) knocked out the bridge, the other five airplanes went after targets of opportunity. They decided to attack the railroad yards at Mokpalin, despite a considerable amount of anti-aircraft guns surrounding the yards. Going in at 300 feet, they dropped their bombs on the yards, smashing up the tracks and some rolling stock, and escaped without getting hit. Coming off the target, two Japanese fighters intercepted the bombers, getting a few hits in the empennage of a few airplanes before breaking off the attack.[48]

Another joint AAF/RAF mission took place on November 16th, against targets along the Bangkok-Chiengmai railroad line. While the Liberators attacked the railroad station and yards at Pitsanuloke, some 250 miles southeast of Chiengmai, the 436th Squadron bombed the railroad yards at Uttaradit, about 40 miles to the northeast on the railroad line to Chiengmai. Six aircraft from the 436th attacked the yards at low level, coming in singly at 300 feet. The airplanes dropped nine 500-pound bombs at 20-foot intervals in the face of light anti-aircraft fire. Lt. Tesh, in the second element, was crossing the railroad yards on his bomb run when a huge explosion, possibly from another bomb or from supplies detonating, damaged his airplane severely. The explosion blew out the nose wheel tire, smashed the glass in the bombardier's position, and warped the fuselage aft of the waist gun positions. The same blast damaged the bomber's elevators, cut the trim tab cables, and severed two hydraulic lines. Tesh flew his badly damaged B-24 back to Madhaganj, where he made a successful landing with no brakes. Col. Alness accompanied the 492nd to the Kaeng Luang Bridge, to the north of Uttaradit. Having tried unsuccessfully to knock out the bridge in a low level attack, the Squadron tried bombing from 3,400 feet in individual bombing runs. Approaching the IP, the six airplanes echeloned to the right, going in over the bridge one after the other. The hills surrounding the bridge concealed the bridge until the airplanes were nearby, making it difficult for the bombardiers to line up the target in their sights. The Squadron was dejected to get only one direct hit and several near misses, but photo reconnaissance showed that the attack had in fact knocked the bridge twelve feet out of line, making it impossible for trains to pass over.[49]

The 436th and 492nd Squadrons made two more attacks on railroad targets before they swapped roles with the 9th and 493rd Squadrons and went out for their two weeks of training. On November 19th, the 436th Squadron sent 11 airplanes and the 492nd sent 12 to bomb the railroad repair shops at Mokpalin from medium altitude, while RAF Liberators bombed rolling stock in another part of the railroad yards. Col. Alness again accompanied the 492nd Squadron. On this mission, the 7th Group had an escort of 17 P-38s from the 459th Fighter Squadron, while RAF Thunderbolts (P-47) from Nos. 30 and 135 Squadrons escorted the Liberators. As the bombers passed Zayatkwin airfield en route to the target, a formation from the *50th Sentai* attempted an interception. The 459th drove the Japanese fighters off, losing one P-38 in the exchange.[50] The 436th Squadron recorded that "this mission stands out as a perfect example of precision bombing from medium altitude."[51] Going in at 11,650 feet, the Squadron dropped 132 500-pound bombs on the railroad repair sheds, all but 20 getting in the target area. The 492nd did slightly better, claiming 100 per cent of their bombs on target. The attack completely demolished the railroad repair sheds. The 492nd noted, perhaps a trifle cattily but with evident pride, that their RAF Liberator cousins missed their target alongside. Two days later, on November 21st, the two squadrons went back to Thailand to bomb targets on the Bangkok-Chiengmai railroad line once again. The 492nd sent six airplanes back to the Kaeng Luang Bridge to finish it off and six more to attack the bridge at Ban Mae Jang, southeast of Chiengmai, while the 436th sent six aircraft to bomb the bridge at Ban Mae Mo nearby. Since the

Bombing the Kaeng Luang Bridge on the Bangkok-Chiengmai railroad line from 3,400 feet. (USAF)

attack on the Kaeng Luang Bridge on November 16th, the Japanese had brought in more machine guns to defend the bridge. Lt. Charles Mead was leading the 492nd's formation attacking the bridge at low level. Coming in at 300 feet, machine gun fire knocked out two engines on the left wing of Mead's B-24 and set the left wing on fire. Mead's airplane released a single bomb, then plunged into the ground past the bridge and exploded, killing all on board, including A.G. Duff, a British war correspondent who had joined the mission. The two 492nd Squadron flights dropped all their bombs close to the target, but when the smoke cleared the two bridges were still standing. The 436th had no better luck with its bridge, dropping 25 1,000-pound bombs from 300 feet but failing to knock it down. Pulling away from the bridge, the formation found a train half a mile away. The B-24s promptly went down and strafed, setting the locomotive and six railroad cars on fire.[52]

In early November 1944, a specially-equipped B-24J joined the 436th Squadron to fly radar "ferret" missions, seeking out

Alec Tronix was a late model B-24J-180-CO equipped with instrumentation to locate and identify Japanese radar sites. The airplane and its crew flew radar "ferret" missions on its own and tagged along on regular bombing missions during the first six months of 1945. (Courtesy Jim Augustus)

the locations of Japanese radar stations in Burma. Flooring and racks for electrical countermeasures equipment filled the B-24's rear bomb bay, along with positions for two radar observers, while the forward bomb bay carried two 450-gallon fuel tanks. Lt. Charles Beard was assigned as project manager for "Ferret 12", a B-24J-180-CO dubbed "Alec Tronix", with 2nd Lt. Charles Sheppard as the pilot. Based with the 436th Squadron at Madhaiganj, the ferret airplane began flying missions in early November, carrying a full crew with Beard and two other radar observers on board. At first, these were unescorted night missions, the airplane flying down the Bay of Bengal at an altitude of 6,000 feet and 30 miles off the west coast of Burma, curving around to fly over the Gulf of Martaban toward the southern Burmese coast as far as Mergui. The radar observers found that the Japanese radar positions would quickly shut off when they found they were tracking only one airplane. This made it difficult to precisely locate the stations and determine their frequencies. The ferret aircraft began tagging along on regular bombing missions, going out on the November 19th mission to Mokpalin, as well as continuing to fly solo, unescorted missions for the next several months.[53]

The 436th Squadron began its training program on November 22nd and continued training until December 5th, while the 492nd began the day before on November 21st, finishing up a little earlier on November 30th. Their training programs mirrored what the 9th and 493rd Squadrons had done. During the training period, the 492nd took time off for a Thanksgiving celebration that apparently was memorable for the quantity of alcohol consumed. As the 492nd Squadron history recorded: "...it commenced with a quiet cocktail party at the officer club and as events of that nature have an odd habit of doing turned into a salubrious bibulation capped by singing unmentionable ditties, not songs, and nefarious activities concomitant to the elated emotions of inebriation. Time was called of course to imbibe in delicious vitals. It is remarkable what the U.S. canning industry has done. Our enlisted men were not to be outdone, as similar reports trickled in via the grape vine."[54] Parties at the officers' and enlisted men's clubs were a regular feature for the 7th Group's squadrons. The squadrons went to great lengths to obtain good food, quantities of drink, and whenever possible, young women ("nurses, red cross girls, and damsels of local origin", as the 9th Squadron described them) as honored guests and dancing partners. In off duty hours the clubs provided a place for relaxation, where a man could get a drink at the bar, find a book or magazine to read, or simply sit and chat with friends. With little in the surrounding area to do, the clubs were important to maintaining morale.

The 9th and 493rd Squadrons went back to flying combat on November 23rd, rejoining the Strategic Air Force's campaign against bridges. Both the 9th and the 493rd went out that day

A party at the 492nd Squadron's officer's club in December 1944. Parties were one of the few social events available to the squadrons. (SQ-Bomb-492-HI December 1944, Albert F. Simpson Historical Research Center, Air Force Historical Research Agency, Maxwell AFB, AL)

to bomb bridges on the Pegu-Martaban railroad line, each squadron sending nine aircraft, along with a fighter escort of P-38s and P-47s, to bomb Bypass #2 at Bridge #71 on the line. The airplanes (all but the 493rd's third element, who could not identify the target) bombed from an altitude of 9,000 feet and got excellent patterns near the bridge, but even from 9,000 feet, a 14-foot wide target was exceedingly difficult to hit. To the frustration of the crews, the bridge emerged from the dust and smoke unscathed. On November 26th, while the RAF Liberators went after the railroad yards at Pyinmana, the 9th and 493rd Squadrons bombed bridges on the Bangkok-Chiengmai line, the 9th Squadron bombing Bridge #68 without result, while the 493rd went after Bridge #69 nearby. This time, the 493rd bombed from 4,400 feet, destroying the bridge and as a bonus blowing up a nearby supply dump, sending up a column of black smoke to 4,000 feet. On the next to last day of the month, both squadrons went out to bomb Bridge #277 on the Bangkok-Moulmein railroad line. Bridge #277, or "Old 277", as it came to be called, became infamous within the 7th Group for the number of sorties directed on this target and the bridge's apparent imperviousness to almost every bomb thrown at it. Bridge #277 was a concrete and steel bridge the Japanese had built during the 1943 monsoon season to span a stretch of river known locally as the Mae Klong. Bridge #277 replaced a wooden trestle bridge built at the same location with POW labor. After the war this became famous as the "Bridge Over the River Kwai". Bombing from 8,500 feet, the two squadrons put their bombs in a tight pattern around the bridge but failed to damage it.[55]

Each of the squadrons built an enlisted men's club where the men could go to relax and have a drink. This is the 493rd Squadron's EM club at Pandaveswar with its "Rudder" Bar. (7th Bombardment Group (H) Historical Foundation, USAFA McDermott Library)

The directive to the Strategic Air Force put Japanese naval and merchant vessels as the Force's number one priority, but as targets of opportunity. At this stage of the war, there were few chances to attack shipping in the seas around Burma, but in the first part of November and then again in the first days of December, the 7th Group was altered to possible shipping targets. On November 9th, the 7th Group received word of a reported Japanese convoy off Tavoy, in southern Burma on the Kra Isthmus. The 436th Squadron sent ten aircraft and the 492nd sent 11, but there was no convoy to be found. The squadrons split up to attack alternate targets. Lt. Ray, leading five of the 436th Squadron's aircraft, went after a group of small coastal vessels, claiming some near misses, while Lt. Sims, leading the other flight, went to bomb the small railroad yard at Bassein, getting good hits. Seven minutes later, two Ki-43 Oscars and a Type 3 fighter (Ki-61 Tony), possibly from the *8th Rensei Hikōtai*, an operational training unit based at Rangoon, jumped the formation and made several half-hearted passes. Col. Alness, again flying with the 492nd Squadron as command pilot in Maj. Gandy's airplane, had a similar experience when the flight he was in bombed the landing ground at Bassein after failing to find any shipping off Tavoy. Four fighters, reportedly three Type 2 Fighters (Ki-44 Tojo) and a single Oscar, attacked Maj. Gandy's formation, making several passes also described as half-hearted.

December brought two unsuccessful sea searches. The 9th Squadron took on the sea search task on December 1, 1944, looking for a large Japanese Navy vessel reported to be off the coast near Mergui. After hours of searching, the Squadron found nothing more than a few small coastal ships and fishing boats. As one of the Squadron's bombardiers said, "We sighted the Japanese Navy and they threw down their paddles and swam like hell."[56] Fortunes had changed dramatically in two years of war. The 9th Squadron received an urgent summons on December 5th, again for reported large naval vessels. Six aircraft were hurriedly prepared and took off at 0100 to land at Chittagong, where the crews were to await orders, but nothing happened. Instead, the airplanes bombed the road between Prome and Taungup. The squadrons also went out on sea searches for missing aircrews, the Strategic Air Force having been given responsibility for Air-Sea Rescue over the Bay of Bengal. These searches cost the Group two airplanes in the space of one month. Shortly before the first sea search mission in November, the 493rd Squadron lost an airplane and crew during a search for a missing B-29 crew that had gone down in the Bay of Bengal. Six aircraft took off from Panda at 1500 on November 5, 1944, and returned the next morning having found nothing. After the flight went through a band of weather, Lt. Thomas Cheany, flying a newly-arrived B-24L, veered away from the formation and headed off into clouds to the right. His airplane was later found to have crashed in the foothills southwest of Udala, in the Indian state of Orissa, around 170 miles southwest of Calcutta, with the loss of the entire crew. Nearly a month later, on December 1st, 2nd Lt. Stanton Phillips was one of four aircraft from the 436th Squadron on a search for another ditched B-29. Not long after take-off Phillips had to make a forced landing, setting his B-24 down in a stretch of rice paddies. All his crew survived, though several were injured in the crash.[57]

The 7th Group spent much of its effort during December attacking stores dumps in Burma in support of the British and Indian Army units advancing down the Arakan and toward the Chindwin River. The Group sent bombers to hit the stores areas at Sagaing, west of Mandalay; the dumps at Maymyo, the supply point for the Japanese *33rd Army* resisting the Chinese divisions on the Salween front; and Akyab, and participated in a major effort by all but one of the Strategic Air Force's squadrons against the dumps at Taungup supplying the Japanese *28th Army* fighting in the Arakan. The RAF sent 48 Liberators and the 7th Group 22 B-24s on missions to Taungup on December 21st and 23rd with excellent results. Near the end of the month, the 7th Group bombed the Prome dumps on December 27th and the Pyinmana dumps on December 30th. Several of these targets were from the Strategic Air Force's list of targets for operational training. They proved to have been good for building needed experience. The bombing results were reported to be excellent, with almost all bombs on target.[58]

Loading fragmentation bombs on a 492nd Squadron B-24J. These were often used for attacks on air fields and supply dumps. (SQ-Bomb-492-HI January 1945, Albert F. Simpson Historical Research Center, Air Force Historical Research Agency, Maxwell AFB, AL)

The railroad system was subject to four attacks during the month. On December 7, 1944, the 436th and 492nd Squadrons bombed the railroad yards at Maymyo. Clouds obscured the target, but the lead bombardier in the 436th Squadron's flight of five aircraft correctly identified the railroad yards and bombed them successfully. The next day, the target was rolling stock, installations, and sidings on the Burma-Thailand railroad line between Thanbyuzayat and Kanchanburi. All four squadrons went on the mission, 19 aircraft bombing the yards at Thanbyuzayat and Phadaw, closer to the Burma-Thai border. Thanbyuzayat was the target again two days later for the 9th and 493rd Squadrons, while the 436th and 492nd went back to Phadaw. The 436th and 492nd bombed their target successfully, but due to poor visibility and despite recent practice, the lead navigator and the lead bombardier for the 9th and 492nd formations misidentified the target, bombing Anankwin, another nearby town.[59]

To knock out the key Bridge #277 once and for all, the 7th Group planned a coordinated attack combining high level and low level bombing runs. Six aircraft each from the 9th and 493rd Squadrons, with four from the 492nd Squadron, were to bomb the bridge with 1,000-pound bombs from 8,000 to 8,500 feet, while one aircraft from each squadron went in at low level. The 9th Squadron's low-level bomber would carry two 2,000-pound bombs, while the 493rd Squadron's low-level aircraft would have four 1,000-pound bombs. Just before the bombers went in, the 436th Squadron was to plaster anti-aircraft positions to the northwest of the bridge with incendiaries and fragmentation bombs. The squadrons began taking off a little after 0937 on the morning of December 13, 1944, reaching the target area around 1645. Leading the 436th Squadron's formation, Lt. Mueth arrived to find his target covered in rain and cloud, forcing the formation to make a second run from the opposite direction. The second run unfortunately placed the 436th on a collision course with the airplanes from the 492nd Squadron, who had to break off their bomb run on the bridge and go after secondary targets. The 436th dropped its bombs on the designated anti-aircraft positions, but unknown to the bomber formations, the Japanese had moved a number of guns to new positions. When they went in, the B-24s came under intense and accurate anti-aircraft fire. As Lt. Duderstadt, leading the 436th Squadron's second element, came in over the target, a large-caliber shell hit his B-24 just below the left waist gun position. The explosion nearly severed the right leg of the left waist gunner, S/Sgt. John Holick, mortally wounding him. His crew did everything they could to try to save him, but Holick died 4 ½ hours later on the return flight. The high level bombers came in through the anti-aircraft fire to drop their bombs, most landing within 300 feet of the bridge. Lt. Col. Kyes, Group Operations Officer, flying one of the 9th Squadron's B-24s, went in at 200 feet to drop his two 2,000-pound bombs; the lone 492nd Squadron bomber came in after him. When the smoke and dust had cleared, Old #277 was still standing. The mission of December 13, 1944, demonstrated, as so many other similar missions had in the past, how difficult it was to destroy a bridge, even from medium altitudes. Low altitude runs were challenging to execute, but had greater success, but also a higher probability of losses if there were any anti-aircraft guns present. Two weeks later, the 7th Group had an answer to the problem.[60]

Azon Bombing

The Azon (*Azimuth Only*) bomb, with radio-controlled, steerable tail fins, gave unprecedented precision bombing. The can-like object attached to the tail fin was the flare that burned intensely once ignited. (7th Bombardment Group (H) Historical Foundation, USAFA McDermott Library)

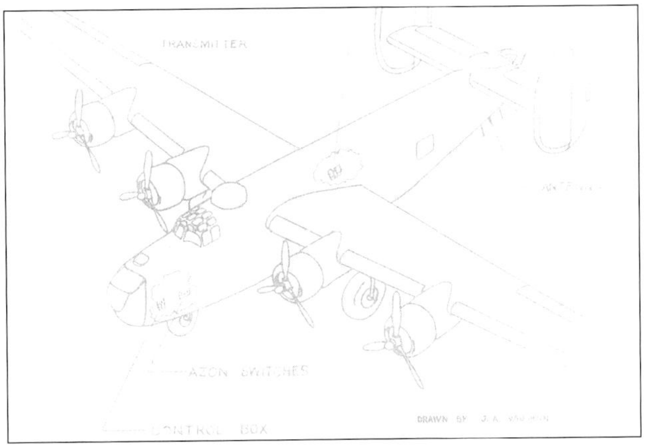

An illustration showing the location of the Azon electrical and radio control equipment. (Via the author)

"There is probably no bombardier in the world", wrote the March 1945 issue of *Impact*, the Army Air Forces' confidential intelligence magazine, "who, having made an imperfect release, has not watched his bombs go down wide of the target without wishing there were some way he could change their course in the air. This is now made possible with the controllable Azon..."[61] The Azon bomb came out of the Army Air Forces' research in guided missiles begun a few years before America's entry into the war.[62] Developed by the National Defense Research Committee, the Azon was a "controlled vertical bomb" that could be controlled in *az*imuth *on*ly (hence its name); that is, could be maneuvered only from left to right in the direction of the bomb's trajectory.[63] The core of the Azon bomb was a controllable tail fin unit that contained a servo motor connected to four movable tail fins, a gyroscope to prevent the bomb from rolling in flight, and a radio receiver to pick up radio signals from the bombardier that activated the servo motor controlling the movable tail fins. To make the Azon visible in flight, a large 800,000 candle power flare was attached to the end of the tail fin unit. The flare would ignite automatically eight to ten seconds after leaving the bomb bay, leaving an easy to track red, white, green, or yellow smoke trail as it fell. For added visibility, the bombs were sometimes painted yellow or white. The Azon tail fin unit was normally attached to a standard AN-M65 1,000-pound bomb and could be carried in a B-24's bomb bay without any modification. A B-24 could be converted relatively easily to using Azon bombs by adding a radio transmitter, additional batteries to power the transmitter, and three transmitting antenna at the rear of the airplane.[64]

The Azon bomb was relatively straightforward to use. The bombardier used a regular Norden bomb sight on his bomb run to pick up the target and drop a single Azon bomb. Once the flare had ignited, he could follow the Azon as it travelled, using a small toggle switch alongside to control the bomb's movement to the left and right through radio signals sent to the receiver in the movable tail unit. An Azon bomb could be steered within a 2,000 to 3,000 foot band to the left or right of the target. Since the Azon could be maneuvered in azimuth only, the ideal targets were ones that were long and straight, where the bomber could make a long straight approach to the target, giving the bombardier the maximum amount of time to direct the Azon onto the target, making small adjustments to move the bomb to the left or right of its path. Bridges were ideal targets. In most cases, the bombardier could simply follow a road or rail line to track the fall of the bomb toward the bridge. The radio control system had six channels, allowing up to six Azon bombs to be dropped and guided at the same time. Guiding an Azon bomb to a direct hit required skill and concentration, but with practice it became achievable. Weather was a critical issue, as the bombardier required clear weather

Hap Arnold Special/Spirit of Ft. Worth was the last B-24J built at Consolidated's Ft. Worth plant. Arriving in India in December 1944, the airplane was assigned to the 493rd Bomb Squadron and converted to an Azon aircraft, with three Azon antenna under the rear fuselage. (3A-33638, RG 342FH, NARA)

to follow the smoke trail the Avon's flare produced as it fell. Following development work at the Army Air Forces' Air Technical Service Command, the Azon went into production in the fall of 1943.[65]

In February 1944, Maj. Gen. Howard Davidson, then the Tenth Air Force and Strategic Air Force commander, met with a visiting representative of the Army Air Forces' Office of Commitments and Requirements for Heavy Bombers, who briefed him on the new Azon bomb. On March 3, 1944, the Tenth Air Force submitted a request to the Army Air Forces to provide 300 Azon tail units and to assign ten B-24 bombers equipped for dropping Azon bombs, ten Azon-trained bombardiers and crews, and a project officer with maintenance technicians.[66] In August 1944, 2nd Lt. E.M. Buyer arrived at Tenth Air Force Headquarters with an advance team of ten maintenance men. A month later, ten B-24Js equipped for dropping Azon bombs, with crews who had undergone a six-week training program at Ft. Dix, New Jersey, began arriving at 7th Group bases, but without badly needed test equipment. As sometimes happens, the plans to assign Azon aircraft to the 7th Group had not reached the Group's commander, Col. Dodson, or his Operations staff. They knew nothing about the Azon program and did not have much interest or enthusiasm for the Azon bomb. Up to that time, Azon bombs had been used with only limited success in Europe. The 7th Group Operations staff may simply have been skeptical of its possible application in the India-Burma Theater. 2nd Lt. Buyer tried to persuade Col. Dodson and his staff to group the Azon bombers in a single squadron, but they refused.[67] The Azon B-24s were distributed among the Group's four squadrons, the Azon equipment removed, and the Azon-trained crews put to hauling gasoline over the Hump. Buyer found his Azon equipment scattered all over the airfield among the armament, ordnance, communications, and engineering departments; one department was using a special Azon battery to power a radio. Over the next three months, three of the Azon B-24s were lost on regular operations. The lack of progress was due in part to: "...the lack of test equipment, inexperience, and perhaps a little timidity on the part of the Azon ground maintenance officer, as well as the lack of enthusiasm on the part of the 7th Bomb Group staff..."[68]

Buyer sent repeated requests to Washington for the test equipment he needed. In the meantime, he went to Pandaveswar to round up all the Azon equipment he could

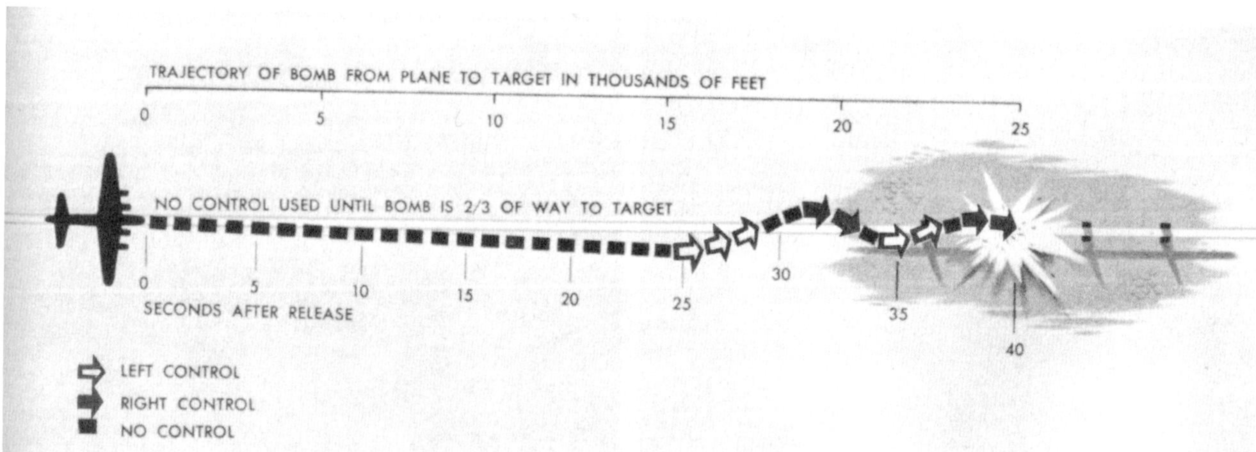

An illustration taken from *Impact* magazine showing how a bombardier could adjust the path of an Azon bomb to the right or left of a straight line to the target. (Via the author)

With their flares ignited, two 1,000-pound Azon bombs head toward the Pyinmana railroad bridge. (3A-37736, RG 342FH, NARA)

One of the Azon bombs scores a direct on the Pyinmana bridge. Note the explosion of one of the conventional bombs in the riverbed above the bridge. (3A-37737, RG 342FH, NARA)

Four conventional 1,000-pound bombs head for the railroad bridge at Pyinmana, the target for the first Azon bomb attack on December 27, 1944. (3A-37735, RG 342FH, NARA)

find and arranged for shipping Azon tail units from Calcutta to Panda. On December 10, 1944, Maj. William Donics, representing the Army Air Forces' Special Projects Office in Washington, arrived in India with a technical observer to find out what had happened to the Azon program. Both men were highly trained on the Azon bomb and brought with them the needed test equipment. Donics and his colleague immediately launched an intensive "sales pitch" for the Azon, briefing senior commanders in the India-Burma Theater on the Azon bomb and its capabilities. The two men finally won support for the Azon project, including, apparently, the support of Col. Alness and his Operations staff. Donics arranged for three of the Azon-trained crews to be pulled off another assignment and transferred to the 493rd Squadron. Three of the remaining seven Azon B-24Js had all the Azon equipment reinstalled and the first Azon bombing mission was set for December 27, 1944. Just before the mission, Maj. Donics called the three crews together and told them: "...it was up to them to prove what Azon could do, that on the basis of their efforts its success or failure in this theater might depend."[69]

The target for the first Azon bombing mission was the railroad bridge at Pyinmana, on the Rangoon-Mandalay railroad line. Pyinmana had been the target on numerous previous missions. The area around the bridge was pockmarked with bomb craters. Six aircraft from the 493rd Squadron began taking off from Panda at 0900. The three Azon B-24s led the flight, each carrying four AN-M65 1,000-pound bombs fitted with Azon tail fin units (as such they were designated VB-1) and six standard AN-M65 1,000-pound bombs. The second element of three standard B-24s carried four 2,000-pound bombs each. The formation arrived over the target at 1313 and began their bombing runs. Each bombardier in the Azon B-24s dropped one Azon bomb and one standard bomb on the rail line approaching the bridge for practice. On the first proper run against the bridge, bombing from between 8,880 and 9,450 feet, the bombardier in the lead Azon bomber scored a direct hit with his first Azon bomb, knocking one span of the bridge askew at a 45° angle. The other Azon bombs fell nearby. The second element dropped its 2,000-pound standard bombs on this first pass, hitting between 50 and 100

Another photograph from *Impact* magazine showing Azon bombs getting three direct hits on the Taungup road bridge while conventional bombs hit wide of the bridge. (Via the author)

feet from the bridge but failing to knock it down. On the second run over the bridge, another Azon bomb scored a direct hit, sending the middle span into the dry river bed below. On their third pass, the Azon B-24s got at least one more hit on the bridge.[70]

The second Azon bombing mission on December 30, 1944, was an even more dramatic demonstration of the Azon bomb's capabilities. In the interim, one more Azon B-24 had its Azon bombing equipment reinstalled. The target on this mission was the Nyaungchidauk Bridge, a 225-foot long wooden trestle road bridge on the road from the rail head at Prome to the Japanese Army supply dumps at Taungup. The bypass bridge next to the main bridge was the first alternate and the Taungup Bridge was the second alternate target. The bridges were not ideal Azon targets, as none of them had long straight approaches. The 493rd sent out four Azon B-24s, each with seven Azon bombs and one 1,000-pound standard bomb, and two standard B-24s with two 2,000-pound bombs each. Five aircraft from the 9th Squadron went out to bomb the Okshitpin road bridge, located a few miles away. Bombing from 10,000 feet, the Azon B-24s made four passes on the main bridge, getting six hits, the lead bombardier getting the final hit that destroyed the bridge on the fourth pass. The bombardier in the No.2 aircraft had just released his Azon bomb when he saw the lead bombardier's bomb hit the main bridge. He quickly maneuvered his bomb toward the nearby bypass bridge, getting a direct hit, as did the bombardier in the No.3 airplane. The 9th Squadron, meanwhile, had bombed the Okshitpin Road Bridge with 2,000-pound bombs without success. As the 9th Squadron's history recorded: "No one was surprised when the 14' structure remained standing after the bomb run at 10,000 feet. This mission, following several highly successful raids against stores areas, seemed to emphasize the importance of the right targets for the right planes."[71] The Azon crews might have amended this statement to read "the right targets for the right bombs". Seeing the Okshitpin Bridge still standing, the 493rd Squadron's Azon B-24s flew over and in two passes, with each aircraft dropping one Azon bomb on each pass, dislocated one span of the bridge and knocked a second into the river. The Azon aircraft still had seven Azon bombs left, so for good measure they flew on and bombed the Taungup Road Bridge, getting three direct hits on their first pass. Four Azon B-24s had knocked out four bridges on a single mission. Writing to the head of the Army Air Forces' Special Projects Office, Maj. Donics said: "The destruction of four bridges on a much attacked supply line by only four Azon aircraft may be said to give an indication of the possible effectiveness of Azon in this theater."[72]

The 493rd Squadron's Azon B-24s went out again on January 1, 1945, bombing two bridges near Phadaw, while the 9th Squadron bombed the Phadaw railroad yards with standard bombs. The Azon bombers got direct hits on one bridge but failed to damage the other. Still, many of those who had been skeptical of the Azon bomb at first were quickly becoming converted. Col. Alness was one of the converts. In a message he sent directly to General Arnold on January 7,

While two Azon bombs strike near the Phadaw Bridge, one Azon gets a direct hit in the center of the bridge and another direct hit on the approach. (SQ-Bomb-493-HI January 1945, Albert F. Simpson Historical Research Center, Air Force Historical Research Agency, Maxwell AFB, AL)

1945, Alness said: "That all our aircraft should be equipped with Azon equipment is indicated by the proven success attained by the use of this equipment."[73] Alness requested that all replacement aircraft for the 7th Group be equipped for Azon bombing and that all replacement crews be trained in using Azon bombs—a strong vote of confidence in the new weapon. While not the complete answer to destroying bridges, the Azon bomb gave the 7th Group a weapon that greatly increased the probability of success. High altitude bombing with standard bombs had proved inefficient and rarely effective. Using Azon bombs, the probable error—a measure of bombing accuracy—was reduced from 140 feet or more to around 75 feet. Low altitude bombing would prove to be the most effective method of destroying a bridge, but the presence of anti-aircraft guns in any number made this method exceptionally dangerous for a low-flying B-24. With the Azon bomb, the 7th Group could attack more well-defended bridges with greater likelihood of success and at lower risk. The other Azon-trained crews were hastily recalled from other missions and assigned to the 493rd Squadron. The 493rd became the 7th Group's specialized Azon bombing squadron. The Squadron set up a ground school to train the other squadron bombardiers in the technique of Azon bombing. In the coming months, the 493rd and its Azon bombs would play a vital role in the Battle of the Bridges.[74]

A China Interlude

In December 1944, the Fourteenth Air Force once again called on the Tenth Air Force for help. By this date, the Japanese *Ichi-go* offensive had succeeded in establishing an overland link between Manchuria and Indochina. Japanese Army forces moving south from Hankow had met up with Japanese forces moving west from Canton, in the process occupying the Fourteenth Air Force's main airfields in central China and cutting off several remaining airfields to the east of the Japanese corridor from their sources of supply. The eastern airfields at Suichwan, Kanchow, Namyung, and Kukong, near China's coast, were critical to maintaining attacks on Japanese shipping in the South China Sea and as bases for fighters attacking the Japanese forces surrounding these bases and the new Japanese communications line. In November 1944, Maj. Gen. Chennault organized the East China Air Task Force, consisting of one fighter squadron, a tactical reconnaissance squadron, and a detachment of B-24s from the 308th Bombardment Group to operate from these eastern airfields. The problem was to keep this force supplied with gasoline, ammunition, and spare parts. The difficulty was that the flight from the main Fourteenth Air Force base at Kunming to Suichwan, a distance of over 700 miles, now involved a flight across Japanese-held territory with the risk of Japanese fighter interception. These were not conditions suited to unarmed transports, so the 7th Bombardment Group was ordered to send a detachment of B-24s to China to fly aviation gasoline from Luliang, a base 60 miles east of Kunming, to Suichwan.[75]

On December 12, 1944, the 7th Group formed Detachment 7th Bomb Group (H) to organize and operate the fuel run from Luliang to the bases in eastern China. The first Group personnel flew up to Luliang the next day, and the first gas hauling flights took off from Luliang on December 16th.[76] The Detachment drew combat crews, maintenance and support personnel, and airplanes from the Group's four squadrons, each squadron designating ten combat crews and four or five aircraft for the Detachment. The airfield at Luliang was at an altitude of 6,000 feet, with a 10,500 foot long runway. According to the Tech Orders for the B-24J, a take-off at 63,000 pounds—the maximum load specified—at an altitude of 6,000 feet required a runway 9,500 feet long and an additional 2,000 feet to get to flying speed and clear a 50-foot obstacle. The 7th Group's B-24s were fitted with three bomb bay fuel tanks carrying 1,200 gallons of gasoline. The airplanes frequently operated out of Luliang with a gross weight of 68,000 to 70,000 pounds, leaving very little margin for error on take-off. To compound the difficulty of getting off safely, three small buttes or knolls lay about three miles from the end of the runway with no lights to indicate their location. Bradley Hamlett was a newly-arrived copilot in the 436th Squadron when his crew was alerted for duty in China: "The 7th Bomb Group was notorious for exceeding the recommended gross weight of 65,000 lbs on their '24s," he recalled. "Flying out of Luliang we were

B-24s unloading gas at Kunming. (3A-00980, RG 342FH, NARA)

grossed at 68,500lbs. We would set the turbos to develop 51in of manifold pressure. The manual recommended 40. The book also said to raise the nose at 80 m.p.h. and it would start flying. Being over-grossed, in order to get the '24 to fly we had to get all the airspeed we could. We did this by raising the nose just enough for the nose wheel to clear the runway. At the end of the runway, you would gently ease back on the control column and hope the S.O.B. would fly. If you came back too fast on the control, it could develop a high speed stall that you would not be able to recover from."[77]

Lt. Robert Jordan and his crew were forced to bail out over China on one of the 9th Bomb Squadron's gas hauling missions. Landing behind Japanese lines, Jordon and his men made their way back with the help of the local Chinese. (SQ-Bomb-9-HI-January 1945, Albert F. Simpson Historical Research Center, Air Force Historical Research Agency, Maxwell AFB, AL)

The flight from Luliang to Suichwan was no picnic either. On roughly 80% of the flights between the two bases the weather was solidly overcast, eliminating the ability to navigate using checkpoints along the way. For night flights, the navigators had to rely on celestial navigation and the radio operators, who concentrated on holding on to a radio bearing. Weather predictions for the route were a "best guess". Poor weather, coupled with "...high winds up to 75 mph, icing, severe turbulence, night flying in poorly charted country, and high mountains made navigation and flying extremely hazardous."[78] Fighters were a constant worry, but although seen on a number of sorties during daylight hours, the 7th Group's bombers never came under attack. Another risk was radar-directed anti-aircraft fire in certain areas, sometimes difficult to avoid when navigation was not exactly precise. Once on the ground at a forward airfield, the crews ran the risk of Japanese air attack. During the six weeks the Detachment operated in China, the airfield at Suichwan came under attack 17 times. Bombers had to get away from the field during "bombing time" (1800 to 2200), adding to the pressure. Often the crews would return to Luliang to find the field covered in an overcast, requiring an instrument let down. To cap all, the Detachment had to go back to India to load up on gasoline for the eastern airfields, shuttling back and forth between Luliang and the Air Transport Command airfields in Assam, and then Luliang to Suichwan or Kanchow. With these conditions maintenance was critical. The small number of maintenance crews did a superb job keeping the airplanes in condition. The squadrons tended, for obvious reasons, to send their better aircraft to the China Detachment, relying on some of the older aircraft for combat missions into Burma and Thailand and inadvertently causing a higher than usual number of aborts for mechanical reasons during the month of January.[79]

Living and working conditions were basic. The men working in the Detachment lived in tents with charcoal stoves to provide some heat in the freezing temperatures. The mess was a wooden shack. As the 436th Squadron recorded: "a constant 35-40 mile-per-hour wind gave the base a miserable dust cover which permeated every opening."[80] The wind, sand, and cold made life for the maintenance crews miserable. And there was next to nothing to do at Luliang, except read, play cards, or visit the small Red Cross Club. The Detachment spent six weeks in China hauling gasoline to the eastern airfields until they fell in a renewed Japanese offensive. The Chinese Government refused to release badly needed supplies to the General commanding the Chinese troops defending the area.[81] Suichwan fell on January 27, 1945, and Kanchow on February 7, 1945. The 7th Group Detachment returned to India at the end of January 1945, to the great joy of the assigned crews and ground staff, who delighted in taking hot baths, having clean quarters again, and hot, decent food.[82]

Not surprisingly, there were losses. Oddly, each squadron lost one airplane during their time with the detachment. On December 17, 1944, the day after the Detachment started hauling gasoline to Suichwan, 2nd Lt. Hugh Murrell and his crew from the 492nd Squadron had to bail out of their B-24 200 miles northeast of Luliang—behind Japanese lines—when they became lost and ran out of fuel after running into severe icing and engine problems.[82] Murrell and his crew evaded the

Japanese and returned to Luliang with the help of local Chinese, though it took them a month to do so. The day after Murrell's loss, Lt. Joseph Richards was making a night take-off from Luliang when he crashed into the small knolls a few miles from the end of the runway, apparently unable to gain sufficient air speed. Richards and his entire crew from the 436th Squadron were killed. Six days later, the 9th Squadron took its turn. Lt. Robert Jordan and his crew were forced to bail out, but like Muller and his crew, made it back to friendly lines after a journey of 31 days using pack horses, a river boat, sedan chairs, and GI boots to return to Luliang. The most tragic loss occurred over Suichwan on January 20, 1945. Two B-24s arrived over the airfield just as a Japanese bomber launched an attack. The airfield lights were quickly turned off and the B-24s were told to circle in the area. A P-61 Black Widow night fighter had taken off to intercept the Japanese bomber. After losing the enemy aircraft on their radar, the night fighter crew picked up another contact. Calling the base to ask if any friendly aircraft were in the area, for some inexplicable reason they were told no. The Black Widow opened fire, shooting down Lt. Richard Embury's B-24; only Lt. Billy Ingram, Embury's navigator, and S/Sgt. Julian Zdep, one of his gunners, bailed out and survived.[83]

B-24J *Pecker Red* abandoned on an airfield in Burma. (7th Bombardment Group (H) Historical Foundation, USAFA McDermott Library)

Moving supplies from Luliang back to Madhaiganj, the 436th Squadron said goodbye to an old war horse. On January 28, 1945, Bradley Hamlett and his pilot, Chuck Linamen, were ordered to fly to Luliang to pick up a load of equipment and 12 passengers and return to Madhaiganj. The aircraft assigned to them was No. 67, a B-24J recently transferred over from the 493rd Squadron. No. 67, named "Pecker Red", was a long-serving combat veteran, one of the first B-24J models assigned to the 493rd. The bomber had accumulated around 89 combat missions, beginning with the hard-fought battles over Rangoon during November-December 1943. Her gunners had claimed eight Japanese fighters. Somehow she had made it through fourteen months of combat and was still flying, though nearly worn out. The engines had over 500 hours of flying time on them and should have been changed. Flying up to Luliang, Linamen and Hamlett noticed that No. 1 and No. 2 engines were throwing oil. On the flight back to Madhaiganj the next day, the crew noticed the oil pressure dropping on No. 2 engine. Hamlett shut down the engine and feathered the propeller. Deciding that discretion was the better part of valor, Lt. Linamen landed at Imphal, rather than attempt to fly back on three tired engines. After landing, a British officer came up and asked Hamlett to park his airplane over by the side of the airfield. It took a while for the crew to get picked up, but on their third day at Imphal two B-24s flew in to take on the equipment and passengers. As the Group was now getting a regular supply of brand new B-24s there was no need or reason to repair Old 67, so the airplane was left at Imphal, a sad end to a gallant warrior.[84]

The Battle of the Bridges

At the beginning of 1945, the Strategic Air Force turned to the interdiction of the supply routes running into Burma with full force, in what the 7th Group squadrons had come to call the "Battle of the Bridges". By January, all the Royal Air Force's Liberator squadrons, as well as the 7th Bombardment Group, had completed periods of intensive training and returned to operations. The Strategic Air Force now had a nominal strength of 128 heavy bombers, though the 7th Group still had over a dozen aircraft on detachment in China. The Force had an added and potent weapon in the Azon bombs concentrated in the 493rd Squadron. At a conference at Eastern Air Command held on December 20, 1944, a decision was reached to concentrate the Strategic Air Forces' entire effort during the first ten days of January against the railroad line from Bangkok to Moulmein through to Pegu, with additional attacks on the Bangkok-Chiengmai railroad line. The objective was to cause as many severe breaks in the lines as possible and delay the flow of supplies to *Burma Area Army*.[85] Since November, the Japanese armies had steadily fallen back toward the defensive line they intended to hold along the Irrawaddy River, offering little resistance to the 14th Army's advance beyond the Chindwin into Burma. Lt. Gen. Sir William Slim, 14th Army commander knighted in December, had wanted to bring the Japanese armies to battle on the Shwebo Plain, west of the Irrawaddy River, and destroy them. From intelligence reports and the lack of resistance, he now realized that the Japanese would

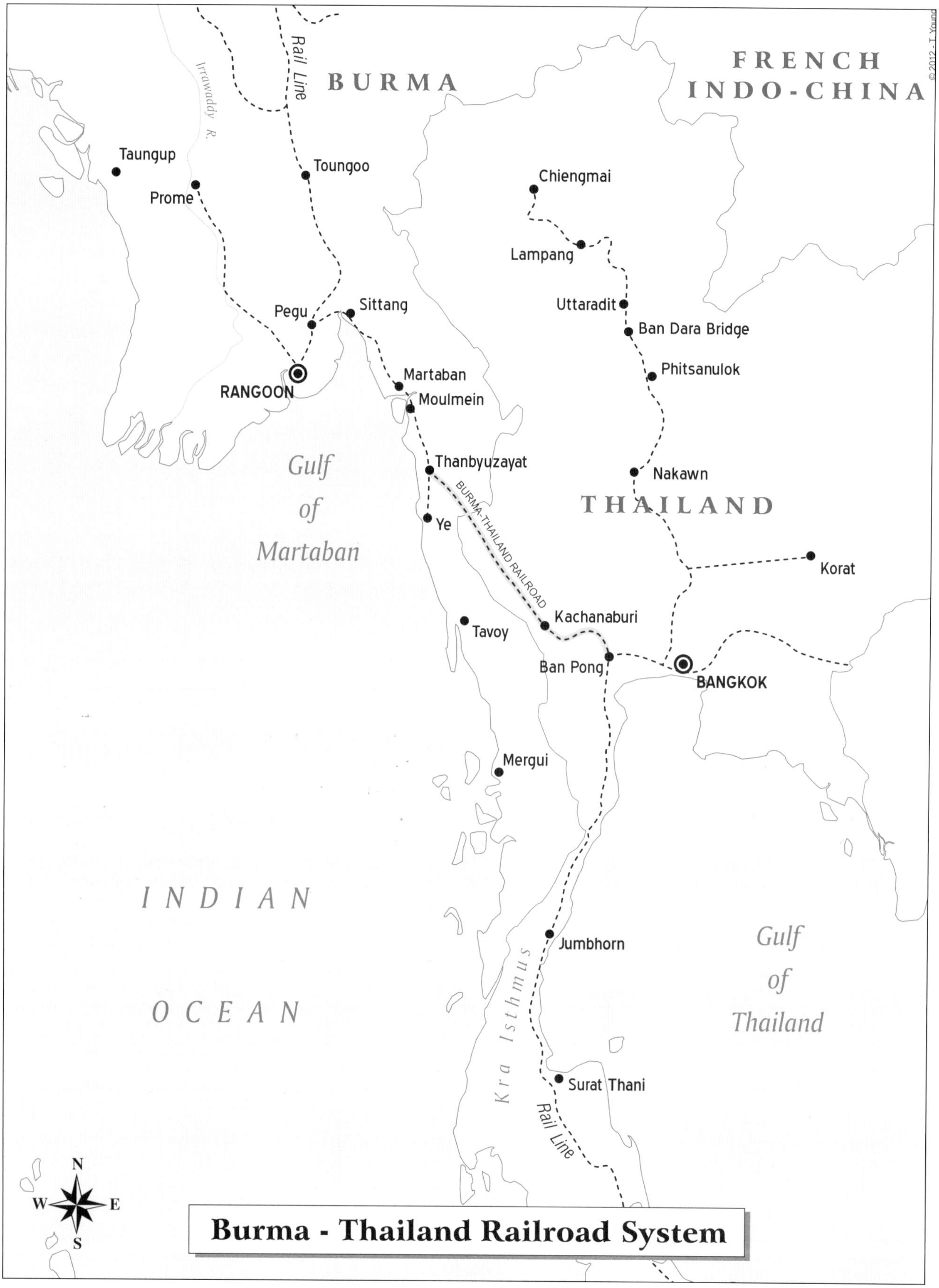

Burma - Thailand Railroad System

The 493rd Squadron attacking the Bridge #71 bypass with Azon bombs on January 11, 1945. (3A-37567, RG 342FH, NARA)

not give battle where he wanted them to and might well continue withdrawing into southern Burma. Slim developed a new plan, called "Extended Capital", he hoped would force the Japanese to give battle on grounds of his own choosing.[86] Extended Capital called for the 14th Army to place a force south of Mandalay to block a Japanese withdrawal toward Rangoon. Slim chose as his target the town of Meiktila, the Japanese Army's administrative and supply center for central Burma, sitting on the main road and railroad lines to the south. Slim knew the Japanese would have to fight to clear their route of withdrawal and to preserve the supplies held at Meiktila. He planned to have his XXXIII Corps capture Mandalay to distract the Japanese while his IV Corps seized Meiktila, with a target date of mid-February 1945. In the Arakan, XV Corps was planning for an amphibious landing on Ramree Island later in January to establish a port and airfields to support the advance in central Burma. In the Northern Combat Area Command, General Sultan's Chinese divisions had captured Bhamo and by the middle of the January, the Ledo Road would be linked up with the Myitkyina-Bhamo road. By the end of January, truck convoys would be rolling from Ledo to Kunming, finally establishing the land route to China.[87]

The attacks on the Burma-Thailand railroad began on January 1, 1945. The RAF sent 39 Liberators to join the 7th Bombardment Group's effort that day. Two days later, on January 3rd, 41 Liberators bombed railroad tracks, sidings, and bridges along the railroad line while the 7th Group sent 24 aircraft to hit Bridge #121, a bridge viaduct at MS 99, and to create breaks in the tracks nearby using Azon and regular bombs. Clouds over Bridge #121 interfered with the bombing, but with the Azon bombs the 493rd Squadron destroyed the south end of the bridge. With several Azon bombs remaining, the 493rd attacked a second bridge nearby, without success on this occasion, but got three probable hits on the railroad line. Using conventional bombs and bombing from around 7,500 feet, the 9th, 436th, and 492nd Squadrons bombed the tracks and the viaduct. The 436th's mission was to hopefully start a landslide to cover the railroad tracks near MS 99, but the lead bombardier misidentified the target and bombed the tracks near MS 95 instead, all other bombardiers dropping on the leader. Unfortunately, the bombs fell wide of the target area. There was another all-out effort on January 8, 1945, with the five Liberator squadrons joining the 7th Group in attacks on the Burma-Thailand railroad line again. The 7th Group split its force, the 9th and 493rd Squadrons going after two bridges (#83 and #97) on the Burma-Thailand line south of Thanbyuzayat, while the 436th and 492nd Squadrons went out to bomb Bridges #151 and #163 on the Thanbyuzayat-Ye rail line. As the 493rd Squadron history described the mission: "It was a very good day for Azon...The weather was clear and the bombardiers had a field day."[88] Making individual runs from 10,000 feet, the 493rd's bombardiers destroyed two spans on Bridge #97 with two to three direct hits out of nine Azons dropped on the bridge and blew out sections on the north and south ends of the approaches to Bridge #83 with the help of 18 standard 1,000-pound bombs from the 9th Squadron. With some extra Azon bombs, the 493rd went after a secondary target, knocking down Bridge #95. The 436th and 492nd

The 9th Bomb Squadron's B-24J *Hot to Go* still going strong in January 1945. (SQ-Bomb-9-HI-January 1945, Albert F. Simpson Historical Research Center, Air Force Historical Research Agency, Maxwell AFB, AL)

Squadrons had no luck this day. Coming in at 300 feet, the squadrons dropped their bombs close to the two bridges but failed to damage them, hitting the approaches instead. A smaller effort against the Burma-Thailand railroad the next day, with only 11 airplanes, brought more success. Using standard 1,000-pound bombs and Azon bombs, the four squadrons made the southern approach to Bridge #83 unserviceable and got additional hits on the center section

Shackrat Special, a late-model B-24J that joined the 9th Bomb Squadron toward the end of 1944. (SQ-Bomb-9-HI-January 1945, Albert F. Simpson Historical Research Center, Air Force Historical Research Agency, Maxwell AFB, AL)

while knocking Bridge #68 out of line. The squadrons split up on January 11, 1945, with five aircraft from the 436th and three from the 492nd Squadrons attacking Bridge #47 on the Bangkok-Chiengmai railroad. Bombing from 475 to 525 feet, the two squadrons dropped 40 1,000-pound bombs on the bridge, knocking down the south span and damaging an abutment and the approaches to the bridge. The bombers ran into small arms fire from nearby trains, but the B-24 gunners quickly silenced this. The 9th and 493rd Squadrons sent six airplanes each to bomb Bypass #2 near Bridge #71 on the railroad line from Pegu to Martaban. The 9th Squadron dropped 27 1,000-pound bombs on anti-aircraft positions defending the bridge, though the remaining anti-aircraft guns put up an accurate barrage that damaged one of the 493rd's airplanes. Using Azon bombs, the 493rd Squadron got six hits on the bypass bridge, knocking it out. The squadrons went on to Bridge #41—the secondary target—and destroyed that bridge with a combination of Azon and standard bombs.[89]

Lt. Harold Nadin was a bombardier with the 493rd Squadron on the mission that day and recorded his impressions in his diary, providing a vivid description of a typical 7th Group Azon bombing mission:

> Got up at 5:00 AM. Had breakfast at 5:15, went to briefing at 6:00. Drew our money belts and glasses. Today we were told of our target being Bridges #71 and 41. The first target was the bypass RR bridge which we low leveled Nov. 14. This time we were to go in at 10,000 feet. Were briefed in the usual fashion. Had pictures of targets etc. Also told we would have top cover of around 50 fighters as they expected P shooters from Rangoon to intercept us. We then drew our target folders and off to the trenches.
>
> We started engines at 7:30 and took off at 7:55. We were #3 ship in the first element and Gordon on our right wing. We had five Azon planes and one regular. Also six planes from the 9th with regular GI bombs. We flew a controlled ground speed as we were to meet the fighters over the target at 1300 and leave by 1330. We had to fly at 10,000 feet all the way and was quite comfortable. We flew almost direct, went just west of Akyab, the harbor was full of boats. We came just south of Toungoo and could see the airfield there but the fighters have left a long time ago. We were early so the lead ship flew due east to loose time. We came down East of the Salween River in Siam. Hit our I.P. and went on our run.
>
> Here we first saw our top cover of around nineteen P-38's and 47's, up higher as top cover for them. Our

Azon bombs going down on the jetties at Moulmein, January 13, 1945. (7th Bombardment Group (H) Historical Foundation, USAFA McDermott Library)

> I.P. was Damanaung and flew a Mag [magnetic] heading of 253 [degrees] to Hminpale. We could see our target as it was clear with no clouds. On our run, they were

> firing HAA [heavy anti-aircraft] at us and was pretty accurate. One hit just in front of the lead ship and put a hole in the nose turret but no further damage. You could hear them going off and sounded like a dull thud or someone banging on the nose wheel doors.
>
> On this run, there were all near misses, my first bomb hit just short on the tracks on the approach. There were no direct hits on the bridge; so we made a second run and the AA was getting too close. One hit about 40 feet low of us but no damage. On this run, my second bomb hit in the middle of the bridge putting it out. I dropped two bombs each time at 50 second intervals.
>
> Then we went to bridge #41 just south of Mokpalin. We made two runs on this, but only one of my bombs hit the tracks but the other boys got it. We got HAA fire from Mokpalin around the Sittang Bridge, but it was short and low as we were too far away from them. You could see the flashes on the ground, then the flak burst, like a big black mushroom.
>
> We then headed home and had fighter escort for a-ways. We came home direct and in formation all the way. We let down on our homeward leg and hit our field on the nose. Landed about 1830. We were interrogated and had our shot of combat whiskey. Time 11:10.[90]

The 7th Group took a hiatus from bombing bridges for the next two weeks, striking at other targets. On January 13, 1945, at the request of the 14th Army and in support of a crossing of the Irrawaddy River by XXXIII just above Mandalay, the Strategic Air Force sent all six RAF Liberator squadrons to bomb Japanese Army positions around Mandalay, while the 7th Bombardment Group went after Japanese troop concentrations at Sagaing, across the Irrawaddy River a few miles to the southwest. Six aircraft from the 436th Squadron, with the Squadron's B-24 ferret airplane tagging along, and six from the 492nd dropped strings of 480 120-pound fragmentation bombs and 24 228-pound incendiary bombs in and around the town. British Army intelligence later learned that possibly as many as 1,000 Japanese troops were killed in the attack on Sagaing. The bombers ran into intense anti-aircraft fire in the area. Escorting P-47s watched for AA fire, then went down to strafe the anti-aircraft positions. The 492nd maneuvered away from the AA fire, but two airplanes in the 436th Squadron got hit. Lt. Osborne, flying B-24 #64, had his hydraulic system knocked out by the AA fire. Returning to Madhaiganj, he made a safe landing using parachutes deployed from the waist gun windows. The 9th and 493rd Squadrons were to have bombed Sagaing as well, but at the last minute the 7th Group received a report of possible Japanese shipping at Mergui. The two squadrons put up twelve B-24s who searched the area around Mergui but found nothing. Instead, they bombed the jetties in Mergui harbor. Several of the 493rd's Azon bombs got direct hits on one of the main jetties.[91]

Maj. Charles Craig, CO of the 493rd Bomb Squadron in early 1945. (SQ-Bomb-493-HI-January 1945, Albert F. Simpson Historical Research Center, Air Force Historical Research Agency, Maxwell AFB, AL)

To disrupt Japanese fighter forces still active over central Burma, now reduced to around 20 Ki-43 Oscars from the long-serving *64th Sentai* with the withdrawal of other units to French Indochina and the Philippines, in mid-January the Strategic Air Force launched an offensive against the main Japanese airfields in central and southern Burma. The heavy bombers took on the airfields around Rangoon. While a formation of RAF Liberators bombed the nearby airfield at Zayatkwin, the 7th Group sent 27 airplanes in its largest mission of the year to bomb Mingaladon with another group of RAF Liberators. In an attack that would have been inconceivable two years earlier, the bombers went in at 11,000 feet, getting hits all over the intersection of Mingaladon's two runways and damaging other buildings against meager anti-aircraft fire. Though the bombers had an escort of P-47s, no Japanese fighters came up to intercept them. On January 18th, the Strategic Air Force bombed the airfields around Meitkila, in central Burma, assigning the satellite airfield at Thedaw to the 7th Group. The Group sent 27 airplanes on the mission. There were a number of airfields in the area, making it difficult to identify the Group's target. Leading the 7th Group formation, the 492nd Squadron picked out Thedaw at nearly the last minute, allowing only a short bomb run at around 8,300 feet. The Squadron dropped its bombs when the B-24s were in a 15° bank, but still got their bombs down on the runway and nearby revetments, as did the following squadrons. The 493rd Squadron had a different view of the success of the mission, stating in the Squadron's Flight Intelligence Report: "...it is the opinion of the Azon trained crews on this mission that had they been sent out with Azon bombs the target could have

The 436th Bomb Squadron approaches a bridge target on the Burma-Thailand Railroad on January 25, 1945. (SQ-Bomb-436-HI-January 1945, Albert F. Simpson Historical Research Center, Air Force Historical Research Agency, Maxwell AFB, AL)

Two bombs explode near the bridge and its approach as smoke drifts away from a previous attack. (SQ-Bomb-436-HI-January 1945, Albert F. Simpson Historical Research Center, Air Force Historical Research Agency, Maxwell AFB, AL)

Following the attack, one span of the bridge lies in the water below. (SQ-Bomb-436-HI-January 1945, Albert F. Simpson Historical Research Center, Air Force Historical Research Agency, Maxwell AFB, AL)

been knocked out by this squadron alone. A runway makes an ideal target for this type of bombing being wide enough to allow for more than the maximum error factor for the majority of Azon bombs dropped by this squadron with singular success in its previous missions."[92]

After bombing a Japanese supply area in support of the amphibious landing on Ramree Island, on the Burmese coast south of Akyab, on January 21, 1945, costing the 9th Squadron 2nd Lt. Roy Howser and his entire crew, the 7th Group went back to bombing bridges. Bad weather prevented a renewed attack on Bridge #277 on January 23rd—the 9th Squadron's favorite "grudge target"—but two days later, the Group had what the 436th Squadron called "sweet revenge". The targets on January 25th were bridges #82, #97, #151, and #163 on the Burma-Thailand railroad south of Thanbyuzayat and on the Thanbyuzayat-Ye line bombed two weeks previously. On this mission, the 7th Group rendered all four bridges unserviceable. The 436th Squadron, with Col. Alness flying as copilot in Capt. Nemecek's airplane, went after Bridge #163, and in a low level attack knocked out three spans and did extensive damage to the tracks leading to the bridge. Making up for their near misses on the January 8th attack on Bridge # 151, the 492nd Squadron came in at 300 feet and knocked down the southern span of the bridge using 1,000-pound bombs. The 9th and 493rd Squadrons successfully bombed #82 and #97. Weather, in the form of low clouds drifting over the target, made bombing difficult for the 493rd Squadron two days later on January 27th, but the Squadron got several Azon bombs onto the northern half of Bridge #83, knocking it out, then damaged the southern approach to Bridge #97. The 9th Squadron destroyed Bridge #148 in a low level attack at 300 feet and demolished the south end of the nearby bypass bridge with standard 1,000-pound bombs, then strafed a nearby train.[93]

For the mission on January 27th, the 436th and 492nd Squadrons tried out a new strategy for attacking bridges, targeting Bridges #147 and #148 that day. The Japanese Army had brought up more heavy, medium, and light anti-aircraft guns to defend the key bridges along the railroad lines. These guns needed to be taken out before the B-24s went in at low level. On the January 27th mission, the 492nd Squadron went in first at 3,500 feet to draw the anti-aircraft fire, dropping fragmentation bombs on the gun emplacements on subsequent bomb runs. The tactic, though dangerous, worked. On the first run, the Squadron's six aircraft counted an estimated 50 to 60 moderate but accurate bursts of AA fire. After the second bombing run the bursts were down to 20 to 30, and on the Squadron's last three runs there were only five bursts that could be seen; two aircraft received slight damage. After bombing the anti-aircraft positions, the high flight continued making dry runs over the bridge to draw off any fire aimed at the bombers coming in at low level. Taking out the anti-aircraft guns enabled two aircraft from the 436th Squadron to come in at 330 feet to knock out the bridges. Three of the 436th Squadron's airplanes were to have joined the 492nd Squadron's attacks on the anti-aircraft emplacements, but two had to abort with mechanical problems. The 436th attributed this complication to the fact that its better airplanes were all in China hauling gasoline. The two squadrons switched roles on January 29th in attacks on Bridges #18 and #19 on the Burma-Thailand railroad line, south of Thanbyuzayat. That day, the 9th and 493rd Squadrons went after another set of old favorites: Bridges #41 and #71 on the Pegu-Martaban line, with an escort of P-47s and P-38s. On this occasion, the 436th Squadron provided the high flight to knock out the anti-aircraft guns. Three aircraft bombed the AA positions from 6,500 feet with fragmentation bombs. With the guns knocked out at each bridge, the two low-level bombers from the 436th joined the 492nd Squadron's traffic pattern around the bridges, each airplane coming in at 350 to 450 feet, dropping 1,000-pound bombs at 25-foot intervals. When they finished their bomb runs, they had destroyed both #18 and #19 and damaged the tracks approaching two other nearby bridges. The new strategy had worked, but it was not without risk; attacking bridges from low level had multiple dangers. As the 492nd Squadron wrote in its monthly history: "As long as the Japs don't catch on to our tactics this is a very effective way of protecting low level ships. Even at 180-190 mph indicated, B-24s are simply huge clay pigeons. A machine gun scored two hits on the right wing of two 492nd airplanes as it was. Another problem on such attacks is the spacing of individual planes in the bombing pattern. We peeled off at twenty second intervals, whereas the bombs had 8-11 second delay fuses. The gaining of just nine seconds in the pattern would be disastrous. One ship did gain about seven seconds and was nearly lost due to flying debris (wooden pieces of bridge)."[94]

The 493rd Squadron had a successful but frustrating mission against Bridges #41 and #71. These bridges had stronger anti-aircraft defenses, so were better targets for medium altitude bombing with the Azon bombs. But on this

Bridge #151 on the Burma-Thailand railroad line, taken from a 492nd Bomb Squadron B-24 on January 25, 1945, after the Squadron had knocked it down. (SQ-Bomb-492-HI-January 1945, Albert F. Simpson Historical Research Center, Air Force Historical Research Agency, Maxwell AFB, AL)

The 9th Bomb Squadron took out Bridge #148 on January 27, 1945. (SQ-Bomb-9-HI-January 1945, Albert F. Simpson Historical Research Center, Air Force Historical Research Agency, Maxwell AFB, AL)

B-24 #88 from the 492nd Bomb Squadron pulls away after bombing Bridge #18 on January 29, 1945. (SQ-Bomb-492-HI-January 1945, Albert F. Simpson Historical Research Center, Air Force Historical Research Agency, Maxwell AFB, AL)

A reconnaissance photo of the railroad yards and roundhouse at Jumbhorn, in southern Thailand, target of the long mission of February 3, 1945. (SQ-Bomb-492-HI-February 1945, Albert F. Simpson Historical Research Center, Air Force Historical Research Agency, Maxwell AFB, AL)

The 436th Bomb Squadron over Jumbhorn on February 3, 1945, the 7th Bomb Group's longest mission of the war up to that time. (SQ-Bomb-436-HI-February 1945, Albert F. Simpson Historical Research Center, Air Force Historical Research Agency, Maxwell AFB, AL)

A post-strike photo of the demolished railroad yards at Jumbhorn. (SQ-Bomb-492-HI-February 1945, Albert F. Simpson Historical Research Center, Air Force Historical Research Agency, Maxwell AFB, AL)

mission the 493rd had a lot of problems with its Azon bombs and equipment. Coming in at 10,540 feet, the 493rd made two runs over the bypass bridges at #71, only to have several Azon bombs hang up on the bomb racks. Other Azon bombs dropped, but failed to respond to the control commands from the bombardier. In two instances the flares on the tail fin failed to ignite. Still, using the Azons the Squadron knocked out the central span of Bypass #2 at Bridge #71 with a direct hit, knocked Bypass #1 out of line, and destroyed the northern end of Bridge #41, the tertiary target. On the way back to Pandaveswar, the airplanes with bombs that had hung up dropped them in salvos over the Mokpalin railroad yards. The first month of the year ended with an attack on a Japanese headquarters in the town of Kyaukse, south of Mandalay, again at the request of the 14th Army.[95]

It was difficult for Allied intelligence to determine with any precision the effect the bombing campaign was having on the flow of supplies into Burma, but the estimate was that the average daily tonnage over the Burma-Thailand railroad dropped from about 700/800 tons a day to perhaps a third of this amount during January—far less than what the *Burma Area Army* required. The Strategic Air Force's operations resulted in an average of 3.3 cuts along the line from Pegu to Thanbyuzayat and 4.1 cuts on the line from Thanbyuzayat to Bangkok on any given day, with a peak of five and nine cuts, respectively. As previously noted, the Japanese became adept at making rapid repairs to bridges and tracks, so that few bridges along the main line were out for much longer than a week. Still, the necessity of making constant repairs on the railroad system represented a drain on Japanese resources at a time when *Burma Area Army* needed everything available for the defense of southern Burma.[96]

During February, the 7th Bombardment Group set two records: one for the longest combat mission flown and one for the heaviest bomb load carried in the Army Air Forces India-Burma Sector. The records reflected the Group's effort during the month: continued attacks on the Japanese line of communications into Burma and tactical missions flown in support of the 14th Army's advance. February also saw the 7th Group break all its previous bomb records. The Group was operational on 20 out of 28 days during the month and dropped 1,580 tons of bombs; greater than the tonnage the Group dropped during all of 1942 and 178% greater than the prior month.[97] The month began with the longest mission the 7th Group had ever flown, a round trip of close to 2,500 miles

The 493rd Bomb Squadron got a direct hit on a railroad bridge on the Bangkok-Singapore railroad line near Jumbhorn on the mission of February 3, 1945. (SQ-Bomb-493-HI-February 1945, Albert F. Simpson Historical Research Center, Air Force Historical Research Agency, Maxwell AFB, AL)

Capt. William Dabney (left), CO of the 9th Bomb Squadron, observes the final formation briefing for pilots and copilots before the start of a mission. (SQ-Bomb-9-HI-February 1945, Albert F. Simpson Historical Research Center, Air Force Historical Research Agency, Maxwell AFB, AL)

to bomb the important railroad switching center and railroad yards on the Bangkok-Singapore railroad line, located at the town of Jumbhorn, in southern Thailand. Jumbhorn was only a few hundred miles from the Malaya border. This mission, on February 3, 1945, was a combined Strategic Air Force effort with 72 RAF Liberators and 7th Group B-24s participating, flying in formation from their bases in India to Jumbhorn. The 9th, 436th, and 492nd Squadrons sent seven aircraft each to bomb the locomotive round house and nearby transshipment warehouse buildings at the Jumbhorn railroad yards. The four RAF Liberator squadrons bombed the main railroad station. Lt. Gene Jacobus was flying as lead aircraft in the 492nd Squadron's second element on the way to the target at low altitude over the ocean and 1,000 miles from base when one of the engines on his B-24 exploded and burst into flames. With commendable alacrity, Jacobus and his copilot, Lt. Elmer Smith, immediately executed emergency procedures: they feathered the propeller on the burning engine, activated the fire extinguisher to put the fire out, and jettisoned the bombs and bomb bay tanks. On three engines and a long way from base, Jacobus instructed the crew to throw out all ammunition and any loose items to lighten their load. They made it back to Madhaiganj and landed safely. Jacobus and Smith were awarded the Distinguished Flying Cross for their skill in saving their airplane and crew. The rest of the formation flew on without incident. Coming in on the target across the Kra Isthmus, the three squadrons found a front of cumulonimbus clouds ahead of them blocking their route. The formation continued east to go out over the Gulf of Thailand, letting down to 6,500 feet and turning around to the west to come back in over land. The bombers had to thread their way through

Throwing their gear onto the truck, combat crews from the 9th Bomb Squadron head out to the line for a mission in February 1945. (SQ-Bomb-9-HI-February 1945, Albert F. Simpson Historical Research Center, Air Force Historical Research Agency, Maxwell AFB, AL)

the thunderclouds to the railroad yards, bombing from 4,500 feet. There was no anti-aircraft fire and the bombing was near perfect, demolishing the round house. The only regret the squadrons had was the decision not to go down and strafe the more than 200 railroad cars they saw in the yards. While the other squadrons were bombing the yards, the 493rd carried out an Azon attack against a railroad bridge on the main Bangkok-Singapore line. Each of the B-24s carried two bomb bay fuel tanks and four 1,000-pound Azon bombs. Two of the Azon bombs hit dead center on the bridge, while another direct hit and two near misses at the southern end of the bridge knocked the tracks out of line. The damage made the bridge unserviceable. The squadrons returned to Pandaveswar and Madhaiganj after flying nearly 16 hours.[98]

The 7th Group kept up the attacks on the railroad bridges every few days for the remainder of the month. On February 5th, the Group went back to Bridge #277 at Kanchanaburi,

A 9th Bomb Squadron crew prepare to board their airplane. (SQ-Bomb-9-HI-February 1945, Albert F. Simpson Historical Research Center, Air Force Historical Research Agency, Maxwell AFB, AL)

Thailand. The 9th Squadron's history for the month recorded the sentiments that the other squadrons must have shared. "To all men in the Ninth", the Squadron wrote, "there must come at one time or another a mission to Bridge Q654 (old 277) at Kanchanaburi. On 5 February another attempt was made to knock out this seemingly indestructible span, and again the attempt was unsuccessful. Some of the crews have been to this particular target five times, and one lad volunteered to parachute out and dynamite the damn thing."[99] On this mission, the 492nd Squadron went in first to neutralize the anti-aircraft positions, dropping fragmentation bombs in and around the gun positions guarding the bridge and the nearby bypass bridge. The 9th and 436th Squadrons circled out of range until the 492nd had finished bombing. After the 492nd Squadron hit the guns, the other squadrons headed south of the target for a few miles, descending to low altitude for their bombing runs. Each B-24 peeled off at intervals of 20 seconds, then headed toward the bridge and the bypass to bomb at 500 feet, with the nose and top turret gunners spraying the approaches as they went in. The copilot held the speed at 180 mph while the pilot concentrated on the approach. The first few airplanes had a clear run in, but those following had to drop their bombs into the cloud of dust of previous explosions. Six aircraft from the 493rd Squadron arrived an hour later after the dust had cleared to make individual runs on the bridge and the bypass with their Azon bombs. Clouds in the area interfered with the bombing runs. Once again, Old 277 survived, though the low level attack and the Azon bombs did do some damage to the approaches to both the bridge and the bypass.[100]

The 7th Group went after bridges again on February 7, 1945. The 436th Squadron had an exceptionally productive day. The Squadron's primary target was a railroad cut, where the line went between two steep inclines at MS 41 south of Thanbyuzayat. The Squadron's first section of four airplanes successfully bombed the cut, demolishing the railroad line, then destroyed nearby Bridge #68. The second section of four bombers diverted to other bridges, knocking out Bridges #83 and #97. The Squadron's radar ferret aircraft again went on the mission. The bombing was, as the Squadron recorded, "to perfection".[101] The Eager Beavers of the 492nd Squadron sent eight aircraft to bomb the railroad line near MS 41 and Bridges #120 and #121. While one airplane bombed the anti-aircraft positions, the first element knocked out the southwestern and northern approaches to Bridge #120—a road bridge—and possibly knocked out one or two spans of the bridge, as well as bombing nearby warehouses. At #121, the Squadron got several hits on the northern approach but no other damage. The Squadron's second element destroyed lengths of track around MS 41 and caused a small landslide. The 493rd Squadron sent two sections of four aircraft to bomb Bridge #121 after the 492nd had completed its attack, one section taking off an hour after the first. The first section bombed

Old #91 B-24J *Jungle Jig*, the oldest airplane in the 492nd Squadron. This airplane flew 80 combat missions and 35 Hump flights before being retired to second line duties in May 1945. (SQ-Bomb-492-HI-May 1945, Albert F. Simpson Historical Research Center, Air Force Historical Research Agency, Maxwell AFB, AL)

from 5,280 feet—not a normal bombing altitude for the Azon bomb—while the second section came in at 8,250 feet an hour later. Despite having a number of dud Azon bombs that either failed to explode or respond to control, the two sections got

17 direct hits on the bridge and its approaches with Azon and standard 1,000-pound bombs, destroying two-thirds of the bridge, knocking several spans into the river below, and demolishing the northern and part of the southern approaches.[102]

Success against Old 277 finally came on February 13, 1945. The 9th and 493rd Squadrons were the instruments of the bridge's destruction. Five days before, on February 9th, the 9th Squadron had gone after Bridge #227 from medium and low altitude, getting two direct hits and knocking out two sections, while the 493rd went after the long Bridge #600 on the Burma-Thailand railroad, knocking out half the main span with Azon bombs. With this warm up exercise behind them, the 9th and 493rd Squadrons went back to Bridge #277. The plan called for the two squadrons to attack #277 and its wooden trestle bypass bridge at low level (Bridge #277 and its bypass bridge had been redesignated Q654). The 436th Squadron went in first, four B-24s bombing the steel and concrete #277 at 450 feet with 1,000-pound bombs and getting six to eight direct hits on the northern approach to the bridge. The bombers ran into intense but inaccurate machine gun fire. The two aircraft going after the bypass bridge got three probable hits on the northern approaches. The 9th Squadron went in an hour later. Four airplanes went after #277 at 420 to 450 feet, knocking two central spans of the bridge into the river and one of the northern spans, while one aircraft knocked holes in the center and northern spans of the bypass bridge. To suppress the anti-aircraft guns, the gunners on the B-24s fired off 12,500 rounds during the low level passes on the bridges. To get around the destruction of the main bridge and its bypass bridge, the Japanese built a causeway across the river bed—mostly dry in this season—about 200 yards from the bypass bridge. A short section of wooden trestle went over the narrow river, allowing bullock carts to transport supplies from the railroad line on one side to the railroad line on the other while the two bridges were under repair. The 7th Group would come back to the Old 277 again.[103]

From the middle of February, the 7th Group divided its effort between the bridges and the battle front. While the Azon-equipped 493rd Squadron continued to go after bridges on the Burma-Thailand railroad, the Group's other three squadrons flew tactical missions in support of the 14th Army's advances on Mandalay and Meiktila. As Lt. Gen. Slim intended, the 14th Army's XXXIII Corps advance on Mandalay gave the Japanese *Burma Area Army* the impression that the sole objective of the 14th Army was to capture the ancient and symbolic capital of Burma through a double envelopment using one division to attack from the north and one division to cross the Irrawaddy and attack from the south. The attack on Mandalay from the north by the 19th Indian Infantry Division began on February 10th. Two days later, the 20th Indian Infantry Division began crossing the Irrawaddy to the south. Then, on February 14, 1945, with the Japanese Army's attention focused on holding Mandalay, Slim launched what came to be considered his master stroke of the Burma campaign: the capture of Meiktila. In the early hours of the morning, the 7th Indian Infantry Division crossed the Irrawaddy River at Nyaungu, southwest of Mandalay, and captured a bridgehead. Three days later, the 17th Indian Infantry Division and the 255th Armored Brigade began their crossing. On February 21st, the 17th Division and the 255th Armored Brigade launched their advance on Meiktila, capturing the town on March 3, 1945, after heavy fighting. With a British force sitting on their main supply base and astride their supply lines to the south, the Japanese *15th* and *33rd Armies* had to retake Meiktila while fighting off the British divisions pressing on Mandalay. Slim had maneuvered the Japanese Army into giving battle to hold on to central Burma and now he intended to destroy it.[104]

Maj. Harry Alexander took command of the 436th Bomb Squadron in February 1945. (SQ-Bomb-436-HI-February 1945, Albert F. Simpson Historical Research Center, Air Force Historical Research Agency, Maxwell AFB, AL)

Eastern Air Command had alerted the Strategic Air Force to be prepared to support the 14th Army's attack on Mandalay and the advance on Meiktila from February 11th to the 26th. The campaign against the railroad line from Thailand into Burma had to be maintained as well. The tactical missions began on February 11th, in the largest heavy-bomber mission undertaken over Burma. The Strategic Air Force sent out 84 RAF Liberators and 7th Bombardment Group B-24s with 59 B-29s from the XX Bomber Command to bomb the important Japanese Army supply dumps at Victoria Lake, near Rangoon.

The 7th Bomb Group heads toward Ramree Island to support the amphibious landing on February 21, 1945. (3A-33601, RG 342FH, NARA)

These dumps held an estimated 50% to 75% of the Japanese Army's supplies in Burma. With the campaign against the bridges severely disrupting the flow of supplies, the destruction of supply dumps in Burma had a direct impact on the Japanese forces fighting against the 14th Army.[105] The bombers had an escort of RAF Thunderbolts and P-38s from the 459th Squadron. Japanese fighters attempted to intercept the RAF Liberators, but the escorts drove them off. The 7th Group ran into nothing more than anti-aircraft fire. Bombing was considered excellent. The tactical strikes continued for the next two weeks, the 7th Group bombing Japanese artillery positions around Myinmu, on the west bank of the Irrawaddy River, on February 12th; supply dumps on February 15th and 16th (the 492nd Squadron's lead bombardier deemed the latter mission perfect); Heho airfield on February 17th; and troop concentrations around Yenangyaung on February 18th. After a three-day pause to rest the crews and do needed maintenance, the 7th Group went back to bombing Japanese Army supply dumps supporting the *15th* and *33rd Armies* fighting around Mandalay and Meiktila. In the course of these missions, the 7th Group set a record for the heaviest bomb load carried by a B-24 in the India-Burma Sector. In an attack on dumps around the town of Myittha, south of Mandalay, on February 21st, the 436th sent three B-24s and the 492nd Squadron sent nine bombers each with a load of 10,400 pounds of bombs: twelve 500-pound bombs, four 1,000-pound bombs, and four 100-pound bombs. Bombing between 8,000 and 9,000 feet, the squadrons got most of their bombs in the area of the dumps. Two days later, the two squadrons carried the same load of bombs to cover the dumps at Mahlaing, while the 9th Squadron bombed dumps at Kuanghmudaw and Myinggan on February 22nd and 24th. Then, on February 25th, 436th Squadron broke the weight lifting record established just a few days earlier on a mission to bomb a Japanese Army headquarters and the dumps at Taunggyi. The 436th sent three airplanes carrying a staggering load of 11,000 pounds of bombs, on this occasion adding four 250-pound bombs in place of the four 100-pound bombs. Five airplanes carried 228-pound incendiary clusters. Once again bombing from medium altitude, the Squadron got an excellent pattern in the designated area. The next day, the 9th Squadron carried a load of 10,400 pounds of bombs to hit Taunggyi again. As they turned for base, the nine aircraft could see a column of smoke and dust behind them rising to 8,000 feet.[106]

While the other squadrons flew tactical missions, the 493rd Squadron continued the battle of the bridges, with occasional assistance from the 9th Squadron. The 493rd sent small formations of four to six aircraft on five missions to bomb bridges on the Burma-Thailand railroad and the Bangkok-Chiengmai railroad line. On one mission clouds obscured the bridges, forcing a diversion to bomb a Japanese landing ground, but on the other four missions the 493rd Squadron obtained direct hits, destroying the bridge or rendering it unserviceable. The Squadron's best day was on February 17, 1945, when four bridges on the railroad line from Moulmein to Ye-u were destroyed or severely damaged. On February 25th, the Squadron went back to the key Ban Dara Bridge in Thailand. Using Azon bombs, the 493rd destroyed the newly-built bypass bridge with four direct hits that knocked down the bridge's eastern and western sections. By this time, the 493rd Squadron had worked out the best tactics for using Azon bombs. On missions where there was little chance of interception, as the flight approached the first initial point the airplanes would go into a trail formation with a 30-second interval between airplanes. At the second initial point leading to the target, each airplane would turn in to make its own run. The flight would set up a circular pattern around the bridge target, with each bomber making individual runs, dropping one Azon bomb on each run. The airplane would make a normal approach to the target, usually flying in line with the axis of the bridge, often flying along the railroad line or road leading to the bridge. The bombardier used his Norden bomb sight to line up correctly on the bridge and to make corrections as needed before dropping a single Azon bomb. Once the flare on the tail fin had ignited, the bombardier steered the bomb onto the target while the pilot kept the airplane on a straight course in level flight. With experience, the Squadron found that the best altitude for Azon bombing was between 8,000 to 10,000 feet. Bombing from this altitude gave the bombardier sufficient time to take over control of the Azon bomb and steer it to the target, but was not so high that range to the target became a problem. It was best for the bombardier to concentrate on one bomb at a time; dropping more than one Azon bomb proved too difficult to control. The results were, for the time, impressive, leading one report on the Azon to state that "...their use has resulted in the most accurate medium altitude bombing attained in the 7th Bomb Group and possibly in the IB [India-Burma] Theater."[107] Statistically, the Azon was a vast improvement over conventional bombing. In an analysis of conventional versus Azon attacks during the period, it was found that in conventional attacks, the 7th Group's squadrons got eight hits on bridges out of 225 bombs dropped, for a hit rate of 2.6 per cent. At that rate it took 33

A B-24 formation about to drop their bombs on a mission in early 1945. B-24J #43 is an Azon airplane from the 493rd Bomb Squadron. (SQ-Bomb-493-HI-March 1945, Albert F. Simpson Historical Research Center, Air Force Historical Research Agency, Maxwell AFB, AL)

sorties to knock out a bridge. In contrast, using Azon bombs the 493rd Squadron had a hit rate of 21 per cent, nearly ten times better. Azon bombs were not perfect, and it took an average of 18.5 Azon bombs to destroy a bridge or make it unserviceable, but it required only 3.3 sorties to do so. In attacks on 36 bridges, the Azon bombs knocked out or made unserviceable 23 bridges. Interestingly, the introduction of the Azon bomb had a salutary effect on the other 7th Bombardment Group squadrons. Bombing accuracy improved, as the non-Azon bombardiers took up the challenge of matching the results of their Azon-bombing colleagues.[108] By the end of February, the 7th Group had destroyed 50 bridges since the Battle of the Bridges began on November 1, 1944.[109]

The squadrons came back together for the last two missions of the month. On February 27th, the 7th Group went back to bombing bridges: the 9th and 492nd Squadrons going after the bypass at Bridge Q195, while the 436th and 493rd went out to bomb the bypass at Bridge Q167. The 9th and 492nd Squadrons got good hits and near misses on their targets, destroying both the bypass and the bridge. After bombing, the 492nd went down to strafe rolling stock along the railroad line. The 436th got several near misses on its target, but failed to knock it down. The 493rd Squadron came in 40 minutes later and in six individual runs got direct hits on the center of the bypass bridge and the northern and the southern approaches, rendering it unserviceable. The last mission of the month on February 28th was a massive raid against Mingaladon airfield by 102 RAF Liberators and 7th Group B-24s. Coming in over the airfield between 10,000 and 12,000 feet to drop loads of fragmentation bombs, the squadrons ran into accurate heavy anti-aircraft fire that damaged a number of airplanes. The 436th Squadron sent up a record 13 bombers for the mission. One of the Squadron's B-24s (No. #62) had a narrow escape when a shell hit the supercharger on one engine and continued on through the wing without exploding.[110]

For their efforts in support of the 14th Army, the 7th Group received the following letter from Air Cdre Mellersh, Air Officer Commanding, Strategic Air Force:

My Dear Alness,

1. On completion of the recent sustained effort put out by the Strategic Air Force in support of the 14th Army during their crossing of the Irrawaddy River in their operations for the capture of Mandalay, I want to send you my thanks and congratulations for the really fine show all squadrons have put up. The fact that you have succeeded in meeting all our demands, and have carried out the tasks given you with such skill and precision has been most gratifying to me personally and reflects the very greatest credit on your personnel, both air crews and ground crews.
2. I shall be glad if you will pass on my congratulations to all concerned and will let them know that I realize what a great deal of hard work this has meant for them and how much I appreciate their efforts."[111]

Nearing the End in Burma

As March began, the 14th Army's IV and XXXIII Corps were engaged in heavy fighting around Mandalay and Meiktila. By the end of the month, Lt. Gen. Sir William Slim's British and Indian divisions had captured both. The shattered remnants of the Japanese *15th* and *33rd Armies* were in headlong retreat to the south. As the month drew to a close, the 14th Army was poised to begin the advance on Rangoon. Released from supporting the 14th Army's advance, the Strategic Air Force returned to bombing the Japanese lines of communications and supply dumps in southern Burma and Thailand. Within the 7th Bombardment Group, the 9th, 436th, and 492nd Squadrons flew a mix of missions, bombing bridges and dumps, while the 493rd Squadron concentrated almost exclusively on attacking bridges. The month saw the Group surpass the records for longest mission and heaviest bomb load established the month before. And after a hiatus of nearly two months, the Group suffered several combat losses, the unfortunate 9th Squadron losing three aircraft during the month.

Major William Dabney, CO of the 9th Bomb Squadron, congratulates Cpl. Howard Stordahl, crew chief on *Shackrat Special*, after the bomber successfully completed 50 missions without an abort. Capt. Dow Martin, Jr., Squadron Engineering Officer, looks on. (SQ-Bomb-9-HI-March 1945, Albert F. Simpson Historical Research Center, Air Force Historical Research Agency, Maxwell AFB, AL)

The 492nd Bomb Squadron's *Cabin in the Sky* gets a new propeller. (SQ-Bomb-492-HI-March 1945, Albert F. Simpson Historical Research Center, Air Force Historical Research Agency, Maxwell AFB, AL)

During March, the 7th Group flew three long missions into Thailand, beginning with an attack on the railroad yards at Korat, in central Thailand, on March 2, 1945, following a night attack by RAF Liberators a day earlier. The Group sent 24 aircraft carrying a 10,000-pound load of two bomb bay tanks and eight 500-pound bombs. For the first hour or so, the airplanes were so heavy that flying in formation proved difficult. The bombing was excellent, the bombers going in at 5,000 feet to complete the destruction of the yards, hitting the tracks, repair sheds, rolling stock, and warehouses. Two days later, the 7th Group flew a night mission, the first for several months, to bomb the warehouses alongside the Klong Toei docks on the Chao Phya River in Bangkok, while RAF Liberators bombed other targets in the city. The aircraft took off and bombed the target individually, dropping 65 tons of incendiaries. Flying with the 492nd Squadron, Maj. Jensen, Squadron S-3, tried out one of the Group's newly-acquired airplanes equipped with radar for navigation and bombing. The radar was a great help in locating the target alongside the river. Painted in black, the airplane proved to be more difficult for the anti-aircraft guns to acquire than the standard un-camouflaged metal B-24s. The 7th Group went back to Bangkok on March 27, 1945, in the Group's first daylight raid over the city. Four RAF Liberator squadrons were on the mission as well. There was some trepidation about going over the city during the day, but the mission proved uneventful. The squadrons took off at night and formed up at a designated rendezvous point. On the way to Bangkok they picked up an escort of P-51D Mustangs from the 2nd Air Commando Group who were disappointed not to run into any Japanese fighters. The targets that day were the Klong Toei docks again and Japanese supply dumps at Klong Bang Chak. Smoke and clouds made some of the targets difficult to pick out, interfering with the bombing.[112]

The key supply dumps at Victoria Lake in Rangoon were the target for three Strategic Air Force missions during the month on March 9th, 11th, and 17th. As the 9th Squadron recorded, the missions to Rangoon saw many new crews initiated into the "Goon at Noon" Club. The mythical club was, as the Squadron's history explained: "...a relic of 1943 when Rangoon was so tough and our noonday attacks were made without benefit of top cover."[113] On each of the three Rangoon missions the Japanese responded with intense anti-aircraft fire, but unlike in 1943, no Japanese fighters rose up to intercept the bombers, giving the P-38, P-47, and P-51 escorts little to do. Weather on the first mission on March 9th was poor, with 8/10ths cloud covering the 7th Group's target area. There were 70 RAF Liberators and 7th Group B-24s over Rangoon that day. Only five aircraft in the 436th Squadron's formation

The 7th Bomb Group bombing the jetties at Martaban on March 7, 1945. (SQ-Bomb-436-HI-March 1945, Albert F. Simpson Historical Research Center, Air Force Historical Research Agency, Maxwell AFB, AL)

dropped their bombs in the target area, the other seven going on to bomb the dumps at Prome, the secondary target. In the 492nd Squadron, the first flight of six airplanes was unable to locate the target through the clouds. The first element decided that making a second run over the target and giving the anti-aircraft guns a chance to correct their aim was probably not

On March 19, 1945, the 7th Bomb Group flew what was believed to be the longest B-24 formation flight to bomb bridges in the Kra Isthmus area of southern Thailand. (SQ-Bomb-492-HI-March 1945, Albert F. Simpson Historical Research Center, Air Force Historical Research Agency, Maxwell AFB, AL)

a good idea. The flight headed off to the secondary target at Prome, but neglected to inform the 492nd Squadron's second flight of their intentions. The second flight found a break in the clouds and dropped their bombs on another area of the dumps. Assuming the Squadron's first flight was on its way back to base, the second flight followed dutifully behind the first flight on its bomb run over Prome, needlessly flying through more intense AA fire, fortunately without incurring any casualties. The 492nd Squadron's history did not record what was said after the two flights landed back at the base. A return visit to the dumps on March 11th saw better weather over the target and much better bombing. On this mission, 34 7th Group B-24s joined 36 RAF Liberators. There were 32 heavy anti-aircraft guns in range as the formation came in on the target at 11,000 feet, with another 22 heavy and 21 light AA guns within a four-mile radius and still effective. The anti-aircraft fire was described as intense and accurate. The 436th Squadron had five aircraft damaged and one crewman wounded, while the 9th and 492nd Squadrons escaped injury, the 492nd recording that "...the flak was as close as possible without being fatal to any of our planes."[114] The third visit to the Victoria Lake dumps that month on March 17th was another large mission, comprising 63 RAF Liberators and 7th Group B-24s with 70 B-29s from the XX Bomber Command. While the B-29s bombed from 27,000 to 30,000 feet, the B-24s went in at medium altitude. The 9th and 492nd Squadrons bombed from 14,900 feet into the target area, apparently

Results of a low-level bombing and strafing attack on the Burma-Thailand Railroad on March 22, 1945. (SQ-Bomb-436-HI-March 1945, Albert F. Simpson Historical Research Center, Air Force Historical Research Agency, Maxwell AFB, AL)

without difficulty, but when the 436th Squadron's formation of nine aircraft came in they found the target covered in clouds and smoke. There was flak over the target, but on this occasion it was meager in intensity and inaccurate, so the 436th decided to go around again. Making a 360° turn and climbing to 14,000 feet, the formation used check points to locate their assigned target area and bombed through the smoke.[115]

The main effort continued to be against the Japanese line of communications. To compound the difficulty of maintaining the flow of supplies into Burma, the Strategic Air Force arranged strikes on the jetties and marshaling yards at Martaban, on the opposite side of the Salween River estuary from Moulmein. The Burma-Thailand railroad ended at Moulmein, where supplies were unloaded and transported by ferry across to Martaban to be put back on trains traveling into Burma. On March 7, 1945, 74 RAF Liberators and three squadrons from the 7th Group (9th, 436th, and 492nd) struck Martaban, severely damaging the jetties and yards and creating another bottleneck in the flow of supplies. On this occasion, the 436th Squadron used one of its radar planes to set up the correct course for the bombing run, the prominent headlands of Martaban and Moulmein providing sharp features on the radar scope. Seventy-five per cent to 90 per cent of the bombs hit in the marshaling yards and gutted the transshipment warehouses alongside. For their next mission against the Japanese line of communications, the 7th Group's squadrons attacked bridges on the Bangkok-Singapore railroad line on the Kra Isthmus, near the town of Surat Thani, more than a hundred miles beyond Jumbhorn, in what the Group believed was the longest mission by a B-24 formation in WWII. This was a round trip of over 2,700 miles, the equivalent of a flight from Boston to Kansas City and back. The 9th and 493rd Squadrons went first, setting out on March 19, 1945, with two bomb bay tanks and four 1,000-pound regular or Azon bombs. That same day, 48 RAF Liberators went out to bomb the railroad at Ban Na Nian, near Jumbhorn. Eight aircraft from the 493rd scored direct hits on Bridge TG 40 and the road bridge next to it, dropping the central spans of both bridges into the river. The 9th Squadron sent 13 B-24s to bomb four bridges at low level, the bombers making their runs at 300 feet. As one of the B-24s went over a target, small arms fire killed the navigator—Lt. Becker, a recent addition to the Squadron, who was observing the bomb run from the astrodome in front of the cockpit; ground fire wounded the navigator and a bombardier in another airplane. The squadrons returned to Pandaveswar, having spent nearly nineteen hours in the air. The next day, March 20th, the 436th and 492nd Squadrons took their turn, flying the 2,700 miles to bomb bridges and strafe locomotives and rolling stock along the

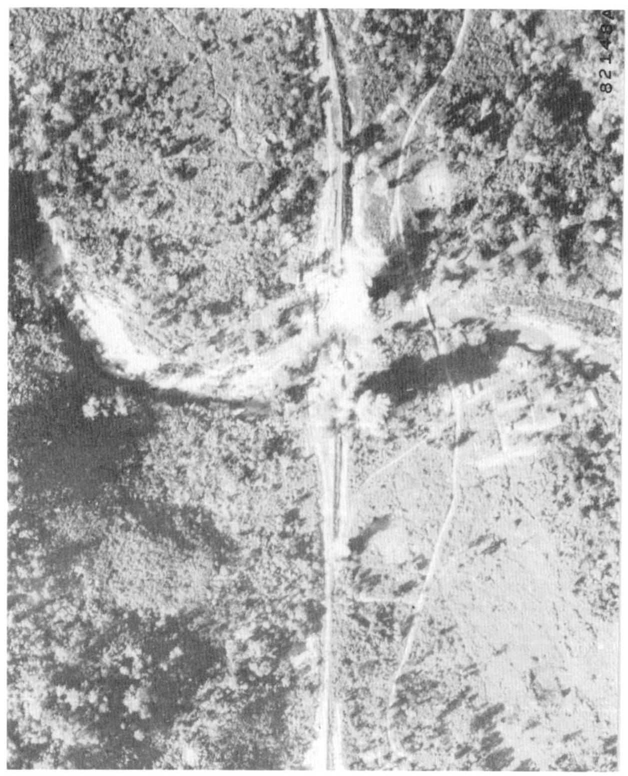

Part of the Burma-Thailand railroad line torn up during low-level attack on March 22, 1945. A knocked-out locomotive can be seen at the lower left of the photo. (SQ-Bomb-436-HI-March 1945, Albert F. Simpson Historical Research Center, Air Force Historical Research Agency, Maxwell AFB, AL)

Singapore-Bangkok railroad line near Ban Don, close to the Thai town of Surat Thani. The 492nd destroyed one bridge, and between them the two squadrons damaged and displaced the railroad tracks on several more. One fighter plane attempted an interception on one of the 492nd's bombers, possibly a Royal Thai Air Force Ki-43 Oscar, but didn't inflict any damage. In the 436th Squadron's formation, ground fire shot out an engine on Lt. Kline's airplane, but he made it back to base on three engines. The 436th lost one aircraft on the mission (a B-24L), but the crew survived. Lt. Oscar Larson and his crew were forced to bail out on the return flight when they ran out of fuel late at night searching for Madhaganj in poor visibility.[116] For successfully completing this mission of an unprecedented distance for a formation of airplanes (the squadrons noted with pride that the distance was only 300 miles shorter than the longest B-29 mission flown up to that time), the 7th Bombardment Group was awarded its second Distinguished Unit Citation.

A 436th Bomb Squadron B-24J undergoing maintenance in March 1945. (SQ-Bomb-436-HI-March 1945, Albert F. Simpson Historical Research Center, Air Force Historical Research Agency, Maxwell AFB, AL)

On March 22, 1945, the Strategic Air Force launched a major attack on locomotives, rolling stock, and other railroad targets on sections of the Burma-Thailand railroad and sections on the Bangkok-Chiengmai railroad line. The 436th Squadron was apparently the only 7th Bombardment Group squadron to participate in the mission of March 22nd, but had great success, covering a section from Nakorn Sawarn to Uttaradit in Thailand. Eight aircraft went out that day, splitting into two sections of four aircraft to cover separate lengths of the railroad line. Sweeping in at low level, the B-24s acted like fighter-bombers, strafing locomotives and rolling stock, bombing and strafing railroad installations, blowing up railroad tracks, and dropping the span on one bridge. One bomber even strafed and destroyed an airplane on the airfield at Nakorn Sawarn. Lt. Bradley Hamlett was flying as copilot in Lt. Linaman's airplane that day, destroying two locomotives and damaging a bridge. On the return flight one of the crew reported smelling gasoline. Looking into the bomb bay, Hamlett saw gasoline pouring out of one of the wing tanks. Bill Nations, the flight engineer, transferred the fuel from the leaking tank to another and opened the bomb bay doors for ventilation. The flight home was without incident. The next day, the ground crew found a live 20mm shell in a wing spar. The shell had grazed the tire in the wing and penetrated the fuel tank. This type of Japanese 20mm shell was set to explode when the attached tracer burned out. Somehow the fuel in the tank extinguished the tracer, allowing Hamlett and his fellow crew members to survive.[117]

On a separate mission that day to the Grand Cocos Islands in the Bay of Bengal, the 9th Squadron destroyed the main Japanese radar site on the islands and damaged two other radar sites. Coming in on the bomb run at 350 feet, machine gun fire hit Lt. Francis Murphy's airplane in the No. 4 engine. As the formation pulled off the target, the other crews saw Murphy's No.4 engine smoking badly. Flames burst from the engine and then a fire erupted in the bomb bay area. Murphy's airplane turned over, crashed into the sea and exploded, killing the crew. The 492nd Squadron went out on March 23rd to cover a section of the line north of Bangkok, having success equal to the 436th the day before. The Squadron's nine aircraft left behind a trail of destroyed locomotives, railroad cars, and bridges. One Oscar and one Ki-27 Nate fighter from the Royal Thai Air Force attempted an interception, inflicting minor damage on one bomber. All four squadrons went out on March 24th to bomb bridges on the Burma-Thailand railroad, each

Combat crew officers of the 492nd Bomb Squadron in April 1944, when the Squadron was at less than full strength. (SQ-Bomb-492-HI-April 1945, Albert F. Simpson Historical Research Center, Air Force Historical Research Agency, Maxwell AFB, AL)

airplane loaded with six 1,000-pound bombs and a bomb bay tank. The main target was Q633, a 1,680-foot long viaduct curving above a river bed west of Kanchanaburi. Because of the topography, the squadrons bombed from higher altitude in individual runs using standard and Azon bombs, getting at least five breaks in the viaduct of various lengths. The 493rd Squadron got several direct hits on the main structure with its Azon bombs. On the way to the target, Lt. Nathan Margolies's aircraft, in the 9th Squadron's formation, had an engine failure. The propeller wouldn't feather, so the crew got rid of the bomb load and the bomb bay tank. When the airplane continued to lose altitude Margolies ordered the crew to bail out. Margolies, his navigator Lt. Edwin Scranton, and two of his gunners (S/Sgts. Edward Reed and John Cunningham) failed to make it. The plane crashed in the Ganges Delta, where the rest of the crew were rescued.[118]

Combat crew officers of the 492nd Bomb Squadron in April 1945. By this point in the war, the 7th Bomb Group had more than a full complement of combat crews in each squadron. (SQ-Bomb-492-HI-April 1945, Albert F. Simpson Historical Research Center, Air Force Historical Research Agency, Maxwell AFB, AL)

While the other squadrons were bombing a variety of targets during the month, the 493rd had continued its own relentless campaign against bridges. Between March 3rd and 31st, the 7th Group bombed 30 bridges, destroying 12 and severely damaging an additional 12, mostly through the efforts of the 493rd Squadron and its Azon bombs.[119] The 493rd flew 11 missions against bridges during the month, the two best missions taking place on March 11th and 21st. The targets on March 11th were bridges Q338 and the bypass bridge at Q195 on the Burma-Thailand railroad. Four airplanes went out loaded with six 1,000-pound Azon bombs each, with an additional six aircraft carrying a load of six standard 1,000-pound bombs. Coming in over Q338, the Squadron got two direct hits on the center of the bridge and two or three hits on the northern approach, destroying it. Moving on to the bypass bridge at Q195, the Squadron destroyed it with ten hits on the bridge and its approaches, then got more hits on the main Q195 bridge as well. With the two main targets knocked out and bombs left over, the ten aircraft attacked five other bridges, destroying three more for a total of five for the day. On March 21st, the 493rd went after four bridges on the Moulmein-Ye railroad line, again with a mix of Azon and standard bombs. Attacking bridge H-64, the seven aircraft on the mission destroyed it with two direct hits in the center and one hit on the eastern and western approaches. Moving on to bridge H-64A, the Squadron took this out with two to three direct hits. Bridges H-41 and H-41A were nearby. Four direct hits on each bridge destroyed them both. At the end of the month, nine aircraft went back to complete the destruction of bridge Q338, getting two direct hits on the northern approach and two direct hits on the southern approach to knock it out of service.

Turning to Q297, the formation destroyed the north section of the bridge and damaged the northern and southern approaches.[120] By the end of March, the 7th Group had destroyed 75 bridges, prompting Col. Alness to write to Maj. Gen. Stratemeyer on the importance of the Azon bomb in the 7th Group's success and the Group's role in developing the techniques and tactics for Azon bombing. "We feel," Alness wrote, "that, coupled with good bombardiers, the guided missiles are most successful and valuable in our work against railroads, bridges, and other line targets. It is requested that strongest support be given to continue the development of this weapon, and that Army Air Forces will insure continued, adequate supply of AZON equipment to this theater."[121]

The 436th Squadron set another record for the heaviest

The 493rd Squadron takes out Bridge H-21 and Bypass H-21A on the Pegu-Moulmein line with Azon bombs on April 2, 1945. (SQ-Bomb-493-HI-April 1945, Albert F. Simpson Historical Research Center, Air Force Historical Research Agency, Maxwell AFB, AL)

bomb load on a mission on March 29th. The standard view of the B-24 was that its maximum bomb load was 8,000 pounds. During February 1945, the 7th Group's Armament Section and squadron armament sections had pushed this to first 10,400 pounds and then 11,000 pounds for short range, medium-altitude missions. In early March, with the near absence of Japanese fighters on almost all missions and the availability of long-range escort fighters when needed, the 7th Group began taking out all the belly turrets from its B-24s. This removed 1,000 pounds of weight that could go to additional fuel or bomb load. The opportunity to try an even heavier load came when Allied intelligence identified what was believed to be the headquarters of *Burma Area Army* in Rangoon. The 9th, 436th, and 492nd Squadrons joined RAF Liberators in bombing the suspected area. The 436th Squadron sent out ten aircraft, each loaded with 12,000 pounds of bombs, believed to be a record for the B-24 in any theater of war. A number of the aircraft had to release their bomb loads manually when the bomb racks malfunctioned, but the 436th's formation still got its string of bombs right across the target area.[122] The 9th Squadron suffered its last combat loss on this mission. Flying in the 9th Squadron's formation, Lt. Charles Wiley's B-24 apparently took some anti-aircraft fire, knocking out the No. 2 engine. On the return flight to base, his airplane steadily dropped behind the formation until it was lost in the haze and failed to return to base, with the loss of Wiley and his crew.[123]

April brought a return of the pre-monsoon weather, oppressive heat and humidity, early and violent thunderstorms over the bases, and more cloud cover over the targets that interfered with bombing. There were several administrative changes within the squadrons. The 7th Group still did not appear to have adopted a formal standard for rotation back to the United States. Rotation seems to have depended on the arrival of replacement crews, prompting one crew to name their B-24 *Slower Than Rotation*. Replacement crews did, however, continue to come in each month, allowing the longer-serving men to return home. Two veterans that departed were Capts. James Nemecek and Charles Meuth from the 436th Squadron, both of whom had been in combat for over 14 months. In another move, the 436th's Operations Officer, Capt. John Sims, moved over to the 7th Group Headquarters as Assistant S-3 to Lt. Col. Kyes. Sims had flown 70 combat missions and accumulated 609 combat hours. This total may have been a record for the 7th Group. Maj. Hilliard Gandy, another long-serving veteran who had commanded the Eager Beavers in the 492nd Squadron since April 1944, left the Group to take a position with the Operations staff at the Strategic Air Force. His replacement was Maj. Ralph Jensen, who had joined the Squadron the previous November and had been serving as Operations Officer. All the 7th Group squadrons were now at full strength with a full complement of crews and airplanes, a dramatic improvement over the prior year. Each

Before the Azon bombers went in to bomb Bypass #1 and #3 at Bridge #71 on the Pegu-Moulmein line, a single B-24 hit the anti-aircraft gun emplacements around the bridge with fragmentation bombs. (SQ-Bomb-493-HI-April 1945, Albert F. Simpson Historical Research Center, Air Force Historical Research Agency, Maxwell AFB, AL)

squadron had around 28 combat crews, with an average of 18 to 22 crews available for combat. In regards to aircraft, the squadrons now had a complement of 14 B-24s and normally

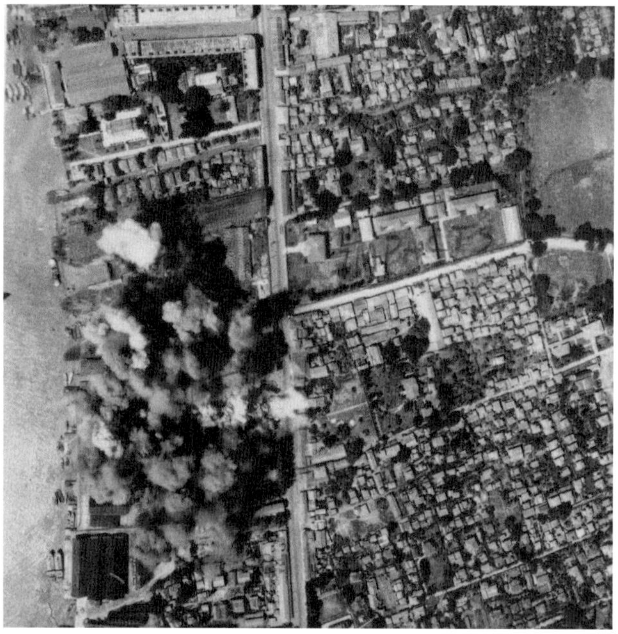

Coming in over Bangkok at low altitude on April 18, 1945, the 7th Bomb Group severely damaged the Borneo Wharves along the Chao Phya River. (SQ-Bomb-492-HI-April 1945, Albert F. Simpson Historical Research Center, Air Force Historical Research Agency, Maxwell AFB, AL)

had ten airplanes available for operations. The B-24J model still predominated, with some of the earliest arrivals still in service, but newer B-24L and B-24M models arrived at the rate of two or three a month.[124]

Shortly after midnight on the morning of April 1, 1945, the 7th Group sent 23 aircraft on what was the beginning of 12 days of continuous attacks on the Burma-Thailand railroad. Because of the frequency and risk of air attack, the Japanese had drastically cut back on the operation of trains along the route by day. Instead, the trains traveled at night, hiding during the daylight hours under camouflage. To counter this, the 9th, 436th, and 492nd Squadrons took off at night to arrive over the Burma-Thailand railroad just after dawn to catch trains before they were hidden. Each squadron took a section of the railroad line and then assigned shorter sections to each individual airplane. The 436th and 492nd Squadrons had good hunting, destroying a number of locomotives and rolling stock and tearing up the track at many places along the route. The 436th added two bridges when one aircraft bombed them at low altitude and damaged both. The 9th Squadron had a harder time, running into cloud cover that made bombing difficult, but did get down low enough to strafe several trains and destroy at least one locomotive. The 493rd went out the next day to bomb Bridge H-21 on the Pegu-Moulmein section of the line with eight aircraft. Dropping 24 1,000-pound Azon bombs and 32 1,000-pound standard bombs, the Squadron destroyed H-21, getting three direct hits in the center section and more hits and near misses on the approaches and the tracks leading up to the bridge. As they flew away, the crews could see the spans sitting in the river. On April 3rd, the 436th and 492nd Squadrons went back to Kanchanaburi to ensure that the wooden bypass bridge (Q654) remained knocked out. The 436th Squadron sent six aircraft, with one aircraft loaded with fragmentation bombs going in ahead of the rest to take out the anti-aircraft guns around the bridge. In low level attacks, the two squadrons knocked out several spans on the bypass bridge and damaged the northern and southern approaches, tearing up several thousand feet of railroad track as well. The 492nd went on to hit the viaduct at Q633, getting six breaks in the railroad line. Despite dropping fragmentation bombs on the gun emplacements around the bridge, enough guns survived to shoot holes in three of the 436th Squadron's aircraft and for Lt. Charles Linamen to shoot what would be the first of two aircraft out from under him.[125]

Just as Linamen's bombardier dropped their last two bombs on the bridge, four anti-aircraft shells hit the B-24, cutting the aileron cables and jamming the ailerons in the full up position. As Linamen's copilot, Bradley Hamlett recalled in his memoire:

During the hot season, the temperatures inside a B-24 could get up to 100 degrees or more, so the crews wore what was comfortable. (Courtesy Jim Augustus)

> The ship started vibrating (indicating a stall) and rolled hard to the left into a spiral. The instrument panel was a blur. Reaching forward, I steadied the panel to check the gauges, which indicated no engine problems. My left-seater, Chuck Linamen, called for power and help

on the controls. By this time the ground was rotating. I let go of the wheel and with both Chuck and I on the rudder, we were unable to stop the spiral. Like the flip of a switch, the spiral stopped. We were 180 degrees off course for home base. We realized there was no aileron control. The ship, with the left wing still down, was wallowing. The nose was in an elliptical orbit. We were not able to get enough pressure on the rudder to turn right. Chuck began using rudder trim to help us, and as the ship was still in a stall, it went over the top with us—or did what is known as a vertical reversement.

This maneuver did improve the situation, turning us right in the general direction of home base. With the right wing down about 15 degrees, one man could keep the ship straight. Torque was now working in our favor. Chuck and I could now trade off on the controls every three to four minutes.[126]

Linamen and Hamlett struggled with their airplane until they were finally able to engage the automatic pilot on the return flight. They did not have the fuel to get back to Madhaiganj, so they opted to make an emergency landing at Cox's Bazar on the Bengalese coast, south of Chittagong. But to land their damaged bomber they had to maintain a speed of 175 mph to keep it from stalling. At that speed their landing run would cover more than the 3,500-foot long runway at Cox's Bazar. The tower suggested they try a landing on the hard sand beach near the runway. Dropping the gear, Linamen brought the airplane down on the water line. The nose gear broke off, filling the nose compartment with sand. When the plane came to a stop the crew got out and walked away. Years later, Hamlett learned that Bill Nation, the flight engineer, had saved their airplane. Standing in the top turret when the flak hit, Nation could see that both ailerons were in the full up position, but on one aileron the trim tab was up and on the other aileron the trim tab was fully down, causing the spiral. Hurrying into the bomb bay, he grabbed the trim tab cables running across the top of the bomb bay and kept pulling on them until they came loose. With the aileron trim tabs in their normal position, Linamen and Hamlett brought the airplane out of its spriral.[127] For his exceptional piloting skills, Linamen was later awarded the Distinguished Flying Cross, while Hamlett received an Oak Leaf Cluster to the Air Medal.

The next day, the 9th and 493rd Squadrons went out to bomb Bridge TE152, lying 80 miles east of Bangkok. At this distance, the aircraft could carry only 4,000 pounds of bombs. For this mission, the 493rd took two 1,000-pound bombs and one 2,000-pound bomb. Four aircraft attacked the bridge from low level, failing to get any direct hits but damaging the approaches. The 9th Squadron appears to have had better luck, dropping delayed action bombs that took out the bridge. For the next two weeks, while the other 7th Group squadrons went to other targets, the 493rd kept up the attacks on the bridges, flying a mission every two days. In four missions relying primarily on Azon bombs, the 493rd claimed ten bridges destroyed and another seven rendered unserviceable, in addition to damaging several more with hits on the bridge structure or the approaches.[128] For the month of April 1945, there were an average of 11.7 breaks a day on the railroad line from Bangkok to Thanbyuzayat, with a peak of 24 breaks on the line in one day from the destruction of bridges and railroad tracks; there had been no through train along the entire line since February.[129] Despite the best efforts of the Japanese to repair the damage as quickly as possible, the flow of supplies into Burma slowed to a crawl.

Cutting the flow of supplies into Burma made the destruction of the Japanese Army supply dumps all the more imperative. Having beaten the Japanese *15th* and *33rd Armies* around Meiktila, the 14th Army had begun its advance on Rangoon and was now in a race against time, or more specifically, the arrival of the monsoon. The IV and XXXIII Corps were entirely dependent on air transport for 90 per cent of their supplies. The Army Air Forces and Royal Air Force transports were flying into fair weather fields that would disintegrate into a morass of mud when the rains came. If it was to survive so far from its base of supply during the monsoon, the 14th Army had to capture the port of Rangoon. To ensure Rangoon's capture, a modified Operation Dracula

The post-strike photo shows the extent of the damage to the Borneo Wharves in Bangkok. (SQ-Bomb-492-HI-April 1945, Albert F. Simpson Historical Research Center, Air Force Historical Research Agency, Maxwell AFB, AL)

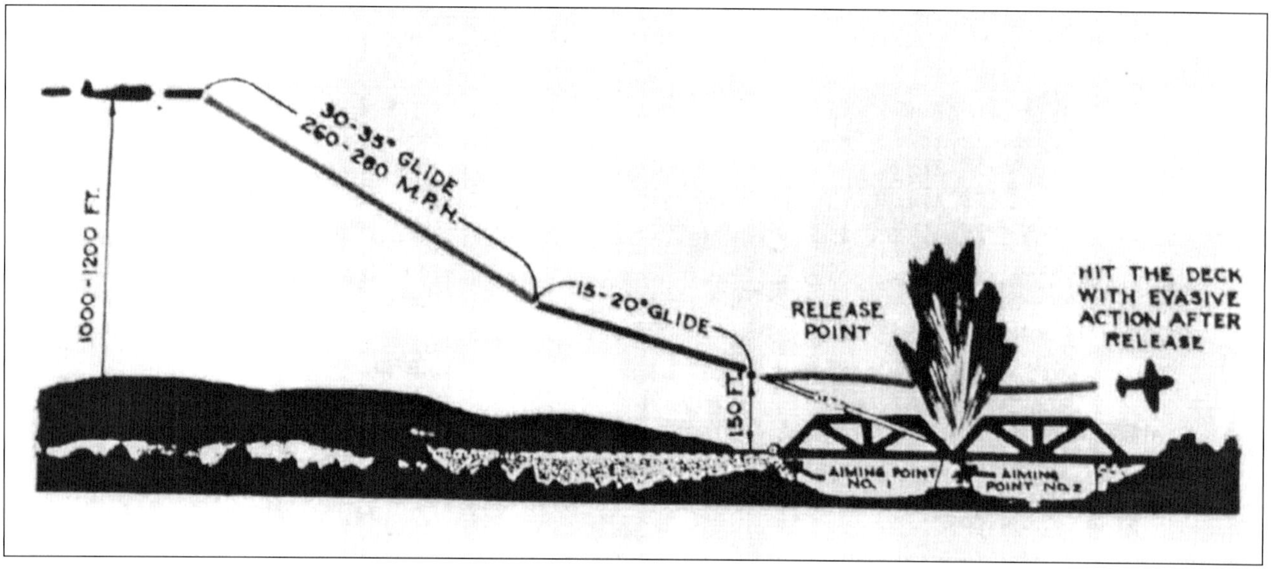

A diagram showing the "glip" low-altitude bombing method the 7th Bomb Group tried out on April 24, 1945, with excellent results. (Via the author)

was resurrected to capture Rangoon by an amphibious landing up the Rangoon River, tentatively scheduled for early May.[130] In the dumps around Victoria Lake in Rangoon, under heavy attack since February, the Japanese Army had the major portion of the six months' worth of supplies held in lower Burma.[131] During April, the Strategic Air Force carried out five attacks on the Rangoon dumps, with the 7th Group participating in the first two missions on April 5th and 11th, and the last mission on April 27th. Though the mention of a mission over Rangoon could still evoke a nervous shudder, the contrast with the 7th Group's missions of previous years was striking. As the 492nd Squadron commented: "There once was a thing called 'Rangoon-jitters', but that feeling has been put away with moth balls for historical purposes only. Our former respect for this Burma 'hotspot' has dwindled to a low ebb and our bombing altitude over this target has taken a similar nosedive. We began the current Rangoon campaign in February from a height of 16,000 feet, but this mission [April 5, 1945] found us poking our noses in at 9,000 feet in spite of accurate flak."[132] The 9th Squadron, originators of the "Goon at Noon Club", expressed similar sentiments, adding: "...there has been a great deal of satisfaction on the part of all personnel that we are now able to 'Drive over the Goon' just about any time we feel like it without encountering a swarm of enemy fighters—a situation that used to obtain during the hectic months of November and December 1943. One begins to see real progress in the war, and our part becomes more real."[133]

The 9th, 436th, and 492nd Squadrons bombed the Rangoon dumps on April 5, 1945. The 436th Squadron, to their surprise, found no anti-aircraft fire over the target, though two airplanes from the 492nd came back with minor damage. Two days later, the attacks on Japanese supply dumps continued with a mission to bomb a dump at Moulmein, and then, on April 9th, an attack on supplies at the railroad sidings at Sittang, where the Japanese kept supplies before ferrying them across the Sittang River. At the 14th Army's request, the 7th Group went out on April 8th and 10th to bomb a section of the road from Prome to Toungup that the Japanese Army was using in their retreat. Then it was back to Rangoon again to hit the Victoria Lake dumps once more, this time going in at only 7,000 feet. To their intense embarrassment, the 492nd dropped their bombs early when the lead bombardier accidently triggered his bomb release, the other eight aircraft in the formation dutifully following suit. The 436th made up for this with a perfect run on the assigned target area, once again without any opposition. Moving farther afield, on April 14th, the 9th and 436th Squadrons accompanied RAF Liberators to bomb the two main power stations in Bangkok with a fighter escort of 2nd Air Commando Group P-51D Mustangs. The squadrons bombed from a remarkable altitude of 2,800 feet and absolutely plastered the target, which was the Samsen Power Station. The three squadrons sent 20 airplanes back to Bangkok on April 18th with a fighter escort to bomb the Borneo Wharves and the warehouses of the Bangkok Dock Company. Clouds over Bangkok forced the bombers down to 3,000 feet to get over the target area. As the 492nd Squadron commented: "To many crew members who had been shot up over Bangkok in the past, this daylight attack at such low altitude seemed to be the height of daring and disregard of safety factors. But in contrast, they afterward described the mission as somewhat akin to a Sunday School picnic."[134] With no flak to distract them and bombing from such a low altitude, the bombardiers got 95 per cent of their bombs onto the docks and warehouses.

The crews had the odd experience of seeing people on the streets below running away in desperation as the bombers flew low over the city.[135]

In sharp contrast with the difficulties the 7th Group had experienced regaining its bombing skills in October 1944, the two missions to Bangkok of April 14 and 18, 1945, earned the Group special praise and a commendation from the Strategic Air Force. Col. Roy Lynn, Army Air Forces, Deputy Air Commander, Strategic Air Force, sent the following letter to Col. Alness:

1. Accurate bombing by the squadrons of the 7th Bomb Group has become so habitual that there is a tendency to forget that excellent bombing does not "just happen", but rather is the result of thorough training, proper planning, capable leadership and a sincere effort on the part of everyone concerned.
2. Occasionally a mission occurs of even more than usual excellence. Emphasizing these facts and calling attention to the high degree of proficiency attained by your organization in precision bombing.
3. Two such missions were recently executed by squadrons of the 7th Bomb Group, and call for the commendation of this headquarters. These attacks were made against the Government Power Station in north Bangkok on 14 April 1945, by the 9th, 436th, and 492nd Bomb Squadrons and against the Bangkok docks on 18 April by the 9th and 436th Bomb Squadrons [leaving out the 492nd Squadron for some reason, who also participated in the mission]. On both occasions the bombing was of such extreme accuracy that virtually all the installations and facilities in the target area were completely destroyed.
4. All the officers and men who participated in the preparation or execution of these missions are to be congratulated and can be justly proud of the resulting destruction which has undoubtedly caused great discomfort and anguish to the Jap and his rapidly increasing ancestors.[136]

The entire 7th Group flew a complicated mission on April 21st to bomb troop concentrations and supply dumps at Toungoo at the 14th Army's request. The Army's forward units were less than 25 miles away from the town. The airfield at Toungoo was vital to maintaining the air supply to the 14th Army, and there was a concern that the Japanese would make a stand at the town to halt the 14th Army's drive toward Rangoon. Each squadron contributed two sections of three to six aircraft for the attack, with each section assigned a particular area around the town. The number of aircraft in each section was based on the size of the target areas the squadron had been assigned. The mission was an extreme test of timing and bombing accuracy. The Strategic Air Force's plan called for the sections to take off at five minute intervals, fly to the Toungoo area independently, and bomb the precisely designated targets at exactly five minute intervals. As the squadrons neared Toungoo, they could see the tanks and vehicles of the 14th Army's advance patrols beneath them. The bombing was as precise as could be expected, with almost all bombs getting into the selected areas.[137]

While all four of the 7th Group squadrons were active flying missions to bomb bridges or supply dumps, in mid-April, Col. Alness and his Operations staff came up with a new technique for attacking bridges. Alness came up with the idea during a bull session with his S-3, Lt. Col. William Kyes; Capt. Edward Thielen, Assistant S-3; Capt. Harold Leffel, Group Navigator; and Capt. Stanley Britten, Group Bombardier. The five men were discussing the problem of bombs bouncing off bridge structures during low level attacks. Experience had proven that low level attacks were the most effective method of destroying bridges, as long as anti-aircraft fire was negligible.

One of the more than 30 bridges destroyed and damaged on April 24, 1945; the 492nd Bomb Squadron took out this one. (SQ-Bomb-492-HI-April 1945, Albert F. Simpson Historical Research Center, Air Force Historical Research Agency, Maxwell AFB, AL)

The major drawback of low level attacks was the likelihood that the bombs would ricochet off the bridge structure or even from water or soil alongside. Increasing the height of the approach or decreasing the airplane's speed could reduce the chance of having a ricochet, but increased the vulnerability to any anti-aircraft defenses. Experience had also shown that bridges had to be attacked repeatedly to keep them unserviceable. Up to mid-April, the 7th Bombardment Group had accounted for 98 bridges destroyed, but there were hundreds more along the railroad lines into Burma. Col. Alness wanted a better method of knocking out bridges—many more bridges—and knocking them out for longer periods of time.

Sitting around discussing the pros and cons of different bombing techniques, Alness hit on the idea of using the B-24 as a dive bomber, something that had never been tried before in the theater in a bomber that big. The 490th Bombardment Squadron (M) had, a year earlier, accidently hit on a technique of bombing bridges the 490th dubbed "glip" bombing, a combination of glide bombing and skip bombing. During a "glip" bombing run, a B-25 would approach the long axis of a bridge in a steep 30 to 35 degree glide. At an altitude of around 450 feet, the B-25 would flatten out the glide and just before going over the bridge release a single bomb. The technique was extremely successful, earning the 490th Squadron the nickname "The Burma Bridge Busters". Putting a heavy B-24 through the same maneuvers a smaller and more nimble B-25 could do with relative ease was a problem of an altogether different magnitude. Alness proposed a variation of this method. He proposed having a B-24 enter a 20 to 25 degree glide from around 1,500 feet, rolling in from medium altitude, aiming directly at the bridge, and releasing one or more bombs at around 200 feet while at the same time pulling out of the dive.[138]

Lt. Col. Kyes and Capt. Thielen tried out the new technique on several practice missions with excellent results. Based on

The 7th Bomb Group's 100th Bridge, destroyed during the mass attack on April 24, 1945. (GP-7-HI-(Bomb)-April 1945, Albert F. Simpson Historical Research Center, Air Force Historical Research Agency, Maxwell AFB, AL)

these tests, Col. Alness ordered all pilots in the Group to undertake training in the new bombing method. For two weeks in April, in between missions, the 7th Group had the squadron pilots practice the technique in secret, using a mock-up of a 200 foot long bridge built on the 7th Group's bombing range as a target. The Armament Sections rigged up a button on the B-24's control wheel so that the pilot could release the bombs using a specially-built sight mounted above

Lt. Col. Stevens, Group Executive Officer, Col. Harvey Alness, CO 7th Bomb Group, and Maj. Ralph Jensen, CO 492nd Bomb Squadron, at a celebration of the destruction of the Group's 100th bridge. (7th Bombardment Group (H) Historical Foundation, USAFA McDermott Library)

the instrument panel. In practice flights, the pilots got to drop 30 bombs on the bridge mock-up. Col. Alness sought and received permission from the Strategic Air Force to undertake a full-scale mission using the dive bombing technique.[139]

The first opportunity to try out the new bombing technique came on April 24, 1945, in an operation the Eastern Air Command's *Weekly Intelligence Summary* said "...may well be described as the most effective bomber mission ever staged in this Theater."[140] That morning, the 7th Group sent 41 B-24s to attack the bridges on the Burma-Thailand railroad. The 9th, 436th, and 492nd Squadrons would try the new dive bombing technique, while the 493rd Squadron bombed selected targets with its Azon bombs. For the test, the Group selected a 210-mile stretch of the railroad line between Thanbyuzayat in Burma and Kanchanaburi in Thailand, each squadron taking its own segment of the line. The results were little short of remarkable. At the end of the day the squadrons returned, claiming 30 bridges destroyed or rendered unserviceable, six more probably destroyed or damaged, the approaches to seven bridges severely damaged, and substantial cuts made in the railroad line at four other locations. The 436th Squadron claimed 19 bridges destroyed or damaged; every one of the eleven pilots the squadron sent out that day claimed hits on a bridge, and one pilot, a Lt. Mills, claimed three destroyed for the high score. The 9th Squadron claimed eleven bridges, the 493rd Squadron claimed ten destroyed or damaged with their Azon bombs, and the 492nd claimed nine. What many considered the most successful day in the 7th Group's history had a decided impact on morale. Air Cdre Mellersh sent his praise for the achievement, saying: "This mission, planned and executed by the 7th Bomb Group (H), is deserving of the highest praise. Undoubtedly the resulting damage and destruction to the rail line surpassed all previous records for an equal number of sorties on similar targets in this or any other theater."[141] In the context of the overall campaign to defeat the Japanese Army in Burma, the 7th Group's devastating attack on the Burma-Thailand railroad took place just eight days before the amphibious invasion of Rangoon, cutting off supplies to Burma at a critical moment.

For the second time in the month, Lt. Charles Linamen from the 436th Squadron had his airplane shot up and had to make another emergency landing at Cox's Bazar. Pulling up after his bomb run on a line of railroad track, Linamen banked to his left to get a look at where his bombs had hit, and at that moment several anti-aircraft bullets hit the airplane in the nose, blowing out the nose wheel tire and wounding his copilot, Bradley Hamlett, in the leg. Another bullet smashed into the mag switch panel, exposing the wires controlling the magnetos on the No. 1 and 2 engines; a short circuit would have knocked out both engines. Lt. Bill Henderson, the navigator, administered first aid to Hamlett, then took his seat to help Linamen get the bomber to Cox's Bazar. Linamen landed the airplane at the very edge of the runway, keeping the nose high until the last possible minute as he rolled down the strip. As the nose came to rest on the field, Henderson cut all four engines. The crew walked away and took another 436th Squadron B-24 back to base, landing in Calcutta to get Hamlett to a hospital.[142]

A 7th Bomb Group B-24 flies past a Japanese air field at the close of the Burma campaign, a result of Allied air superiority. (7th Bombardment Group (H) Historical Foundation, USAFA McDermott Library)

There was a growing sense within the 7th Group that the end in Burma was near. In the 9th Squadron, and no doubt the others, the men began to speculate about their future. As the 9th viewed the question: "It seems evident that a move is likely within a few months if not a few weeks. Reasons for this run the full gamut from the fact that we are running out of suitable heavy bomber targets to the fact that Tokyo Rose says we are moving. Good bets are the Philippines and China; Tokyo Rose's guess of Siberia is running a poor fourth to these two and the one that has us returning to the U.S. to re-equip with B-32s or B-29s. It will seem peculiar, when the time does come, not to call Pandaveswar home."[143] If any additional evidence was needed, the mission of April 27, 1945, to the dumps in Rangoon provided confirmation of how badly the Japanese had been beaten. The 9th and 492nd Squadrons accompanied RAF Liberators to Rangoon, the 7th Group squadrons bombing this once feared target from 2,300 to 3,300 feet. The altitude alone served as a "signpost" pointing to the end. While the other squadrons went to Rangoon, the 493rd flew one last Azon bombing mission for the month, destroying the H-41 bypass bridge and damaging several others. When the No.4 engine on Lt. Morrell's B-24 started cutting out he turned back to base, but on reaching the Bengal coast the No. 1 engine quit as well. Putting the airplane on autopilot, Morrell ordered the crew to bail out. The local Bengal police helped them find transportation back toward Calcutta.[144] The last Group mission of the month, on April 29, 1945, was to the airfield at Moulmein to make it unserviceable before the scheduled amphibious assault on Rangoon. The squadrons made individual runs over the airfield, each airplane taking a section of the runway or the field installations. To keep the Japanese uncertain, the B-24s dropped bombs with 36-hour delayed fuses. So ended the 7th Bombardment Group's last full month of bombing in WWII.[145]

CHAPTER EIGHT

VICTORY IN BURMA

The Fall of Rangoon

By April 30, 1945, advance elements of the 14th Army were at Pegu, 50 miles away from Rangoon. Operation Dracula, the assault on Rangoon, began the next morning when a battalion from the 50th (P) Brigade dropped five miles west of Elephant Point at the mouth of the Rangoon River. The battalion marched east and stopped two and a half miles away from Japanese positions while these positions came under a devastating air bombardment. The Strategic Air Force sent in 82 RAF Liberators and 7th Group B-24s on May 1, 1945, to bomb the gun positions at Elephant Point. All four 7th Group squadrons participated in the attack, the airplanes taking off at one-minute intervals and bombing their selected target areas individually. Eastern Air Command had launched a massive attack to ensure the safe passage of Allied landing craft up the river to Rangoon. As the 492nd Squadron recorded, the sky over Elephant Point was "...filled to the brim with planes of all sorts. Libs, B-24s, Beaufighters, P-47s, and Mosquitos flew madly about the I.P. It was not an uncommon sight to see 4 A/C to come out of the clouds, each headed for

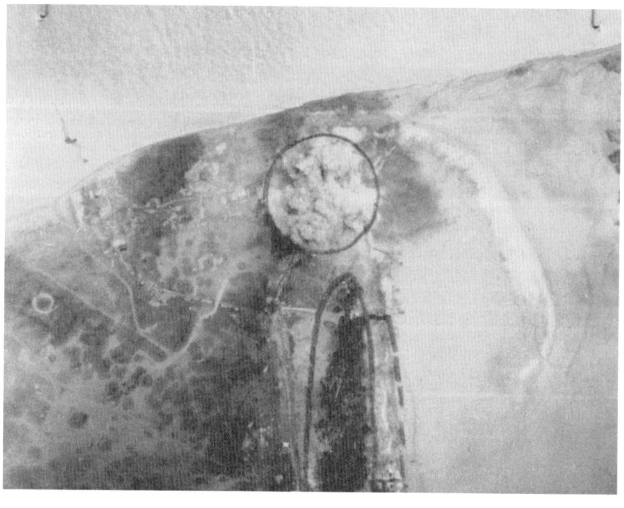

Bombing gun positions around Elephant Point, south of Rangoon, in preparation for Operation Dracula, May 1, 1945. (SQ-Bomb-492-HI-May 1945, Albert F. Simpson Historical Research Center, Air Force Historical Research Agency, Maxwell AFB, AL)

the same target, at different altitudes and different angles. Nobody got hurt—a miracle in itself. On that day, 26 tons were dropped as well as 2 tons of sweat."[1] The next morning, May 2nd, the Strategic Air Force returned to bomb Japanese gun positions in the landing areas between 0500 and 0630. Taking off at 0100, the 7th Group's squadrons arrived shortly before dawn, each squadron's aircraft bombing its assigned area individually. Clouds in the area made it difficult to pick out the targets. As on the day before, the bombers constantly dodged other aircraft as they weaved in and out of the cloud cover. The landings that began half an hour after the end of the bombardment were an anti-climax; the Japanese had already withdrawn from Rangoon three days before.[2]

With the capture of Rangoon on May 3, 1945, just as the monsoon rains arrived, attention shifted to disrupting the retreat of the Japanese Army, whose shattered remnants were withdrawing into Thailand to regroup. The Strategic Air Force was called on to attack the smaller harbors and transshipment points down the Burmese coast. For all but the 493rd Squadron, these attacks were the 7th Bombardment Group's last bombing missions of the war. On May 3rd, the 9th, 436th, and 492nd Squadrons went to Moulmein to bomb shipping and the jetties in the harbor. The bombers plowed through fronts and dodged thunderstorms in and around Moulmein, the kind of weather, as the 492nd put it, "...best observed lying on your back in the sack."[3] Bombing from 500 to 3,700 feet, the squadrons hit the jetties and several smaller coastal vessels in the harbor, the 436th Squadron sinking an 80-foot long coaster and damaging four larger 150-foot long ships. The bombers ran into heavy and accurate fire from machine guns and light and heavy anti-aircraft guns. In the 492nd Squadron, Lt. Robeson's ship returned with 46 holes and one tire shot out. Robeson made a safe landing, but by the end of the day his aircraft and two others sat at the end of the runway at Madhaiganj, all with flak damage. In the 436th Squadron, of the six aircraft that attacked Moulmein three returned with major damage, two had minor damage, and the airplane flown by 2nd Lt. J.P. Osborne failed to return from the mission. Osborne's B-24 was seen to enter a cloud bank with one engine knocked out and the propeller feathered from AA fire. In all likelihood, Osborne crashed into the ocean while returning to base, as neither the airplane nor the crew were ever found.[4] This was the 436th Squadron's first aircraft lost in combat since January 1944 and its last B-24 combat loss. The squadrons went to Mergui and Tavoy the next day. Clouds in the area made it difficult to pick out targets. The 436th Squadron bombed two small coastal vessels they found and dropped their remaining bombs on the railroad jetties at Moulmein, while the 492nd Squadron, finding no shipping at either harbor, bombed supply dumps around Mergui. The squadrons returned to Mergui once again on May 5th to search for shipping, destroying or damaging several coastal vessels and dropping bombs on the shipyards in the town. In deference to the heavy machine gun and light AA fire, the bombers went in at 7,000 feet. On the way to Mergui, Lt. W.R. Smith had an engine failure over the Gulf of Martaban. Feathering the propeller, he jettisoned his bombs and turned for base, only to have another engine start to falter. Smith decided to land at the first Allied airfield he could find and ended up on a dirt strip carved out of dry rice paddies 12 miles north of Pegu. The crew lived in their airplane for a week with an armed guard around the airplane day and night. Japanese troops, holed up in woods a mile away, made frequent attempts to infiltrate the British lines at night. Smith's crew lived on their emergency rations until they ran out. The British soldiers gave them British Army rations for the remainder of their stay. The bombardier apparently got bored and hitched a ride to Toungoo, where he caught a C-46 to Chittagong and hopped a 492nd Squadron B-24 back to Madhaiganj. The rest of the crew came out on a Strategic Air Force B-25 loaded down with Japanese flags and rifles as souvenirs.[5]

After two days of rest and maintenance on their aircraft, the squadrons headed out again on May 8th to bomb troop concentrations around Martaban. The airplanes took off at night to arrive over Martaban at dawn, running into heavy but inaccurate anti-aircraft fire from gun positions in the town and from Moulmein across the way. The bombers made individual runs on the barracks area, a large white pagoda providing a perfect aiming point. In what was one of the 492nd Squadron's best missions, the squadron's bombardiers got over 90 per cent of their bombs in the designated target area. It was, however, hard work, even with the pagoda as an aiming point. The weather was bad, with lots of clouds in the area, and the I.P. was "...a nameless piece of sandbar in the Salween River."[6] Taking off for this mission, 2nd Lt. Eugene William's B-24 crashed at the end of the runway and exploded, killing the crew; this was the 492nd Squadron's last combat loss of the war.[7] Two days later, on May 8, 1945, the day the war in Europe ended, the 9th, 436th, and 492nd flew what was to be their last combat mission. Mergui was the target again, with all four squadrons in the 7th Group joining 12 Liberators from No. 99 Squadron, Royal Air Force, to attack supply dumps around the town. Despite the cloud cover, the bombers found the target and did an excellent job of getting 90 per cent of their fragmentation bombs in and around the dumps, causing large fires. The 493rd Squadron sent out seven aircraft that morning, but only six bombed Mergui with loads of incendiaries. The bomb bay doors on the seventh aircraft failed to open. The incendiaries had to be carefully removed from their bomb bay shackles and carried, one by one, to the waist gun windows, where they were tossed out into the ocean. One 493rd aircraft had its No. 4 engine shot out by flak over

Mergui; the crew made an emergency landing at Cox's Bazar, where they counted 20 flak holes in their airplane. On their return to base, the squadrons were put on alert for an anti-shipping strike. RAF reconnaissance patrols had spotted a Japanese Navy cruiser and destroyer at Port Blair, in the Andaman Islands. After four days of waiting, the Strategic Air Force sent off 42 Liberators and B-24s to attack the ships reported at Port Blair, but three hours before reaching the Andaman Islands all the bombers were recalled and brought their bombs back to base. The next day, the entire 7th Bombardment Group stood down from operations.[8]

With the capture of Rangoon, the campaign to liberate Burma had effectively ended, and with it, the rationale for maintaining Army Air Forces units in the India-Burma Sector. The divergent strategic objectives between the United States and Great Britain emerged once more. British forces were now preparing for an invasion of Malaya and the re-conquest of Singapore, while the American Joint Chiefs of Staff wanted to re-orient the American air effort in Asia toward China. There was still some consideration given to a possible landing on the China coast as a preliminary step toward the ultimate invasion of Japan.[9] Early in 1945, the Joint Chiefs had decided that with the recapture of Rangoon all Army Air Forces units operating over Burma would be withdrawn to China. In January, Maj. Gen. Stratemeyer's planning staff worked out proposals to redeploy the Tenth Air Force to China and to move General Stratemeyer's headquarters to China as well, to command both the Tenth and Fourteenth Air Forces.[10] The Tenth Air Force was to become a purely tactical air force, supporting the Chinese armies in a planned advance against Japanese forces. The Fourteenth Air Force would be restructured as a strategic air force, based around the former B-29 base complex at Chengtu to conduct strategic operations in concert with the Far East Air Forces based in the Philippines and Okinawa, both air forces in China operating under a new organization (Army Air Forces, China Theater). As part of this reorganization, in May, Stratemeyer was promoted to Lt. Gen.[11]

The decision to move the Tenth Air Force and all its units to China ended the joint Royal Air Force-Army Air Forces command structure created under Air Command, South East Asia. Over the previous eleven months, the tactical units in Eastern Air Command had been completely reorganized. The Tenth Air Force was reconstituted in June 1944 as an operational unit to provide tactical air support to the Chinese divisions fighting in the Northern Combat Area Command. The Third Tactical Air Force disbanded at the end of 1944, so that its two component groups (Nos. 221 and 224 Groups, RAF) could be closely integrated with their 14th Army counterparts (IV Corps and XV Corps, respectively). Now the entire Eastern Air Command was set for disbandment on June 1, 1945, with its remaining components—the Strategic Air Force, the Combat Cargo Task Force, and the Photo Reconnaissance force—disbanding as well, the RAF units returning to the newly-established HQ, RAF Burma, while the American units reverted to the Tenth Air Force. With the end of the Strategic Air Force, the 7th Bombardment Group would take on a new and different role.[12]

After the 7th Group went non-operational, the squadrons resumed an intensive training program for all air crews while the Group waited for a decision on its future. Rumors were rife, most believing (and hoping) that the Group would be sent back to the United States to re-equip with the B-32, with a move to China the second favorite bet.[13] Newly-arrived crews began a program of operational training, while the older crews returned to training in each of their specialty areas, the Group setting up a Gunnery School, Bombardier's School, and Radio Operator's School, while the pilots and flight engineers undertook daily practice flights to sharpen their skills. The Group's navigators received extensive training in the use of radar for navigation, a new addition too many of the newer B-24s arriving for the Group and in the newly-introduced use of Loran (Long range navigation). Bombardiers received training twice a week on the bomb trainers, while the gunners went to the ranges for skeet shooting and ground firing from turrets set up on the range. Each of the squadrons conducted additional training as they saw fit. Maj. Jensen, in the 492nd Squadron, put his pilots through intensive instrument training in the monsoon weather, while in the 493rd Squadron the new bombardiers trained in Azon bombing and the newer dive bombing techniques. As a relief for the ground crews, who had worked so hard maintaining the aircraft during an intensive period of operations, the squadrons arranged for B-24s to make aerial flights over the Taj Mahal.[14]

Toward the end of May the blow fell: the 9th, 436th, and 492nd Squadrons and 7th Group Headquarters were to be taken off bombing and sent to Tezpur, a former Air Transport Command base in Assam, to haul gasoline to China for the Fourteenth Air Force. Only the 493rd Squadron would remain at Pandaveswar as an operational bomber squadron. The reaction in the three squadrons selected was intense disappointment. As the 9th Squadron recorded: "No single order ever has effectively depleted, in one stroke, the morale of a unit. Every concerted effort which went to make the Group and the Squadrons a "Crack" fighting unit, culminating in the virtual destruction of the Burma-Siam Railway in a single mission, seemed to collapse. Not that the worked ceased, but the light and the spirit went out."[15] The other squadrons had similar sentiments, the 436th Squadron commenting on the "...disappointment and distinct lowering of morale occasioned by the announcement that we were leaving bombardment work...", while the 492nd joked about the "fighting sahibs" become the "freighting sahibs".[16] There was a grudging realization that hauling gas was important work and a sense of resignation, but it was not the mission that the men had trained for and devoted their energy to. The most disappointed and indignant, once again, were the bombardiers, who would no longer have a role in the squadrons, and the gunners, who in the absence of Japanese fighter aircraft were no longer needed.

In farewell, Air Cdre Mellersh, Air Commander, Strategic Air Force, wrote a heartfelt letter of appreciation to Co. Alness and the squadron commanders in the 7th Group:

> 1. It is a great blow to me that the 7th Group has been relieved from the operational control of the Strategic Air Force. I am writing you a line to thank you for the magnificent work which your Group has done whilst it has been under my control and also in order to say goodbye to you all.
> 2. I need hardly tell you how extremely proud I have been to have had the 7th Group as part of my command. The work you have carried out has been absolutely grand and I have the greatest admiration for your own outstanding leadership of the Group and also for the courage and skill of all those serving under you.
> 3. I feel certain that history will prove that the work of the Heavy Bombers of the Strategic Air Force has been one of the major factors in the victorious campaign which is now reaching its conclusion in Burma. The constant hammering of their lines of communications made it impossible for the Japanese to retain their positions in Burma and, I am certain, contributed in no small measure to the final victory.
> 4. During the time the 7th Group has been operating under my control there has existed between us an extremely happy spirit of co-operation. I have found at all times the utmost willingness on your part and on the part of all your officers to carry out in every way possible the desires of this Headquarters. It has been the greatest pleasure to work with you in such an harmonious atmosphere.
> 5. I would like to wish you and all the Officers and Enlisted Men serving under you, the very best of good luck and success in your future tasks. Will you very kindly pass on to all of them a personal message from me of thanks for their grand work in the past and my very best wishes for their success in the future.[17]

Col. Alness added his own comments to this letter, distributed throughout the Group, saying: "It is with pride and pleasure that I forward this message. It is indeed a privilege to serve with an organization which deserves such praise and wish to take this opportunity to commend each and every member of this command for a superb job."[18]

Hauling Gas, Again

With their fate decided, the 9th, 436th, and 492nd Squadrons got ready for their next task. There was much to be done; the squadrons had to move lock, stock, and barrel to their new base at Tezpur, prepare their B-24s to haul gas, and train the crews for flying over the Hump. The move to Tezpur was scheduled for the first week of June. Using a combination of their own B-24s and assigned C-46 transports, the 436th and 492nd Squadrons said goodbye to Madhaiganj and the 9th said goodbye to Pandaveswar and moved everything to Tezpur. What couldn't go by airplane went by truck convoy. The gunners and bombardiers went up on the first few flights and supervised the unloading of the incoming aircraft, each bombardier in charge of a team of six to eight gunners. The move was complicated, as unlike in the previous year, the squadrons had to completely uproot, take every piece of equipment and squadron department, and set them up again from scratch at the new base. Before leaving, each individual was assigned to a barracks building and each department to its own new building, so that on arrival they could move in

Preparing a 492nd Bomb Squadron B-24J for the move to Tezpur. (SQ-Bomb-492-HI-May 1945, Albert F. Simpson Historical Research Center, Air Force Historical Research Agency, Maxwell AFB, AL)

The 7th Bomb Group's new headquarters building at Tezpur. (GP-7-Bomb-HI-June 1945, Albert F. Simpson Historical Research Center, Air Force Historical Research Agency, Maxwell AFB, AL)

Officer's bashas at Tezpur. (GP-7-Bomb-HI-June 1945, Albert F. Simpson Historical Research Center, Air Force Historical Research Agency, Maxwell AFB, AL)

"Old 91", B-24J-15-CO 42-73160 *Jungle Jig*. One of the first B-24J models assigned to the 7th Bomb Group, *Jungle Jig* flew over 80 combat missions and 35 Hump flights with the 492nd Squadron. (SQ-Bomb-492-HI-June 1945, Albert F. Simpson Historical Research Center, Air Force Historical Research Agency, Maxwell AFB, AL)

7th Bomb Group B-24s at Tezpur, ready to begin hauling aviation gasoline to China. (SQ-Bomb-492-HI-June 1945, Albert F. Simpson Historical Research Center, Air Force Historical Research Agency, Maxwell AFB, AL)

directly. A thousand and one details had to be resolved, not to mention an attempt to set up some of the amenities and creature comforts the squadrons had carefully built up at their old bases and become used to.[19]

Tezpur was located in northern Assam, and in contrast to Madhaiganj and Pandaveswar was much wetter, with lush vegetation. The foothills of the Himalayan mountain range lay 30 miles to the north. The airfield had one runway 6,000 feet long by 150 feet wide, with ample hard stand areas for all three squadrons and full radio communications and its own radio beacon. The living quarters were three miles from the airfield, and here the men were housed in 18 by 30-foot bashas, four men to a basha. Within a short time, the Group and the Squadrons were installed in their new quarters with a newly-built ice making plant and a coca-cola bottling plant. A new officers club arose, featuring a bar, soda-making machine built from spare parts, and an air conditioning unit. The squadrons combined to organize a single PX facility for everyone on the base to provide longer hours and more service. Tezpur quickly became home. After a month or so of settling in, the 492nd described their new base as having "...showers, a Red Cross club, beer, ice cream, coca-cola, a few cool nights, good shows, good friends, and soft mattresses.[20]

The gas hauling B-24s had all excess weight removed. *Cabin in the Sky* has had the top and belly turrets removed and the guns stripped from the nose and tail turrets. (SQ-Bomb-492-HI-June 1945, Albert F. Simpson Historical Research Center, Air Force Historical Research Agency, Maxwell AFB, AL)

After stripping excess equipment from the B-24s, three bomb bay tanks were installed. (SQ-Bomb-492-HI-June 1945, Albert F. Simpson Historical Research Center, Air Force Historical Research Agency, Maxwell AFB, AL)

The B-24s underwent a radical transformation to convert them to tanker aircraft, an approximation of the C-109 (the tanker conversion of the standard B-24). To reduce weight, the Engineering departments removed all top turrets and any remaining ball turrets and their assemblies. The nose and tail turrets were stripped of their guns and internal parts and locked in the neutral position. The maintenance crews took out all the armor plate, the flak vests that accompanied the bombers on missions, and any other extraneous equipment not needed for hauling gas. Each B-24 was fitted with three bomb bay tanks. With the severe weather expected over the Hump route at any time of year, those airplanes that did not have heaters in the wings and tails had their de-icer systems reinstalled. This was a complicated task, as the leading edges of the wings had to be removed and de-icer boots put back in and de-icer fluid tanks for the propellers re-fitted. All this equipment had been taken out at modification centers in India when the airplanes had arrived.[21]

With no need for bombardiers or gunners, and no doubt mindful of the loss of too many crews the year before, the crews for the Hump flights were cut back to pilot, copilot, navigator, flight engineer, and radio operator. To prepare for flying the Hump route, all pilots in the squadrons received eight hours of instrument flying instruction with a rated instrument instructor and then an instrument flight test. Training covered instrument take-offs and landings, spiral climbs, banking turns, steep banks, stalls, and recovery from unusual maneuvers, with particular emphasis on flying by radio compass. Pilots had to make instrument landings with one of the outboard engines feathered. The navigators received extra training in the use of Loran navigation. The 7th Group obtained the loan of a special Loran training airplane, a C-47 fitted out with six Loran sets and with two instructors: one a WAC and the other a Lt. Col. The C-47 could take twelve navigators at a time on missions out over the Hump using Loran to get back to Tezpur for practice. As the 492nd commented, "the WAC was nice, but too heavily chaperoned by the Lt. Colonel."[22]

The final phase of training involved check flights with Air Transport Command pilots over the Hump. The ATC crews did not impress the men of the 492nd, whose somewhat scathing comments are worth recording in full:

> We of the 7th Bomb Group use the word "hump" as an ordinary noun without capital letters and without undue emphasis. Not that we don't respect the dangers of hump flying, for we are quite aware of all its peculiarities. Many of us had already flown the route several times...The next phase of pilot training was a big treat, ah yes. We were sent to Jorhat to fly two missions each with A.T.C. pilots. Now as everyone knows, the A.T.C. spells 'hump" like this—"HUMP!"—with apologies for not having typewriters that can write the word in italics.
>
> On the credit side of the ledger we must say that our experience with the A.T.C. was invaluable as far as learning the routes and the radio procedures were concerned. Many of the pilots we rode with were not only fine fliers but fine fellows as well.
>
> But we got more than route experience. A.T.C. went out of its way to make out grade slips on our flying ability too. And these were later sent to our own

Col. Harvey Alness welcomes his replacement as commander of the 7th Bomb Group, Col. Howard Bronson. (GP-7-Bomb-HI-June 1945, Albert F. Simpson Historical Research Center, Air Force Historical Research Agency, Maxwell AFB, AL)

operations office. Although these were meant to be helpful, we really hadn't looked to A.T.C. for this sort of aid. And after flying with them our opinion remains unchanged.

It seems that the 7th Bomb Group's record gas haul a year ago was not enough to convince them that anyone besides the A.T.C. can fly the hump and do it well. We will have to convince them again.

And it seems someone should talk to them about their flying technique. We can't go into detail over each grade slip that was issued to our pilots, but we can't help but mention this one—"Fair pilot, but he cracks his nose wheel on takeoff at 85 miles per hour." A.T.C. pilots take off with an average gross weight of 60,000 pounds. They charge the full length of the runway with their nose wheel on the ground—if they can, they remain on the runway until they reach 140 miles per hour. They don't know what it is like to take off with a gross weight of 70,000 lbs. or over. They don't know that it is a necessity to crack the nose wheel as soon as possible on a heavy-loaded takeoff. For raising the nose wheel off the ground removes the rolling friction of the nose wheel, removes the possibility of the nose wheel collapsing, alters the tendency of the plane to fly into the ground, and places the plane in a flying attitude.

So to the A.T.C. and its "HUMP!" we must say, quote, "HUMPH!" ...just watch our steam, that's all", unqote.[23]

During the 7th Group's transition to its new mission there were several command changes. A new Group commander arrived to replace Col. Alness. After eight months in command, he was ordered to return to the United States for reassignment. Alness had taken over the Group as it was making an unsteady transition back to bombing. Over the following months, he and his operations staff and squadron commanders had built the 7th Group into the most accurate heavy bomber unit in the Strategic Air Force. An operational analysis of the Strategic Air Force's campaign against bridges from November 1944 to May 1945 compared the results of the 7th Bombardment Group to the Liberator squadrons in No. 231 Group, RAF, commenting that "...the standard of medium level bombing is not as high as the 7th Group...", noting that while No. 231 Group's squadrons had not made as many medium attacks on bridges, the average line error during May 1945 was 318 feet, "...which does not compare very favorably with that of the 7th Group for bridges viz: 228 ft".[24] Under Alness' leadership the 7th Group had received its second Distinguished Unit Citation and had developed a new and dramatically effective bombing method for destroying bridges, proven in the record

The cover of the 492nd Bomb Squadron's history for the month of June. Although the shift to hauling gas was a disappointment, like the "Eager Beavers" of the 492nd, the men of the 9th and 436th Squadrons made the best of their new assignment. (SQ-Bomb-492-HI-June 1945, Albert F. Simpson Historical Research Center, Air Force Historical Research Agency, Maxwell AFB, AL)

destruction of the mission of April 24, 1945. It was a record to be proud of. In recognition of the 7th Group's contribution to the success of the Strategic Air Force, the Royal Air Force awarded Col. Alness the Distinguished Service Order (DSO) on his departure from the Group. Informing the 7th Group's personnel of the award, Alness said, "it is not the custom of the RAF to award unit citations, but it is my feeling that this DSO is to be regarded as such...as a commemoration of the fine period of operations the Seventh Group has had while serving under an RAF commander."[25] In his own farewell letter to the officers and men of the 7th Group, Alness said: "It is with much reluctance that I am completing my second tour with the 7th Bombardment Group (H). I am particularly mindful of your fine efforts and achievements. Working with you has been all one could ask for and I'm sure you know my pride in all of you and the 7th Bombardment Group."[26]

Col. Alness' replacement was Col. Howard Bronson, another prewar 7th Bombardment Group veteran who transferred from Headquarters, Army Air Forces, India-Burma Sector. Bronson formally took command of the 7th Group on June 24, 1945. Lt. Col. William Kyes, Group Operations officer, was also reassigned to the United States. Maj. Harry Alexander, commander of the 436th Squadron, was promoted to Lt. Colonel and appointed Kyes' replacement at the end of the month. Capt. Walter Rector, who had joined the Group in November 1944 as an instrument flying instructor and had then become Director of Training and Flying Safety took over command of the 436th Squadron; Rector was promoted to Major in July. In the 9th Squadron, now-Maj. William Dabney, another long-serving 7th Group veteran, got his chance to return to the longed-for Zone of Interior, Capt. John Dozier replacing him. A number of 7th Group staff and administrative officers left the Group as well. Among them was Lt. Col. Eugene Stevens, the Group Executive Officer, who had joined the 88th Reconnaissance Squadron in 1935 as a Sergeant and had served with the 7th Group continuously since that time, going overseas in November 1941 as a Sargent Major and rising rapidly after receiving a direct commission as a 2nd Lieutenant. In order to provide the 493rd Squadron, left at Pandaveswar, with more stability in its roster of crews, the 492nd Squadron sent six of its newest crews to the 493rd, taking in return six of the 493rd Squadron's oldest crews who were more likely to be sent home.[27]

At Tezpur, the three 7th Group squadrons came under the operational control of the India-China Division, Air Transport Command, who supervised the delivery of aviation gasoline to the Fourteenth Air Force's bases in China. The 436th Squadron had the honor of undertaking the first gas hauling flight to China, Lt. Warren Lippitt and his crew flying a load of aviation gasoline to the former B-29 base at Hsinching, near Chengtu, the home of the 312th Fighter Wing and its component units—the 81st and 311th Fighter Groups and the 490th Bombardment Squadron (M), old friends from Burma. The other 7th Group squadrons followed over the next few days. Maj. Ralph Jensen, CO of the 492nd Squadron, made the first flight over the Hump on June 20th, his experience illustrating what the pilots had to cope with on these flights. Taking off from Tezpur under a low ceiling of cloud, he went on instruments and did not get into the clear until he had reached his cruising altitude of 19,500 feet and had flown through a thunderstorm. The capture of Myitkyina almost a year earlier enabled the A.T.C. to start flying lower altitude routes across the Himalayan mountain ranges and to establish more radio beacons along the route. Arriving over Chengtu, Jensen was assigned a nearby field to land on and unload his gasoline. This required an instrument let-down through 8,000 feet of overcast. Unloading the gasoline at the field took two hours. Jensen took the northernmost A.T.C. route over the mountains on his way back, flying at 19,500 feet in clear weather, returning to Tezpur after 13 hours. By the end of June, the Group had flown 105 sorties to China and delivered 103,270 gallons of gasoline. Initially the Group pooled all aircraft and had Group Operations schedule crews and assign aircraft, but beginning in July airplanes and operations returned to the squadrons, with each squadron receiving a quota for the amount of gasoline to be taken to China that

2nd Lt. George Olsen, in the 492nd Bomb Squadron, was a talented cartoonist who drew several humorous cartoons of real concerns on the Hump flights. (SQ-Bomb-492-HI-July 1945, Albert F. Simpson Historical Research Center, Air Force Historical Research Agency, Maxwell AFB, AL)

Another of 2nd Lt. Olsen's cartoons. (SQ-Bomb-492-HI-July 1945, Albert F. Simpson Historical Research Center, Air Force Historical Research Agency, Maxwell AFB, AL)

month. This encouraged a healthy competition between the squadrons as to who could not just meet, but exceed their monthly quota.[28]

During July—the first full month of hauling gas—the 9th Squadron placed first, delivering 147,800 gallons in 166 trips over the Hump. The 436th Squadron was second, carrying 143,700 gallons in 155 Hump trips. Both accomplishments were due in large measure to a great deal of hard, sweaty, hot work on the part of the squadron Engineering departments and the maintenance crews who serviced the airplanes. Morale gradually improved with a general acceptance, on the part of older crews, of the work that needed to be done and the changing tenor of the squadrons as more and more combat veterans left to return to the United States. The newer crews arriving had no other frame of reference, so simply adjusted to the new routine. As the 492nd Squadron's history for July recorded: "The swaggering Rangoon Ramblers are all gone but a few. 14 crews have never seen a burst of flak. 19 crews made their first trip to China. It's a new 'Eager Beaver' outfit, but a good one. Somehow, it's this newness, this fresh spirit, that's bound to survive the future troubles when the weather gets worse and the planes get more ragged."[29] But there was still an underlying disappointment and frustration with the Group's new role, despite the brave face the 492nd tried to put on it. The same monthly squadron history commented: "It's been a rough month, full of hard work, heart break, and bad weather. It is easily evident that there is nothing inspiring about Hump flying. That fact alone cuts off half the incentive necessary for an 'Eager Beaver' squadron. As one of the linemen said, 'We shoulda stood wid bombing.' How right."[30]

The weather over the Hump during the monsoon season as well as over China was awful. The flying was demanding and unforgiving. The 7th Group lost four airplanes and three crews during the month of July; the 492nd lost more airplanes over the Hump that month than it had during five months of combat. The weather made navigation critical. The 492nd Squadron's history recorded: "the weather at present makes the navigator's job quite touchy, with fingertips on dials at all times. Usually the Loran or radio compass is working. If neither is, Jow Grope does push-ups while squinting through the bombardier's peep hole for check points. Such is a job."[31] Good navigation and good weather were not all that was needed to fly the Hump safely. When the weather went bad flying skill, a fully functioning airplane, and sometimes a healthy dose of luck were often required.

The 436th Squadron suffered the loss of two aircraft during July. The experiences of the two crews illustrate the dangers and the risks they faced flying the Hump and across China in bad weather. On July 11, 1945, Lt. Donald Landin and his crew had a narrow escape returning to Tezpur in the early morning from a flight to China. Visibility over the airfield was poor due to the darkness, ground fog, and rain. Landin made two passes over the field but could not make out the runway. Worried that his fuel would soon be exhausted, Landin decided to put his B-24M down on his next pass, even if he couldn't see the runway. He landed 200 yards away in the grass and mud, ripping off his left main landing gear and narrowly missing the airfield tower as his bomber slid on its belly for another 500 feet, miraculously failing to explode. His airplane (#66) was a wreck, but Landin and his crew walked away from

Lt. Donald Landin and his crew had a narrow escape, landing at Tezpur in bad weather. (SQ-Bomb-436-HI-July 1945, Albert F. Simpson Historical Research Center, Air Force Historical Research Agency, Maxwell AFB, AL)

the crash. Ten days later, Lt. Gustav Schneider and his crew took off for a routine flight to Chengtu over the Hump route. Arriving over Chengtu, Schneider was ordered to take his airplane to another nearby airfield where he ran into thunderstorms, severe turbulence, and electrical disturbances that made it impossible for the radio operator to contact the tower below. After circling for 30 minutes, Schneider contacted Chengtu for a bearing to return to that field. Given a new heading for Chengtu, he climbed to 27,000 feet to get above the bad weather and find calmer air. At the worst possible time the airplane's radio gave out with blue flames arcing through the wiring. With no radio contact with the ground and bad weather below, the pilot alerted the crew to prepare to bail out. As a result of the severe turbulence the radio operator had become violently air sick and was throwing up in the bomb bay. Having taken off his oxygen mask, he passed out from lack of oxygen. Seeing this, the Flight engineer went back to give him his own mask, but for some reason, possibly fatigue, failed to take along a hand-held oxygen bottle. The engineer passed out, too, as did Schneider, who got out of his seat to help him. In the confusion that followed while trying to revive the engineer and the pilot, the radio operator somehow fell out of the airplane, though no one on the crew saw him leave. With the pilot and engineer revived, the crew started bailing out. Schneider put the airplane on autopilot in a gentle bank and at 27,000 feet the navigator went first, followed by the engineer, then the copilot, then Schneider. All the crew but the radio operator landed safely, though the copilot lost several teeth and the navigator suffered a cracked knee cap. Local Chinese later found the radio operator dead with his chute unopened.[32] Other crews were not as fortunate. The 9th Squadron lost Lt. Hugh Sheldon and his veteran crew on July 11th while trying to land on an airfield in China during a rain storm. Flying Officer Harold Sheldon and his crew and 2nd Lt. Norman Rosengren and his crew, both in the 492nd Squadron, were lost on July 7 and 28, 1945, while flying gas into China.[33]

The Longest Paper Route in the World

After the Strategic Air Force disbanded on June 1, 1945, the 493rd Squadron remained non-operational, its bombing skills no longer called for over Burma with the reorientation of the Tenth Air Force towards China. There was some thought that the 493rd would move to China to undertake operations there, but logistical problems delayed the movement of many Tenth Air Force squadrons to new China bases. In addition, the Fourteenth Air Force had decided that medium bombers and fighters were better suited to the interdiction and close support missions then being flown more than the gas-guzzling B-24s of its own 308th Bombardment Group.[34] Three of the 308th Group's squadrons were shifted, like the 7th Group, to hauling gasoline over the Hump from India, while its fourth squadron that specialized in low-level radar bombing was transferred to Okinawa, effectively leaving the new Army Air Forces, China Theater, with one available heavy bomber squadron, the 493rd.[35] While the other three squadrons in the 7th Group were setting up at Tezpur during the first few weeks of June, the 493rd began an intensive training program for all combat crews in order to maintain its proficiency. Newly-arrived crews started a three-month air crew training syllabus involving 136 hours of ground training and 90 hours of flight training for every pilot during the course. The course covered basic flying proficiency, squadron and group formation tactics, dive bombing, Azon and radar bombing, and cruise control techniques for obtaining maximum range. In separate courses navigators received training in standard navigation, but also training in the newer Loran and radar navigation methods, while bombardiers trained on Norden bomb sights, Azon bombing, and radar bombing, with each bombardier allowed

Preparing a 493rd Squadron B-24 a mission to drop leaflets over Thailand. (SQ-Bomb-493-HI-July 1945, Albert F. Simpson Historical Research Center, Air Force Historical Research Agency, Maxwell AFB, AL)

two 1,000-pound Azon bombs for practice using an uninhabited island in the Bay of Bengal. The Squadron began, for the first time, an intensive radar training course for radar operators (a new crew position), navigators, and bombardiers.[36]

During June, the 493rd Squadron took up a new mission, working with the United States Office of War Information

A propaganda leaflet in Burmese. The 7th Group dropped these type of leaflets regularly on bombing missions over Burma. (Author's collection)

A propaganda leaflet in Thai showing a B-24. The caption reads "News from the pilot who is always on time." (Author's collection)

(OWI) to distribute propaganda leaflets throughout Thailand. With the defeat of Germany, the OWI stepped up the propaganda campaign throughout Asia and the Pacific, aiming at not just the Japanese, but also the peoples of China and Southeast Asia.[37] At the start of the Pacific War, Thailand had allied itself with Japan and had, controversially, declared war on Great Britain and the United States, though the United States, unlike Great Britain, chose to view Thailand as an occupied country and did not reciprocate Thailand's declaration of war. Opposition within Thailand to the declaration of war resulted in the formation of the Free Thai underground movement. By 1945, the Free Thai were working actively with the United States and Britain against the Japanese, providing valuable intelligence for Strategic Air Force bombing missions into Thailand against Japanese facilities.[37] As Japan's fortunes declined, conditions worsened in Thailand and opposition to the Japanese grew. The fall of Burma set the stage for expanded operations against Japanese forces in other parts of Southeast Asia, principally through the invasion of Malaya, scheduled for the fall, but also the potential seizure of vital areas within Thailand.[39] To broaden support for the Allies among the Thai people and provide them with more accurate news and information on the state of the war and Japan's precarious position, the OWI enlisted the help of the 493rd Squadron to distribute Thai language propaganda leaflets over key population centers within Thailand.

The 493rd began working with the OWI in mid-June and continued leaflet dropping missions over Thailand for the next three months, the propaganda mission gradually taking the place of bombing missions. The first OWI mission took place on June 18, 1945, and may well have been undertaken at the request of the Free Thai underground, or in cooperation with them. Lt. Col. Charles Craig, Squadron commander, led three B-24s out from Pandaveswar on the mission to Bangkok with an escort of P-38s. Descending to 400 feet, the bombers flew over the Pramane Grounds (Sanam Luang in Thai), a large open area near the Royal Palace used for parades and ceremonies, and dropped loads of medical supplies onto the center of the grounds. No anti-aircraft guns fired on the bombers as they came in over the city. Pulling away from the drop zone, the bombers and their escorts saw two submarines moored in the Chao Phya River and immediately went down to strafe them; reports indicated one of the subs may have been sunk. It is possible these were two of four submarines the Royal Thai Navy had ordered from the Mitsubishi Corporation before the outbreak of the war. In addition to dropping the medical supplies, the three airplanes distributed 150,000 OWI leaflets over Bangkok and villages in the surrounding area. The 493rd scheduled a regular bombing mission against the airfield at Ban Takli, an airfield 150 or so miles north of Bangkok, by a single B-24 on June 26th, but severe weather en route forced the pilot to abandon the mission. The Squadron tried again the next day, sending one B-24 to drop leaflets over Bangkok while a second airplane attacked Ban Takli as a diversion. 2nd Lt. Wesley Sommers was the pilot of the B-24 bombing Ban Takli. He apparently

Another photo from the same *Phoenix* article shows bombardier Lt. Glen Brownfield making sandwiches for the rest of the crew on the return flight back to Pandaveswar. Food was welcome on these 13-16 hour missions over Thailand. (Via the author)

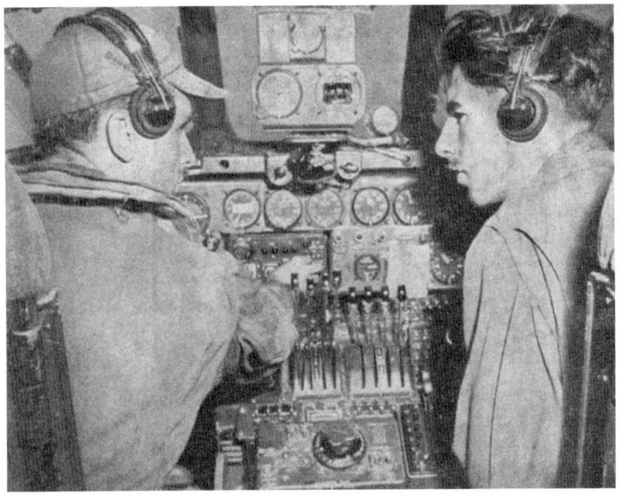

A photograph taken from the July 14, 1945, issue of *Phoenix*, a magazine for SEAC forces featuring an article on the 7th Bomb Group. The photo shows Lt. Sheppard Cummings of the 493rd Bomb Squadron with his copilot, Lt. Julian Christopher. (Via the author)

completed his mission, but on the return flight back to base the airplane disappeared after contacting Calcutta with an E.T.A.[40]

The leaflet dropping missions into Thailand continued through July. These missions were grueling and involved, as the 493rd Squadron's history noted, "...practically every hazard of normal combat operations...", in addition to the necessity of plowing through the monsoon weather over Burma to reach Thailand.[41] The missions were long, averaging around 13 hours, the longest mission that month occurring when Lt. Dan Shendeldecker and his crew returned, having spent 18 hours and 10 minutes in the air. The B-24s normally carried 24 M-55 propaganda bombs in the bomb bays to drop over a city area, the bombs falling open to release the leaflets. More leaflets were carried in cartons in the waist section for the gunners to toss out the waist windows. One airplane could carry between 150,000 to 180,000 leaflets on a single mission. The crews were assigned a specific area within Thailand on each leaflet-dropping mission, usually covering some of the larger towns and cities as well as rural areas, often along the railroad lines. By this stage in the war, the Japanese Army Air Force had less than 200 airplanes in Southeast Asia outside the Netherlands East Indies, and not all of these were serviceable.[42] Although the Squadron's aircraft had all had the undersurfaces of the wings and fuselages painted black for night missions, during July, the 493rd began flying their leaflet dropping missions into Thailand during daylight. The bombers took off from Pandaveswar before dawn, cruising over the Thai countryside during the day and getting back to base in the evening with little risk of interception. Only occasionally did the Squadron's airplanes run into anti-aircraft fire. The crews joked that they were operating the longest paper route in the world.

The 493rd carried out the 7th Bombardment Group's last bombing mission of the war on July 3, 1945, when a single B-24M bombed Ban Takli airfield. Over the target area, the bombardier couldn't locate the field due to haze and the airplane's new radar equipment malfunctioned. Returning to the initial point, the town of Nakorn Sawarn, the bombardier used check points along the way and dropped his bombs on his ETA over what he hoped was the airfield. A second airplane had been sent out to bomb the airfield at Koke Kathiem, but had to turn back with mechanical problems. The rest of the missions the Squadron flew that month were to drop leaflets, covering cities and towns in central Thailand and along the Bangkok-Chiengmai railroad line. Single B-24Ms went out on July 4th, 6th, and 7th. A week later, on July 14th, three aircraft went to Bangkok and towns to the north and west of the city. Flying over Kanchanaburi (the 7th Group's old stomping grounds during the bridge busting days) Lt. Jones' B-24 ran into some anti-aircraft fire, machine gun bullets punching a few holes in his airplane. Despite the presence of anti-aircraft guns, when he saw a locomotive below him he took his B-24 down on a strafing run, punching holes in the engine and setting fire to several flat cars. Over Bangkok four days later, one of three B-24s on a leaflet mission ran into heavy flak over the city, returning with several holes but no injuries. A similar encounter took place on July 25th—the last mission of

A series of photos showing a leaflet dropping mission the 493rd Bomb Squadron undertook in July 1945. Here the crews get briefed on their destinations in Thailand. (SQ-Bomb-493-HI-July 1945, Albert F. Simpson Historical Research Center, Air Force Historical Research Agency, Maxwell AFB, AL)

While the crews are at the briefing, the crew chiefs prepare the airplanes for the mission. (SQ-Bomb-493-HI-July 1945, Albert F. Simpson Historical Research Center, Air Force Historical Research Agency, Maxwell AFB, AL)

Going out to the line. (SQ-Bomb-493-HI-July 1945, Albert F. Simpson Historical Research Center, Air Force Historical Research Agency, Maxwell AFB, AL)

The crew arrives at the airplane. (SQ-Bomb-493-HI-July 1945, Albert F. Simpson Historical Research Center, Air Force Historical Research Agency, Maxwell AFB, AL)

Dropping propaganda leaflet bombs over Chiengmai, Thailand. (SQ-Bomb-493-HI-July 1945, Albert F. Simpson Historical Research Center, Air Force Historical Research Agency, Maxwell AFB, AL)

Throwing propaganda leaflets out the waist windows over Thailand. (SQ-Bomb-493-HI-July 1945, Albert F. Simpson Historical Research Center, Air Force Historical Research Agency, Maxwell AFB, AL)

Returning to Pandaveswar from a long mission over Thailand. (SQ-Bomb-493-HI-July 1945, Albert F. Simpson Historical Research Center, Air Force Historical Research Agency, Maxwell AFB, AL)

Unloading the airplane after landing back at Pandaveswar. (SQ-Bomb-493-HI-July 1945, Albert F. Simpson Historical Research Center, Air Force Historical Research Agency, Maxwell AFB, AL)

Interrogation after the mission. (SQ-Bomb-493-HI-July 1945, Albert F. Simpson Historical Research Center, Air Force Historical Research Agency, Maxwell AFB, AL)

the month—when four airplanes went to Thailand, one airplane again running into heavy flak over Bangkok and picking up a few more holes. Apart from these three incidents, the 493rd ran into no other opposition, and in a month of flying in daylight over Thailand never even saw a Japanese airplane.[43]

The combat crew training program begun in June continued at full tilt during July, with both new and older combat crews making regular training flights. The radar training courses provided instruction for radar operators and navigators in the AN/APS-15A search radar and how this equipment could be used for bombing and navigation. The newer B-24M models then arriving for the squadron had the search radar fitted and this equipment was soon put to work as an aid to navigation, helping at least one navigator locate his position when he was lost. The 493rd Squadron also received the AN/APQ-5 low altitude bombing radar. This equipment had been used successfully against shipping in the Pacific and in China. The Squadron's bombardiers received training in how to use this bombing radar against ground targets, but the war ended before they had a chance to try their new skills.[44]

Finale

The end of the war with Japan found the 7th Group's squadrons engaged in the same efforts as the month before: the squadrons at Tezpur flying gas over the Hump and the 493rd dropping leaflets over Thailand. Then came the electrifying news of the first atomic bomb attack on Hiroshima on August 6, 1945, with the second atomic bomb attack on Nagasaki and the Russian entry into the war against Japan following three days later. As professional airmen, the men of the 7th Group instantly became fascinated with the atomic bomb and scoured news reports for any scraps of information on its size, weight, and destructiveness. Debates on its use flourished, but the general feeling was that if the atomic bomb helped to shorten the war its use was justified. Rumors started flying about when the war would officially end. The premature announcement on August 11th of Japan's intention to surrender caused an uproar among every man in the Group. In the 9th Squadron, the "Cobra Club" held an open house for all the enlisted men with all drinks on the house. An uproarious party ensued and in other squadrons, surpassed only by the explosion of uncontained joy when the 7th Group received confirmation of

Japan's actual surrender early in the morning of August 15, 1945. Sirens went off, jeep and truck horns blared, and when darkness fell flare guns and bon fires filled the sky with light.

The 493rd Bomb Squadron painted many of its B-24s black in anticipation of flying night missions. (SQ-Bomb-493-HI-August 1945, Albert F. Simpson Historical Research Center, Air Force Historical Research Agency, Maxwell AFB, AL)

Within the 436th Squadron: "...long hoarded 'bottles' were broken out and many a man drank his months' beer ration in one sitting."[45]

As the men recovered from their celebrations over the next several days, they learned to their dismay that their work would continue, though Group Operations ordered that there would be no flights over the Hump unless conditions were good and no night flights.[46] The news that the squadrons at Tezpur would continue flying gas to China caused an immediate drop in morale. With the war at an end, the question in many minds was "why bother?" and more critically, "When are we going home?" The squadrons went back to hauling gas. With four airplanes stuck in China awaiting engine changes and no engines available, the 9th Squadron was down to five operational aircraft. The 436th Squadron took the gas hauling honors that month, flying 138 trips over the Hump and delivering 125,315 gallons of gas. Tragically, now that the war was over, the 492nd Squadron lost an airplane and crew on August 19, 1945, despite the restrictions on Hump flying. Lt. John Stulz and his crew became the 7th Bombardment Group's final loss in a long war when they took off from Tezpur on a flight to Kunming and disappeared. The 493rd Squadron kept on flying leaflet missions, sending out 12 sorties during the month on even longer missions, the average flying time going up to 16 hours, with a new record of 19 hours in the air for one mission.[47]

The squadrons continued their work while undergoing a rapid turnover in personnel. Three days after the end of the war, 80 per cent of the bombardiers and gunners serving with the squadrons at Tezpur were transferred out and sent on their way back to the United States. More men left under the new points system the War Department had implemented to determine the order in which men would return to the United States: in the 9th Squadron, 29 officers and 120 enlisted men left; 26 officers and 116 enlisted men left the 436th; and 154 officers and enlisted men from the 492nd. A smaller number of new five-man crews arrived as replacements, but the three squadrons all had to scramble to ensure that their departments would still function efficiently. There were changes in command as well. In the 492nd Squadron, Maj. Ralph Jensen received orders transferring him back to the Zone of Interior the day the war ended. Capt. Brad Chase, Operations officer in the 493rd Squadron, moved over to replace him. In the 493rd, Lt. Col. Charles Craig handed over the Squadron to Lt. Col. James McKee on August 17th.[48]

There was one final push before the end. The 493rd Squadron flew its last combat mission, and the last combat mission for the 7th Bombardment Group, on September 3, 1945, three years, eight months, and 27 days since the attack on Pearl Harbor. Four B-24s took off from Pandaveswar to drop leaflets over 17 cities and towns in Thailand, ranging from Chiengmai down to Bangkok, to the south as far as Jumbhorn—the site of the 7th Group's longest mission—and east past Bangkok to Ubon. The crews completed the mission without incident. The squadrons at Tezpur continued what they had come to call "Hump jumping" when the happy news

Lt. Dan Shindeldecker (kneeling second from the right) and his crew after returning from a near 15-hour mission over Thailand in August 1945. (SQ-Bomb-493-HI-August 1945, Albert F. Simpson Historical Research Center, Air Force Historical Research Agency, Maxwell AFB, AL)

arrived on September 9, 1945, that the War Department had placed the 7th Bombardment Group on Category IV status, indicating a unit that had been designated to return to the United States earlier than others. The second part of the good

After the end of the war, the squadrons made sure the record of each aircraft was properly recorded beneath the cockpit. This 436th Bomb Squadron B-24M was named *Home Stretch*. (Author's collection)

news was that once a certain amount of gasoline had been delivered to China, the gas hauling operations would cease. The squadrons kept up a fast pace of Hump flights until even better news came on September 18th. The men learned that the Theater commander had terminated the 7th Group's Hump operations and that the Group had received orders to return to the United States for reassignment as a unit, the aircrews flying their own aircraft back while the ground echelons went by sea. By then, the 492nd had done 94 trips over the Hump, delivering 122,699 gallons of gasoline, compared to 87 trips for the 436th and 84 for the 9th Squadron. The final total for the three months of Hump operations put the 436th Squadron on top, as it had been the year earlier, with a total of 401,044 gallons of gasoline delivered. The 492nd Squadron took second place and the 9th was third. Between June and September, the three squadrons delivered 1.1 million gallons of aviation gasoline to China. With their gas hauling days over, on September 19th, the 7th Group held a special ceremony to mark the end of the Group's participation in WWII.[49]

The next few weeks were a frenzied round of activity as the Group prepared for the return to "Shangri La". The airplanes to be flown back to the States underwent a thorough inspection. New engines and new tires were installed, new life rafts put in, baggage racks built in the bomb bays, and every airplane was test flown to ensure it was in perfect working order for the long journey. As each airplane was to carry fifteen men, comprising the combat crew, crew chief and maintenance men, and additional passengers, the Engineering departments scrounged discarded or salvaged rows of metal seats from C-47s and C-87s and installed them in the waist areas on the B-24s. Once the bombers were equipped, inspected, tested, and cleaned and polished, the crews took time to add more personal touches. As the 9th Squadron described the process: "Artists sprang up overnight and all rushed to the line to beautify the planes with pictures and a record of their bombing and hump missions at the same time keep the Pin-ups of their choice within the dictates of decorum dictated by Higher Headquarters."[50] In the 492nd Squadron, two veteran B-24Js were added to the airplanes designated for the flight to the United States. "Old 86" had accumulated 1,477:55 hours of flying time, but "Old 91", *Jungle Jig*, had even more. A Consolidated-built B-24J-15 and one of the first B-24Js assigned to the 492nd back in November 1943, *Jungle Jig* had flown 1,623:85 hours during 80 combat missions and 35 Hump flights, participating in every kind of mission the 7th Group had flown, from high altitude battles over Rangoon, bombing bridges from medium altitudes, to dive bombing on the mission of April 24, 1945.[51] It was altogether fitting that this should be one of the airplanes to return home.

Throughout this last month there were a flurry of personnel moves. Men with enough points headed back to the United States, while a new War Department order that all men over the age of 35 could return saw more members of the Group depart. Men without enough points and those who had only recently arrived were transferred to other Army Air Forces units within the India-Burma Theater, while some high-point men from other units shifted to the 7th Group to return to the

Many B-24s also had images of scantily clad young women painted on before departing for the United States. This 493rd Bomb Squadron B-24L or M was later named *Lascivious Lil*. (SQ-Bomb-493-HI-September 1945, Albert F. Simpson Historical Research Center, Air Force Historical Research Agency, Maxwell AFB, AL)

States. Each squadron had a net decrease in personnel of around 200 men during the month. This complicated the task of shutting down the Group's activities. There were personnel files to be updated and completed, equipment to be sorted, turned in, packed up, or disposed of, and a thousand other

The 9th Bomb Squadron's B-24J *Cute Lil' Lass* having just landed at West Palm Beach, Florida, in November 1945. (7th Bombardment Group (H) Historical Foundation, USAFA McDermott Library)

The 9th Bomb Squadron's B-24L/M *Luscious Lace* in the United States. (Author's collection)

tasks. But the work got done and then the planes started leaving, flying west across the Middle East and Africa to Brazil along the route their B-17E forbearers had pioneered in 1942. The ground echelons closed down operations at Tezpur and Pandaveswar, moving to temporary quarters near Calcutta. On December 6, 1945, the men boarded the USS *General W.M. Black*, a U.S. Navy transport ship, for the long voyage home. Arriving in New York on January 5, 1946, the men traveled to Camp Kilmer in New Jersey, where the 7th Bombardment Group (H) and its component squadrons were formally inactivated the next day.[52]

Before their departure from India, the men of the 7th Group received the following letter of commendation from Lt. Gen. Raymond A. Wheeler, the last commander of the India-Burma Theater:

1. In reviewing the activities of the 7th Bomb Group (H), I find that the Group has played a conspicuous part in the defeat of the enemy and the achievement of victory. Arriving in this theater on 12 March 1942, the Group applied itself assiduously to the task of bringing destruction of the enemy and demolishing their lines of communication. In 1943 it was instrumental in denying to the Japanese the use of Rangoon as a port of entry into Burma. During the Monsoon of 1944, the Group air-lifted over two million gallons of high octane gasoline across the hazardous "Hump" route to support the operations of the 14th Air Force in China, which was then being threatened by advancing Japanese forces.
2. In the course of the Group's operations, the enemy was denied the use of over 100 bridges which were destroyed by low level bombing attacks. An outstanding achievement of the Army Air Forces in this theater was the mission made on 19 March 1945 when elements of the 7th Bombardment Group flew over 2,700 miles without benefit of fighter escort, to disrupt Japanese communications on the Bangkok-Singapore and Kra-Isthmus Railroads in the face of extremely adverse weather and heavy anti-aircraft fire. This 18 hour airborne mission was accomplished with distinction and outstanding bombing results.
3. Before leaving his theater I desire to commend the officers and men of the 7th Bombardment Group (H) for their distinguished record of achievement which will remain indelibly inscribed in the history of this theater as a tribute to their determination and outstanding devotion to duty.[53]

A Summing Up

The 7th Bombardment Group was one of the few Army Air Forces units of WWII that could claim to have been present at the start of America's war with Japan and to have still been flying missions at war's end. As Lt. Gen. Wheeler's letter attests, the 7th Group compiled an impressive record during nearly four years of combat in Java and over Burma. The war the 7th Group ended up fighting was different from the war the Group had trained for. As Gen. Stratemeyer had said to the men of the Group on his visit in November 1944, the 7th Bombardment Group had been instrumental in developing the tactics and techniques necessary to carry out the core mission of the Army Air Corps and soon the Army Air Forces: unescorted daylight precision strategic bombing with the objective of forcing "...the capitulation of an enemy nation by air action applied directly against the vital points of its national structure."[54]

This was the doctrine, and the mission, that had guided the 7th Group's training in peace time and that the Group took to war. The 7th Group's experience flying missions into Burma, however, mirrored that of other Army Air Forces heavy bomber units, as the Army Air Forces' prewar doctrine confronted its first test in a real war. The air power theorists who developed the doctrine of strategic bombing in the Army Air Corps and went on to put this doctrine into practice against Germany and Japan had overestimated the defensive capability of bomber formations and the ability of these formations to fly unescorted missions over enemy territory, the ability of bombardiers to destroy targets from actual combat altitudes, and the resilience of the enemy in the face of air attack.[55] The 7th Group was fortunate that during most of its first year in combat over Burma the Japanese Army Air Force's fighter defenses were relatively weak, allowing the Group to undertake unescorted bombing missions with light losses. Once the Japanese increased the number of fighters defending the Rangoon area, however, losses increased dramatically, even with an escort of long-range fighters.

With few "strategic" targets in Burma, apart from the oil fields that contributed to the enemy's ability to prosecute the war, the logical target for heavy bombers was the Japanese line of communications system that was essential to supplying the armies in Burma. This objective was in line with prewar doctrine and the campaign the 7th Group, and later the full Strategic Air Force undertook mirrored the comments of Lt. Kenneth Walker, the early air power advocate, in his 1933 article in *U.S. Air Services*, where he wrote: "...destruction of the means by which any armed force is supplied, moved, and made ready to operate, eliminates that force as a threat."[56] The technology the 7th Group deployed for high altitude bombing, though arguably the best in the world at that time, proved to be effective against large, stationary targets like dock areas and railroad marshaling yards, but was inadequate against smaller targets like ships and bridges.[57] High altitude attacks against bridges in Burma were singularly ineffective, with the 7th Group getting one hit for every 81 sorties during 1943. The Japanese Army proved surprisingly adept at making rapid repairs to the railroad system, demonstrating a resilience that was frustrating to the bomber squadrons, who came to see themselves in a race between their ability to continue bombing a bridge and the ability of the Japanese engineers to effect repairs on it.

What ultimately brought about success in the campaign against the Japanese communications system was a combination of a relentless battle of attrition against shipping and the railroad system, a battle that the formation of the Strategic Air Force greatly enhanced, a change in tactics, and new bombing technology. The two latter factors only became possible once Allied fighters had decimated the Japanese Army Air Force and established air superiority over Burma. The 7th Bombardment Group made an outstanding contribution to the campaign's success. For most of 1943, the 7th Group constituted the core of the strategic bombing effort out of India, as only the B-24s had the range to bomb targets deep in Burma. During much of this period, the 7th Group was short of both combat crews and airplanes, yet the constant attacks on shipping and the docks and warehouses in Rangoon did disrupt the flow of supplies into Burma's main port. The mining campaign the 7th Group initiated in early 1943 and then continued throughout the year and into 1944, aided by growing numbers of RAF Liberators, in combination with the continued bombing of port facilities, resulted in the Japanese effectively abandoning the ports of Rangoon and Bangkok by

7th Bomb Group pilots from the 9th Bombardment Squadron in 1932. (SQ-Bomb-9-SU-PH-1932, Albert F. Simpson Historical Research Center, Air Force Historical Research Agency, Maxwell AFB, AL)

early 1944 and sharply reducing the size of the cargo ships they would risk sending to Burma's smaller southern ports. The attacks on rail facilities and marshaling yards in Burma, coupled with the efforts of the medium bomber squadrons against bridges, knocked out roughly 65% of the Burmese railroad system by the end of 1943.[58]

During the first half of 1944, attacks on railroad installations accounted for 22.6% of the tonnage dropped on targets in Burma and attacks on bridges amounted to a mere 5.5%, in large measure due to the need to support the 14th Army's response to the Japanese Army's offensives.[59] The shift in the

Thirteen years later: a 7th Bomb Group Azon crew from the 493rd Bomb Squadron in 1945. (7th Bombardment Group (H) Historical Foundation, USAFA McDermott Library)

7th Group's mission during the 1944 monsoon to hauling gasoline to China and the need for additional training for the 7th Group and the RAF Liberator squadrons at the end of the year delayed a renewed and sustained attack on the Japanese communication system until the beginning of 1945. Beginning in January 1945, in the Battle of the Bridges the Strategic Air Force turned its full weight against the Burma-Thailand railroad and the rail line that ran from Bangkok to Chiengmai. Taking the period from November 1944 to April 1945, the 7th Bombardment Group played the most significant role in the campaign, flying twice the number of sorties against bridge targets and dropping nearly twice the bomb tonnage of the RAF Liberator squadrons.[60] It should be remembered that these missions took place over long distances. As an operational analysis report noted: "none of the bridges attacked were less than 700 miles from the nearest H.B. base, and the majority of the attacks were carried out between 800 and 1000 miles from base. In Europe this is equivalent, in radius of action, to interdicting the rail communications from Rome southwards by means of Heavy Bombers based in East Anglia!"[61] As described, the renewed offensive against the railroad system began just as the first Azon bombs came into use. The Azon, though by no means a perfect answer, did finally give the 7th Group a means to undertake "precision" bombing. The other solution to the problem of destroying bridges was the switch to low altitude attacks and ultimately to the dive, or "glip" bombing technique Col. Harvey Alness and his operational staff worked out. It is ironic that the 7th Group's most important contribution to the Allied victory in Burma was achieved through low level attacks, and not through the high altitude precision bombing that American bomber groups were trained for. It seems highly unlikely that any of the instructors at the Air Corps Tactical School ever envisioned four-engine bombers attacking targets at 300 feet, much less going down to strafe trains. To his credit, Col. Alness became an enthusiastic supporter of Azon bombing once its potential had been demonstrated and was willing to abandon prewar doctrine and adopt other bombing methods in pursuit of the principal objective: destroying the railroad lines into Burma. The combination of low level bombing where anti-aircraft fire was minimal and Azon bombing for targets that were well-defended proved to be the winning combination, while Azon and conventional bombing used in combination brought the best results of any bombing method, destroying 68% of the bridges attacked.[62] But neither method would have been possible without Allied air superiority. By early 1945, the heavy bombers could range deep into Thailand with near impunity, often without fighter escort, thanks to the excellent work of the AAF and RAF fighters the year before and to the appalling losses the Japanese Army Air Force suffered in other theaters of war; losses the Japanese aviation industry was incapable of replacing.

While the Strategic Air Force's campaign against the Japanese lines of communication into Burma never achieved complete success—the flow of supplies was never brought to a complete halt—the results were still remarkable and did have a decided impact on the Japanese Army and Air Force units fighting in Burma. The Army Air Forces and the Royal Air Force in the Theater learned through experience that to be effective, attacks on the line of communications system

A Ki-43 Oscar abandoned at an airfield in central Burma. (SQ-LIA-5-HI-May 1945, Albert F. Simpson Historical Research Center, Air Force Historical Research Agency, Maxwell AFB, AL)

had to be relentless and that certain key targets had to be attacked again, and again, and again. The number of heavy bombers in the Theater remained roughly the same from March 1944 to March 1945, but the cumulative impact increased dramatically. During the Strategic Air Force's first period of action from December 15, 1943, to May 31, 1944, the Force dropped 6,859 tons of bombs; during the last period, from December 1, 1944, to April 30, 1945, the tonnage had nearly doubled to approximately 13,000 tons. Though not all this bomb tonnage was directed at the railroad systems, the results of attacks on the lines of communication were impressive. By March 1945, continuous bombing had forced the Japanese to abandon the Bangkok-Chiengmai railroad line as a supply line, while the average tonnage along the vital railroad line from Bangkok to Pegu dropped from an estimated 600/700 tons a day to an estimated 100/150 tons a day by April 1945. As one example of the impact of the interdiction campaign and the disruption of the flow of supplies to Japanese units in Burma, advancing Allied troops captured 40 unserviceable Japanese fighters at an airfield in north Burma in January 1945 and a further 26 airplanes at the airfields around Meiktila in March 1945, airplanes that had been grounded due to lack of spare parts.[63] As the last battles in Burma got underway, the Japanese Army was short of medical and other military supplies, could only transport supplies by night, had difficulties deploying troop units where needed, had fewer airfields in use due to the inability to bring up supplies, and had only sixty fighters available to counter the nearly 1,000 Allied aircraft undertaking attacks all across Burma.[64]

Summarizing the vital role of air power in the Burma campaign in his final report to the Combined Chiefs of Staff, Admiral Lord Louis Mountbatten said:

> Air operations—striking at the enemy's airfields; at his supply centres; at his ports and shipping; at his rail and road communications; at his forward concentrations, and also at his front-line positions—formed the background and the unceasing accompaniment to the land fighting. Land advances depended for their success on air protection from enemy interference. In most cases, the air forces provided the spearhead of the attack; during the operations they fought the enemy in the air and harried him on the ground; and after the battle they continued to attack his communications and bases, and to weaken his fighting organization.[65]

The men of the 7th Bombardment Group fought a long and tiring, but ultimately successful war. Their effort and sacrifice was little-known and even less well recognized; their colleagues in the RAF called themselves "the Forgotten Air Force", akin to the 14th Army's moniker "the Forgotten Army".[66] The 7th Group was at the end of the longest supply line in the world, and up until nearly the end of the war had the lowest priority for aircraft, personnel, and equipment. The Group never suffered the severe losses inflicted on many of the heavy bomber units operating in Europe, but the Group's own losses—48 aircraft lost on combat missions and a further 23 lost hauling gas to China—were no less painful. Living conditions on the bases were adequate, but rarely more, and the amenities were few. The men worked, flew, and fought in often appalling weather, over vast distances, for hours on end, knowing that if they went down in enemy territory their chances of survival were slim. They built a proud record of achievement.

> Old men forget; yet all shall be forgot,
> But he'll remember, with advantages,
> What feats he did that day.
> *The Life of King Henry the Fifth*
> Act 4, Scene 3

CHAPTER NINE:

NOSE ART GALLERY

One of the 11th Bombardment Squadron's Curtiss B-2 Condors showing the brightly-colored markings on the nose and the Squadron's famous "Mr. Jiggs" insignia. (7th Bombardment Group (H) Historical Foundation, USAFA McDermott Library)

B-17E *Jungle Jim* at Karachi in June 1942. (7th Bombardment Group (H) Historical Foundation, USAFA McDermott Library)

A Douglas B-18 with the 7th Bombardment Group insignia on the nose. (3B-25021, RG 342FH, NARA)

B-17E *Sea Breeze*, from the 9th Bombardment Squadron in the Middle East in 1942. (7th Bombardment Group (H) Historical Foundation, USAFA McDermott Library)

B-24D 41-23879 *Apocalypse* 436th Bomb Squadron. (Author's collection)

B-24D *The Captain and the Kids* 492nd Bomb Squadron. (Courtesy Col. Tom Sledge, USAF Ret'd)

B-24J *Lady Luck II* 436th Bomb Squadron. (7th Bombardment Group (H) Historical Foundation, USAFA McDermott Library)

B-24D *The Butcher* 493rd Bomb Squadron. (7th Bombardment Group (H) Historical Foundation, USAFA McDermott Library)

B-24J 42-73057 *Half Ass* 9th Bomb Squadron. (7th Bombardment Group (H) Historical Foundation, USAFA McDermott Library)

B-24J 42-73067 *Rangoon Rosie* 436th Bomb Squadron. (7th Bombardment Group (H) Historical Foundation, USAFA McDermott Library)

B-24J 42-73299 *Little Lass* 436th Bomb Squadron. (7th Bombardment Group (H) Historical Foundation, USAFA McDermott Library)

B-24J 42-xxxxx *SNAFU* 493rd Bomb Squadron. (Courtesy Jim Augustus)

B-24J 44-40282 *Shoot You're Covered* 9th Bomb Squadron. (7th Bombardment Group (H) Historical Foundation, USAFA McDermott Library)

B-24J 44-40819 *Bar Made* 493rd Bomb Squadron. (Courtesy Jim Augustus)

B-24J 44-40857 *Cactus Kid/Rangoon Rangler* 9th Bomb Squadron. (7th Bombardment Group (H) Historical Foundation, USAFA McDermott Library)

B-24J 44-40857 *Cactus Kid/Rangoon Rangler* 9th Bomb Squadron. (7th Bombardment Group (H) Historical Foundation, USAFA McDermott Library)

B024J 44-40985 *Shy Ann* 436th Bomb Squadron. (Author's collection)

B-24J 44-40989 *Double Trouble* 493rd Bomb Squadron. (Author's collection)

B-24J 44-44501 *Loveable Lorena* 492nd Bomb Squadron. (7th Bombardment Group (H) Historical Foundation, USAFA McDermott Library)

B-24J/L 44-4xxxx *Miss Manookie* (Author's collection)

B-24J/L 44-41xxx *Mission Completed* 9th Bomb Squadron. (Author's collection)

B-24L 44-49504 *Boomerang, Back Again* 493rd Bomb Squadron. (Courtesy Jim Augustus)

B-24J/L 44-4xxxx *The Angry Angel* 9th Bomb Squadron. (Courtesy Jim Augustus)

B-24L 44-4xxxx *Fabulous Fannie* 492nd Bomb Squadron. (Courtesy Jim Augustus)

B-24L 44-4xxxx *Lassie, I'm Home* 436th Bomb Squadron. (Courtesy Jim Augustus)

B-24M 44-42273 *Hot to Go* 9th Bomb Squadron. (Author's collection)

B-24M 44-42460 *Hello-ver Burma* 436th Bomb Squadron. (Author's collection)

B-24M 44-42275 *Kentucky Kloud Hopper*. 436th Bomb Squadron (Author's collection)

B-24M 44-50792 *Bachelor's Playmate* 493rd Bomb Squadron. (Courtesy Jim Augustus)

B-24M 44-50857 *Home Stretch* 436th Bomb Squadron. (Courtesy Jim Augustus)

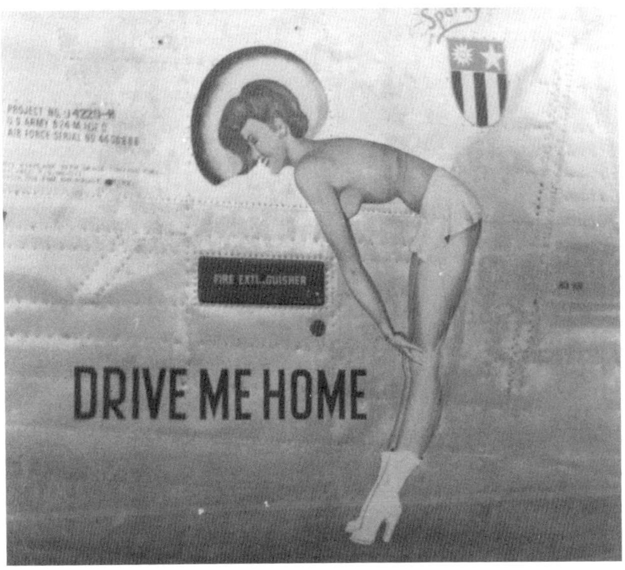

B-24M 44-50866 *Drive Me Home* 492nd Bomb Squadron. (Author's collection)

B-24M 44-51030 *Sleepy Time Gal* 493rd Bomb Squadron. (Courtesy Jim Augustus)

B-24M 44-51040 *Homesick Angel* 493rd Bomb Squadron. (Courtesy Jim Augustus)

B-24L/M 44-4xxxx *Eager Beaver Bombing Company* 492nd Bomb Squadron. (Author's collection)

B-24M 44-51054 *Flame of the Squadron* 493rd Bomb Squadron. (Courtesy Jim Augustus)

B-24L/M 44-xxxxx *Dangerous Dance* 493rd Bomb Squadron. (7th Bombardment Group (H) Historical Foundation, USAFA McDermott Library)

B-24L/M 44-xxxxx *Wandering Wanda* 493rd Bomb Squadron. (7th Bombardment Group (H) Historical Foundation, USAFA McDermott Library)

B-24L/M 44-4xxxx *Blind Date* 493rd Bomb Squadron. (Author's collection)

B-24L/M 44-xxxxx *Donna D Wanna* 493rd Bomb Squadron. (Author's collection)

B-24L/M 44-xxxxx *McSwine's Flying Comet* 493rd Bomb Squadron. (Author's collection)

B-24L/M 44-xxxx *Lascivious Lil* 493rd Bomb Squadron. (Author's collection)

B-24L/M 44-4XXXX *Mors Ab Alto* (Death From Above, the motto of the 7th Bombardment Group), 493rd Bomb Squadron. (Author's collection)

B-24L/M 44-xxxxx *Black Magic* 493rd Bomb Squadron? Note the comment to the right of the nose art stating "Censored by India-Burma Theater". (Author's Collection)

B-24L/M 44-xxxxx *Southern Comfort*. (Author's collection)

B-24L/M 44-4xxxx *Luscious Lace*, 493rd Bomb Squadron. (Author's collection)

B-24J-CO 44-40XXX *Reddy Teddy*. (Author's collection)

APPENDICES

Appendix A
Commanders

7th Bombardment Group
Maj. Albert L. Snead 1 June 1928-10 July 1928
Capt. H. M. Elmendorf 10 July 1928-5 May 1929
Capt. Frank H. Pritchard 10 July 1928-5 May 1929
Maj. Carl A. Spatz 6 May 1929-29 October 1931
Maj. Joseph T. McNarney 29 October1929-3 July 1933
Maj. Leo A. Walton 3 July 1933-11 May 1934
Maj. Charles T. Phillips 11 May 1934-8 October 1934
Capt. Lewis R.P. Reese 8 October 1934-5 November 1934
Lt. Col. Clarence L. Tinker 5 November 1934-31 August 1936
Col. Davenport Johnson 31 August 1936-17 November 1936
Lt. Col. George E. Stratemeyer 17 November 1936-15 August 1938
Lt. Col. Joseph T. McNarney 15 August 1938-5 March 1939
Maj. Earl H. Deford 5 March 1939-26 August 1939
Lt. Col. Ralph Royce 26 August 1939-7 April 1941
Maj. Earl H. Deford 7 April 1941-5 October 1941
Maj. Stanley K. Robinson 6 October 1941-29 January 1942
Maj. Austin A. Straubel 30 January 1942-3 February 1942
Maj. Kenneth B. Hobson 4 February 1942-20 March 1942
Maj. Cecil E. Combs 22 March 1942-30 June 1942
Lt. Col. Conrad F. Necrason 1 July 1942-8 February 1944
Maj. William A. Delahay 8 February 1944-26 March 1944
Col. Aubrey K. Dodson 27 March 1944-5 November 1944
Col. Harvey T. Alness 6 November 1944-24 June 1945
Col. Howard F. Bronson 25 June 1945-Unknown

9th Bombardment Squadron
Capt. Leo F. Post 1 April 1931-1 October 1931
Capt. Younger A. Pitts 1 October 1931-29 July 1932
Capt. Harold D. Smith 29 July 1932-23 September 1933
Maj. Charles T. Phillips 23 September 1933-11 May 1934
Lt. John G. Moore 11 May 1934-12 December 1934
Capt. John g. Moore 12 December 1934-14 October 1936
Capt. Kenneth N. Walker 14 October 1936-21 January 1938
Capt. Wilfred J. Paul 21 January 1938-1 March 1938
Maj. Thad V. Foster 1 March 1938-September 1939
Maj. Elmer E. Adler September 1939-February 1941
Maj. Julius T. Flock February 1941-23 July 1941
Maj. Richard H. Carmichael 23 July 1941-5 October 1941
Maj. Conrad F. Necrason 5 October 1941-15 March 1942
Maj. Donald M. Kaiser 15 March 1942-3 August 1942
Maj. Max R. Fennell 3 August 1942-3 November 1942
Maj. Willard A. Fountain 3 November 1942-3 January 1943
Capt. Homer E. Adams 3 January 1943-February 1943
Maj. William Stark February 1943-6 April 1943
Maj. Joseph S. Pirruccello 6 April 1943-21 October 1943
Capt. Allan A. Lathan 21 October 1943-29 December 1943
Capt. David N. Kellogg 29 December 1943-5 May 1944
Maj. William b. Kyes 5 May 1944-November 1944
Capt. William C. Dabney November 1944-7 June 1945
Capt. John M. Dozier 7 June 1945-Unknown

11th Bombardment Squadron
Capt. Edward O. Black 1 June 1928-20 July 1929
Lt. Francis B. Valentine 20 July 1929-28 April 1930
Lt. Frederick P. Kenny 28 April 1930-1 May 1930
Lt. Charles H. Howard 1 May 1930-30 July 1933
Capt. Robert E. Selff 30 July 1933-2 October 1934
Maj. Arthur g. Hamilton 2 October 1934-19 October 1935
Maj. Carlyle Ridenour 20 October 1935-14 June 1937
Capt. Edgar T. Noyes 14 June 1937-7 July 1937
Maj. Dale V. Gaffney 7 July 1937-2 September 1937
Capt. Donald W. Benner 2 September 1937-11 July 1938
Capt. Joseph H. Atkinson 11 July 1938-January 1940
Unknown January 1940-1 May 1940
Maj. John W. Warren 1 May 1940-January 1941
Unknown January 1941-
Maj. Austin A. Straubel 1941-3 February 1942
Capt. Elbert Helton 4 February1942-30 March 1942
Maj. Gordon C. Leland 26 April 1942-3 June 1942
Maj. William E. Bayse 4 June 1942-15 September 1942
22nd Bombardment Squadron
Maj. John A. Warren 1 February 1940-1 May 1940
Capt. Joseph J. Ladd 1 May 1940-May 1941
Capt. Kenneth B. Hobson May 1941-15 September 1942

31st Bombardment Squadron
Capt. Earl G. Harper 1 April 1931-14 October 1931
Capt. Devereaux Myers 14 October 1931-2 November 1931
Capt. Earl G. Harper 2 November 1931-1 December 1931
Capt. Harold W. Beaton 1 December 1931-29 June 1932
1sr Lt. Ralph Snavely 29 June 1932-6 January 1934
Maj. Harold D. Smith 6 January 1934-16 November 1936
Maj. James G. Taylor 16 November 1936-1 February 1938
88th Reconnaissance Squadron
Maj. Newton Longfellow 6 October 1936-1 December 1941
Capt. Richard Carmichael 1December 1941-16 March 1942
Capt. William E. Bayse 16 March 1942-22 April 1942

436th Bombardment Squadron
Capt. William E. Bayse 16 March 1942-15 June 1942
Capt. John M. Toomy 15 June 1942-28 June 1942
Lt. Daniel E. Braswell 28 June 1942-22 August 1942
Capt. Earl R. Tash 22 August 1942-4 February 1943
Maj. Harvey J. Watkins 4 February 1943-12 August 1943
Lt. Col. Clyde Box 13 August 1943-6 October 1943
Capt. Richard T. Henning 7 October 1943-7 January 1944
Capt. James C. Griffith, Jr. 8 January 1944-1 April 1944
Lt. Col. John T. Fixwater 2 April 1944-31 October 1944
Capt. David Brown 1 November 1944-30 November 1944
Maj. Raymond E. Holsey 30 November 1944-14 January 1945
Capt. James J. Nemecek, Jr., 15 January 1945-31 January 1945
Maj. Harry S. Alexander 1 February 1945-30 June 1945
Maj. Walter S. Rector 1 July 1945-Unknown

492nd Bombardment Squadron
Lt. Herbert C. Boettcher 25 October 1942-13 January 1943
Capt. Joeseph S. Pirruccello 13 January 1943-9 April 1943
Capt. William A. Delahay 9 April 1943-28 December 1943
Capt. John Stephens 28 December 1943-8 April 1944
Capt. Hilliard L. Gandy 8 April 1944-15 April 1945
Maj. Ralph A. Jensen 15 April 1945-15 August 1945
Capt. Brad M. Chase 15 August 1945-6 January 1946

493rd Bombardment Squadron
Lt. Harold K. Trinkle 25 October 1942-10 January 1943
Capt. Wesley L. Werner 10 January 1943-14 November 1943
Capt. Robert G. Bailey 14 November 1943-21 June 1944
Capt. Frank J. Maholchic 21 June 1944-23 August 1944
Capt. Jack Bradford 23 August 1944-1 January 1945
Maj. Charles Cf. Craig 1 January 1945-17 August 1945
Lt. Col. James T. McKee 17 August 1945-Unknown

Appendix B

Missions With the Tenth Air Force Out of India

	Date	Target
1.	April 2, 1942	Port Blair, Andaman Islands
2.	April 3, 1942	Rangoon docks
3.	April 15, 1942	Sea reconnaissance-Karachi
4.	April 16, 1942	Rangoon docks
5.	April 18, 1942	Sea reconnaissance-Karachi
6.	April 19, 1942	Sea reconnaissance-Karachi
7.	April 20, 1942	Sea reconnaissance-Karachi
8.	April 22, 1942	Sea reconnaissance-Karachi
9.	April 24, 1942	Sea reconnaissance-Karachi
10.	April 25, 1942	Sea reconnaissance-Karachi
11.	April 26, 1942	Sea reconnaissance-Karachi
12.	April 27, 1942	Sea reconnaissance-Karachi
13.	April 29, 1942	Rangoon docks
14.	April 30, 1942	Rangoon docks
15.	May 1, 1942	Rangoon docks
16.	May 2, 1942	Rangoon docks
17.	May 3, 1942	Rangoon docks
18.	May 4, 1942	Rangoon docks
19.	May 5, 1942	Rangoon docks
20.	May 7, 1942	Rangoon docks
21.	May 12, 1942	Mingaladon airfield
22.	May 25, 1942	Mingaladon airfield
23.	May 29, 1942	Myitkyina
24.	May 30, 1942	Myitkyina
25.	May 31, 1942	Rangoon docks
26.	June 4, 1942	Rangoon docks
27.	June 7, 1942	Akyab
28.	July 4, 1942	Rangoon docks
29.	Oct. 21, 1942	Lin-hsi Mines
30.	Oct. 29, 1942	Rangoon dock
31.	Nov. 6, 1942	Rangoon docks
32.	Nov. 9, 1942	Rangoon docks
33.	Nov. 20, 1942	Mandalay railway yards
34.	Nov. 22, 1942	Mandalay railway yards
35.	Nov. 25, 1942	Bangkok, Thailand
36.	Nov. 29/30, 1942	Rangoon
37.	Nov. 30, 1942	Port Blair, Andaman Is.
38.	Dec. 4, 1942	Pyawbe truck park
39.	Dec. 7, 1942	Mandalay
40.	Dec. 7, 1942	Rangoon
41.	Dec. 11, 1942	Rangoon docks
42.	Dec. 11, 1942	Port Blair, Andaman Is.
43.	Dec. 20, 1942	Rangoon railway yards
44.	Dec. 20, 1942	Mingaladon airfield
45.	Dec. 22, 1942	Rangoon docks
46.	Dec.26/27, 1942	Bangkok, Thailand
47.	Dec. 29, 1942	Shipping-Rangoon
48.	Jan. 3, 1943	Mandalay railroad yards
49.	Jan. 3, 1943	Rangoon, shipping
50.	Jan. 4, 1943	Mandalay railroad yards
51.	Jan. 7, 1943	Sea search
52.	Jan. 10, 1943	Myitnge railroad bridge
53.	Jan. 15, 1943	Convoy off Rangoon
54.	Jan. 16, 1943	Rangoon shipping
55.	Jan. 19, 1943	Thazi railroad junction
56.	Jan. 24, 1943	Rangoon wharves/shipping
57.	Jan. 26, 1943	Rangoon wharves/shipping
58.	Feb. 1, 1943	Rangoon docks/shipping
59.	Feb. 2, 1943	Port Blair, shipping
60.	Feb. 4, 1943	Myitnge railroad bridge
61.	Feb. 5, 1943	Myitnge railroad bridge
63.	Feb. 8, 1943	Mingaladon airfield
64.	Feb. 12, 1943	Myitnge railroad bridge
65.	Feb. 12, 1943	Mahlwagon marshaling yards
66.	Feb. 15, 1943	Myitnge railroad bridge
67.	Feb. 20, 1943	Gokteik Viaduct
68.	Feb. 22/23, 1943	Mining Rangoon estuary
69.	Feb. 22/23, 1943	Rangoon, Mingaladon
70.	Feb. 25, 1943	Myitnge railroad bridge
71.	Feb. 27, 1943	Shipping and reconnaissance
72.	Feb. 27, 1943	Pazundaung railroad bridge
73.	Mar. 3, 1943	Pazundaung railroad bridge, Rangoon docks, Mahlwagon yards
74.	Mar. 6, 1943	Pazundaung railroad bridge
75.	Mar. 6, 1943	Myitnge railroad bridge
76.	Mar. 6, 1943	Moulmein
77.	Mar. 6, 1943	Mahlwagon marshaling yards
78.	Mar. 8, 1943	Sea search Gulf of Martaban
79.	Mar. 10, 1943	Mingaladon airfield
80.	Mar. 10, 1943	Pazundaung railroad bridge
81.	Mar. 12, 1943	Pazundaung bridge
82.	Mar. 13, 1943	Pazundaung railroad bridge
83.	Mar. 14, 1943	Moulmein docks
84.	Mar. 16, 1943	Pazundaung railroad bridge
85.	Mar. 18, 1943	Pazundaung railroad bridge
86.	Mar. 21, 1943	Gokteik Viaduct
87.	Mar. 24, 1943	Myitnge railroad bridge
88.	Mar. 26/27, 1943	Mining Rangoon estuary
89.	Mar. 26/27, 1943	Mingaladon, Rangoon
90.	Mar. 29, 1943	Sea search, bomb Tavoy
91.	Mar. 31, 1943	Pyinmana railroad bridge
92.	Apr. 4, 1943	Rangoon Thilawa refinery
93.	Apr. 5, 1943	Prome
94.	Apr. 5, 1943	Rangoon Mahlwagan yards
95.	Apr. 6, 1943	Pazundaung railroad bridge, Mahlwagon yards
96.	Apr. 7, 1943	Toungoo Japanese HQ
97.	Apr. 15, 1943	Rangoon Thilawa Refinery
98.	Apr. 15, 1943	Prome
99.	Apr. 16, 1943	Bassein jetty area
100.	Apr. 17, 1943	Pazundaung railroad bridge
101.	Apr. 18/19, 1943	Rangoon central railroad yards
102.	Apr. 20/21, 1943	Bangkok railroad station, arsenal
103.	Apr. 22/23, 1943	Mahlwagon railroad yards
104.	Apr. 26, 1943	Thilawa refinery
105.	Apr. 26, 1943	Rangoon warehouses
106.	Apr. 28, 1943	Sea sweep
107.	Apr. 29, 1943	Rangoon docks/shipping
108.	Apr. 30, 1943	Rangoon docks/shipping
109.	May 1, 1943	Rangoon shipping
110.	May 4, 1943	Thilama oil refinery
111.	May 4, 1943	Toungoo railroad yards, Japanese HQ
113.	May 5, 1943	Pyinmana railroad yards
114.	May 6, 1943	Pazundaung railroad bridge
115.	May 6, 1943	Namtu smelting plant
116.	May 7, 1943	Toungoo railroad yards
117.	May 7, 1943	Mahlwagon marshaling yards
118.	May 8, 1943	Sinthe Railroad Bridge
119.	May 11, 1943	Syuam Oil Refinery, Rangoon
120.	May 12, 1943	Sinthe Railroad Bridge
121.	May 12, 1943	Wharves Rangoon
122.	May 13, 1943	Sea Search
123.	May 13, 1943	Japanese HQ Myitkyina Mission Abandoned Due to Weather (MADW)
124.	May 14, 1943	Japanese HQ Myitkyina
125.	May 14, 1943	Toungoo Railroad yards
126.	May 14, 1943	Lashio military barracks (MADW)
127.	May 15, 1943	Lashio military barracks
128.	May 18, 1943	Prome railroad yards
129.	May 18, 1943	Thayetmyo town
130.	May 18, 1943	Mullah oil field
131.	May 18, 1943	Numbu town
132.	May 19, 1943	Sea sweep
133.	May 19, 1943	Pyage oil installations
134.	May 19, 1943	Padaukpin oil installations
135.	May 19, 1943	Magwe town
136.	May 19, 1943	Yenanguang oil facilities
137.	May 20, 1943	Sea search Gulf of Martaban
138.	May 20, 1943	Prome railroad warehouses
139.	May 20, 1943	Allanymyo ginning mill
140.	May 20, 1943	Thayetmyo cement plant

141. May 20, 1943 Yenanguang workshops
142. May 21, 1943 Sea search Gulf of Martaban (MADW)
143. May 22/23, 1943 Mining mission
144. May 22/23, 1943 Mining mission (MADW)
145. May 22/23, 1943 Insun military dumps
146. May 22/23, 1943 Pazundaung Motor Truck Depot
147. May 23, 1943 Sea sweep-Rangoon
148. May 24, 1943 Sea search-Rangoon (MADW)
149. May 26, 1943 Sea search Rangoon estuary (MADW)
150. May 30, 1943 Sea search Rangoon estuary (MADW)
151. June 1, 1943 Shweli River Bridge
152. June 2, 1943 Sea search (MADW)
153. June 11, 1943 Sea search Rangoon River
154. June 12, 1943 Thanbyuzayat railroad junction (MADW)
155. June 12, 1943 Thanbyuzayat railroad junction
156. June 13, 1943 Thanbyuzayat railroad junction (MADW)
157. June 13, 1943 Prome railroad yards (MADW)
158. June 15, 1943 Thanbyuzayat railroad yards
159. June 16, 1943 Lashio military barracks
160. June 16, 1943 Mandalay railroad yards
161. June 17, 1943 Thayemyo cement plant (MADW)
162. June 18, 1943 Sea sweep (MADW)
163. June 18, 1943 Yamethin railroad yards
164. June 21, 1943 Ywataung railroad yards (MADW)
165. June 22, 1943 Myingyan (MADW)
166. June 22, 1943 Sea search Rangoon estuary
167. June 22, 1943 Monywa
168. June 24, 1943 Ywataung (MADW)
169. June 24, 1943 Myingyan
170. June 24, 1943 Sea sweep Gulf of Martaban
171. June 25, 1943 Sea search Andaman Sea
172. June 26, 1943 Thanbyuzayat railroad yards
173. June 27, 1943 Thanbyuzayat railroad yards
174. June 27, 1943 Rangoon
175. July 1, 1943 Syaum Oil Refinery
176. July 1, 1943 Rangoon
177. July 2, 1943 Syian Oil Refinery
178. July 3, 1943 Myitnge Bridge
179. July 4, 1943 Shweli River Bridge
180. July 4, 1943 Ywataung railroad yards (MADW)
181. July 4, 1943 Sea search
182. July 9, 1943 Mandalay railroad yards
183. July 12, 1943 Ywataung railroad yards
184. July 13, 1943 Chauk oil fields (MADW)
185. July 13, 1943 Myingyan railroad yards
186. July 13, 1943 Sagaing jetty area (MADW)
187. July 14, 1943 Sagaing jetty area (MADW)
188. July 14, 1943 Pyinmana railroad yards (MADW)
189. July 17, 1943 Sea sweep Andaman Sea (MADW)
190. July 20, 1943 Mandalay railroad yards
191. July 20, 1943 Myitnge Bridge
192. July 21, 1943 Wuntho railroad yards
193. July 21, 1943 Namtie mines
194. July 22, 1943 Ywataung railroad yards
195. July 23, 1943 Shipping off Pagoda Point
196. July 23, 1943 Port Blair, Andaman Islands (MADW)
197. July 23, 1943 Maymyo engine sheds, bombed Kawlin A/F
198. July 24, 1943 Akyab
199. July 24, 1943 Monywa
200. July 25. 1943 Maymyo engine sheds, bombed Japanese barracks
201. July 27, 1943 Sea sweep Andaman Islands
202. July 28, 1943 Pagoda Point
203. July 28, 1943 Sea sweep Andaman Sea
204. July 28, 1943 Shipping Port Blair, Andaman Islands
205. July 29, 1943 Shipping Port Blair, Andaman Islands
206. July 30, 1943 Shipping Rangoon (MADW)
207. July 31, 1943 Mining Rangoon River
208. July 31, 1943 Mining Rangoon River estuary
209. August 3, 1943 Thanbyuzayat
210. August 4, 1943 Shipping-Port Blair (MADW)
211. August 4, 1943 Thanbyuzayat sweep (MADW)
212. August 7, 1943 Shipping-Port Blair (MADW)
213. August 7, 1943 Shipping-Rangoon (MADW)
214. August 12, 1943 Shipping-Port Blair (MADW)
215. August 12, 1943 Sea sweep Ye
216. August 13, 1943 Sea sweep
217. August 14, 1943 Sea sweep
218. August 15, 1943 Shipping Chatham Islands
219. August 16, 1943 Convoy off Tavoy
220. August 16, 1943 Convoy near Rangoon
221. August17, 1943 Shipping-Rangoon (MADW)
222. August 18, 1943 Prome
223. August 19, 1943 Sea sweep Port Blair (MADW)
224. August 21, 1943 Kyaukpyu
225. August 22, 1943 Sagaing railroad yards (MADW)
226. August 22, 1943 Monywa
227. August 22, 1943 Sea sweep Rangoon (MADW
228. August 23, 1943 Meiktila
229. August 23, 1943 Myingyan Railroad Bridge
230. August 23, 1943 Pakokku town
231. August 23, 1943 Shipping
232. August 24, 1943 Pyawbwe and Akyab
233. August 24, 1943 Yamathin
234. August 25, 1943 Sea sweep
235. August 25, 1943 Fable Island
236. August 25, 1943 Shipping Car Nicobar Islands
237. August 26, 1943 Pagoda Point landing ground
238. August 26, 1943 Sea sweep Andaman Islands
239. August 27, 1943 Thazi railroad junction
240. August 28, 1943 Akyab
241. August 29, 1943 Myitkyina
242. August 29, 1943 Monywa
243. August 29, 1943 Shipping-Rangoon (MADW)
244. August 29, 1943 Sea sweep
245. September 1, 1943 Mandalay
246. September 2, 1943 Pyawbwe
247. September 2, 1943 Chauk oil fields
248. September 3, 1943 Car Nicobar Island
249. September 4, 1943 Letpadan
250. September 4, 1943 Rangoon Dule Pagoda docks
251. September 4, 1943 Flatt Islands
252. September 6, 1943 Cargo vessel at Rangoon
253. September 7, 1943 Sea sweep
254. September 7, 1943 Sea sweep Rangoon estuary
255. September 8, 1943 Shipping-Rangoon (MADW)
256. September 9, 1943 Sea sweep (MADW)
257. September 11, 1943 Pyinmana railroad yards
258. September 11, 1943 Lay mines (MADW)
259. September 12, 1943 Kwetnge airfield
260. September 12, 1943 Yamethin railroad
261. September 13, 1943 Sea sweep
262. September 14, 1943 Myitkyina barracks
263. September 14, 1943 Sea sweep
264. September 16, 1943 Sea sweep
265. September 18, 1943 Sea sweep
266. September 19, 1943 Monywa railroad yards
267. September 20, 1943 Sagaing railroad yards
268. September 21, 1943 Ywataung
269. September 21, 1943 Wetlet
270. September 22, 1943 Ross Island
271. September 25, 1943 Thanbyuzayat railroad yards
272. September 26, 1943 Sea sweep
273. September 26, 1943 Letpadan
274. September 26, 1943 Sea sweep Rangoon
275. September 27, 1943 Sea sweep Andaman Sea
276. September 27, 1943 Akyab
277. September 29, 1943 Rangoon railroad station (MADW)
278. September 29, 1943 Akyab
279. October 1, 1943 Sea sweep Rangoon and Andaman Sea
280. October 1, 1943 Bassein
281. October 3, 1943 Shipping-Rangoon, Mingaladon airfield
282. October 4, 1943 Shipping-Rangoon
283. October 7, 1943 Pyinmana railroad yards
284. October 8, 1943 Lashio barracks
285. October 9, 1943 Sea sweep, Kanbauk mines
286. October 9, 1943 Sagaing railroad yards
287. October 10, 1943 Meza Railroad Bridge

288. October 11, 1943 Sagaing railroad yards
289. October 13, 1943 Toungoo railroad yards
290. October 14, 1943 Ramree Island
291. October 14, 1943 Rangoon docks
292. October 17, 1943 Naba railroad yards
293. October 18, 1943 Heho airfield
294. October 19, 1943 Monywa railroad yards
295. October 20, 1943 Kanbalu railroad yards
296. October 21, 1943 Myingyan railroad yards
297. October 22, 1943 Prome railroad yards
298. October 23, 1943 Kanbalu railroad yards
299. October 26, 1943 Shipping-Rangoon, dock area
300. October 28, 1943 Toungoo Japanese HQ, railroad yards
301. October 30, 1943 Lashio airfield
302. November 2, 1943 Myitnge railroad yards
303. November 3, 1943 Loiwing airfield
304. November 5, 1943 Akyab
305. November 6/7, 1943 Mining Rangoon River
306. November 8/9, 1943 Mining Rangoon River
307. November 9/10, 1943 Mingaladon airfield
308. November 11, 1943 Heho airfield
309. November 12/13, 1943 Mining
310. November 13, 1943 Myitnge carriage shop
311. November 13/14, 1943 Mining
312. November 14, 1943 Maymyo barracks
313. November 16, 1943 Meiktila cantonment area
314. November 18, 1943 Pyinmana railroad yards and bridge
315. November 20, 1943 Chiengmai, Lampang
316. November 25, 1943 Mingaladon and Zayatkwin airfields
317. November 27, 1943 Insein Locomotive Works, Rangoon
318. November 28, 1943 Botataung docks, Rangoon
319. December 1, 1943 Insein Locomotive Works, Rangoon
320. December 4/5, 1943 Mining Rangoon estuary
321. December 6, 1943 Chatham Island
322. December 12, 1943 Myittha Railroad Bridge
323. December 13/14, 1943 Heho airfield
324. December 15, 1943 Chauk oil fields
325. December 16, 1943 Thayitmyo cement plant
326. December 19/20, 1943 Bangkok docks
327. December 23/24, 1943 Bangkok railroad station
328. December 30, 1943 Monywa railroad yards
329. January 4, 1944 Yenangyaung oil installations
330. January 3, 1944 Yenangyaung oil installations
331. January 4, 1944 Sea sweep Andaman Islands
332. January 5, 1944 Sea sweep (MADW), bombed Akyab
333. January 10/11, 1944 Bangsue railroad yards, mining Chao Phya River
334. January 15, 1944 Kyaukchaw (MADW)
335. January 17, 1944 Kyaukchaw (MADW)
336. January 18, 1944 Kyaukchaw
337. January 19/20, 1944 Bangkok, Don Muang airfield
338. January 22, 1944 Prome camp area
339. January 23, 1944 Mergui
340. January 26, 1944 Japanese ground installations Razabil and Maungdaw
341. January 29, 1944 Yenangyaung oil installations, N.O.C. Refinery
342. January 31, 1944 Mingaladon airfield
343. February 4/5, 1944 Aungban airfield
344. February 5/6, 1944 Heho and Aungban airfields
345. February 10/11, 1944 Bangkok Ban Mah Arsenal, Don Muang airfield
346. February 13/14, 1944 Heho airfield
347. February 23, 1944 Akyab airfield
348. February 24/25, 1944 Moulmein and Martaban
349. February 28/29, 1944 Mandalay railroad yards
350. March 3, 1944 Loiwing airfield
351. March 4/5, 1944 Mingaladon, Zayatkwin, Hlegu airfields
352. March 6/7, 1944 Prong Island oil tanks, mining Gulf of Thailand
353. March 7/8, 1944 Shipping Gulf of Thailand
354. March 8/9, 1944 Shipping Gulf of Thailand
355. March 9, 1944 Kamaing, Moguang dumps
356. March 10, 1944 Mogaung dumps
357. March 14/15, 1944 Victoria Lake dumps, Rangoon
358. March 17, 1944 Kongyi dumps
359. March 18, 1944 Kalewa dumps
360. March 23, 1944 Kalewa dumps
361. March 23, 1944 Shwebo railroad yards
362. March 23/24, 1944 Moulmein jetties
363. March 24, 1944 Pyingaing dumps
364. March 25, 1944 Mogaung dumps
365. March 26, 1944 Tiddam-Imphal road
366. March 27, 1944 Kamaing dumps
367. March 28, 1944 Kamaing dumps
368. April 1, 1944 Lanywa Power Station (MADW)
369. April 3, 1944 Chauk BOC Oil Refinery
370. April 3, 1944 Lanywa Power Station
371. April 5, 1944 Burma-Thailand railroad
372. April 8/9, 1944 Mergui mining
373. April 11, 1944 Tavoy mining
374. April 13, 1944 Kongyi dumps
375. April 15, 1944 Shipping-Port Blair
376. April 18, 1944 Yenangyaung gas plant
377. April 21, 1944 Lashio
378. April 23/24, 1944 Moulmein jetties and railroad yards
379. April 25, 1944 Monywa railroad yards, Alon railroad sidings
380. April 29, 1944 Kongyi dumps
381. May 1, 1944 Yenangyaung oil installations
382. May 4, 1944 Mandalay railroad yards
383. May 5/6, 1944 Mining Koh Si Chang, Gulf of Thailand
384. May 6/7, 1944 Mining Koh Si Chang, Gulf of Thailand
385. May 7/8, 1944 Mining Sattahip harbor, Gulf of Thailand
386. May 8, 1944 Japanese troop concentrations Moirang
387. May 9, 1944 Japanese troop concentrations Ningthoukong
388. May 10/11, 1944 Myitkyina
389. May 15/16, 1944 Myitkyina
390. May 18, 1944 Myitkyina and Kalewa
391. May 20, 1944 Yenangyaung, bombed secondary
392. May 23, 1944 Naba railroad junction, bombed Homalin
393. May 25, 1944 Naba railroad junction, bombed Indaw railroad yards
394. May 27, 1944 Yenangyaung, bombed Pakkoku
395. May 28, 1944 Tiddim-Imphal road, bombed Kalemyo
396. May 29, 1944 Tiddim-Imphal road, bombed Kalemyo
397. May 31, 1944 Ye-U
398. June 2, 1944 Yenangyaung oil installations
399. June 7, 1944 Kalemyo
400. June 7, 1944 Wuntho railroad yards
401. June 8/9, 1944 Mergui harbor mining
402. June 8/9, 1944 Bangkok mining Chao Phya River
403. June 10, 1944 Yenangyaung N.O.C. Oil Refinery
404. October 19, 1944 Moulmein jetties
405. October 22, 1944 Moulmein jetties
406. October 25, 1944 Paleik railroad yards, bombed Ye-U
407. October 26, 1944 Sinde dump area
408. October 27, 1944 Pakkoku
409. October 29, 1944 Taungup dump area
410. November 1, 1944 Ban Dara Bridge
411. November 4, 1944 Sea search for B-29 crew
412. November 5, 1944 Bangkok-Chiengmai railroad line tunnels
413. November 8, 1944 Tavoy reported convoy
414. November 9, 1944 Tavoy reported convoy
415. November 13, 1944 Hninpale bridge
416. November 16, 1944 Uttaradit, Thailand railroad yards
417. November 16, 1944 Kaeng Luang Bridge, Thailand
418. November 19, 1944 Mokpalin railroad yards
419. November 21, 1944 Ban Mea Mo, Thailand railroad bridge
420. November 23, 1944 Pegu-Martaban railroad line by-pass bridge #2
421. November 26, 1944 Bangkok-Chiengmai railroad line Bridges #59, #68
422. November 29, 1944 Burma-Thailand railroad Bridge #277
423. December 1, 1944 Mergui reported naval vessel
424. December 3, 1944 Hnohngpladuk supply dumps
425. December 4, 1944 Sagaing jetties and railroad sidings
426. December 5, 1944 Reported naval vessels
427. December 7, 1944 Maymyo railroad yards

428. December 8, 1944 — Burma-Thailand railroad locomotives and rolling stock
429. December 10, 1944 — Thanbyuzayat railroad yards
430. December 10, 1944 — Phadaw railroad yards
431. December 13, 1944 — Burma-Thailand railroad Bridge #277
432. December 17, 1944 — Myabin supply dumps
433. December 19, 1944 — Maymyo supply dumps
434. December 21, 1944 — Taungup supply dumps
435. December 21, 1944 — Taungup supply dumps
436. December 27, 1944 — Prome supply dumps
437. December 27, 1944 — Pyinmana railroad bridge (first Azon mission)
438. December 30, 1944 — Prome-Taungup road Okahitpin bridge (second Azon mission)
439. January 1, 1945 — Burma-Thailand railroad Bridge #95 and #97
440. January 3, 1945 — Burma-Thailand railroad Bridge Mile Stone 95 ½
441. January 3, 1945 — Burma-Thailand railroad Bridge #121
442. January 8, 1945 — Burma-Thailand railroad Bridge #83 and #97
443. January 8, 1945 — Thanbyuzayat-Ye railroad line Bridge #151 and #163
444. January 9, 1945 — Burma-Thailand railroad Bridge #62, #68, and #83
445. January 11, 1945 — Bangkok-Chiengmai railroad line Bridge #47
446. January 13, 1945 — Sagaing jetties
447. January 13, 1945 — Mergui shipping, jetties
448. January 16, 1945 — Mingaladon airfield
449. January 18, 1945 — Meiktila airfield, Thedaw landing ground
450. January 21, 1945 — Ramree Island support for landings
451. January 23, 1945 — Burma-Thailand railroad Bridge #277 (MADW)
452. January 25, 1945 — Thanbyuzayat-Ye railroad line Bridge #163
453. January 27, 1945 — Burma-Thailand railroad Bridge #147 and #148
454. January 29, 1945 — Burma-Thailand railroad Bridge #18 and #19
455. January 31, 1945 — Kyaukse Japanese HQ
456. February 3, 1945 — Jumbhorn, Thailand railroad yards and bridges
457. February 4, 1945 — Jumbhorn, Thailand railroad yards
458. February 5, 1945 — Burma-Thailand railroad Bridge #277
459. February 7, 1945 — Burma-Thailand railroad Bridge #68, #83, and #97
460. February 7, 1945 — Burma-Thailand railroad Bridges #120, #121
461. February 8, 1945 — Twingan Japanese barracks
462. February 9, 1945 — Burma-Thailand railroad Bridge #277
463. February 9, 1945 — Burma-Thailand railroad Bridge #600
464. February 11, 1945 — Rangoon-Mandalay railroad Bridge #453
465. February 11, 1945 — Rangoon Victoria Lake supply dumps
466. February 12, 1945 — Mandalay Japanese artillery positions
467. February 13, 1945 — Burma-Thailand railroad Bridge #277
468. February 13, 1945 — Burma-Thailand railroad Bridge #654
469. February 14, 1945 — Tigaing supply dumps and troop concentrations
470. February 15, 1945 — Mandalay area supply dumps and troop concentrations
471. February 15, 1945 — Burma-Thailand railroad Bridge #51 by-pass and #57
472. February 16, 1945 — Mandalay Japanese troop positions at 14th Army request
473. February 17, 1945 — Moulmein-Ye railroad Bridge #147 and #148
474. February 17, 1945 — Heho airfield
475. February 18, 1945 — Yenangyaung troop concentrations
476. February 20, 1945 — Singaingmyo supply dumps
477. February 21, 1945 — Burma-Thailand railroad Bridge #71 by-pass
478. February 21, 1945 — Myittha supply dumps
479. February 22, 1945 — Kaungmaw supply dumps
480. February 23, 1945 — Mahlaing supply dumps
481. February 23, 1945 — Burma-Thailand railroad, attacked secondary
482. February 25, 1945 — Ban Dara by-pass A-51
483. February 25, 1945 — Taungyi supply dumps
484. February 25, 1945 — Myingyan supply dumps (11,000-pound of bombs)
485. February 27, 1945 — Burma-Thailand railroad Bridge #167 by-pass
486. February 27, 1945 — Burma-Thailand railroad Bridge #195
487. February 28, 1945 — Mingaladon airfield
488. March 2, 1945 — Korat, Thailand railroad yards
489. March 3, 1945 — Burma-Thailand railroad Bridge Q-297 and Q-338
490. March 4/5, 1945 — Bangkok Klong Toei Docks
491. March 5, 1945 — Moulmein-Ye railroad By-pass H-147A and H-148A
492. March 7, 1945 — Burma-Thailand railroad Bridge Q-379 and Q-390
493. March 7, 1945 — Martaban jetties
494. March 9, 1945 — Pegu-Martaban railroad line Bridge #41 and #64
495. March 9, 1945 — Rangoon Victoria Lake supply dumps
496. March 11, 1945 — Burma-Thailand railroad Bridge Q-195 and Q-338
497. March 11, 1945 — Rangoon Victoria Lake supply dumps
498. March 13, 1945 — Burma-Thailand railroad Bridge Q-577 and Q-578
499. March 17, 1945 — Rangoon Victoria Lake supply dumps
500. March 19, 1945 — Kra Isthmus, Thailand railroad bridges
501. March 21, 1945 — Pegu-Moulmein-Ye railroad line H-41, H-41A, H-64, H-64A
502. March 22, 1945 — Bangkok-Chiengmai railroad locomotives and rolling stock
503. March 23, 1945 — Bangkok-Chiengmai railroad bridges, locos, rolling stock
504. March 24, 1945 — Burma-Thailand railroad Bridge Q-633, Q-635
505. March 27, 1945 — Bangkok Klong Toei, Klong Bang Chak docks
506. March 29, 1945 — Rangoon Japanese Army HQ
507. March 29, 1945 — Burma-Thailand railroad Bridge Q-577, Q-578, Q-579
508. March 30, 1945 — Burma-Thailand railroad Bridge Q-397 and Q-338
509. April 1, 1945 — Burma-Thailand railroad locomotives and rolling stock
510. April 2, 1945 — Pegu-Moulmein railroad Bridge H-21 and H-21A by-pass
511. April 3, 1945 — Burma-Thailand railroad Bridge Q-629, Q-633, Q-654
512. April 3, 1945 — Burma-Thailand railroad By-pass Q-654A, Kanchanburi
513. April 4, 1945 — East of Bangkok Bridge TE 152
514. April 5, 1945 — Rangoon Victoria Lake supply dumps
515. April 6, 1945 — Pegu-Moulmein railroad H-71 by-pass #1 and #3
516. April 7, 1945 — Moulmein supply dumps
517. April 8, 1945 — Prome-Taungup road
518. April 8, 1945 — Burma-Thailand railroad Bridge Q-167 and Q-195
519. April 9, 1945 — Sittang railroad sidings
520. April 10, 1945 — Burma-Thailand railroad road bridges
521. April 11, 1945 — Rangoon Victoria Lake supply dumps
522. April 12, 1945 — Prome-Taungup road
523. April 14, 1945 — Burma-Thailand railroad Bridge Q-297, Q-338, Q-390, Q-398
524. April 14, 1945 — Bangkok Samsen Power Station
525. April 15, 1945 — Amherst Point, defensive positions
526. April 17, 1945 — Pegu-Moulmein railroad Abya Chaung road bridge
527. April 18, 1945 — Bangkok Borneo Wharves
528. April 20, 1945 — Amherst Point supply dumps
529. April 21, 1945 — Toungoo supply dumps
530. April 24, 1945 — Burma-Thailand bridges mass attack
531. April 27, 1945 — Pegu-Moulmein railroad Bridge H-41 by-pass, H-64, H-71
532. April 27, 1945 — Rangoon Victoria Lake supply dumps
533. April 27, 1945 — Rangoon radar station
534. April 29, 1945 — Moulmein airfield
535. May 1, 1945 — Elephant Point gun positions
536. May 2, 1945 — Rangoon River gun positions
537. May 3, 1945 — Moulmein shipping
538. May 4, 1945 — Mergui and Tavoy shipping
539. May 5, 1945 — Martaban jetties
540. May 5, 1945 — Mergui shipping and shipyards

541.	May 8, 1945	Martaban Japanese troop concentrations
542.	May 10, 1945	Mergui supply dumps
543.	May 14, 1945	Port Blair Japanese naval vessels, recalled
544.	June 18, 1945	Bangkok dropping medical supplies
545.	June 26, 1945	Ban Takli airfield (MADW)
546.	June 27, 1945	Ban Takli airfield
547.	June 27, 1945	Thailand OWI leaflet dropping
548.	July 1, 1945	Ban Takli airfield (MADW)
549.	July 2, 1945	Sea search for missing B-24
550.	July 3, 1945	Ban Takli airfield
551.	July 3, 1945	Koke Kathiem airfield (MADW)
552.	July 4, 1945	Thailand OWI leaflet dropping
553.	July 6, 1945	Thailand OWI leaflet dropping
554.	July 7, 1945	Thailand OWI leaflet dropping
555.	July 14, 1945	Thailand OWI leaflet dropping
556.	July 18, 1945	Thailand OWI leaflet dropping
557.	July 25, 1945	Thailand OWI leaflet dropping
558.	August, 1945	Thailand OWI leaflet dropping
559.	August, 1945	Thailand OWI leaflet dropping
560.	August, 1945	Thailand OWI leaflet dropping
561.	August, 1945	Thailand OWI leaflet dropping
562.	August, 1945	Thailand OWI leaflet dropping
563.	August, 1945	Thailand OWI leaflet dropping
564.	August, 1945	Thailand OWI leaflet dropping
565.	August, 1945	Thailand OWI leaflet dropping
566.	August, 1945	Thailand OWI leaflet dropping
567.	August, 1945	Thailand OWI leaflet dropping
568.	August, 1945	Thailand OWI leaflet dropping
569.	August, 1945	Thailand OWI leaflet dropping
570.	September 3, 1945	Thailand OWI leaflet dropping

Appendix C

Distinguished Unit Citations

Award of December 20, 1942:

The 7th Bombardment Group (H), United States Army Forces in the Far East, is cited for outstanding performance in action during the period January 14 to March 1 1942. Opposing the full force of the numerically superior Japanese with all available aircraft, the 7th Bombardment Group participated daily in attacking the enemy whenever they found him during his prolonged drive through the Philippines and Netherlands Indies to Java. Long range bombing attacks were executed in the face of heavy antiaircraft fire and large concentrations of enemy fighters over the target areas. Despite extremely adverse weather and dangerous field conditions, hampered by lack of adequate personnel to maintain aircraft in continuous combat condition, many successful missions were performed by crews fatigued from daily flights against the numerically dominant enemy. During this period great damaged was inflicted against enemy aircraft, ground installations, warships and transports. Combat crews exhibited the greatest bravery and resourcefulness; the ground units, in the face of heavy enemy fire, performed all duties with utter disregard of personal safety. The superior courage and devotion to duty shown by this bombardment Group will always be worth of emulation.

Award of May 5, 1945:

The 7th Bombardment Group (H) , Air Force, is hereby cited for outstanding performance of duty in action on 19 March 1945. Upon the denial of Rangoon, Burma as a major port of entry for Japanese supplies due to constant bombardment, harbor-mining and sea sweeps by bombardment units in the India-Burma Theater, the enemy was forced to utilization of Bangkok, Thailand as the main receiving point for supplies, equipment and personnel. Two methods were available to him for transportation to Bangkok; one by sea through that port and the other overland by railroad and road running down the Kra Isthmus through Jumbhorn, Thailand and extending to receiving ports along the Gulf of Siam and to the large enemy base at Singapore. Previous mining of Bangkok harbor had effectively denied the use of the first method. Only the overland route remained available. To interdict, destroy and disrupt this most vital line of supply, the 7th Bombardment Group (H) undertook on 19 March 1945 the longest known attack mission by formations of heavy bombers in WWII. Thirty-seven (37) heavy bombardment aircraft of this group, all squadrons participating, carried out a 2,700 mile round trip to strike the enemy's rail and road bridges ranging from Bandon to Jumbhorn, Thailand. All personnel of this group extend maximum effort in the planning and preparation for this mission. Meticulous calculations were made as to fuel and bomb loads. Maintenance crews spent inordinately long hours preparing the aircraft to operate to peak efficiency. Taking off from bases in India, aircraft of this group were airborne for approximately eighteen (18) hours. The flight being made almost entirely over water with the major portion of it over hostile waters. Outstanding bombing results were accomplished, one road and four rail bridges being either destroyed or severely damaged. The attack on the Ban Tak Kan bridge, of heavy steel and concrete construction, lifted the bridge eight feet in the air and threw it six feet out of line, destroying the railroad trackage and severely weakening the structure. All strikes were made without benefit of fighter escort and in the face of enemy automatic weapons and machine gun fire. In order to achieve maximum results, several bombing runs were made on each bridge although heavy anti-aircraft fire was being encountered. Only one aircraft was lost, that due to a shortage of fuel, its air crew successfully parachuting to safety. On this occasion, all personnel of the 7th Bombardment Group (H) displayed exceptional determination, aggressiveness, courage, and flying skill, attaining results so outstanding as to seriously curtail the enemy's line of supply in Southeast Asia and to aid greatly the conduct of the Allied war effort in Burma. This group's superior performance of duty in action against an armed enemy is worthy of the highest traditions of the military service and reflects great credit in the highest degree upon the Armed Forces of the United States.

Appendix D

Named Aircraft of the 7th Bombardment Group (H)

B-17E Name	Serial Number	Squadron
Calamity Jane	41-2440	
El Toro	41-2461	
Fennel vs Rommel	41-9029	
Gem of the Mountains	?	
Guinea Pig	41-2472	
Jungle Jim	?	
Malicious	?	
Mormon Meteor	?	
Naughty But Nice	41-2430	
Per Diem	41-2457	
Queenie	41-2464	
San Antonio Rose	41-2416	
Sea Breeze	?	
Sky Witch	?	
The Yankee Rebel	?	
LB-30		
Gopher Gus/Kangaroo Kate	AL573	
Minnie From Trinidad	AL608	
B-24D-M		
The Lone Wolf	B-24D 41-11757	9th
Blond Bomber	B-24D 41-11895	?
We'rewolves	B-24D 41-11925	492nd
Poison Ivy	B-24D 41-23660	?
Rangoon Rambler II	B-24D 41-23702	436th
Apocalypse	B-24D 41-23879	436th
Susie's Sister	B-24D 41-23893	493rd
Destiny's Tot	B-24D 41-23865	9th
Sittin' Bull	B-24D 41-23921	493rd
The Butcher	B-24D ?	493rd
The Squaw	B-24D 41-24220	493rd
Corporal Gee-Eye	B-24D ?	436th
Battlin' Bitch	B-24D 41-24237	9th
Special Delivery	B-24D 41-24274	492nd
Boisterous Bitch	B-24D 41-24302	493rd
The Captain and the Kids	B-24D ?	492nd
Hairless Joe	B-24D 42-41252	?
Nightmare Express	B-24D 42-63778	?

B-17E Name	Serial Number	Squadron
Frozen, Hot To Go	B-24D 42-72803	9th
Burma Roadster	B-24D ?	492nd
Burma Bitch	B-24D ?	9th
Baby Me	B-24D ?	?
Lil Deicer	B-24D/J ?	?
Half Ass	B-24J 42-73057	9th
H2O Eleanor	B-24J 42-73063	493rd
Rangoon Rosie	B-24J 42-73067	436th
Star Duster	B-24J 42-73072	493rd
Lady Be Good	B-24J 42-73074	492nd
Double Trouble	B-24J 42-73079	493rd
Pecker Red	B-24J 42-73158	493rd
Tough Baba	B-24J 42-73159	493rd
Jungle Jig	B-24J 42-73160	492nd
Little Lass	B-24J 42-73299	436th
Leaping Lena	B-24J 42-73302	9th
Hot To Go	B-24J 42-73303	9th
Earthquake Express	B-24J 42-73448	436th
Miss Tennessee	B-24J 42-73xxx	9th
Paulette	B-24J 42-100239	492nd
Outlaw Chief	B-24J 42-xxxxx	436th
SNAFU	B-24J 42-xxxxx	493rd
Shoot You're Covered	B-24J 44-40282	9th
Pennsylvania Polecat	B-24J 44-40318	9th
Pal Joey	B-24J 44-40590	?
Cabin In The Sky	B-24J 44-40810	492nd
Bar Made	B-24J 44-40819	493rd
Babe	B-24J ?	492nd
Little Princess	B-24J ?	492nd
Lady Luck II	B-24J ?	436th
Alec Tronix	B-24J 44-40815	436th
Cactus Kid/Rangoon Rangler	B-24J 44-40857	9th
Miss Hilda	B-24J 44-40859	9th
Shy Ann	B-24J 44-40985	436th
Double Trouble	B-24J 44-40989	493rd
Lost Angel	B-24J 44-40xxx	436th
Crusader	B-24J 44-40xxx	436th
Cute Lil Lass	B-24J 44-41085	9th

B-17E Name	Serial Number	Squadron
Loveable Lorena	B-24J 44-41222	492nd
Spirit of Ft. Worth	B-24J 44-44501	493rd
Pride of the Fleet	B-24J 44-xxxxx	493rd
Shackrat Special	B-24J ?	9th
Miss Manookie	B-24J/L 44-4xxxx	?
Nut-cracker Sweet	B-24J/L 44-4xxxx	9th
Mission Completed	B-24J/L 44-41xxx	9th
Miss Guided Miss	B-24J/L ?	493rd
Erotic Edna	B-24J/L 44-xxxxx	492nd
Boomerang, Back Again	B-24L 44-49504	493rd
The Angry Angel	B-24L? 44-4xxxx	9th
Fabulous Fannie	B-24L 44-4xxxx	492nd
Lassie I'm Home	B-24L 44-4xxxx	436th
Calamity Jane	B-24M 44-42019	9th
Slower Than Rotation	B-24M 44-42251	436th
Hot To Go	B-24M 44-42273	9th
Kentucky Kloud Hopper	B-24M 44-42275	436th
Mary	B-24M 44-42454	436th
Hello-ver Burma	B-24M 44-42460	436th
Bachelor's Playmate	B-24M 44-50792	493rd
Big Camahooch	B-24M 44-50809	436th
Home Stretch	B-24M 44-50857	436th
Drive Me Home	B-24M 44-50866	492nd
Sleepy Time Gal	B-24M 44-51030	493rd
Homesick Angel	B-24M 44-51040	493rd
Flame of the Squadron	B-24M 44-51054	493rd
Luscious Lace	B-24L/M 44-4xxxx	9th
Mors Ab Alto	B-24L/M 44-4xxxx	493rd
Eager Beaver Bombing Company	B-24L/M 44-4xxxx	492nd
Blind Date	B-24L/M 44-4xxxx	493rd
Black Magic	B-24L/M 44-xxxxx	493rd
Dangerous Dance	B-24L/M 44-xxxxx	493rd
Donna D Wanna	B-24L/M 44-xxxxx	493rd
Lascivious Lil	B-24L/M 44-xxxxx	493rd
McSwine's Flying Comet	B-24L/M 44-xxxxx	493rd
The Walden Belle	B-24L/M 44-xxxxx	493rd
Wandering Wanda	B-24L/M 44-xxxxx	493rd
Southern Comfort	B-24L/M 44-xxxxx	?
Black Magic V2	B-24L/M 44-xxxxx	?
Thai Times	B-24L/M 44-xxxxx	493rd

ENDNOTES

Endnotes

Introduction

1. See Biddle, Tami Davis: *Rhetoric and Reality in Air Warfare: The Evolution of British and American Ideas About Strategic Bombing, 1914-1945*. (Princeton: Princeton University Press, 2002), pp. 205-08; Greer, Thomas H.: *The Development of Air Doctrine in the Army Air Arm 1917-1941* (Washington, D.C.: Office of Air Force History, 1985), pp. 123-26.
2. Biddle, *Rhetoric and Reality in Air Warfare: The Evolution of British and American Ideas About Strategic Bombing, 1914-1945*, P.207; McFarland, Stephen L.: *America's Pursuit of Precision Bombing, 1910-1945* (Washington, D.C.: Smithsonian Institution Press, 1995), pp.100-104; Greer, *The Development of Air Doctrine in the Army Air Arm 1917-1941*, P.125.
3. Biddle, *Rhetoric and Reality in Air Warfare: The Evolution of British and American Ideas About Strategic Bombing, 1914-1945*, Chapter Three for a discussion of Army Air Corps' theories on strategic bombing.
4. McFarland, *America's Pursuit of Precision Bombing, 1910-1945*, P. 190.

Chapter One: A Laboratory for Air Power: Building the 7th Bombardment Group

1. Maurer, Maurer, Ed.: *Air Force Combat Units of WWII*. Washington: Office of Air Force History, 1983. P.43; Air Force Historical Research Agency, "7th Operations Group Fact Sheet", 1 December 2006.
2. Maurer, *Aviation in the U.S. Army 1919-1939* (Washington: U.S. Government Printing Office, 1987) P.455; "7th Operations Group Fact Sheet".
3. Maurer, *Aviation in the U.S. Army 1919-1939*, P.70.
4. "7th Operations Group Fact Sheet".
5. Maurer, *Aviation in the U.S. Army 1919-1939*, P.4.
6. Maurer, *Aviation in the U.S. Army 1919-1939*, P.9.
7. Maurer, *Aviation in the U.S. Army 1919-1939*, P.44.
8. Maurer, *Aviation in the U.S. Army 1919-1939*, pp.72-74, 191.
9. Maurer, *Aviation in the U.S. Army 1919-1939*, pp.196-97.
10. *Oakland Tribune*, April 9, 1928.
11. *Air Corps News Letter*, Volume XII, No. 8, June 5, 1928, P.204.
12. Wagner, Ray: *American Combat Airplanes of the 20th Century: A Comprehensive Reference* (Reno, Nevada: Jack Bacon & Co., 2004), pp.48-49.
13. *Air Corps News Letter*, Volume XII, No. 8, June 5, 1928, P.209.
14. *Air Corps News Letter*, No. 10, July 10, 1928, P.267.
15. *Air Corps News Letter*, No. 12, August 29, 1928, P.311.
16. *Air Corps News Letter*, No. 12, August 29, 1928, P.311.
17. *Air Corps News Letter*, Vol. XIV, No.9, July 28, 1930, P.203-04; Rathbun, CWO Gail D.: "History of the Eleventh Bombardment Squadron", no date, copy in the collection of the Hamilton Field Military Museum; Thomas, Gerald C., Jr.: *The First Team: Thornton D. Hooper and America's First Bombing Squadrons* (Dallas, TX: The League of WWI Aviation Historians, 1992), pp.49-56.
18. *Western Flying*, Vol. IV, No. 8, August 1928, P.80; No. 9, September 1928, P.258.
19. *Air Corps News Letter*, Vol. XII, No. 12, August 29, 1928, P.311.
20. *Air Corps News Letter*, Vol. XII, No. 16, September 13, 1928, P.318.
21. *Air Corps News Letter*, Vol. XII, No. 16, November 24, 1928, P.429.
22. At this time, he spelled his name "Spatz", changing it to "Spaatz" at the end of the 1930's at the insistence of his wife and daughter. I have used the latter spelling as it is more familiar to readers. See Mets, David R.: *Master of Air Power: General Carl A. Spaatz* (Novato, CA: Presidio Press, 1988), P.104.
23. *Air Corps News Letter* Vol. XII, No.17, December 18, 1928, P.449; Vol. XIII, No.2, January 31, 1929, pp.22-27; Mets, *Master of Air Power*, pp.69-73.
24. *Air Corps News Letter* Vol. XII, No. 3, February 23, 1929, P.73.
25. *Air Corps News Letter* Vol. XII, No. 4, March 15, 1929, P.100.
26. *Air Corps News Letter* Vol. XII, No.7, May 16, 1929, P.191.
27. *Air Corps News Letter* Vol. XII, No.7, May 16, 1929, P.190.
28. *Air Corps News Letter* Vol. XII, No.7, May 16, 1929, P.188.
29. *Los Angeles Times*, August 6, 1927.
30. Wagner, *American Combat Airplanes of the 20th Century*, P. 49.
31. Wagner, *American Combat Airplanes of the 20th Century*, P.48.
32. Bowman, Harold W.: *Birds of a Feather: A Memoir* (no date) P. 13.
33. Hansell, Maj. Gen. Haywood S., Jr. USAF (Ret.): "The Keystone Bombers: Unhonored and Unloved", *Air Force Magazine*, September 1977, P.132.
34. *Air Corps News Letter* Vol. XII, No. 8, June 7, 1929, P.211.
35. Mets, David R.: *Master of Air Power*, P. 75.
36. *Air Corps News Letter* Vol. XII, No. 8, June 7, 1929, P.201.
37. Gardner, George: "The Army Air Corps Maneuvers", *Aero Digest*, Vol. 14, No.6, June 1929, P. 50.
38. *Plain Dealer*, May 28, 1929.
39. Gardner, "The Army Air Corps Maneuvers", P.51.
40. Maurer, *Aviation in the U.S. Army 1919-1939*, P.244; Gardner, "The Army Air Corps Maneuvers", P.51; *Plain Dealer*, " Planes Off Today on Refueling Trip", May 21, 1929; *Air Corps News Letter* Vol. XII, No. 8, June 7, 1929, P.209-10.
41. *The New York Times*, May 23, 1929, P.1.
42. *Air Corps Aerial Gunnery and Bombing*, Training Regulations TR 440-40, (Washington: War Department, March 11, 1929), pp.10-18.
43. Shiner, John F.: "The Coming of the GHQ Air Force, 1925-1935", in Nalty, Bernard C.: *Winged Shield, Wing Sword: A History of the United States Air Force*, Vol. I 1907-1950 (Washington: United States Air Force 1997), P.113.
44. *Air Corps News Letter*, Vol. XIII, No.9, June 29, 1929, P.235.
45. *Air Corps News Letter*, Vol. XIII, No.9, June 29, 1929, P.235.
46. *Air Corps News Letter*, Vol. XIII, No.11, August 12, 1929, P.287; No. 14, October 17, 1929, P.367.
47. *Air Corps News Letter*, Vol. XIII, No.14, October 17, 1929, P.365; *Pacific Flyer*, February 1930, P.25.
48. *Air Corps News Letter*, Vol. XIII, No.14, October 17, 1929, P.365; No. 15, November 9, 1929, P.386.
49. Mets, David R.: *Master of Air Power*, P.79.
50. *Air Corps News Letter*, Vol. XIII, No.17, December 21, 1929, P.443.
51. *Air Corps News Letter*, Vol. XIV, No.4, March 31, 1930, pp.86-87.
52. *Air Corps News Letter*, Vol. XIV, No.4, March 31, 1930, pp.75-77; "The Army Air Corps Maneuvers", *Pacific Flyer*, April 1930, pp.6-7.
53. Maurer, *Aviation in the U.S. Army 1919-1939*, P.231.
54. "Army Maneuvers on Coast Completed", *Aviation*, Vol. 28, No.18, May 3, 1930, P.911.
55. Mets, David R.: *Master of Air Power*, P.80.
56. *Air Corps News Letter*, Vol. XIV, No. 1, January 16, 1930, pp.16, 20.
57. *Air Corps News Letter*, Vol. XIV, No. 1, January 16, 1930, pp.16, 20.
58. "Army Maneuvers on Coast Completed", *Aviation*, Vol. 28, No.18, May 3, 1930, P.910; *Air Corps News Letter*, Vol. XIV, No.4, March 31, 1930, pp. 77, 83-84; No.5, April 18, 1930, P.107.
59. *Aviation*, Vol.28, No.16, April 19, 1930, P.820; No.17, April 26, 1930, P.854; No.18, "Army Maneuvers on Coast Completed", P.907-911; *Air Corps News Letter*, Vol. XIV, No. 6, May 13, 1930, pp.126-29.
60. *Air Corps News Letter*, Vol. XIV, No.4, March 31, 1930, P.92; No. 6, May 13, 1930, P.143; Wagner, *American Combat Airplanes of the 20th Century*, P.50; Lt. Col. H.H. Arnold, Material Division, Wright Field, to Chief of the Air Corps, July 15, 1931, Aircraft Allotment Tables for Fiscal Year 1932, Aircraft Allotment for Bombardment Airplanes as of July 1, 1931, Entry 166, 452.1A, Allocation of Airplanes, Record Group 18, General Records of the Army Air Forces, National Archives and Records Administration.
61. Wagner, *American Combat Airplanes of the 20th Century*, P.48.
62. Mets, David R.: *Master of Air Power*, P.79.
63. *Air Corps News Letter*, Vol. XIV, No. 7, June 9, 1930, P.159.
64. *Air Corps News Letter*, Vol. XIV, No. 7, June 9, 1930, P.153.
65. *Air Corps News Letter*, Vol. XIV, No. 12, October 20, 1930, pp.298-99,

301-02; No. 13, November 14, 1930, P.330; No. 14, December 8, 1930, P.345.
66. Maurer, *Aviation in the U.S. Army 1919-1939*, pp.216-20.
67. Maurer, *Air Force Combat Units of WWII*, P.373.
68. *Air Corps News Letter*, Vol. XV, No.6, May 7, 1931, P.163.
69. *Air Corps News Letter*, Vol. XX, No. 6, March 15, 1937, P.10.
70. *Air Corps News Letter*, Vol. XX, No. 10, May 15, 1937, P.11-12.
71. *Air Corps News Letter*, Vol. XX, No. 6, March 15, 1937, P.10.
72. *Air Corps News Letter*, Vol. XV, No. 7, June 5, 1931, P.221.
73. Wagner, *American Combat Airplanes of the 20th Century*, pp.96-7.
74. Maurer, *Aviation in the U.S. Army 1919-1939*, P.206.
75. Maurer, *Air Force Combat Units of WWII*, P. 61-62; Maurer, Maurer: Ed.: *Combat Squadrons of the Air Force, WWII* (Washington: Office of Air Force History, 1983), pp.163-64, 268-69, 316-317.
76. "The First Provisional Air Division", *Air Corps News Letter*, Vol. XV, No. 7, June 5, 1931, P.190-195; *The New York Times*, December 28, 1930.
77. *Air Corps News Letter*, Vol. XV, No.1, January 15, 1931, P.28.
78. *Air Corps News Letter*, Vol. XV, No. 3, February 28, 1931, P.74.
79. *Air Corps News Letter*, Vol. XV, No. 3, February 28, 1931, P.74.
80. *Air Corps News Letter*, Vol. XV, No. 1, January 15, 1931, P.19; No. 6, May 7, 1931, P.171.
81. *Air Corps News Letter*, Vol. XV, No. 6, May 7, 1931, P.173-74.
82. "The First Provisional Air Division", *Air Corps News Letter*, Vol. XV, No. 7, June 5, 1931, P.190-195.
83. "The First Provisional Air Division", *Air Corps News Letter*, Vol. XV, No. 7, June 5, 1931, P.190-195.
84. Maurer, *Aviation in the U.S. Army 1919-1939*, P.246.
85. *Dallas Morning News*, May 12, 1931.
86. *Air Corps News Letter*, Vol. XV, No.8, June 30, 1931, P.224.
87. *Dallas Morning News*, May 22, 1931.
88. ; "The Air Division And Coast Defense", Vol. XV, No.9, July 21, 1931, pp.252-254.
89. Trest, Warren A.: *Air Force Roles and Missions: A History* (Washington, D.C.: Air Force History and Museums Program, 1998), pP. 48-55.
90. "The First Provisional Air Division, 1931, Concluded", *Air Corps News Letter*, Vol. XV, No.8, June 30, 1931, pp.224-28; "The Air Division And Coast Defense", Vol. XV, No.9, July 21, 1931, pp.252-254; *Air Corps News Letter*, Vol. XV, No.8, June 30, 1931, P.245.
91. Spaatz, Major Carl: "Radio-Controlled Sky Battles of the Next Great War", *The Salt Lake Tribune*, June 7, 1931, P.9.
92.. Harley, Dr.R. Bruce: *The March Field Story: 50th Anniversary 1918-1968* (March Field, CA: 1968), P.34; *The Laredo Times*, September 27, 1931.
93. Biography of General Joseph T. McNarney, U.S. Air Force Historical Research Agency.
94. *Air Corps News Letter*, Vol. XVI, No. 1, January 25, 1931, P.10.
95. *Air Corps News Letter*, Vol. XVI, No. 1, January 25, 1931, P.26.
96. *Air Corps News Letter*, Vol. XVI, No. 1, January 25, 1931, P.26.
97. Lt. Col. H.H. Arnold, Material Division, Wright Field, to Chief of the Air Corps, July 15, 1931, Aircraft Allotment Tables for Fiscal Year 1932, Aircraft Allotment for Bombardment Airplanes as of June 30, 1932, Entry 166, 452.1A, Allocation of Airplanes, Record Group 18, General Records of the Army Air Forces, National Archives and Records Administration.
98. Bowman, Harold W.: *Birds of a Feather: A Memoir*, P.22.
99. This data comes from the website www.Accident-Report.com, which contains a list of aircraft accidents by air field for the 1930s.
100. *Air Corps News Letter*, Vol. XVI, No.3, March 15, 1932, P.108.
101. *Air Corps News Letter*, Vol. XVI, No.2, February 18, 1932, pp.39-40; No. 3, March 15, 1932, pp.86-87.
102. Maurer: *Aviation in the U.S. Army 1919-1939*, P.250.
103. Arnold, General of the Air Force H.H.: *Global Mission* (New York: Harper Brothers 1949), P. 134.
104. *Western Flying*, Vol. 12, No. 6, June 1932, P.46.
105. *Air Corps News Letter*, Vol. XVI, No. 11, September 21, 1932, P.375, 382, 389.
106. *Air Corps News Letter*, Vol. XVI, No. 7, June 27, 1932, P.247; No. 9, August 13, 1932, P.307.
107. *Air Corps News Letter*, Vol. XVI, No. 14, November 30, 1932, pP. 461, 472.
108. Shiner, "The Coming of the GHQ Air Force, 1925-1935", P.123.
109. Shiner, "The Coming of the GHQ Air Force, 1925-1935", P.124.
110. Coffman, Edward M.: *The Regulars: The American Army 1898-1941* (Cambridge, MA: The Belknap Press, 2004), pp.239-41.
111. Maurer, *Aviation in the U.S. Army 1919-1939*, P. 218, 220.
112. Maurer, *Aviation in the U.S. Army 1919-1939*, P.199.
113. Maurer, *Aviation in the U.S. Army 1919-1939*, pP. 200-201.
114. Maurer, *Aviation in the U.S. Army 1919-1939*, pP. 200.
115. Maurer, *Aviation in the U.S. Army 1919-1939*, pP. 219-21.
116. Operations Report of Airplanes as of July 31, 1932, Operations Reports of Airplanes 1932, Office of the Chief of the Air Corps, Training and Operations Division, Entry 227, Record Group 18 (Army Air Forces), NARA.
117. *Western Flying*, January 1933, P.46.
118. Wagner, *American Combat Airplanes of the 20th Century*, pp.175-76, 221-22; Pelletier, Alan J.: "Bombers As Postmen: Douglas YO-35 and Y1B-7", *Air Enthusiast*, Vol. 122, March/April 2006, pp.30-32, 35; *Air Corps News Letter*, Vol. XVII, No.1, January 31, 1933, P.16; No.2, February 24, 1933, P.44.
119. Maurer, *Aviation in the U.S. Army 1919-1939*, P.414; *The New York Times*, April 2, 1933.
120. Maurer, *Aviation in the U.S. Army 1919-1939*, P.414; *The New York Times*, April 2, 1933 ; *Air Corps News Letter*, Vol. XVII, No. 6, June 30, 1933, P.153.
121. *Air Corps News Letter*, Vol. XVII, No. 5, May 29, 1933, P.127; Pelletier, Alan J.: "Bombers As Postmen: Douglas YO-35 and Y1B-7", P.35.
122. Maurer, *Aviation in the U.S. Army 1919-1939*, P.416.
123. Maurer, *Aviation in the U.S. Army 1919-1939*, P.416.
124. Maurer, *Aviation in the U.S. Army 1919-1939*, P.416.
125. Maurer, *Aviation in the U.S. Army 1919-1939*,pp.283-84.
126. Shiner, "The Coming of the GHQ Air Force, 1925-1935", P.118.
127. Ibid, pP. 119-20; Maurer, *Aviation in the U.S. Army 1919-1939*, pP. 288-90; Trest, Warren A.: *Air Force Roles and Missions: A History* (Washington, D.C.: Air Force History and Museums Program, 1998), pP. 55-59.
128. "The Air Corps' West Coast Exercises-1933" *Air Corps News Letter*, Vol. XVII, No. 6, June 30, 1933, pp.138-42.
129. *Los Angeles Times*, May 16, 1933, P.A2.
130. *The Seattle Daily Times*, June 1, 1933, p.11.
131. "The Air Corps' West Coast Exercises-1933", pp.142-44.
132. Arnold, *Global Mission*, pp.140-141.
133. Maurer, *Aviation in the U.S. Army 1919-1939*, P.349.
134. Arnold, *Global Mission*, P.141.
135. Mets, David R.: *Master of Air Power*, P.89; see also "The Air Corps' West Coast Exercises-1933", P.139.
136. See Clay, *U.S. Army Order of Battle 1919-1941: Volume 3: The Services-Air Service, Engineers, and Special Troops 1919-1941*, pp.1242, 1301, 1377, 1378, 1397; Biography of General Joseph T. McNarney, U.S. Air Force Historical Research Agency.
137. Borden, Norman E., Jr.: *Air Mail Emergency 1934*, (Freeport, Maine: Bond Wheelwright Company, 1968), pp.2-9.
138. Shiner, "The Coming of the GHQ Air Force, 1925-1935", P.124.
139. Borden, Norman E., Jr.: *Air Mail Emergency 1934*, pP. 29, 36-7; Shiner, "The Coming of the GHQ Air Force, 1925-1935", pp.123-24; Arnold, *Global Mission*, P.143.
140. *Los Angeles Times*, February 15, 1934, P.A1.
141. *Los Angeles Times*, February 15, 1934, P.A1.
142. *The Seattle Daily Times*, February 14, 1934, P.2.
143. *The Seattle Daily Times*, February 17, 1934, P.12; Pelletier, Alan J.: "Bombers As Postmen: Douglas YO-35 and Y1B-7", P.36.
144. Shiner, "The Coming of the GHQ Air Force, 1925-1935", P.125.
145. Maurer, *Aviation in the U.S. Army 1919-1939*, P.316-17.
146. Shiner, "The Coming of the GHQ Air Force, 1925-1935", P.133.
147. *Air Corps News Letter*, Vol. XVII, No. 9, September 30, 1933, P.217.

Chapter Two: A Laboratory for Air Power: Bigger and Better Bombers

1. Anderson, John D., Jr.: *The Airplane: A History of its Technology* (Reston, VA: American Institute of Aeronautics and Astronautics, 2002), see the discussion in Chapter 6: The First Design Revolution: The Era of the Mature Propeller-Driven Airplane, pp.183-282; Munson, Kenneth: "The Biplane's Fall from Favor", in Jarrett, Philip, Ed.: *Biplane to Monoplane: Aircraft Development 1919-1939* (London: Putnam Aeronautical Books, 1997), pP. 11-28.
2. Wagner, *American Combat Airplanes of the 20th Century*, pP. 223-

26; Shiner, "The Heyday of the GHQ Air Force, 1935-39", ", in Nalty, Bernard C.: *Winged Shield, Wing Sword: A History of the United States Air Force*, Vol. I 1907-1950 (Washington: United States Air Force 1997), pp.138-40.

3. Futrell, Robert F.: *Ideas, Concepts, and Doctrine, Volume I: Basic Thinking in the United States Air Force 1907-1960* (Maxwell AFB, AL: Air University Press, 1989), pp.28-30.
4. Futrell, *Ideas, Concepts, and Doctrine, Volume I: Basic Thinking in the United States Air Force 1907-1960* pp.62-63; see also Air Service Tactical School: *Bombardment* (Washington, D.C.: Government Printing Office 1926), P.2.
5. Biddle, Tami Davis: *Rhetoric and Reality in Air Warfare: The Evolution of British and American Ideas About Strategic Bombing, 1914-1945* (Princeton, NJ: Princeton University Press, 2002), pP. 132-35;
6. Finney, Robert T.: *History of the Air Corps Tactical School 1920-1940* (Washington, D.C.: Center for Air Force History, 1992), P.63.
7. Finney, *History of the Air Corps Tactical School 1920-1940*, pp.56-57.
8. Walker, Lt. Kenneth N.: "Bombardment Aviation—Bulwark of National Defense", *U.S. Air Services*, Vol. XVIII, No. 8, August, 1933, P.15.
9. Walker, "Bombardment Aviation—Bulwark of National Defense", P.15.
10. Walker, "Bombardment Aviation—Bulwark of National Defense", P.16.
11. Finney, *History of the Air Corps Tactical School 1920-1940*, P.67; Greer, Thomas H.: *The Development of Air Doctrine in the Army Air Arm 1917-1941* (Washington, D.C.: Office of Air Force History,1985), P.47.
12. Greer, Thomas H.: *The Development of Air Doctrine in the Army Air Arm 1917-1941*, P.57.
13. Biddle, *Rhetoric and Reality in Air Warfare: The Evolution of British and American Ideas About Strategic Bombing, 1914-1945*, pP. 143; Trest, Warren A.: *Air Force Roles and Missions: A History*, P.60.
14. Biddle, *Rhetoric and Reality in Air Warfare: The Evolution of British and American Ideas About Strategic Bombing, 1914-1945*, pP. 143.
15. Biddle, *Rhetoric and Reality in Air Warfare: The Evolution of British and American Ideas About Strategic Bombing, 1914-1945*, pp.164-70; Greer, *The Development of Air Doctrine in the Army Air Arm 1917-1941*, pP. 80-83.
16. *Air Corps News Letter*, Vol. XVII, No. 7, July 31, 1933, P.169.
17. The *San Antonio Express* of June 20, 1934, noted on page 8 the arrival at Kelly Field of eight new Army bombing planes on their way to March Field. Photos show B-12s from the 11th Bombardment Group flying around the March Field area during July 1934.
18. Virgin, Edward W.: "The Martin Bomber B-10, B-12, B-10B", in Higham, Robin and Carol Williams, Eds.: *Flying Combat Aircraft of the USAAF-USAF*, Vol. 2, (Ames, Iowa: The Iowa State University Press, 1978), pp.27, 29-30.
19. Virgin, "The Martin Bomber B-10, B-12, B-10B", pP. 28-31.
20. Arnold, Lt. Col. Henry H.: "Employment of Tactical Units Equipped with Modern Pursuit and Bombardment Airplanes", November 26, 1934, MilSpecManuals.com, No.007822, P.1.
21. Arnold, "Employment of Tactical Units Equipped with Modern Pursuit and Bombardment Airplanes", P.5.
22. Arnold, "Employment of Tactical Units Equipped with Modern Pursuit and Bombardment Airplanes", P.17; Greer, *The Development of Air Doctrine in the Army Air Arm 1917-1941*, P.59.
23. Arnold, "Employment of Tactical Units Equipped with Modern Pursuit and Bombardment Airplanes", P.10.
24. Arnold, "Employment of Tactical Units Equipped with Modern Pursuit and Bombardment Airplanes", pP. 10-11, 17.
25. *Nevada State Journal*, October 3, 1934; *The Galveston Daily News*, October 3, 1934; *Oakland Tribune*, November 28, 1934.
26. *Air Corps News Letter*, Vol. XVIII, No.2, February 1, 1935, P.33.
27. *The New York Times*, October 2, 1934, P.1.
28. "Hamilton Air Force Base, California: Its First Thirty Years", copy at the Albert F. Simpson Research Center, Air Force Historical Research Agency, Maxwell AFB, AL.
29. "Hamilton Air Force Base, California: Its First Thirty Years".
30. *Oakland Tribune*, November 18, 1934.
31. *Oregonian*, December 2, 1934.
32. *Air Corps News Letter*, Vol. XVIII, No.2, February 1, 1935, P.33.
33. *Air Corps News Letter*, Vol. XVIII, No. 4, March 1, 1935.
34. *Air Corps News Letter*, Vol. XVIII, No. 4, March 1, 1935, P.91.
35. *Air Corps News Letter*, Vol. XVIII, No. 3, February 15, 1935, pp.48-49; No. 4, March 1, 1935, P.86; No.6, April 1, 1935, P.154; *The New York Times*, February 26, 1935, P.1, March 3, 1935, P.28.
36. Maurer, *Aviation in the U.S. Army 1919-1939*, P.328.
37. Clay, Lt. Colonel Steven E. (Ret'd): *U.S. Army Order of Battle 1919-1941: Volume 3: The Services-Air Service, Engineers, and Special Troops 1919-1941*, P.1432; *Air Corps News Letter*, Vol. XVIII, No. 7, April 15, 1935, P.177.
38. Maurer, *Aviation in the U.S. Army 1919-1939*, P.329; *Air Corps News Letter*, Vol. XVIII, No. 8, May 1, 1935, P.11.
39. "The Air Force Crucible", *Air Corps News Letter*, Vol. XVIII, No. 11, June 15, 1935, P.1.
40. "The Air Force Crucible", P. 5.
41. "The Air Force Crucible", P.1.
42. *Air Corps News Letter*, Vol. XVIII, No. 11, June 15, 1935, P.5; No. 8, May 1, 1935, P.21.
43. *Air Corps News Letter*, Vol. XVIII, No. 7, April 15, 1935, P.170; No. 8, May 1, 1935, P.14; No. 9, May 15, pP. 8, 11; No. 12, July 1, 1935, P.7; No. 14, August 1, 1935, P. 16; No. 15, August 15, 1935, P. 13; *Salt Lake Tribune*, July 16, 17, 19, 22, 24, 25, 1935.
44. *Air Corps News Letter*, Vol. XVIII, No. 11, June 15, 1935, P. 4.
45. *Morning News, Florence, S.C.*, May 29, 1935.
46. *Air Corps News Letter*, Vol. XVIII, No. 17, September 15, 1935, P.5; Vol. XIX, No. 11, June 1, 1936, pp.12-13.
47. Maurer, *Aviation in the U.S. Army 1919-1939*, P.377.
48. Maurer, *Aviation in the U.S. Army 1919-1939*, pp.378-79.
49. "Bombing Activities of the 7th Bombardment Group", *Air Corps News Letter*, Vol. XVIII, No. 11, June 1, 1936, P.15.
50. "Seventh Bombardment Group Completes Training for F.Y. 1935-36", *Air Corps News Letter*, Vol. XIX, No. 17, September 1, 1936, pp.10-11.
51. "Seventh Bombardment Group Completes Training for F.Y. 1935-36", P.11.
52. Ibid, P.11; "The Seventh Bombardment Group", *Air Corps News Letter*, Vol. XVIII, No. 11, June 1, 1936, P.13.
53. Crowder, James L., Jr.: *Osage General: Major General Clarence L. Tinker* (Tinker Air Force Base, OK: Officer of History, Oklahoma City Air Logistics Center 1987), pP. 227-32.
54. *The Bakersfield Californian*, November 13, 1935.
55. " The Seventh Bombardment Group", *Air News Letter*, Vol. XVIII, No. 11, June 1, 1936, pP. 12, 16-17.
56. *Air Corps News Letter*, Vol. XIX, No.2, January 15, 1936, pp.11-15.
57. *The New York Times*, December 15, 1935, P.29.
58. *Air Corps News Letter*, Vol. XIX, No.1, January 1, 1936, P.20.
59. *Air Corps News Letter*, Vol. XIX, No. 15, August 1, 1936, pp.6, 18.
60. McFarland, Stephen L.: *America's Pursuit of Precision Bombing, 1910-1945* (Washington, D.C.: Smithsonian Institution Press, 1995), P.93.
61. McFarland, *America's Pursuit of Precision Bombing, 1910-1945*, P.96.
62. McFarland, *America's Pursuit of Precision Bombing, 1910-1945*, P.96.
63. McFarland, *America's Pursuit of Precision Bombing, 1910-1945*, P.95.
64. Lt. Col. H.R. Harmon, Executive Officer, 1st Wing, G.H.Q. Air Force, Operations Memo, February 13, 1936, Field Exercises, 1st Wing, GHQ Air Force, March 1936, in Files 360.07 (1930) to 361 (1936), Box 689, Sarah Clark Correspondence Files, Entry P-26, Record Group 342, Records of United States Air Force Commands, Activities, and Organizations, NARA.
65. *Air Corps News Letter*, Vol. XIX, No. 6, March 15, 1936, P.16.
66. Operations Memo, February 28, 1936, Field Exercises, 1st Wing, March 1936: Tactical Missions, 7th Bombardment Group, in Files 360.07 (1930) to 361 (1936), Box 689, Sarah Clark Correspondence Files, Entry P-26, Record Group 342, Records of United States Air Force Commands, Activities, and Organizations, NARA.
67. *Air Corps News Letter*, Vol. XIX, No. 18, September 15, 1936, P.6.
68. *Air Corps News Letter*, Vol. XIX, No.21, November 1, 1936, P.9.

69: *Air Corps News Letter*, Vol. XIX, No. 17, September 1, 1936, P.22.

70. Headquarters 7th Bombardment Group, Officer of the Operations Officer, November 18, 1936, "Report of Joint Coastal Frontier Defense Exercise No.2", in GP-7-SU (Bomb) November 1936, Albert F. Simpson Historical Research Center, Air Force Historical Research Agency, Maxwell AFB, AL.
71. "Report of Joint Coastal Frontier Defense Exercise No.2".
72. Headquarters 7th Bombardment Group, Officer of the Operations Officer, November 18, 1936, "Report of Joint Coastal Frontier Defense Exercise No.2", in GP-7-SU (Bomb) November 1936, Albert F.

Simpson Historical Research Center, Air Force Historical Research Agency, Maxwell AFB, AL, P.43.

73. Clay, *U.S. Army Order of Battle 1919-1941: Volume 3: The Services-Air Service, Engineers, and Special Troops 1919-1941*, P.1630; *Air Corps News Letter*, Vol. XIX, No. 17, September 1, 1936, pp.4-6.
74. Clay, *U.S. Army Order of Battle 1919-1941: Volume 3: The Services-Air Service, Engineers, and Special Troops 1919-1941*, P.1432; *Air Corps News Letter*, Vol. XIX, No. 17, September 1, 1936, P.5.
75. Clay, *U.S. Army Order of Battle 1919-1941: Volume 3: The Services-Air Service, Engineers, and Special Troops 1919-1941*, pP. 1242, 1301, 1377, 1397, 1432; *Air Corps News Letter*, Vol. XX, No. 10, May 15, 1937, P.14; Byrd, Martha: *Kenneth N. Walker: Airpower's Untempered Crusader* (Maxwell AFB, AL: Air University Press, 1997), pP. 50-51.
76. *Air Corps News Letter*, Vol. XX, No. 2, January 15, 1937, P.18.
77. *Air Corps News Letter*, Vol. XX, No. 2, January 15, 1937, P.18; No.3, February 1, pP. 13-15; No. 5, March 1, P. 13; No. 7, April 1, P.3, 5, 23.
78. "Variety is the Spice of Life", *Air Corps News Letter*, Vol. XX, No. 9, May 1, 1937, pp.7-8.
79. *Los Angeles Times*, May 10, 1937.
80. "Army Air Force Combat Units to Concentrate in California", *Air Corps News Letter*, Vol. XX, No. 8, April 15, 1937; "The General Headquarters Air Force Exercises", *Air Corps News Letter*, Vol. XX, No. 11, June 1, 1937, pp.1-4; "The GHQ Air Force Maneuvers on the West Coast", *Air Corps News Letter*, Vol. XX, No. 12, June 15, 1937, pp.5-6, 16-17; Maurer: *Aviation in the U.S. Army 1919-1939*, P.401-02.
81. I am indebted to Dan Hagedorn, Sr., Senior Curator at the Museum of Flight, for providing me with a copy of his forthcoming history of the Douglas B-18, *The Douglas B-18 and B-23: America's Forsaken Warriors*. I have relied heavily on Dan's study in preparing this section on the B-18.
82. USAF Historical Studies No. 6: *The Development of the Heavy Bomber* (Historical Division, Air University, U.S. Air Force 1951), P.74.
83. *The New York Times*, December 22, 1935, P.24.
84. Johnson, David E.: *Fast Tanks and Heavy Bombers: Innovation in the U.S. Army 1917-1945* (Ithica, NY: Cornell University Press, 1998), P.163.
85. See particularly Greer, *The Development of Air Doctrine in the Army Air Arm 1917-1941*, pP. 89-94.
86. *The New York Times*, December 9, 1935, P.1; Maurer, *Aviation in the U.S. Army 1919-1939*, P. 360.
87. Maurer, *Aviation in the U.S. Army 1919-1939*, P. 360.
88. *Air Corps News Letter*, Vol. XX, No. 20, October 15, 1937, P.17.
89. *Oakland Tribune*, January 31, 1937, P.4C.
90. *Air Corps News Letter*, Vol. XXI, No.14, July 15, 1938.
91. *Air Corps News Letter*, Vol. XX, No. 22, November 15, 1937, P.21.
92. *Air Corps News Letter*, Vol. XX, No. 20, October 15, 1937, P.17.
93. *Air Corps News Letter*, Vol. XX, No. 22, November 15, 1937, P.27.
94. Close, Winton R.: "The B-18—A Reminiscence", in Higham, Robert and Carol Williams, Eds.: *Flying Combat Aircraft of the USAAF-USAF*, Volume III (Manhattan, KS: Sunflower University Press, 1981), pP. 110, 113.
95. *Air Corps News Letter*, Vol. XX, No. 22, November 15, 1937, P.8; No. 24, December 15, 1937.
96. *Air Corps News Letter*, Vol. XXI, No. 3, February 1, 1938, P.13; No. 6, March 15, 1938, P.6; . Clay, *U.S. Army Order of Battle 1919-1941: Volume 3: The Services-Air Service, Engineers, and Special Troops 1919-1941*, pP. 1377-78.
97. *Air Corps News Letter*, Vol. XXI, No. 4, February 15, 1938, P.18.
98. *The New York Times*, May 12, 1938, P.1.
99. Operating Instructions No. 1, GHQ Air Force, 25 April 1938, File 354.2 Orders, Etc., Box 632, Army Air Forces Central Decimal Files 1917-38, Record Group 18, NARA; *Seattle Daily Times*, May 2, 1938, P.22.
100. War Department Press Release, April 30, 1938, in File 354.2, Orders, Etc., Box 632, RG 18, NARA.
101. *The New York Times*, May 12, 1938, P.1; May 13, P.3; May 17, P.1; May18, P. 8.
102. Baldwin, Hanson: "War Games Show Air Force is Weak", *The New York Times*, May 15, 1938, P.1.
103. Memorandum to the Chief of the Air Corps, from Lt. Col. H.C. Davidson, Chief, Training and Operations Division, May 26, 1938, File 354.2 Orders, Etc., Box 632, Army Air Forces Central Decimal Files 1917-38, Record Group 18, NARA, P.5.
104. Caldwell, Cy: "Knighthood in Flower", *Aero Digest*, Vol. , No. (June 1938), p.99.
105. For the 1st Wing maneuvers, see *Seattle Daily Times*, July 20, 1938, P.2, August 9, P.2; August 10, P.2; August 11, P.2; August 12, P.4; *Air Corps News Letter*, Vol. XXI, No. 19, October 1, 1938, P.10. For the B-18 transcontinental flight, see *Air Corps News Letter*, Vol. XXI, No. 17, September 1, 1938, P. 5; *Berkeley Daily Gazette*, August 20, 1938, P.2.
106. *Air Corps News Letter*, Vol. XXI, No. 7, April 1, 1938, P.21; Clay, *U.S. Army Order of Battle 1919-1941: Volume 3: The Services-Air Service, Engineers, and Special Troops 1919-1941*, P. 1301.
107. Shiner, "The Heyday of the GHQ Air Force", P.148; see also Maurer, *Aviation in the U.S. Army 1919-1939*, pp.406-8.
108. Shiner, "The Heyday of the GHQ Air Force", P.148; Maurer, *Aviation in the U.S. Army 1919-1939*, pp.408-9
109. Greer, *The Development of Air Doctrine in the Army Air Arm 1917-1941*, P.99.
110. Greer, *The Development of Air Doctrine in the Army Air Arm 1917-1941*, P.99.
111. Wagner, *American Combat Airplanes of the 20th Century*, P.233.
112. Greer, *The Development of Air Doctrine in the Army Air Arm 1917-1941*, P.100.
113. Brendon, Piers: *The Dark Valley: A Panorama of the 1930s* (London: Jonathan Cape, 2000), P.533.
114. Dallek, Robert: *Franklin D. Roosevelt and American Foreign Policy, 1932-1945*. New York, NY: Oxford University Press, 1979, P.171.
115. Ibid, P.172; Greer, *The Development of Air Doctrine in the Army Air Arm 1917-1941*, P.100; Shiner, "The Heyday of the GHQ Air Force", P.154.
116. Greer, *The Development of Air Doctrine in the Army Air Arm 1917-1941*, P.100.
117. Greer, *The Development of Air Doctrine in the Army Air Arm 1917-1941*, P.100.
118. Shiner, "The Heyday of the GHQ Air Force", pp.155-56.
119. *The New York Times*, January 13, 1939, pp.1, 8.
120. Maurer, *Aviation in the U.S. Army 1919-1939*, pp.436.
122. Maurer, *Aviation in the U.S. Army 1919-1939*, pp.436.
123. *The New York Times*, April 18, 1939.
124. *San Antonio Express*, April 26, 1939, P.9.
125. Maurer, *Aviation in the U.S. Army 1919-1939*, pp.436.
126. Wagner, *American Combat Airplanes of the 20th Century*, pP. 234-35, 238, 244.
127. *Air Corps News Letter*, Vol. XXI, No. 7, April 1, 1938, P.14; Vol. XXII, No. 17, September 1, 1939, P.14.
128. *Air Corps News Letter*, Vol. XXII, No. 17, September 1, 1939, P.14.
129. Maurer, *Aviation in the U.S. Army 1919-1939*, pp.437; *The New York Times*, May 30, P. 1; October 22, 1939, P.21.
130. *Marin Journal*, August 24, 1939.
131. *Air Corps News Letter*, Vol. XXII, No. 18, September 15, 1939, P. 11.
132. Ibid.
133. *Air Corps News Letter*, Vol. XXII, No. 21, October 15, 1939, P.8; *Oregonian*, September 29, 1939.
134. Maurer, *Combat Squadrons of the Air Force, WWII*, P.115; *Air Corps News Letter*, Vol. XXIII, No. 4, February 15, 1940, P.6.
135. *Air Corps News Letter*, Vol. XXIII, No. 2, January 15, 1940, P.12.
136. *Los Angeles Times*, January 15, 1940, P.B; *The New York Times*, February 25, 1940, P. 35.
137. *Los Angeles Times*, January 7, 1940, P.A1; *Oakland Tribune*, January 21, 22, 1940; *Air Corps News Letter*, Vol. XXIII, No. 3, February 1, 1940, P.19; No. 5, March 1, 1940, P.24.
138. *Air Corps News Letter*, Vol. XXIII, No. 11, June 1, 1940, P.21.
139. Craven, Wesley Frank, and James Lea Cate, Eds.: *The Army Air Forces in WWII*, Volume One: *Plans and Early Operations January 1939 to August 1942*. (Chicago, Il: The University of Chicago Press 1948), P.105.
140. Army Air Force Historical Studies No.5: *Individual Training of Bombardiers*. P. 2; Army Air Force Historical Studies No. 27: *Individual Training of Navigators in the AAF*. P. 3, Maxwell AFB, AL: USAF Historical Division, Research Studies Institute, Air University, 1944 and 1945.
141. Craven and Cate, *The Army Air Forces in WWII*, Vol. One, P.106.
142. U.S. Air Force Historical Study No.5: *Individual Training of Bombardiers*. pp.18-22; U.S. Air Force Historical Study No. 27: *Individual Training of Navigators in the AAF*. pP. 43-49.
143. "Hamilton Air Force Base, California: Its First Thirty Years", pp.19-20.

144. *Air Corps News Letter*, Vol. XXIII, No. 17, September 1, 1940, P.21.
145. *Air Corps News Letter*, Vol. XXIII, No. 19, October 1, 1940, P.10; No. 21, November 1, 1940, P. 6; No. 22, November 15, 1940, P.15.
146. *Salt Lake Telegram*, September 2, 3, 1940.
147. *Air Corps News Letter*, Vol. XXIII, No. 21, November 1, 1940, P. 6.
148. *Air Corps News Letter*, Vol. XXIII, No. 21, November 1, 1940, P. 6.
149. This information is from Dan Hagedorn's research on the B-18.
150. *Air Corps News Letter*, Vol. XXIII, No. 21, November 1, 1940, pp.6, 17; No. 23, December 1, 1940, P.21-22; Vol. XXIV, No.5, March 1, 1941, pp.13-14; Maurer, *Air Force Combat Units of WWII*, pP. 95, 99.
151. Clay, *U.S. Army Order of Battle 1919-1941: Volume 3: The Services-Air Service, Engineers, and Special Troops 1919-1941*, pp.1377, 1378.
152. Greer, *The Development of Air Doctrine in the Army Air Arm 1917-1941*, P.123.
153. Greer, *The Development of Air Doctrine in the Army Air Arm 1917-1941*, P.123.
154. Greer, *The Development of Air Doctrine in the Army Air Arm 1917-1941*, P.123.
155. Ibid, P.125; Biddle, *Rhetoric and Reality in Air Warfare: The Evolution of British and American Ideas About Strategic Bombing, 1914-1945*, P.206.
156. Biddle, pP. 206-08; Nalty, Bernard C.: "Reaction to the War in Europe", in Nalty, Bernard C.: *Winged Shield, Winged Sword: A History of the United States Air Force*. Volume I, *1907-1950*. Washington, D.C. Air Force History and Museums Program 1997, pp.187-191.
157. Dallek, Robert: *Franklin D. Roosevelt and American Foreign Policy, 1932-1945*. New York, NY: Oxford University Press, 1979, pP. 300-03; Craven and Cate, *The Army Air Forces in WWII*, Vol. One, pp.176-78. See also Williford, Glen: *Racing the Sunrise: Reinforcing America's Pacific Outposts, 1941, 1942*.Annapolis, MD: Naval Institute Press, 2010, Chapter 1.
158. Craven and Cate, Vol. One, P.178; USAF Historical Study No. 111: *Army Air Action in the Philippines and Netherlands East Indies 1941-1942*. USAF Historical Division, Research Studies Institute, Air University. Maxwell AFB, AL. P. 24.
159. Dallek, Robert: *Franklin D. Roosevelt and American Foreign Policy, 1932-1945*. P.303; Williford, Glen: *Racing the Sunrise: Reinforcing America's Pacific Outposts, 1941, 1942*. P.112.
160. Bowers, Peter M.: *Fortress in the Sky*. California: Sentry Books, Inc. 1976, pp.76, 94-95.
161. Craven and Cate, Vol. One, P.178.
162. Craven and Cate, Vol. One, pp.178-79; Williford, *Racing the Sunrise: Reinforcing America's Pacific Outposts, 1941, 1942*. pp.112-13.
163. Williford, *Racing the Sunrise: Reinforcing America's Pacific Outposts, 1941, 1942*. pp.118-20.
164. USAF Historical Study No. 111: *Army Air Action in the Philippines and Netherlands East Indies 1941-1942*. P.31.
165. Mayhew, Wilbur W.: *Battlefields Galore*. Private memoir, courtesy of Jim Augustus, pp.2-3;
166. "S-3 Diary for the 7th Bombardment Group, December 1 1941-February 27, 1942", Folder 6, Box 1, MS 60, Series 1, United States Air Force Academy, McDermott Library Collection.
167. Arakaki, Leatrice r. and John R. Kuborn: *7 December 1941: The Air Force Story*. Hickam Air Force Base, Hawaii: Pacific Air Forces Office of Air Force History 1991, P.72.
168. "S-3 Diary for the 7th Bombardment Group, December 1 1941-February 27, 1942"
169. Arakaki and Kuborn, *7 December 1941*, P.73.
170. Arnold, *Global Mission*, P.268.
171. Arakaki and Kuborn, *7 December 1941*, P.73.
172. Arakaki and Kuborn, *7 December 1941*, P.73; Prange, Gordon W.: *At Dawn We Slept: The Untold Story of Pearl Harbor* (New York: McGraw-Hill Book Company 1981), P.476; Arakaki and Kuborn, *7 December 1941*, P.157.
173. Prange, *At Dawn We Slept: The Untold Story of Pearl Harbor*, P.480-81, 501.

Chapter Three: To War in Java

1. Prange, *At Dawn We Slept*, P.522.
2. Arakaki and Kuborn, *7 December 1941*, pP. 73, 158.
3. Arakaki and Kuborn, *7 December 1941* pP. 75-6, 157.
4. Dorr, Robert F.: *7th Bombardment Group/Wing 1918-1995*. Paducah, KY: Turner Publishing Company 1996, P.52.
5. McPherson, Irene W.: *Four Decades of Courage: Development of United States Air Power and the 7th Bombardment GrouP.* (Bloomington, IN: AuthorHouse 2006), P. 223-24.
6. Craven and Cate, Vol. One, pp.278, 294.
7. "S-3 Diary for the 7th Bombardment Group, December 1 1941-February 27, 1942"; McPherson, *Four Decades of Courage*, pp.255-54.
8. "S-3 Diary for the 7th Bombardment Group, December 1 1941-February 27, 1942".
9. "S-3 Diary for the 7th Bombardment Group, December 1 1941-February 27, 1942".
10. Williford, *Racing the Sunrise*, P.153.
11. Williford, *Racing the Sunrise*, pP. 158-66; Mayhew, *Battlefields Galore*, pp.5-8.
12. USAF Historical Study No. 111: *Army Air Action in the Philippines and Netherlands East Indies 1941-1942*. P.1; Wilmott, H.P.: *Empires in the Balance: Japanese and Allied Pacific Strategies to April 1942*. (Annapolis, MD: Naval Institute Press, 1982), P. 148.
13. USAF Historical Study No. 111: *Army Air Action in the Philippines and Netherlands East Indies 1941-1942*, pp.53-58; Bartsch, William H.: *December 8, 1941: MacArthur's Pearl Harbor*. (College Station, TX: Texas A & M University Press, 2003), P. 409.
14. Bartsch, William H.: *December 8, 1941: MacArthur's Pearl Harbor*. (College Station, TX: Texas A & M University Press, 2003), pp.68-73.
15. Craven and Cate, Vol. One, *Plans and Early Operations*, P.223.
16. USAF Historical Study No. 111: *Army Air Action in the Philippines and Netherlands East Indies 1941-1942*. Pp.83-84.
17. As stated in McPherson, *Four Decades of Courage*, pp.256-57.
18. "Unit Diary of Composite 11th Bombardment Squadron Beginning December 14, 1941—March 1942", SQ-Bomb-11-SU-RE-D December 1941-March 1942, Albert F. Simpson Historical Research Center, Air Force Historical Research Agency, Maxwell AFB, AL.
19. Bowman, Martin W.: *Consolidated B-24 Liberator*. London: The Crowood Press, 1998, P.10.
20. "S-3 Diary for the 7th Bombardment Group, December 1 1941-February 27, 1942"; Craven and Cate, Vol. One, *Plans and Early Operations*, P. 333.
21. See "Aircraft Arrivals in Java from the U.S.: 11 January- 20 February 1942", Folder 9, Box 1, MS 60, Series 1, United States Air Force Academy, McDermott Library Collection; Dorr, *7th Bombardment Group/Wing 1918-1995*, P. 59; USAF Historical Study No. 111: *Army Air Action in the Philippines and Netherlands East Indies 1941-1942*, pp.104-05.
22. Wilmott, *Empires in the Balance*, pP. 153, and 172.
23. Wilmott, *Empires in the Balance*, pp.66-70.
24. Kirby, Major-General S. Woodburn: *The Loss of Singapore*, Vol. I of *The War Against Japan* (London: Her Majesty's Stationary Office, 1957), P.89.
25. Kirby, *The Loss of Singapore*, pp.92-93; Wilmott, *Empires in the Balance*, pp.73-74.
26. Wilmott, *Empires in the Balance*, P.172.
27. Wilmott, *Empires in the Balance*, P.177.
28. Kirby, *The Loss of Singapore*, P.291.
29. Kirby, *The Loss of Singapore*, P.291; www.niehorster.orbat.com, "WWII Armed Forces: Orders of Battle and Organizations".
30. Wilmott, *Empires in the Balance*, P.95.
31. Wilmott, *Empires in the Balance*, pp.257-259; Kirby, *The Loss of Singapore*, pp.263-267.
32. Kirby, *The Loss of Singapore*, P.265.
33. Kirby, *The Loss of Singapore*, pp.292-93.
34. USAF Historical Study No. 111: *Army Air Action in the Philippines and Netherlands East Indies 1941-1942*, P.102.
35. USAF Historical Study No. 111: *Army Air Action in the Philippines and Netherlands East Indies 1941-1942*, P.103.
36. Mitchell, John H.: *In Alis Vicimus-On Wings We Conquer: The 19th and 7th Bombardment Groups of the United States Air Force in the Southwest Pacific in the first year of World War Two* (Springfield, MO: G.E.M. Publishers, 1990), pP. 73-75.
37. Mitchell, *On Wings We Conquer*, pp.76-77.
38. The Joint Army-Navy Assessment Committee set up after the war to determine Japanese navy and merchant shipping losses does not confirm these claims, nor many other claims of ships sunk by either the 7th or the 19th Bombardment Groups. Shipping targets proved far more difficult to hit from 20,000-25,000 feet than the Army Air Force had estimated prior to the war.

39. Mitchell, *On Wings We Conquer*, pp.79-80; see also U.S. Air Force Historical Study No.29: *Summary of Air Action in the Philippines and Netherlands East Indies 7th December 1941-26th March 1942* (USAF Historical Division, Research Studies Institute, Air University. Maxwell AFB, AL), P.86.
40. Edmonds, Walter D.: *They Fought With What They Had* (Boston: Little, Brown and Company, 1951), P. 300.
41. Dorr, *7th Bombardment Group/Wing 1918-1995*, P.76.
42. Mitchell, *On Wings We Conquer*, P.75.
43. Edmonds, *They Fought With What They Had*, P.300.
44. USAF Historical Study No. 111: *Army Air Action in the Philippines and Netherlands East Indies 1941-1942*, P. 124.
45. Edmonds, *They Fought With What They Had*, P. 304.
46. Edmonds, *They Fought With What They Had*, pP. 304-05; "Unit Diary of Composite 11th Bombardment Squadron Beginning December 14, 1941—March 1942".
47. Edmonds, *They Fought With What They Had*, pP. 304-05; "Unit Diary of Composite 11th Bombardment Squadron Beginning December 14, 1941—March 1942".
48. Pajdosz, Waldemar R. and Andre R. Zbiegniewski: *Kagero Air Minatures No. 20: 3/202 Kokutai* (Lublin, Poland: Kagero Publishing, 2003), pP. 25-26.
49. Pajdosz and Zbiegniewski, *3/202 Kokutai*, P.26.
50. Edmonds, *They Fought With What They Had*, pp.305-06; Dorr, *7th Bombardment Group/Wing 1918-1995*, P. 84.
51. Edmonds, *They Fought With What They Had*, P.306; Pajdosz and Zbiegniewski, *3/202 Kokutai*, P.26.
52. Pajdosz and Zbiegniewski, *3/202 Kokutai*, P.26; "Unit Diary of Composite 11th Bombardment Squadron Beginning December 14, 1941—March 1942".
53. "Unit Diary of Composite 11th Bombardment Squadron Beginning December 14, 1941—March 1942".
54. "Unit Diary of Composite 11th Bombardment Squadron Beginning December 14, 1941—March 1942".
55. Edmonds, *They Fought With What They Had*, pP. 305-07.
56. This information is drawn primarily from "Unit Diary of Composite 11th Bombardment Squadron Beginning December 14, 1941—March 1942" and U.S. Air Force Historical Study No.29: *Summary of Air Action in the Philippines and Netherlands East Indies 7th December 1941-26th March 1942*,pP. 128-29. Data on aircraft arrivals comes from "Aircraft Arrivals in Java from the U.S.", Folder 9, Box 1, MS 60, Series 1, United States Air Force Academy, McDermott Library Collection.
57. Edmonds, *They Fought With What They Had*, P.302 and P.308.
58. Dorr, *7th Bombardment Group/Wing 1918-1995*, P.86.
59. Edmonds, *They Fought With What They Had*, P.302.
60. Edmonds, *They Fought With What They Had*, P.302.
61. Edmonds, *They Fought With What They Had*, P.302.
62. U.S. Air Force Historical Study No.29: *Summary of Air Action in the Philippines and Netherlands East Indies 7th December 1941-26th March 1942*, pp.107-110.
63. Wilmott, *Empires in the Balance*, pp.288, 292.
64. Hata, Ikuhiko, Yasuho Izawa, and Christopher Shores: *Japanese Naval Air Force Fighter Units and Their Aces 1932-1945* (London: Grub Street, 2011), pp.20, 163.
65. Dorr, *7th Bombardment Group/Wing 1918-1995*, P.87.
66. The information on the combat missions comes from U.S. Air Force Historical Study No.29: *Summary of Air Action in the Philippines and Netherlands East Indies 7th December 1941-26th March 1942*, pP. 111-126, and a daily summary of the activities of the V Bomber Command, "V Bomber Command Journal January 13, 1942-March 19, 1942" (hereinafter referred to as "V Bomber Command Journal"), in Folder 7, Box 1, MS 60, Series 1, United States Air Force Academy, McDermott Library Collection.
67. Edmonds, *They Fought With What They Had*, P.310.
68. Edmonds, *They Fought With What They Had*, P.309.
69. "Unit Diary of Composite 11th Bombardment Squadron Beginning December 14, 1941—March 1942".
70. Bartsch, William H.: *Every Day a Nightmare: American Pursuit Pilots in the Defense of Java, 1941-1942* (College Station, TX: Texas A & M University Press, 2010), P.44.
71. Edmonds, *They Fought With What They Had*, pp.176-77.
72. Bartsch, *Every Day a Nightmare*, P.66; "Second Anniversary", in GP-7-HI(Bomb) 1917 to 1947, Albert F. Simpson Historical Research Center, Air Force Historical Research Agency, Maxwell AFB, AL.
73. Edmonds, *They Fought With What They Had*, pP. 309-10; "Second Anniversary".
74. U.S. Air Force Historical Study No.29: *Summary of Air Action in the Philippines and Netherlands East Indies 7th December 1941-26th March 1942*, P.132.
75. U.S. Air Force Historical Study No.29: *Summary of Air Action in the Philippines and Netherlands East Indies 7th December 1941-26th March 1942*, pP. 129-38; "V Bomber Command Journal"; Dorr, *7th Bombardment Group/Wing 1918-1995*, pP. 88-89.
76. Kirby, *The Loss of Singapore*, pP. 347, 349-50.
77. The history of Far East Air Force fighter operations has been told in great detail in William Bartsch's *Every Day a Nightmare: American Pursuit Pilots in the Defense of Java, 1941-1942*.
78. Kirby, *The Loss of Singapore*, P.351.
79. Shores, Christopher, Brian Cull, and Yasuho Izawa: *Bloody Shambles*, Volume Two: *The Defence of Sumatra to the Fall of Burma* (London: Grub Street, 1993), P. 150.
80. Shores, Christopher, Brian Cull, and Yasuho Izawa: *Bloody Shambles*, Volume Two: *The Defence of Sumatra to the Fall of Burma*, P. 150.
81. Shores, et al, *Bloody Shambles*, Volume Two: *The Defence of Sumatra to the Fall of Burma*, pp.151-58; Womack, Tom: *The Dutch Naval Air Force Against Japan: The Defense of the Netherlands East Indies, 1941-1942* (Jefferson, NC: MacFarland and Company, Inc., 2006), P.98; Pajdosz and Zbiegniewski, *3/202 Kokutai*, pP. 29-33; Bartsch, *Every Day a Nightmare*, pP. 115-121.
82. Edmonds, *They Fought With What They Had*, P.313; "19th Bombardment Group History".
83. Shores, et al, *Bloody Shambles*, Volume Two: *The Defence of Sumatra to the Fall of Burma*, pp.156-57.
84. Edmonds, *They Fought With What They Had*, P.313; "19th Bombardment Group History"; U.S. Air Force Historical Study No.29: *Summary of Air Action in the Philippines and Netherlands East Indies 7th December 1941-26th March 1942*, pP. 139-42; "S-3 Diary for the 7th Bombardment Group, December 1 1941-February 27, 1942".
85. "19th Bombardment Group History"; U.S. Air Force Historical Study No.29: *Summary of Air Action in the Philippines and Netherlands East Indies 7th December 1941-26th March 1942*, pP. 139-42; "S-3 Diary for the 7th Bombardment Group, December 1 1941-February 27, 1942"; "Aircraft Arrivals in Java from the U.S.".
86. Hata, Izawa, and Shores: *Japanese Naval Air Force Fighter Units and Their Aces 1932-1945*, P.345.
87. Naoki, Koudachi: *Reisen: Saigo no Shogen (Reisen: The Last Testimony)* (Tokyo: Kojinsha 2011 edition), pp.134-35. A book of reminiscences by former Zero pilots, this book contains a brief description of former Imperial Japanese Navy Ensign Kuniyoshi Tanaka's experiences fighting the B-17s in Java.
88. Shores, et al, *Bloody Shambles*, Volume Two: *The Defence of Sumatra to the Fall of Burma*, pp.160-61.
89. Edmonds, *They Fought With What They Had*, P.329; "V Bomber Command Journal".
90. This and the following paragraph are drawn from Edmonds, *They Fought With What They Had*, P.330-31, the description of the mission of February 8, 1942, in "V Bomber Command Journal", Shores, Christopher, Brian Cull, and Yasuho Izawa: *Bloody Shambles*, Volume Two: *The Defence of Sumatra to the Fall of Burma*, pp.166-67, and Kuniyoshi Tanaka's remembrances in Naoki, Koudachi: *Reisen: Saigo no Shogen (Reisen: The Last Testimony)*, pp.134-35.
91. See Edmonds, *They Fought With What They Had*, P.330-31, the description of the mission of February 8, 1942, in "V Bomber Command Journal", Shores, Christopher, Brian Cull, and Yasuho Izawa: *Bloody Shambles*, Volume Two: *The Defence of Sumatra to the Fall of Burma*, pp.166-67, and Kuniyoshi Tanaka's remembrances in Naoki, Koudachi: *Reisen: Saigo no Shogen (Reisen: The Last Testimony)*, pp.134-35; "S-3 Diary for the 7th Bombardment Group, December 1 1941-February 27, 1942".
92. Edmonds, *They Fought With What They Had*, P. 333.
93. Report on the mission of February 8, 1942, in "V Bomber Command Journal".
94. Report on the mission of February 8, 1942, in "V Bomber Command Journal".
95. Report on the mission of February 8, 1942, in "V Bomber Command Journal".
96"V Bomber Command Journal"; Shores, Cull, and Izawa: *Bloody*

Shambles, Volume Two: *The Defence of Sumatra to the Fall of Burma*, pP. 213-14.

97. "V Bomber Command Journal"; "Aircraft Arrivals in Java from the U.S."
98. U.S. Air Force Historical Study No.29: *Summary of Air Action in the Philippines and Netherlands East Indies 7th December 1941-26th March 1942*, pp.171-190; "V Bomber Command Journal". The details of Captain Strother's suicide come from "S-3 Diary for the 7th Bombardment Group, December 1 1941-February 27, 1942".
99. Edmonds, *They Fought With What They Had*, pp.337.
100. Edmonds, *They Fought With What They Had*, P.334-37
101. Edmonds, *They Fought With What They Had*, P.336.
102. U.S. Air Force Historical Study No.29: *Summary of Air Action in the Philippines and Netherlands East Indies 7th December 1941-26th March 1942*, pp.183-94; "V Bomber Command Journal"; Wilmott, *Empires in the Balance*, pP. 297-300.
103. U.S. Air Force Historical Study No.29: *Summary of Air Action in the Philippines and Netherlands East Indies 7th December 1941-26th March 1942*, pp.199-206; "V Bomber Command Journal"; Edmonds, *They Fought With What They Had*, P. 340; Shores, Cull, and Izawa: *Bloody Shambles*, Volume Two: *The Defence of Sumatra to the Fall of Burma*, pp.196-98.
104. Brereton, Lt. General Louis H.: *The Brereton Diaries: The War in the Air in the Pacific, Middle East, and Europe, 3 October 1941-8 May 1945* (New York, NY: William Morrow and Company, 1946), P.93.
105. Brereton, *The Brereton Diaries*, P.94.
106. Kirby, *The Loss of Singapore*, P.424.
107. Kirby, *The Loss of Singapore*, P.424.
108. Interview with Captain H.C. Smelser, conducted April 6, 8, 9, 1942, and one undated. This interview was one of a series that Walter Edmonds used to prepare his book on the Far East Air Force, *They Fought With What They Had*. The Smelser interview was located in File 168.7022-5, 1941-42, Volume 2, Albert F. Simpson Historical Research Center, Air Force Historical Research Agency, Maxwell AFB, AL.
109. Edmonds, *They Fought With What They Had*, P.364.
110. Smelser interview.
111. U.S. Air Force Historical Study No.29: *Summary of Air Action in the Philippines and Netherlands East Indies 7th December 1941-26th March 1942*, pp.208-16; "V Bomber Command Journal"; Shores, Cull, and Izawa: *Bloody Shambles*, Volume Two: *The Defence of Sumatra to the Fall of Burma*, pP. 174-82, 207-08.
112. Brereton, *The Brereton Diaries*, P.95.
113. Edmonds, *They Fought With What They Had*, P.367.
114. Edmonds, *They Fought With What They Had*, P.362.
115. "V Bomber Command Journal"; Shores, Cull, and Izawa: *Bloody Shambles*, Volume Two: *The Defence of Sumatra to the Fall of Burma*, pP. 213-14.
116. "V Bomber Command Journal"; Shores, Cull, and Izawa: *Bloody Shambles*, Volume Two: *The Defence of Sumatra to the Fall of Burma*, pP. 219 20; U.S. Air Force Historical Study No.29: *Summary of Air Action in the Philippines and Netherlands East Indies 7th December 1941-26th March 1942*, pp.223-26.
117. Craven and Cate, Vol. One, *Plans and Early Operations*, P. 395-97.
118. Brereton, *The Brereton Diaries*,P.97.
119. Brereton, *The Brereton Diaries*, P.98.
120. Edmonds, *They Fought With What They Had*, P.402.
121. Kirby, *The Loss of Singapore*, P.429.
122. Edmonds, *They Fought With What They Had*, pp.368-69.
123. Brereton, *The Brereton Diaries*, P.99.
124. Edmonds, *They Fought With What They Had*, pp.370.
125. "V Bomber Command Journal"; Shores, Cull, and Izawa: *Bloody Shambles*, Volume Two: *The Defence of Sumatra to the Fall of Burma*, pP. 221-26; U.S. Air Force Historical Study No.29: *Summary of Air Action in the Philippines and Netherlands East Indies 7th December 1941 26th March 1942*, pp.227-36.
126. Edmonds, *They Fought With What They Had*, pp.404 15. Edmunds describes the evacuation of the ground echelons of the Far East Air Force in detail.
127. Kirby, *The Loss of Singapore*, pp.434-35.
128. "V Bomber Command Journal"; Shores, Cull, and Izawa: *Bloody Shambles*, Volume Two: *The Defence of Sumatra to the Fall of Burma*, pP. 233-41; U.S. Air Force Historical Study No.29: *Summary of Air Action in the Philippines and Netherlands East Indies 7th December 1941-26th March 1942*, pp.237-44.
129. Shores, Cull, and Izawa: *Bloody Shambles*, Volume Two: *The Defence of Sumatra to the Fall of Burma*, pP. 243.
130. Smelser interview.
131. Smelser interview.
132. Edmonds, *They Fought With What They Had*, P.431.
133. Bartsch, *Every Day a Nightmare*, P. 317.
134. Bartsch, *Every Day a Nightmare*, pp.319-20.
135. Edmonds, *They Fought With What They Had*, pp.430-31.
136. Bartsch, *Every Day a Nightmare*, pp.320.
137. Bartsch, *Every Day a Nightmare*, pp.320.
138. Bartsch, *Every Day a Nightmare*, pp.320; Smelser interview.
139. Dorr, *7th Bombardment Group/Wing 1918-1995*, P.95.
140. Wilmott, *Empires in the Balance*, P.361.
141. Wilmott, *Empires in the Balance*, P.334.
142. USAF Historical Study No. 111: *Army Air Action in the Philippines and Netherlands East Indies 1941-1942*, P.178.
143. These estimates are from Wilmott, *Empires in the Balance*, American and British official histories of the campaigns, and data from articles on the campaigns in Wikpedia.
144. Wilmott, *Empires in the Balance*, P.436.
145. USAF Historical Study No. 111: *Army Air Action in the Philippines and Netherlands East Indies 1941-1942*, P.195.
146. USAF Historical Study No. 111: *Army Air Action in the Philippines and Netherlands East Indies 1941-1942*, P.200.
147. USAF Historical Study No. 111: *Army Air Action in the Philippines and Netherlands East Indies 1941-1942*, P.201.
148. "History of the Tenth Air Force Headquarters for the Calendar Year 1942", File 830.1 Tenth Air Force History 1942, Albert F. Simpson Historical Research Center, Air Force Historical Research Agency, Maxwell AFB, AL.
149. "V Bomber Command Journal".
150. Craven and Cate, Vol. One, *Plans and Early Operations*, P.413; Mitchell, *In Alis Vicimus-On Wings We Conquer*, pP. 101,103.
151. Mitchell, *In Alis Vicimus-On Wings We Conquer*, pP. 103-4.
152. *The New York Times*, December 9, 1942; Maurer, *Air Force Combat Units of WWII*, P.67.

Chapter Four: India and the Tenth Air Force

1. Craven and Cate, Vol. One, *Plans and Early Operations*, pp.388, 395.
2. Craven and Cate, Vol. One, *Plans and Early Operations*, P.492.
3. Wilmott, *Empires in the Balance*, pp.419-21; Kirby, Major-General S. Woodburn: *The War Against Japan*, Volume II: *India's Most Dangerous Hour*, (London: Her Majesty's Stationary Office, 1958), pP. 79-104 on the evacuation of Rangoon.
4. Kirby, *India's Most Dangerous Hour*, pP. 150-51, 156-7, 195.
5. Romanus, Charles F., and Riley Sunderland: *Stilwell's Mission to China*, United States Army in WWII: China-Burma-India Theater, (Washington, D.C.: Office of the Chief of Military History, Department of the Army, 1953), pP. 7-21; Dallek, *Franklin Roosevelt and American Foreign Policy, 1932-1945*, P.273.
6. Romanus, Charles F., and Riley Sunderland: *Stilwell's Mission to China*, pP. 29-31.
7. Romanus, Charles F., and Riley Sunderland: *Stilwell's Mission to China*, P.49.
8. Wilmott, *Empires in the Balance*, P.73; Dallek, *Franklin Roosevelt and American Foreign Policy, 1932-1945*, pp.328-32.
9. Romanus, Charles F., and Riley Sunderland: *Stilwell's Mission to China*, pP. 61-63.
10. Craven and Cate, Vol. One, *Plans and Early Operations*, P. 493; Romanus, Charles F., and Riley Sunderland: *Stilwell's Mission to China*, pp.78-79; Pound, Merritt B.: *History of the United States Army Air Forces, India-Burma Sector, China-Burma-India Theater (From Activation through April 1944)* (Pound Report), File 825.0115, Albert F. Simpson Historical Research Center, Air Force Historical Research Agency, Maxwell AFB, AL., P.9.
11. Lt. General Henry Arnold, Deputy Chief of Staff for Air, to Colonel Caleb V. Haynes, February 21, 1942, in File 830.1, Tenth Air Force, February 1942-March 1943, Albert F. Simpson Historical Research Center, Air Force Historical Research Agency, Maxwell AFB, AL., P.9.
12. Craven and Cate, Vol. One, *Plans and Early Operations*, P. 493; Romanus, Charles F., and Riley Sunderland: *Stilwell's Mission to China*, pp.78-79.
13. Craven and Cate, Vol. One, *Plans and Early Operations*, P. 493.

14. Pound Report, P.3.
15. U.S. Air Force Historical Study No. 12: *The Tenth Air Force 1942*, (USAF Historical Division, Research Studies Institute, Air University. Maxwell AFB, AL, 1944), P.12.
16. U.S. Air Force Historical Study No. 12: *The Tenth Air Force 1942*, pp.11-17 discusses these and other problems the Tenth Air Forced faced in India.
17. Kirby, *India's Most Dangerous Hour*, P.213.
18. "Consolidated History of the Seventh Bombardment Group (H), AFF, Ground and Air Echelons for the Year 1942", Headquarters 7th Bombardment Group (H) AAF, GP-7-HI(Bomb) Year 1942 Pt-1, Albert F. Simpson Historical Research Center, Air Force Historical Research Agency, Maxwell AFB, AL; Mayhew, personal memoir.
19. "Consolidated History of the Seventh Bombardment Group (H), AFF, Ground and Air Echelons for the Year 1942".
20. Mayhew memoir, P.11; Scott, Colonel Robert L.: *God is My Co-pilot* (New York, NY: Charles Scribner's & Sons, 1943), pP. 50, 82-3.
21. Mayhew memoir, P.11.
22. U.S. Air Force Historical Study No. 12: *The Tenth Air Force 1942*, P.23.
23. U.S. Air Force Historical Study No. 12: *The Tenth Air Force 1942*, P.21.
24. U.S. Air Force Historical Study No. 12: *The Tenth Air Force 1942*, P.21.
25. "Unit History Covering Period From June 26, 1917 to June 1, 1943", 11th Bombardment Squadron (M), 341st Bombardment Group (M), SQ-11-HI-16 June 1917-May 1943; "Historical Data, 22nd Bombardment Squadron (M), 341st Bombardment Group (M)" SQ-22-HI-November 1938-December 1943, Albert F. Simpson Historical Research Center, Air Force Historical Research Agency, Maxwell AFB, AL.
26. "Unit History Covering Period From June 26, 1917 to June 1, 1943", 11th Bombardment Squadron (M), 341st Bombardment Group (M), SQ-11-HI-16 June 1917-May 1943; "Historical Data, 22nd Bombardment Squadron (M), 341st Bombardment Group (M)" SQ-22-HI-November 1938-December 1943.
27. Probert, Air Commodore Henry: *The Forgotten Air Force: The Royal Air Force in the War Against Japan 1941-1945*, (London: Brassey's, 1995), pp.90-94.
28. Brereton, *The Brereton Diaries*, P.113.
29. Brereton, *The Brereton Diaries*, pp.114-15.
30. "History of the Tenth Air Force Headquarters for the Calendar Year 1942".
31. Dorr, *7th Bombardment Group/Wing 1918-1995*, P.120.
32. Brereton, *The Brereton Diaries*, pp.116-17.
33. Brereton, *The Brereton Diaries*, pp.117-18; Rowan, Captain Thomas T.: *Born in Battle: Round the World Adventures of the 513th Bombardment Squadron* (Philadelphia, PA: The John C. Winston Company, 1944), P.69.
34. "U.S. Air Attacks-By Date, April-October 1942", File 830.308-4 2 April 1942-31 July 1942, Albert F. Simpson Historical Research Center, Air Force Historical Research Agency, Maxwell AFB, AL.
35. Rowan, *Born in Battle*, P.70.
36. Rowan, *Born in Battle*, P.73.
37. Rowan, *Born in Battle*, pp.81-82.
38. "Consolidated History of the Seventh Bombardment Group (H),
39. Mayhew Memoir, P.13.
40. Form Orange 2 (Bomber), dated 14/5/42, in Allied Air Forces-Reports on Raids, Air 23/5062, Air Ministry and Ministry of Defence: Royal Air Force Overseas Commands: Reports and Correspondence, Public Records Office, United Kingdom.
41. The information about the 9th Squadron's bombing missions during May 1942 comes from "U.S. Air Attacks-By Date, April-October 1942"; "Bombing Operations 1941-1942 by R.A.F. and U.S.A.A.F. Units Based in India and Burma", Air Command, South East Asia, Bombing Operations Air 23/2855, Air Ministry and Ministry of Defence: Royal Air Force Overseas Commands: Reports and Correspondence, the National Archives, Kew, United Kingdom; and "History- 9th Bombardment Squadron (H) 1942", SQ-Bomb-9-HI-Jan-Dec 1942. There is some discrepancy among these three sources, but "Bombing Operations 1941-1942", seems to have the most details.
42. Romanus and Sunderland. *Stilwell's Mission to China*, P.143. For the retreat from Burma see *Stilwell's Mission to China*, pP. 125-48, and Kirby, *India's Most Dangerous Hour*, pP. 199-220.
43. Kirby, *India's Most Dangerous Hour*, P.220.
44. "Consolidated History of the Seventh Bombardment Group (H), AFF, Ground and Air Echelons for the Year 1942"; "Operations of the Tenth Air Force 12 Feb 1942-Jan 43", File 830.306 12 Feb 1942-Jan 1943, Albert F. Simpson Historical Research Center, Air Force Historical Research Agency, Maxwell AFB, AL.
45. This account of the mission comes from Rowan, *Born in Battle*, pp.118-126.
46. Shores, Christopher: *Air War Over Burma: The Allied Air Forces Fight Back in South-east Asia 1942-1945* (London: Grub Street, 2005), P. 16.
47. Shores, *Air War Over Burma: The Allied Air Forces Fight Back in South-east Asia 1942-1945*, P.16.
48. Rowan, *Born in Battle*, pp.118-126; Dorr, *7th Bombardment Group/ Wing 1918-1995*, P. 125.
49. "Bombing Operations 1941-1942 by R.A.F. and U.S.A.A.F. Units Based in India and Burma".
50. "Operations of the Tenth Air Force 12 Feb 1942-Jan 43".
51. *The Record: The 11th Bombardment Squadron (M)* (Richmond, VA: 1947), P.36.
52. *The Record: The 11th Bombardment Squadron (M)*, P.36; "Bombing Operations 1941-1942 by R.A.F. and U.S.A.A.F. Units Based in India and Burma".
53. "Historical Data, 22nd Bombardment Squadron (M) AAF, 341st Bombardment Group (M) AAF, Squadron History", SQ-Bomb-22-HI-Nov 1938-Dec 1943, Albert F. Simpson Historical Research Center, Air Force Historical Research Agency, Maxwell AFB, AL; Dorr, *7th Bombardment Group/Wing 1918-1995*, P.125.
54. Brereton, *The Brereton Diaries*, pP. 130-31; Craven and Cate, Vol. One, *Plans and Early Operations*, pp.512-13.
55. Porch, Douglas: *Hitler's Mediterranean Gamble: The North African and Mediterranean Campaigns in WWII* (London: Weidenfeld & Nicolson, 2004), pP. 265-85.
56. Craven and Cate, Vol. One, *Plans and Early Operations*, P. 512.
57. "Operations of the Tenth Air Force 12 Feb 1942-Jan 43". This document states that only eight B-17s went to the Middle East, but Wilbur Mayhew recalls that twelve B-17s went out from Karachi.
58. "Operations of the Tenth Air Force 12 Feb 1942-Jan 43".
59. Mayhew Memoir, P.16.
60. Craven, Wesley Frank, and James Lea Cate, Eds.: *The Army Air Forces in WWII*, Volume Two: *Europe: Torch to Pointblank, (August 1942 to December 1943)* (Chicago, IL: University of Chicago Press, 1949), P.10.
61. "Chronological Historical Record Ninth Air Force Aug 42-Aug 43", File 533.052, Part 1, Aug1942-Aug 1943; "History 9th Bombardment Squadron (H) 1942", File SQ-Bomb-9-HI-Jan-Dec 1942, Albert F. Simpson Historical Research Center, Air Force Historical Research Agency, Maxwell AFB, AL.
62. Craven and Cate, *Europe: Torch to Pointblank*, P.20.
63. Craven and Cate, *Europe: Torch to Pointblank*, P.20.
64. Walker, James W.: *The Liberandos: A WWII History of the 376th Bombardment Group and its Founding Units* (Waco, TX: 376th Heavy Bombardment Group Veterans Association, Inc. 1994), P.64.
65. Walker, *The Liberandos*, P.68.
66. "Chronological Historical Record Ninth Air Force Aug 42-Aug 43"; "History 9th Bombardment Squadron 1942".
67. "Chronological Historical Record Ninth Air Force Aug 42-Aug 43"; "History 9th Bombardment Squadron 1942".
68. Walker, *The Liberandos*, P.73.
69. U.S. Air Force Historical Study No. 8: *The AAF in the Middle East: A Study in the Origins of the Ninth Air Force* , (USAF Historical Division, Research Studies Institute, Air University. Maxwell AFB, AL, 1945), P.85.
70. "History 9th Bombardment Squadron 1942".
71. Walker, *The Liberandos*, pp.73-74.
72. "Operations of the Tenth Air Force 12 Feb 1942-Jan 43".
73. Freeman, Roger A.: *B-17 Flying Fortress at War* (New York, NY: Charles Scribner's and Sons, 1977), P.24.
74. "Operations of the Tenth Air Force 12 Feb 1942-Jan 43"; "Bombing Operations 1941-1942 by R.A.F. and U.S.A.A.F. Units Based in India and Burma".
75. "Operations of the Tenth Air Force 12 Feb 1942-Jan 43"; "Bombing Operations 1941-1942 by R.A.F. and U.S.A.A.F. Units Based in India and Burma"; *The Record: The 11th Bombardment Squadron (M).*
76. Craven and Cate, *Plans and Early Operations*, pp.566-69.
77. Craven and Cate, *Plans and Early Operations*, P.569.

78. Craven, Wesley F. and James L. Cate: *The Army Air Forces in WWII*, Volume Four, *The Pacific: Guadalcanal to Saipan August 1942 to July 1944* (Chicago, IL: The University of Chicago Press, 1950), p.420.
79. Craven and Cate, *The Pacific: Guadalcanal to Saipan*, P.420; Beauvais, Charles J.: *Plum to Dacca* (Privately published, 1986), P. 37.
80. Craven and Cate, *The Pacific: Guadalcanal to Saipan*, P.420.
81. Beauvais, *Plum to Dacca*, pP. 64-65.
82. See "Tenth Air Force Operational Diary", File 830.305-1, 1 June 1942-1 June 1943, Albert F. Simpson Historical Research Center, Air Force Historical Research Agency, Maxwell AFB, AL, entry for September 24, 1942.
83. "Operations of the Tenth Air Force 12 Feb 1942-Jan 43".
84. Captain James E. Tull interview, in McCulloch and Hubbard Interviews, #1 (Nos. 1-25), File 168.2022-5 1941-42 V.1, Albert F. Simpson Historical Research Center, Air Force Historical Research Agency, Maxwell AFB, AL. Walter Edmonds drew on these interviews for his book *They Fought With What They Had*.
85. Beauvais, *Plum to Dacca*, P.56.
86. "Consolidated History of the Seventh Bombardment Group (H), AFF, Ground and Air Echelons for the Year 1942"; "History 436th Bombardment Squadron (H) 1942 and 1 January 1943 to 31 May 1943", SQ-Bomb-436-HI Jan-May 1943, Albert F. Simpson Historical Research Center, Air Force Historical Research Agency, Maxwell AFB, AL.
87. Craven and Cate, *The Pacific: Guadalcanal to Saipan*, P.414.
88. Craven and Cate, *The Pacific: Guadalcanal to Saipan*, pP. 431-32.
89. "Consolidated History of the Seventh Bombardment Group (H), AFF, Ground and Air Echelons for the Year 1942"; "History 436th Bombardment Squadron (H) 1942 and 1 January 1943 to 31 May 1943"; "History of the 492nd Bombardment Squadron (H), 7th Bombardment Group (H), AAF, for the Year 1942", SQ-Bomb-492-HI Jan 1942-May 43"; "History 493rd Bombardment Squadron (H) 1942 and 1 January 1943 to 31 May 1943", SQ-Bomb-493-HI Oct 42-May 43, Albert F. Simpson Historical Research Center, Air Force Historical Research Agency, Maxwell AFB, AL.

Chapter Five: India Air Task Force

1. Howard, Michael: *History of the Second World War: Grand Strategy*, Volume IV: *August 1942-September 1943* (London: Her Majesty's Stationary Office, 1970), P. 79.
2. Kirby, *India's Most Dangerous Hour*, P.426.
3. Kirby, *India's Most Dangerous Hour*, P.427.
4. Howard, *Grand Strategy*, Volume IV: *August 1942-September 1943*, P.83; Romanus and Sunderland, *Stilwell's Mission to China*, P.201.
5. Howard, *Grand Strategy*, Volume IV: *August 1942-September 1943*, P.101. See also Romanus and Sunderland, *Stilwell's Mission to China*, Part Two, Chapters V-VIII.
6. Howard, *Grand Strategy*, Volume IV: *August 1942-September 1943*, P.95; Romanus and Sunderland, *Stilwell's Mission to China*, pp.178-79.
7. Romanus and Sunderland, *Stilwell's Mission to China*, pp.32-36, 89-90, 183-84, 186.
8. Howard, *Grand Strategy*, Volume IV: *August 1942-September 1943*, P.104.
9. Howard, *Grand Strategy*, Volume IV: *August 1942-September 1943*, P.104.
10. Howard, *Grand Strategy*, Volume IV: *August 1942-September 1943*, pp.83-87.
11. Howard, *Grand Strategy*, Volume IV: *August 1942-September 1943*, P. 438.
12. Howard, *Grand Strategy*, Volume IV: *August 1942-September 1943*, pp.83-87, 99-101, 399-401.
13. Howard, *Grand Strategy*, Volume IV: *August 1942-September 1943*, pp.437-47, 571-80; Romanus and Sunderland, *Stilwell's Mission to China*, pP. 320-41, 355-59.
14. Craven and Cate, *The Pacific: Guadalcanal to Saipan*, pp.460-61.
15. Romanus and Sunderland, *Stilwell's Mission to China*, P.201.
16. Romanus and Sunderland, *Stilwell's Mission to China*, P.201.
17. Air Officer Commanding-in-Chief, Air Forces in India, to Air Officer Commanding, Bengal, 18 October 1942, "Bombing Policy in N.E. India Winter 1942/43: Directive to Air Officer Commanding, Bengal", Air Command, South East Asia, Bombing Targets-Policy, Air 23/2413, Air Ministry and Ministry of Defence: Royal Air Force Overseas Commands: Reports and Correspondence, the National Archives, Kew, United Kingdom;
18. Air Historical Branch (1), Air Ministry: *R.A.F. Narrative: The Campaigns in the Far East*, Volume III, *India Command: September 1939 to November 1943* (London: Royal Air Force Air Force Centre for Air Power Studies, MLRS Books edition), pP. 115-16.
19. Brigadier General Clayton Bissell, Commanding General, Tenth Air Force, to Brigadier General C.V. Haynes, Commanding General, India Air Task Force, October 2, 1942, copy in "History of United States Army Air Forces, India-Burma Sector, China-India-Burma Theater", File 825.0115 20 Aug 1943-Apr 1944, Albert F. Simpson Historical Research Center, Air Force Historical Research Agency, Maxwell AFB, AL, entry for September 24, 1942.
20. War Department: *Air Corps Field Manual: Tactics and Technique of Air Attack* (Washington, D.C.: Government Printing Office, 1940), P.2.
21. Walker, Lt. Kenneth N.: "Bombardment Aviation—Bulwark of National Defense", *U.S. Air Services*, Vol. XVIII, No. 8, August, 1933, P.15.
22. Craven and Cate, *The Pacific: Guadalcanal to Saipan*, P.469.
23. Craven and Cate, *The Pacific: Guadalcanal to Saipan*, pp.468-76.
24. Craven and Cate, *The Pacific: Guadalcanal to Saipan*, P.430.
25. Mayhew, *Battlefields Galore*, P. 21.
26. Mayhew, William: "The China Trip for the Linsi (Lin-hsi) Mine Raid", no date, 7th Bombardment Group (H) Historical Foundation, Folder 19, Box 3, MS 60, Series 1, United States Air Force Academy, McDermott Library Collection.
27. Mayhew, "The China Trip for the Linsi (Lin-hsi) Mine Raid".
28. Cunningham, Sgt. Ed: "Jinx Flight: Nine Men Played Peek-a-Boo with Death Over Rangoon-And Lived to Tell the Tale", *Yank*, January 20, 1943, pP. 20-21.
29. Craven and Cate, *The Pacific: Guadalcanal to Saipan*, pp.475-76.
30. Craven and Cate, *The Pacific: Guadalcanal to Saipan*, pp.475.
31. "Tenth Air Force Operational Diary", File 830.305-1 1 June 1942-1 June 1943, Albert F. Simpson Historical Research Center, Air Force Historical Research Agency, Maxwell AFB, AL, entries for November 6 and 9, 1942.
32. "Consolidated History of the Seventh Bombardment Group (H), AFF, Ground and Air Echelons for the Year 1942"; "Operations of the Tenth Air Force 12 Feb 1942-Jan 43"; *The Tenth Air Force 1942*, P.121.
33. "Tenth Air Force Operational Diary", entry for November 20 and 22, 1942; "Headquarters India Air Task Force 1942 & 1 January to 31 May 1943", File 827.01 30 October 1942-May 1943, Albert F. Simpson Historical Research Center, Air Force Historical Research Agency, Maxwell AFB, AL.
34. *The New York Times*, November 27, 1942, P.6.
35. "Tenth Air Force Operational Diary", entry for November 27, 1942; "History 436th Bombardment Squadron 1942 & 1 January 1943 to 31 May 1943", SQ-Bomb-436-HI Jan-May 1943, Albert F. Simpson Historical Research Center, Air Force Historical Research Agency, Maxwell AFB, AL.
36. Shores, *Air War Over Burma*, P.36.
37. "Tenth Air Force Operational Diary", entry for November 27, 1942; "History 436th Bombardment Squadron (H) 1942 & 1 January 1943 to 31 May 1943", SQ-Bomb-436-HI Jan-May 1943.
38. "Tenth Air Force Operational Diary", entry for December 4, 1942; "History 436th Bombardment Squadron (H) 1942 & 1 January 1943 to 31 May 1943", SQ-Bomb-436-HI Jan-May 1943.
39. "Tenth Air Force Operational Diary", entry for December 4, 1942; "History 436th Bombardment Squadron (H) 1942 & 1 January 1943 to 31 May 1943",
40. Probert, *The Forgotten Air Force: The Royal Air Force in the War Against Japan 1941-1945*, P.214.
41. "Consolidated History of the Seventh Bombardment Group (H), AFF, Ground and Air Echelons for the Year 1942"; Beauvais, *Plum to Dacca*, pP. 49-54, 63-64.
42. Interview with Colonel Thomas E. Sledge, U.S.A.F. (Ret'd), October 2 and October 7, 2010.
43. "Tenth Air Force Operational Diary", entries for December 22 and 23, 1942; Sledge interview.
44. Sledge interview.
45. *The New York Times*, December 29, 1942, P.4.
46. *CBI Roundup*, Vol. I, No.16, December 31, 1942.
47. "Tenth Air Force Operational Diary", entry for January 1, 1943; "History 436th Bombardment Squadron (H) 1942 & 1 January 1943 to 31 May 1943".

48. "Tenth Air Force Operational Diary", commentary for November-December 1942.
49. "Tenth Air Force Operational Diary", commentary for November-December 1942.
50. U.S. Air Force Historical Study No. 12: *The Tenth Air Force 1942*, P. 128.
51. U.S. Air Force Historical Study No. 104: *The Tenth Air Force 1942 1 January-10 March 1943*, (USAF Historical Division, Research Studies Institute, Air University. Maxwell AFB, AL), P. 1.
52. Kirby, *India's Most Dangerous Hour*, P. 299-302.
53. "Tenth Air Force Operational Diary", entries for January 6, 11, 12, 1943.
54. Sledge interview.
55. "Tenth Air Force Operational Diary", entry for January 18, 1943.
56. "History 492nd Bombardment Squadron (H) 1 January 1943 to 31 May 1943", SQ-Bomb-492-HI Jan 42-May 43; "History 493rd Bombardment Squadron (H) 1 January 1943 to 31 May 1943", SQ-Bomb-493-HI Oct 42-May 43, Albert F. Simpson Historical Research Center, Air Force Historical Research Agency, Maxwell AFB, AL.
57. "History 492nd Bombardment Squadron (H) 1 January 1943 to 31 May 1943"; Sledge interview.
58. Anabuki, Satoru: *Aozora no Kawa: Anabuki Gunso Hayabusa Kusen (The Blue Sky River: Sergeant Anabuki's Hayabusa Air Battle Chronicle)* (Tokyo: Kojinsha, 1985), pp.294-99; Shores: *Air War Over Burma: The Allied Air Forces Fight Back in South-east Asia 1942-1945*, P.55.
59. "History 493rd Bombardment Squadron (H) 1 January 1943 to 31 May 1943".
60. "History 493rd Bombardment Squadron (H) 1 January 1943 to 31 May 1943"; "Tenth Air Force Operational Diary", entries for January 26, 1943.
61. Memorandum from Brigadier General C.V. Haynes to Lt. General Arnold, February 9, 1943, File 827.306-2, 9 Feb 1943, Albert F. Simpson Historical Research Center, Air Force Historical Research Agency, Maxwell AFB, AL.
62. U.S. Air Force Historical Study No. 104: *The Tenth Air Force 1942 1 January-10 March 1943*, P. 41.
63. U.S. Air Force Historical Study No. 104: *The Tenth Air Force 1942 1 January-10 March 1943*, pp.20-21; "Tenth Air Force Operational Diary", entries for January 10 and 12, 1943.
64. "Tenth Air Force Operational Diary", entries for January 22, 1943.
65. U.S. Air Force Historical Study No. 104: *The Tenth Air Force 1942 1 January-10 March 1943*, P.46.
66. "Tenth Air Force Operational Diary", entries for February 12, 15, 25, 1943; "History 436th Bombardment Squadron (H) 1 January 1943 to 31 May 1943"; "History 492nd Bombardment Squadron (H) 1 January 1943 to 31 May 1943"; "History 493rd Bombardment Squadron (H) 1 January 1943 to 31 May 1943".
67. Craven and Cate, *The Pacific: Guadalcanal to Saipan*, pp.488-89.
68. "Tenth Air Force Operational Diary", entries for March 24, 1943; ; "History 436th Bombardment Squadron (H) 1 January 1943 to 31 May 1943"; "History 492nd Bombardment Squadron (H) 1 January 1943 to 31 May 1943"; "History 493rd Bombardment Squadron (H) 1 January 1943 to 31 May 1943".
69. Craven and Cate, *The Pacific: Guadalcanal to Saipan*, pp.484-85.
70. Craven and Cate, *The Pacific: Guadalcanal to Saipan*, P.489.
71. Craven and Cate, *The Pacific: Guadalcanal to Saipan*, P.489.
72. "Tenth Air Force Operational Diary", entries for February 20 and March 21, 1943; ; "History 436th Bombardment Squadron (H) 1 January 1943 to 31 May 1943"; "History 492nd Bombardment Squadron (H) 1 January 1943 to 31 May 1943"; "History 493rd Bombardment Squadron (H) 1 January 1943 to 31 May 1943".
73. "Tenth Air Force Operational Diary", entry for February 27, 1943; "History 436th Bombardment Squadron (H) 1 January 1943 to 31 May 1943".
74. "Tenth Air Force Operational Diary", entries for February 27, March 3, 10, 18, April 17, 1943; ; "History 436th Bombardment Squadron (H) 1 January 1943 to 31 May 1943"; "History 492nd Bombardment Squadron (H) 1 January 1943 to 31 May 1943"; "History 493rd Bombardment Squadron (H) 1 January 1943 to 31 May 1943".
75. McFarland, *America's Pursuit of Precision Bombing, 1910-1945*, P. 170.
76. McFarland, *America's Pursuit of Precision Bombing, 1910-1945*, P. 169-70.
77. McFarland, *America's Pursuit of Precision Bombing, 1910-1945*, P. 224-225.
78. Craven and Cate, *The Pacific: Guadalcanal to Saipan*, P.492.
79. Craven and Cate, *The Pacific: Guadalcanal to Saipan*, P.473.
80. Colonel Harold Wright, A-2, Tenth Air Force, to Commanding General, Tenth Air Force, January 13, 1943, Project Low, File 830.322-6, Jan-Mar 1943, Albert F. Simpson Historical Research Center, Air Force Historical Research Agency, Maxwell AFB, AL.
81. See Colonel Wright to General Bissell, January 28, 1943, "Mining of RANGOON RIVER"; Colonel Harold Wright, A-2, to General Bissell, January 29, 1943; General Bissell to A-2, January 31, 1943; Colonel Wright to General Bissell, "Project Low", February 1, and 11, 1943, Project Low, File 830.322-6, Jan-Mar 1943, Albert F. Simpson Historical Research Center, Air Force Historical Research Agency, Maxwell AFB, AL.
82. "Tenth Air Force Operational Diary", entries for February 22, 1943; ; "History 436th Bombardment Squadron (H) 1 January 1943 to 31 May 1943"; "History 492nd Bombardment Squadron (H) 1 January 1943 to 31 May 1943"; "History 493rd Bombardment Squadron (H) 1 January 1943 to 31 May 1943"; Colonel Harold Wright to Brigadier General Bissell, March 6, 1943, "Follow up of "Low" Project", Project Low, File 830.322-6, Jan-Mar 1943, Albert F. Simpson Historical Research Center, Air Force Historical Research Agency, Maxwell AFB, AL.
83. "History 436th Bombardment Squadron (H) 1 January 1943 to 31 May 1943"; "History 492nd Bombardment Squadron (H) 1 January 1943 to 31 May 1943"; "History 493rd Bombardment Squadron (H) 1 January 1943 to 31 May 1943".
84. Shores, *Air War Over Burma*, pp.56-7; Kirby, *India's Most Dangerous Hour*, P.451; Hata, Izawa, and Shores: *Japanese Army Air Force Fighter Units and Their Aces 1931-1945*, pP. 141-44, 156-59.
85. Kuroe, Yasuhiko: *Ah, Hayabusa Sentotai* (Ah, the Hayabusa Fighter Unit) (Tokyo: Kojinsha, 1984), pp.181-82.
86. In his book *Air War Over Burma*, Christopher Shores states that the *64th Sentai* returned to Burma from Japan on February 10, 1943, but as he also states that the *50th Sentai* withdrew from Burma to re-equip with the Ki-43-II on February 4, 1943, it seems more likely that the Oscar fighters that intercepted the 436th Squadron on this date came from the *64th Sentai* and not the *50th*.
87. "History 436th Bombardment Squadron (H) 1 January 1943 to 31 May 1943".
88. This mission on February 12 is something of a conundrum. The "Tenth Air Force Operational Diary" carries a detailed description of the mission in its entry for February 12, 1943, but the 492nd Squadron history does not mention it. The Squadron's history for 1 January to 31 May 1943 does, however, contain a chart of ammunition expenditure for the first quarter of 1943 which lists the expenditure of 4,000 rounds during the mission of February 12, as well as dropping 45 500 pound bombs on the mission, which tallies with the Tenth Air Force Operational Diary. I have proceeded on the assumption that the Tenth Air Force Operational Diary is correct, and for some reason the mission of February 12 simply missed inclusion in the 492nd Squadron's records.
89. "Tenth Air Force Operational Diary", entries for February 22, 1943; ; "History 436th Bombardment Squadron (H) 1 January 1943 to 31 May 1943"; "History 492nd Bombardment Squadron (H) 1 January 1943 to 31 May 1943"; "History 493rd Bombardment Squadron (H) 1 January 1943 to 31 May 1943".
90. Izawa, Yasuho: "64th Flying Sentai, Part 2", *Aero Album*, Vol. 4, No. 3 (Fall 1971), P.7.
91. "Tenth Air Force Operational Diary", entry for March 10, 1943; "History 492nd Bombardment Squadron (H) 1 January 1943 to 31 May 1943".
92. "Tenth Air Force Operational Diary", entry for March 12, 1943; "History 436th Bombardment Squadron (H) 1 January 1943 to 31 May 1943".
93. "Tenth Air Force Operational Diary", entry for March 13, 1943; *CBI Roundup*, Vol. I, No. 28, March 25, 1943, P.1.
94. Shores, *Air War Over Burma*, pp.76-7; "History 493rd Bombardment Squadron (H) 1 January 1943 to 31 May 1943".
95. Shores, *Air War Over Burma*, P.77; Dorr, *7th Bombardment Group/ Wing 1918-1995*, pp.153, 155.
96. Hinoki, Yohei: *Tsubasa no Kessen: Kaerazaru Hayabusa* (The Bloody War of Wings: Hayabusa Fighting Unit of No Return) (Tokyo: Kojinsha, 1984), P.179.

97. Kuroe, *Ah, Hayabusa Sentotai*, pP. 251-55; Miyabe, Hideo: *Kato Hayabusa Sentotai no Saigo* (Last Days of the Kato Hayabusa Sentai) (Tokyo: Kojinsha, 1986), pP. 46-50.
98. *Air Corps Field Manual FM 1-10: Tactics and Technique of Air Attack*, P. 8.
99. *Air Corps Field Manual FM 1-10: Tactics and Technique of Air Attack*, P. 69.
100. See Freeman, Roger A.: *Mighty Eighth War Diary* (New York, NY: Jane's Publishing Incorporated, 1981), P.152, the date for the December 10, 1943 mission to Bremen which saw 631 bombers take off from 23 bomb groups.
101. United States. Army Air ForcE. Intelligence ServicE. *Informational Intelligence Summary*, No. 44-7, 29 February 1944 (Washington, D.C.: U.S. Army Air Forces, 1944), P. 3.
102. *Informational Intelligence Summary*, No. 44-7, 29 February 1944 P. 4.
103. *Informational Intelligence Summary*, No. 44-7, 29 February 1944 P. 3.
104. Duncan, Charles V., Jr.: *B-24 Over Burma* (privately published 1986), pp.59-60.
105. "Tenth Air Force Operational Diary", entries for April 17, 19, 21, 22, 26, 1943; "History 492nd Bombardment Squadron (H) 1 January 1943 to 31 May 1943".
106. Shores, *Air War Over Burma*, P.86; "History 492nd Bombardment Squadron (H) 1 January 1943 to 31 May 1943"; Dorr, *7th Bombardment Group/Wing 1918-1995*, P.239.
107. Perez, Alfonso B.: *A B-24 Bombardier 'Over Burma': The Personal Diary of Lt. Alfonso B. Perez* (Privately published) copy in Folder 26, Box 3, MS 60, Series 1, 7th Bombardment Group (H) Historical Foundation, United States Air Force Academy, McDermott Library Collection, pP. 22-24.
108. Shores, *Air War Over Burma*, P.89; "Tenth Air Force Operational Diary", entries for May 8, 11, 1943; "History 436th Bombardment Squadron (H) 1 January 1943 to 31 May 1943"; "History 492nd Bombardment Squadron (H) 1 January 1943 to 31 May 1943".
109. *R.A.F. Narrative: The Campaigns in the Far East*, Volume III, *India Command: September 1939 to November 1943*, P.83.
110. *R.A.F. Narrative: The Campaigns in the Far East*, Volume III, *India Command: September 1939 to November 1943*, P.85.
111. "Tenth Air Force Operational Diary", entries for May 14-23, 1943; "History 436th Bombardment Squadron (H) 1 January 1943 to 31 May 1943"; "History 492nd Bombardment Squadron (H) 1 January 1943 to 31 May 1943"; "History 493rd Bombardment Squadron (H) 1 January 1943 to 31 May 1943".
112. "History Headquarters India Air Task Force 1942 & 1 January to 31 May 1943".
113. Duncan, *B-24 Over Burma*, P.71.
114. Duncan, *B-24 Over Burma*, P.71.
115. "India Air Task Force: Bombing Activity Jun-Sep 1943", File 827.306 Jun-Sep 1943; "History of the 492nd Bombardment Squadron (H) for the Month of June 1943", SQ-Bomb-492-HI- June 1943; "History of the 493rd Bombardment Squadron (H) for the Month of June 1943", SQ-Bomb-493-HI- June 1943, Albert F. Simpson Historical Research Center, Air Force Historical Research Agency, Maxwell AFB, AL.
116. "India Air Task Force: Bombing Activity Jun-Sep 1943".
117. Dorr, *7th Bombardment Group/Wing 1918-1995*, P.239.
118. "History of the 493rd Bombardment Squadron (H) for the Month of July 1943", SQ-Bomb-493-HI- July 1943, Albert F. Simpson Historical Research Center, Air Force Historical Research Agency, Maxwell AFB, AL.
119. "India Air Task Force: Bombing Activity Jun-Sep 1943".
120. "History of the 436th Bombardment Squadron (H) for the Month of June, July 1943"; "History of the 492nd Bombardment Squadron (H) for the Month of June, July 1943", "History of the 493rd Bombardment Squadron (H) for the Month of June, July 1943".
121. "History of the 436th Bombardment Squadron (H) for the Month of June, July 1943"; "History of the 492nd Bombardment Squadron (H) for the Month of June, July 1943", "History of the 493rd Bombardment Squadron (H) for the Month of June, July 1943".
122. Duncan, *B-24 Over Burma*, P.75.
123. "History of the 9th Bombardment Squadron (H) for the month of June, July, August, 1943"; "History of the 436th Bombardment Squadron (H) for the Month of June, July, August, 1943"; "History of the 492nd Bombardment Squadron (H) for the Month of June, July, August, 1943", "History of the 493rd Bombardment Squadron (H) for the Month of June, July, August, 1943"; Duncan, *B-24 Over Burma*, P.76.
124. U.S. Air Force Historical Study No. 117: *The Tenth Air Force 1943* (USAF Historical Division, Research Studies Institute, Air University. Maxwell AFB, AL), P. 76.
125. "History of the 436th Bombardment Squadron (H) for the Month of July, 1943".
126. "History of the 493rd Bombardment Squadron (H) for the Month of June, July, August, 1943"; Joint Army-Navy Assessment Committee (JANAC): *Japanese Naval and Merchant Shipping Losses During WWII by All Causes*, (Washington DC: U.S. Government Printing Office, NAVEXOS P-468, 1947). Copy available at Hyperwar.com.
127. "History of the 9th Bombardment Squadron (H) for the month of July, August, 1943"; "History of the 436th Bombardment Squadron (H) for the Month of July, August, 1943"; "History of the 492nd Bombardment Squadron (H) for the Month of July, August, 1943", "History of the 493rd Bombardment Squadron (H) for the Month of July, August, 1943"; Shores, *Air War Over Burma*, P.98; Izawa, Yasuho: "64th Flying Sentai, Part 3", *Aero Album*, Vol. 5, No. 4 (Winter 1972), P. 8.
128. "History of the 493rd Bombardment Squadron (H) for the Month of August, 1943".
129. Perez, *A B-24 Bombardier 'Over Burma': The Personal Diary of Lt. Alfonso B. Perez*, pP. 59-60.
130. Joint Army-Navy Assessment Committee (JANAC): *Japanese Naval and Merchant Shipping Losses During WWII by All Causes*; "India Air Task Force: Bombing Activity Jun-Sep 1943"; "I.A.T.F. Bombing Missions", File 827.308 Dec 42-Sept 43, Albert F. Simpson Historical Research Center, Air Force Historical Research Agency, Maxwell AFB, AL.
131. "History of the 492nd Bombardment Squadron (H) for the Month of September, 1943".
132. Perez, *A B-24 Bombardier 'Over Burma': The Personal Diary of Lt. Alfonso B. Perez*, pP. 60-61.
133. "History of the 492nd Bombardment Squadron (H) for the Month of September, 1943"; "History of the 493rd Bombardment Squadron (H) for the Month of September, 1943"; Shores, *Air War Over Burma*, P.98.
134. "India Air Task Force: Bombing Activity Jun-Sep 1943".
135. "India Air Task Force: Bombing Activity Jun-Sep 1943".
136. "India Air Task Force: Bombing Activity Jun-Sep 1943"; "History of the 9th Bombardment Squadron (H) for the month of September, 1943"; "History of the 436th Bombardment Squadron (H) for the Month of September, 1943"; "History of the 492nd Bombardment Squadron (H) for the Month of September, 1943", "History of the 493rd Bombardment Squadron (H) for the Month of September, 1943".

Chapter Six: Strategic Air Force

1. Pound, Merritt B.: *History of the United States Army Air Forces, India-Burma Sector, China-Burma India Theater (From Activation through April 1944)*, 825.0115, Albert F. Simpson Historical Research Center, Air Force Historical Research Agency, Maxwell AFB, AL, P.12.
2. Craven and Cate, *The Pacific: Guadalcanal to Saipan*, pp.439-41, 449-50.
3. Craven and Cate, *The Pacific: Guadalcanal to Saipan*, P.450.
4. Craven and Cate, *The Pacific: Guadalcanal to Saipan*, P.451-52.
5. Kirby, *India's Most Dangerous Hour*, P. 421-24.
6. Craven and Cate, *The Pacific: Guadalcanal to Saipan*, P.453-57; Kirby, Major-General S. Woodburn: *The War Against Japan*, Vol. III: *The Decisive Battles* (London: Her Majesty's Stationary Office, 1961), pp.47-8; Probert, *The Forgotten Air Force*, P.151.
7. Kirby, *India's Most Dangerous Hour*, P. 428-32.
8. Kirby, *India's Most Dangerous Hour*, P. 432-33; Kirby, *The Decisive Battles*, P.43.
9. Air Historical Branch (1), Air Ministry: *R.A.F. Narrative: The Campaigns in the Far East*, Volume IV, *South East Asia (November 1943 to August 1945)* (London: Royal Air Force Air Force Centre for Air Power Studies, MLRS Books edition), pP. 30-31.
10. *R.A.F. Narrative: The Campaigns in the Far East*, Volume IV, *South East Asia (November 1943 to August 1945)*, pp.29-32; Kirby, *India's Most Dangerous Hour*, pP. 432-33; Kirby, *The Decisive Battles*, P.43.
11. Kirby, *India's Most Dangerous Hour*, P.433.
12. *R.A.F. Narrative: The Campaigns in the Far East*, Volume IV, *South East Asia (November 1943 to August 1945)*, pP. 29-32, Appendix No.

19; Hata, Izawa, and Shores, *Japanese Army Air Force Fighter Units and Their Aces 1931-1945*, pP. 55, 136-37, 179; Izawa, "64th Flying Sentai, Part 3", P. 8.

13. Young, Edward M.: Osprey Duel No. 41: *B-24 Liberator vs Ki-43 Oscar: China and Burma 1943* (Oxford, UK: Osprey Publishing, Ltd., 2012), P.74.
14. Young, *B-24 Liberator vs Ki-43 Oscar: China and Burma 1943*, pP. 64-65.
15. "Operations Analysis Report: Study of 7th Bomb Group Operations from 1 February 1943 to 31 March 1944", 27 May 1944, File 830.310, Albert F. Simpson Historical Research Center, Air Force Historical Research Agency, Maxwell AFB, AL.
16. "History of the 436th Bombardment Squadron (H) for the Month of September, 1943".
17. "History of the 493rd Bombardment Squadron (H) for the Month of September, 1943".
18. "History of the 436th Bombardment Squadron (H) for the Month of October, 1943".
19. "History of the 9th Bombardment Squadron (H) for the month of October, 1943".
20. "History of the 9th Bombardment Squadron (H) for the month of October, 1943".
21. Ichimura, Hiroshi: *Ki-43 'Oscar' Aces of World War 2*, Osprey Aircraft of the Aces No. 85, (Oxford, UK: Osprey Publishing, Ltd., 2009), P.34.
22. Perez, *A B-24 Bombardier 'Over Burma': The Personal Diary of Lt. Alfonso B. Perez*, P. 67.
23. "History of the 9th Bombardment Squadron (H) for the month of October, 1943"; "History of the 436th Bombardment Squadron (H) for the Month of October, 1943"; "History of the 492nd Bombardment Squadron (H) for the Month of October, 1943"; "History of the 493rd Bombardment Squadron (H) for the Month of October, 1943".
24. "History of the 9th Bombardment Squadron (H) for the month of October, 1943"; "History of the 493rd Bombardment Squadron (H) for the Month of October, 1943"; Shores, *Air War Over Burma*, P. 104.
25. Perez, *A B-24 Bombardier 'Over Burma': The Personal Diary of Lt. Alfonso B. Perez*, pP. 68-69.
26. Perez, *A B-24 Bombardier 'Over Burma': The Personal Diary of Lt. Alfonso B. Perez*, P. 70.
27. "History of the 9th Bombardment Squadron (H) for the month of October, 1943"; "History of the 493rd Bombardment Squadron (H) for the Month of October, 1943"; "History of the 436th Bombardment Squadron (H) for the Month of October, 1943"; "History of the 492nd Bombardment Squadron (H) for the Month of October, 1943".
28. "History of the 9th Bombardment Squadron (H) for the month of October, 1943"; "History of the 493rd Bombardment Squadron (H) for the Month of October, 1943"; Dorr, *7th Bombardment Group/Wing 1918-1995*, P.239.
29. U.S. Air Force Historical Study No. 117: *The Tenth Air Force 1943*, P.100.
30. History of the 436th Bombardment Squadron (H) for the Month of October, 1943".
31. "History of the 9th Bombardment Squadron (H) for the month of October, 1943"; "History of the 436th Bombardment Squadron (H) for the Month of October, 1943"; "History of the 492nd Bombardment Squadron (H) for the Month of October, 1943"; "History of the 493rd Bombardment Squadron (H) for the Month of October, 1943".
32. "History of the 493rd Bombardment Squadron (H) for the Month of October, 1943"; Swanborough, Gordon, and Peter M. Bowers: *United States Military Aircraft Since 1909*, New Edition (London: Putnam Aeronautical Books, 1989), P. 186, gives the empty weight of the B-24D as 32,605 pounds and the empty weight of the B-24J as 36,500 pounds, and gross weights of 60,000 and 65,000 pound respectively.
33. "History of the 9th Bombardment Squadron (H) for the month of October, 1943".
33. Army Air ForcE. Intelligence ServicE. *Informational Intelligence Summary*, No. 44-7, 29 February 1944, P.4.
34. "History of the 492nd Bombardment Squadron (H) for the Month of October, 1943".
35. Sledge interview.
36. Army Air ForcE. Intelligence ServicE. *Informational Intelligence Summary*, No. 44-7, 29 February 1944, pp.2-3.
37. Fielder, James M.: *459th Fighter Squadron: the Twin Dragons CBI 1943-1945* (Privately published 1993), P.98.
38. Fiedler, *459th Fighter Squadron: the Twin Dragons CBI 1943-1945*, P. 1; U.S. Air Force Historical Study No. 117: *The Tenth Air Force 1943*, P.54.
39. U.S. Air Force Historical Study No. 117: *The Tenth Air Force 1943*, P.54.
40. The 493rd Bombardment Squadron's history for October refers to "messages received as prearranged from an F-5 reconnaissance ship". "History of the 493rd Bombardment Squadron (H) for the Month of October, 1943".
41. "History of the 9th Bombardment Squadron (H) for the month of October, 1943"; "History of the 436th Bombardment Squadron (H) for the Month of October, 1943"; "History of the 492nd Bombardment Squadron (H) for the Month of October, 1943"; "History of the 493rd Bombardment Squadron (H) for the Month of October, 1943".
42. Ichimura, *Ki-43 'Oscar' Aces of World War 2*, P. 36.
43. "History of the 9th Bombardment Squadron (H) for the month of October, 1943"; "History of the 436th Bombardment Squadron (H) for the Month of October, 1943"; "History of the 492nd Bombardment Squadron (H) for the Month of October, 1943"; "History of the 493rd Bombardment Squadron (H) for the Month of October, 1943"; Shores, *Air War Over Burma*, P. 108; Dorr, *7th Bombardment Group/Wing 1918-1995*, P.239.
44. "History of the 436th Bombardment Squadron (H) for the Month of October, 1943"; Dorr, *7th Bombardment Group/Wing 1918-1995*, P.239.
45. "Operations Analysis Report: Study of 7th Bomb Group Operations from 1 February 1943 to 31 March 1944", P.4.
46. "History of the 9th Bombardment Squadron (H) for the month of October, 1943".
47. "Operations Analysis Report: Study of 7th Bomb Group Operations from 1 February 1943 to 31 March 1944", P.4.
48. "Operations Analysis Report: Study of 7th Bomb Group Operations from 1 February 1943 to 31 March 1944", P.4.
49. *CBI Roundup*, Vol. II, No. 9, November 12, 1943.
50. "History of the 9th Bombardment Squadron (H) for the month of October, 1943"; "History of the 436th Bombardment Squadron (H) for the Month of October, 1943"; "History of the 492nd Bombardment Squadron (H) for the Month of October, 1943"; "History of the 493rd Bombardment Squadron (H) for the Month of October, 1943".
51. "History of the 9th Bombardment Squadron (H) for the month of November, 1943".
52. "History of the 9th Bombardment Squadron (H) for the month of November, 1943".
53. "History of the 9th Bombardment Squadron (H) for the month of November, 1943"; "History of the 436th Bombardment Squadron (H) for the Month of November, 1943"; "History of the 492nd Bombardment Squadron (H) for the Month of November, 1943"; "History of the 493rd Bombardment Squadron (H) for the Month of November, 1943".
54. Sledge interview; History of the 436th Bombardment Squadron (H) for the Month of November, 1943"; "History of the 492nd Bombardment Squadron (H) for the Month of November, 1943".
55. Guelich, Capt. Robert V. and Sgt. William G Mors: "One Man Crew", *Air Force*, Vol. 27, No. 2, February 1944, P.22.
56. Duncan, *B-24 Over Burma*, P.88.
57. Guelich and Mors: "One Man Crew", P. 22.
58. Guelich and Mors: "One Man Crew", pP. 23-24.
59. History of the 436th Bombardment Squadron (H) for the Month of November, 1943"; "History of the 492nd Bombardment Squadron (H) for the Month of November, 1943".
60. "History of the 9th Bombardment Squadron (H) for the month of November, 1943"; "History of the 492nd Bombardment Squadron (H) for the Month of November, 1943"; Dorr, *7th Bombardment Group/Wing 1918-1995*, pP. 160, 239.
61. "History of the 9th Bombardment Squadron (H) for the month of November, 1943".
62. "History of the 9th Bombardment Squadron (H) for the month of November, 1943"; "History of the 436th Bombardment Squadron (H) for the Month of November, 1943"; "History of the 492nd Bombardment Squadron (H) for the Month of November, 1943"; "History of the 493rd Bombardment Squadron (H) for the Month of November, 1943".
63. Major General George E. Stratemeyer, Headquarters, Army Air Forces, India-Burma Sector, China-India-Burma Theater, to Commanding

General, Army Air Forces, Washington, D.C., 27 December 1943, File 825.306B, Albert F. Simpson Historical Research Center, Air Force Historical Research Agency, Maxwell AFB, AL.

64. Stratemeyer to Commanding General, Army Air Forces, 27 December 1943.
65. "History of the 492nd Bombardment Squadron (H) for the Month of November, 1943"; Glines, Carroll V.: *Chennault's Forgotten Warriors: The Saga of the 308th Bomb Group in China* (Atglen, PA: Schiffer Publishing Ltd., 1995), P. 100.
66. *The Tenth Air Force 1943*, P.81.
67. *The Tenth Air Force 1943*, pP. 81-83.
68. *The Tenth Air Force 1943*, pP. 83-84. This history lists the Insein Locomotive Works as the 7th Bombardment Group's target on November 25, but all the individual squadron histories list the airfields at Mingaladon and Zayatkwin as their targets.
69. "Organizational History of the 308th Bombardment Group (H), AAF, GP-308-HI (Bomb), Albert F. Simpson Historical Research Center, Air Force Historical Research Agency, Maxwell AFB, AL.
70. Glines, *Chennault's Forgotten Warriors*, P.101.
71. "History of the 9th Bombardment Squadron (H) for the month of November, 1943"; "History of the 436th Bombardment Squadron (H) for the Month of November, 1943"; "History of the 492nd Bombardment Squadron (H) for the Month of November, 1943"; "History of the 493rd Bombardment Squadron (H) for the Month of November, 1943"; "Organizational History of the 308th Bombardment Group (H), AAF; Shores, *Air War Over Burma*, pP. 115-17; *The Tenth Air Force 1943*, P.85.
72. *The Tenth Air Force 1943*, pP. 85-6.
73. "History of the 9th Bombardment Squadron (H) for the month of November, 1943"; "History of the 436th Bombardment Squadron (H) for the Month of November, 1943"; "History of the 492nd Bombardment Squadron (H) for the Month of November, 1943"; "History of the 493rd Bombardment Squadron (H) for the Month of November, 1943"; "Organizational History of the 308th Bombardment Group (H), AAF; Shores, *Air War Over Burma*, pP. 118-19; *The Tenth Air Force 1943*, P.86.
74. "History of the 9th Bombardment Squadron (H) for the Month of November, 1943"; "History of the 436th Bombardment Squadron (H) for the Month of November, 1943"; "History of the 492nd Bombardment Squadron (H) for the Month of November, 1943"; "History of the 493rd Bombardment Squadron (H) for the Month of November, 1943"; "Organizational History of the 308th Bombardment Group (H)", AAF; Shores, *Air War Over Burma*, P. 119; *The Tenth Air Force 1943*, pP. 86-7.
75. Shores, *Air War Over Burma*, pp.123-24.
76. *The Tenth Air Force 1943*, P. 87.
77. "History of the 9th Bombardment Squadron (H) for the Month of December, 1943"; Shores, *Air War Over Burma*, P. 124; *The Tenth Air Force 1943*, pP. 87; Dorr, *7th Bombardment Group/Wing 1918-1995*, P.241.
78. "History of the 436th Bombardment Squadron (H) for the Month of December 1943"; "History of the 492nd Bombardment Squadron (H) for the Month of December 1943"; "History of the 493rd Bombardment Squadron (H) for the Month of December 1943"; Shores, *Air War Over Burma*, P. 124; Dorr, *7th Bombardment Group/Wing 1918-1995*, pp.241-42.
79. "Organizational History of the 308th Bombardment Group (H)".
80. "Organizational History of the 308th Bombardment Group (H)"; Shores, *Air War Over Burma*, P. 124.
81. *The Tenth Air Force 1943*, P.89.
82. *The Tenth Air Force 1943*, P.91.
83. "History of the 492nd Bombardment Squadron (H) for the Month of December, 1943".
84. "History of the 9th Bombardment Squadron (H) for the month of December 1943"; "History of the 436th Bombardment Squadron (H) for the Month of December 1943"; "History of the 492nd Bombardment Squadron (H) for the Month of December 1943"; "History of the 493rd Bombardment Squadron (H) for the Month of December 1943".
85. *The Tenth Air Force 1943*, P.90.
86. United States Strategic Bombing Survey, Military Analysis Division: *Air Operations in China, Burma, India WWII* (Washington, D.C. 1947), P.22.
87. *Air Operations in China, Burma, India WWII*, P.22.
88. Craven and Cate, *The Pacific: Guadalcanal to Saipan August 1942 to July 1944*, P.493.
89. *The Tenth Air Force 1943*, pp.33-37; Probert, *The Forgotten Air Force: The Royal Air Force in the War Against Japan 1941-1945*, pp.151-52.
90. *The Tenth Air Force 1943*, P.38.
91. "Dispatch of Operations of Strategic Air Force, Eastern Air Command for the Period 15 December to 31 May 1944", File 821, Albert F. Simpson Historical Research Center, Air Force Historical Research Agency, Maxwell AFB, AL, P.2
92. "Operations of the Strategic Air Force 15 December 1943-3 May 1945", File 821, Albert F. Simpson Historical Research Center, Air Force Historical Research Agency, Maxwell AFB, AL, P.25.
93. *Air Operations in China, Burma, India WWII*, P.22.
94. "Operations of the Strategic Air Force 15 December 1943-3 May 1945", P.25.
95. "Operations of the Strategic Air Force 15 December 1943-3 May 1945", P.25.
96. "Operations of the Strategic Air Force 15 December 1943-3 May 1945", P.2.
97. "Operations of the Strategic Air Force 15 December 1943-3 May 1945", P.11.
98. "Operations Analysis Report: Study of 7th Bomb Group Operations from 1 February 1943 to 31 March 1944".
99. *R.A.F. Narrative: The Campaigns in the Far East*, Volume IV, *South East Asia (November 1943 to August 1945)*, Appendix No. 10.
100. "History of the 9th Bombardment Squadron (H) for the month of January, 1944".
101. "History of the Headquarters 7th Bombardment Group (H), AAF, for the month of February 1944", GP-7-Hi-(Bomb) 1917-to-1947, Albert F. Simpson Historical Research Center, Air Force Historical Research Agency, Maxwell AFB, AL.
102. "History of the 436th Bombardment Squadron (H) for the Month of January, 1944".
103. Col. M.F. Summerfelt, HQ, AAF, to Commanding General, Tenth Air Force, 14 February 1944, "Report on Visit to 10th A.F. Stations", Tab "A" in Bombardment Reports-China-Burma-India Theater: Bombing Tactics (General), File 825.153, March 1944, Copy 1, Albert F. Simpson Historical Research Center, Air Force Historical Research Agency, Maxwell AFB, AL.
104. "History of the 9th Bombardment Squadron (H) for the Month of December 1943 and January 1944"; "History of the 436th Bombardment Squadron (H) for the Month of December 1943 and January 1944"; "History of the 492nd Bombardment Squadron (H) for the Month of December 1943 and January 1944"; "History of the 493rd Bombardment Squadron (H) for the Month of December 1943 and January 1944"; "History of the Headquarters 7th Bombardment Group (H), AAF, for the month of January and February 1944".
105. "History of the 436th Bombardment Squadron (H) for the Month of December 1943"; "History of the 492nd Bombardment Squadron (H) for the Month of January 1944".
106. *Air Operations in China, Burma, India WWII*, P.22.
107. *Air Operations in China, Burma, India WWII*, P.22.
108. *Air Operations in China, Burma, India WWII*, P.22.
109. "History of the 9th Bombardment Squadron (H) for the Month of January 1944"; "History of the 436th Bombardment Squadron (H) for the Month of January 1944"; "History of the 493rd Bombardment Squadron (H) for the Month of January 1944".
110. "History of the 9th Bombardment Squadron (H) for the Month of January 1944"; "History of the 436th Bombardment Squadron (H) for the Month of January 1944"; "History of the 492nd Bombardment Squadron (H) for the Month of January 1944"; "History of the 493rd Bombardment Squadron (H) for the Month of January 1944"; Dorr, *7th Bombardment Group/Wing 1918-1995*, P.242; *Japanese Naval and Merchant Shipping Losses During WWII by All Causes*.
111. "History of the 9th Bombardment Squadron (H) for the Month of April 1944"; "History of the 436th Bombardment Squadron (H) for the Month of April 1944"; "History of the 492nd Bombardment Squadron (H) for the Month of April 1944"; "History of the 493rd Bombardment Squadron (H) for the Month of April 1944"; Dorr, *7th Bombardment Group/Wing 1918-1995*, P.242.
112. "Operations of the Strategic Air Force 15 December 1943-3 May 1945", P.28.
113. "History of the 9th Bombardment Squadron (H) for the Months of

December 1943, February and April 1944"; "History of the 436th Bombardment Squadron (H) for the Month of December 1943 and April 1944"; "History of the 492nd Bombardment Squadron (H) for the Month of December 1943 and February 1944".

114. "Dispatch of Operations of Strategic Air Force, Eastern Air Command for the Period 15 December to 31 May 1944", P.3.
115. Craven and Cate, *The Pacific: Guadalcanal to Saipan August 1942 to July 1944*, P.513.
116. "History of the 9th Bombardment Squadron (H) for the Months of January and April 1944"; "History of the 436th Bombardment Squadron (H) for the Months of January and April 1944"; "History of the 492nd Bombardment Squadron (H) for the Months of January and April 1944"; "History of the 493rd Bombardment Squadron (H) for the Months of January and April 1944".
117. "History of the 9th Bombardment Squadron (H) for the Month of May 1944".
118. "History of the 9th Bombardment Squadron (H) for the Months of May and June 1944"; "History of the 436th Bombardment Squadron (H) for the Months of May and June 1944"; "History of the 492nd Bombardment Squadron (H) for the Month of May 1944"; "History of the 493rd Bombardment Squadron (H) for the Month of May 1944"; Dorr, *7th Bombardment Group/Wing 1918-1995*, P.243.
119. "History of the 436th Bombardment Squadron (H) for the Month of April 1944".
120. *Air Operations in China, Burma, India WWII*, P.21.
121. "History of the 9th Bombardment Squadron (H) for the Months of December 1943 and January 1944"; "History of the 436th Bombardment Squadron (H) for the Months of December 1943 and January 1944"; "History of the 492nd Bombardment Squadron (H) for the Months of December 1943 and January 1944"; "History of the 493rd Bombardment Squadron (H) for the Months of December 1943 and January 1944".
122. "History of the 436th Bombardment Squadron (H) for the Month of February 1944".
123. "History of the 9th Bombardment Squadron (H) for the Months of December 1943 and February to May 1944"; "History of the 436th Bombardment Squadron (H) for the Months of December 1943 and February to May 1944"; "History of the 492nd Bombardment Squadron (H) for the Months of December 1943 and February to May 1944"; "History of the 493rd Bombardment Squadron (H) for the Months of December 1943 and February to May 1944".
124. Office of the Assistant Chief of Air Staff, Intelligence: *Impact*, Vol. 2. No. 7, (July 1944), pp.48-49; Major General Howard Davidson to Assistant Chief of Staff, Intelligence, "Spike Bombs", 28 May 1944, File 830.310 Tabs, Albert F. Simpson Historical Research Center, Air Force Historical Research Agency, Maxwell AFB, AL.
125. "History of the 9th Bombardment Squadron (H) for the Month of February 1944".
126. Maj. Gen. Davidson's report on spike bombs of 28 May 1944 refers to the 7th Group using spike bombs against bridges.
127. "History of the 9th Bombardment Squadron (H) for the Month of March 1944"; "History of the 436th Bombardment Squadron (H) for the Month of March 1944"; "History of the 492nd Bombardment Squadron (H) for the March of January 1944"; "History of the 493rd Bombardment Squadron (H) for the Month of March 1944".
128. "History of the 436th Bombardment Squadron (H) for the Month of April 1944"; "History of the 492nd Bombardment Squadron (H) for the March of April 1944".
129. Dorr, *7th Bombardment Group/Wing 1918-1995*, P.242.
130. "History of the 9th Bombardment Squadron (H) for the Month of April 1944".
131. "History of the 493rd Bombardment Squadron (H) for the Month of April 1944".
132. "History of the 436th Bombardment Squadron (H) for the Month of May 1944".
133. *Air Operations in China, Burma, India WWII*, P.12.
134. "History of the 9th Bombardment Squadron (H) for the Month of January 1944"; "History of the 436th Bombardment Squadron (H) for the Month of January 1944"; "History of the 492nd Bombardment Squadron (H) for the Month of January 1944"; "History of the 493rd Bombardment Squadron (H) for the Month of January 1944".
135. "History of the 9th Bombardment Squadron (H) for the Months of February and March 1944"; "History of the 436th Bombardment Squadron (H) for the Months of February and March 1944"; "History of the 492nd Bombardment Squadron (H) for the Months of February and March 1944"; "History of the 493rd Bombardment Squadron (H) for the Months of February and March 1944"; *Air Operations in China, Burma, India WWII*, pp. 14-15.
136. "History of the 9th Bombardment Squadron (H) for the Months of January to June 1944"; "History of the 436th Bombardment Squadron (H) for the Months of January to June 1944"; "History of the 492nd Bombardment Squadron (H) for the Months of January to June 1944"; "History of the 493rd Bombardment Squadron (H) for the Months of January to June 1944"; "Dispatch of Operations of Strategic Air Force, Eastern Air Command for the Period 15 December to 31 May 1944", P.5.
137. "Dispatch of Operations of Strategic Air Force, Eastern Air Command for the Period 15 December to 31 May 1944", Appendix H.
138. Kirby, *The Decisive Battles*, pp. 53-70, 73-81.
139. Kirby, *The Decisive Battles*, pp.125-26; "History of the 9th Bombardment Squadron (H) for the Month of January 1944"; "History of the 436th Bombardment Squadron (H) for the Month of January 1944"; "History of the 492nd Bombardment Squadron (H) for the Month of January 1944"; "History of the 493rd Bombardment Squadron (H) for the Month of January 1944".
140. Kirby, *The Decisive Battles*, P.174.
141. "History of the 9th Bombardment Squadron (H) for the Month of March 1944"; "History of the 436th Bombardment Squadron (H) for the Month of March 1944"; "History of the 492nd Bombardment Squadron (H) for the Month of March 1944"; "History of the 493rd Bombardment Squadron (H) for the Month of March 1944".
142. "History of the 9th Bombardment Squadron (H) for the Month of March 1944"; "History of the 436th Bombardment Squadron (H) for the Month of March 1944"; "History of the 492nd Bombardment Squadron (H) for the Month of March 1944"; "History of the 493rd Bombardment Squadron (H) for the Month of March 1944".
143. Kirby, *The Decisive Battles*, P. 81.
144. Kirby, *The Decisive Battles*, P. 80.
145. "History of the 9th Bombardment Squadron (H) for the Month of March 1944"; "History of the 436th Bombardment Squadron (H) for the Month of March 1944"; "History of the 492nd Bombardment Squadron (H) for the Month of March 1944"; "History of the 493rd Bombardment Squadron (H) for the Month of March 1944".
146. Romanus, Charles F., and Riley Sunderland: *Stilwell's Command Problems*, United States Army in WWII: China-Burma-India Theater, (Washington, D.C.: Office of the Chief of Military History, Department of the Army, 1956), pp. 204-15.
147. "History of the 9th Bombardment Squadron (H) for the Month of May 1944".
148. "History of the 9th Bombardment Squadron (H) for the Month of May 1944"; "History of the 436th Bombardment Squadron (H) for the Month of May 1944"; "History of the 492nd Bombardment Squadron (H) for the Month of May 1944"; "History of the 493rd Bombardment Squadron (H) for the Month of May 1944".
149. "Dispatch of Operations of Strategic Air Force, Eastern Air Command for the Period 15 December to 31 May 1944", P.7.
150. Kirby, *The Decisive Battles*, P.389.
151. "History of the 436th Bombardment Squadron (H) for the Months of April and May 1944".
152. "History of the 9th Bombardment Squadron (H) for the Month of April 1944".
153. "History of the 9th Bombardment Squadron (H) for the Month of May 1944".
154. "History of the 9th Bombardment Squadron (H) for the Month of April 1944".
155. "History of the 9th Bombardment Squadron (H) for the Month of April 1944".
156. "History of the 436th Bombardment Squadron (H) for the Months of April 1944".
157. "History of the 436th Bombardment Squadron (H) for the Months of April and May 1944"; "History of the 492nd Bombardment Squadron (H) for the Months of April and May 1944"; "History of the 493rd Bombardment Squadron (H) for the Months of April and May 1944".
158. Office of Statistical Control, Headquarters, Army Air Force: *Army Air Force Statistical Digest, WWII*, Table 46. Copy available at the Air Force Historical Research Agency website, www.afhra.mil.
159. "History of the 9th Bombardment Squadron (H) for the Months of May and June 1944"; "History of the 436th Bombardment Squadron (H) for

the Months of May and June 1944"; "History of the 492nd Bombardment Squadron (H) for the Months of May and June 1944"; "History of the 493rd Bombardment Squadron (H) for the Months of May and June 1944".
160. "History of the 9th Bombardment Squadron (H) for the Months of May and June 1944"; "History of the 436th Bombardment Squadron (H) for the Months of May and June 1944"; "History of the 492nd Bombardment Squadron (H) for the Months of May and June 1944"; "History of the 493rd Bombardment Squadron (H) for the Months of May and June 1944".
161. "History of the 9th Bombardment Squadron (H) for the Month of June 1944"; "History of the 436th Bombardment Squadron (H) for the Month of June 1944"; "History of the 492nd Bombardment Squadron (H) for the Month of June 1944"; "History of the 493rd Bombardment Squadron (H) for the Month of June 1944".
162. Romanus and Sunderland, *Stillwell's Mission to China*, pp. 252-53.
163. Romanus and Sunderland, *Stillwell's Mission to China*, pp. 280-81, 322-24.
164. Romanus and Sunderland, *Stillwell's Mission to China*, P. 320; Byrd, Martha: *Chennault: Giving Wings to the Tiger* (Tuscaloosa, AL: University of Alabama Press, 1987), P. 222.
165. Byrd, *Chennault: Giving Wings to the Tiger*, P. 222.
166. Byrd, *Chennault: Giving Wings to the Tiger*, P. 223.
167. Romanus, and Sunderland, *Stilwell's Command Problems*, P. 316.
168. Craven, Wesley Frank and James Lea Cate, Eds.: *The Army Air Forces in WWII*, Volume Five, *The Pacific: Matterhorn to Nagasaki June 1944 to August 1945* (Chicago, IL: The University of Chicago Press, 1953), P. 219.
169. Craven and Cate, *The Pacific: Matterhorn to Nagasaki June 1944 to August 1945*, pp.220-21; *Army Air Force Statistical Digest, WWII*, Table 129.
170. "History of the 9th Bombardment Squadron (H) for the Month of June 1944"; "History of the 436th Bombardment Squadron (H) for the Month of June 1944"; "History of the 492nd Bombardment Squadron (H) for the Month of June 1944"; "History of the 493rd Bombardment Squadron (H) for the Month of June 1944"; "Summary of Gasoline Hauling Activities During Period 20 June thru 30 September 1944", 1 November, 1944, GP-7-HI-(Bomb)-1917 to 1947.
171. "History of the 9th Bombardment Squadron (H) for the Month of June 1944".
172. "History of the 9th Bombardment Squadron (H) for the Month of June 1944".
173. "History of the 9th Bombardment Squadron (H) for the Month of June 1944".
174. Dorr, *7th Bombardment Group/Wing 1918-1995*, P.171.
175. Office of Flying Training, Office of Assistant Chief of Staff, Training, Headquarters, AAF: *Pilot Training Manual for the B-24 Liberator* (October 1944), P. 59.
176. Dorr, *7th Bombardment Group/Wing 1918-1995*, P.171.
177. "History of the 9th Bombardment Squadron (H) for the Month of July 1944".
178. Dorr, *7th Bombardment Group/Wing 1918-1995*, P.171.
179. "Summary of Gasoline Hauling Activities During Period 20 June thru 30 September 1944", 1 November, 1944, GP-7-HI-(Bomb)-1917 to 1947.
180. Fritsche, Carl: "B-24 Liberator", in Higham, Robin and Carol Williams, Eds.: *Flying Combat Aircraft of the USAAF-USAF*, Volume 2 (Ames, Iowa: The Iowa State University Press, 1978), pp. 49-50.
181. "Summary of Gasoline Hauling Activities During Period 20 June thru 30 September 1944", 1 November, 1944, GP-7-HI-(Bomb)-1917 to 1947.
182. "Summary of Gasoline Hauling Activities During Period 20 June thru 30 September 1944", 1 November, 1944, GP-7-HI-(Bomb)-1917 to 1947.
183. "History of the 436th Bombardment Squadron (H) for the Month of September 1944".
184. "History of the 436th Bombardment Squadron (H) for the Months of July, August, and September 1944".
185. See Dorr, *7th Bombardment Group/Wing 1918-1995*, pp. 243-45 for a list of airplanes and men lost on the gas hauling operation.
186. "History of the 436th Bombardment Squadron (H) for the Month of September 1944".
187. "History of the 9th Bombardment Squadron (H) for the Month of September 1944".
188. Lt. Col. Joe Mountain to Lt. Col. Payne Jennings, October 30, 1944, "Status of Crew Training in the 7th Bombardment Group", GP-7-HI-(Bomb)-1917 to 1947.
189. Dorr, *7th Bombardment Group/Wing 1918-1995*, P.179.
190. "History of the 436th Bombardment Squadron (H) for the Month of September 1944".
191. "Summary of Gasoline Hauling Activities During Period 20 June thru 30 September 1944", 1 November, 1944, GP-7-HI-(Bomb)-1917 to 1947.
192. "History of the 436th Bombardment Squadron (H) for the Month of September 1944".
193. "History of the 436th Bombardment Squadron (H) for the Month of September 1944".
194. Romanus and Sunderland, *Time Runs Out in CBI*, P.4.

Chapter Seven: Back to Bombing

1. Slim, Field Marshal Sir William: *Defeat Into Victory* (London: Cassell and Company Ltd, 1956), P.246, quoted in Allen, Louis: *Burma: The Longest War 1941-45* (New York, NY: St. Martin's Press, 1984), P. 188.
2. Allen, Louis: *Burma: The Longest War 1941-45*, P. 193;
3. Romanus, Charles F., and Riley Sunderland: *Time Runs Out in CBI*, United States Army in WWII: China-Burma-India Theater, (Washington, D.C.: Office of the Chief of Military History, Department of the Army, 1959), pp.77-79.
4. Kirby, Major-General S. Woodburn: *The War Against Japan*, Vol. IV: *The Reconquest of Burma* (London: Her Majesty's Stationary Office, 1965), pp. 1-13; Romanus and Sunderland, *Time Runs Out in CBI*, pp. 81-87.
5. Kirby, *The Reconquest of Burma*, pp. 53-61; Allen, *Burma: The Longest War 1941-45*, pp. 390-92.
6. Craven and Cate, *The Pacific: Matterhorn to Nagasaki June 1944 to August 1945*, P. 234.
7. Headquarters, Eastern Air Command, *Weekly Intelligence Summary*, Number 11, 10 November 1944, File 820.607, Albert F. Simpson Historical Research Center, Air Force Historical Research Agency, Maxwell AFB, AL.
8. Craven and Cate, *The Pacific: Matterhorn to Nagasaki June 1944 to August 1945*, P. 205.
9. Kirby, *The Reconquest of Burma*, P.403.
10. "Dispatch on Operations Against the Japanese by the Strategic Air Force (E.A.C.) From 1st June, 1944 to 26th November, 1944", File 821, Albert F. Simpson Historical Research Center, Air Force Historical Research Agency, Maxwell AFB, AL, P.14.
11. "Dispatch on Operations Against the Japanese by the Strategic Air Force (E.A.C.) From 1st June, 1944 to 26th November, 1944", P.15.
12. Allen, *Burma: The Longest War 1941-45*, P.207.
13. "History of the 9th Bombardment Squadron (H) for the Month of October 1944".
14. "History of the 9th Bombardment Squadron (H) for the Month of October 1944"; "History of the 436th Bombardment Squadron (H) for the Month of October 1944"; "History of the 492nd Bombardment Squadron (H) for the Month of October 1944"; "History of the 493rd Bombardment Squadron (H) for the Month of October 1944".
15. See Notes of conference held by Brigadier General Ray H. Clark, Air Inspector, AAF, India-Burma Sector, at Headquarters, 7th Bombardment Group (H), 1 November 1944, in GP-7-HI-(Bomb)-1917 to 1947.
16. See Notes of conference held by Brigadier General Ray H. Clark, Air Inspector, AAF, India-Burma Sector, at Headquarters, 7th Bombardment Group (H), 1 November 1944, in GP-7-HI-(Bomb)-1917 to 1947.
17. See Notes of conference held by Brigadier General Ray H. Clark, Air Inspector, AAF, India-Burma Sector, at Headquarters, 7th Bombardment Group (H), 1 November 1944, in GP-7-HI-(Bomb)-1917 to 1947.
18. "History of the 9th Bombardment Squadron (H) for the Month of October 1944"; "History of the 436th Bombardment Squadron (H) for the Month of October 1944"; "History of the 492nd Bombardment Squadron (H) for the Month of October 1944"; "History of the 493rd Bombardment Squadron (H) for the Month of October 1944"; See Notes of conference held by Brigadier General Ray H. Clark, Air Inspector, AAF, India-Burma Sector, at Headquarters, 7th Bombardment Group (H), 1 November 1944, in GP-7-HI-(Bomb)-1917 to 1947.

19. "History of the 9th Bombardment Squadron (H) for the Month of October 1944"; "History of the 436th Bombardment Squadron (H) for the Month of October 1944"; "History of the 492nd Bombardment Squadron (H) for the Month of October 1944"; "History of the 493rd Bombardment Squadron (H) for the Month of October 1944"; See Notes of conference held by Brigadier General Ray H. Clark, Air Inspector, AAF, India-Burma Sector, at Headquarters, 7th Bombardment Group (H), 1 November 1944, in GP-7-HI-(Bomb)-1917 to 1947; "Dispatch on Operations Against the Japanese by the Strategic Air Force (E.A.C.) From 1st June, 1944 to 26th November, 1944", P.15.
20. "History of the 9th Bombardment Squadron (H) for the Month of October 1944"; "History of the 436th Bombardment Squadron (H) for the Month of October 1944"; "History of the 492nd Bombardment Squadron (H) for the Month of October 1944"; "History of the 493rd Bombardment Squadron (H) for the Month of October 1944"; Shores, *Air War Over Burma: The Allied Air Forces Fight Back in South-east Asia 1942-1945*, P.275; Izawa, "64th Flying Sentai, Part 3", P.13.
21. "History of the 493rd Bombardment Squadron (H) for the Month of October 1944"; Shores, *Air War Over Burma: The Allied Air Forces Fight Back in South-east Asia 1942-1945*, P.275; the comment on the Group's gunnery on the mission of October 22, 1944, comes from Lt. Col. Joe Mountain to Lt. Col. Payne Jennings, dated October 30, 1944, "Status of Air Crew Training of the 7th Bombardment Group", included in Notes of conference held by Brigadier General Ray H. Clark, Air Inspector, AAF, India-Burma Sector, at Headquarters, 7th Bombardment Group (H), 1 November 1944, in GP-7-HI-(Bomb)-1917 to 1947.
22. "History of the 436th Bombardment Squadron (H) for the Month of October 1944"; "History of the 493rd Bombardment Squadron (H) for the Month of October 1944".
23. 7th Bomb Group War Diaries, Lt. Donald Young, 493rd BS, P. 29, courtesy of Jim Augustus.
24. "History of the 436th Bombardment Squadron (H) for the Month of October 1944"; "History of the 492nd Bombardment Squadron (H) for the Month of October 1944"; See Notes of conference held by Brigadier General Ray H. Clark, Air Inspector, AAF, India-Burma Sector, at Headquarters, 7th Bombardment Group (H), 1 November 1944, in GP-7-HI-(Bomb)-1917 to 1947.
25. See Notes of conference held by Brigadier General Ray H. Clark, Air Inspector, AAF, India-Burma Sector, at Headquarters, 7th Bombardment Group (H), 1 November 1944, in GP-7-HI-(Bomb)-1917 to 1947.
26. "History of the 9th Bombardment Squadron (H) for the Month of October 1944"; "History of the 436th Bombardment Squadron (H) for the Month of October 1944"; "History of the 492nd Bombardment Squadron (H) for the Month of October 1944"; "History of the 493rd Bombardment Squadron (H) for the Month of October 1944"; See Notes of conference held by Brigadier General Ray H. Clark, Air Inspector, AAF, India-Burma Sector, at Headquarters, 7th Bombardment Group (H), 1 November 1944, in GP-7-HI-(Bomb)-1917 to 1947.
27. See the entry for Monday 30 October 1944 in Lt. General George Stratemeyer's Personal Diary for 1 January 1944 thru 31 December 1944, copy at the United States Air Force Academy, McDermott Library Collection.
28. See the entry for Tuesday 31 October 1944 in Lt. General George Stratemeyer's Personal Diary for 1 January 1944 thru 31 December 1944.
29. See letter Brigadier General Charles B. Stone to Air Inspector, Army Air Force, India-Burma Sector, 30 October 1944 and Notes of conference held by Brigadier General Ray H. Clark, Air Inspector, AAF, India-Burma Sector, at Headquarters, 7th Bombardment Group (H), 1 November 1944, in GP-7-HI-(Bomb)-1917 to 1947.
30. "Status of Air Crew Training of the 7th Bombardment Group".
31. Brigadier General Ray Clark to Commanding General, Army Air Force, India-Burma Sector, 4 November 1944, in GP-7-HI-(Bomb)-1917 to 1947.
32. Included in Notes of conference held by Brigadier General Ray H. Clark, Air Inspector, AAF, India-Burma Sector, at Headquarters, 7th Bombardment Group (H), 1 November 1944, in GP-7-HI-(Bomb)-1917 to 1947.
33. Included in Notes of conference held by Brigadier General Ray H. Clark, Air Inspector, AAF, India-Burma Sector, at Headquarters, 7th Bombardment Group (H), 1 November 1944, in GP-7-HI-(Bomb)-1917 to 1947.
34. "History of the 9th Bombardment Squadron (H) for the Month of November 1944"; "History of the 492nd Bombardment Squadron (H) for the Month of November 1944"; "History of the 493rd Bombardment Squadron (H) for the Month of November 1944".
35. "History of the 436th Bombardment Squadron (H) for the Month of November 1944".
36. "History of the 436th Bombardment Squadron (H) for the Month of January 1945".
37. "History of the 436th Bombardment Squadron (H) for the Month of January 1945".
38. "Dispatch on Operations Against the Japanese by the Strategic Air Force (E.A.C.) From 1st June, 1944 to 26th November, 1944", P.17.
39. "History of the 436th Bombardment Squadron (H) for the Month of November 1944".
40. "History of the 436th Bombardment Squadron (H) for the Month of November 1944".
41. "History of the 493rd Bombardment Squadron (H) for the Month of November 1944"; 7th Bomb Group War Diaries, Lt. Donald Young, 493rd BS, P. 29, courtesy of Jim Augustus; Dorr, *7th Bombardment Group/Wing 1918-1995*, P.246.
42. "History of the 9th Bombardment Squadron (H) for the Month of November 1944"; "History of the 436th Bombardment Squadron (H) for the Month of November 1944"; "History of the 492nd Bombardment Squadron (H) for the Month of November 1944"; "History of the 493rd Bombardment Squadron (H) for the Month of November 1944".
43. "History of the 436th Bombardment Squadron (H) for the Month of November 1944".
44. "History of the 9th Bombardment Squadron (H) for the Month of November 1944"; "History of the 436th Bombardment Squadron (H) for the Month of November 1944"; "History of the 492nd Bombardment Squadron (H) for the Month of November 1944"; there is a short biography of William Dabney in the 7th Bombardment Group (H) Historical Foundation Newsletter of November 2003, P.4.
45. Craven and Cate, *The Pacific: Matterhorn to Nagasaki June 1944 to August 1945*, pp. 225-32; Romanus and Sunderland, *Time Runs Out in CBI*, pp. 4-15.
46. Operational Research Section, Air Command, South East Asia: Report No. S.45 "Six Months of Bridge Bombing by the Strategic Air Force, Including the Use of Azon", Section V, Operational Use of Azon, Air 23/2842, National Archives, Kew, United Kingdom.
47. "History of the 9th Bombardment Squadron (H) for the Month of November 1944"; "History of the 436th Bombardment Squadron (H) for the Month of November 1944"; "History of the 492nd Bombardment Squadron (H) for the Month of November 1944"; "History of the 493rd Bombardment Squadron (H) for the Month of November 1944".
48. "History of the 436th Bombardment Squadron (H) for the Month of November 1944"; "History of the 492nd Bombardment Squadron (H) for the Month of November 1944".
49. "History of the 436th Bombardment Squadron (H) for the Month of November 1944"; "History of the 492nd Bombardment Squadron (H) for the Month of November 1944".
50. Shores, *Air War Over Burma: The Allied Air Forces Fight Back in South-east Asia 1942-1945*, P. 285.
51. "History of the 436th Bombardment Squadron (H) for the Month of November 1944".
52. "History of the 436th Bombardment Squadron (H) for the Month of November 1944"; "History of the 492nd Bombardment Squadron (H) for the Month of November 1944"; Dorr, *7th Bombardment Group/ Wing 1918-1995*, P.246.
53. "History of the 436th Bombardment Squadron (H) for the Month of November 1944". There is a brief description of radar counter-measures in CBI and Lt. Charles Beard's role at the China-Burma-India: Remembering a Forgotten Theater website, www.cbi-theater.home.
54. "History of the 492nd Bombardment Squadron (H) for the Month of November 1944".
55. "History of the 9th Bombardment Squadron (H) for the Month of November 1944"; "History of the 493rd Bombardment Squadron (H) for the Month of November 1944". Information on the origins of Bridge #277 came from an article on Wikpedia on the WWII Burma

Railway.

56. "History of the 9th Bombardment Squadron (H) for the Month of December 1944".
57. "History of the 9th Bombardment Squadron (H) for the Month of December 1944"; "History of the 436th Bombardment Squadron (H) for the Month of December 1944"; "History of the 492nd Bombardment Squadron (H) for the Month of December 1944"; "History of the 493rd Bombardment Squadron (H) for the Month of December 1944"; Dorr, *7th Bombardment Group/Wing 1918-1995*, P.246.
58. "History of the 9th Bombardment Squadron (H) for the Month of December 1944"; "History of the 436th Bombardment Squadron (H) for the Month of December 1944"; "History of the 492nd Bombardment Squadron (H) for the Month of December 1944"; "History of the 493rd Bombardment Squadron (H) for the Month of December 1944".
59. "History of the 9th Bombardment Squadron (H) for the Month of December 1944"; "History of the 436th Bombardment Squadron (H) for the Month of December 1944"; "History of the 492nd Bombardment Squadron (H) for the Month of December 1944"; "History of the 493rd Bombardment Squadron (H) for the Month of December 1944".
60. "History of the 9th Bombardment Squadron (H) for the Month of December 1944"; "History of the 436th Bombardment Squadron (H) for the Month of December 1944"; "History of the 492nd Bombardment Squadron (H) for the Month of December 1944"; "History of the 493rd Bombardment Squadron (H) for the Month of December 1944"; Flight Intelligence Report, 14 December 1944, Headquarters Seventh Bombardment Group (H), GP-7-SU-OP-S, Albert F. Simpson Historical Research Center, Air Force Historical Research Agency, Maxwell AFB, AL.
61. "New Bombing Techniques", *Impact*, Volume III, No. 3, March 1945, P.33.
62. Craven, Wesley Frank and James Lea Cate: *The Army Air Forces in WWII*, Volume Six: *Men and Planes* (Chicago, Il: The University of Chicago Press, 1955), pp. 253-62.
63. Craven and Cate, *Men and Planes*, P.259.
64. "Azimuth Only", Ordnance Technical Digest, Headquarters C.B.I. Air Service Command, File 835.813 V.1 No.6, July 1945, Albert F. Simpson Historical Research Center, Air Force Historical Research Agency, Maxwell AFB, AL; "Mechanical Details and Flight Characteristics of the Azon Bomb", copy in the papers of Frank F. Nelson, Jr., in the 7th Bombardment Group (H) Historical Foundation papers, United States Air Force Academy, McDermott Library Collection.
65. See sources listed in footnote 64 above, and in addition Headquarters Eastern Air Command South East Asia, *Weekly Intelligence Summary*, Number 34, 20 April 1945, pp. 1-4; Kopp, Dr. Carlo: "The Dawn of the Smart Bomb", Air Power Australia, 26 March 2011. For those interested, there are some fascinating movies of 7th Bomb Group B-24s dropping Azon bombs available on You Tube.
66. "Azon in the India Burma Theater", Office of the Historical Officer, Headquarters, Tenth Air Force, 20 March 1945, File 830.04-3 February-March 45, Albert F. Simpson Historical Research Center, Air Force Historical Research Agency, Maxwell AFB, AL.
67. 2nd Lt. E.M. Buyer to Major William Donics, November 1944, Appendix "D" in "Azon in the India Burma Theater".
68. "Notes on Briefed History of the Azon Project", Merrill B. Lamont to Col. Wm. H. Knowles, Jr., 14 January, 1945, Appendix "B" in "Azon in the India Burma Theater".
69. "Azon in the India Burma Theater".
70. "Azon in the India Burma Theater"; "Azon Dropping Report, Mission #1, 27 December 1944", Appendix "F" in "Azon in the India Burma Theater"; "History of the 493rd Bombardment Squadron (H) for the Month of December 1944".
71. "History of the 9th Bombardment Squadron (H) for the Month of December 1944".
72. "Azon in the India Burma Theater", P.5; "Azon Dropping Report, Mission #2, 30 December 1944", Appendix "G" in "Azon in the India Burma Theater".
73. "Azon in the India Burma Theater", P.6.
74. "Azon in the India Burma Theater", P.5.
75. Craven and Cate, *The Pacific: Matterhorn to Nagasaki June 1944 to August 1945*, pp. 252-53, 259-60.
76. Captain Lawrence Paulson to Commanding Officer, HQ. 7th Bomb Group (H), AAF, 1 January 1945, "History of Detachment", GP-7-HI-(Bomb)-1917 to 1947.
77. Hamlett, T. Bradley: *Bombing the Death Railroad* (Sun River, MT: Hamlett Ranch Company, 2002), P. 46.
78. "History of the 492nd Bombardment Squadron (H) for the Month of January 1945".
79. "History of the 9th Bombardment Squadron (H) for the Months of December 1944 and January 1945"; "History of the 436th Bombardment Squadron (H) for the Months of December 1944 and January 1945"; "History of the 492nd Bombardment Squadron (H) for the Months of December 1944 and January 1945"; "History of the 493rd Bombardment Squadron (H) for the Months of December 1944 and January 1945".
80. "History of the 436th Bombardment Squadron (H) for the Month of January 1945".
81. Craven and Cate, *The Pacific: Matterhorn to Nagasaki June 1944 to August 1945*, pP. 260-261.
82. "History of the 493rd Bombardment Squadron (H) for the Month of January 1945".
83. "History of the 9th Bombardment Squadron (H) for the Month of December 1944"; "History of the 436th Bombardment Squadron (H) for the Month of December 1944"; "History of the 492nd Bombardment Squadron (H) for the Month of December 1944"; "History of the 493rd Bombardment Squadron (H) for the Month of January 1945"; Dorr, *7th Bombardment Group/Wing 1918-1995*, P.247; Hamlett, *Bombing the Death Railroad*, P. 60.
84. Hamlett, *Bombing the Death Railroad*, P. 66.
85. "Dispatch on Operations Against the Japanese by the Strategic Air Force (E.A.C.) From 27th NoV. 1944 to 31st May 1945", File 821, Albert F. Simpson Historical Research Center, Air Force Historical Research Agency, Maxwell AFB, AL, P.3.
86. Kirby, *The Reconquest of Burma*, pP. 163-65.
87. Romanus and Sunderland, *Time Runs Out in CBI*, pP. 114-41.
88. "History of the 493rd Bombardment Squadron (H) for the Month of January 1945".
89. "History of the 9th Bombardment Squadron (H) for the Month of January 1945"; "History of the 436th Bombardment Squadron (H) for the Month of January 1945"; "History of the 492nd Bombardment Squadron (H) for the Month of January 1945"; "History of the 493rd Bombardment Squadron (H) for the Month of January 1945"; Flight Intelligence Reports for 8 January, 9 January, and 11 January 1945, Headquarters Seventh Bombardment Group (H), GP-7-SU-OP-S.
90. *Diary of: 1st Lt. Harold W. Nadin (aka Pappy) 436th and 493rd Bomb Squadrons, 7th Bombardment Group (H), 10th Air Force Based in India WW II*, (copy courtesy of Jim Augustus)
91. "History of the 9th Bombardment Squadron (H) for the Month of January 1945"; "History of the 436th Bombardment Squadron (H) for the Month of January 1945"; "History of the 492nd Bombardment Squadron (H) for the Month of January 1945"; "History of the 493rd Bombardment Squadron (H) for the Month of January 1945"; Flight Intelligence Report for 13 January 1945, Headquarters Seventh Bombardment Group (H), GP 7 SU OP-S.
92. "History of the 9th Bombardment Squadron (H) for the Month of January 1945"; "History of the 436th Bombardment Squadron (H) for the Month of January 1945"; "History of the 492nd Bombardment Squadron (H) for the Month of January 1945"; "History of the 493rd Bombardment Squadron (H) for the Month of January 1945"; Flight Intelligence Reports for 18 January 1945, Headquarters Seventh Bombardment Group (H), GP-7-SU-OP-S; "Dispatch on Operations Against the Japanese by the Strategic Air Force (E.A.C.) From 27th NoV. 1944 to 31st May 1945", P.7.
93. "History of the 9th Bombardment Squadron (H) for the Month of January 1945"; "History of the 436th Bombardment Squadron (H) for the Month of January 1945"; "History of the 492nd Bombardment Squadron (H) for the Month of January 1945"; "History of the 493rd Bombardment Squadron (H) for the Month of January 1945"; Flight Intelligence Reports for 25 and 27 January 1945, Headquarters Seventh Bombardment Group (H), GP-7-SU-OP-S.
94. Quote from "History of the 492nd Bombardment Squadron (H) for the Month of January 1945"; "History of the 436th Bombardment Squadron (H) for the Month of January 1945".
95. "History of the 9th Bombardment Squadron (H) for the Month of January 1945"; "History of the 493rd Bombardment Squadron (H) for the Month of January 1945"; Flight Intelligence Reports for 29

January 1945, Headquarters Seventh Bombardment Group (H), GP-7-SU-OP-S.

96. "Dispatch on Operations Against the Japanese by the Strategic Air Force (E.A.C.) From 27th NoV. 1944 to 31st May 1945", P.25.

97. February Operational Summary, Headquarters, 7th Bombardment Group (H), AAF, GP-7-HI-(Bomb)-1917 to 1947.

98. "History of the 9th Bombardment Squadron (H) for the Month of February 1945"; "History of the 436th Bombardment Squadron (H) for the Month of February 1945"; "History of the 492nd Bombardment Squadron (H) for the Months of February and April 1945"; "History of the 493rd Bombardment Squadron (H) for the Month of February 1945".

99. "History of the 9th Bombardment Squadron (H) for the Month of February 1945".

100. "History of the 9th Bombardment Squadron (H) for the Month of February 1945"; "History of the 436th Bombardment Squadron (H) for the Month of February 1945"; "History of the 492nd Bombardment Squadron (H) for the Month of February 1945"; "History of the 493rd Bombardment Squadron (H) for the Month of February 1945"; Hamlett, *Bombing the Death Railroad*, P. 73-74.

101. "History of the 436th Bombardment Squadron (H) for the Month of February 1945".

102. "History of the 436th Bombardment Squadron (H) for the Month of February 1945"; "History of the 492nd Bombardment Squadron (H) for the Month of February 1945"; "History of the 493rd Bombardment Squadron (H) for the Month of February 1945"; Flight Intelligence Report for 7 February 1945, Headquarters Seventh Bombardment Group (H), GP-7-SU-OP-S.

103. "History of the 9th Bombardment Squadron (H) for the Month of February 1945"; "History of the 436th Bombardment Squadron (H) for the Month of February 1945"; Flight Intelligence Reports for 9 and 13 February 1945, Headquarters Seventh Bombardment Group (H), GP-7-SU-OP-S; Kratoska, Paul H., Ed.: *The Thailand-Burma Railway, 1942-1946: Documents and Selected Writings,* Volume 6 (London: Routledge, 2006), P. 24.

104. Kirby, *The Reconquest of Burma*, pP. 253-63.

105. Craven and Cate, *The Pacific: Matterhorn to Nagasaki June 1944 to August 1945*, P.161.

106. "History of the 9th Bombardment Squadron (H) for the Month of February 1945"; "History of the 436th Bombardment Squadron (H) for the Month of February 1945"; "History of the 492nd Bombardment Squadron (H) for the Month of February 1945"; Flight Intelligence Reports for 21, 23, and 25 February 1945, Headquarters Seventh Bombardment Group (H), GP-7-SU-OP-S.

107. "Azon in the India Burma Theater".

108. "Azon in the India Burma Theater"; "History of the 493rd Bombardment Squadron (H) for the Month of February 1945"; "Azon (VB-1) in India-Burma Sector", Operations Analysis Section, India-Burma Theater, 29 March 1945, File 825.3101-7, Albert F. Simpson Historical Research Center, Air Force Historical Research Agency, Maxwell AFB, AL, P.7.

109. February Operational Summary, Headquarters, 7th Bombardment Group (H), AAF,

110. "History of the 9th Bombardment Squadron (H) for the Month of February 1945"; "History of the 436th Bombardment Squadron (H) for the Month of February 1945"; "History of the 492nd Bombardment Squadron (H) for the Month of February 1945"; "History of the 493rd Bombardment Squadron (H) for the Month of February 1945"; Flight Intelligence Report for 28 February 1945, Headquarters Seventh Bombardment Group (H), GP-7-SU-OP-S.

111. Copy of Air Commodore Mellersh's letter is in "History of the 492nd Bombardment Squadron (H) for the Month of February 1945".

112. "History of the 9th Bombardment Squadron (H) for the Month of March 1945"; "History of the 436th Bombardment Squadron (H) for the Month of March 1945"; "History of the 492nd Bombardment Squadron (H) for the Month of March 1945".

113. "History of the 9th Bombardment Squadron (H) for the Month of March 1945".

114. "History of the 492nd Bombardment Squadron (H) for the Month of March 1945".

115. "History of the 9th Bombardment Squadron (H) for the Month of March 1945"; "History of the 436th Bombardment Squadron (H) for the Month of March 1945"; "History of the 492nd Bombardment Squadron (H) for the Month of March 1945".

116. "History of the 9th Bombardment Squadron (H) for the Month of March 1945"; "History of the 436th Bombardment Squadron (H) for the Month of March 1945"; "History of the 492nd Bombardment Squadron (H) for the Month of March 1945"; "History of the 493rd Bombardment Squadron (H) for the Month of February 1945".

117. Hamlett, *Bombing the Death Railroad*, P. 84.

118. "History of the 9th Bombardment Squadron (H) for the Month of March 1945"; "History of the 436th Bombardment Squadron (H) for the Month of March 1945"; "History of the 492nd Bombardment Squadron (H) for the Month of March 1945"; "History of the 493rd Bombardment Squadron (H) for the Month of March 1945"; Dorr, *7th Bombardment Group/Wing 1918-1995*, P.248.

119. "Dispatch on Operations Against the Japanese by the Strategic Air Force (E.A.C.) From 27th Nov. 1944 to 31st May 1945", P.13.

120. "History of the 493rd Bombardment Squadron (H) for the Month of February 1945".

121. "History of Headquarters, 7th Bombardment Group (H), AAF for the Month of March 1945".

122. "History of the 436th Bombardment Squadron (H) for the Month of March 1945".

123. Dorr, *7th Bombardment Group/Wing 1918-1995*, P.248.

124. "History of the 436th Bombardment Squadron (H) for the Months of March and April 1945"; "History of the 492nd Bombardment Squadron (H) for the Months of March and April 1945".

125. "History of the 9th Bombardment Squadron (H) for the Month of April 1945"; "History of the 436th Bombardment Squadron (H) for the Month of April 1945"; "History of the 492nd Bombardment Squadron (H) for the Month of April 1945"; "History of the 493rd Bombardment Squadron (H) for the Month of April 1945".

126. Hamlett, *Bombing the Death Railroad*, pp.85-86.

127. Hamlett, *Bombing the Death Railroad*, P. 88.

128. "History of the 9th Bombardment Squadron (H) for the Month of April 1945"; "History of the 493rd Bombardment Squadron (H) for the Month of April 1945".

129. "Dispatch on Operations Against the Japanese by the Strategic Air Force (E.A.C.) From 27th Nov. 1944 to 31st May 1945", P.25.

130. Kirby, *The Reconquest of Burma*, pp. 327-32.

131. "Dispatch on Operations Against the Japanese by the Strategic Air Force (E.A.C.) From 27th Nov. 1944 to 31st May 1945", P.29.

132. "History of the 492nd Bombardment Squadron (H) for the Month of April 1945".

133. "History of the 9th Bombardment Squadron (H) for the Month of April 1945".

134. "History of the 492nd Bombardment Squadron (H) for the Month of April 1945".

135. "History of the 9th Bombardment Squadron (H) for the Month of April 1945"; "History of the 436th Bombardment Squadron (H) for the Month of April 1945"; "History of the 492nd Bombardment Squadron (H) for the Month of April 1945"; "History of the 493rd Bombardment Squadron (H) for the Month of April 1945".

136. Col. Roy Lynn, Deputy Air Commander, Strategic Air Force, to Commanding Officer, Headquarters, 7th Bomb Group, 25 April 1945, copy in "History of the Headquarters 7th Bombardment Group (H) for the Month of April 1945".

137. "History of the 9th Bombardment Squadron (H) for the Month of April 1945"; "History of the 436th Bombardment Squadron (H) for the Month of April 1945"; "History of the 492nd Bombardment Squadron (H) for the Month of April 1945"; "History of the 493rd Bombardment Squadron (H) for the Month of April 1945"; Kirby, *The Reconquest of Burma*, pp. 385-86.

138. "History of the 436th Bombardment Squadron (H) for the Month of April 1945"; "History of the Headquarters 7th Bombardment Group (H) for the Month of April 1945"; Craven and Cate, *The Pacific: Guadalcanal to Saipan August 1942 to July 1944*, P.492.

139. "History of the 436th Bombardment Squadron (H) for the Month of April 1945"; "History of the Headquarters 7th Bombardment Group (H) for the Month of April 1945";

140. Eastern Air Command *Weekly Intelligence Summary*, Number 35, 27 April 1945, P. 2.

141. Air Commodore Mellersh to Commanding Officer, 7th Bombardment Group, 30 April 1945, copy in "History of the Headquarters 7th Bombardment Group (H) for the Month of April 1945".

142. Hamlett, *Bombing the Death Railroad*, pp. 94-100.

143. "History of the 9th Bombardment Squadron (H) for the Month of April 1945".

144. "History of the 493rd Bombardment Squadron (H) for the Month of April 1945".
145. "History of the 9th Bombardment Squadron (H) for the Month of April 1945"; "History of the 436th Bombardment Squadron (H) for the Month of April 1945"; "History of the 492nd Bombardment Squadron (H) for the Month of April 1945"; "History of the 493rd Bombardment Squadron (H) for the Month of April 1945".

Chapter Eight: Victory in Burma

1. "History of the 492nd Bombardment Squadron (H) for the Month of May 1945".
2. Kirby, *The Reconquest of Burma*, pp. 394-97.
3. "History of the 492nd Bombardment Squadron (H) for the Month of May 1945".
4. Dorr, *7th Bombardment Group/Wing 1918-1995*, P.249.
5. "History of the 9th Bombardment Squadron (H) for the Month of May 1945"; "History of the 436th Bombardment Squadron (H) for the Month of May 1945"; "History of the 492nd Bombardment Squadron (H) for the Month of May 1945"; "History of the 493rd Bombardment Squadron (H) for the Month of May 1945".
6. "History of the 492nd Bombardment Squadron (H) for the Month of May 1945".
7. "History of the 492nd Bombardment Squadron (H) for the Month of May 1945"; Dorr, *7th Bombardment Group/Wing 1918-1995*, P.249.
8. "History of the 9th Bombardment Squadron (H) for the Month of May 1945"; "History of the 436th Bombardment Squadron (H) for the Month of May 1945"; "History of the 492nd Bombardment Squadron (H) for the Month of May 1945"; "History of the 493rd Bombardment Squadron (H) for the Month of May 1945"; "Dispatch on Operations Against the Japanese by the Strategic Air Force (E.A.C.) From 27th Nov. 1944 to 31st May 1945", P.22.
9. Craven and Cate, *The Pacific: Matterhorn to Nagasaki June 1944 to August 1945*, P.267.
10. Craven and Cate, *The Pacific: Matterhorn to Nagasaki June 1944 to August 1945*, P.268.
11. Craven and Cate, *The Pacific: Matterhorn to Nagasaki June 1944 to August 1945*, P.268-69.
12. *R.A.F. Narrative: The Campaigns in the Far East*, Volume IV, *South East Asia (November 1943 to August 1945)*, pp. 305-09.
13. "History of the 9th Bombardment Squadron (H) for the Month of May 1945".
14. "History of the 9th Bombardment Squadron (H) for the Month of May 1945"; "History of the 436th Bombardment Squadron (H) for the Month of May 1945"; "History of the 492nd Bombardment Squadron (H) for the Month of May 1945"; "History of the 493rd Bombardment Squadron (H) for the Month of May 1945"; "History of the Headquarters 7th Bombardment Group (H) for the Month of May 1945".
15. "History of the 9th Bombardment Squadron (H) for the Month of May 1945".
16. "History of the 436th Bombardment Squadron (H) for the Month of May 1945"; "History of the 492nd Bombardment Squadron (H) for the Months of May and June 1945".
17. Col. Harvey Alness to Commanding Officers, All Squadrons, 7th Bomb Group (H), 21 May 1945, "History of the Headquarters 7th Bombardment Group (H) for the Month of May 1945".
18. Col. Harvey Alness to Commanding Officers, All Squadrons, 7th Bomb Group (H), 21 May 1945, "History of the Headquarters 7th Bombardment Group (H) for the Month of May 1945".
19. "History of the 9th Bombardment Squadron (H) for the Month of June 1945"; "History of the 436th Bombardment Squadron (H) for the Month of June 1945"; "History of the 492nd Bombardment Squadron (H) for the Month of June 1945"; "History of the 493rd Bombardment Squadron (H) for the Month of June 1945"; "History of the Headquarters 7th Bombardment Group (H) for the Month of June 1945"; "History of the Headquarters 7th Bombardment Group (H) for the Month of June 1945".
20. "History of the 9th Bombardment Squadron (H) for the Month of June 1945"; "History of the 436th Bombardment Squadron (H) for the Month of June 1945"; "History of the 492nd Bombardment Squadron (H) for the Months of June and July 1945"; "History of the 493rd Bombardment Squadron (H) for the Month of June 1945"; "History of the Headquarters 7th Bombardment Group (H) for the Month of June 1945".
21. "History of the 492nd Bombardment Squadron (H) for the Month of June 1945"; "History of the Headquarters 7th Bombardment Group (H) for the Month of June 1945".
22. "History of the 492nd Bombardment Squadron (H) for the Month of June 1945".
23. "History of the 492nd Bombardment Squadron (H) for the Month of June 1945".
24. "Six Months of Bridge Bombing by the Strategic Air Force, Including the Use of Azon", P.9.
25. Col. Harvey Alness to Officers and Men of the Seventh Bombardment Group, 25 June 1945, copy in "History of the Headquarters 7th Bombardment Group (H) for the Month of June 1945".
26. Col. Harvey Alness to Officers and Enlisted Men of the 7th Bombardment Group (H), 23 June 1945, copy in "History of the Headquarters 7th Bombardment Group (H) for the Month of June 1945".
27. "History of the 9th Bombardment Squadron (H) for the Month of June 1945"; "History of the 436th Bombardment Squadron (H) for the Month of June 1945"; "History of the 492nd Bombardment Squadron (H) for the Month of June 1945"; "History of the 493rd Bombardment Squadron (H) for the Month of June 1945"; "History of the Headquarters 7th Bombardment Group (H) for the Month of June 1945"; "History of the Headquarters 7th Bombardment Group (H) for the Month of June 1945".
28. "History of the 9th Bombardment Squadron (H) for the Month of June 1945"; "History of the 436th Bombardment Squadron (H) for the Month of June 1945"; "History of the 492nd Bombardment Squadron (H) for the Month of June 1945"; "History of the 493rd Bombardment Squadron (H) for the Month of June 1945"; "History of the Headquarters 7th Bombardment Group (H) for the Month of June 1945".
29. "History of the 492nd Bombardment Squadron (H) for the Month of July 1945".
30. "History of the 492nd Bombardment Squadron (H) for the Month of July 1945".
31. "History of the 492nd Bombardment Squadron (H) for the Month of July 1945".
32. "History of the 436th Bombardment Squadron (H) for the Month of July 1945".
33. "History of the 9th Bombardment Squadron (H) for the Month of July 1945"; "History of the 492nd Bombardment Squadron (H) for the Month of July 1945"; Dorr, *7th Bombardment Group/Wing 1918-1995*, P.249.
34. Glines, *Chennault's Forgotten Warriors: The Saga of the 308th Bomb Group in China*, pp.198-99.
35. Glines, *Chennault's Forgotten Warriors: The Saga of the 308th Bomb Group in China*, pp.198-99.
36. "History of the 493rd Bombardment Squadron (H) for the Month of June 1945".
37. Winkler, Allan M.: *The Politics of Propaganda: The Office of War Information 1942-1945* (New Haven, CT: Yale University Press, 1978), P.137.
38. Wyatt, David K.: *Thailand: A Short History* (New Haven, CT: Yale University Press, 1984), pp. 256-60.
39. Kirby, Major-General S. Woodburn: *The War Against Japan*, Vol. V: *The Surrender of Japan* (London: Her Majesty's Stationary Office, 1969), P.225.
40. "History of the 493rd Bombardment Squadron (H) for the Month of June 1945".
41. "History of the 493rd Bombardment Squadron (H) for the Month of July 1945".
42. Kirby, *The Surrender of Japan*, P.64.
43. "History of the 493rd Bombardment Squadron (H) for the Month of July 1945".
44. "History of the 493rd Bombardment Squadron (H) for the Month of July 1945".
45. "History of the 436th Bombardment Squadron (H) for the Month of August 1945".
46. "History of the Headquarters 7th Bombardment Group (H) for the Month of August 1945".
47. "History of the 9th Bombardment Squadron (H) for the Month of August 1945"; "History of the 436th Bombardment Squadron (H) for the Month of August 1945"; "History of the 492nd Bombardment Squadron (H) for the Month of August 1945"; "History of the 493rd

Bombardment Squadron (H) for the Month of August 1945"; Dorr, *7th Bombardment Group/Wing 1918-1995*, P.250.

48. "History of the 9th Bombardment Squadron (H) for the Month of August 1945"; "History of the 436th Bombardment Squadron (H) for the Month of August 1945"; "History of the 492nd Bombardment Squadron (H) for the Month of August 1945"; "History of the 493rd Bombardment Squadron (H) for the Month of August 1945".
49. "History of the 9th Bombardment Squadron (H) for the Month of September 1945"; "History of the 436th Bombardment Squadron (H) for the Month of September 1945"; "History of the 492nd Bombardment Squadron (H) for the Month of September 1945"; "History of the 493rd Bombardment Squadron (H) for the Month of September 1945".
50. "History of the 9th Bombardment Squadron (H) for the Month of September 1945".
51. "History of the 492nd Bombardment Squadron (H) for the Month of September 1945".
52. "History of the 9th Bombardment Squadron (H) for the Month of September 1945"; "History of the 436th Bombardment Squadron (H) for the Month of September 1945"; "History of the 492nd Bombardment Squadron (H) for the Month of September 1945"; "History of the 493rd Bombardment Squadron (H) for the Month of September 1945"; Maurer, *Combat Squadrons of the Air Force WWII*, pp. 50, 539, 592, 593; Dorr, *7th Bombardment Group/Wing 1918-1995*, P. 195.
53. A copy of Lt. General Wheeler's letter of September 8, 1945, is attached to "History, 1917-1945, 7th Bomb. Group (H) A.A.F.", GP-7-HI-(Bomb) 31 May 1917-30 June 1945.
54. United States Strategic Bombing Survey, Military Analysis Division: *Air Operations in China, Burma, India WWII*, P. 50.
55. Biddle, *Rhetoric and Reality in Air Warfare*, P. 291.
56. Walker, "Bombardment Aviation—Bulwark of National Defense", P. 15.
57. McFarland, *America's Pursuit of Precision Bombing, 1910-1945*, P. 190.
58. United States Strategic Bombing Survey, Military Analysis Division: *Air Operations in China, Burma, India WWII*, pp. 22, 24.
59. "Dispatch of Operations of Strategic Air Force, Eastern Air Command for the Period 15 December to 31 May 1944", Appendix H.
60. Operational Research Section, Air Command, South East Asia: Report No. S.45 "Six Months of Bridge Bombing by the Strategic Air Force, Including the Use of Azon", P. 5.
61. Operational Research Section, Air Command, South East Asia: Report No. S.45 "Six Months of Bridge Bombing by the Strategic Air Force, Including the Use of Azon", P. 5.
62. Operational Research Section, Air Command, South East Asia: Report No. S.45 "Six Months of Bridge Bombing by the Strategic Air Force, Including the Use of Azon", P. 6.
63. United States Strategic Bombing Survey, *Air Operations in China, Burma, India WWII*, P.14.
64. United States Strategic Bombing Survey, *Air Operations in China, Burma, India WWII*, P.14.
65. Vice-Admiral the Earl Mountbatten of Burma, *Report to the Combined Chiefs of Staff by the Supreme Allied Command South-East Asia 1943-1945* (London: His Majesty's Stationary Office, 1951), P. 31.
66. This is the title of Air Commodore Henry Probert's history of the Royal Air Force in Burma.

Bibliography

Government Documents

Air Historical Branch (1), Air Ministry: *R.A.F. Narrative: The Campaigns in the Far East,* Volume III, *India Command: September 1939 to November 1943* (London: Royal Air Force Air Force Centre for Air Power Studies, MLRS Books edition)

Air Historical Branch (1), Air Ministry: *R.A.F. Narrative: The Campaigns in the Far East,* Volume IV, *South East Asia (November 1943 to August 1945)* (London: Royal Air Force Air Force Centre for Air Power Studies, MLRS Books edition)

Air Service Tactical School: *Bombardment* (Washington, D.C.: Government Printing Office 1926)

Air Corps Aerial Gunnery and Bombing, Training Regulations TR 440-40, (Washington, D.C.: War Department, March 11, 1929)

"Bombing Operations 1941-1942 by R.A.F. and U.S.A.A.F. Units Based in India and Burma", Air Command, South East Asia, Bombing Operations Air 23/2855, Public Records Office, United Kingdom.

"Chronological Historical Record Ninth Air Force Aug 42-Aug 43", File 533.052, Part 1, Aug1942-Aug 1943, Albert F. Simpson Historical Research Center, Air Force Historical Research Agency, Maxwell AFB, AL.

"Dispatch on Operations of Strategic Air Force, Eastern Air Command for the Period 15 December to 31 May 1944", File 821, Albert F. Simpson Historical Research Center, Air Force Historical Research Agency, Maxwell AFB, AL.

"Dispatch on Operations Against the Japanese by the Strategic Air Force (E.A.C.) From 1st June 1944 to 26th November 1944", File 821, Albert F. Simpson Historical Research Center, Air Force Historical Research Agency, Maxwell AFB, AL.

"Dispatch on Operations Against the Japanese by the Strategic Air Force (E.A.C.) From 27th Nov. 1944 to 31st May, 1945", File 821, Albert F. Simpson Historical Research Center, Air Force Historical Research Agency, Maxwell AFB, AL.

Headquarters 7th Bombardment Group (H) AAF, "Consolidated History of the Seventh Bombardment Group (H), AFF, Ground and Air Echelons for the Year 1942", GP-7-HI(Bomb) Year 1942 Pt-1, Albert F. Simpson Historical Research Center, Air Force Historical Research Agency, Maxwell AFB, AL.

Headquarters 7th Bombardment Group, Officer of the Operations Officer, November 18, 1936, "Report of Joint Coastal Frontier Defense Exercise No.2", in GP-7-SU (Bomb) November 1936, Albert F. Simpson Historical Research Center, Air Force Historical Research Agency, Maxwell AFB, AL.

"History of the 7th Bombardment Group (H)", GP-7-HI(Bomb)-1942-1945, Albert F. Simpson Historical Research Center, Air Force Historical Research Agency, Maxwell AFB, AL.

"History of the 9th Bombardment Squadron (H)", SQ-9-HI (Bomb)-1942-1945, Albert F. Simpson Historical Research Center, Air Force Historical Research Agency, Maxwell AFB, AL.

"History of the 436th Bombardment Squadron (H), SQ-436-HI(Bomb)-1942-1945, Albert F. Simpson Historical Research Center, Air Force Historical Research Agency, Maxwell AFB, AL.

"History of the 492nd Bombardment Squadron (H)", SQ-492-HI (Bomb)-1942-1945, Albert F. Simpson Historical Research Center, Air Force Historical Research Agency, Maxwell AFB, AL.

"History of the 493rd Bombardment Squadron (H)", SQ-493-HI(Bomb)-1942-1945, Albert F. Simpson Historical Research Center, Air Force Historical Research Agency, Maxwell AFB, AL.

"History Headquarters India Air Task Force 1942 & 1 January to 31 May 1943", File 827.01 30 October 1942-May 1943, Albert F. Simpson Historical Research Center, Air Force Historical Research Agency, Maxwell AFB, AL,

"History of United States Army Air Forces, India-Burma Sector, China-India-Burma Theater", File 825.0115 20 Aug 1943-Apr 1944, Albert F. Simpson Historical Research Center, Air Force Historical Research Agency, Maxwell AFB, AL, entry for September 24, 1942.

"I.A.T.F. Bombing Missions", File 827.308 Dec 42-Sept 43, Albert F. Simpson Historical Research Center, Air Force Historical Research Agency, Maxwell AFB, AL.

Joint Army-Navy Assessment Committee (JANAC): *Japanese Naval and Merchant Shipping Losses During WWII by All Causes*, (Washington DC: U.S. Government Printing Office, NAVEXOS P-468, 1947). Copy available at Hyperwar.com.

Office of the Assistant Chief of Air Staff, Intelligence: *Impact*, Vol. 2. No. 7, (July 1944) (New York, NY: James Parton and Company, Inc., 1980)

"Operations Analysis Report: Study of 7th Bomb Group Operations from 1 February 1943 to 31 March 1944", 27 May 1944, File 830.310, Albert F. Simpson Historical Research Center, Air Force Historical Research Agency, Maxwell AFB, AL.

"Operations of the Strategic Air Force 15 December 1943-3 May 1945", File 821, Albert F. Simpson Historical Research Center, Air Force Historical Research Agency, Maxwell AFB, AL.

Pound, Merritt B.: *History of the United States Army Air Forces, India-Burma Sector, China-Burma-India Theater (From Activation through April 1944)*, 825.0115, Albert F. Simpson Historical Research Center, Air Force Historical Research Agency, Maxwell AFB, AL.

"S-3 Diary for the 7th Bombardment Group, December 1, 1941-February 27, 1942", Folder 6, Box 1, MS 60, Series 1, 7th Bombardment Group (H) Historical Foundation, United States Air Force Academy, McDermott Library Collection.

"Tenth Air Force Operational Diary", File 830.305-1, 1 June 1942- 1 June 1943, Albert F. Simpson Historical Research Center, Air Force Historical Research Agency, Maxwell AFB, AL

"Unit Diary of Composite 11th Bombardment Squadron Beginning December 14, 1941—March 1942", SQ-Bomb-11-SU-RE-D December 1941-March 1942, Albert F. Simpson Historical Research Center, Air Force Historical Research Agency, Maxwell AFB, AL.

"V Bomber Command Journal, January 13, 1942-March 19, 1942", Folder 7, Box 1, MS 60, Series 1, United States Air Force Academy, McDermott Library Collection.

War Department: *Air Corps Field Manual FM 1-10: Tactics and Technique of Air Attack* (Washington, D.C.: Government Printing Office, 1940)

Books, Articles, and Memoirs

Allen, Louis: *Burma: The Longest War 1941-45* (New York, NY: St. Martin's Press, 1984)

Anabuki, Satoru: *Aozora no Kawa: Anabuki Gunso Hayabusa Kusen (The Blue Sky River: Sergeant Anabuki's Hayabusa Air Battle Chronicle)* (Tokyo: Kojinsha, 1985)

Anderson, John D., Jr.: *The Airplane: A History of its Technology* (Reston, VA: American Institute of Aeronautics and Astronautics, 2002)

Arakaki, Leatrice R. and John R. Kuborn: *7 December 1941: The Air Force Story*. (Hickam Air Force Base, Hawaii: Pacific Air Forces Office of Air Force History 1991)

Arnold, General of the Air Force H.H.: *Global Mission* (New York: Harper Brothers 1949)

Bartsch, William H.: *December 8, 1941: MacArthur's Pearl Harbor*. (College Station, TX: Texas A & M University Press, 2003)

——— *Every Day a Nightmare: American Pursuit Pilots in the Defense of Java, 1941-1942* (College Station, TX: Texas A & M University Press, 2010)

Beauvais, Charles J.: *Plum to Dacca* (Privately published, 1986) Copy courtesy of Jim Augustus.

Biddle, Tami Davis: *Rhetoric and Reality in Air Warfare: The Evolution of British and American Ideas About Strategic Bombing, 1914-1945*. (Princeton: Princeton University Press, 2002)

Borden, Norman E., Jr.: *Air Mail Emergency 1934*, (Freeport, Maine: Bond Wheelwright Company, 1968)

Bowers, Peter M.: *Fortress in the Sky*. (California: Sentry Books, Inc. 1976)

Bowman, Harold W.: *Birds of a Feather: A Memoir* (no date)

Bowman, Martin W.: *Consolidated B-24 Liberator*. (London: The Crowood Press 1998)

Brendon, Piers: *The Dark Valley: A Panorama of the 1930s* (London: Jonathan Cape, 2000)

Brereton, Lt. General Louis H.: *The Brereton Diaries: The War in the Air in the Pacific, Middle East, and Europe, 3 October 1941-8 May 1945* (New York, NY: William Morrow and Company, 1946)

Byrd, Martha: *Chennault: Giving Wings to the Tiger* (Tuscaloosa, AL: University of Alabama Press, 1987)

——— *Kenneth N. Walker: Airpower's Untempered Crusader* (Maxwell AFB, AL: Air University Press, 1997)

Cea, Eduardo: *Japanese Military Aircraft*, No. 5: *Aircraft of the Imperial Japanese Navy. Land-based aviation, 1929-1945 (II)* (Valaldolid, Spain: AF Editions, 2010)

Clay, Lt. Colonel Steven E. (Ret'd): *U.S. Army Order of Battle 1919-1941: Volume 3: The Services-Air Service, Engineers, and Special Troops 1919-1941* (Fort Leavenworth, KS: Combat Studies Institute Press, 2010)

Close, Winton R.: "The B-18—A Reminiscence", in Higham, Robert and Carol Williams, Eds.: *Flying Combat Aircraft of the USAAF-USAF*, Volume III (Manhattan, KS: Sunflower University Press, 1981)

Craven, Wesley Frank, and James Lea Cate, Eds.: *The Army Air Forces in WWII*, Volume One: *Plans and Early Operations January 1939 to August 1942* (Chicago, Il: The University of Chicago Press, 1948)

——— *The Army Air Forces in WWII*, Volume Two: *Europe: Torch to Pointblank, August 1942 to December 1943* (Chicago, IL: University of Chicago Press, 1949)

——— *The Army Air Forces in WWII*, Volume Four: *The Pacific: Guadalcanal to Saipan August 1942 to July 1944* (Chicago, IL: University of Chicago Press, 1950)

——— *The Army Air Forces in WWII*, Volume Five, *The Pacific: Matterhorn to Nagasaki June 1944 to August 1945* (Chicago, IL: The University of Chicago Press, 1953)

Crowder, James L., Jr.: *Osage General: Major General Clarence L. Tinker* (Tinker Air Force Base, OK: Officer of History, Oklahoma City Air Logistics Center 1987), pp. 227-32.

. Dallek, Robert: *Franklin D. Roosevelt and American Foreign Policy, 1932-1945* (New York, NY: Oxford University Press, 1979)

Daso, Dik Alan: *Hap Arnold and the Evolution of American Air Power* (Washington, D.C.: Smithsonian Institution Press, 2000)

Dorr, Robert F.: *7th Bombardment Group/Wing 1918-1995*. (Paducah, KY: Turner Publishing Company 1996)

Duncan, Charles V., Jr.: A B-24 Over Burma (privately published 1986) Copy courtesy of Jim Augustus.

Edmonds, Walter D.: *They Fought With What They Had* (Boston: Little, Brown and Company, 1951)

Fielder, James M.: *459th Fighter Squadron: the Twin Dragons CBI 1943-1945* (Privately published 1993)

Finney, Robert T.: *History of the Air Corps Tactical School 1920-1940* (Washington, D.C.: Center for Air Force History, 1992)

Fritsche, Carl: "B-24 Liberator", in Higham, Robin and Carol Williams, Eds.: *Flying Combat Aircraft of the USAAF-USAF*, Volume 2 (Ames, Iowa: The Iowa State University Press, 1978)

Futrell, Robert F.: *Ideas, Concepts, and Doctrine, Volume I: Basic Thinking in the United States Air Force 1907-1960* (Maxwell AFB, AL: Air University Press, 1989)

Glines, Carroll V.: *Chennault's Forgotten Warriors: The Saga of the 308th Bomb Group in China* (Atglen, PA: Schiffer Publishing Ltd., 1995)

Greer, Thomas H.: *The Development of Air Doctrine in the Army Air Arm 1917-1941* (Washington, D.C.: Office of Air Force History,1985)

Guelich, Capt. Robert V. and Sgt. William G Mors: "One Man Crew", *Air Force*, Vol. 27, No. 2, February 1944

Hamlett, T. Bradley: *Bombing the Death Railroad* (Sun River, MT: Hamlett Ranch Company, 2002)

. Hansell, Maj. Gen. Haywood S., Jr. USAF (Ret.): "The Keystone Bombers: Unhonored and Unloved", *Air Force Magazine*, September 1977

Harley, Dr. R. Bruce: *The March Field Story: 50th Anniversary 1918-1968* (March Field, CA: 1968)

Hata, Ikuhiko, Yasuho Izawa, and Christopher Shores: *Japanese Army Air Force Fighter Units and Their Aces 1931-1945* (London: Grub Street, 2002)

Hata, Ikuhiko, Yasuho Izawa, and Christopher Shores: *Japanese Naval Air Force Fighter Units and Their Aces 1932-1945* (London: Grub Street, 2011)

Howard, Michael: *History of the Second World War: Grand Strategy*, Volume IV: *August 1942-September 1943* (London: Her Majesty's Stationary Office, 1970)

Ichimura, Hiroshi: *Ki-43 'Oscar' Aces of World War 2*, Osprey Aircraft of the Aces No. 85, (Oxford, UK: Osprey Publishing, Ltd., 2009)

Izawa, Yasuho: "64th Flying Sentai, Part 2", *Aero Album*, Vol. 4, No. 3 (Fall 1971)

Izawa, Yasuho: "64th Flying Sentai, Part 3", *Aero Album*, Vol. 5, No. 4 (Winter 1972)

Jarrett, Philip, Ed.: *Biplane to Monoplane: Aircraft Development 1919-1939* (London: Putnam Aeronautical Books, 1997)

Johnson, David E.: *Fast Tanks and Heavy Bombers: Innovation in the U.S. Army 1917-1945* (Ithica, NY: Cornell University Press, 1998)

Kirby, Major-General S. Woodburn: *The War Against Japan*, Vol. I.: *The Loss of Singapore*, (London: Her Majesty's Stationary Office, 1957)

——— *The War Against Japan*, Vol. II: *India's Most Dangerous Hour*, (London: Her Majesty's Stationary Office, 1958)

——— *The War Against Japan*, Vol. III: *The Decisive Battles* (London: Her Majesty's Stationary Office, 1961)

——— *The War Against Japan*, Vol. IV: *The Reconquest of Burma* (London: Her Majesty's Stationary Office, 1965)

——— *The War Against Japan*, Vol. V: *The Surrender of Japan* (London: Her Majesty's Stationary Office, 1969)

Kratoska, Paul H., Ed.: *The Thailand-Burma Railway, 1942-1946: Documents and Selected Writings*, Volume 6 (London: Routledge, 2006)

Maurer, Maurer, Ed.: *Air Force Combat Units of WWII* (Washington: Office of Air Force History, 1983)

——— *Aviation in the U.S. Army 1919-1939*. (Washington, D.C.: U.S. Government Printing Office, 1987)

——— *Combat Squadrons of the Air Force WWII* (Washington, D.C.: Office of Air Force History, 1982)

Mayhew, Wilbur W.: *Battlefields Galore*. Private memoir, copy courtesy of Jim Augustus.

McFarland, Stephen L.: *America's Pursuit of Precision Bombing, 1910-1945* (Washington, D.C.: Smithsonian Institution Press, 1995)

Mets, David R.: *Master of Air Power: General Carl A. Spaatz* (Novato, CA: Presidio Press, 1988)

Mitchell, John H.: *In Alis Vicimus-On Wings We Conquer: The 19th and 7th Bombardment Groups of the United States Air Force in the Southwest Pacific in the first year of World War Two* (Springfield, MO: G.E.M. Publishers, 1990)

Nalty, Bernard C.: "Reaction to the War in Europe", in Nalty, Bernard C.: *Winged Shield, Winged Sword: A History of the United States Air Force*. Volume I, *1907-1950*. (Washington, D.C. Air Force History and Museums Program 1997)

------.: *Winged Shield, Wing Sword: A History of the United States Air Force*, Vol. I *1907-1950*. (Washington, D.C. Air Force History and Museums Program, 1997)

Pelletier, Alan J.: "Bombers As Postmen: Douglas YO-35 and Y1B-7", *Air Enthusiast*, Vol. 122, March/April 2006, pp.30-32.

Perez, Alfonso B.: *A B-24 Bombardier 'Over Burma': The Personal Diary of Lt. Alfonso B. Perez* (Privately published) copy in Folder 26, Box 3, MS 60, Series 1, 7th Bombardment Group (H) Historical Foundation, United States Air Force Academy, McDermott Library Collection.

Prange, Gordon W.: *At Dawn We Slept: The Untold Story of Pearl Harbor* (New York: McGraw-Hill Book Company 1981)

Probert, Air Commodore Henry: *The Forgotten Air Force: The Royal Air Force in the War Against Japan 1941-1945*, (London: Brassey's, 1995)

Romanus, Charles F., and Riley Sunderland: *Stilwell's Mission to China*, United States Army in WWII: China-Burma-India Theater, (Washington, D.C.: Office of the Chief of Military History, Department of the Army, 1953)

——— *Stilwell's Command Problems*, United States Army in WWII: China-Burma-India Theater, (Washington, D.C.: Office of the Chief of Military History, Department of the Army, 1956)

——— *Time Runs Out in CBI*, United States Army in WWII: China-Burma-India Theater, (Washington, D.C.: Office of the Chief of Military History, Department of the Army, 1959)

Rowan, Captain Thomas T.: *Born in Battle: Round the World Adventures of the 513th Bombardment Squadron* (Philadelphia, PA: The John C. Winston Company, 1944)

Shiner, John F.: "The Coming of the GHQ Air Force, 1925-1935", in Nalty, Bernard C.: *Winged Shield, Wing Sword: A History of the United States Air Force*, Vol. I 1907-1950 (Washington, D.C.: United States Air Force 1997)

——— "The Heyday of the GHQ Air Force, 1935-39". Nalty, Bernard C.: *Winged Shield, Wing Sword: A History of the United States Air Force*. Vol. I, *1907-1950* (Washington, D.C.: Air Force History and Museums Program, 1997)

Shores, Christopher, Brian Cull, and Yasuho Izawa: *Bloody Shambles*, Volume Two: *The Defence of Sumatra to the Fall of Burma* (London: Grub Street, 1993)

Shores, Christopher: *Air War Over Burma: The Allied Air Forces Fight Back in South-east Asia 1942-1945* (London: Grub Street, 2005)

Slim, Field Marshal Sir William: *Defeat Into Victory* (London: Cassell and Company Ltd, 1956)

The Record: The 11th Bombardment Squadron (M) (Richmond, VA: 1947)

Thomas, Gerald C., Jr.: *The First Team: Thornton D. Hooper and America's First Bombing Squadrons*. (Dallas, TX: The League of WWI Aviation Historians, 1992)

Trest, Warren A.: *Air Force Roles and Missions: A History* (Washington, D.C.: Air Force History and Museums Program, 1998)

U.S. Air Force Historical Study No. 6: *The Development of the Heavy Bomber* (USAF Historical Division, Research Studies Institute, Air University. Maxwell AFB, AL)

U.S. Air Force Historical Study No. 8: *The AAF in the Middle East: A Study in the Origins of the Ninth Air Force* , (USAF Historical Division, Research Studies Institute, Air University. Maxwell AFB, AL, 1945)

U.S. Air Force Historical Study No. 12: *The Tenth Air Force 1942*, (USAF Historical Division, Research Studies Institute, Air University. Maxwell AFB, AL, 1944)

U.S. Air Force Historical Study No.29: *Summary of Air Action in the Philippines and Netherlands East Indies 7th December 1941-26th March 1942* (USAF Historical Division, Research Studies Institute, Air University. Maxwell AFB, AL)

U.S. Air Force Historical Study No. 104: *The Tenth Air Force 1 January-10 March 1943* (USAF Historical Division, Research Studies Institute, Air University. Maxwell AFB, AL)

U.S. Air Force Historical Study No. 111: *Army Air Action in the Philippines and Netherlands East Indies 1941-1942* (USAF Historical Division, Research Studies Institute, Air University. Maxwell AFB, AL)

U.S. Air Force Historical Study No. 117: *The Tenth Air Force 1943* (USAF Historical Division, Research Studies Institute, Air University. Maxwell AFB, AL)

United States Strategic Bombing Survey, Military Analysis Division: *Air Operations in China, Burma, India WWII* (Washington, D.C. 1947)

Virgin, Edward W.: "The Martin Bomber B-10, B-12, B-10B", in Higham, Robin and Carol Williams, Eds.: *Flying Combat Aircraft of the USAAF-USAF*, Vol. 2, (Ames, Iowa: The Iowa State University Press, 1978)

Wagner, Ray: *American Combat Airplanes of the 20th Century: A Comprehensive Reference* (Reno, Nevada: Jack Bacon & Co., 2004)

Walker, James W.: *The Liberandos: A WWII History of the 376th Bombardment Group and its Founding Units* (Waco, TX: 376th Heavy Bombardment Group Veterans Association, Inc. 1994)

Walker, Lt. Kenneth N.: "Bombardment Aviation—Bulwark of National Defense", *U.S. Air Services*, Vol. XVIII, No. 8, August, 1933.

Williford, Glen: *Racing the Sunrise: Reinforcing America's Pacific Outposts, 1941, 1942*.(Annapolis, MD: Naval Institute Press, 2010)

Wilmott, H.P.: *Empires in the Balance: Japanese and Allied Pacific Strategies to April 1942*. (Annapolis, MD: Naval Institute Press, 1982)

Winkler, Allan M.: *The Politics of Propaganda: The Office of War Information 1942-1945* (New Haven, CT: Yale University Press, 1978),

Womack, Tom: *The Dutch Naval Air Force Against Japan: The Defense of the Netherlands East Indies, 1941-1942* (Jefferson, NC: MacFarland and Company, Inc., 2006)

Wyatt, David K.: *Thailand: A Short History* (New Haven, CT: Yale University Press, 1984)

Young, Edward M.: Osprey Combat Aircraft 87: *B-24 Liberator Units of the CBI* (Oxford: Osprey Publishing Ltd., 2011)

——— Osprey Duel No. 41: *B-24 Liberator vs Ki-43 Oscar: China and Burma 1943* (Oxford, UK: Osprey Publishing, Ltd., 2012)

INDEX